The Wilson Chronology of the World's Religions

Other Titles in the Wilson Chronology Series

The Wilson Chronology of the World's Religions

David Levinson

with contributions from
John Bowman
C. Roger Davis
Michael Golay
Eva Weber

The H.W. Wilson Company

New York · Dublin

2000

Library of Congress Cataloging-in-Publication Data

The Wilson chronology of the world's religions / edited by David
Levinson
    p. cm.
  Includes bibliographical references and index.
  ISBN 0-8242-0978-8 (alk. paper)
    1. Religion—History—Chronology. I. Levinson, David, 1947– . II.
H. W. Wilson Company.

BL 80.2 .W55 1999
200'.2'02—dc21
99-052362

CIP

Printed in the United States of America

08 07 06 05 04 03 02 01 00 99   10 9 8 7 6 5 4 3 2 1

The H. W. Wilson Company
950 University Avenue
Bronx, NY 10452

www.hwwilson.com

Contents

Introduction

The purpose of *The Wilson Chronology of the World's Religions* is to provide readers with a reasonably complete record of the major events in the development and spread of religions around the world. The chronology begins with religion in prehistoric times, dating to 100,000 B.C.E., and ends in 2000. This chronology is primarily a chronology of events, with each entry listing and describing a specific event or series of events that took place in a specific year or span of years.

Our compilation of this chronology was guided by four primary beliefs about the nature of religion and the history of religion. First, despite the inability of experts to agree on exactly what is and what is not religion, religion can be defined broadly as beliefs and actions that take place within the context of the relationship between the human and supernatural worlds. This broad definition had the practical advantage of allowing us to cover of religion in the chronology as broadly as possible. Thus, we include not just organized religions or world religions but also such topics as spirituality, witchcraft, the personal growth movement, and alternatives to religion, such as deism and atheism. Our second guiding belief was that religion, as a societal institution, has never existed in isolation from other societal institutions. Rather, the situation is quite the opposite, and as many entries throughout the chronology show, religion throughout human history and across cultures has almost always influenced and been influenced by social, economic, and political developments, events, trends, and contexts. Our third guiding principle was that as religion has been the subject of interdisciplinary study, this chronology must also be interdisciplinary; we have therefore relied on a broad range of sources from history, anthropology, religious studies, sociology, political science, and the humanities. The fourth principle is that all religious beliefs and practices are equally valid and are entitled to respect and acceptance. Thus, in compiling the chronology we have tried to be fair and nonjudgmental. Adherence to these four principles has allowed us to compile a chronology that has considerable historical depth, is cross-cultural, and contains information about how and why particular events, trends, and developments took place, in addition to the what, when, where, and who of these events.

The chronology is meant to serve readers in a variety of ways. First, it provides a general history of the origins, development and spread of religion and thus allows readers to learn when and where particular events took place and what effect those events had on subsequent events. Second, it provides general histories of the origin, development, and spread of specific religions and sects and thus enables readers to learn when and where a particular religion began, how it developed, when and where it spread, and its status in the 1990s. Third, it allows readers to compare the development and spread of different religions by comparing events for each religion of interest in specific years, decades, or spans of years or centuries. Fourth, it gives readers an opportunity to learn how different religions have influenced one another. Fifth, it enables readers to understand the development and roles of religion and religions in their political, social, and economic contexts. And, sixth, it explores topics related to religion that cut across various religions; these topics include fundamentalism, creationism, African-American religion, Native American religion, and religious rights.

Coverage

The entries in the chronology cover seven major themes in the prehistory and history of religion:

(1) Religion in the prehistoric world; that is, religions about which we know through the study of the archaeological record. Coverage of these is slight compared to coverage of religion in the historic period, as information is limited by the absence of written records and the need to base interpretations on a less than full archaeological record.

(2) Religion in the ancient world, with an emphasis on the religions of major civilizations in China, Japan, Southeast Asia, Mesopotamia, Egypt, Africa, India, Greece, Rome, and the Americas. Information about these religions comes from both the archaeological and often written records.

(3) Major world religions; religions whose followers are widely distributed throughout the world and/or religions that have influenced other religions in significant ways. The world religions covered here are Judaism, Roman Catholicism, Protestantism (Baptist, Churches of God, Episcopalian, Anglican, Evangelical and Pentecostal Christianity, Pentecostal, Lutheran, Methodist, Congregational, Presbyterian, and the Salvation Army), Eastern Orthodoxy, Eastern Christianity, Mormonism, Islam, Buddhism, Confucianism, Daoism, Shinto, Hinduism, Jainism, Sikhism, Zoroastrianism, Baha'i, Coptic Christianity, Mormonism, Seventh-Day Adventist, Society of Friend (Quakers), Christian Science, Moravians, and the Unitarians.

(4) Other religions, including the Shakers, Anabaptists (Amish, Hutterites, and Mennonites), Rosicrucians, Gnostics, Unification Church, Hare Krishna, Brethren, Japanese new religions, and Scientology.

(5) Religious sects and cults, including mystical orders of the Middle Ages, spiritual groups of the nineteenth and twentieth centuries, New Thought

and New Age groups, witchcraft, astrology, apocalyptic and millenarian groups, and the personal growth movement.

(6) Religious tolerance and intolerance, including ecumenicism, missionary activity, relations among denominations and sects within a religion, relations between and among different religions and relations between the church and state. One major theme in the history of religion is both intolerance and tolerance by governments of religion or specific religions; therefore, the relationship between religion and the state is afforded much attention here.

(7) Special topics, including Native American religion, African-American religion, atheism, creationism, missionary activity, televangelism, the role of women in religion, and ecumenicism.

As much as possible we have tried to make coverage of each religion parallel while also including information about unique features of each religion. For each religion covered in the chronology we provide information on the following: origin; development and refinement of major beliefs and practices; origin and revision of major texts; major founding individuals, leaders, and reformers; designation of important places; tolerance or intolerance by others; major denominations or sects; and geographical spread.

Structure

The heart of the volume is the chronology itself. It is supplemented by about 250 information sidebars which describe all of the major and minor religions covered in the chronology, provide biographical sketches of major religious figures, define and frame major issues or events, and in general provide context to the information provided in the chronology. The volume also includes a bibliography and an index.

To aid readers in working through the chronology, nineteen subject codes are used to indicate the topic or topics covered in each entry. Other religions and topics, as well as specific topics within these general categories, are listed in the index. In addition, cross-references are included in the entries to direct users to other relevant entries.

AFRICAN	African and African-American Religions
BUDD	Buddhism
CATH	Roman Catholicism
CHRIS	Christianity, general
CIVIL	Religion in prehistoric times and in ancient civilizations
CONF	Confucianism
DAO	Daoism

EVAN	Evangelical and Pentecostal Christianity
HIND	Hinduism
JAIN	Jainism
JUD	Judaism
ISLAM	Islam
MISC	General information about religion in general
NATIV	Native American religions
ORTHO	Eastern Orthodoxy
PROT	Protestantism
SECT	Other religions, sects, and cults
SHINTO	Shinto
TOL	Religious tolerance and intolerance

A number of special decisions were made about how to best handle and present the information in the chronology. Perhaps the most difficult issue was how to present information that is dated at one point in time by adherents of a religion and at a different point in time by such experts as archaeologists or historians. In many religions it is not unusual for followers of the religion to date early events at earlier dates than do scholars. When there is a conflict in dates of this type, we have indicated that the date is one supported by religious belief by saying that it is the "traditional" date and that it is one supported by experts by saying it is the date assigned by "experts." Readers are free to choose whichever date, or both, as they prefer. Our goal is to be respectful of all religious beliefs while at the same time providing an accurate statement of the historical record.

A second issue that required special consideration was how to direct readers to entries that specifically relate to other entries that may be years or even centuries apart in the chronology. Of course, the index and the nineteen subject codes help, but for some entries we have also added cross-references or references in the text to the year where related information may be found.

The other decisions were more technical. They include the following:

(1) presenting all events in the present tense with events that take place later presented in the future tense or with information about when they occur;

(2) presenting all B.C.E. dates with a preceding – (minus) sign;

(3) not using C. (circa) with B.C.E. dates; as many B.C.E. dates are not exact, it is to be understood that sources often differ in the dates listed for these events;

(4) using C. (circa) to indicate that the date is approximate in the C.E. section of the chronology;

(5) using parentheses, as in (St.) Peter, to indicate that sainthood has been conferred on an individual at some later point in time.

Acknowledgments

A number of people not listed as contributors deserve mention and special thanks for their help with this work. First, I want to thank Michael Schulze, vice president and director of General Reference at H.W. Wilson, for his support of the idea and bringing the concept to a project with a minimum of fuss. I also want to thank the editorial staff at H.W. Wilson, including Gray Young, Lynn Messina, and Jacquelene Latif, as well as Hilary Claggett for supplying useful tips about reliable sources of information related to religion as the project progressed.

David Levinson

B.C.E.

-100,000– 75,000 B.C.E.	During the middle Paleolithic period in Europe, hunting and gathering peoples are engaging in ritual behavior, including burials and the extraction of the brains of the dead, perhaps for ritual use. In Germany during this period, bear skulls are collected in caves suggesting the worship of bears or other animals. **MISC**
-50,000– 6500 B.C.E.	During this period people enter North America from northeast Asia. By about 12,000 B.C.E. they have settled the entire Americas from west to east and north to south, with the exception of the extreme north, which is settled by about 3000 B.C.E. These peoples are hunter-gatherers whose religions are centered on shamans, religious specialists who communicate with the spirit world, and rites centered on animals. **MISC**
-40,000– 10,000 B.C.E.	During the Upper Paleolithic period in Europe, people are making clay and stone figurines of mammoth, bear, and the human female figure and engraving animal bones. In western Europe people are engraving and painting the walls and ceilings of caves. The figurines may indicate worship of specific animals, women, or fertility and the cave paintings indicate similar beliefs, with the caves serving as the locale for the performance of rituals. Near the close of the period in northern Europe, hunters are participating in annual sacrifices of reindeer, perhaps as a ritual means to ensure a productive hunt. **MISC**
-10,500	Japanese archaeological sites from around this time (the end of the Paleolithic era) yield burial sites containing grave offerings and evidence of cultural and trade exchanges with mainland Asia. **SHINTO**
-10,500– 400 B.C.E.	In the Jomon Neolithic period in Japan, nomadic bands begin the inhabitation of villages, leaving behind evidence of ceremonial pit houses and ritual objects, including earthen human and animal figures probably used in fertility and hunting rites. Drums and masks from the later part of the period are indicators of shamanism. Communal cemeteries emerge as well. All these artifacts and remains indicate that indigenous religious practices, as precursors of Shinto, are well developed. **SHINTO**
-10,000– 5000 B.C.E.	During the Mesolithic period in Europe, people make ritual objects out of bone that depict animals that are used for ritual purposes. Burials are more elaborate than in the past, with the dead buried with grave goods including stone tools and remains of animals and in some places, burials that are accompanied by ritual activity. **MISC**

-10,000– 200 B.C.E.	During the Jomon Neolithic period in Japan, people live by hunting, fishing, and gathering wild plants for food. The religious practices that emerge during this period include burials in which the bodies were arranged with jewelry, body mutilations such as teeth removal as part of initiation rites, and the production of clay figurines in human form, often with a body part missing, signifying the use of the figurines for magical purposes, most likely the curing of illnesses. **MISC**
-9000– 7000 B.C.E.	During the Mesolithic period in Mesopotamia, hunter-gatherers bury their dead on stone platforms. The dead wear ornamental stone and bone ornaments that perhaps served as amulets, and during the end of the period as more people are living in permanent settlements, people worship at shrines in their dwellings. **CIVIL**
-8500	Hallucinogenic drugs are being used by Native Americans in northern Mexico, although it is not known if they are used for religious purposes. **NATIV**
-7000– 6000 B.C.E.	During the Neolithic period in Mesopotamia, when people live in permanent farming villages, the dead are buried under the floors of houses and clay figurines of animals and pregnant women are made, perhaps reflecting the presence of animal cults and the worship of a god or forces related to fertility. **CIVIL**
-6500– 2500 B.C.E.	Native Americans in Mexico and parts of Central America begin to live in settled communities based on the growing of corn, beans, squash, cotton, and other crops. In these communities new religious beliefs and practices emerge with rituals enacted to ensure a steady supply of food. Ritual specialists, ancestor worship, sacrifice, and a belief in the afterlife were all present by about 2500 B.C.E. **NATIV**
-6000	At Jericho in the Middle East, skulls of the deceased are fashioned into masks, suggesting a belief that dead ancestors influence the lives of the living. **CIVIL**
-6000– 4200 B.C.E.	During the Ubaid period in Mesopotamia, temples are built on raised brick platforms. The temples are places of worship to local deities. Religion plays a major role in village life, as priests own much land and thereby also exercise considerable political power. **CIVIL**
-6000– 3500 B.C.E.	During the early Neolithic period in Europe, people across the continent from south to north gradually shift from a nomadic hunter-gatherer way of life to one supported by farming in settled communities. Settled living is accompanied by an increase in ritual activity, including worship in special buildings in some places; the making of clay figurines, especially of the female form, for ritual worship or use; and animal sacrifice, especially of dogs. In southeastern Europe the ritual use of female figurines is especially common and widespread, suggesting the worship of goddesses. **MISC**

-5000	With people now living in settled communities in the Middle East, priests have become important as community leaders. Their authority is based on their ability to mediate between the human and supernatural worlds and to influence the gods and spirits to provide rain and ample harvests. **CIVIL**
-5000	Pedomancy, a form of divining done by reading the contours, shape, and lines of the feet, is practiced in China. **SPIR**
-5000– 3100 B.C.E.	During the Predynastic period in Egypt, people believe in an afterlife that is much like life on earth. Burials are elaborate, with many grave goods included, probably to make life comfortable for the deceased in the afterlife. People also worship in animal cults devoted to jackals, sheep, cows, and dogs. These animals are sacrificed and buried with humans and represented in pottery decorations. There is also local worship of various gods and goddesses, including Ptah and possibly Re, the Sun God, who are important later in Egypt. Religious worship is both private and conducted in public sanctuaries by priests. **CIVIL**
-4200– 3100 B.C.E.	During the Uruk period in Mesopotamia, civilization emerges with the appearance of cities, states, and writing. From the cities the rulers control the economy, government, and religion. The temples are the largest and most elaborately decorated structures, with temples dedicated to the worship of deities, such as Anum, the god of the firmament, and Inanna, the goddess of love and war. The temples own much land, employ many people, collect payments, and are the repositories of myths recorded on clay tablets. Priests are politically powerful and rulers cannot gain or maintain power without the support of the priests. **CIVIL**
-3761	According the Jewish tradition, this is the year of creation and the first year in the Jewish calendar. **JUD**
-3500	The legendary kings Yao and Shun create a civilized world through moral persuasion, providing the basis for *ju-chia* (scholarly tradition), according to Chinese historians, which forms the cultural basis for Confucius's hero models, the sage-kings of antiquity. **CONF**
-3500– 3000 B.C.E.	During the middle Neolithic period in Europe, large stone monuments called megaliths are erected across much of Europe. Some are freestanding stones, others are arranged in circles, and others are built as above-ground burial chambers. The deceased are often buried with objects they were associated with in life: men with animals and women with pottery. In southern Europe the use of female figurines in rituals continues, suggesting fertility rites or the worship of goddesses. **MISC**
-3114	According to the Mayan long count calendar, this is the first year of the current Cosmic era. **NATIV**

-3100– 2686 B.C.E.	During the early Dynastic period in Egypt, the belief in the divine source of kingship emerges, as reflected in the building of royal tombs for the rulers of the Egyptian dynasties. People continue to worship various deities, priests conduct public services in public sanctuaries, and funerals and burials become more elaborate, with grave goods (including slaves and servants) buried with the wealthy and powerful. CIVIL
-3000– 1700 B.C.E.	During this time, when the Indus Valley civilization flourishes at such sites as Harappa and Mohenjo-Daro, there are elements of religious life that later Jains will cite as proof that Jainism can be traced back to the earliest pre-Vedic days of India's past. One such example are figures of men in what is claimed to be the yoga posture for meditation that the Jains will practice. Beyond such specifics, Jains will claim that the early inhabitants of India generally practiced a faith that is closer to Jainism than the Vedic Brahmanism that is introduced by the Aryans. CIVIL, JAIN
-3000	Writing and the compilation of written records has become an important component of political power in the Middle East, and in many communities it is the priests who control record keeping and thereby wield much political influence. CIVIL
-3000	In Greece Zeus is worshiped as the god of the day. Over the next several thousand years, beliefs in his power grow, and by 300 B.C.E. he has become the supreme god of the Greek pantheon and the ruler of all humans. CIVIL
-2900– 2335 B.C.E.	During the early Dynastic period in Mesopotamia, Sumer emerges as the dominant state in southern Mesopotamia. The region contains over 12 major cities, each with a large and elaborate central temple where residents worship the patron god of the city. The most important god is Enlil, the patron of the centrally located city of Nippur. Royalty are buried in elaborate graves accompanied by rich burial goods and sometimes human sacrifices as well. MISC
-2800– 1100 B.C.E.	Stonehenge is built in southern England. Although not actually used as a place of worship by Druids, in the 19th century it becomes the locale for pagan festivals. SPIR
-2686– 2181 B.C.E.	During the Old Kingdom period in Egypt, religion became closely linked to the divine concept of the kingship. Pharaohs are believed to be and portray themselves in grand public spectacles as the sons of the Sun God who rule on earth supported by the priesthood and after death become stars in the sky. Great earth and then stone pyramids, including those at Giza, are constructed as stairways that the deceased pharaohs can take to the sky. Under pharaonic rule Egyptian government is centralized, local pantheons of deities are structured, and a wisdom literature is written that provides rules for daily life based in part on religion. CIVIL

-2675   An epic is written about the legendary Mesopotamian king Gilgamesh. The epic contains an account of a great flood that is quite similar to and is later believed to be the basis of the story of the Noahian Flood in the Book of Genesis in the Bible.   **CIVIL**

-2600–
1800 B.C.E.   During the late Neolithic period in Europe, religious practices of the preceding period continue, with the erection of megaliths, burials in above-ground stone chambers, and burial goods buried with the dead. Animals, including pigs, sheep, and goats, are also buried with the dead, indicating the use of animals in religious rituals and sacrifice. People live in tribal societies, and it is likely that public rituals serve the purpose of bringing together different kinship groups within the tribe.   **MISC**

Ancient Greek Religion

The religion of ancient or classical Greece was polytheistic, with Greeks worshiping a hierarchy of gods and other supernatural beings all of whom were believed to directly influence life on earth. At the top of the pantheon of major gods was Zeus, the king of the gods, and then his wife Hera, the goddess of marriage and birth. The other 10 major gods were Poseidon, Hades, Demeter, Artemis, Ares, Aphrodite, Athena, Hephaestus, Hermes, and Hestia. In addition, the Greeks worshiped many lesser gods (such as Dionysus, who controlled specific items such as wine), gods and goddesses of cities and towns, family gods, spirits of ancestors, and heroes, such as the Spartan general Lysander. Depending on their influence, gods and goddesses were worshiped at temples built in their honor, at festivals such as the Olympics (for Zeus), and at altars in the home. The Greeks did not have religious texts in the modern sense but instead relied on myths for the stories of their gods and information about the supernatural world. Considerable time was spent in religious activities, with festivals held throughout the year in many communities and people often involved in cults devoted to a particular god. In some cults members were required to perform secret rituals known as mysteries through which they appealed to the god of their devotion. The best known of the mysteries was the Eleusinian Mysteries, whose members worshiped the goddess Demeter, who they believed would protect them in the afterlife. Priests served as intermediaries between the human and supernatural worlds, especially in important matters, and were consulted for advice about major matters such as waging war. Such priests were called oracles as were the places where the gods were invoked. Greeks also relied on various methods of divination, such as peering into still water for signs from the gods in order to predict the future. Greek religion influenced and was influenced in turn by the various peoples who came under Greek rule. Perhaps most important, Greek religion influenced the Roman Empire, with the pantheon of 12 major gods "borrowed" and renamed by the Romans.

| -2500 | During the Archaic period Native Americans in California bury their dead in burial mounds, indicating a belief in the afterlife and the worship or veneration of ancestors. **NATIV** |

| -2500–2000 B.C.E. | At Mohenjo-Daro, the center of the Indus Valley civilization in southern Asia, female terra-cotta figurines are produced. They may be used for religious purposes and may represent the worship of goddesses. **CIVIL** |

| -2500–1500 B.C.E. | The Indus Valley civilization in what is later Pakistan and India is at its height. Although the civilization has declined by the time Indo-Iranian peoples from central Asia begin migrating into the region and then to the south and east, the religious beliefs and practices of the civilization likely influence the migrants. In the 20th century experts do not agree about what influence, if any, the Indus Valley civilization had on the development of Hinduism in southern Asia. **HIND** |

| -2500–1500 B.C.E. | In the Andean highlands of South America, the Kotash religious tradition, which is marked by terraced platform mounds, small ceremonial rooms, burial chambers, and friezes with religious themes, develops and flourishes. **NATIV** |

Pyramids of Giza

The Pyramids of Giza, now located in a suburb south of Cairo, Egypt, are one of the greatest achievements in the construction of monumental religious architecture in human history. The three large pyramids, several smaller ones, the temples, and the Sphinx were built between about 2528 B.C.E. and 2465 B.C.E. by three Egyptian kings, Khufu, Khafre, and Menkaure, as burial tombs for themselves, their queens, and other family members. The Great Pyramid built by Khufu is the largest of the three and is considered one of the Seven Wonders of the Ancient World. The pyramids were constructed from limestone blocks so massive as to suggest they reach up to the sun, whose god Re was manifested on earth in the form of the divine kings. The exterior blocks were of light-colored limestone that reflected the sun's rays, adding to the symbolism of the king as a manifestation of Re. One of the great questions that has faced archaeologists, architects, and engineers is how the pyramids were built in the absence of nonhuman forms of energy and even such basic lifting devices as the tackle and pulley. The answer is most likely the Egyptian genius for organizing and managing the labor of huge numbers of laborers, in this case farmers who could not farm during the months when the Nile flooded. They were worked long and hard, with much of the effort going to cutting the huge blocks and moving them up a ramp made from mud, brick, and sand. Once the pyramid was complete, the ramp was removed and the outside stones worked by masons. Although the grave goods in the tombs were looted and the same exterior stones were removed later for other uses, the Pyramids of Giza remain an architectural wonder and a major tourist attraction.

-2500– 1500 B.C.E.	In the Indus Valley civilization of southern Asia, clay seals with figures in yoga postures suggest the practice of yoga as a religious ritual. CIVIL
-2334– 2230 B.C.E.	The Akkadians come to power in southern Mesopotamia, and during the rule of Naram-Sin (r. -2254–2217 B.C.E.) the basis of the kingship is redefined, with the king now seen as a god, rather than as an agent of the gods. CIVIL
-2250	In Egypt the scarab beetle symbol is used as a good luck charm. CIVIL
-2112– 2004 B.C.E.	During the Imperial period in the Mesopotamian city of Ur, the great ziggurat (mound and temple complex) is expanded as a center for the worship of Nanna, the Moon God. The ziggurat, standing high above the city, also serves a political purpose as the symbol of the power of Ur over the surrounding region. CIVIL
-2000	Native Americans in what would become Louisiana begin living in settled villages supported by agriculture and make ritual objects in the shape of clams, falcons, and owls, suggesting a veneration of nature. NATIV
-2000– 1000 B.C.E.	During the Formative period in Mesoamerica, distinctive communities led by chiefs emerge. The chiefs derive some of their authority from their knowledge of and ability to communicate with the supernatural world. Rituals that include bloodletting are practiced, perhaps as a form of sacri-

Ziggurats

The most conspicuous element of Mesopotamian religions were the ziggurats, the large towers crowned by a temple found in all major cities. The best known ziggurats in modern times are the Tower of Babylon, known only from early descriptions, such as that by the Greek historian Herodotus and the ziggurat at Ur, the remains of which were excavated by British archaeologist Sir Leonard Woolley in the 1930s. Most ziggurats in Mesopotamia have disappeared, their stone and clay platforms and stairways turned into dust or plundered for use elsewhere. Ziggurats consisted of a series of brick platforms, one on top of and smaller than the one below. The levels were joined by a series of stairways, and the entire structure was probably topped by a temple. The ziggurat, which could be seen by travelers from miles across the desert, marked the location of major cities and was where the priests conducted the most important rituals. Only the wealthy and powerful could climb the ziggurat; the masses were restricted to observing from below. Although ziggurats were perhaps the first example of this style of religious architecture, the religious monument built to reach toward the sky, the home of the spirits and gods in many religions, is not unique in human history. The pyramids of Egypt, Mesoamerica, and South America; the mounds of North American Indians; the great cathedrals of Medieval Europe; and even the church spires of New England also display this common theme.

fice to the gods, and some houses have small shrines, suggesting the worship of personal or family spirits or deities. **NATIV**

-1991–
1786 B.C.E.

During the middle Kingdom period in Egypt, which follows the decline of the First Intermediate period (-2181–1991 B.C.E.), the kingship is humanized, with the pharaohs no longer seen as remote gods. Orisis replaces Re, the Sun God, as the chief god, and massive temples and stone statues are built. **CIVIL**

-1800

Scribes in Mesopotamia complete the King-list, a sketchy chronological account of the rulers of the region in the third and second millennia B.C.E. Included in the list is reference to rulers before the flood. Floods are a common theme in Mesopotamian myths and legends and it is likely that the biblical Flood is derived from these earlier Mesopotamian sources. **CIVIL**

-1800

The Israelites, a number of loosely affiliated tribes, migrate into Palestine from Mesopotamia. The region is under Egyptian control at this time and remains so until about 1200 B.C.E. About this time, according to Jewish tradition, Abraham, one of the forefathers of Judaism, recognizes the existence of a supreme god, marking the emergence of Judaism as a monotheistic religion, and also leads his people to Palestine. Abraham is considered to be the ancestor of Jews and is also a major figure in Christianity and Islam. Along with his son Isaac and Isaac's son Jacob, he is considered one of the forefathers of the Jewish community. Their wives Sarah, Rebekah, Leah, and Rachel are considered the matriarchs of the Jewish community. **JUD**

-1800–
800 B.C.E.

During the Initial period of the development of Andean civilization in South America, ceremonial centers become larger and more elaborate with sunken courtyards, temples, mounds, plazas, and religious carvings. **NATIV**

-1800–
300 B.C.E.

The Olmec culture develops, flourishes, and then declines on the Gulf Coast of Mexico. Various religious beliefs and practices of the Olmec form the basis of later religions in Mesoamerica. Most important is the link between nature and religion, with the Olmecs using caves, hills, earth mounds, and stone carvings to represent religious themes. **NATIV**

-1800–
200 B.C.E.

During the Formative period of the Maya civilization in Mesoamerica, ceremonial cities with large temples develop and by the end of the period some of these centers such as El Mirador have become major political centers as well. **NATIV**

-1790

In Babylonia Hammurabi creates a separation of church and state when he differentiates between the responsibilities of priests and government officials and when he suggests that he is not a god but merely the "favorite of the gods." **CIVIL**

-1786–
1567 B.C.E.

During the Second Intermediate period in Egypt, lower Egypt comes under the control of the Hyksos, a people who have immigrated into the region from the east. They adopt the existing Egyptian religion. **CIVIL**

-1700–
600 B.C.E.
During this period the Aryans move into northern and central India and bring their Vedic Brahmanic religion that tends to drive the indigenous religious practices underground. The Vedic Brahmanic religion stresses rituals, animal sacrifice, priests, and elitism; it also encourages the active life, a life of heroic struggle, wealth, power, and plentiful food and drink. It is against such practices and beliefs that the founders of Indian faiths such as Jainism will rebel. **HIND, JAIN**

-1600
The Minoan civilization on the island of Crete in the Mediterranean Sea is at its height. The religion centers on the worship of a "mother earth" goddess, veneration of the bull, perhaps as a symbol of the power of nature, and animal and human sacrifice. **CIVIL**

-1600
An early form of Judaism begins to develop in Palestine with an emphasis on spirits, ritual cleanliness, and rites for the dead. **JUD**

-1570–
1528 B.C.E.
As Egypt declines as a regional power, the void in the southern reaches of the empire in Nubia is filled by black African rulers in the city of Kerma in the Kingdom of Kush. It is the first African state, and the rulers borrow many practices, including religious ones from Egypt. The rulers are buried under large mounds accompanied by grave goods, including large numbers of sacrificial victims. **AFRICAN**

-1567–
1085 B.C.E.
During the New Kingdom period in Egypt the Hyksos are defeated and Egypt is reunited under Egyptian rule. Thebes is the capital city, with religious worship centered on Anum-Re, the Sun God, and the Temple of Anum. Religious celebrations are now controlled by the royalty, as the priests have lost power to bureaucrats, soldiers, and political officials. During the rule of Pharaoh Akhenaten (-1353–1336 B.C.E.), the Great Disk of Amun-Re, called Aten, is elevated to the status of the supreme god, the ruler of all other gods. Experts disagree in the 1990s as to whether this is the first recorded instance of monotheism in human history or whether it is a modified form of Egyptian polytheism. **CIVIL**

-1500
Poverty Point Mounds are built and then expanded in subsequent years by Native Americans of the Mississippian cultural tradition in what would later be Louisiana. The mounds and earthworks are likely influenced by Mesoamerican peoples from the south and include temple platforms, wood temples, and enclosures with the space inside considered sacred. **NATIV**

-1500
From the sixteenth century B.C.E. on, Rosicrucians attribute the birth of Rosicrucianism to Egyptian pharaoh Thutmose III (-1500–1447 B.C.E.), who they believe organized a group that studied mysticism in a way similar to that later adopted by adherents of Rosicrucianism. Rosicrucians in the 20th century do not see Rosicrucianism as a religion but rather as a method of study and learning based on ancient mysticism and metaphysics, designed to enhance personal, spiritual, physical, intellectual, and psychic well-being. **SECT**

-1500– 1200 B.C.E.	During this period Indo-European/Aryan peoples migrate into northwestern India. They are tribes of pastoral nomads from central Asia who in later centuries are called Aryans and are the ancestors of many Asian Indians. **HIND**
-1500– 1200 B.C.E.	By this time the Mesoamerican ball game is being played in Mexico. Played by nearly all men and some women in Mexican groups across Mexico, it reaches its most highly developed form in major ceremonial centers where the game is played on permanent stone courts and has much ritual importance with losers often sacrificed to the gods. **SEE 1585, NATIV.** **NATIV**
-1500– 563 B.C.E.	The Indo-European/Aryan people who come to dominate much of northern and central India during this period impose their Vedic Brahmanic religion on native Indians. Their stress on rituals, including sacrifices, elites and the caste system, royal power, and military force, leaves many Indians dissatisfied with Vedic and Brahmanic authority. By at least 600 B.C.E., various reformist individuals and movements are emerging in India, especially in the north; they share a rejection of elaborate rituals, a return to simpler faith, and a call for more meaningful devotion. In a related development, many wandering ascetic teachers claim to have found the way of escape from life's sufferings and win converts among the people. **BUDD, HIND**
-1300– 1200 B.C.E.	This is the traditional time frame cited in Judaism for when Moses led the Hebrew people out of slavery in Egypt to the border of Palestine. It is likely that these people joined with Hebrew peoples already resident in Palestine. Moses declares Yahweh (God) to be liberator of his people. At this time, Judaism develops further with the Ten Commandments, which are at once a criminal code and a liturgical code. Graven images (representations

---

Moses

Moses is perhaps the most venerated figure in Jewish history and one of the most important figures in the history of religion in general. Within Judaism and Christianity he is the individual who led the Israelites out of Egypt, guided their journey across the wilderness, and brought them the laws of God. His impact was so central to Judaism that the basic laws of Judaism are called the Mosaic Law. His story is told in four of the five books of the Torah. Moses was also held up by some later Jewish and Christian theologians as the model human being. Despite his centrality in the origin of Judaism, little is actually known with any certainty about Moses, who he was, where he came from, and what he actually accomplished. Most scholars do not accept much of the biblical version of his story, as it is not supported by other archaeological or historical evidence. In a historical sense Moses is seen by many scholars as a composite figure whose life, events, and contributions as depicted in the Bible, which were recorded 1,000 or more years after they took place, are based on an amalgam of themes, events, and individual stories drawn from a number of cultural and religious traditions in the Middle East.

of God) are prohibited.   JUD

-1250–
1020 B.C.E.   During the Period of Judges, the Israelites are living mainly in Samaria and Bethel and the idea of a single all-powerful god emerges. During this period the god, named Yhwh, is seen as the god of Israel and the protector of the Israelites. Although the name for the Hebrew god is subsequently given as Yahweh, YHWH, or Jehovah, Jews since the sixth century B.C.E. have not used these renderings. Rather, God is referred to by the Hebrew word *Adonai* (my Lord) or the Hebrew word *Elohim* (majesty). In writing Jews also do not spell out names for their God. Thus, in English usage, *God* is spelled *G-d*.   JUD

-1230   The first written reference to Israel appears on a stela (inscribed stone slab on a column) record of Egyptian Pharaoh Merneptah.   JUD

Hinduism

The Hindu religion is the most complex of the world's religions. Actually, it is so complex that there is some question as to whether it is really a single religion or instead a large number of related religions that share many common elements. Nearly all Hindus (about 700 million) live in India, where Hinduism emerged over 3,000 years ago and where it has continued to evolve. There are also about five million Hindus who live in many other nations around the world. Although Hinduism is the predominant religion in India, it also had an early influence on Buddhism as it is now practiced in Thailand and Vietnam and Islam as it is practiced in India and Indonesia. In India Hinduism is closely tied to Indian nationalism, and a significant segment of the population believes that India should be an officially Hindu nation. Hinduism is a mix of beliefs, rituals, festivals, sects, cults, gods (over one million), shrines, temples, and texts distributed across India. India has always been and remains largely a nation of small villages, and each village has over time tended to develop its own form of Hinduism, with its own gods, festivals, temples, shrines, and rituals. Nonetheless, there are several unifying forces in Hinduism that create unity across this diversity. First, there is a large quantity of religious texts considered sacred by all Hindus. Second, there is the caste system that organizes Indian society into discrete social units in accord with Hindu beliefs. Third, there are basic beliefs, such as those in rebirth, *karma*, and *dharma*, that are widely shared. Fourth, in the pantheon of one million gods, there are some (Shiva, Vishnu, and Brahma) who are most important. Fifth, there is the concept of *ashrama* (life stages) and the ritual requirements one must meet to achieve liberation from the cycle of rebirth, something very few actually achieve. Finally, there are the Hindu rituals and pilgrimages to shrines that play a central role in the daily life of Hindus. Many of these rituals and restrictions on behavior concern Hindu concepts of ritual pollution and purity and the desire to engage in pure behaviors.

-1200	Egypt enters a period of decline as political instability ends effective centralized government control and many ancient temples and tombs are looted for their valuable grave goods, carvings, and precious metals. CIVIL
-1200	The Philistines, a people from Crete, settle in Palestine and emerge as the dominant group in Palestine. It is their threat to the tribes of Judah and Israel that later encourages the two tribes to unite. JUD
-1200	The Phoenicians, a trading people who have cooperative relations with the Israelites, establish the city of Tyre as the center of their operations. Their religious system has some influence on emerging Judaism, including the structure of the temple with a shrine and anteroom and the concept of a superior god. JUD
-1200	At the Olmec ceremonial center of San Lorenzo in Mexico, perhaps the first representations of Mesoamerican deities appear in the form of large, carved stone heads. NATIV
-1200	The prophet Zoroaster (Zarathustra) founds the Zoroastrianism religion in Persia through his preaching in northeast Iran. It closely resembles the Vedic beliefs of ancient Hinduism, which is practiced to the east of Persia in northern India. In the twentieth century there is much controversy among scholars as to the dates when Zoroaster lived (placed anywhere from -1400 to 500 B.C.E.) and some question whether he actually lived at all. SECT
-1200–900 B.C.E.	The Hindu *Yajurveda, Samaveda,* and *Atharvaveda* are composed. They are religious texts that reinforce the *Rigveda,* the oldest and most important of the *Vedas* of ancient Hinduism. They also provide instructions for rituals of Hinduism as it is practiced in southern Asia. During this period the Vedic religion emerges with the compilation of the *Vedas* (knowledge), which are transmitted orally from generation to generation before they are first written down beginning in about 100 B.C.E. Key elements of the Vedic religion are the creation of the world from a cosmic being, the renewal of life from cosmic energy, and the use of sacred food and plants in ritual sacrifices. The Vedic supernatural and human world is organized into three categories—priest, warrior, and food producer—a system that is the precursor of the Hindu caste system that emerges centuries later. HIND
-1200–-200 B.C.E.	The Vedic *Rigveda* hymns are composed by the Aryans of northern India. They are a collection of 1,028 hymns devoted to numerous gods, including Indra, the warrior god; Varuna, the guardian of the universe; Agni, the sacred fire; and the Ashvin twins, pastoral horsemen. HIND
-1100	Heavenly columns associated with religious and community festivals are in use in Germany. These are the forerunners of maypoles still in use throughout Europe in the 20th century. MISC

-1100– 350 B.C.E.	With the end of Egyptian rule, Nubia comes under the rule of indigenous leaders who establish a kingdom similar to the Egyptian kingdom. Priests play a major role in governing the kingdom and maintain the religion of Egypt, including the worship of Amun, the concept of the divine kingship, and the burial of rulers under stone pyramids. The priests often interact with the common people and as such reinforce the divine basis of the rule of the kings, who remain remote. **AFRICAN**
-1040– 256 B.C.E.	The Zhou dynasty, the third of the ancient dynasties, rules in China. The Zhou is the classical age of Confucius and Laozi, by tradition the founder of Daoism. It is also a period of general political turbulence and instability. **CONF, DAO**

Hindu Texts

Hinduism has an exceedingly ancient, rich, long, and complex set of religious texts. They fall into two general categories: *sruti* and *smrti*. *Sruti*, which means "that which is heard," are considered by Hindus to be revealed text. They include the following:

Vedas—the oldest and most important of texts that are considered to be eternal and are comprised of the *Rigveda* (*Hymns of Gods*), *Samaveda* (*Musical Instructions for the Hymns*), *Yajurveda* (*Ceremonies*), and *Atharvaveda* (*Hymns and Spells*).

Brahmanas—ancient writings that deal with ritual sacrifice.

Upanisads and Aranyakas—collections of wisdom and philosophy and the doctrines of various schools of Hinduism.

Agamas—texts considered to be revealed by some but not all Hindu sects and that usually cover doctrine, ritual, and rules for daily life.

Smrti means "that which has been remembered," and in this category are texts that mainly concern matters of daily life and conformity to Hindu rituals. Not all Hindu sects agree on what texts belong in this category, and some assign certain texts that they consider to be revealed to the *sruti* category. The major *smrti* texts are as follows:

Puranas—mythical accounts of ancient times

Dharmasatra—religious laws and rules of personal conduct

Itihasa—poems, legends, and epics

In addition to texts in these two categories are others that defy easy classification. The most important are the *sutras*, collections of religious instructions, and the *Mahabharata* and *Ramayana*, collections of *sruti* and *smrti* texts that are often consulted by Hindus.

-1030– 1010 B.C.E.	Saul, the first king of Israel, reigns. He is successful in wars with neighboring groups, such as the Ammonites and Moabites, and establishes the boundaries of the small Kingdom of Israel. **JUD**
-1010– 970 B.C.E.	These years cover the reign of David (c. -1037–970 B.C.E.), who unites the Israelite tribes into one political unit and displaces rival groups in the region. **JUD**
-1000	What is to become the first Greek god appears in the belief system of the people of the island of Crete. Known as Britomartis, Dictynna, or Ariande, she is believed to rule all of nature and is later known in Greece as Demeter. **CIVIL**
-1000	In Greece the dead are usually buried in small graves lined with stones. **CIVIL**
-1000	Tradition claims that about this time in China, the *Zhouyi* (*Changes of Zhou*), the core text of what will become known as the *I Ching*, or *Yijing*, is codified by diviners serving the royal court of the Zhou dynasty. The text is probably passed on orally until it is written down about 500 B.C.E. **DAO**
-1000–	The Maya ceremonial center of Cuello is built and goes through a series of expansions in Mesoamerica. It contains a temple platform and temple and is the locale for Mayan rituals including human sacrifices. **NATIV**
-1000– 700 B.C.E.	The Hindu *Brahmanas* and *Aranyakas* (forest books) are composed. These sacred oral texts provide details about the conduct of Vedic sacrifices and discussions of the meaning of the sacrifices. **HIND**

David

David, who was born c. 1037 B.C.E. and died c. 967 B.C.E., is a central figure in Jewish history and Jewish consciousness. He is considered the most important king of ancient Israel, the unifier of Israel and Judah, and a figure of much symbolic importance as a link between the Jewish nation and God. Jews believe that he was chosen by God through the Prophet Samuel to be the King of Israel, that all kings of Israel must be descended from David, and that the Messiah will also come from his line. As a leader he was most effective, deposing his political enemies, defeating or forming alliances with other states in the region, unifying Israel and Judah, expanding Israel's boundaries, and organizing the priesthood. He is also credited as the author of the Book of Psalms, although scholarly research has shown that most of these psalms were actually written by someone else after his death. As a human being he is praised for being brave, loyal, and devoted to God but is also criticized for being too self-interested and for committing adultery.

-1000– 200 C.E.	The Maya cities of Nakbé and Mirador are built, expand, and then collapse in Guatemala. They are both centers of Maya religion, with Maya rulers creating a theocracy in which they portray themselves as living manifestations of the gods. The cities are major ceremonial centers with temples, plazas, and pyramids. **NATIV**
-970– 932 B.C.E.	These years include the reign of Solomon (c. -986–932 B.C.E.), during which the First Temple is built in Jerusalem. Solomon forges diplomatic ties with the neighboring states, expands trade, builds seaports, and increases the wealth of the nation. **JUD**
-965– 587 B.C.E.	The First Temple period in Jewish history begins with the building of the Temple in Jerusalem during the reign of Solomon and ends with the destruction of the Temple by the Babylonians. Prior to and during this period, the prophets known to scholars as the former, or oral, prophets are active. They include Joshua, Samuel, Nathan, and Gad, and they set forth two ideas that remain central to subsequent human history: first, that historical events do not occur randomly but are determined by God; and second, that if people follow the laws of God they will be rewarded in this and future days. **JUD**
-950	The island of Delos in the Cyclades Islands in Greece is settled by the Greek Ionians, who make it a major locale for the worship of their gods. Especially important is Apollo, who is honored by a large festival held on the island each year. **CIVIL**

Major Deities of Ancient Greece and Rome

Greek Name	Roman Name	Domain
Zeus	Jupiter	supreme god
Hera	Juno	marriage and childbirth
Poseidon	Neptune	sea, horses, earthquakes
Hades	Pluto, Orcus	underworld
Ares	Mars	war
Demeter	Ceres	fertility
Artemis	Diana	animals and hunting
Aphrodite	Venus	love
Athena	Minerva	wisdom, war
Hephaestus	Vulcan	fire
Hestia	Vesta	hearth and home
Dionysus, Bacchus	Liber, Bacchus	wine, festivals
Hermes	Mercury	travel
Apollo	Apollo	prophecy, music

-950   According to the traditional beliefs of the Falasha (Ethiopian Jews, Beta Israel), their ancestors arrive at about this time in Ethiopia as emissaries from King Solomon's court. Historians dispute this view and believe that the Falasha appeared as a distinct group with some Jewish customs no earlier than the 14th century. They were a people of local origin who adopted Jewish customs from Jewish travelers and traders in East Africa and resisted conversion to Christianity and Islam.   **JUD**

-931   Israel splits into the Kingdom of Judah (in the south, with the capital at Jerusalem) and the Kingdom of Israel (in the north with the capital at Samaria). For the next 150 years there is conflict between the north and south and with the Assyrians and other rivals.   **JUD**

-900–
200 B.C.E.   During the early Horizon period in the development of Andean civilization in South America, cult and pilgrimage centers develop, myths center on anthropomorphic gods, rituals performed in temples become more complex, and religious specialists use hallucinogenic drugs to communicate with the spirit world.   **NATIV**

- 900   Codification of Jewish law begins with focus on laws that eventually appear in the Book of Exodus.   **JUD**

-800s   The Prophet Elijah redefines the role of the prophet in ancient Israelite society. Up to this time prophets had been members of the ruling class and were closely aligned with the king, although they might criticize him. Elijah was from outside the ruling class and established the prophets as a more independent category of religious specialists who provided guidance on moral, legal, ethical, and religious issues.   **JUD**

-876   This is the end of the time frame, according to the Jains, of the first 22 of the 24 *tirthankaras* (literally "makers of the river crossing," and referring to

---

Tirthankaras

In Jainism the *tirthankaras* are people who have crossed the river of life to attain a higher state and are the forerunners of Jainism. The actual years when this took place are unknown because they involve the Jains' theory of cyclic periods of the universe; in any case, these are almost certainly purely mythical beings. The first of these 22 *tirthankaras* is Rishabha; the last is Nemi Bharat (or Nemi-natha). They practice the eternal principles of Jainism, attain the state of *kevalin* (completed soul), and preach the true word. For this reason they are given the title of *jina* (victor, in the spiritual sense); *Jain* is derived from this word. In Jain literature and art of later centuries, the *tirthankaras'* life stories will be embellished with miraculous events that are clearly allegories or direct borrowings from age-old Indian metaphysical concepts.

those who have crossed the river of life to attain a higher state), who are the forerunners of Jainism (also known as Jinism). **JAIN**

-876–776 B.C.E. According to Jain tradition, this is the lifespan of Parsvanatha—the 23d of the *tirthankaras*, or holy guides. (This belief is based on the claim that Parsvanatha lived some 250 years before the traditional dates for Mahavira.) In some accounts he is credited with teaching many of the doctrines of what will become Jainism; in this view, Mahavira is more like a reformer and organizer of the teachings of Parsvanatha, not the founder of a faith. (In some accounts Gautama Buddha starts out as a follower of the teachings of Parsvanatha.) Virtually nothing with any historical evidence is known of this Parsvanatha, but Jain legend claims that he is the son of King Asvasena and Queen Vama of Varanasi; that at age 30 he renounces the world and becomes an ascetic; that he practices extreme austerities for 83 days and then on the 84th attains omniscience (as *kevalin* is often translated); that he then preaches his doctrines for 70 years; and that finally, at age 100 he attains nirvana. **BUDD, JAIN**

-800 The Hindu Shrauta Sutras are composed. These sacred texts provide instructions on conducting major Vedic sacrifices. **HIND**

-800–700 B.C.E. According to Zoroastrian tradition, the Prophet Zoroaster lives, is trained as a priest, has revelations, and begins preaching a new religion that becomes Zoroastrianism. **SECT**

-800–600 B.C.E. Religious, philosophical, and social reaction against orthodox sacrificial Brahmanism is emerging in the Gangetic plain of eastern India. Mysticism and meditation fundamental to this movement are to become central to Indian religious thought and practice. The new approach leads to the rise of hermits, itinerant mendicants, and ascetics *(munis)*, who gradually supplant *brahmans*, the Vedic priests, as holders of spiritual knowledge. In particular, in the east-central region (which includes the modern states of Bihar and eastern part of Uttar Pradesh), where the Aryan civilization and Brahmanical religion probably arrive relatively late, the people still practice much of the pre-Aryan religion. This is probably why Jainism and Buddhism emerge here. **HIND, JAIN**

-800–500 B.C.E. In India the idea develops in Hinduism that humans are reincarnated again and again and that one's actions in the current life (*karma*) determine one's fate in the next life. Suffering is the major characteristic of the rebirth process, with suffering alleviated by engaging in correct ritual behavior. **HIND**

-800–400 B.C.E. In India the *sramana* traditions develop in Hinduism. These traditions emphasize knowledge rather than behavior as the means to end suffering. Adherents engage in ascetic behaviors and remove themselves from society as itinerants or hermits. **HIND**

-700s	A belief in immortality is attested in Zhou dynasty China. It will become a characteristic feature of Daoism. **DAO**
-776	A festival, later labeled the first Olympic games, in honor of the Greek god Zeus is held at Mount Olympus. Such festivals are commonly held in Greece to honor deities, although this is possibly the first one in which an athletic event—a race of about 200 meters—is held and the results recorded as part of the festival. **CIVIL**
-771– 111 B.C.E.	Feudal states in China are ruled by lords who pay homage to the king of Chou. Education for the nobility consists of the six arts: rituals, music, archery, charioteering, writing, and mathematics. Mere memorization is condemned. Confucius will refer approvingly to the ancient spirit of such learning as including thought. **CONF**
-771	The benevolent Chou kings of China, virtuous rulers for centuries previous, under pressure of barbarian attacks from Central Asia, move their capital eastward to the area later called Lo-yang and cede power to the regional lords. This begins an undermining of the feudal system and a moral decline in leadership that by 521 B.C.E. inspires Confucius to revitalize the institutions central to political stability and social order. **CONF, TOL**
-750	In Greece the practice of burying the dead in graves has been replaced by cremation, with the ashes saved in pottery containers that are buried. **CIVIL**
-750	The *Iliad* is written by the Greek poet Homer. It is an epic poem that recounts the exploits of Greek gods, goddesses, and heroes during the Trojan War. Later in the century he writes the *Odyssey*, another epic poem, that tells the story of the travels of the mythical hero Odysseus after the war. **CIVIL**
-750	Ceremonial centers with large earthen temple mounds and earthworks enclosing sacred grounds are built by the Native Americans of the Adena/Hopewell cultural tradition in the Ohio River Valley. Some mounds contain elaborate tombs for the ruling class and priests. **NATIV**
-750– 550 B.C.E.	The so-called literary, latter, or classical prophets emerge and are active in the Jewish world. They include Amos, Hosea, Isaiah, Micah, Jeremiah, Nahum, Uriah, Ezekiel, Zechariah, and Malachi. They act as spokesmen for God, transmitting his word to Jews and non-Jews. Their authority comes from the belief that God is universal, and therefore, his message is for all people. **JUD**
-722	Israel (the northern kingdom) is conquered and destroyed by the Assyrians under Saragon II. Judah is not destroyed but comes under Assyrian rule. Under Assyrian rule the Jewish community is splintered into groups that resist Assyrian rule, groups that accept it, and groups that support it. The Israelites are dispersed to Babylon, Chaldea, the Caucasus, and Turkey. **JUD**

-720 | In the Middle East Assyria enters a period of dominance and prosperity. Assyrian religion centers on the supreme god Ashur, whose symbol, the winged disk, leads the Assyrians in battle. To a great extent Assyrian religious practice focuses on communicating with the gods in order to prevent harm and win their support. **CIVIL**

-720– 700 B.C.E. | The traditional time period cited by Bukharan Jews of central Asia for their arrival in what is now Bukhara in central Asia. Bukharan Jews claim their ancestors were members of the Lost Tribes of Israel. Scholars believe that the Bukharan Jews arrived or became distinct from other Jews in the region no earlier than the sixth century C.E. and perhaps as late as the eighth or ninth century. **JUD**

-700 | The Greeks build temples of brick and wood with a statue of a god placed inside. Actual worship of the god is conducted at an altar outside the temple. The oracle at Delphi is the most important religious center in Greece. It houses a temple supported by the Greek states and the oracle is consulted by Greek leaders about matters of state and by individuals seeking divine guidance on personal matters. The oracle remains in use for state matters until the 300s B.C.E. and is closed in 390 C.E. by the Roman emperor Theodosius. **CIVIL**

-700– 500 B.C.E. | In India the idea of a supreme god (*Bhagavan*) or goddess (*Bhagavati*) who has created the universe and has power over humans develops in Hinduism. The two gods who occupy this role are Shiva (previously called Rudra) and Vishnu. Adherents of Shiva are called Shaivas and adherents of Vishnu are called Vaisnavas. **HIND**

-700– 200 B.C.E. | The 13 core Vedic *Upanishads* are composed in northern India. These oral collections of prose and verse are philosophical and symbolic discussions of the earlier religious texts dealing with Vedic sacrifice and stress the development of individual insight and knowledge rather than ritual alone in achieving salvation. They are also called Vedanta (the end of the Vedas) because they mark the end of the Vedic sacred texts, and they play a major role in the development of Hindu yoga and meditation traditions and the emergence of Buddhism and Jainism as alternatives to Hinduism. **HIND**

-600s | Guanzi (d. 645 B.C.E.) is minister of state in the Chinese kingdom of Qi. He is regarded as a model minister; the *Guanzi*, a collection of essays on political, social, and religious themes dating from the Warring States and Han periods, will be named for him. **CONF, DAO**

-660 | This is the legendary date for the start of the reign of Jimmu, the first emperor of Japan. This ancestry for the imperial line originating from the sun goddess Amaterasu is created in 603 C.E. to legitimize the political power of the then ruling family. This date is reinforced in the Meiji era by the Imperial Edict of 1881. In reality, this dating is probably at least six centuries too early. According to the legend, Amaterasu Omikami, from whom the unbroken line of emperors descends, commands her grandson Ningi no Mikoto to rule over Japan and presents him with the Imperial Regalia—the sword, mirror, and sacred jewel. These ritual objects become part of the accession ceremony of each new emperor.   SHINTO, TOL

-660–
30 B.C.E.

According to the chronicle of ancient times, *Nihongi*, many shrines devoted to *kami*—spirits and divinities of natural places, forces of nature, and mythological deities—are established throughout Japan during the time of the legendary early emperors. The name *Shinto* (the way of the *kami*) will not be used until the sixth century C.E.   SHINTO

-640–
609 B.C.E.

Judah is ruled by Josiah. During his rule Judaism experiences a number of important developments, including a restructuring of the temple staff, official recognition of the celebration of Passover, the establishment of Jerusalem as the center of Jewish worship, and the linking of Jewish kingship to knowledge of Jewish law.   JUD

-600

The Romans begin building temples to their gods around the forum, the public square and marketplace in Rome. The first temple is devoted to Vesta, the goddess of the home.   CIVIL

-600

In northern India new Hindu sacred texts appear. These differ from older ones in that they emphasize introspection rather than the Vedic sacrifices.
                    HIND

-600–
300 B.C.E.

At the Zapotec Monte Albán ceremonial center in Oaxaca, Mexico, buildings are aligned with astronomical events such as solstices and equinoxes, indicating a belief that the human world and the natural world are interrelated and should be in harmony with one another.   NATIV

-500s

The first temples are built by the Greeks on the Acropolis in Athens. The temples are used to worship major Greek gods, including Athena, the goddess of Athens.   CIVIL

-500s

According to tradition, a meeting occurs between Laozi (Lao-tzu), original name Li Erh, deified as Lao-chun, T'ai-shang Lao-chun, also called Lao Tun or Lao Tan (500s B.C.E.), and Confucius (-551– 479 B.C.E.). Sources are inconsistent and contradictory. During the interview, Laozi accuses Confucius of pride and ambition, and Confucius, impressed, compares Laozi to a dragon that rises to the sky, borne on winds and clouds.   CONF, DAO

-500s

By tradition, the *Dao De Jing* (*The Classic of the Way and Its Power*) appears in China during the late Zhou dynasty. Often known as the *Laozi*, the name of its alleged author, the possibly legendary Laozi (the name means "old master"), this short work, which runs to around 5,000 Chinese characters, is regarded as the founding document of Daoism, the origin of what will become an organized religion with a 2,000-year tradition of ordained priests, a vast scriptural canon, a liturgy based on ritual texts, and distinctive techniques for achieving a transcendent immortality.   CONF, DAO

-595   The Great Sacred War takes place in Greece. It pits the Athenians against the Phocians as the Athenians seek to keep the oracle at Delphi, which is in Phocian territory, open to Athenians.   CIVIL

-587   The Babylonians under Nebuchadnezzar, King of Chaldea, conquer and destroy Judah and exile many of the people to Babylon. The Temple in Jerusalem is destroyed. During the Babylonian Captivity, which lasts until 529 B.C.E., the synagogue develops as a central place of worship, study, and assembly and remains so even after the Temple is rebuilt in Jerusalem. The Sabbath and ritual circumcision also develop during this period as Jewish customs.   JUD

Laozi

Little is known of the philosopher/recluse Laozi's life. He may have been an archivist and a soothsayer. Tradition has him contemporaneous with Confucius (-551–479 B.C.E.), though a little older. One legend has Confucius visiting him to ask him about rites (*li*). Another has Laozi leaving China for the West astride a purple buffalo. Some texts place the year of Laozi's birth as far back as 1331 B.C.E. In some legends he is born, returns to the womb, and is born again. He is said to have recited the *Scripture of the Three Terraces* from the womb. (Only a fragment of this text survives.) Modern scholars question whether Laozi existed and whether, if he actually lived, he wrote the work tradition credits to him. In any case, they fix the date of the *Dao De Jing* at two to three centuries later than Laozi's supposed life span and speculate that several scholars contributed to it.

Laozi's philosophical system, with its emphasis on personal spiritual freedom, is a contrast to and a chief rival of Confucianism. Next to Confucianism, Daoism is the most important and influential indigenous Chinese philosophy. In some ways the two are complementary, appealing as they do to two distinct aspects of Chinese character. Confucianism is solemn, responsible, mundane. Daoism is a flight from responsibility that offers a transcendental vision of worlds of the spirit. The *Dao De Jing* (otherwise known as the *Laozi*) proposes a philosophy and a way of life for China's ruling elite. The Way (*dao*), the source of all being and the regulator of all life, is passive; there is no conflict, no coercion, and actions are spontaneous and effortless. The sage understands the mystic principle of the Way and bends his life to it. In the *Dao De Jing*, Laozi instructs the ruler/sage to refrain from meddling in his subjects' lives, to avoid warfare, to forswear luxurious living, and to lead his people into a state of harmony with the Way. A wise ruler simply leaves things alone. The writings attributed to Laozi were witty, full of paradox, and so vague as to give rise to sometimes widely differing interpretations. The *Laozi* is said to have influenced even the 20th-century Communist Mao Zedong.

-586	Only after this year do ancient historians begin referring to the Jews. Before this year they were called Hebrews or Israelites. Thus, this year marks the emergence— at least in the eyes of others—of the Jews as a distinct religious group. **JUD**
-582	The Greeks begin organizing athletic games as part of festivals honoring their gods, including Zeus, Apollo, and Poseidon. The games are held every two or four years as part of large festivals. **CIVIL**
-563	According to most 20th-century scholars, this is the probable birth year of Siddhartha Gautama (-563–483 B.C.E.), eventually to be known as the Buddha ("the awakened one"); the traditional dates are -623–544 B.C.E. or 543 B.C.E. (Another, "short chronology," prefers the dates -445–365 B.C.E.) **BUDD**
-551– 479 B.C.E.	This is the lifespan of Confucius, a Latinized form of Chinese (Wade-Giles) K'ung-Fu-Tzu, or K'ung-Tzu, or (Pinyin) Kongfuzi, or Kongzi, or Kong Qiu, "the Master Kong," originally named K'ung Ch'iu, with the literary name Chung-Ni. A sage of ancient China, he is its most revered philosopher and political theorist. He is born in Qufu (Ch'u-fu or Ku-fow) in the duchy of Lu, which will later become Shantung Province. The tradi-

Confucius

Confucius is the Latinized version of K'ung-Fu-Tzu, or K'ung-Tzu, or (Pinyin) Kongfuzi, or Kongzi, or Kong Qiu, "the Master Kong," the name of China's most revered philosopher. The name Confucius was used by Jesuit priests in the 16th century and has been used in the West ever since, but not in China. In China Confucius is revered as a great sage and teacher. As with many early religious leaders whose biographies were written by followers centuries later, very little about his life is known with any certainty. Much of what is known about him comes from the *Analects*, compiled and written by his followers many years after his death. What seems most likely is that he was born in 551 B.C.E. in Qufu, Lu (the modern province of Shandong), to a family that had fallen from the aristocracy, was orphaned while quite young, and grew up in poverty. He received no formal education but was self-taught and earned a living as a tutor to the sons of the wealthy. He also spent some time employed as a low-level civil servant. At the age of 56, he began a period of travel in which he offered advice to local rulers in an effort to end the hostility between various states as the Zhou declined. The rulers ignored him but he attracted followers estimated at as many as 3,000 but more likely numbering only 72. They continued to discuss his ideas about creating a better, more just society after his death in 479 B.C.E. and eventually recorded them in the *Analects* as a series of dialogues between Confucius and his followers. Throughout his life Confucius saw himself as a teacher, and once his ideas took root in Chinese society several hundred years after his death, he became renowned as the model teacher and a sage. Although there were efforts among some later followers to deify him, he is not considered a god nor a supernatural figure in China.

tional claim that he is born on the 27th day of the eighth lunar month is questioned by historians, but to the end of the 20th century September 28 is still widely observed as his birthday. He focuses his teaching on virtue and finds models of inspiration in legendary sage-kings who ruled by moral suasion rather than might. He is said to attract 3,000 students, of whom 72 are close disciples. His philosophy becomes the traditional sub-

Buddha

The term *buddha* can be used in three ways in Buddhism. First, it is a generic term that can be used in reference to any individual who is enlightened and has found the path to truth, the goal of Buddhist belief and practice. Second, *Buddha* (with a capital *B*) is used as the title for specific personages who are fully enlightened and in the absence of the Truth are able to rediscover the path to it. Third, *Buddha* is used to refer to Gautama (Gotoma), the founder of Buddhism in its current forms. However, in Buddhist belief, he is not the only Buddha; in Theravada Buddhism there are six Buddhas who preceded him (with more to follow) and in Mahayana Buddhism there are numerous other individuals referred to as Buddha. Little is actually known of the life of Gautama. Depending on the chronology followed, he lived either from about -566 to 486 B.C.E. (Long Chronology) or -448 to 368 B.C.E. (Short Chronology) and was born in what is now southern Nepal.

In a common version of his story, Buddha was born Siddhartha into a wealthy, aristocratic family of the *kshatriya* clan (a caste of warriors) known as the Sakyas; his birth village, Lumbini, later became part of southern Nepal. His father was Suddhodana, and his mother was Maya. Siddhartha means "he who has accomplished his aim"; Gautama (Gotama) is the family name. He was raised within the Brahmanic faith, married the Princess Yasodhara, and had a son, Rahula. Throughout Buddha's youth he was literally isolated from the world's problems and the sufferings of others, but when he was 29 the gods conspired to expose him to the "four great visions" (an old person, a diseased person, a corpse, and then a serene, mendicant holy man). Buddha fled from his family, cut off his hair, exchanged his fine clothing for rags (the "Great Renunciation"), and adopted the wandering life to seek the truth and salvation. He studied meditation under two teachers, then adopted the life of the extreme ascetics; he eventually rejected such conduct and adopted a more moderate "middle path." At age 35 he achieved true enlightenment while sitting under an Indian fig tree at Bodh Gaya, near Patna in the state of Bihar in northeastern India; this tree was hereafter known as the Bodhi ("awakening") Tree. From that time on he lived as an itinerant preacher, wandering around northern India, gaining converts to his way of life and his views; his followers eventually formed the first Sangha ("community"), an order of monks and nuns. At the age of 80, he died at Kusinara, thereby attaining *nirvana*, or cessation of suffering and rebirth. His body was cremated (although his bones survived and became sacred relics among Buddhists.) The survival of the sect was problematic, as Gautama left no written teachings, but he did leave behind five disciples and many monks, nuns, and lay believers.

stance of learning, source of values, and social code of the Chinese people for over 2,000 years. It affects the daily life and culture of Daoists, Buddhists, and Christians, and its influence extends to Korea, Japan, and the West. **CONF, TOL**

-550 In Greece cremation, which has replaced burial as the primary means of disposing of the dead, is now replaced by burial or burial/cremation with the bodies cremated inside graves. **CIVIL**

-550 Divisions emerge in India as new sects begin to appear in opposition to the priests (Brahmans) in Hinduism. The two most succesful splinters are those led by Siddhartha Gautama (c. -563–c. 483 B.C.E.), which becomes Buddhism and Nataputta Vardhamana (c. -599–527 B.C.E.), which becomes Jainism. **HIND**

-550–
330 B.C.E. The Persian Empire, which spreads from Greece to Egypt and east to North India, is ruled by the Achaemenid dynasty. In the 20th century some scholars believe that the rulers of the dynasty adopted Zoroastrianism as the state religion. Others argue that only some rulers such as Darius (-522–486 B.C.E.) did so, and still others believe that Zoroastrianism remained a minority religion, while the official religion resembled the Vedic religion of northern India. **SECT**

-540–
468 B.C.E. This is the lifespan of Vardhamana Mahavira, according to modern historians. (His traditional dates are -599–527 B.C.E., and these are still preferred by followers of Jainism.) He is recognized as the 24th and final Jain. **JAIN**

-539–
322 B.C.E. The Babylonians are defeated by the Persians and under the rule of Cyrus II the Jews are allowed to return to Palestine. In 538 B.C.E. they rebuild the Temple in Jerusalem. Under Persian rule they enjoy considerable political and religious freedom and Jews serve in high government offices. They are taxed heavily to support the Persian Empire. **JUD**

-538–
70 C.E. The Second Temple period in Jewish history begins with building of the Second Temple in Jerusalem and ends with its destruction in 70 C.E. **JUD**

-520–
512 B.C.E. Confucius begins a brilliant teaching career based on his mastery of the six arts and the classical traditions, particularly poetry and history. He devotes his life to learning and teaching in order to transform and improve society through not only the transmission of knowledge but also the building of character. He seeks to make education available to all and to establish teaching as a vocation. **CONF**

-512 According to tradition, this is the year when Sun Tzu Wu leads an army of Ho Lu (r. -514–496 B.C.E.), king of Wu in China, and using the principles he has set forth in his *Art of War* defeats a much larger force. Although not directly linked to Daoism in any specific way, the *Art of War* is adopted by

Daoists in later centuries as a text consistent with certain basic elements of Daoism. It stresses rational deliberation and planning in all aspects of warfare and in particular stresses the importance of rapid and decisive action. Little solid evidence exists to establish the facts about Sun Tzu Wu, but he is alleged to have lived during this time and to have written the basic 13 chapters of this classic Chinese text.   **DAO, TOL**

-510–
498 B.C.E.

At the age of 30, and being of a reflective mind, Mahavira, the founder of Jainism, leaves his family and relatives and retires to the solitude of the forest at the edge of his town. There he begins to mediate on the misery that fills the lives of most people on earth and he seeks to find some means of permanent release from the eternal and inevitable passions and suffering. He knows the traditional ways of the Vedas and the Hindu rituals of sacrifice that promise release from *karma* but is unsatisfied with these. He has already given away all his wealth and now he discards all his clothing and wanders about naked. During this time people call him Sramana—"the ascetic." **JAIN**

Mahavira

In Jainism Mahavira is considered to be the 24th and final *tirthankara* (person who has crossed the river of life and reached a higher state) of this cycle of time. As the final *tirthankara* he also considered to be the founder of Jainism. His role in this regard is suggested by his original name Vardhamana, meaning "bringer of prosperity." Many years later his followers will call him Mahavira, meaning "great hero." He was born into the family of a ruling chief of the Naya, or Natri, a clan of the *kshatriya* (the princely or warrior caste in Hinduism). In early Buddhist texts he is called *Nigantha Nataputta*, meaning "the naked ascetic of the clan of the jnatrikas." (Although Mahavira and his followers are mentioned in Buddhist texts, early Jain texts do not refer to Buddha or Buddhists.) His father was Siddhartha. His mother was Trishala, sister of Chetaka, chief of the larger kindred tribe of the Licchavis. (In some accounts his parents are said to have been followers of the teachings of Parsvanatha.) Both tribes lived around the city of Vaishali (about 27 miles north of Patna in the modern state of Bihar); hence Mahavira is sometimes called Vaishalika. As the son of a clan chieftain and a member of the warrior caste (*kshatriya*), Mahavira was raised in the Hindu-Vedic religion. The Digambara sect of Jains claims he never married but remained celibate throughout his life. The Svetambara sect of Jains claims he married Yasoda, daughter of King Samaravira, had a daughter, and lived with them for some years; in this account, his son-in-law and nephew Jamali later left Mahavira's order to found a new sect known as Bahurata. Among other special characteristics, Mahavira's speech is said to have been intelligible to all living creatures—including all animals, even the lowliest. During his wanderings he attracted both monks and lay followers to his teachings. At his death some accounts claim his followers numbered some 50,000 monks and nuns and 480,000 lay followers.

-509 –31 B.C.E.	During the period of the Roman Republic, cremation is the primary means of disposing of the dead, with the wealthy burying the ashes of their ancestors in family burial plots. The plots are marked by gravestones. **CIVIL**
-508– 503 B.C.E.	Confucius serves as magistrate, then assistant minister of public works, then minister of justice in the state of Lu, China. **CONF**
-500	The Eleusinian Mysteries are a popular cult in Greece. Cult members worship Demeter, the goddess of fertility and harvest. Such worship, conducted in secret in temples at night, is meant to ensure prosperity on earth and happiness in the afterlife. **CIVIL**
-500	In China the *Zhouyi* (*Changes of Zhou*), which has been codified since about 1000 B.C.E. by diviners serving the royal court of the Zhou dynasty (and the core text of which will become known as the *I Ching* or *Yijing*), is first written down. For several hundred years after that, there will be commentaries and additions until about 100 B.C.E. **DAO**

Jainism

Jainism is a southern Asian religion that emerged in northern India in the sixth century B.C.E. as an alternative to Hinduism and then to Buddhism. Jainism takes it name from the word *jina* which means "conqueror" and refers to the need of individuals to conquer their own desires and wishes. Jainism is based on ethical and moral principles and requires much personal sacrifice on the part of the adherent. For the most devout this involves ascetic behavior, and Jainism is the oldest ascetic religion in the world.

Jainism was founded by the ascetic Mahavira, who lived in the sixth century B.C.E. and is considered by Jains to be the 24th and final *tirthankara* (person who has crossed the river of life and reached a higher state) of this cycle of time. In the third century B.C.E., the Jain community in India divided into two groups over differences in doctrine and practice. The Svetambaras are dominant in northern India and the Digambaras in southern India. Jains believe that all living things have immortal souls that can be liberated through correct religious belief and behavior, including not killing any living thing; avoiding immoral behaviors, such as lying, being angry, stealing; renouncing sexual pleasure; and avoiding relationships that involve intense emotional attachments. While the most devout seek to achieve these goals through ascetic behaviors, such as going naked, avoiding many foods, filtering water, and being celibate, the acceptable code of conduct for most Jains is more relaxed and stresses generosity, meditation, a period of monkhood, periods of self-denial, and causing no harm to others. There are about five million Jains, with nearly all in India save for about 25,000 each in Great Britain and the United States. In India they form a distinct religious minority, although some Jains also practice Hinduism and identify themselves as both Jains and Hindus. The Jain community is wealthy, with many Indian professionals and business leaders coming from this community.

-500   Reference to yoga as a method of achieving control of the mind first appears in Hinduism, in the Upanishads.   **HIND**

-500   In India the ritual sacrifices that are a major component of the Vedic religion dwindle in importance and through a process that lasts some 1,500 years, *bhakti* (devotion) as expressed through rituals meant for personal gods or goddesses becomes a core element of Hinduism.   **HIND**

-500   In the *Svetashvatara Upanishad* Hindu religious text, the god Shiva is marked for the first time as the supreme god. This marks the emergence of Shaivism, a Hindu sect devoted to the worship of Shiva. It is possible that the belief in Shiva as a supreme god dates to earlier times.   **HIND**

-500   Vedic society in northern India has become more complex: people are now tied to occupational groups that are ordered by rank based on degree of

Ancient Roman Religion

It is impossible to describe ancient Rome as having a single, unified religion, since the religions of the Roman Republic (-509–31 B.C.E.) and the Roman Empire (31 B.C.E. –476 C.E.) changed as new beliefs and practices were taken from conquered peoples and also because the expanse of lands under Roman rule meant that people in wide-ranging places practiced differing religions. In the early years of the Republic, Roman religion was heavily animistic as Romans believed that living things and natural places were imbued with supernatural spirits that could influence human affairs. Therefore, much effort was given to the performance of rituals that would please these spirits so they would cause no harm. As the Romans adopted gods from conquered peoples such as the Etruscans and the Greeks, these spirits diminished in importance and a pantheon of gods emerged who were worshiped in order to win their support in important matters like marriage, war, or long journeys. In addition, many local and family gods were worshiped as well. By the 200s B.C.E. the Greek gods became prominent and eventually the pantheon of the 12 major gods was taken over by the Romans, as were gods also borrowed from Egypt and Persia. The appearance of Christianity complicated the situation as Christians now competed with non-Christians (called *pagans* by Christians) for religious dominance in the Roman Empire. At times Christianity was accepted, repressed, or merely tolerated by the rulers, but until the early fifth century C.E., paganism and Christianity existed together. The pagan religion centered on communication with the gods through oracles, divination, and especially animal sacrifice. In ancient Rome religion was a political matter. The rulers closely controlled religious belief, consulted oracles for advice, and were served by priests during the Republic. With the appearance of the Empire in 31 B.C.E., emperor worship began, with the emperor considered a god. With the official acceptance of Christianity in the fourth century, paganism declined and emperor worship disappeared and what had been the Roman world became largely Christian, although some pagan practices survived and were merged with Christianity.

ritual purity. This structure marks the emergence of the Hindu caste system.

HIND

-500   By this time the Babylonians have developed a list of constellations, an 18-group zodiac, and lunar mansions, all of which are later used by the Greeks in the development of astrology.

SPIR

-500–
300 B.C.E.   The *Ramayana*, the Hindu epic poem written in Sanskrit, is composed in India. It is also called the *Valmiki-Ramayana* to distinguish from later versions, which are written in other Indian languages. It contains about 24,000 verses in seven volumes and is a popular text in India. It also influences lit-

---

Caste

Caste is the name given to a particular form of social organization found among Hindus in India. Caste is often discussed in comparison to the social class organization found in Western societies, with class considered to be less rigid, less formal, and more amenable to change. In the Hindu caste system, a person is born into a social category and remains in it for life. People marry within their own caste, derive their status from the relative status of their caste, and work at the occupation traditionally held by members of their caste. There are two major, interrelated caste systems in Hindu India. The first, called the *varna* system, divides Hindu society into five social categories: Brahman, who traditionally were priests and now are often professionals, government officials, and landowners; Kshatriya, who were traditionally warriors and now are often professionals and landowners; Vaisya, who were traditionally and are still farmers, traders, and merchants; Sudra, who were and remain mainly farmers; and Untouchables, who are outside the caste system and perform work that is considered ritually polluting by Hindus, such as working with leather. The second caste system is called the *jati* system and refers to the thousands of occupational working-class castes, such as carpenters, barbers, traders, and priests found across Hindu India. The *jati* system is especially significant in rural India, where people are born into their *jati* and marry others from the same *jati*. In Indian cities and for Hindus outside India, the caste systems are less important. Caste is closely linked to Hindu beliefs and practices. Every individual's caste position is determined by his or her *karma* and *dharma*. *Karma* is one's behavior in a previous life and it determines one's current caste position. *Dharma* is one's behavior in his or her current life and it determines caste in the next life. Thus, in accord with the cyclical Hindu view of time and belief in reincarnation, every Hindu's caste position and therefore status can change over time. The caste hierarchy and relations between castes are governed by Hindu notions of ritual purity and pollution. The higher the caste, the purer it is thought to be and the less contact is allowed with members of lower castes who are considered to be ritually polluting. "Purer" activities include praying in Sanskrit, using the services of Brahman priests, and consuming a vegetarian diet. While individuals cannot "become purer" during their current life, occupational castes can change their group status by switching to less polluting occupations or by emulating the ritual behavior of higher castes.

erary forms and provides the basis for epics in Thailand, Java, Malaysia, Vietnam, Laos, and Cambodia.   **HIND**

-400s   The worship of the goddess Cybele spreads from Asia Minor to Greece, where she is named Meter Oreia and then by the 200s B.C.E. to Rome and then to North Africa. Associated with fertility, she is considered the mother of the gods.   **CIVIL**

-400s   The Acropolis in Athens, which was destroyed by the Persians in 480 B.C.E., is rebuilt during the rule of Pericles. It contains temples to Greek gods, including the Parthenon with its stature of Athena, the goddess of Athens. Also built on the Acropolis is the Theater of Dionysus, which seats 15,000 people who attend plays that are staged as part of religious festivals honoring the gods.   **CIVIL**

-400s–
300s B.C.E.   This is the probable date of settlement by Dravidian-speaking people from Kerala, south India; they introduce Buddhism, which is well established there by the fourth century C.E.   **BUDD**

-400s–
300s B.C.E.   The followers of Confucius split into eight schools shortly after his death, according to Han Fei-tzu (d. 233 B.C.E.). The second generation of Confucius's students includes Yen Yuan, Tseng-tzu, Tzu Kung, and Tzu-hsia.

Astrology

Astrology is a belief system in which people seek to predict events or states on earth through analysis of the position and movement of the stars and planets. (So defined, astrology is a sophisticated form of divination.) The prediction of events based on the position, alignment, and appearance of heavenly bodies is a common feature of many religions, although such practices do not constitute astrology, as they do not form unified systems of belief. However, it is likely that modern astrology, which emerged in the centuries before and following the birth of Christ in the Greek Near East and Egypt, is based to some extent on such practices in Mesopotamia and perhaps Egypt as well. Although some modern astrologers point to ancient Egypt as a major source of astrology, there is actually little evidence to support this assumption. It is far more likely that modern astrology was developed by Greeks in Egypt and that both modern Western and Indian astrology reflect Greek influences. Astrology is condemned in Judaism, Christianity, Islam, Sikhism, and some schools of Buddhism. It is more widely tolerated in Hinduism. Its condemnation by many religious leaders led to its disappearance—at least from public view—from about the fifth century C.E. until a revival occurred as part of the emergence of spiritualism in the late 19th century in Europe and the United States. It has remained popular ever since, although few now view it as a system of religious belief. There are now dozens of astrological systems used to predict one's life course, gain information about specific events, answer specific questions, locate buildings, provide advice, and even help people with personal problems.

They generate enthusiasm, but the attempt to moralize politics is not successful. **CONF, TOL**

-498–
468 B.C.E.

At the age of 42, after 12 years of meditation and hardships, Mahavira, the founder of Jainism, feels that he has attained his own personal enlightenment and become a "completed soul" (*kevalin*) and a *jina*, a "victor" in the spiritual sense. He now spends 30 years wandering through much of northern India. (Jains believe these years to be -557–527 B.C.E.) **JAIN**

-495

Confucius realizes that his superiors are not interested in his moral rectitude and goes into voluntary exile with an expanding circle of students for 12 years. **CONF**

Confucianism

Confucianism is a system of ethical and moral thought that developed in China beginning about 500 B.C.E. Experts do not agree on whether Confucianism is a religion, a philosophy, or some combination of both. There is no doubt that Confucius, the ancient Chinese scholar who organized the ideas and texts that became Confucianism, was a follower of the spirit and ancestor worship of his time and that he also saw a supernatural force called heaven as the inspiration of his work. In addition, Confucius was a codifier of numerous rules of behavior governing both ritual and temporal matters. On the other hand, Confucianism seems more like a philosophical system because of its emphasis on ethics, morality, proper behavior, and making the world a more peaceful place and because it differs from many other major religions in offering neither a clear vision of God nor a revealed doctrine. Although it came to be used as a political and social ideology first in China and then in Korea, Vietnam, and Japan, Confucianism is a moral ideology that stresses the need for the "good" person and the "good" government. Developed by Confucius at a time of political turmoil in China, it was meant as a set of guiding principles for maintaining order in society. Thus, it set forth principles and rules to establish and maintain harmonious social relations and a moral order, to control self-interest, to provide education for all, to encourage the government to be generous to the people, and to develop citizens who were just, moral, loyal, brave, and trustworthy. Although repressed and in competition at times with Daoism and Buddhism, Confucianism and later neo-Confucianism served as a basic organizing principle of Chinese society for nearly 2,000 years. Because the basic texts (the *Five Classics* and later the *Four Books*) served as the basis for the government civil service test until the test was eliminated in 1905, Confucianism had a major effect on government. It also, through the model of Confucius as a great teacher, had a major effect on teaching in China. In the 20th century Confucianism was repressed in China and was criticized by the Communist government as a conservative ideology that interferes with progress.

-484   Confucius is welcomed back to Lu, the state of his birth, by the reigning prince. He spends his remaining years editing classical texts and teaching.

CONF

-484   Makkhali Gosala dies. He begins as an associate of Mahavira but breaks off to found the Ajivika sect, a rival to Jainism and Buddhism based on strict determinism and extreme self-mortification. The sect flourishes in Gujarat (now central Pakistan) c. -300–100 B.C.E. under patronage of the Mauryan dynasty. **JAIN**

-483   Tradition claims that the First Buddhist Council is held at Rajagraha (in the modern state of Bihar, India) immediately after Buddha's death to recite his teachings in order to guarantee accurate oral transmission of doctrine. According to another tradition, two of the major parts of the *Tripitaka* (three baskets), the oldest Buddhist scriptural canon, are standardized; these are the *Sutra* and the *Vinaya*, the former being the sermons or discourses of Buddha, the latter being the rules for monks and nuns. (The third part is the *Abhidharma*; it contains philosophical and psychological texts that are considered extremely complex; although attributed to the Buddha, these writings were actually penned by later Buddhist scholars according to modern historians.) In other versions these teachings are written down in the Pali language about 400 B.C.E.; in fact, the *Tripitaka* is first recorded in Sri Lanka in the first century C.E. **BUDD**

-483   A Sri Lankan tradition claims that, on the very day the Buddha attains nirvana, Prince Vijaya arrives on Sri Lanka at the head of a group of Indo-Europeans and introduces their culture, including Buddhism, to the aborigines on the island. **BUDD**

-480   The Persians invade Greece and destroy the buildings on the Acropolis in Athens, including the temples of the Greek gods. **CIVIL**

-479   Confucius dies largely unknown; his ideas are spread by his followers, said to number 3,000, the most influential of whom were Mencius (-390–305 B.C.E.) and Xunzi (third century B.C.E). A temple dedicated to Confucius will eventually be found in every one of China's 2,000 counties. **CONF**

-475   By tradition, "Immortals" in the east China states of Yan and Qi are granted longevity by the taking of certain drugs. Many of them will enter the Daoist hagiographies. **DAO**

-475–
221 B.C.E.   During this time known to historians of China as the period of Warring States, the preaching of Mencius and other Confucians to princes concerning virtuous personal conduct and humane government are largely ignored. **CONF, TOL**

-468   At age 72 Mahavira reaches his final liberation, or *nirvana*, at Pava-puri in modern Bihar (Pava-puri will become a place of pilgrimage for Jains, with temples and a resting house for pilgrims. The day of his *nirvana* will become a major feast—it comes early in the Indian winter.) The main temple at Pava-puri contains the sacred footmarks of Mahavira. **JAIN**

-468–
404 B.C.E.

During his lifetime Mahavira had 11 main disciples known as *ganadharas* ("supporters of the communities," in reference to the groups of believers they attract), all of whom have memorized his sacred teachings; nine pre-deceased Mahavira. In the years following his death, Jainism does not flourish, but it is kept alive by two of Mahavira's disciples, Indrabhuti (Gautama) and Sudharman. (In the main temple at Pava-puri, side niches contain the sacred footmarks of Indrabhuti and Sudharman.) Sudharman is regarded as head of the church and spiritual father of all Jain monks since. At his death he turns over charge of the faith to Jambuswami. Jambuswami attains *nirvana* 64 years after the *nirvana* of Mahavira. **JAIN**

-468–
376 B.C.E.

This is the lifespan of Mozi, philosopher of the Warring States period and an early rival of Confucius. A "utilitarian" philosopher, he is interested in practical economic matters and is critical of extravagant funerals and other elaborate rituals. He advocates peaceful relations between competing Chinese states and decries war as wasteful. **CONF**

-450

The Torah is written in Hebrew and declared to be the full and final word of God by the prophets Ezra and Nehemiah in Jerusalem. From this point on Jewish theology and philosophy is concerned with interpreting and commenting on the Torah, as it cannot be added to or changed. **JUD**

-426–
423

The Greeks order all inhabitants of the island of Delos, a major religious center for 500 years, to leave the island so that it may be used solely as a place of worship. **CIVIL**

Hebrew Bible

The Hebrew Bible, or Jewish Bible, consists of 24 books categorized into three groupings. The Pentateuch, or Torah, consists of the Books of Genesis, Exodus, Leviticus, Numbers, and Deuteronomy. For Jews this is the most sacred section of the Bible and the only section that is considered to be of divine origin. It is also called the Five Books of Moses. During the Jewish year the five books are read in their entirety, with passages read each week during synagogue services. It is a great honor in Judaism to be asked to read from the Torah and also an honor to be asked to recite the prayers that precede and follow each Torah reading. Reading the Torah is accompanied by much ritual, and strict rules govern the copying of the Torah, which must be done on parchment by trained scribes. The second section is the Prophets, which covers the Former, Latter, and Twelve prophets in eight books. The third section is the Writings, consisting of the books of Psalms, Proverbs, Job, Song of Songs, Ruth, Lamentations, Ecclesiastes, Esther, Daniel, Ezra-Nehemiah, and Chronicles. Christians refer to the Hebrew Bible as the Old Testament.

**-404–
300 B.C.E.**

During these years, five *kevalins* (completed souls)—Vishnu-nandin, Nandi-mitra, Aparajita, Go-vardhana, and Bhadra-bahu—are credited with carrying on the tradition of Mahavira's Jainism. But even during his lifetime, there are those who differ from Mahavira and who split off to establish separate schools. Of seven principal ones, known as Nihnavas, two are founded during his lifetime (one by Jamali, Mahavira's son-in-law and nephew), and the other five break away in later centuries. In later centuries numerous schools and orders of Jains come into existence. The two main sects will be known as the Svetambaras and Digambaras **(SEE 79, JAIN)**. These two sects in turn later divide into hundreds of orders and suborders. They disagree over matters of doctrine, practice, and interpretation, but many simply become followers of a particular teacher/monk—hardly different from students of a particular professor or devotees of a particular priest. **JAIN**

**-403–
221 B.C.E.**

During this era in China, known as the Warring States period, seven major rivals vie for supremacy. One state, Qin, emerges as the most powerful and defeats the others one by one. The first emperor of the Qin dynasty in China will show a great interest in Daoism. **DAO**

-400

Celtic peoples in Europe are wearing the torc, a circular band of metal worn as a bracelet amulet. Pagan people living on the island of Gotland off the coast of Sweden begin erecting large memorial stones that become more elaborate with symbolic carvings over the next 1,000 years. **MISC**

-400

In Babylon a system of proto-astrology has emerged, with the position of the stars and planets seen as omens of events on earth. The system is taken up by the Greeks at about this time and is first mentioned by the Greek physician Hippocrates in his book *On Diets*. At this time, astronomy and astrology are not distinguished from one another and both are called "astrologia." **SPIR**

**-400–
400 C.E.**

The *Mahabharata*, the Hindu epic of war written in Sanskrit, is composed in India. In its finished form it contains over 100,000 verses in 18 volumes and is a rich source of information on Vedic culture and religion. Although it does not have the same sacred status of earlier texts, it enjoys great popularity in Hinduism and functions as a basic guide to Hinduism. Contained in the sixth book is the Bhagavad Gita, a dialogue between the god Krishna and the warrior Arjuna. This passage is one of the most important in all Hindu texts and has been subject to interpretation by writers and philosophers ever since. **HIND**

**-400–
300 B.C.E.**

In Japan during the initial Yayoi period, the introduction of rice paddy cultivation in northwest Kyushu leads to new seasonal traditions, including agricultural festivals and the adoption of deities from mainland Asia by way of the Korean peninsula. **SHINTO**

-400– -200	The *Midrash*, a method of studying the Torah to interpret legal points and lessons for life, is begun by Jewish scholars. During this period there are many interpretations of the Torah required by new and changing conditions of Jewish life during the period of Greek rule. JUD
-400– 250 C.E.	With the spread of rice agriculture during Japan's Yayoi period, a wide range of artifacts indicates the increasing complexity of religious life. Archaeologists have found wooden anthropomorphic statuettes, cups and jars for food offerings, oracular bones, and burial sites, which have yielded relics, such as metal weapons and mirrors. All these suggest institutionalized shamanism, fertility rites, agricultural festivals, and offerings of food to divinities, still a feature of Shinto. SHINTO, TOL
-300s	Tradition claims that the *Khandhaka* is written down, regulating the fundamental institutions of Buddhist monastic life (such as admission to the order, clothing, food and drugs for the sick, and so on). BUDD
-300s	Rulers of the state of Yan in China dispatch expeditions to search for the "isles of immortality." They are in quest of the Daoist aim of longevity. DAO
-300s	The century sees the probable first appearance, in east coastal China, of the Huang Lao philosophical-political movement, out of which first philosophical and later religious-messianic forms of Daoism will develop. DAO
-383	(Some claim 373 B.C.E or 350 B.C.E.) This is the traditional date for the Second Buddhist Council, which meets at Vaishali, India, amid deepening rifts over lack of discipline by many monks. Some claim that as many as 10,000 monks, led by the monk Mahadeva, split off to form a separate sect, the *Mahasanghika* ("majority group") Buddhists; they will later be seen as the forerunners of one of the two major divisions of Buddhists, the Mahayana ("great vehicle") Buddhists (SEE -100–150 C.E., BUDD). Those who claim to be holding fast to the true teachings of the Buddha are known as the Sthaviras or Theras (elders), and they are regarded as the founders of Theravada Buddhism. Theravada, meaning "way of the elders," will remain the core of the other of the two major divisions of Buddhism; later it will become widely known as Hinayana, "small vehicle," Buddhism, but this is a somewhat demeaning term; a more acceptable alternative name is Nikaya Buddhism, although in its fullest sense this term also includes schools related to Theravada Buddhism that have died out over the centuries. BUDD
-370– 300 B.C.E.	This is the lifespan of Mencius (Mengzi or Meng-tzu, original name Meng K'o, posthumous name Tsou Kung or Duke of Tsou), the "Second Sage" of the Confucian heritage. He is born in the ancient state of Tsou, China. His mentor is a pupil of Tzu Su, the grandson of Confucius. As counsel to various princes, he holds to the intrinsic goodness of human nature and the value of kingly government based on moral virtue. He performs as social critic, moral philosopher, and courageous political activist, becoming a champion of the common people and an advocate of democratic principles

in government. He also argues that cultivating scholar-officials not directly involved in agriculture, industry, or commerce is vital to the state. His basic text is known only by his name, the *Mencius*, and like Confucius's *Analects* is a record of the philosopher's conversations. In later years Mencius comes to be revered as the cofounder of Confucianism, second only to Confucius himself. **CONF, TOL**

-360   This is the approximate peak time of Gongsun Yang (Lord Shang), the traditional author of one of the two surviving treatises of the Legalist school of government. In legalism the government punishes and rewards, in contrast to the Confucian emphasis on ritual and the virtue of rulers. **CONF**

-350   An important collection of Buddhist discourses attributed to Buddha himself but probably not written down until about this time is the *Digha Nikaya* ("long group" of discourses). In these, reference is made to six unorthodox teachers of the time around Buddha. One among them is referred to as Nigantha Nataputta; this is Vardhamana Mahavira, the leader of the Jains. From this and other references to Nataputta in Buddhist scripture, it is clear that the Buddhists regard Jainism as only one of several competing belief

---

Theravada and Mahayana Buddhism

Theravada and Mahayana Buddhism are the two major traditions within Buddhism. Theravada means "way of the elders" and refers to the more traditional focus of the tradition. Theravada is also called the "Small Vehicle" by Mahayana Buddhists, who call their own tradition the "Great Vehicle." These labels are rejected by Theravada Buddhists as insulting to their tradition. Mahayana Buddhism developed in northwest and southern India and was probably influenced to some extent by these regions' contacts with foreigners. The early Mahayana Buddhists created their own texts, which they claim to be the words of the Buddha himself. One major distinction between the two schools is that the Mahayana Buddhists stress the role of *Bodhisattvas*, or enlightened beings, individuals who strive to become Buddhas; Mahayana Buddhists see Gautama Buddha as simply one earthly manifestation of a cosmic Buddha essence, and people are encouraged to believe they can attain salvation by faith in an individual *Bodhisattva*. Eventually, Mahayana Buddhists came to treat the Buddha and *Bodhisattvas* as deities while Theravada Buddhists considered Buddha to be a man who showed other humans the route to salvation. Gradually, two main philosophical branches of Mahayana Buddhism emerged: the *madhyamaka* (dialectical) and *vijnanavada* (consciousness) schools. In general, Mahayana Buddhism is more personal, more open to change, and more responsive to the laity, while Theravada Buddhism is more conservative and more rigid, with greater emphasis on the monastic life and monks as being the central figures in Buddhist communities. Although their doctrines differ in important ways and look to different canonical scriptures, the two schools coexist throughout Asia as broad and sometimes overlapping movements.

systems at that time—all sharing their rejection in various ways of the orthodox Vedic Brahmanic Hinduism. **JAIN, BUDD**

-350–
300 C.E.
The kingdom of Meroe is a regional power in Lower Nubia in northeastern Africa. The religion is a mix of elements from the ancient Egyptian religion to the north and from African religions to the east and south. At least in public manifestations of the religion, it closely resembles Egyptian religion with a divine kingship, worship of Egyptian gods, the building of grand temples, and burial of rulers in pyramids. **AFRICAN**

-333–
332 B.C.E.
The Greeks under Alexander the Great conquer Judea and other districts. Judeans are granted Greek citizenship and thrive. **JUD**

-330–
247 B.C.E.
The Persian Empire is conquered by the Greeks under Alexander the Great and ruled by his generals in the Seleucid dynasty. Although the Greeks adopt some aspects of Zoroastrianism, which may have been the Persian state religion, Zoroastrianism is repressed and the definitive copy of the *Avesta*, the Zoroastrian sacred text, destroyed. Zoroastrians refer to Alexander as Alexander the Accursed. **SECT**

Mencius

After Confucius himself, Mencius is considered to be the second most important Confucian scholar. Mencius is the English rendering of Men Gzi, which means Master Meng. Mencius was born in about 370 B.C.E. in Zhou, in the modern-day province of Shandong, China. He studied philosophy under the Zi Si, the grandson of Confucius. Like Confucius, Mencius spent much of his career traveling about China, offering advice to the rulers in an attempt to end the conflict of the Warring States period (-403–222 B.C.E.). Mencius argued for a return to the traditional way of life and looked to former rulers and the Confucian Classics as models of government and thought that could be used by the rulers of his time. He believed that a ruler should be just and moral, ruling for the benefit of the people rather than for his own personal gain. Further, he believed that the people had the right to revolt against a ruler who did not meet this standard. Mencius also believed that people were inherently good and that the role of society was to help people develop their full potential through education. Mencius's ideas were generally ignored by the rulers whom he counseled and also by other philosophers of his time and the following centuries. After his death, Mencius's thoughts were compiled by his students in the form of a series of dialogues. It is not clear if he actually wrote any of the material himself. His work did not become central to Confucianism until the Song dynasty when the great scholar Chu Hsi included *Mencius* (the name of his work) as one of the *Four Books* of the Confucian Classics. In 1315 the Mongol rulers of China added the book to requirements of the civil service exam, cementing its importance in Chinese society.

-326	Alexander the Great invades northern India (modern Pakistan) and encounters naked monks who are assumed by later historians to be Jains. One of these monks, Kalyana (Kalanos in Greek accounts), accompanies Alexander on his trip back; but when Kalyana becomes ill in Persia, he immolates himself. **JAIN**
-321– 297 B.C.E.	Chandragupta Maurya, founder of the Mauryan dynasty (c. -321– 184 B.C.E.) and the first great Indian empire, reigns. Based in the modern state of Bihar, the Mauryan Empire eventually extends its rule across much of India and into central Asia. Jain tradition maintains that Chandragupta is a patron of Jainism. The Digambara sect even claims that he ultimately renounces the throne and becomes a Jain monk, under the influence of the 11th in the succession of Ganadharas, Bhadrabahu. Some Jains, however, remain behind under the influence of another Ganadhara, Sthulabhadra; they will become the nucleus of the Svetambara sect of Jains **(SEE 79, JAIN)**. According to the Svetambara sect, Bhadrabahu goes to Nepal and there ends his days in solitude and fasting. **JAIN**
-320– 198 B.C.E.	Palestine is taken by Ptolemy and his successors in Egypt and then by the Seleucids from Babylonia. During this period Jewish dispersion continues and Jewish communities exist in major cities including Alexandria, Antioch, Damascus, and Ephesus. **JUD**
-310	The *Zhuangzi*, the second (along with the *Dao De Jing*, or *Laozi*: **(SEE 500s B.C.E., DAO)** of the two important early tracts of Daoism, circulates in China. Its author is the Late Zhou philosopher Zhuangzi (c. -369–286 B.C.E.), a contemporary of the Confucian successor Mencius (-372–289 B.C.E.). At one time, Zhuangzi served as a minor imperial official in what would

---

The *Zhuangzi*

The *Zhuangzi* is regarded as one of the great imaginative works of Chinese literature. It introduced what became such essential features of Daoism as inner cultivation and the quest for immortality. Unlike the *Laozi*, which recommends styles of behavior (gentleness, humility) for survival in the world, the *Zhuangzi* is indifferent to human relations and disdains conventional values. The author seeks to rise above the world, rather than reform it or even accept it as it is. (The philosopher Xunjing will attack *Zhuangzi*, saying the author was "so clouded over by heaven that he knew nothing of man.") The *Zhuangzi* argues, in opposition to Confucius, that efforts to improve the world are useless, even harmful. It offered spiritual freedom, the limitless possibilities of the Way, in contrast to the circumscribed potential of the material world. The *Zhuangzi* emphasized the Daoist affinity for confusion. "The sage," writes Zhuangzi (c. -369–286 B.C.E.), "steers by the torch of chaos and doubt." Neither founding Daoist text lays out a systematic and logical set of philosophical ideas. Thus, both the *Laozi* and the *Zhuangzi* allow for a broad range of commentary and interpretation.

become Henan province, but he retired early to private life. Little is known about him otherwise except that he lived the latter part of his life as a recluse. Recent scholarship suggests the *Zhuangzi* is a combination of the philosopher's own essays and those of some of his disciples. Zhuangzi wrote the first seven chapters of the work attributed to him. Chapters 8–10 and part of chapter 11 were added around 205 B.C.E. The other part of chapter 11 and chapters 12–14 and 33, date to the second century B.C.E. Chapters 28–31 appeared around 200 B.C.E. No dates have been assigned to the other chapters.   **CONF, DAO**

-310–
220 B.C.E.

This is the lifespan of Xun-zi (Hsun-tzu), original name Hsun K'uang, principal transmitter of Confucian scholarship. He is born in Chao, north central China. Like Mencius, the "Second Sage" of the Confucian heritage, he believes in humane government, social harmony, education, and the perfectibility of all people through self-cultivation. In contrast to Mencius, he claims that human nature is evil and needs ritual and authority for the well-being of society. Xun stresses the sublimation of individual instinctual demands for the public good. Rather than mere sayings or conversations, his 32-chapter work, the *Xunzi (Hsun-tzu),* is a milestone in Chinese philosophy, with well-organized essays characterized by sustained reasoning, detail, and clarity.   **CONF**

-300

This is the traditional date for the writing down of the *Dhammapada*, which contains teachings of the Buddha, recorded by his disciples. A popular and enormously influential text in Pali verse, it is a foundation text of Theravada Buddhism.   **BUDD**

-300

The Greeks begin worshiping the Egyptian goddess Isis, a major deity who is believed to be the mother of Horus, the Egyptian sun god. Many cults develop around Isis, and the Romans adopt her as a major deity as well, with many temples built in her honor.   **CIVIL**

-300

The Hindu codes of law, the *Dharma Sutras* and *Dharma Shastras,* are compiled. The laws explain and institutionalize the Hindu caste system in which people are born into specific occupational groups and must marry within that group and retain the group status for their current life.   **HIND**

-300–
250 B.C.E.

According to 20th-century scholars, the *Dao De Jing* is written in China. Two silk manuscripts of the work, one dating before 206 B.C.E. and the other between 206 B.C.E. and 194 B.C.E., will be excavated from a tomb in Hunan province in 1973.   **DAO**

-300–
200 B.C.E.

Like so much associated with the early centuries of Jainism, there is no certainty about exactly when its founder Mahavira's teachings are written down and systematized , but some scholars believe it may have begun during this century. In particular, Svetambara Jains date the initial 11 Angas religious texts to this period.   **JAIN**

-300–
150 B.C.E.

During these centuries Jainism is kept alive and propagated by a series of *ganadharas* (supporters of the communities). They are known as Dasa-Purvins, Ekadasa-Angins, Catur-Angins, and Eka-Angins.   JAIN

-200s

Buddhism, established in Kathmandu Valley, Nepal, introduces elements that become central to Nepalese culture, including architectural forms such as *stupas* (Buddhist domed temples), and such ideas as the king as upholder of cosmic law.   BUDD

-200s

Jainism is introduced to south India during this century. It will play a part in introducing northern Indian culture into the Deccan (south-central) and Tamil (southern) regions. Jainism flourishes in southern India until the 11th century, often with the support of regional kings. Probably during this century as well, the Jains begin to introduce images of their holy men—first figurines and statues, then paintings.   JAIN

-200s–
100s B.C.E.

Living in harmony with nature, a minor issue for Confucius, emerges as an important theme in Confucian thought.   CONF

-285–
246 B.C.E.

During the reign of Ptolemy II, it is believed that the *Septuagint*, the Greek language translation of the Torah, is written by Jewish scholars. The Greek version is revised numerous times over the next centuries and serves as the Bible for the Jews in Egypt and other areas where Greek is the primary language. It differs from the Hebrew version in various ways and is the version of the Bible used by the early Christians. The *Apocrypha*, which appear in the *Septuagint* but not in the Hebrew version, are accepted by Catholics but not by Jews and Protestants.   JUD

-280

Another sect of Buddhists led by a monk named Vatsiputriya breaks away from the Theravada Buddhists. They become known as Pudgalavadins, "those who affirm the person." They later become known as the Sammitiyas.) They argue that there is a "self" or personality, and although this is regarded as heretical by most Buddhists, some of their beliefs gradually become absorbed by Mahayana Buddhists.   BUDD

-270–
221 B.C.E.

During the time of Shih Huang Ti of the Ch'in dynasty, Confucian texts are ordered destroyed. However, a descendant of Confucius hides books in the walls of his house and later, during the Western Han dynasty (-202–9 B.C.E.), the books are recovered.   CONF

-269–
233 B.C.E.

India's Mauryan Emperor Ashoka reigns. He is said to have converted to Buddhism c. 260 B.C.E.; whether or not this is true, Buddhism is a pervasive influence on Ashoka's reign. While also supporting Jains and Ajivikas, he promulgates Buddhist teachings of righteousness, compassion, and reverence and makes the first recorded pilgrimage to Buddhist holy sites in about 249 B.C.E. His ethical teachings are carved on rocks, cave walls, and pillars. By this century Jainism is gaining in adherents throughout northern India;

most are of the *kshatriya* class merchants and landowners. Several orders of Jain monks also emerge.   **BUDD**

-250

A group of Buddhist monks in India breaks away from the Theravada School and forms the Sarvastivada school. Their differences involve interpretations of the early texts. In particular, the Sarvastivadins believe that certain texts were the work of disciples of Buddha, where the Theravadins believe that the Buddha himself wrote them. There are also complex philosophical disagreements over the reality of past, present, and future events. The Sarvastivada monks will eventually settle in Kashmir but they remain an important influence in Indian Buddhism for another 1,000 years. **BUDD**

-250

Tradition claims that Ashoka sends missions to the successors of Alexander the Great in central Asia, the Middle East, even northern Greece and North Africa, but there is no contemporary record of this. Buddhism does begin to spread across much of India and most likely into Indonesia; there is some evidence suggesting Buddhism has made its way into central Asia by 200 B.C.E. Sri Lankan and other Theravada Buddhists claim that about this time King Ashoka sponsors a Buddhist council, at Pataliputra; but it is not recognized by Mahayana Buddhists; such differences reflect the growing sectarianism among Buddhists.   **BUDD, TOL**

-250

This year marks the probable first appearance in China of the core of the *Guanzi*, a collection of essays dealing with political, social, and economic theory. Named for a model minister of the state of Qi in the 600s B.C.E., the *Guanzi* combines various strains of thought, such as Confucianism, Legalism, and Daoism. Among other matters, the work takes up *yin-yang* theory, military history, and Huang Lao philosophy. It is one of the oldest and most extensive of surviving pre-Han and early Han works.   **CONF, DAO**

-247–
227 C.E.

During the rule of Parthian dynasty in Persia, repression of Zoroastrianism ends and it draws more adherents, although it is not the majority religion nor the religion of the rulers. According to Zoroastrian tradition, during the reign of King Vologasses I (51–80 C.E.), the *Avesta* (sacred text) that was destroyed by Alexander the Great is reconstructed.   **SECT**

-240

India's Emperor Ashoka sends his son Mahinda, a Buddhist monk, to Sri Lanka where he converts the king, Tissa (r. -250–c. 207 B.C.E.), to Buddhism; Ashoka assigns Tissa the title Devanampiya, "dear to the gods." Another tradition claims that Ashoka's daughter, the Buddhist nun Sanghamitta, brings a cutting from the Bodhi tree under which the Buddha attained enlightenment; she plants this at the island's then capital, Anuradhapura. It is claimed that the tree still growing there in the 1990s is the original one, making it the oldest identifiable living organism on earth. In any case, it remains venerated by all Buddhists. (In the 1800s a cutting from this tree is planted at Bodhi Gaya, the site in India of the original tree, which had been cut down by Hindus c. 600 C.E.) The king founds a monastery at

Mahavihara ("great monastery"), and Theravada Buddhism becomes the state religion; royal patronage will embed it deeply in Sri Lankan culture, and Theravada Buddhism will eventually trace many of its roots to the texts found on Sri Lanka. **BUDD, TOL**

-240–
184 B.C.E.

Throughout the Mauryan Kingdom, Ashoka and later rulers erect thousands of *stupas* (mound-shaped religious structures), monasteries, and monumental freestanding stone pillars incised with lengthy Buddhist inscriptions, most erected along major trade and pilgrimage routes. The excavation of chambers in living rock to be used for meditation or religious retreat (such as the Barabar Caves, Bihar) begins a millennium-long Indian tradition. **BUDD**

-230

Xun-zi (Hsun-tzu), Confucian philosopher, dies in Lan-ling, Chu Kingdom. Surviving their author and his era, the Warring States period, a time of great instability, are his seminal works promoting ritual practices, *li*, as a culturally binding force to build the ideal society. Among other essays, his *Discussion of Music* reveals the importance of music as a vehicle for expressing emotions without generating interpersonal conflict. **CONF**

-221

With the defeat of the last of the rival Warring States, the state of Qin forcibly unifies China. Qin Shih Huang-ti—the "August Lord of Qin"—rules as the First Emperor. The rise of religious Daoism accompanies the establishment of the short-lived Qin dynasty (-221–206 B.C.E.). **DAO, TOL**

-221–
-206

The first Qin emperor imposes centralized bureaucratic rule in China and standardizes the law code for all the empire. Daoism becomes a major intellectual current in Qin China; Daoist thought deeply influences the First Emperor, who becomes a quasi-Daoist. The admixture of sorcery, shamanism, and philosophical Daoism centering on the search for an elixir of immortality particularly attracts him. Adherents of this Daoist cult believe that such an elixir can either be found or created. Those fortunate enough to quaff it will live as immortals on island-mountains at sea or atop mountains on land. **DAO, TOL**

-220–
211 B.C.E.

Contacts between Rome and Carthage in North Africa lead some Romans to adopt some Carthaginian religious beliefs, including the worship of the god Baal. **CIVIL**

-219

China's first Qin emperor tours Shandong in the northeast and leaves an inscription at Langye. It bears Legalist and Confucian sentiment, but also contains a strong Daoist allusion within these words: "He who embodies the Way (*dao*) and practices its power (*de*)." The emperor sends a magician and hundreds of followers in search of the island-mountains and the immortality plant, thought to be a mushroom, that is said to grow there. They never return; by tradition, the seekers settled in Japan. **CONF, DAO**

-219	China's Qin dynasty establishes an academy of 70 scholars expert in all important areas of knowledge, including Daoist arcana. **DAO**
-215	China's first Qin emperor, on his third trip to China's coast, sends another party of magicians in search of the elixir. Like the first expedition, it fails in its quest. **DAO**
-213	Shih Huang-ti, the First Emperor of Qin China, orders his chief minister to carry out a widespread "Burning of the Books," including the archives of vanquished rival Warring States. The motive is to enforce a monopoly of learning for the imperial Chinese court; surviving material is available only to court academicians. **CONF, DAO**
-210	The Qin First Emperor dies at age 49 while on a trip to eastern China, supposedly to seek an elixir of immortality from Daoist magicians, bringing his 37-year reign to a close. Many of his concubines and those who had worked on his tomb are buried with him in what is said to be one of the last recorded instances of human sacrifice in China. Also buried are 7,500 terra-cotta soldiers. Ancient historians will portray the Daoist First Emperor as something of a barbarian, ruthless and crude, and will not be kind to his memory. **DAO, TOL**
-206	Four years of civil war in China end with the establishment of the Han dynasty (206 B.C.E.–220 C.E.) on the ruins of the Qin Empire. The first Han emperor, Gaodi, shifts his capital to Chang'an (near modern Xian), issues a general amnesty, and moves to restore order throughout China. **DAO, TOL**
-206–195 B.C.E.	The founder of the Han dynasty in China, Gaodi, is much influenced by the Daoist sage Zhang Liang (d. 189 B.C.E.), who confirms the ruler's mandate and presents auguries of success to him. Zhang, regarded as the master or teacher of the Han ruling house, persuades Gaodi to adopt an imperial posture of pliancy and outward humility. **DAO, TOL**
-206–136 B.C.E.	Han Empire rulers of China summon Confucian scholars to court, but overall imperial patronage favors Daoist adepts associated with Huang-Lao, who follows techniques and doctrines of the Yellow Emperor and Lao-tzu. **CONF, DAO**
-206–8 B.C.E.	During the first half of the Han dynasty in China, the Confucian canon stabilizes in the tradition of Confucius and Mencius yet includes portions indicating the influence of Daoism represented by the texts *Lao-tzu* and *Chuang-tzu*. **CONF, DAO**
-206–220 C.E.	During the Han dynasty in China, Confucius and his family receive special honors. Confucianism is slowly adopted as an ideology and provides the officially accepted norms, morals, and ritual and social behavior regulating relations between ruler and subject. The mastery of Confucian literature

becomes the basis for a civil service examination system that survives until the end of the Ch'ing dynasty in the 20th century. **CONF, TOL**

-202 –
25 C.E.
Early varieties of religious Daoism flourish in China. Daoism is in favor among the empresses and concubines of the imperial harem, and Daoist beliefs prevail among China's lower classes. In Han texts Laozi, author of the founding work of Daoism, is often associated with the mythical Yellow Emperor, an august figure. **DAO**

-200
Fangshi practitioners—magicians—are active in coastal northeast China. The *fangshi* will gradually disappear early in the current era with the development of Celestial Masters Daoism. **DAO**

-200
A compilation of the *Mishnah* begins as Jewish scholars and rabbis begin collecting and recording the various rules and laws governing Jewish life that have existed apart from the Torah. **JUD**

-200
Greek astronomy is introduced to the Romans when Roman soldiers come into contact with Greeks in southern Italy. **SPIR**

-200–
1 B.C.E.
Many *viharas* dedicated to the Jain faith are built during this time at Udayagiri, near Bhuvanesvar in Orissa, east-central India. A *vihara* is a monastic structure cut out of rock—usually associated mostly with Hinayana Buddhism; some are little more than verandahs cut out of rock; other, more elaborate types are large halls. Udayagiri *viharas* follow no regular plan; some have elaborate carvings and architectural elements, such as columns, doorways, and cornices. **JAIN**

-200–
70 C.E.
The second half of the Second Temple period in Jewish history is marked by much political and religious turmoil in the Jewish communities of Palestine. Various groups, such as the Samaritans, Pharisees, Sadducees, and Judeo-Christians, emerge and compete for political and religious power. The Pharisees, who stress traditional Jewish law, are dominant, and their influence is central in the development of rabbinic Judaism, with rabbis serving as the interpreters of Jewish law. **JUD**

-200–
600 C.E.
During the early Intermediate period in Andean civilization in South America the image of the rulers is transformed, with rulers now portraying themselves as agents of the gods who rule by divine right. Various myths, ceremonial centers, and rituals develop to support this religio-political structure. **NATIV**

-200–
700 C.E.
In the southern Andean region in western South America, the Nazca state emerges with its major ceremonial center at Cahuachi. The center contains a large temple, mounds, burial grounds, and shrines. Public rituals are led by priests and concern rain, water, and fertility, while families conduct rites for ancestors. Of particular interest in later centuries are the Nazca lines, markings in the desert that represent birds, monkeys, insects, and plants.

Such geoglyphs are common in western South America but their purpose remains unknown in the 20th century. **NATIV**

-193   Cao Shen becomes chancellor of the Han China state. He is influenced by a form of Daoist thought known as Huang-Lao. This form, which may have emerged as early as the 300s B.C.E. in the east coastal state of Qi, combines some of Laozi's principles with those attributed to the mythical Yellow Emperor of China's prehistory. The proper ruler seeks a compromise between the respect due the individual and the compulsion sometimes necessary for effective governance. Rulers who act in accord with natural principles will succeed in finding the compromise between the freedom of the Dao and imperial control. Cao Shen attempts to translate this doctrine into government policies of inaction. **DAO**

-184
145 B.C.E.   Pusyamitra Sunga, commander in chief of the last of the Mauryan kings, Brhadratha, usurps the throne. His rule over north central India is marked by wars. A devoted Brahmin, Pusyamitra persecutes both Jains and Buddhists, and they are forced to move from east central India (modern Bihar) to a west-central part of India (the modern state of Gujarat); neither Jainism nor Buddhism will ever again be that strong in their native region. **JAIN, TOL**

-180–
157 B.C.E.   The Han dynasty Emperor Wendi reigns in China. His empress, Dou, is a devotee of Daoist writings and she directs her son, the future emperor Jingdi, in Huang-Lao Daoist studies. Father and son become Daoists. **DAO**

-175–
105 B.C.E.   Tung Chung-shu (Dong Zhonhshu) (-195–105 B.C.E.), a Chinese scholar and statesman of the Han dynasty, lives. He is born in Kuang-ch'uan, later to be Hopei Province. During his lifetime, he articulates a Confucian ideal of Chinese political culture. His commentary on the spring and autumn *Annals* contains an important series of short essays on political philosophy, including his vision of the ruler as a fount of wisdom able to align the empire with Heaven and Earth. He becomes a grand synthesizer of several Chinese schools of thought—*yin-yang*, Huang Law, Legalist five-phase cosmology, and Confucianism—primarily responsible for the rise of Han Confucianism as an imperial philosophy and cult. **CONF, TOL**

-175   According to their tradition, Bene Israel arrive and settle on the west coast of India near Bombay. They claim to be members of the Lost Tribes of Israel. Until the 18th century they live isolated from other Jewish communities and develop their own version of Judaism, which is much influenced by Hinduism. After the 18th century they are influenced by the Indian Cochin Jews to the south and adopt more mainstream Jewish customs. In 1948 most of the community of 30,000 began immigrating to Israel. **JUD**

-168   In China silk manuscripts of the *Dao De Jing* are buried with the occupant of the Mawangdui tomb in what is today Hunan Province. The tomb will be excavated in 1973. **DAO**

-167   The Jews revolt against the Seleucid ruler Antiochus, who represses Judaism, and in 164 B.C.E. drive his forces from Jerusalem and rededicate the Temple. The revolt is lead by the Maccabees, whose triumph is celebrated by the festival of Hanukkah. From about 167 B.C.E. until 130 B.C.E., Jewish society experiences much religious growth and change, with three religious sects—the Pharisees, Sadducees, and Essenes—competing for religious and political power. It is during this period that modern Judaism takes shape as the Pharisees, whose views encourage rabbinic Judaism, hold sway.   JUD

-157–
141 B.C.E.   Jingdi reigns in Han China. His mother, the Daoist empress Dou, has taught him to rule according to Laozi's principle of quiescence, or *wu wei*, in which a person's goal of man is to achieve conformity with the Way and in consequence attain a state of happiness and well-being. In practical terms, this means a passive imperial rule.   DAO, TOL

-155–
130 B.C.E.   This is the approximate period when Milinda, or Menandros, a Greek, rules the territory of northwestern India and Afghanistan. He is said to have held a three-day discussion with a Buddhist monk, Nagasena, whose answers to the king's questions about life, recorded in the *Milinda Panha* (questions of King Milinda), converted the king to Buddhism. Milinda thereafter supported Buddhism throughout his realm.   BUDD, TOL

-150   Buddhist art in India, particularly stone sculpture, flourishes under the Sunga and Satavahana dynasties. Relief carvings on balustrades and *toranas*, or gateways, at the monastery at Bharhut, Madhya Pradesh, are major examples of Sunga art. Images include complex narrative reliefs, iconic representation of deities, and symbolic representations of Buddha. Sunga art is also notable for terra-cotta figures and monumental Buddhas.   BUDD

-150   The Han China philosopher Dong Zhongshu uses Daoist numerology and astrology to develop a theory of the dynastic cycle that links the reign of a ruler to certain colors and natural elements. Green is the color of the Han dynasty, for example; yellow is associated with the mythical Yellow Emperor, a deified sage of Daoism.   DAO

-150   By tradition, three brothers named Mao go to a mountain in what is today Jiangxi Province in China to cultivate the Dao. The three peaks are each named for a brother, and the site becomes known as Three-Mao Mountain, Mount Mao for short. It will become an important Daoist holy place.   DAO

-150   The *Salmeschiniaka*, a general discussion of astrology, is written by Greeks in Egypt. It combines Babylonian and Egyptian beliefs about astrology. By about this time Greek astrology includes the birth chart; the zodiac; the positioning of the sun, moon, and five planets; and houses. But the system is still quite primitive and calculations are imprecise.   SPIR

-150   Astrology is criticized by a number of schools of Greek philosophy, including the Stoics, Epicureans, Skeptics, and Cynics.   SPIR

-150– 141 B.C.E.	Tung Chung-shu embraces teaching and scholarly tasks in the capital of China with Confucian colleagues and begins doctrinal expositions of the *Ch'un-ch'iu fan-lu* (Luxuriant gems of the spring and autumn), which through its metaphysical and spiritual dimensions acquires over time a similar authority to that of Christian scripture. He pursues the meaning of the five agents (metal, wood, water, fire, and earth), numerical categories, and human correspondences, and he promotes the view that human actions have cosmic consequences. **CONF**
-140– 134 B.C.E.	Tung Chung-shu urges Emperor Wu to institute reforms in line with the techniques of Confucius and establish a Grand Academy to attract the best and brightest candidates from outlying areas for study and government service. Wu promotes Tung. **CONF**
-140– 87 B.C.E.	Emperor Wudi (Wu-ti, original name Liu Ch'e) (-156–87 B.C.E.) reigns. He assumes the throne of China at 17 and immediately seeks out and favors scholars who wish to implement reforms based on the teachings of Confucius, though Huang-Lao practitioners and Daoist adepts (**SEE -206–136 B.C.E, CONF, DAO**) continue to fill posts under his regent, Empress Dowager Dou. Emperor Wudi vastly increases the range and authority of the Han dynasty through military conquest, extends Chinese influence abroad, and establishes Confucianism as the state orthodoxy of China. Daoism will wane in influence. A Daoist practitioner at the imperial court of Wudi, Dongfang Shuo (-154–93 B.C.E.), argues against the grain of Dao belief that one does not need to withdraw from the world but can find immortality anywhere, even at court. **CONF, DAO**

Huainanzi

The *Huainanzi* is a collection of Daoist essays. *Huainanzi* means "master of Huainan." The author, Liu An, was a prince of Huainan, a small kingdom in east China south of the Huai River. The work itself is a collection or summary of extant knowledge of philosophy, astronomy, geography, zoology, botany, government, history, and myth. Although Daoist in outlook, it refers to other schools and aims to synthesize previous Chinese thought. A long text divided into 21 chapters, it contains essays on mythology and religious devotion along with a systematic explanation of the universe in accord with Daoist principles. The *dao*, according to the *Huainanzi*, operates in the linked realms of heaven, earth, and man through the media of the polar concepts of *yin* and *yang* and the Five Agents. All things are created through the interaction of *yin* and *yang*, which operate through the Five Agents or five kinds of essences—wood, fire, earth, metal, and water—and their correlates. Man's ideal should be to live in harmony with the rhythms of nature, and he must always take care not to disrupt the balance of the natural world. When man attempts to control or conquer nature, imbalance occurs, and calamity results.

-139   The Daoist essays known as the *Huainanzi,* one of the most important philosophical works of Early Han China, is completed. Liu An (-180–122 B.C.E.), a grandson of China's first Han emperor, Gaodi, is the patron of the scholars who compile the *Huainanzi* and an important sponsor of Huang-Lao Daoism. He presents a copy of the work to the emperor Wudi.   **DAO**

-139   Astrologers are expelled from Rome and Roman Italy. The rulers fear their influence on slaves, but it is likely that the use of court astrologers continues.   **SPIR**

-136   Wudi, the Martial Emperor, establishes at court five Erudites of the *Wu Ching,* the *Five Classics,* the core curriculum for Confucian education. They are the *I Ching,* combining divining with numerology and ethics; the *Shu Ching,* presenting kingship as the virtuous foundation for humane government; the *Shih Ching,* a poetic vision of honest and evocative responsiveness; the *Li Chi,* a vision of society organized by the four functional occupations—scholar, farmer, artisan, and merchant; and the *Ch'un-ch'iu,* emphasizing historical consciousness.   **CONF**

-136   The emperor Wudi of Han dynasty China decrees Confucianism the orthodox religion of China, relegating its rival Daoism to secondary status.   **CONF, DAO**

Confucian Classics

The Confucian Classics were a collection of texts associated with Confucianism in China. To the Chinese the texts were equivalent to the ancient Greek and Roman classics for Westerners and had authority similar to that of the Christian Bible. The collection includes texts that preceded Confucius, texts purported to have been written by Confucius, and additional texts. The original texts were *Shih* (*Song Lyrics*), *Shu* (*Ancient Historical Documents*), *I* (*Change*), *Ch'un-ch'iu* (*Spring and Autumn*), *Li Chi* (texts setting forth correct ritual behavior), and *Yüeh Ching* (*Ritual Music*). The last of these were lost some 2,300 years ago, but their existence is known from references in other texts. The collection is called the Confucian Classics because it is believed that Confucius had a role in organizing and editing all of them. For some 2,000 years, the Classics formed the basis of Chinese intellectual life and provided the guiding principles for Chinese philosophy, education, and government. Every student was required to memorize them, those seeking employment in the government had to pass an examination on them, and government decisions and documents often referred to them as the basis for government action. Over the course of Chinese history, the Classics were edited, interpreted, printed in new editions, and added to by Chinese philosophers. During the Sung dynasty (960–1279), neo-Confucian scholars produced the *Four Books,* which became the core of the Classics from then on, with interpretations added by the scholar Chu Hsi. The *Four Books* or *Books of the Great Philosophers* are the *Analects, Mencius, Ta Hsüeh,* and *Chung Yung.*

-135   The dowager empress Dou dies, and the once-strong Huang-Lao Daoist influence on the governance of Han China continues to wane. The authority of the imperial government increases, more intrusive government policies are imposed, and the bureaucracy expands.   DAO

-133   The Han China emperor Wudi sends the *fangshi* ("men of techniques," magicians or shamans) in search of the Immortals, those granted longevity or even eternal life, of Daoist legend.   DAO

-130–
122 B.C.E   Han dynasty disciples of Confucian scholar and statesman Tung Chung-shu include Wu-Ch'iu Shou Wang, commander-in-chief of Tung Commandery and palace attendant to the Grand Master for Splendid Happiness; Chu Ta, administrator to the Kingdom of Liang; Yin Chung; Lu Pu-shu, administrator to the counselor-in-chief; and Yin Kung, Grand Master of Remonstrance under Emperor Chao.   CONF

-128   The power of the Seleucids is now greatly reduced and the Jews achieve independence. They are ruled by the Maccabees, who begin the Hasmonean dynasty. Hasmonean rule is marked by much conflict and factionalism and the expansion of the Kingdom to include much of ancient Israel and Judea.   JUD

-124   Emperor Wudi in China assigns 50 students to study with five Erudites of the *Five Classics*, creating in effect an imperial university based on Confucian precepts. By 50 B.C.E. enrollment is 3,000. By the year 1 a hundred people enter government service every year through state examinations based on Confucian principles.   CONF, TOL

-122   Emperor Wudi directs debate of scholar duke Chiang of Hsia-ch'iu with Tung Chung-shu, whose views and eloquence mark the prominence of Confucian Kung-yang learning. The emperor directs the heir apparent to receive instruction from Tung based on the *Ch'un-ch'iu* (*Spring and Autumn*).   CONF

-122   The Daoist patron Liu An, associated with the compilation of the *Huainanzi*, commits suicide when he is accused of plotting against China's imperial throne. Daoist legend ignores the suicide story and has Liu assumed into heaven after his alchemical researches reveal the secret of immortality.   DAO

-120   A major temple to Apollo, the god of prophecy, is built by the Romans at Pompeii.   CIVIL

-119–
105 B.C.E.   Tung Chung-shu continues to teach, write, and exert great influence at the central court in China with recommendations based on the teachings of Confucius ranging from the optimal planting time for winter wheat and spring grain to aspects of filial piety, greedy officials, land ownership, taxation, and slavery.   CONF

-110   Emperor Wudi sets out for the sacred Mount Tai near Confucius's birthplace to perform the *feng* and *shan* ceremonies dating from early Zhou times. These rites are supposed to make him immortal and allow him to ascend to heaven. **CONF, TOL**

-101–
59 B.C.E.   Dutthagamani (r. -101–77 B.C.E.) and his brother-successor Saddhatissa (r. -77–59 B.C.E.) are probably the first truly historical kings of Sri Lanka. Both are strongly committed to Buddhism, and while unifying the island they build many of the great Buddhist structures at their capital, Anuradhapura. **BUDD, TOL**

-100s–
1 C.E.   The great Buddhist *stupa* (circular structure) at Sanchi, India, is totally rebuilt, its original Ashokan *stupa* doubled in size to 120 feet in diameter; it is now enclosed by a stone railing and *toranas* (gates) elaborately carved with religious narratives and cosmological symbolism. *Stupas*, the most characteristic Buddhist and Jain art form from Ashoka onward, are the earliest surviving forms of religious architecture in India. During this period clockwise circumambulating of *stupas* becomes central to the Buddhist devotional rite. **BUDD**

-100s–.
200s C.E.   A major southern Indian art school flourishes under Satavahana patronage at Amaravati, in modern-day Andhra Pradesh, India. Great *stupas* and some of India's finest sculptures are produced, generally in limestone or marble, and carved with tremendous vitality, complexity, and flow. Major Buddhist sites develop at Nagarjukonda and Amaravati, where a magnificent *stupa* is completed c. 200 C.E. This school greatly influences Southeast Asian art. **BUDD**

-100   In China the *I Ching* (*Book of Changes*) is codified in the form known in the 20th century. Originally simply a manual for diviners or soothsayers to predict the outcome of their patrons' planned actions, the commentators of later centuries reinterpreted the "changes" in moral and metaphysical terms. The basis of the *I Ching* is a set of 64 six-line diagrams known as hexagrams; each symbolizes a different human situation, and within each there are numerous other symbolic variations; to make a divination, the diviner randomly sorts 50 small sticks (originally plant stalks) to form a hexagram, which is then interpreted. Although strictly speaking not a Daoist text or system, in the 20th century the *I Ching* will be adopted by many Westerners as embodying certain principles consistent with Daoism. **DAO**

-100   In India the Hindu idea that life consists of suffering, an extension of the earlier doctrine that suffering is the key element of the rebirth process, is developed. It is an important belief in yoga traditions, some Hindu sects, and in Buddhism. **HIND**

-100	Native Americans of the Adena/Hopewell cultural tradition in Ohio build the large Serpent Mound. The mound is in the shape of a serpent, but its symbolism and use remain unknown in the 20th century. **NATIV**
-100	Hallucinogenic drugs including peyote are being used by Native Americans in northern Mexico, very likely as part of religious rituals, a use that continues into the 20th century. **NATIV**
-100– 70 B.C.E.	A new generation of Confucian disciples of Tung Chung-shu in China includes Sui Meng, manager of credentials; Yen P'eng-tzu, governor of Honan and grand mentor of the heir apparent; and Yen An-le, aide to the governor of Ch'i Commandery. All serve under Emperor Hsuan. **CONF**
-100– 1 B.C.E.	According to one tradition, the Jain monk Kalakacarya causes the overthrow of King Gardabhilla of Ujjain in central India, which results in his replacement by Saka (or Scythian) rulers. The earliest traces of paintings in Jain caves, those in Orissa, east central India, date from this period. Also from this century comes the oldest known Jain bronze, a figurine of Parasvanatha. **JAIN**
-100– 100 C.E.	During Japan's middle Yayoi period, bronze mirrors arrive from China by way of the Korean peninsula. The mirrors are valued as cult objects. The Japanese begin the domestic production of bronze artifacts, mainly ritual objects, such as wide-bladed daggers and large decorated bells (*dokatu*). **SHINTO**
-100– 150 C.E.	Mahayana (great vehicle) Buddhism begins to emerge as an alternative to Theravada Buddhism in northwest and southern India. **BUDD**
-100– 400 C.E.	Composition in south India of *Prajnaparamita* (perfection of wisdom) *Sutras*, a central text on enlightenment and one of the earliest scriptures of Mahayana Buddhism. **BUDD**
-100– 500 C.E.	The *Cankam* literary tradition of bardic poetry develops and thrives among the Tamil culture of southern India. The literature contains a number of religious themes, such as emotional worship, the god Murukan, and sacrifice, which allow for a merging with the Hinduism that has developed in northern India. **HIND**
-100– 500 C.E.	In the Hindu *Yoga Sutra*, details about the practice of yoga are provided, although yoga had begun as a religious practice hundreds of years earlier. The religious text describes yoga as a form of mind control involving restraint, discipline, posture, breath control, sense withdrawal, concentration, and meditation. **HIND**
-97– 30 B.C.E.	According to tradition, until the reign of Japan's legendary 10th emperor, Sujin (r. -97–30 B.C.E.), the emperor's residence is also the shrine of his divine ancestors. To protect the Imperial Regalia, or Three Sacred

Treasures—the mirror, sword, and jewel—Sujin has copies made of the mirror and sword and keeps these replicas in the palace along with the original jewel. He sends the original sword and mirror to Kasanui in Yamato, where a shrine is built for them. He sends his daughter Princess Toyosuki Iri-hime to be in charge of worship at the shrine and to guard the treasures with her life. **SHINTO**

-97–
30 B.C.E.

This is the traditional Japanese date for the origin of the Shinto rite of *Toshigoi-no-matsuri*, the spring prayer for a good rice harvest in autumn. More likely the rite originates from Emperor Temmu's reign (672–686 C.E.). According to tradition, Emperor Sujin also builds the Tatsuta shrine at Nara to end a series of natural disasters and gain power over destructive winds. **SHINTO**

-90

The early Han Chinese historian Sima Qian (c. -145–90 B.C.E.) narrates the Laozi legend in his *Historical Documents*. In reaction to Daoist influence at the imperial court, he criticizes the *Zhuangzi*, one of the Daoist scriptures, as a selfish vision of little or no practical use to men of affairs. Later scholars will regard it as subversive of the Confucian order. **CONF, DAO**

-80–
60 B.C.E.

A textbook is written on astrology by Nechepso and Petosiris, purported to be an ancient Egyptian pharaoh and an Egyptian high priest. The book, which exists only in fragments, is in later centuries often cited as proof of the Egyptian origins of astrology, although it is more likely that the authors were Greeks in Alexandria, Egypt, and that the book is based on Babylonian, Egyptian, and Greek ideas about astrology. **SPIR**

-63

The Romans intervene in Hasmonean affairs under Pompey, conquer Jerusalem, and reduce the Hasmonean ruler to a puppet under the Roman governor of Syria. **JUD**

-53–
18 C.E.

The Chinese Daoist Yang Xiong, author of the Daoist *Classic of the Great Way*, lives. He draws inspiration from Laozi but calls the other great Daoist Zhuangzi a "fomenter of disorder and enemy of the laws." **DAO**

-47

Jews in communities outside Palestine are allowed by Julius Caesar to provide financial support for the Temple in Jerusalem. **JUD**

-37

Under Herod the Great, who now rules Palestine for Rome, the Romans take full control of Jerusalem and the Jews are persecuted. **JUD**

-34–
33 B.C.E.

As part of his attempt to revitalize Rome, Octavian (who later rules as the emperor Augustus) rebuilds many temples in Rome and appoints priests. **CIVIL**

-31

The Olmecs on the Gulf Coast of Mexico have by this time developed the long count calendar system, later refined by the Mayans and widely used in pre-Columbian Mesoamerica to schedule religious and other events. **NATIV**

-30– 100 C.E.	The major texts that come to be known as the canon of Theravada Buddhism are written in the ancient Pali language in Sri Lanka. It is claimed that these texts have been transmitted orally from the Buddha himself, but most scholars reject this (SEE **483** B.C.E., BUDD). **BUDD**
-29 70 C.E.	Under the legendary Japanese emperor Suinin, the original sword and mirror of the Imperial Regalia are moved from Kasanui to Ise's Inner Shrine. His daughter is appointed the priestess charged with their worship. This position of emperor's daughter as priestess at the Ise Shinto shrine becomes customary. Some specify the date for this event as 4 B.C.E. **SHINTO, TOL**
-25– 1000 C.E.	In about 25 B.C.E. a group of monks breaks away from the Mahavihara Monastery on Sri Lanka, the main seat of Theravada Buddhism; these monks found the Abhayagiri Monastery. For the next 1,000 years, these two monasteries carry on their disputes, which often center on the sacred texts, and the Abhayagiri monks effectively become part of the Mahayana school of Buddhism. Beyond such religious quarrels, however, the two monasteries contend for influence and power with the secular rulers of Sri Lanka, and over the centuries successive kings favored one or the other monastery. By about 1000, as Buddhism is on the decline throughout India, the Abhayagiri/Mahayana monks will also vanish, and Sri Lanka survives as the center of Theravada Buddhism. **BUDD**
-23	In the Roman Empire the practice of deifying the emperor begins to emerge with the appearance of the cult of Augustus et Roma devoted to Emperor Augustus. **CIVIL**
-15	Philo of Alexandria (c. 15 B.C.E.–50 C.E.) is born. He is a leading scholar, writer, and philosopher of the Greek-speaking Jewish community in Alexandria, Egypt. His writings on religion, Judaism, and Greek philosophy are admired by leaders of the early Christian community and influence their theology. **JUD**
-12	State and religious authority are merged in the Roman Empire when Emperor Augustus is made the leader of the state religion with the title Pontofex Maximus. **CIVIL**
-4	Jews in Palestine mount an unsuccessful revolt against the Romans. **JUD**
-2	A Chinese text, *Wei-lueh*, not written until the third century C.E., claims that Buddhist scriptures are being transmitted orally into China by this year. Modern scholars believe that Buddhism was in fact being introduced into China by at least 50 B.C.E. by traveling merchants, if not by missionaries. Other Chinese quasi-historical sources date the introduction as early as the third century B.C.E. **BUDD**

C.E.

1	The beginning of the Christian era. **CHRIS**
1	China's Emperor P'ing inaugurates the practice of awarding Confucius posthumous titles by naming him a duke. **CONF**
c. 4	Jesus of Nazareth is believed to have been born in Bethlehem. Experts do not agree on the exact date of his birth and variously place it between 7 B.C.E. and 8 C.E. **CHRIS**
6	The Roman emperor Augustus makes Palestine a Roman province. The Roman rulers repress Judaism. **JUD**
c. 9– 15	A textbook on astrology is written as a long poem by the philosopher Manilius in Rome. Although astrology was introduced to Rome by the Greeks some 200 years earlier, the book sets forth a unified system of astrology that appeals to Roman intellectuals. **SPIR**
11	In Rome astrology is banned by the emperor Augustus and by subsequent emperors over the next 100 years. The ban is generally applied only to astrologers who serve the common people, while court astrologers, who rely on Greek systems of astrology, often continue to serve the emperors. **SPIR**
14	Upon his death Roman emperor Augustus is deified, a temple is built in his honor, and priests are appointed to serve worshipers. This initiates the practice of deifying all Roman emperors. **CIVIL**
c. 24– 26	Jesus of Nazareth begins preaching and attracts a small following of people who find appeal in his words and deeds. **CHRIS**
25– 220	In China some Confucian scholars of the later Han dynasty reject Tung Chung-shu's worldview for a more rational and moralistic approach to the Confucian Classics. The works of Yang Hsiung (-53–18 B.C.E.)—*fa-yen* (model sayings) in the aphoristic style of the *Analects* and the *T'ai-hsuan Ching* (*Classic of the supremely profound principle*), cosmological speculations similar to the *I Ching*—are widely accepted, even as examination of the Classics becomes more elaborate. **CONF**

c. 27	(St.) John the Baptist (?–c. 30) begins preaching and baptizing people in the River Jordan. He meets Jesus and baptizes him and recognizes him as the Christ. **CHRIS**
c. 28	Jesus is crucified as an enemy of the Roman state. His adherents claim that he is resurrected and has appeared among them, marking the beginning of the Christian religion. His teachings are spread by St. Peter (?–64). **CHRIS**
c. 30	(St.) John the Baptist is executed by Roman ruler Herod for his criticism of Herod and religious leaders. **CHRIS**
c. 33	Saul of Tarsus (St. Paul, ?–c. 65), a persecutor of Christians, encounters the risen Christ while traveling in the desert to Damascus, Syria, and then converts to Christianity. He becomes known as Paul (his Latin name) and becomes Christianity's most successful early missionary and most influential theologian. **CHRIS**
c. 35–40	The term *Christian* is first used in reference to Christians in Antioch, Syria. The word *Christos* is the Greek translation of the Hebrew word for messiah, used by Christians in reference to Jesus of Nazareth. **CHRIS**

Sainthood

Reverence for people who are considered to be especially holy is found in all religions. However, sainthood as a religious institution is most elaborated in Christianity and especially in Roman Catholicism. The Christian concept of sainthood dates to the second century of Christianity, when martyrs were venerated. For the first few centuries, the conferring of sainthood was mainly a local matter, wherein a cult would develop following the death of a martyr or another individual who displayed great devotion to Christianity. The relics of saints were collected and kept in sacred places and the saints worshiped and prayed to. Saints were believed to have performed miracles and were often seen as sources of healing. As control of the Church centralized, it became common for local cults to appeal to the pope to approve or canonize their saint, and Pope Gregory IX (1227–1241) made it mandatory that the pope canonize individuals nominated for sainthood. Some Protestant reformers rejected the worship of saints, and since then sainthood has been more important in Roman Catholicism and Eastern Orthodoxy than in Protestantism. The exact number of Christian saints is unknown, but one attempt to list and describe all of them filled 12 volumes. Modern requirements for canonization are rigorous and require careful study of the deeds or pattern of holy behavior that are grounds for sainthood and also evidence that the individual performed a miracle. In 1969 the Catholic Church revised the official list of saints, eliminated some, and reduced the number of saints' days worthy of official recognition. Nonetheless, saints remain important sacred figures, and many Christians take seriously the worship of their patron saints. The study of the lives of saints, called hagiography, remains a popular activity in Christianity.

c. 35   (St.) Stephen (?–c. 35) is killed on the orders of the Jewish council in Jerusalem for his preaching of Jesus as the Messiah. He is considered to be the first martyr of Christianity.   **CHRIS**

35   Christians in Asia Minor and North Africa begin meeting in small groups. There are no churches; groups meet in homes to worship, and people sometimes enlarge rooms to hold the entire group assembled there.   **CHRIS**

c. 44   (St.) James the Great (?–c. 44) is beheaded by the Romans. He and his brother John were close friends and followers of Jesus and he accompanied Jesus on his travels. He is the first apostle to be martyred and is later made the patron saint of Spain, pilgrims, and laborers. A cult to him develops in Spain in the ninth century based on the (erroneous) belief that his body is buried there.   **CHRIS**

c. 47–49   (St.) Paul becomes the leading early missionary of Christianity when he seeks converts to Christianity among the peoples of Asia Minor, Greece, and Cyrus and establishes churches. He preaches to Jews and pagans alike but is often criticized and driven off by the Jews and draws more support from the

Paul of Tarsus

Saint Paul is generally considered to be the most important of the first Christians. His importance is based on his devotion as an apostle, his success as a missionary, and his teachings and writings as a theologian. Paul was born of Jewish parents in Tarsus shortly after the birth of Jesus. They were Roman citizens, a status that later in life afforded him some protection from Jewish critics. He was educated in Jerusalem and after Christ's death was a major persecutor of Christians and volunteered to oversee Christian refugees in Damascus. While traveling there he experienced a vision of Christ, converted, was baptized, and then spent several years in isolation, praying and meditating. He was then accepted with some wariness by the apostles in Jerusalem and in 44 C.E., was recruited as a missionary by Barnabas. His travels took him to Greece and Asia Minor. He preached to Jews and pagans but was mostly successful with the pagans and established several churches for the newly converted Christians. His ideas on Christian theology are set forth in his Thirteen Epistles, or Letters, to the churches he established. Experts believe that seven of these were certainly written by Paul, but the authorship of the others is a matter of dispute. Paul's major argument to converts was that salvation no longer depended on one's deeds on earth but rather on devotion to Jesus Christ and God's mercy. Paul also was the first to set forth the basic Christian doctrines of predestination, grace, free will, and justification by faith that were developed later by theologians such as Augustine and Martin Luther. Paul's preaching was resisted by both the Jews and Romans, and around 60 C.E. he was arrested, detained for several years, perhaps freed to preach again, and then executed during Nero's persecution of the Christians. The Church of St. Paul outside Rome is built over his burial site.

pagans. He teaches a form of Christianity separate from Judaism and thus is influential in establishing Christianity as a distinct religion.   **CHRIS**

49   A council of leaders of the emerging Christian community is held in Jerusalem. The major issue is the extent to which the emerging new religion must adhere to the beliefs and practices of Judaism. A decision, supported by (Sts.) Peter and Paul, is made not to require pagan converts to be circumcised but to maintain some other Jewish practices, such as certain dietary restrictions.   **CHRIS**

c. 50–
150   This is the approximate period of Asvaghosha, Mahayana Buddhist scholar and saint and one of the earliest known poets and dramatists of classical Sanskrit literature. He is claimed by some to flourish at Kanishka's court at

---

Christianity

Christianity is the largest religion, with some two billion adherents around the world. Christianity takes its name from Jesus Christ, believed by Christians to be the Messiah. *Christos* is a Greek translation of the Hebrew word for Messiah used by Jews and the first Christians, and the label "Christian" was probably first used between 35 and 40 C.E. in reference to followers of Jesus living in the city of Antioch in Syria. Christians in the modern world are generally divided into three major categories: Roman Catholics (one billion), Orthodox (220 million), and Protestant (405 million), with Anglicans (the Church of England, 70 million) sometimes treated as a distinct category and other times lumped with Protestants. In addition, there are about 300 million Christians who belong to churches outside these major categories. These include Eastern Christians, Pentecostalists, and other groups, such as Jehovah's Witnesses, Mormons, Seventh-Day Adventists, Unitarians, and others who not all other Christians consider to be Christians. Christianity can also be subdivided on the basis of culture and geography, with groups such as African-American, Latin American, African, and southern Asian Christians seen as distinct in some ways. As a worldwide religion that has existed for 2,000 years, Christianity displays considerable diversity in religious practice and belief and lacks any central unifying structure. The most successful unifying institution has been the World Council of Churches, which includes most Protestant denominations and Orthodoxy, but not Roman Catholicism. Despite the variations, unity is created at the theological level across denominations by adherence to a number of basic beliefs. These include a belief in a supreme god, who is also the god worshiped by Jews and Muslims; a belief that God is active in and influences the human world; a belief that Jesus is the Messiah who rose, body and soul, from the dead; a belief that the Old and New Testaments are sacred and are the core texts of Christianity; a belief that Christians have a special relationship with God; a belief that they have an obligation to convert others to Christianity; the use of prayer to communicate with God; and the use of bread, wine, and water in religious rituals. Christianity has become the largest world religion both through the migration of Christians to other parts of the world and through the missionary activity that is supported by many denominations and churches.

Peshawar. He helps to establish the canon of Mahayana Buddhism. His great literary work is *Buddhacarita*, an epic poem that claims to recount the life of the Buddha.   **BUDD**

50–
200

Under influence of Mahayana Buddhism, the earliest anthropomorphic representations of Buddha appear c. 50. Appearing more or less simultaneously in Gandhara and Mathura, they already incorporate the elongated earlobes, third eye, and cranial protuberance that are to become conventions in depicting Buddha. These iconic Buddhist images that spread along the Silk Road throughout central Asia into China contribute significantly to the spread of Buddhism during this period.   **BUDD**

c. 51–
54

(St.) Paul conducts his second missionary journey and preaches the gospel for the first time in Europe, at Philippi in Greece. He and his companion Silas are imprisoned but are then released and continue preaching mainly in Greece.   **CHRIS**

c. 51–
c. 58

(St.) Paul writes the seven letters that 20th-century scholars believe to have been actually written by him and appear in the New Testament as Romans, 1–2 Corinthians, Galatians, Philippians, 1 Thessalonians, and Philemon. Six other letters that appear in the New Testament and are attributed to Paul are believed by scholars to have been written by others. Paul's writing and his theology, as expressed by others in his name, are the basis of many key Christian beliefs, including the doctrines of predestination, grace, free will, and justification by faith alone.   **CHRIS**

52

According to Syrian Christian tradition, (St.) Thomas, a disciple of Jesus Christ, arrives in southwestern India and converts some Hindus to Christianity. They use the Syriac liturgy and are called Syrian Christians or Thomas Christians after their founder. Syrian Christians live apart from their Hindu neighbors. The community survives and, at times, thrives and in the 1990s numbers some five million people in India.   **CHRIS, HIND**

c. 53–
c. 60

(St.) Paul undertakes his third missionary journey to Asia Minor and then to Jerusalem.   **CHRIS**

57–
75

Emperor Mingdi reigns in China. A Chinese text dated to 65 C.E. refers to the half-brother of the emperor adopting Buddhist practices; this is the first documented mention of Buddhism in China. A later Chinese text claims that Mingdi sees the Buddha in a dream and then sends emissaries to India to inquire after his doctrines. They return (67 C.E.) bringing texts and statues, as well as two Indian monks, Kasyapa Matranga and Gobharana, who set about translating the Buddhist writings into Chinese; traditionally the first of these is the *Sutra in Forty-two Sections*. It is generally conceded that, along with the continuing decay of Confucian values and a developing surge of popular religious Daoism, foreign merchants on the Silk Road have introduced Buddhism to China, and a cult of the Buddha is thought to be active in the capital, Luoyang, by this time.   **BUDD**

59	China's Emperor Mingdi recognizes Confucius as patron of scholars and orders that sacrifices be offered to him in all government schools. The sacrifice consists of a solemn banquet to honor venerated figures and instill reverence and propriety among believers rather than to propitiate spirits. The elite pay strict attention to such rituals, but they are largely ignored by the masses. CONF, TOL
c. 60	(St.) Paul comes to Jerusalem and is criticized by the leaders of the Jewish community. He is rescued but then imprisoned by the Roman rulers who evidently view him as the potential leader of a revolt. He spends two years imprisoned in Caesarea and then another two years under house arrest while awaiting trial in Rome. CHRIS
c. 60	(St.) Andrew (?–c. 60) dies. He is a friend and the first follower of Jesus and is instrumental in having his brother Simon (St. Peter) baptized by Jesus. He is also the first missionary of the Christian church, but claims that he was directly or indirectly involved in bringing Christianity to Russia and Scotland are shown by scholars in later centuries to be false. He is venerated as the patron saint of Russia, Scotland, and fishermen, after his profession and that of his father and brother. CHRIS

Gospels

In Christianity the Gospels are the early and authoritative (canonical) works of Matthew, Mark, Luke, and John that form the first four books of the New Testament. Some experts believe that the term *Gospel* should be applied only to these four works and not to other Christian writings that preceded or followed them. Some other experts take a broader view and consider some other writings to be part of the Gospel as well. Although they vary in content and style and expected audience, all four Gospels recount the story of Jesus Christ: his birth, teachings, miracles, travels, death, and resurrection. Thus, they provide the basic story of Christianity as told by associates of Jesus or people alive during his lifetime. As they were written from 30 to 60 years after his death, it is likely that they were recorded to provide a permanent record of his life as his contemporaries who carried forth the oral tradition of his life became fewer and fewer. Although they appear in the Bible in the order listed above, experts believe that Mark was written first (about 65 C.E.), Matthew and Luke, which are based in part on Mark, about 10 years later, and John not until near the end of the first century. As with early religious texts in many religions, experts have spent much time trying to identify the sources of the Gospels. It is generally believed that Mark is based in part on earlier writings, such as stories about and the sayings of Jesus. Matthew and Luke are based on Mark and also on the so-called Q document. The Q document is the name given by scholars to a hypothetical source that they believe contains sayings of Jesus. John is based on a broader range of sources, including the earlier Gospels, the author's personal knowledge, other Christian writings, and even materials from the Dead Sea Scrolls.

c. 60s	The Gospel according to Mark is written by (St.) Mark (?–c. 74), one of the Twelve Apostles and one of the Four Evangelists of Christianity, and later becomes the second book of the New Testament. The Gospel covers John the Baptist and Jesus's life, work, travels, death, and resurrection. Scholars in the 20th century consider it to be the oldest of the three synoptic Gospels (Mark, Matthew, and Luke) and a partial source of the other two. **CHRIS**
64	Christianity is subject to official persecution in the Roman Empire for the first time when Christians are persecuted by Nero (r. 54–69) in Rome. At the time Christians are a small minority and are attacked by pagans, who form the majority of the population. **CHRIS**
64–70	The Jews revolt against Roman rule under Nero. The revolt is put down and the Temple destroyed. The day on which the Temple is destroyed becomes and remains a day of prayer and fasting for Jews. In 70 C.E. the Jewish Diaspora to Europe and elsewhere in the Middle East intensifies, and soon all major cities in the Roman Empire have Jewish populations. Babylon replaces Jerusalem as the center of Jewish religion and culture over the next four centuries. **JUD**
c. 65	St. Paul, the most important early Christian missionary and theologian, is executed by the Romans in Rome. It is not clear to 20th-century experts if his execution followed some four years of imprisonment and confinement as a potential leader of a revolt against Roman rule or if he enjoyed a few years of freedom and missionary work following his arrest and before his execution. **CHRIS**
65–100	A surge of popular religious Daoism accompanies the introduction of Buddhism from India into late Han dynasty China. **DAO, BUDD**
66	One tradition claims that a Jain monk, Arhadbali, convenes a council of the Jain monks of southern India at Mahima (in Maharashtra, India). This event is alleged to have contributed to the major schism among the Jains. **JAIN**
c. 70s	The Gospel according to Matthew is written by (St.) Matthew, one of the Twelve Apostles and Four Evangelists of Christianity, and later becomes the first book of the New Testament. The Gospel covers John the Baptist and Jesus's life, work, travels, death, and resurrection. It seeks to combine the new Christian teachings with established Jewish belief and practice and represents, to some extent, the viewpoint of the Jewish Christian Church. **CHRIS**
c. 70s	The Gospel according to Luke is written by (St.) Luke, one of the Twelve Apostles and Four Evangelists of Christianity, and later becomes the third book of the New Testament. The Gospel covers Jesus's life, work, travels, death, and resurrection and attempts to separate emerging Christianity from politics in the Roman Empire. **CHRIS**

70–77	Liu Ying, a half-brother of the late Han China emperor Mingdi, is accused of a Daoist conspiracy and driven into exile. Liu eventually commits suicide. Thousands of his supposed followers are tried and executed on charges they used magic for subversive purposes. **DAO**
c. 74	(St.) Mark (?–c. 74), an early follower of Jesus and a disciple of St. Peter, dies in Alexandria. He is the author of the Gospel according to Mark, the first Gospel written after Christ's death. **CHRIS**
75	King Gogidubnus of Britain shows his allegiance to Rome by building temples to honor the Roman gods Minerva and Neptune. **CIVIL**
c. 78–123	King Kanishka, the first great Kushan emperor, reigns; Kushans are central Asians, known to the Chinese as the Yue Zhi. Kanishka extends the Kushan rule across present-day Afghanistan, Pakistan, much of central Asia, northern India, and even parts of eastern and central India. (The Kushan empire declines in the late second century C.E. and submits to the Sassanid dynasty of Persia c. 260.) Kanishka is a Buddhist convert and assumes the Buddhist title *Devaputra* (son of Divine Being). He is credited with advancing Mahayana Buddhism throughout central Asia and into China. One tradition claims that he summons a fourth Buddhist Council to Jalandhara, Kashmir; it is dominated by Theravada followers, who authorize commentaries on Buddhist canon. **BUDD, TOL**
c. 79	According to Jain tradition, this is the time when the Jains split into their two principal sects: the Digambaras ("sky-clad," meaning "naked") and the Svetambaras ("white-clad," meaning "white clothing"). (There is said to have been a third sect, the Yapaniya, who lived naked like Digambaras and eventually merged with Digambara sect.) All such claims (including the names of the sects) are based on testimony written many centuries later— the earliest is dated about 500 C.E. In fact, modern historians are inclined to trace this split back to the time of Bhadrabahu, when he goes south with his followers and they remain naked monks, while those who stay behind, the followers of Sthulabhadra, take to wearing white robes **(SEE 321–297 B.C.E., JAIN)**. Other historians believe that the roots of such a division existed even in the time of Mahavira himself. The most important of several schisms within Jainism was the split into Digambaras and Svetambaras sects dated to about 79 C.E. in Jain traditions. The more liberal Svetambara monks wear white clothing, open their ranks to admit women and declare them capable of securing *nirvana*. The strict Digambara monks believe in absolute poverty to the extent that they refuse to own or wear clothing (although most abandon this requirement in 20th-century India); they maintain an exclusive male monastic order. Also, whereas the Svetambaras accept the 11 *Angas* as sacred scripture, the Digambaras do not accept their full authority. For many centuries there is not a clear division between these two groups; only with the passage of time and changed conditions do the two sects really draw distinct lines around their separate doctrines. **JAIN**

c. 85 — The Jewish Christianity espoused by Jewish converts to Christianity is rejected by leaders of the Jewish community and is officially condemned. Jewish Christianity is also rejected by many Christians and the movement disappears over the next several decades. **CHRIS**

c. 90 — Buddhist monks establish a monastery at China's imperial capital, Luoyang. **BUDD**

c. 96 — A special ministry is emerging in the Christian church, and in this year the First Epistle of Clement is written. It is a letter from the Church in Rome to the Church in Corinth which deals with the issue of replacing prophets and teachers with elders. The letters argue for a policy of electing elders who are descendants of the Apostles. **CHRIS**

c. 100 — The basilica, a large, rectangular building with a high, vaulted roof, comes into use in Rome as a marketplace and meeting hall. In the 400s Christians adopt the basilica as the basic form of the church, adding later an apse (niche) at one end. **CHRIS**

c. 100 — The Gospel according to John is written by (St.) John, one of the Twelve Apostles. This Gospel differs from the earlier synoptic Gospels (Mark, Matthew, and Luke) in its greater breadth of coverage, various details of Jesus's work, and its emphasis on spiritual devotion. Because of the emphasis on spiritual devotion, it has become a more popular reading than the other Gospels. **CHRIS**

c. 100 — Easter, the feast celebrating Christ's resurrection, is celebrated by Christians. It combines elements from Christianity, paganism, and Judaism. It is to some extent a Christian version of Passover, although in the second century efforts are made to separate it from the Jewish celebration and its date, in the west, is moved to the Sunday following Passover. **CHRIS**

c. 100 — Catacombs, underground chambers and passageways, are used in Rome and other Italian cities as burial places for the dead. Burial of the dead is replacing cremation as the primary means of disposal of the dead, perhaps due to the influence of Christians who do not believe in cremation. **CIVIL**

c. 100 — The Mandeans, a Gnostic sect that develops in the first century in the Jordan Valley, moves to a region along the modern border of Turkey and Syria. They later migrate into Mesopotamia and in the 1990s remain a small religious minority of about 25,000 in Iraq and Iran. They are the only one of the many Gnostic sects of the first few centuries C.E. to survive into modern times. Their religion combines elements from early Christianity and magic but rejects Judaism. **SECT**

c. 100 — The *Anthology* of astrology is written by Vettius Valens, probably a Greek who writes in Greek and lives in Alexandria, Egypt. The book mainly summarizes existing knowledge and beliefs about astrology in the Greek and

Roman worlds but also admonishes astrologers to keep their knowledge and methods secret, an indication that astrology is of considerable importance to the Romans. **SPIR**

100s–
200s

Mathura is the center of finest Kushan dynasty art production, particularly sculpture. Supernatural beings, *bodhisattvas*, and ancient fertility goddesses are incorporated into Buddhist iconography. Patrons are typically monks or nuns. It is probably during this time, too, that a major Buddhist temple is erected at Bodh Gaya, the site (in northern India) where the Buddha first attained enlightenment. Since the time of Ashoka (c. 250 B.C.E.) there has been a Buddhist shrine here, but now a large temple, known as the Mahabodhi temple, is erected; over the centuries that follow it will be greatly enlarged. **BUDD**

100

Historical evidence suggests that Jews (later called Cochin Jews) establish a community on the southwestern coast of India. Other accounts of their arrival suggest they may have arrived as much as 1000 years later. Those who settle there are probably the Jews who fled Palestine after the Second Temple was destroyed in 70 C.E. **JUD**

100

The Passover rite is transformed into its modern form as the seder meal, with the Jewish Exodus from Egypt recounted through the reading of the *Haggadah*. **JUD**

100

At about this time the Samaritans emerge as a distinct religious group in Palestine. It is unclear whether they were a sect of Judaism or were a group who arrived from elsewhere. In the 1990s a community of about 500 Samaritans still exists in Israel. It differs from other Jews (not all Jews consider Samaritans to be Jews) in the belief in the divine origin of only the first five books of the Bible, strict religious observances regarding the Sabbath, and veneration of Mount Gerhizim as their holy site. **JUD**

100–
200

Religious Daoism evolves in China, with the elaboration of rites, exercises, and disciplines. Popular Daoist religious organizations concerned with faith healing begin to appear. Educated Chinese who are anti-Confucius begin to eschew from involvement in public affairs in order to immerse themselves, as the Daoist sages Laozi and Zhuangzi teach, in their inner lives. Zhuangzi, heretofore regarded in Han China as a "fomenter of disorder," is restored to a high place in the canon. **CONF, DAO**

100–
200

Astrology is popular in Greece and especially so in Egypt, where Greek astrology developed, and in the Greek Near East. There is no unified system, and astrologers use their own systems, with horoscopes prepared for all levels of citizens. **SPIR**

100–300	Jews had arrived in Spain centuries earlier, and during this period distinctive Jewish communities emerge. **JUD**

100–400 Sometime during this period lives Kundakunda, the famous Jain mystic/teacher of the Digambara sect. His most famous work is the *Pravacanasara* (*Essence of the Doctrine*), a versified outline of Jainism's main doctrines and ethics. Also during this period another Jain teacher, Samantabhadra, writes several important works on the philosophy of Jainism. **JAIN**

100 - 700 The Moche Civilization develops and flourishes in the northern Andean region of western South America. The empire is governed from major ceremonial centers with elaborate burial grounds, pyramids, platforms, and temples. Considerable power is held by warrior-priests, called the Lords of Sipán, who oversee the capture and sacrifice of prisoners. **NATIV**

100 - 1100 The city of Aksum is a major trading center on the African coast of the Red Sea and exerts influence over the adjacent region in North Africa. Trade is primarily with Arabs and other peoples in Arabia, and Aksum religion is much influenced by the indigenous religions of Arabia. Arabian-style temples and shrines are built and Arabian gods, such as the moon and war gods, are worshiped. The kings build large stone stelae as symbols of their power and the divine source of their power. The kingdom comes under the influence of Rome, Christianity, and Islam before it dissolves. In the fourth century King Ezana converts to Christianity, which survives in the region as Coptic Christianity. After 700 C.E. the Coptic community comes under attack by the Muslims from Arabia. **AFRICAN**

112 A report by Pliny the Younger, governor of the Roman province of Bithynia in northwest Asia Minor, indicates what is probably the first large-scale conversion to Christianity, with many of the people in the region following Christian teachings and abandoning the worship of pagan gods. **CHRIS**

c. 120 The Pantheon is built in Rome by the emperor Hadrian. It became a model of early Roman temples; it is circular and is built of brick, with marble columns and a high, vaulted roof. **CIVIL**

c. 130 The New Testament canon (authoritative religious writings accepted as such by the Church) begins to form when the Four Gospels and the 13 letters of Paul are accepted by Church scholars and leaders. **CHRIS**

132–135 The Jews revolt again against Roman rule during the reign of Hadrian. The revolt fails and Jerusalem is destroyed, Judaism is severely repressed, and many Jews are killed or flee the region. The region is now named Syria Palestina. **JUD**

135 Valentinus (110–175), an early and influential Gnostic poet and teacher from Alexandria, settles in Rome and seeks a role in the Christian Church.

He is rejected as his views combine Christianity and magic but gains a number of followers who in turn create a number of Gnostic sects that survive into the early third century C.E. SECT

138–
212

Following Hadrian's death a series of more moderate Roman emperors rule Palestine, and the restrictions on Jews and Judaism are gradually relaxed. In 212 Jews, like all other free persons in the empire, are granted Roman citizenship. JUD

142

By tradition, Laozi appears to a small landowner of Sichuan in China named Zhang Daoling. In an encounter on Mount Heming in Sichuan, Laozi hands Zhang a new law, the Zhengi ("correct unity"). This is the founding event of the Five Pecks of Rice (later, Celestial Masters) sect that will spread widely throughout China. DAO

143

Three brothers, Zhang Jue, Zhang Bao, and Zhang Liang (no relation to Zhang Daoling of Sichuan), launch The Way of Great Peace religious movement in central and eastern China. They present the *Scripture of the Great Peace* to the Han imperial court. Developing parallel to the Five Pecks of Rice movement in the west, the movement draws inspiration from philosophical and religious Daoism, among other sources. DAO

c. 150

Nagarjuna, an Indian Buddhist philosopher, founds one of the major schools within Mahayana Buddhism; it is called the Madhyamaka (dialectical) school and is characterized by a fundamental skepticism in which everything is believed to be unreal and illusory. Writings attributed to Nagarjuna (but which probably include works by others, in particular his best known student, Aryadeva) will enter the Tibetan and Chinese Buddhist canons. He is also claimed as the founder of, or the first major figure associated with, the University of Nalanda, in Bihar, India. Whether this is true or not, the University of Nalanda from very early times will be associated with Buddhist scholarship **(SEE 400s–500s, BUDD)**. At about this same time, a Buddhist monk from central Asia, An Shi Gao, appears in China; he assembles a translation team that produces numerous translations of Buddhist texts; this is said to inspire the Chinese practice of translation teams. BUDD

c. 150

In the Christian Church, the monarchial episcopate system of administration is in place, having developed and spread over the past 70 or so years. The bishop is the leader of each church and is solely responsible for leading public worship and for administering the sacraments. Although elected by the community, he has virtually unlimited power in matters of religion. The bishops' authority is derived from their presumed descent from the Apostles and the belief that they will adhere to the original teachings of the Church. CHRIS

150s–
180s

The Daoist Way of Great Peace in eastern China attracts hundreds of thousands of adherents; they become known as the Yellow Turbans for their distinctive headgear. (They choose yellow for its association with the venerated Yellow Emperor of legend.) In Sichuan in the west, the Daoist Five

Pecks of Rice movement spreads, and members recite the "five thousand words" of the *Laozi*, which are widely believed to possess magical powers. A grandson of founding Celestial Master Zhang Daoling will establish an autonomous theocratic state in parts of Sichuan and Shanxi and present himself as the earthly representative of Laozi. A long line of successive celestial masters will be known to Westerners as the "Daoist popes." **DAO**

150   The Greek scientist Ptolemy writes his *Tetrabiblos* in Alexandria, Egypt. In this book he seeks to place astrology within the framework of astronomy and philosophy. He is the best known proponent of astrology during his lifetime and for several centuries thereafter. **SPIR**

150–
250   This is the period of the Gandharan, or Indo-Greek, school of art in India's northwest region. Unique in the long history of Indian art, these works exhibit Buddhist content and classical Greco-Roman modeling and costume. Sculptures predominate; statues, portraits, narrative relief carvings, Mahayana saints, and *bodhisattvas* (enlightened beings who devote themselves to the improvement of humans) are common. Gandharan-style art is produced in some peripheral territories for six centuries. **BUDD**

156   (St.) Polycarp (c. 70–156), the bishop of Smyrna, is killed. He is an early Christian martyr, and the account of his martyrdom in an epistle from the Church of Smyrna is the oldest account of a Christian martyr. As such, it establishes some basic requirements of martyrdom, including that it must follow the suffering of Christ, involve the collection of relics by followers (the cult), and require specific forms of prayer. **CHRIS**

c. 160   The Bible is translated into the Syriac language. This version, known as the Distessaron, is suppressed and largely disappears after the fifth century. **CHRIS**

160–
175   What is perhaps the first synod (meeting of Christian bishops from different communities) takes place in Asia Minor. The bishops meet to discuss common problems and develop shared solutions. The synod becomes an important means of creating unity across the dispersed Christian communities in Asia, Europe, and Africa. **CHRIS**

165   The Feast of Love, the precursor to the Mass, is being used by Christians. In this early form it involves prayer by the assembled, a kiss of peace, a prayer over bread and wine by the leader of the assembly, and the eating and drinking of the bread and wine. **CHRIS**

165–
66   With imperial sanction, Daoists in Han China worship a deified Laozi and make sacrifices to him. He is represented as an eternal god who lives in the heavens and presides over the universe; he appears on earth from time to time to advise the emperors. **DAO**

166	The cult of the Buddha is formally introduced at China's imperial court in Luoyang. **BUDD**
166	The number of Christians in Rome now exceeds the number of Jews, although both groups remain minorities, as most Romans are what are later called pagans. **CHRIS**
c. 170	Lokakshema, a Buddhist monk from Kushan, the Buddhist realm of northern India and central Asia, comes to China and forms a team that translates largely Mahayana Buddhist texts; he is regarded as the founder of Mahayana Buddhism in China. **BUDD**
170–180	The Chinese chronicle *Wei Zhi* (*The Record of Wei* in the *History of the Three Kingdoms*) of 297 C.E. reports warfare among 30 chiefdoms of Wa (Japan), which ends when Priestess-Queen Himiko of Yamatai emerges victorious and unites these factions under her leadership. **SHINTO**
c. 170–220	Mou Zi of China writes a text, known only by his name, that defends Buddhism against Confucian critics. **BUDD**
170–220	The canon of the Christian Church expands when the Four Gospels and the 13 letters of Paul, which were accepted as canon in c. 130, are combined with the Christian version of the Old Testament. The Christian version is based on the Jewish version used in Alexandria, Egypt, and contains writings in addition to those in the other Jewish versions. **CHRIS**
175	After decades of study, scholarly conferences and government-sponsored scholars arrive at an approved version of the Confucian Classics, and the imperial court in China has it carved on large stone tablets. These tablets are later housed in the museum of Xian. **CONF**
c. 178	(St.) Irenaeus (c. 140–c. 200) is elected the bishop of Lyons. He is possibly the first bishop to begin setting forth Church creed—teachings of the bishops—which sets forth basic doctrine that is accepted by all members of the Church. **CHRIS**
180s	The spread of civil war in Han dynasty China spurs the development of religious Daoism. Alongside Buddhism, it will become one of the two great clerical and salvationist religions of China. Features of the Daoist political/utopian movements that spring to life include confession of sins, good deeds such as almsgiving, and abstention from alcohol. **BUDD, DAO**
c. 180–226	About 180 Shih Hsieh, a Chinese, is appointed prefect of a region that includes much of northern Vietnam; he is able to take advantage of the increasingly ineffective Han dynasty to become the *de facto* ruler, which the Han court officially recognizes in 205. Contacts and trade with India thrive; in particular, Buddhism prospers and Buddhist temples are built. **BUDD**

184   The Daoist-inspired Yellow Turban rebellion flares in eastern China, especially in coastal regions. Several hundred thousand peasants rise up when omens and visions persuade them that the Han dynasty should be brought to an end. The *Scripture of the Great Peace,* the Yellow Turbans' textual authority, recommends filial piety, obedience, and loyalty and contains prescriptions for magical cures for disease.   **DAO, TOL**

185   The Montanism movement begins in Asia Minor. It is a Christian millenarian movement whose founder, Montanus, prophesies the approaching end of the world and the arrival of heaven on earth. The movement spreads to Rome and north Africa but is condemned as heresy by the Christian Church in 200 and disappears in the early third century.   **CHRIS**

185   The eunuch-dominated Han imperial court of China, too weak to react to the spread of the Dao-influenced Yellow Turban rebellion, turns to provincial warlords for protection. The warlords swiftly subdue the main Yellow Turban outbreak and kill most of the rebel leaders, including the three Zhang brothers. Minor outbreaks continue, however, until around 207. The religious uprisings effectively bring the Han dynasty to an end, though a figurehead emperor will reign tenuously until 220.   **DAO, TOL**

c. 189   Victor, the bishop of Rome until about 199, is the first Christian leader to write in Latin. Before then, Christian texts were written in Greek, the language of masses, suggesting that Christianity appealed to the common people.   **CHRIS**

The Five Pecks of Rice Daoist State in China

In Shanxi and Sichuan, in the enclave known as Hanzhong, Zhang Lu (r. 190–215), grandson of the Daoist Celestial Master Zhang Daoling, expanded the Five Pecks of Rice sect into a theocratic autonomous state, with the aim of creating a perfect earthly state under the rule of religion and morality. The community adopted many practices of the Yellow Turbans of east central China, including medical cures through confession of sins, recitation of sacred texts, and an ecclesiastical hierarchy. Every believer in Zhang's enclave paid five pecks of rice to his religious leaders. The sect established charity houses and other aid programs and effectively ruled for nearly four decades, remaining strong and influential in western China through the end of the Han dynasty. The government's leading officials, called libationers, handled both religious and administrative duties. They collected tax payments (not just grain, but fabrics, paper, and other products as well) and managed the honor-system inns that provided rice and meat to needy travelers. Misdeeds—drunkenness, adultery, theft—were expiated by public confession and penances that involved public service such as road repair. Sickness was regarded as a punishment for sins. Religious ceremonies included communal meals called "kitchens," consisting of snacks, alcohol, and rice. Festivals of the Three Administrations—Heaven, Earth, and Water—took place three times a year. There were strictly controlled sexual rites that begin with a fast, prayers, and breathing exercises with a ritual dance following.

190s	Daoist groups form protective societies in disturbed areas of China and carry out administrative and military, as well as religious, functions. **DAO**
193	Large communities of Buddhist converts flourish in eastern China. Buddhists build a vast temple in the Chu capital of Pengcheng that stands several stories high and can hold 3,000 devotees. Later this year the warlord Cao Cao sacks Pengcheng, driving a Buddhist community more than 10,000 strong south to the Yangzi, where the Buddha cult is thus introduced. **BUDD**
193–211	During the rule of Septimius Severus, the Roman Empire begins systematic persecution of Christians when an edict is issued that requires governors of Roman territory to persecute Christians. Because of their loyalty to God, Christians are believed to have less than full loyalty to the emperor. **CHRIS**
c. 197	*Apology* is written by the early Christian theologian Tertullian (c. 160–c. 225) in North Africa. He is the first Christian theologian to write in Latin; his other major works include *Against Marcion, Against Praxeas, On the Soul, The Soldier's Crown, On Penitence,* and *On Modesty.* **CHRIS**
c. 200	Christians have grown in number in the Roman Empire and begin meeting outside private homes to worship together. Many of these places of worship are shrines built at places associated with early martyrs of the Church. **CHRIS**
c. 200	Christianity has now spread into southern France (Gaul) and is practiced by both the elite and the common people as indicated by the use of both Latin and Celtic by priests. **CHRIS**
200	By the end of the Han dynasty in China, all public schools offer regular sacrifices to Confucius and many temples are built. Eventually a Confucian temple stands in every one of the 2,000 counties. **CONF**
200	This is the probable rough date of the appearance in China of the commentary on the *Dao De Jing* known as the *Xiang'er*. Ascribed by tradition to Zhang Lu, head of the autonomous Daoist state in Sichuan, it is the earliest such interpretive work. The early Celestial Masters organization uses it as a catechism to be recited by the faithful. **DAO**
200s	The Chinese chronicle *Wei Zhi* carries an account of the Eastern Barbarians, including the "people of Wa," or the Japanese. The religious practices described include divination by baking of bones, purification rites, magic, and taboos. **SHINTO**
200s	The Inner Shrine of Ise, Japan's most important Shinto shrine, is founded as the center of the Yamato clan's worship of its divine ancestors and of the sun goddess Amaterasu Omikami, the mythical ancestor of the imperial

family. The shrine will not be opened to the public until the late 15th century. **SHINTO**

200s–300s Around the southern coast of Cambodia, the Kingdom of Funan has experienced maritime navigators and builders of large ships who trade with India, China, and, indirectly, Rome. During the fourth century, the process of Indianization broadens, perhaps influenced by waves of traders and pilgrims. Temples of brick and stone honor the Hindu gods Siva, and to a lesser extent, Vishnu; the Funanese are also touched by Buddhism. It appears that its main port city Oc Eo goes into decline during the fourth century, when an all-sea route is pioneered between India and China via the Straits of Malacca. **BUDD**

200–300 During this century the Jain holy man Umaswati writes the *Tatvartha-Sutra*, the first work on Jain philosophy; it ranges from logic and epistemology to ethics and cosmology. Its contents are generally accepted by both the Svetambara and the Digambara Jains. **JAIN**

200–750 Teotihuacan, located in central Mexico, houses a population of about 200,000 at its height in 500 C.E. and is the imperial center of Mesoamerica. The city is designed as a religious symbol, with streets and buildings aligned with astronomical features and in accord with beliefs about the structure and nature of the universe. It also contains large monuments and plazas. The worship of various gods, who are later worshiped in other Mesoamerican cultures, including Tlaloc, the Rain God, and Quetzalcoatl, the Feathered Serpent, is institutionalized here. In about 750 the religious center is destroyed, perhaps in a revolt against imperial rule. **NATIV**

200–900 During the Classic period of the Maya of Mesoamerica a number of religious innovations take place. These include the development of a number of calendrical systems designed to align human events with astronomical phenomena. The long count calendar is the most elaborate, a detailed mythology explaining the creation of the universe, a system of writing, and the building of major ceremonial centers. For unknown reasons, the Mayan civilization suddenly collapses about 900 C.E. **NATIV**

200–900 During the Classic period of Maya civilization in Mesoamerica the Maya religion experiences its greatest expression. Major ceremonial centers become the focus of life for surrounding communities, religious calendars reach their highest complexity, and the priests share power with the royalty, who are seen as the manifestations of gods on earth. Maya societies are highly stratified, with the rich and powerful having far more access and involvement in religion than do the mass of people, who are farmers and live outside the ceremonial centers. **NATIV**

200–1000 States appear in the Andean Highlands of South America that are governed from cities that serve as political and economic capitals and also as ceremonial centers with platforms, temples, carved stones, and a concern with alignment with features of the environment. The religion centers on anthropomorphic gods, rituals that venerate the leaders, and human sacrifice to the gods. **NATIV**

200–1200

During this time Jainism flourishes in Karnataka, the southwestern region of India, due to the support given it by a succession of ruling dynasties. In particular, the Gangas dynasty gives great credit to a Jain sage-teacher, Simhanandi, for having influenced the most notable of their early kings, Kongunivarma I. All these dynasties are generous in donating property, food, and other material support to the Jain monks, in serving as patrons of scholars and poets, and in general promoting Jainism; in return, individual Jain gurus advise the kings in both spiritual and worldly matters. During this era, too, Jainism takes hold in Tamiland, the southernmost region of the peninsula. It is the Digambara, or sky-clad Jains, who predominate in southern India. **JAIN**

215

The Daoist Celestial Master Zhang Lu surrenders to the Chinese warlord Cao Cao, who absorbs Zhang's Five Pecks of Rice movement and dismantles his autonomous state. Zhang's heirs will adopt the title of celestial masters. Thousands of members of the Hanzhong Celestial Masters community disperse and resettle, spreading Daoism throughout the realm. **DAO**

215

The Jewish *Mishnah,* a compilation of rabbinic teachings, traditions, and laws, is written down. It covers six matters: agriculture, festivals, women, torts, religious matters, and ritual purity. SEE **250, JUD**. **JUD**

Daoism during the Three Kingdoms and Six Dynasties Era in China

The Yellow Turban and Five Pecks of Rice religious institutions of late Han China were perpetuated in the gradual development of a Daoist church during the Three Kingdoms and Six Dynasties period. Daoism became established as the religion of China, as distinct from the imperial cult, popular religious manifestations, and the foreign religion of Buddhism. The three major scriptural traditions of Daoism took shape: the Celestial Masters, the *Shangqing* (Higher Purity), and the *Lingbao* (Numinous Gem). Rituals, codes, and meditations were expanded and a priesthood was established. Daoist communities divided into parishes that were supported by believers' contributions of grain and other products. Daoists marked important days and events with feasts and fasts, including the "fast of mud and charcoal," a ritual of contrition in which adherents smeared their faces as proof of the expiation of their sins. There were also "union of breath" ceremonies that featured ritual sexual activities in public. These ceremonies were supposed to guarantee a long life. The first Daoist temples appeared during this period. They were usually patterned after Buddhist monasteries, themselves modeled on imperial palace architecture.

215–
250

Heshang Gong's influential commentary on the *Dao De Jing*, the founding text of Daoism, circulates in China. This and other commentaries give rise to the philosophical movement known as neo-Daoism. With the state cult of Confucianism on the wane, intellectual interest in Daoism builds; at the same time Buddhism spreads among the masses, as well as the educated classes. The scholar-officials Wang Bi (226–249) and his friend He Yan (d. 249) are admirers of the *Laozi* and the *Zhuangzi*, but their philosophical aim is to infuse new meaning into Confucian texts and to reinterpret Daoism in terms of Confucian social and moral philosophy. The sage, they argue, does not withdraw from the world, as Dao purists suggest, but rather seeks social and political involvement. **CONF, DAO**

220–
300

After the Han dynasty in China, disenchantment with the excessive scholasticism of earlier Confucianism leads men living in an uncertain era to approach Confucian classics like the *I Ching* in new ways, borrowing from the *Lao-tzu* and *Chuang-tzu*, and creating a synthesis known as *Hsuan-hsueh*, the "Dark Learning." **CONF, DAO**

220–
589

A period of fragmentation known as the Three Kingdoms and Six Dynasties follows the collapse of the Han empire in China. It's a tumultuous era, the longest single stretch of disunion in China's history. Smaller states coexist until reunification under the Sui dynasty near the end of the sixth century. **DAO**

222–
235

During the rule of Alexander Severus, persecution of Christians is temporarily halted in the Roman Empire and Jesus is afforded a place in the pantheon of Roman gods. **CHRIS**

226–
240

According to Zoroastrian tradition, during the reign of King Ardashir I of the Sassanid dynasty, Zoroastrianism is established as the state religion of Persia. In the 20th century scholars believe that it was King Shapur I (r. 224–271) who established a state religion and that it may have been Zoroastrianism, Mazdakism, or Zurvanism. **SECT**

227–
651

During the rule of the Sassanid dynasty in Persia, a state religion is promulgated based on the ancient Zoroastrian sacred text (*Avesta*), with an organized priesthood and the high priest second in power only to the king. At the same time, the rulers persecute followers of other religions, including Judaism, Christianity, Manichaeism, Mazdakism, Hinduism, and Buddhism. **CIVIL**

230

Sun Quan (185–252), founder of the central Chinese Wu Kingdom, orders his leading general to organize an expedition to search for immortality herbs, a feature of Daoism. **DAO**

231

The Christian priest and scholar Origen (c. 185–c. 254) establishes a school at Caesarea in Palestine. His theological interpretations concerning the nature of the soul and resurrection and other issues, known as Origenism, are controversial during and following his lifetime. They are condemned by the Church at the Second Council of Constantinople in 553.   CHRIS

235–
244

Persecution of Christians, which had been halted from 222 to 235, resumes when Maximin becomes Roman Emperor and continues through a series of emperors until 244.   CHRIS

236

The basic form of Eucharistic prayers in Christianity has taken shape, and they are recorded in the *Church Order* by Hippolytus (?–236).   CHRIS

240

The Manichaeist religion is founded by Mani (216–c. 277), a member of the Mandaean sect in Persia. Mani had visions and received revelations beginning at the age of 12, and at the age of 24 began preaching of his new religion. Manichaeism is based on Christianity, Zoroastrianism, Buddhism, local religions, and the teachings of Mani and includes a complex view of the universe, multiple gods, and reincarnation. The religion is spread into central Asia by missionaries.   SECT

Zoroastrianism

Zoroastrianism, which emerged in the Near East (probably in northwest Iran) probably between -400 and 500 B.C.E., is the oldest prophetic religion in the world. It was never a world religion and probably not even a major regional religion, and there are only about 200,000 adherents today. It played a central role in the development of other major religions, however. Jews, Christians, and Muslims in ancient times were in contact with the Zoroastrians of Persia, and from Zoroastrianism these religions took the concepts of a supreme god, the devil, a pantheon of angels and demons, heaven and hell, resurrection, an afterlife, judgment at death, a messianic age, and Armageddon. Very little is known about the emergence and development of Zoroastrianism, and the traditional view of Zoroastrians is often at odds with the interpretations of archaeologists, historians, and religious scholars. It developed as a distinct religion in the first millennium B.C.E. and was an accepted religion and perhaps at times the official religion of the Persian Empire. Zoroastrianism was repressed for some 1,200 years under Muslim rule in Iran and spread to China, where it disappeared, and India, where the Zoroastrians are called Farsis. The Farsis benefitted from British rule and formed a wealthy economic and political elite. In the 20th century there has been some migration to Britain and the United States. Zoroastrians believe in a supreme god (*Ahura Mazada*) who oversees a world of continual conflict between good and evil. Zoroastrians pursue "good thoughts, good words, and good deeds" and at death are judged, with the good going to heaven and the evil to hell. Sacred texts are collected in the *Avesta*, which includes prayers, hymns, and ritual instructions. Fire is an important element in Zoroastrianism as it represents purity, light, warmth, and power, and a fire is kept burning in all temples and in all Zoroastrian homes. The largest populations of Zoroastrians are in India, Iran, and communities in the United States, Great Britain, Australia, and Pakistan.

243 Christian missionary Gregory the Wonderworker arrives in Asia Minor and during the next 30 years is instrumental in converting most of the pagan peoples of the region to Christianity. **CHRIS**

244–
249
During the rule of Philip the Arabian, who is friendly to the Christians, persecution of Christians is again halted in the Roman Empire. **CHRIS**

246 (St.) Cyprian (c. 205–258), a recent convert to Christianity, is made bishop of Carthage, a major center of Christianity in North Africa. He suffers through the repression of Christianity by the Roman Emperor Decius from 249 to 251. After the end of the repression he rebaptizes those who had left the faith and sets forth the doctrine that "Outside the church there is no salvation." **CHRIS**

249–
251
Christians, who have been sporadically persecuted since 64 C.E. by Roman emperors, suffer perhaps the harshest persecution yet during the rule of Decius. Christians are forced by threat of death to abandon Christianity and many do so, although many others are tortured and die as martyrs. From 252 on persecutions abate for 50 years and many people return to Christianity. **CHRIS**

c. 250 Pope Fabian (r. 236–250) divides the Roman Empire into seven regions with a deacon placed in authority in each region, marking the beginning of a centralized administrative structure in the Christian Church. **CHRIS**

250 Work on the Jewish *Mishnah* continues through the adding of wisdom from rabbis and scholars to make it applicable to the situation confronting Jews as they live under Roman rule. This extension of the *Mishnah* is called the *Gemara* and is completed by about 400. **JUD**

250s The Chinese philosopher Ji Kang (223–262) is the leader of a group of neo-Daoist intellectuals known as the Seven Sages of the Bamboo Grove. The group meets regularly in the shade of the bamboo to engage in philosophical discussions inspired by the freedom of Daoist thought. One of the sages, Ruan Ji (210–263), produces a study titled *Toward an Understanding of the Zhuangzi*, an early neo-Daoist commentary. Other members of the group are practicing religious Daoists who cultivate the techniques of longevity. Others, however, are dilettantes who overindulge in drink, drugs, and nudism. They give Daoism a bad name among conservative members of the Confucian ruling class. **DAO**

250s The Chinese scholars Xiang Xiu, a member of the Seven Sages of the Bamboo Grove, and Guo Xiang (d. 312) collaborate on an important commentary on Daoism, part philosophical exegesis and part reconstructed and edited version of the *Zhuangzi*—the version we have today. Xiang Xiu prepared the first commentary. Guo Xiang revised the work, which calls for a compromise and reconciliation between Daoism and Confucianism. Guo stresses Zhuangzi's notions of self-transformation and contentment as his central themes. **DAO**

250–400	Confucian scholar Wani, from the Korean state of Paekche, arrives in Japan with 11 volumes of classic Chinese writings. He becomes tutor to the crown prince and institutes the specialized occupation of scribes, who become essential for keeping accurate records in bureaucratic government. **CONF**
250–600	Japan's Kofun period is named after the era's monumental mounded-earth mausoleum tombs, often encircled with moats and adorned with hollow clay figures of priests, dancers, mourners, animals, servants, and soldiers. The burial objects found by archaeologists include ceremonial swords, bronze mirrors, and curved jewels. These are the source of the tradition of the Imperial Regalia, or Three Sacred Treasures, the ritual objects passed on at the accession of each new emperor, symbolizing the descent of the imperial line from the sun goddess Amaterasu. **SHINTO**
c. 251	(St.) Agatha (? – c. 251), who is later designated the patron saint of Catania, Sicily, as well as wet nurses and bell founders, is executed in Sicily during the general persecution of Christians across the Roman Empire. She is tortured and burned to death after refusing the advances of a Roman consul and refusing to renounce Christianity. **CATH**
255	This is the traditional date for the appearance in China of the *Commands and Admonitions for the Families of the Great Dao*. It contains an account of the origin of the Dao and, in a break with past practice, gives prominence to filiality, loyalty, and other expressly Confucian virtues. The work is sometimes attributed to the Celestial Master Zhang Lu, though it is unlikely to have come from his hand. **DAO**
255	Astrology is criticized by the philosopher Platinus, the developer of the Neoplatonism school of philosophy in Rome. His ideas are influential among Christians who also reject astrology. **SPIR**
261	Roman emperor Gallienus issues an edict of toleration concerning Christians and returns property to them that had been taken earlier. **CHRIS**
266	The Wei Kingdom falls in China. For the next 150 years, historical documentation on Daoism will be scarce. **DAO**
274	Roman emperor Aurelian establishes the worship of the sun (Sol Invictus) as a Roman religious practice and designates December 25 as a day of national celebration. **CIVIL**
c. 277	Mani, the Apostle of Light and founder of Manichaeism, is executed by Sassanid Persian king Bahram I at the urging of Zoroastrian high priest Kartir. **SECT**
288	The Daoist scholar Wang Fu in China prepares his polemic *Laozi Huahujing* (*Book of the Conversion of the Barbarians by Laozi*), a harsh attack on

Buddhism. He claims the Buddha is only one incarnation of Laozi and that Buddhism is merely a coarser form of Daoism. **BUDD, DAO**

c. 290   The *Teachings of the Apostles,* which sets forth instructions for bishops, priests, and deacons of the Christian churches, is written. It is later incorporated into other documents but falls into disuse after the seventh century. **CHRIS**

300   By this time, nearly all pagan peoples along the coast of North Africa have converted to Christianity. **CHRIS**

c. 300–500   The early Hindu *Puranas* are written. They are religious texts of myth, folklore, and legends that concern virtually all matters of the Hindu religion. New *Puranas* are created and old ones revised and amended as Hinduism begins to develop regional and local forms across northern India. **HIND**

300s   A Daoist cult of filial piety appears in China, centered on the Sichuan saint Xu Sun (239–292), a scholar/official. He rids his home region of an evil dragon and other monsters, ends epidemics, and keeps the waterways clean and safe. A shrine is built to him on West Mountain near Nanchang in Jiangxi Province, and Daoist techniques are practiced there. The shrine lapses after a time, only to be revived during the early T'ang dynasty and later eras. **DAO**

300s   The legend of the immaculate conception of the Daoist philosopher Laozi and his birth from his mother's right side is attested to in China in scholarly writings and becomes part of Daoist belief. **DAO**

300s   The revival of Daoism opens the way for the infiltration of Buddhism into China's educated elite. The two religious philosophies will react powerfully on one another, Daoism making Buddhism clearer to the Chinese mind, Buddhism making Daoism more explicit. With the "barbarian" invasions of North China and the retreat of the Chinese imperial court south to the Yangzi River, contacts and exchanges of ideas increase between Daoist and Buddhist intellectuals. **DAO, BUDD**

300s   Japan's Yamato clan gains supremacy over the country's other clans. The Yamato will manipulate Shinto mythology to legitimize their claim to political power. **SHINTO**

300s–400s   Two of the major texts of Theravada Buddhism, the *Dipavamsa* (*Short Chronicle*) and the *Mahavamsa* (*Great Chronicle*) are probably compiled on Sri Lanka. **BUDD**

300s - 600   In Japan Izumo, the main shrine of the Shinto tradition second only to Ise, is established. During this Kofun period, Japanese society is grouped into clans (*uji*) who each worship their own tutelary divinities or *ujigami*. This worship often is carried on through the organization of corporate groups or *be* with distinct rituals and ideology. **SHINTO**

300s– 620	A period of disunity in China follows the end of the Han dynasty (220 C.E.), as non-Chinese peoples invade from the north and a succession of states rise and fall in the south. Confucianism goes into decline, as Buddhism and neo-Daoism spread rapidly throughout much of China, although there are some instances of restrictive legislation and even persecution. Buddhism's appeal lies in its offering of consolations and magical powers; Buddhism appeals to common people as a comfort in times of distress. Buddhist ideas and images open up new imaginative worlds for Chinese artists and thinkers, although Confucian ideas continue to shape the views of the elite on politics, society, ethics, and etiquette, and Confucius continues to be universally honored as a sage. Buddhism becomes established in China in its Mahayana form, the Greater Vehicle, with its worship of the Buddha in various manifestations. Many Buddhist texts are translated into Chinese, including the first Chinese edition of the Tripitaka (518 C.E.). Through translation of the *sutras* (traditional sermons and teachings of the Buddha and successor sages), the Chinese make major adaptations to the Buddhism of India. Non-Chinese invaders, who settle permanently among the Chinese and adopt their ways, are especially quick to accept Buddhism. **BUDD, TOL**
301– 330	Armenia becomes a Christian kingdom when King Trdat is converted to Christianity by missionary Gregory the Enlightener (c. 240–332). Armenia has remained a Christian nation ever since and in the 1990s is the oldest continuously Christian nation in the world. Claims made by some experts that Armenia was the first Christian kingdom are probably erroneous, as the small kingdom of Osrhoene in Mesopotamia probably converted at an earlier date. **CHRIS**
303– 312	Perhaps the harshest and the final persecution of Christians by the Roman Empire begins during the rule of Diocletian (r. 284–305) and continues until 312, although it ends for a brief period in 311 during the rule of Galerius. By official order churches are destroyed, books burned, Christians forbidden to assemble, and first church officials and then commoners tortured and killed. The persecution is motivated in part by threats to the empire from eastern invaders and a resulting disruption of life that is blamed on the Christians. **CHRIS**
c. 304	(St.) Agnes (c. 292–304), who is later designated the patron saint of betrothed couples, gardeners, and virgins, is executed in Rome during the general persecution of Christians across the Roman Empire. A virgin, she is exposed as a Christian and forced into prostitution, although she refuses to renounce Christianity or sacrifice her virginity and is tortured and executed before becoming a martyr. **CATH**
304	(St.) Afra, who is later designated the patron saint of penitent women, is executed in Augsburg, Germany, during the general persecution of Christians across the Roman Empire. A prostitute, she refuses to renounce

Christianity and is executed along with her mother and servants and becomes a martyr. CATH

c. 305 (St.) Alban becomes the first Christian martyr in Britain when he is tortured and executed for refusing to renounce Christianity during the general persecution of Christians throughout the Roman Empire. CATH

305 Christian monasticism is founded by (St.) Antony (251–356), later made the patron saint of basket makers, when he comes out of 20 years of hermitage and establishes a community of monks in Pispir, Egypt. From a wealthy Christian family, he gives away his wealth to the poor upon his parents' death. CHRIS

c. 310 (St.) Catherine (c. 290–c. 310) is beheaded by Roman emperor Maxentius in Alexandria after he holds her responsible for converting his family to Christianity. Her life and devotion to Christ are associated with several miracles, and she is widely worshiped across Europe in the Middle Ages. CATH

c. 310 At the council of Elvira in Spain, representatives from 36 dioceses in Spain are in attendance. Their presence indicates that Christianity has spread widely in Spain, although it has not by this time spread across the entire peninsula nor attracted many common people. CHRIS

312 Roman emperor Constantine (c. 288–337) is the first emperor to accept Christianity. He does so following a dream in which the words "In this sign, you will conquer" on a cross precede his victory over rival Maxentius at the Battle of Milvian Bridge. CHRIS

Catholic Monasticism

During the Middle Ages monasteries and convents in Europe were places where people aspired to lead lives of perfection, prayer, humility, and discipline in the service of God. Monks and nuns took vows of poverty, chastity, and obedience—vows still taken by some Catholic monks today. To permit monks to better fulfill their vows, European monasteries were generally located in the wilderness, far from the worldly presence of the towns. Monks labored to farm the land and convert pagans. Eventually, the monasteries became centers of culture. The monasteries, which provided some of the few available medieval schools, drew people from far away and encouraged the growth of towns around them. Monasteries also served important social functions, offering a respectable retirement for noble widows and noblemen, and an honorable situation for unmarried noblewomen. Powerful families gave financial support to monasteries and convents to guarantee their families a refuge in time of need and expected in return to have relatives appointed as abbots or abbesses in charge of the monasteries.

313   Roman emperors Constantine (of the East) and Licinius (of the West) issue the Edict of Milan, which grants Christians religious freedom throughout the Roman Empire.   **CHRIS**

314   At the Council of Arles in southern France, three bishops from Britain are in attendance. Their presence indicates that Christianity has penetrated into Britain, but when it first arrived is not known.   **CHRIS**

315   Roman emperor Constantine issues edicts designed to repress the Jewish community in Roman lands.   **JUD**

315   Eusebius of Caesarea (c. 265–c. 340) is elected bishop and plays a major role in the establishment of Christianity as the state religion during the rule of Constantine. He is a major theologian and historian whose major works include *Ecclesiastical History, Chronicle, Life of Constantine*, and *Martyrs of Palestine*.   **ORTHO**

317   The Chinese scholar and alchemist Ge Hong (283–343) finishes his *Baopuzi* (*"The Master Who Embraces Simplicity*," a quotation from the *Laozi*), an encyclopedia of Daoist beliefs and knowledge. A member of a south China aristocratic family, Ge is a seeker of immortality through alchemical practices. Though usually regarded as a Daoist, he also propounds Confucian thinking: he divides his *Baopuzi* into two sections, one devoted to Daoism, the other to Confucianism. Each—spiritual Daoism, worldly Confucianism—has its place. The book deals with immortals, medical prescriptions, and methods of prolonging life that combine breathing exercises and sexual practices with drugs and elixirs. It also summarizes Ge's social and political views. With this and other works, Ge develops a new tradition of Daoist thought.   **DAO**

320   A form of Christian monasticism based on prayer, study of the Scriptures, and communal work is established by Pachomius (c. 290–346), a former soldier and monk, when he founds a monastery in Egypt. By the end of his life he has established eight additional monasteries for men and two for women in Egypt.   **CHRIS**

320 - 454   The Golden or Classic Age of Indian civilization occurs during the Gupta Empire (c. 220–647), which is at its most powerful and so controls much of India and influences other regions not under its direct control. During the Classic Age, major advances are made in literature, science, technology, law, drama, dance, and philosophy. During this period, which extends to about 800 C.E., Hinduism achieves its definitive form, with major developments in both the north and south. During this period, as in most others in Indian history, Jain images of the *tirthankaras* reflect a direct dependence on Buddhist prototypes: The statues can easily be mistaken for images of the Buddha, in technical details of the carving, in poses, and in overall style. Buddhism continues to flourish. Sculpture of the Gupta period, known for its elegance and simplicity, is the classical style of plastic art in India. It refines earlier Kushan

conventions, depicting gods and goddesses and narrative legends and myths. Artists in Sarnath, Uttar Pradesh, specialize in Buddhist temple sculpture; the simple, serene style developed there will exert profound influence on sculpture in central and eastern India and Southeast Asia. Workshops in Mathura, by contrast, produce images for Buddhists, Jains, Vaishnavites, and Saivites alike; much of their work is exported. Traders, scholars, and monks from India contribute to the spread of Buddhism in Vietnam, although the mass of Vietnamese do not abandon their traditional belief in the spirits that inhabit natural forms. **BUDD, HIND, JAIN**

325   The (First) Council of Nicaea is held in Turkey by bishops with nearly all representing churches in the east (Asia) and only minimal representation from the west (Europe). The Council is called by Emperor Constantine to resolve disputes over Arianism, the doctrine that Christ is not equal in divinity to God. The council rejects Arianism and uses the word *homoousion* (Greek for "of like substance") to define the relationship between God and Christ, Father and Son. The Council establishes the basic doctrine of Catholic and Orthodox Christianity, as theologians declare that God had three aspects, known as the Trinity: the Father, the Son, and the Holy Spirit. Mary is worshiped as the Mother of God or the "God-Bearer" without the Roman Catholic concept of the Immaculate Conception. The council also establishes the date of Easter and Church sees, and gives the sees in Rome, Alexandria, and Antioch authority over other sees in their regions. In practice Rome enjoys the greatest power due to the earlier presence of (Sts.) Peter and Paul, its ties to the Roman Empire, and the wealth it has amassed. **CHRIS**

c. 330   (St.) Nicholas, who lives in the fourth century, may be the bishop of Myra in southwestern Asia Minor. Little is known of his life, but legends about his charity eventually result in his being made the patron saint of children. Those legends are then combined by Christians in northern Europe with the pagan god Thor to form the figure of Santa Claus. **CHRIS**

330   The Georgian Church, later the Georgian Orthodox Church, is established when King Mirian converts to Christianity. The conversion is effected by one Nina, the Apostle to the Georgians, of whom nothing is known in later centuries. The church is under the authority of the church in Antioch until 506. **ORTHO**

334–361   King Mahasena reigns on Sri Lanka. He forces the Mahavihara monks to flee to the south of the island and establishes a third major monastery, the Jetavana. It will be abolished in the late 1100s by another Sri Lankan king. **BUDD, TOL**

336   Christians in Rome celebrate Christmas, the feast of Jesus's birth, perhaps for the first time. It is celebrated on December 25 in the west and on January 6 in the east. In the fifth century it shifts to December 25 in the east, except for the Armenian Church, which continues to celebrate it on January 6

in the 20th century. In Rome it replaces the pagan festivals, including a national celebration of the sun. **CHRIS**

337   The astrology textbook *Mathesis* is written in Greek by the Sicilian Julius Firmicus Maternus. The book is not especially popular during his lifetime but is rediscovered in Europe in Latin translation in the 11th century and becomes a major source of information about ancient Greek astrology. **SPIR**

341   Frumentius is appointed bishop of the Christian Church in Ethiopia. Earlier in the century he and another young man, named Aedesius, had been shipwrecked off the coast and had begun converting Ethiopians to Christianity. Their work is continued by monks who arrive in the next century. **CHRIS**

341   Christian missionary activity among the Goths of central Europe begins when Ulfilas (c. 311–383), a man from central Turkey, is appointed bishop to the Goths. He translates the New Testament into the Gothic language. **CHRIS**

c. 350   A new school of Mahayana Buddhism, Vijnanavada, or Yogacarin, is taking shape in India. Its chief proponents are the brothers Asanga and Vasubandhu; they stress the quest for achieving pure thought, in part through the practice of meditation and yoga. Their writings, which include the *Mahayana Samgraha*, the *Vimsika*, and the *Trimsika*, will inspire schools of Buddhism in China and eventually in Japan **(SEE 563, BUDD)**. Another work attributed to Vasubandhu, the *Abhidharma Kosa*, will become a major text for the Ju She school of Buddhism **(SEE 563–567, BUDD)**. Monastic Theravada Buddhism continues to prevail, particularly in north India. **BUDD**

350   Constantius (r. 337–361), the son of Constantine, becomes the sole Roman emperor and as a strong supporter of Christianity moves to eradicate paganism by closing temples and banning sacrifices. Paganism survives but only in large cities such as Rome and Alexandria. **CHRIS**

350   Around this time, during Japan's early Kofun period, the Yamato clan establish their court in the Nara region. As the country's single ruling family, the Yamato base their power on descent from the sun goddess Amaterasu. **SHINTO**

350s   Chinese scholars attempt to synthesize the doctrines of Confucianism, Daoism, and Buddhism. However, the Buddhist clergyman Chi Dun (314–366) challenges Confucian interpretations of the Daoist *Zhuangzi*, equating these Confucian interpretations with voluntary servitude. "Let us escape into the infinite," he suggests, "like the phoenix in its prodigious flight, like the Buddhist who frees himself from the world!" **BUDD, DAO**

352–379   King Meghavanna reigns on Sri Lanka, during which time the Tooth Relic, believed to be the tooth of the Buddha, arrives on Sri Lanka; the shrine housing it is attached to the Royal Palace. In the late 1200s the tooth relic will be carried off to India, but it is returned in the early 1300s. In the 1600s it is taken to the then capital of Kandy, where it remains through the 20th century, housed in the Temple of the Tooth (Dalada Maligawa). It is Sri Lanka's greatest treasure and the palladium of the nation of Sri Lanka.   **BUDD, TOL**

357   Astrologers—including court or "scientific" astrologers who practice Greek astrology and those who serve the general population—as well as magicians and diviners are banned by the Eastern Roman emperor Constantine. The ban marks the decline of astrology in the Roman Empire, and within 200 years Greek astrology disappears almost entirely from public view, although it continues to be practiced in private.   **SPIR**

357–
360   A council of Jains meets at Mathura, India; led by the teacher Skandila, they attempt to codify Jainism's essential texts and beliefs. In some accounts another council is held at this same time at Valabhi, presided over by Nagarjunasuri. In any case, the two major sects of Jains, Digambaras and Svetambaras, are unable to agree on the canon of the texts.   **JAIN**

358   (St.) Basil the Great (c. 329–379) settles into the life of a hermit on the River Iris in Asia Minor. From a wealthy and devout family, he attracts some followers and establishes the first monastery in the East, which becomes the model for later Eastern Orthodox monasticism, and is recognized as the patron saint of Russia.   **ORTHO**

360s   (St.) Cyril of Jerusalem (c. 313–c. 386), the archbishop of Jerusalem, establishes a calendar of religious events based on the Scriptures that influences subsequent practice in all Christian churches.   **CHRIS**

361–
363   Christianity is again repressed in the Roman Empire, during the reign of Julian. Although raised a Christian, he has admired paganism since boyhood and seeks to restore paganism as the religion of the Empire. His efforts to restrict Christianity and promote paganism fail, and the Roman persecution of Christians ends with his death in 363.   **CHRIS**

363   Ephrem the Syrian (c. 306–373) settles in Edessa, Syria. A Christian theologian, writer, and poet, he composes poems and hymns that become popular in the Eastern Orthodox Church and remain so in the 20th century. **ORTHO**

363   Christianity is again made the official religion of the Roman Empire by Jovian (r. 363–364) and his successors Valentinian I (r. 364–375) and Valens (r. 364–378).   **CHRIS**

364   Astrology is condemned for the first time by Christians at the Council of Laodicaea. Astrology is seen as a form of paganism and superstition, although it is only astrology as practiced by uneducated practitioners that is banned, while the "scientific" astrology that is based on the Greek system continues.   **SPIR**

| 364–370 | Gods and spirits appearing at night reveal and dictate the Daoist texts known as the *Shangqing* (*Great Purity*) scriptures to a Chinese medium named Yang Xi (330–386). Some of these nocturnal "perfected beings" are legendary immortals of China's Han dynasty; others are local saints. The texts will give rise to the Shangqing movement, with its center on Mao Shan (Mount Mao), a holy peak in southwestern Jiangxi Province, the eighth of 10 Grotto-Heavens in the sacred geography of Daoism. The Shangqing school (also called Mao Shan Daoism) mixes elements of the Celestial Masters and Ge Hong traditions and also adapts some Buddhist practices and Confucian notions. The revealed texts contain a fully realized cosmology and pantheon of gods and include *fangshi* practices such as alchemy. A main innovation of the Shangqing school is a greater emphasis on meditation; also, less importance is placed on the use of herbs and drugs. "Private contemplation," says one adept, "is the root and origin of spiritual immortality." Confession of sins is completely private, sexual practices are condemned, and there is no need to travel in search of truth, for it is found within oneself. **DAO** |

| 367 | The full canon of the Christian Church has now been widely accepted throughout the Christian world, as indicated by reference to it in the *Festal Letter* of (St.) Athanasius (c. 296–373), the bishop of Alexandria and a major theologian. **CHRIS** |

| 370 | The rise of the Shangqing movement is, to an extent, a reaction to the introduction of the Celestial Masters tradition into south China from the north. The south China aristocracy widely embraces the new movement, and it will remain the most influential school through the end of the T'ang dynasty in the 10th century. **DAO** |

| 372 | (St.) Martin of Tours (c. 316–c. 400), a former pagan and soldier, is made bishop of Tours in Gaul (southern France). Since his arrival there in 360 he has played and continues to play a leading role in establishing monasteries and churches and converting pagans to Christianity. He is later made the patron saint of France. **CHRIS** |

| 372 | King Sosurim, 17th ruler of Koguryo (r. 371–384), the largest of the three kingdoms into which ancient Korea is divided, establishes T'aehak, a royal academy for the training of prospective government officials in the Chinese language and the Confucian Classics. During his reign he extends the Chinese-influenced bureaucracy and commissions the *Yugi*, a history of Koguryo. **CONF** |

| 372 | According to Japanese tradition, the ruler of the Korean state of Paekche sends the Seven-Branched Sword to the king of Wa (Japan). Inscribed with the date 369, the sword is now at Isonokami Shrine. **SHINTO** |

| 374 | (St.) Ambrose (c. 339–397), a Roman governor, is elected bishop of Milan. He comes to power during the period of division in the church that pits |

adherents of Arianism against other Christians. He strongly supports the Catholic view of the divinity of Christ and influences Roman emperors Gratian and Valentinian II to repress Arianism. He later is venerated as the patron saint of Milan. **CHRIS**

375 King Sosurium (r. 371–384), the 17th ruler of the Koguryo Kingdom of Korea, establishes Buddhism as the spiritual foundation of the state and Confucius's teachings as its legal basis. **BUDD, CONF**

379 (St.) Gregory of Nazianzus (329–389) is appointed bishop of Constantinople. Renowned as a theologian and a supporter of the Creed of Nicaea, he influences Church doctrine and is later recognized as one of the "Three Hierarchs" of Orthodox Christianity, along with Basil the Great and John Chrysostom. **ORTHO**

c. 380 The expansion of Christianity out of southern France to the north is initiated by (St.) Martin, the bishop of Tours, a former soldier and monk who works among the rural people. **CHRIS**

c. 380 The *Macarian Homilies* are written by an unknown author in Syria. Authorship is initially assigned to Macarius the Great of Egypt, a Christian monk, but scholars who study the documents later reject this view. The doc

Gnosticism

Gnosticism is the name given to a number of related religious movements that came to be seen as an alternative to Christianity in the second and third centuries C.E. in North Africa, west Asia, and southern Europe. The origins of Gnosticism are unclear, but it likely developed within Judaism before and during the first century C.E. and was also influenced by Egyptian mythology, pagan beliefs and practices, and Asian religions, such as Zoroastrianism. After the appearance of Christianity, some Christian elements were added as well, making it a set of beliefs and practices that took various forms, all of which were different from the mainstream Judaism, Christianity, and paganism of the time. The three core beliefs of Gnosticism were a belief in a supreme but distant and remote superior god, the importance of knowledge in personal salvation, and Jesus Christ as God's emissary in human form. Gnostics also used the Bible, although they mistrusted the Old Testament and placed more faith in the New Testament, and their interpretations often differed from those of their Christian contemporaries. They also often allowed women a larger role in religious ritual and were accused by their Christian opponents of engaging in various forms of unacceptable sexual and personal behavior. The Gnostics were seen as heretics by the early Christians and Gnosticism was repressed starting in the second century C.E. It evidently survived in secret at least to the fifth century and perhaps as late as the eighth century. Some experts believe that Gnostic ideas had some influence on other religions, such as Manicheism, Hinduism, and Sufi Islam. Gnostic ideas enjoyed a resurgence during the revival of spiritualism in Europe in the late 19th century.

uments are a collection of sermons and directives that stress the personal and emotional nature of Christian worship and become important in Orthodox Christianity. **ORTHO**

380 Christianity reaches its greatest influence in the Roman Empire when Theodosius I (r. 379–395) bans paganism, declares Christianity the official religion of the empire, and affords special privileges to the clergy. **CHRIS**

380 Priscillian (340–386), the bishop of Avila in Spain, is excommunicated for espousing Gnosticism, a religious system that combines beliefs from Christianity with magic and esoteric beliefs. He is executed in 386, but his cult survives into the following century. **SECT**

381 The (First) Council of Constantinople is held. Although listed as a Christian ecumenical council, only bishops from the east attend. Decisions reached at Nicaea in 325 are ratified, the Arianism controversy ended completely, and the teachings of Apollinarius (c. 310–c. 390), the bishop of Laodicaea, which question the human nature of Christ, are condemned. An expanded version of the Nicene Creed first formulated at the Council of Nicaea in 325 is established. It sets forth that the Godhead of Father, Son, and Holy Spirit is "one in essence" and also establishes the three manifestations of the Godhead. The creed establishes Christ as the Savior. The bishop of Constantinople is made the second-highest official in the Christian Church, following the bishop of Rome. The decision makes Constantinople the effective center of Christianity in the east and the patriarch of Constantinople, later called the ecumenical patriarch, the leader of Orthodoxy. The decision is reaffirmed at the Church council in 451. **ORTHO**

c. 382 The Old and New Testament canon of the Christian Church is established by the church in Rome. **CHRIS**

382 At a Church council, Pope Damascus (r. 366–384) asserts that Rome is the center of the Christian world. **CHRIS**

382– (St.) Jerome (c. 342–420) serves as the secretary to Pope Damascus in
385 Rome. One of the fathers of the Christian Church, who lived as a hermit for five years, he advocates asceticism, urges the use of the Hebrew rather than the Greek version of the Old Testament, and later in life (c. 392) translates the Bible into Latin, producing the Vulgate, the "popular version" of the Bible widely used in the Church. **CHRIS**

384 In Korea a Serindian monk named Malananda introduces Buddhism into Paekche. In the same year Mukhoja, a monk from Koguryo, introduces Buddhism into Silla, but the doctrine is not accepted by the state and adherents suffer persecution. **BUDD**

384–399	Pope Siricius (?–399) continues to assert the primacy of the church in Rome in the Christian world and begins issuing *Decretals*, which set forth his views of church policy on both theological and administrative issues. **CHRIS**
386–535	A barbarian state in China, the Northern Wei, adopts a Sinicization policy chiefly Confucian in character, as Confucian values continue to dominate the central bureaucracy, recruitment of officials, and even local governance. **CONF**
c. 390	Pope Siricius makes celibacy a requirement for the clergy in the western Christian Church. The practice of celibacy by the clergy had begun earlier, perhaps in Spain, and was based on a desire to keep the sacred nature of the clergy distinct from the laity. **CHRIS**
390	The power of the Christian Church in the Roman Empire is displayed publicly when Emperor Theodosius I is rebuked by the bishop for massacring citizens of Thessalonika and does penance outside the door of the Milan cathedral. **CHRIS**
396	(St.) Augustine of Hippo (354–430), is made bishop of Hippo in North Africa. An enormously influential figure in early Christianity, he sets down some of the abiding teachings of Catholic theology, including original sin, predestination, and unity of the Church, that remain influential into the 13th century. His major works are *Confessions* and *The City of God*. **CHRIS**

Lingbao Scriptures

These Daoist texts blended elements of the Celestial Masters and Shangqing schools and absorbed Buddhism's distinctive notion of salvation. They borrowed from Confucianism too, particularly in their respect for Confucian virtues. They were based on a text called the *Wufujong* (*The Text of the Five Talismans*), by tradition the oldest of the Lingbao texts, said to derive from Ge Xuan (164–244), the great-uncle of the Daoist scholar Ge Hong. In fact, a scholar named Ge Chaofu produced the Lingbao scriptures. Little is known of him other than that he belonged to the family of Ge Xuan and Ge Hong. Lingbao represented a new direction in Daoism. The goal of Lingbao Daoism remained to "ascend into heaven in broad daylight," but now the idea of universal salvation was attached. Gymnastics, drug-taking, and alchemy are less important in Lingbao than in Shangqing Daoism, though Lingbao retained some of these elements too. (The Lingbao movement eventually absorbed the Shangqing school.) Lingbao gods appeared. The Celestial Venerable One of the Original Beginning was supreme, with the deified Laozi second in importance. Demon kings and dragon kings also figured in the pantheon. Lingbao rituals were theatrical, accompanied by music, banners, chants, dances, and even pantomime. Scholars later identified Daoist rituals as an important source for the Chinese theater.

399

399–
414
The Buddhist Faxian (Fa-Hsien) is the first Chinese to make a pilgrimage to India. He spends more than 10 years seeking Buddhist texts in north India and Sri Lanka. He returns with Buddhist works that he translates for a Chinese audience; his own chronicle of Buddhist India is a major historical source for the Gupta age. **BUDD**

c. 400
Dignaga, a pupil of Vasubandhu (SEE C. 350, BUDD), establishes the foundations of Mahayana Buddhism and Buddhist logic. **BUDD**

c. 400
With the dominance of Christianity, Romans end the use of catacombs for the burial of the dead. **CIVIL**

400
By now religion in Japan has two aspects. Regional devotees carry on a form of Shinto with their own local myths and divinities, the essence of which is the celebration of agricultural rites and seasonal festivals. The wider aspect of Shinto is associated with the centralization of political power grounded in ritual and myth supporting the legitimacy of the ruling Yamato clan. **SHINTO**

400s
The Malay Peninsula, with its abundance of natural resources, is located on maritime routes that, at least by the fifth century, are used by traders going back and forth between China and India. Most information on the early history of Malaysia is based on accounts of maritime trade travelers and Buddhists on pilgrimage to India. During this period, cultural influences from India in particular are adapted to local custom in the trade centers and courts, where elements of Hinduism and Buddhism are assimilated. **BUDD, HIND**

400s
Ireland comes under the influence of Christianity, and it develops a Christian religious structure based on the monastery, rather than on the church, unlike any other region in Europe. Each monastery is tightly associated with an existing Irish clan. Irish bishops live in the monasteries, but abbots hold most of the power and direct the spiritual life of the Irish community. **CHRIS**

400s
With political power in China shared among many competing centers during the Six Kingdoms and Three Dynasties period (220–589), Dao popular sects remain strong in the countryside. At the same time, religious Daoism, with its emphasis on immortality, gains among the elites of south China. In the north, the sage Kou Qianzhi attacks the excesses of popular Daoism and attempts to establish Daoism as the state religion. **DAO, TOL**

400s–
500s
Buddhism is coming under increasing pressure from the new devotional (*bhakti*) religions. But the major Indian Buddhist university and monastery at Nalanda in Bihar (SEE C. 150, BUDD) flourishes, teaching both Mahayana Buddhist doctrine and Vedic disciplines to students from as far away as China. At its peak it has several thousand monk-students and a library requiring three multistory buildings. It will survive until 1197. SEE **1197–1203, BUDD.** **BUDD**

400s– 500s	In India this is the probable period of collection of verses in the Tamil language, known as the *Naladinannurru* (*The Four Hundred Quatrains*). Although they will always be enjoyed by Tamils of all faiths, they are by tradition written by a large group of Jain monks who have been sheltered and fed by a Tamil king; when they leave his court, each leaves a quatrain as a blessing for his kindness. The verses deal with morality but with warmth and humanity, advocating good conduct in a spirit of true sympathy and love, as opposed to the rather austere advocacy of avoiding evil or just performing charitable acts out of thought for one's soul. This is also the period of Tamil Jain epic *Cilappatikaram*, drawing on folklore and other local Tamil secular sources. It is probably also the period of Devanandin, or Jinendrabuddhi, a famed Jain scholar better known as Pujyyapada; he is best known as the author of the *Jainendravyakarana*, or *Pancadhyayi*, and the *Sarvarthasiddhi*.　　　　　　　　　　　　　　　　**JAIN**
400– 600	In Hinduism the Goddess is venerated in the *Devimahatmya* (*The Glory of the Goddess*) in the Markandeya Purana religious text. The text is recited during the annual festival to the Goddess held each autumn.　　**HIND**
c. 400– 750	The first Nepalese state is ruled by the Licchavi dynasty, descended from a north Indian clan. Hinduism and Buddhism are brought from India and flourish. This is the golden age of Nepalese culture, and it is heavily influenced by north Indian Kushana models. Sanskrit is the official administrative and literary language. Traders, missionaries, and pilgrims spread Buddhism from Nepal throughout Asia.　　**BUDD, HIND**
401	Kumarajiva (334–413), a scholar of Buddhism, arrives in Xi'an, the capital of northern China. Of Indian and central Asian descent, Kumarajiva had become a noted student of Buddhism while still a youth in Kashmir, northeastern India. The emperor of northern China hears of his reputation and invites him to the capital of Xi'an. En route, Kumarajiva is taken prisoner by a Chinese warlord in western China and held for 17 years, during which time he learns Chinese. After finally arriving at Xi'an, Kumarajiva organizes a team of translators, editors, and scribes and oversees the translation of many of the basic Buddhist texts into Chinese. These works, plus his missionary efforts, play a major role in spreading Buddhism in China.　　**BUDD**
402	Hui Yuan (333–416), a convert from Daoism, founds the Jing Tu (Pure Land) school of Buddhism in China. The Pure Land school teaches that the spiritual quality of the world has been in decline since the Buddha's time but that all who meditate on or devote themselves to the Buddha Amitabha (the Buddha of Infinite Radiance) will be reborn into his paradise, "the Pure Land." Pure Land Buddhism, based on the Indian Buddhist text, the *Sukhhavati Vyuha* (*Pure Land Sutra*), will become one of the most important Chinese traditions of Buddhism, especially after the early 700s; Pure Land Buddhism also spreads to Korea and Japan. SEE **1175, BUDD.**　　**BUDD**

| 402 | The Daoist priest Sun En again rises in rebellion in China. After his defeat, Sun drowns himself. Hundreds of his adherents follow his example. They are known later as "water immortals." **DAO, TOL** |

402–
417

Innocent I (360–417) is pope of the church in Rome. During his rule he strengthens the authority of the church in Rome over other Christian communities and requires the clergy to be celibate. **CATH**

403

At the Synod of the Oak, (St.) John Chrysostom (c. 347–407) is deposed as the archbishop of Constantinople by Emperor Theophilus. Although reinstated in 404, he is again banished and dies while being taken into exile in 407. A rigid theologian, powerful speaker, and critic of the state, he angers the wealthy and powerful but draws many followers among the common people. He is considered by the Orthodox Church as one of the "Three Hierarchs" along with Basil the Great and Gregory Nazianzus and is honored in church services. **ORTHO**

409–
431

Reign of King Mahanama on Sri Lanka, during which time the Buddhist monk/scholar Buddhaghosa comes over to the island from India; he immediately sets to work translating and editing many texts in the native Sri Lankan language into the classical Pali language; in so doing, he systematizes Theravada Buddhism's doctrines. He also composes his own major work on Theravada Buddhism, the *Visuddhimagga* (*Path of Purity*). At some point Buddhaghosa returns to India. **BUDD**

410

The New Testament is translated into Armenian, making it available to many common people in Armenia. **CHRIS**

410

Following the withdrawal of the Romans from Britain, Christian missionaries become active in converting the Celtic and Celtic-Roman population to Christianity. Many people convert over the next three centuries. **CHRIS**

411–
484

Spain is conquered and ruled by the Visigoths, who afford the Jews religious freedom. **JUD**

413

The island of Cyprus in the Mediterranean Sea has been the home to Christians since the earliest days of Christianity, and in this year the Church of Cyprus becomes an independent church within Christianity. **ORTHO**

415

The Daoist priest Kou Qianzhi (365–448) in China claims to see a vision of Laozi, who gives him the title of celestial master and charges him with issuing a new Daoist code to replace the old, corrupt way. Laozi hands texts to Kou dealing with talismans (*fu*), breathing exercises, and other matters. He further instructs Kou to stamp out sexual promiscuity and other abuses and to see to the correct use of meditation and dietary techniques that prolong life. In Kou's new Daoist code, sexual practices are dropped, as are the imposition of religious taxes and the inheritance of religious titles. The code also prescribes rules for good behavior. The good will have eternal life; the bad will be reborn as insects or other lower animals. **DAO**

415 Roman law prohibits the building of new temples by Jews. **JUD**

415 The first Hagia Sophia (Church of the Holy Wisdom) is built in Constantinople during the reign of Constantius II. **ORTHO**

416 In *The City of God* Christian theologian St. Augustine criticizes astrology as inconsistent with the beliefs of Christianity. Other Christian writers of the period also equate astrology with paganism and with heresy. Criticism by Christians, along with the general decline in education in Europe during the Middle Ages, leads to a decline in the popularity of astrology, although predictions based on the location or movement of heavenly bodies continue in daily life. **SPIR**

418 Jews living in the western Roman Empire are prohibited from holding public office. Jews on the island of Minorca in the Mediterranean Sea are forced to convert to Christianity. Many die or flee instead. **JUD**

c. 419 The *Lausiac History* is written by Palladius. It contains both a history and biographies of the Christian Desert Fathers (Egyptian monks who established Christian monasticism) and becomes an important record of the emergence of monasticism. **CHRIS**

420 Influenced by the Chinese Buddhist Faxian (**SEE 399–414, BUDD**), 25 Chinese Buddhists set off on a pilgrimage to India. **BUDD**

423 The Daoist celestial master Kou Qianzhi in China has a second vision and encounter with Laozi. A man called Li Buwen, claiming to be a great-grandson of Laozi, gives him a text in 60 chapters and instructs him in alchemy and the summoning of spirits. Li directs him to worship the heavenly gods and to support the emperor of the Northern Wei dynasty (386–534). **DAO**

423 The Temple to Mothers honoring the wives of the Hindu gods is constructed at Gangdhar in northern India. **HIND**

424–28 With the patronage of the powerful minister Cui Hao (381–450), Daoist priest Kou Qianzhi is influential at the Northern Wei imperial court in China. Kou instructs the emperor, and the ruler himself invests Kou as a celestial master. A Daoist shrine is built in the capital, Chang'an, and 120 Daoist priests are invited to settle there. **DAO**

c. 425 The Jewish Palestinian *Talmud* (*Instruction*), which combines the *Mishnah* and *Gemara* is completed. It becomes part of the basis for the more comprehensive Babylonian *Talmud* completed in the sixth century (**SEE C. 550, JUD**). **JUD**

c. 428   Theodore of Mopsuestia (c. 390–c. 428) dies. As the patriarch of
         Constantinople, he had been a fierce supporter of the doctrine of the two
         natures of Christ and an equally fierce opponent of alternative interpreta-
         tions. Although his views were in accord with Church doctrine, they were
         considered extreme by some, and in 553 they were formally condemned by
         the Church. Nonetheless, he remains a revered figure among Eastern Syrian
         Christians.   ORTHO

429–   The Vandals attack North Africa and destroy churches and Christian reli-
431   gious objects in Hippo. In 431 they capture the city and loot it.   CHRIS

431   The Council of Ephesus is held in Turkey. The council holds that divinity
         and humanity are united in Christ. However, it fails to resolve differences
         among Christian bishops and leads to further disagreement when first
         Nestorius is excommunicated by the Eastern bishops, and then Cyril is
         excommunicated by the Western bishops. The conflict is resolved in a sec-
         ond council in 433 but revives in 449.   CHRIS

c. 432   (St.) Patrick (c. 389–461) returns to Ireland (where he had worked as a slave
         for six years after having been taken from Britain) from France and begins
         to convert the Irish to Christianity.   CHRIS

442   The Daoist Kou Qianzhi initiates the emperor of the Northern Wei in
         China, Tai Wudi, confirming his imperial virtue. The ceremony formally
         elevates Daoism to a state religion of China.   DAO

Pope Leo I

Leo I (c. 390–461), later known as Saint Leo and Leo the Great, served as leader of the
Western or Latin Church from 440 until his death in 461. Little is known of his early
life, though it is likely that he was a Tuscan and he served as a deacon and earned
renown as a preacher among rival factions before being elected pope in 440. Leo
ruled during a period of internal dispute over Church doctrine, competition between
cities for primacy over the Christian world, and invasions by the Huns and Vandals.
Leo was considered an especially devout and honorable man who was able to halt the
sacking of Rome by the Huns and then oversaw its rebuilding after it was sacked by
the Vandals in 455. In Church affairs, he established central doctrines that have lasted through the 20th century and also succeeded in establishing Rome and the papacy as the center of Western Christendom. Most important was his work *Tome*, which
was authorized as doctrine by the Council of Chalcedon in 451 and established as
doctrine that "One and the same Christ, Son, Lord, Only-begotten, made known in
two natures [which exist] without confusion, without change, without division, without separation." Leo's importance to Roman Catholicism was so great that he was
made a doctor of the Church by Pope Benedict XIV in 1754. He and Pope Gregory I
are the only popes afforded the title "the Great."

445	Pope Leo I (the Great) (c. 390–461) wins the support of Western Roman emperor Valentian III for the position that the center of the Church is to be in Rome. **CHRIS**
446	The Daoist Tai Wudi, emperor of the Northern Wei dynasty in China, proscribes Buddhism. **BUDD, DAO**
448	The thriving Daoist community of Chang'an, the capital of China's Northern Wei dynasty, begins to decline with the death of Kou Qianzhi. **DAO**
c. 450	A Buddhist monastery at Tuen Mun, on mainland Hong Kong, claims to have been founded about this time. Although this is possible, the first written evidence of the monastery dates from only 950. **BUDD**
450–650	In Myanmar writing in Indian scripts and with verses derived from classical Indian texts that is found on stone, gold plates, silver vessels, burial urns, bronze figurines, coins with traditional Indian motifs, *stupas* and monasteries attest to the strong influences of Hindu, Buddhist, and Jain cultures of India. In particular, Theravada Buddhism is prominent in these cities. Among the remains of many structures are Buddhist *stupas*, the domed temples, and Buddhist monasteries, decorated with carvings depicting traditional episodes in Buddha's life. **BUDD, HIND**

Eastern Christianity

Eastern Christianity is a general label for Christian churches that broke from mainstream Christianity following the Council of Chalcedon in 451 C.E. In a statement of theology, the council differentiated between the divine and human natures of Christ as existing in one person and one substance. The churches that refused to accept or ignored this doctrine were subsequently known as the Eastern, Oriental, or the Monophysite churches, as they continued to worship the Christ of one nature, which differentiated them from the churches centered in Rome and Constantinople. The Eastern churches that have survived into modern times are the Coptic Church in Egypt, the Nestorians, the Jacobites, the Maronites, the Armenian Church, the Church of Ethiopia, and the St. Thomas Christians in India. The Maronites in Lebanon reunited with the Roman Catholic Church in 1182 and thus are now more properly classified as a Uniate church. Other churches, such as the Nestorians in the Middle East and the St. Thomas Christians, have at times been strongly influenced by Orthodoxy or Protestantism, although they have remained independent. Since the 1960s there has been a movement in the Eastern churches to create greater unity and perhaps stronger ties to the Catholic or Orthodox churches, a strategy dictated by their members' minority status in the Middle Eastern and African nations (Egypt, Ethiopia, Iran, Iraq, Lebanon, Syria) where they live and have been subject to persecution.

| 451 | The Council of Chalcedon is held in Turkey. The bishops attempt to end the disputes between the sees in Alexandria and Antioch and the Western bishops. The Creed of Chalcedon sets forth the doctrine of the two natures of Christ, divine and human in one person in two forms. Eastern churches that dispute the two natures doctrine are called Monophysites and include the Coptic Church in Egypt, the Jacobites, the Armenian church, and the Nestorians. The council also marks the beginning of an increase in tension between the Eastern Church in Constantinople and the Western Church in Rome over primacy in the Church. **CHRIS** |

| 451 | (St.) Geneviève (c. 422–c. 500), a nun who entered the church as a young girl, correctly predicts that the Huns will bypass and not destroy Paris. This prediction and others, her love of Paris, and later miracles associated with her relics (ritual objects associated with a person such as clothing, hair, or nail clippings), including the end of a plague in 1129, led her to be considered the patron saint of Paris. **CHRIS** |

| 452 | With the assassination of the Northern Wei emperor Tai Wudi, Buddhism is restored in China. Daoism enters a period of decline. **BUDD, DAO** |

Coptic Church

The Coptic Church is the ancient Christian Church of Egypt and, since the Christian Council of Chalcedon in 451, the distinctive Christian Church of Egypt. The name Copt is derived from the Greek *Aigyptios,* which meant "Egyptians." The origins of the Copts are obscure. Coptic belief cites Saint Mark as the founder of the Coptic Church, but it is more likely that the church emerged in the first few centuries C.E. through an amalgamation of Christian beliefs and Gnostic beliefs then popular in Egypt. The split from mainstream Christianity occurred following the Council of Chalcedon, when the Copts continued to adhere to their beliefs that God and Christ are of the same essence and that Christ's divinity and humanity are one (the monophysite position) and thus became one of the Eastern or Oriental Christian churches. The Copts were persecuted by the rulers of the Byzantine Empire who sought unity among their subjects and have been often persecuted by the Muslim rulers of Egypt since it came under Muslim control in 641 C.E. Nonetheless, the church has survived and in the 1990s numbers perhaps six million in Egypt and several hundred thousand in North America and Europe. The Coptic Church is headed by a pope and the sacraments are performed by priests. The most important religious specialists are the monks, who wield much political influence in Coptic communities and also serve as a symbolic tie to Christian monasticism that began in Egypt in the third century C.E. Within Egypt the Copts form a distinct religious minority who in the 1990s are to a large extent excluded from national life. To some extent they have been able to maintain their identity during centuries of persecution by educating their children in the Coptic religion and by restricting marriage to other Copts, and also because they have been classified as outsiders by their Arab Muslim neighbors.

c. 453 A major council of Svetambara/Jain leaders meets at Valabhi. Jains continue to establish and write down the formal canon of their texts. These consist of 45 texts in prose and verse and include: the 11 original *Angas* (*Limbs*); 12 *Upangas* (*Secondary Limbs*); 10 *Prakirnaka* (*Miscellaneous Texts*); 6 *Chedasutras* (*Separate Texts*); 4 *Mulasutras* (*Basic Texts*); the *Nandisutra* (*Blessing*); and the *Anuyyogadvara* (*Door of Enquiry*). Some of these texts may date to the third century B.C.E., but much of the material probably dates from no older than the first century C.E. Elements within even the more recent texts may well have been handed down over many centuries. The texts are for the most part in the Ardha-Mgadha (or Arsha) dialect of Prakrit; Prakrit is an early derivative of Sanskrit, spoken in Bihar. Dialects sometimes show up in various texts. The early commentaries on the texts are also in Prakrit. Sanskrit, first employed by the Digambaras, will become predominant after about 1000 C.E., although the Prakrit will also continue in use. Of modern dialects, the Marwari, a special form of Hindi, and Gujarati, are preferred. JAIN

455 Rome is attacked and looted by the Vandals. Under Pope Leo I, the city is rebuilt and the church restored. The Vandals are adherents of the Arian form of early Christianity and persecute the Catholics. CHRIS

461 The Daoist priest Lu Xiujing (406–77) retires to Mount Lu in China, establishes a monastery (*kuan*) there, and begins to collect and catalog Daoist scripture. DAO

465– Earliest Gupta cave paintings are drawn at Bagh caves in western Malwa, a
500 monastic settlement consisting of a series of 10 carved and painted sanctuaries cut into rock cliffs. Ajanta cave temples enter their final phase (until the early seventh century): 20 of Ajanta's 30 halls date from the period, with walls, ceilings, and columns painted with anthropomorphic Buddhist images and narratives, especially from *Jakata* tales. Painted caves are widespread and were probably painted by professional artists. BUDD

467 The Daoist author Gu Huan (c. 420–c. 483), the Shangqing school's first historian and bibliographer, characterizes the Buddha as a barbarian, emphasizing the long-simmering feud between Daoists and Buddhists in China. He declares it impossible for Buddhists and Daoists to live in the same world. BUDD, DAO

c. 470 (St.) Brigid (c. 435–c. 523) establishes the first convent in Ireland at Kildare, which becomes a major center for Christianity in Ireland. She comes to be considered the second patron saint of Ireland, after St. Patrick. CHRIS

471 Lu Xiujing completes the first catalog of Daoist scriptures in China, three sections of 1,090 scrolls. He adapts Buddhist concepts and integrates them into the canon and standardizes Daoist ritual. DAO

482 The Western Church in Rome and the Eastern Church in Constantinople sever relations over a dispute about the nature of Christ. The schism is

482

repaired quickly but is another in a continuing series of disagreements
between the two Churches.   **CHRIS**

484   The Indian monk Nagasena is given a commission by the court of Funan to
return to the Chinese court with gifts (including two ivory models of
Buddhist shrines) and complaints about the Chams. Nagasena reports to
the Chinese court that the state religious cult in Funan is addressed to Siva
but that Buddhism is also important.   **BUDD, HIND**

484   The Vandals, who have conquered North Africa and are adherents of the
Arian form of early Christianity, effectively ban Catholicism by forbidding
Catholics to assemble, taking over the churches, and ending the authority
of the bishops.   **CHRIS**

Esoteric (Tantric) Buddhism

Esoteric or Tantric Buddhism can be placed alongside Theravada and Mahayana as a third major stream of Buddhism. In fact, it became the predominant form of Buddhism in Tibet. The mix of Tantra and native Tibetan religion produced Tibetan Buddhism of which the Dalai Lama is the highest representative. From Tibet, Tantra in the form of Lamaism spread to central Asia and Mongolia during the time of the Mongol conquests. Tantra, which had been brought directly from India, was briefly popular in China, and during the early part of the ninth century, Japanese monks studying in China took Tantric teachings back to Japan, where it gained a strong following, especially among the nobility. Known as Shingon, or "True Words," it is still popular there in the 1990s. Tantrism seems to have developed along the northern borders of India and borrows heavily from Hindu Tantrism. The Tantric scriptures are said to have been revealed by divine beings on Mount Sumeru, a mystical mountain in Buddhist and Hindu mythology. These scriptures stress the importance of ritual action and the use of spells, hand gestures, and magic circles or mandalas to achieve control over the forces of the spirit world and provide a shortcut to enlightenment. Mandalas were used in visualization meditation, in which the adept mentally re-created visions of divinities and Buddhas, or perhaps entire worlds populated by thousands of Buddhas. Visualization meditation was believed to bring these divine beings closer to the meditator and to help the individual gain enlightenment. The use of magic was also part of the most ancient teachings. The Buddha had specifically condoned the use of magic for certain purposes. Less orthodox were Tantric rituals involving sexual symbolism and even physical sexual intercourse. These rites were intended to reenact the union of Wisdom, visualized as a female goddess, and Action, or Means, visualized as a male god. The mystic joining of the two elements was believed to lead to enlightenment. Painted images and sculptures of the union of these two divinities may be found in the temples of Tibetan Buddhism in Tibet, Mongolia, and northern China.

492–496	Gelasius I is pope of the church in Rome. He sets forth a model of church-state relations in which the Church has the spiritual authority and the responsibility for moving the people toward eternal salvation, while the state is responsible for caring for the people and maintaining the state polity. **CHRIS**
496	Clovis, king of the Franks, converts to Christianity along with 3,000 of his soldiers following a victory over his German rivals. The Franks are supporters of the Roman form of Christianity and play a role in its rise to prominence in the Church. **CHRIS**
500	The Chinese scholar/alchemist Tao Hongjing (456–536), the successor to Gu Huan as the historian and bibliographer of the Shangqing (or Mao Shan) school of Daoism, prepares his *Zhen Gao* (*Revelations of the Truth*), an encyclopedia of contemporary Daoism. In another of Tao's works, he enumerates some 36,000 Daoist gods inside and outside the human body. He also prepares alchemical concoctions for Emperor Wu of the Southern Liang dynasty. **DAO**
500s	In Sri Lanka Buddhist monks compile the *Mahavansa* (*Great Genealogy*), the Pali chronicle of Sri Lanka's history through first century C.E. Based on fourth-century sources, the work is the beginning of one of the world's oldest continuous written histories. **BUDD**
500s	During this period the Jain philosopher/saint Siddhasena Divakara composes his works on logic and theories of knowledge and judgment. **JAIN**
c. 500–528	Buddhists are persecuted by Hindus in India, leading to a Buddhist migration east into southeastern Asia. **BUDD, HIND**
c. 500–535	According to later tradition, Chan Buddhism (in Japanese, *Zen*) is introduced to China through Bodhidharma, probably a central Asian (possibly an Indian) sage who seeks an audience with Emperor Wudi (of the Liang dynasty), himself a Buddhist. **SEE 675, BUDD.** **BUDD**
c. 500–550	The practice of dating time A.D. (Latin for *anno Domini*, "in the year of our Lord," comes into use in Christian Europe. **CHRIS**
500s–600s	Tantrism, an esoteric, magic-oriented strand of Hinduism and Jainism as well as Buddhism, begins to emerge in India, but it is known that elements of Tantrism have already formed a undercurrent of south Asian religious belief for many centuries. (A Chinese translation of an Indian Buddhist Tantric text dates from the 400s C.E.) Tantrism includes *mantras* (sacred syllables, incantations), *mandalas* (ritual diagrams), *tanghkas* (religious scroll paintings), and explanation of Tantra, the sacred texts; Tantrism also involves strict discipline, including yogic and other practices to attain mastery over oneself and physical phenomena. **BUDD, TOL**

c. 500– 800	The Alvars, Vaisnava Hindu poet/saints, are active in southern India, where they establish temples and pilgrimage sites, spread Hinduism, and combat the spread of Jainism and Buddhism. **HIND**
c. 500s– 800s	By the sixth century, it is believed that Indian traders who are in contact with the Mon people in Thailand introduce Hinduism and Buddhism. In particular, Mon communities from west central to eastern Thailand develop a society and economy and culture with a strong Theravada Buddhist element: these towns and their culture-complex are known as *Dvaravati.* Its presence is indicated by the many monasteries, sculptures made of terracotta or stucco, and inscriptions; the culture-complex is obviously imported from India. What remains unclear is exactly what relationship this Buddhist culture has with the Tai people who are now moving into this region. **BUDD**
500s– 1300s	Buddhism and Hinduism brought to Indonesia from India provide a cultural basis for the governments formed by rulers of the early kingdoms that rise and fall between the 6th and 14th centuries. As early as the 6th and 7th centuries C.E., Chinese chronicles refer to the influence of Buddhism in Indonesia. Although it is believed that villagers practice predominantly traditional religious rituals, the influence of India manifests itself in many ways. Sanskrit inscriptions found far from trade routes suggest the presence of Brahmans or local scholars with some knowledge of India in some royal courts, primarily on Java, where Siva worship is taught to the ruling elite. Sanskrit literature is believed to provide religious and legal guidelines for the formation of the early kingdoms of the archipelago but with considerable adaptation to local conditions. Hindu structure and ritual influence is concentrated at the courts. **BUDD, HIND**
504	Daoism is proscribed in the Southern Liang state of China. **DAO**

Chan Buddhism

Chan—the word derives from the Sanskrit for "meditation"—was distinctively Chinese in style (although in the 20th century it will become better known to the West in its Japanese variety, Zen Buddhism). It is imparted and passed on not from a text but from an already enlightened mind, a teacher-student process that appeals to China's Confucian tradition of thinker and disciples. Bodhidharma, the Chan patriarch, entered a monastery near Luoyang and passed nine years in silent meditation, his face to the wall, before taking on disciples. In Chan Buddhism the goal of meditation is enlightenment, in which all illusions are cleared away and an individual becomes fully aware of wisdom. Chan Buddhism de-emphasizes texts and many of the other elements of more traditional Buddhism, including prayer, asceticism, and good works; it claims that enlightenment comes as the intuition of a moment.

506	The Georgian Orthodox Church becomes independent of the church in Antioch when it joins with the Church of Armenia in resisting Church reforms. **ORTHO**

511   Under the rule of Clovis, most of the people of Gaul have converted to Christianity, and Christianity in its Roman form is the religion of the realm. **CHRIS**

517   The proscription of Daoism is renewed in Southern Liang China. Many practicing Daoists are forced to migrate to the north. The proscription has the unintended consequence of spreading the Shangqing school's teaching throughout China. **DAO**

520   The Daoist Jiang Bin and the Buddhist Tan Wuzui debate their respective religions at the court of the Northern Qi in China. **BUDD, DAO**

523–554   King Song, the 26th ruler of Paekche, one of the Three Kingdoms currently ruling Korea, reigns. He moves the capital to Sabi (modern Puyo) in 538, and forges close ties to the Liang dynasty in southern China and to Japan. Buddhism flourishes and is conveyed to Japan. **BUDD**

c. 527   The Silla Kingdom of Korea recognizes Buddhism. Monks are accepted into highest social order (*hwarang*), and the state, hitherto the least culturally evolved of the Three Kingdoms, strengthens its stability by giving religious justification for the authority of its rulers. **BUDD**

c. 530   (St.) Benedict (c. 480–547) establishes a monastery at Monte Cassino in Italy. His *Rule* establishes the Western form of Catholic monasticism that is centered in the abbey he builds at Monte Cassino. He also plays a leading role in converting the pagans to Christianity and in 1964 is made patron saint of Europe by Pope Paul VI. Benedictine monks are also strong supporters of the Church in Rome and play a role in shifting power there from other church centers. **CHRIS**

c. 530   Mazdak, the leader of the Zoroastrians during the rule of Kawad in Persia, is executed by Crown Prince Khusrau because Mazdak's belief in equality and communal property threatens the royal family and their followers who control the wealth. **SECT**

535   During the rule of Justinian, the eastern Roman Empire drives the Vandals from Rome and reestablishes Christianity. **CHRIS**

537   The Roman emperor Justinian issues an edict that denies Jews civil equality and religious freedom. **JUD**

537   After its destruction during the riots of 532, the Hagia Sophia in Constantinople is rebuilt by Byzantine emperor Justinian. It is a massive structure, with a large dome, and becomes the model for subsequent Orthodox churches. Taken

over by the Muslims after the Ottoman conquest, it is converted to a museum by the Turkish government in the 1920s.   ORTHO

538   According to tradition, Buddhism is introduced in Japan by a delegation from the Korean kingdom of Paekche.   BUDD

538   It is about this time that the name *Shinto* begins to be used to differentiate Japan's ancient indigenous beliefs from the new foreign ones. This is occasioned by the arrival (also held by some to be 552) of Buddhism in Japan. The adoption of the name *Shinto* by the ruling elite leads over the next half century to the end of the indigenous Kofun tomb-building practices and funerary rites, which are deemed inappropriate by the Buddhists. SEE **250–600** SHINTO.   BUDD, SHINTO

Shinto

Shinto is the indigenous religion of Japan. Although the name *Shinto* (which means literally "the divine way") was not used until the sixth century C.E., the basis of Shinto goes back thousands of years earlier to prehistoric Japan and traditional rituals and practices. The core belief of Shinto is *kami*, the divine essence that is found in all living things and inanimate objects as well, and much of Shinto practice is devoted to the ritual worship of *kami*. Shinto is also closely tied to the state in Japan, and until the practice was banned by the United States after World War II, the emperor was seen as both the religious and political leader of the nation. Shinto emerged as a distinct religion only in the sixth century as a reaction to the arrival of Confucianism and Buddhism from China. Over time, elements from these two religions as well as Daoism and ancestor worship were integrated into Shinto, with Shinto in various forms remaining the core religion of Japan and an important element of the social and political structure of society as well. Shinto does not have a clear theology nor a scripture in the sense that other religions do, nor does it have a set of rituals followed by all adherents. Rather, the focus is on the carrying out of the proper ritual in the context of the three major branches of Shinto: Shrine, Sect, and Folk, or popular, Shinto. Shrine Shinto focuses on the worship of supernatural beings, forces, environmental features, individuals, and objects at over 100,000 shrines throughout Japan. The shrines are supported by the voluntary donations of worshipers. Sectarian Shinto is more organized: adherents worship in congregations organized in accord with five major and hundreds of minor sects of Sectarian Shinto. The five major sects are Purification, Pure, Confucian, Faith Healing, and Mountain. Folk Shinto is Shinto as it is practiced at the family level and focuses on the worship of deities at altars in the home. It also emphasizes ancestor worship and the use of offerings to win support from the gods and spirits. About 90 percent of Japan's 130 million people are adherents of Shinto, although many Japanese claim adherence to more than one religion, with an almost equal number also following Buddhism.

539	Korea's oldest extant Buddhist image is cast in bronze. The simple figurine depicts a standing Buddha with eyes closed and one hand raised in the manner of a blessing. Found in Koguryo, South Yonngsang Province, it is unclear where the image was cast. **BUDD**
539	An embassy from Funan, the kingdom in southern Cambodia, reports to the Chinese that Funan possesses a hair relic of the Buddha; this illustrates the importance of Buddhism in Funan. **BUDD**
c. 540	(St.) David (c. 520–c. 589), who is later made the patron saint of Wales, begins his missionary work in Wales and during his lifetime establishes 12 monasteries. **CHRIS**
c. 542	Jacob Baradeus (c. 500–578) is made a bishop in the Christian Church. A supporter of the monophysite interpretation of Christ's divinity, he is persecuted by the Byzantine authorities but succeeds in establishing the Syrian Eastern Christian Church centered in Antioch. **CHRIS**
548	Imperial officials in China order the dispersal of the Daoist community Kou Qianzhi gathered in Chang'an 120 years earlier. **DAO**
c. 550	The Jewish Babylonian *Talmud* (*Instruction*) that combines the *Mishnah* and *Gemara* is completed. The *Talmud* consists of two primary sections: the *Halakhah,* which delineates the laws of the Torah that are binding on all Jews and the *Aggadah,* which consists of stories, fables, and proverbs that illuminate and inspire. The *Talmud* is not a neatly organized or even logical document but rather one filled with information and opinion and sometimes contradictory statements. Thus it is open to the interpretation and codification that begins in the 11th century and continues through the 20th. **JUD**
c. 550	Following persecution in Persia, some Manichaeians flee to central Asia where they settle in Manichaeian communities established in the third century. They form the eastern branch of Manchaeism, with the western branch centered in Babylon. **SECT**
550	Borrowing from Buddhism, the Daoist master Song Wenming imposes celibacy on his followers. With many other adaptations, the Daoist church is practically modeled on the Buddhist church, though Daoists retain their own distinctive doctrines and practices. **BUDD, DAO**
553	The (Second) Council of Constantinople is held. The bishops address the continuing dispute between the Western and Eastern Christian churches over the two natures of Christ. The council also condemns Origenism. **CHRIS**
554	In return for Japan's aid, the Korean kingdom of Paekche sends to Japan specialists in Confucianism, Buddhism, divination, calendars, herbs, and music. Learning is apparently valued by Japanese of the era. **BUDD**

| 555 | Buddhists and Daoists in China are summoned to debate at the court of the Northern Qi. The Daoists are defeated and ordered to become Buddhist monks. **BUDD, DAO** |

| 563 | Some Chinese Buddhists form a new school based on a translation by the Indian scholar Paramartha (498–569) of the *Mahayana Samgraha* into Chinese. This Indian work is attributed to Asanga. In China the text becomes the basis of the Wei Shi school, a variation of the Vijnanavada school with its emphasis on striving for pure thought **(SEE C. 350, BUDD)**. **BUDD** |

| 563– 567 | The Indian scholar Paramartha (498–569) translates the *Abhidharma Kosa* into Chinese. This crucial Buddhist text is a commentary on the *Abhidhara* and is attributed to the Indian monk Vasubandhu **(SEE C. 350, BUDD)**. In China this text becomes the basis of an equivalent school, the Ju She school. **BUDD** |

| 566 | (St.) Columba (c. 521–597), a leading Catholic missionary, leaves Ireland and establishes a monastery on the island of Iona that becomes a center for Christian missionary efforts in Scotland. **CHRIS** |

| 569 | The Wudi emperor of the Northern Zhou (r. 561–578) listens to a debate on the merits of China's Three Teachings and officially ranks them: Confucianism is first, Daoism is second, and Buddhism is third. **DAO, TOL** |

| c. 570 | Muhammad (c. 570–632), the Prophet and founder of Islam, is born in the city of Mecca in Arabia. **ISLAM** |

Muhammad

Muhammad the Prophet, the founder of Islam, was born in about 570 in the city of Mecca in what is today the nation of Saudi Arabia. His father died several months prior to his birth and his mother and paternal grandfather both died when he was still a young child. As a result, Muhammad was raised by his paternal uncle and trained to be a merchant, the occupation of his clan. As he grew older Muhammad became a respected man in the community and developed the practice of retreating to a cave on Mount Hira near Mecca to meditate. On one such occasion the angel Gabriel revealed the will of Allah to him and called upon him to serve as his prophet. The year was 610 and the event became known as the "Night of Power." From then until his death in 632, Muhammad preached the word of Allah. At the same time he continued to receive revelations from Allah, which were organized into the Qur'an shortly after his death. In Islam Muhammad is regarded as the last prophet sent by Allah, and the Qur'an is regarded as the final revealed text. In addition to being the Prophet, Muhammad was also a highly capable politician and military leader, and he was able with a small band of followers to defeat opponents of the emerging Islam religion.

c. 570– 713	Xin Xing, a Chinese Buddhist, founds the San Jie Jiao (Three Ages school) of Buddhism in the late 500s c.e. It teaches that after the first age of *dharma*, or truth, established by the Buddha, the world has deteriorated and now exists in a degenerate age. Because the doctrine is extended to mean that no present-day government is worthy of respect, the Three Ages school comes under attack by the T'ang emperors. In 713 the treasury of its head temple is confiscated and the school is thereafter suppressed. **BUDD**
572	At the council of Braga, Christian bishops formally ban the use of contraception. Although this is the first formal ban, contraception had been discouraged by Church leaders since the earliest days of Christianity, with both marriage and sexual intercourse viewed as primarily for procreation. **CHRIS**
574	The Northern Zhou emperor in China launches an effort to suppress Buddhist and Daoist religious practices in favor of Confucian ritual. Privately, Emperor Wudi (r. 561–578) is interested in magical aspects of Daoism. In practical affairs he remains a Confucian. Buddhist and Daoist temples, scriptures, and images are destroyed in the state of Northern Zhou and clergy are forced to return to lay life. With the death of the emperor, the proscription of Buddhism is relaxed to a degree. **BUDD, DAO**
579	Rome again falls to non-Christians, when it is conquered by the Lombards moving south from Germany. **CHRIS**
580	In China Wudi's successor Yang Jian, who will establish the Sui dynasty and rule as Wendi, lifts the proscription on Daoism in Northern Zhou China. **DAO**
581– 604	Yang Jian, who, with his allies, has toppled the Northern Zhou dynasty and asserted control over north China, reigns. Yang Jian takes the title of Emperor Wendi, holds a dawn audience, declares an amnesty, and proclaims the dynasty of Sui (581–618). Born in 541 in a Buddhist temple and raised by a nun, he is a strong, authoritarian, and successful ruler. Privately a devout Buddhist, among his first acts as emperor are the full restoration of rights to Buddhists and the rehabilitation of the Buddhist clergy; he also lifts the proscription on Daoists. Wendi builds Buddhist monasteries and shrines and sends missionaries to spread Buddhism throughout his realm and even outside it, including to Japan. **BUDD, DAO**
581– 618	The reunification of China by the Sui dynasty assists in the revival of Confucian learning. **CONF**
582	The Wendi emperor of Sui dynasty China establishes a Daoist monastery at Chang'an to cultivate aspects of Daoism that would be useful to the state. It also has the effect of bringing Daoist communities under stricter state control. **DAO**
585	To about this time, the Japanese people believe solely in the power of the *kami*, or native spirits and divinities. The newly arrived Buddhism does not replace Shinto (the Way of the Kami). Instead the two religions begin a form

of coexistence and even cooperation well into modern times. Buddhists often build their temples next to Shinto shrines, and for nearly 1,000 years Buddhist priests frequently carry out their rites, alternating with those conducted by Shinto priests, in Shinto shrines, except at the main Shinto sanctuaries of Ise and Izumo.　**BUDD, SHINTO**

586　In an overture to Daoists, the Wendi emperor of Sui dynasty China orders an inscribed stele to be set up at the supposed birthplace in Anhui of Laozi, whom religious Daoists venerate as their spiritual ancestor. "We honor Laozi's ideal of attaining oneness," the emperor declares. At the same time, he remains alert to the Daoist potential for political trouble; he suppresses alleged black magic and other dangerous practices.　**DAO**

589　At the Synod of Toledo, Recared, the Visigoth ruler of Spain, renounces Arianism and accepts Christianity, opening the way for the conversion of the region to Christianity.　**CHRIS**

589　Bishops of the Western Christian Church meet in Spain and add the word *filioque* ("and from the son") to the Nicene Creed, indicating that the Holy Spirit flows from both God and Christ. Eastern Christians object, claiming that the new wording weakens the authority of God.　**CHRIS**

589–591　The Wendi emperor conquers the south and reunifies China. With a view to the smooth restoration of the empire, the Sui dynasty imposes an easy peace. The emperor's son, installed as the southern viceroy, conciliates Buddhists dispossessed during the upheaval and makes peaceful overtures to Daoists and Confucians as well.　**BUDD, CONF, DAO, TOL**

c. 590　The Chinese Buddhist scholar/monk Zhi Yi (Chih I) is asked by Emperor Wendi to help revive Buddhism. He has already begun to systematize the many and diverse Buddhist texts and doctrines that have been making their way into China. Consistent with Emperor Wendi's desire to use Buddhism to impose some unity throughout China, Zhi Yi founds the Tian Tai school of Chinese Buddhism. While it stresses the devotion as set forth in the *Lotus Sutra*, it attempts to find harmony among the many Buddhist texts and teachings. Although it stresses the need to study the texts, Tian Tai Buddhism also accepts that some Buddhists (even the more ecstatic elements) stress ceremonies and discipline. Thus the Tian Tai Buddhism of China advocates a tolerance that suits the Chinese, and it spreads throughout much of China.　**BUDD**

590–604　Gregory I (the Great) is pope of the church in Rome. During his rule, the influence of the Church expands as Spain is converted to Catholicism and cordial relations established with the Lombards, which later leads to their conversion.　**CHRIS**

593　Shotoku Taishi (523–621) comes to power as prince regent of Japan and immediately proclaims Buddhism the official religion. Although the Shinto priests and the military oppose this, intellectuals and government authorities welcome it, the former because it links them to what they regard as the superior Chinese culture, the latter because they see Buddhism as a means to increase their own authority. Eating of four-legged animals is banned for religious reasons, leading to a decrease in hunting. With the encouragement of prince Shotoku, the Japanese elite begin to vie with each other in constructing Buddhist temples in the Asuka region and commissioning works of art for them. Not only an effective ruler but a religious and scholarly man, Shotoku writes commentaries on Buddhist sutras and supports the foundation of monasteries. In the eighth century he becomes the focus of a religious cult and is held by some to be an incarnation of Buddha. (As an honored cultural icon, he will be portrayed on late-20h-century Japan's 10,000-yen banknote.) **BUDD**

595   Muhammad, the Prophet and founder of Islam, marries his first wife, Khadija, a wealthy widow who later becomes the first convert to Islam. **ISLAM**

596–   Christianity is reintroduced to Britain following nearly two centuries of
597   Anglo-Saxon rule when Pope Gregory sends (St.) Augustine of Canterbury (d. 604) as a missionary to Kent. He is successful in converting Ethelbert, king of Kent, to Christianity and in founding the cathedral at Canterbury. **CHRIS**

c. 600   The Bodhi tree at Bodh Gaya, site of the Buddha's enlightenment, is cut down; a Hindu shrine is erected on the site. **BUDD**

c. 600   Chinese legend attributes the creation of the martial art known as T'ai Chi Ch'uan (supreme ultimate fist) to a quasi-mythological Daoist of this time, Chan San Feng. By stressing the goal of attaining maximum efficiency through integrating the mind and body in harmonious movement, this system is linked to Daoism because it also promotes living in harmony with nature. During the 19th century the Chen family in Henan Province, China, revive and promote T'ai Chi; it is then introduced into Beijing by Yang Lu-chan (1799–1872). His grandson Yang Cheng-fu (1883–1936) choreographed the Yang style widely used in the 20th century; one of Yang Cheng-fu's students, Cheng Man-ch'ing (1901–1975), choreographed the Yang style short form, a somewhat simplified version also practiced in the 20th century. **DAO**

c. 600   The earliest Tantras are produced by Hindus in India with the majority written over the next four centuries. The Tantras are religious texts that are important in some sects of Hinduism and Buddhism. They take the form of a dialogue between the Goddess and the god Shiva, with the former asking the latter questions and receiving answers about a wide range of matters. The dialogue is subject to much interpretation, and Tantric masters base their status on their knowledge and interpretation of the dialogues and their meanings. **HIND**

600	As a result of the Jewish Diaspora there are now major Jewish communities in southern Spain and Italy, the Rhine and Loire valleys in western Europe, Turkey, Mesopotamia, Egypt, and Carthage. **JUD**
600	Native Americans in Oklahoma build a large ceremonial center at Spiro with earth pyramids and elaborate burial chambers. The appearance of ceremonial earth mounds and pyramids in North America is probably a borrowing based on the stone pyramids of Mesoamerica. **NATIV**
c. 600–630	In India's southern peninsula, the Pallava king Mahendravarman I is said to be converted from Jainism to Hindu Saivism by the Saivite saint Appar. His capital at Kanchi becomes a Saivite center, and Saivite temples are erected throughout his kingdom. The royal conversion is a blow to Jainism in southern India. **HIND, JAIN**
c. 600–635	Hindus in India again persecute Buddhists. **BUDD, HIND**
600s	In India there is a rise of heterodox Buddhist cults. The Buddhist philosopher Candrakirti, in his *Prasannapada*, establishes the definitive version of Nagarjuna's school of Madhyamaka Buddhism (SEE C. 150, BUDD). Tradition claims that a council convened by India's Buddhist king Harsha (r. 606–647) at Kanauj is attended by thousands of kings, priests, and representatives of various Buddhist cults. The casting of a life-size statue of Buddha at Sultanganj, Bihar, indicates a thriving tradition of metalwork. **BUDD**
600s	During this century Tibet is only beginning to emerge as a historical entity, as Buddhism and centralized rule, two of Tibet's most enduring institutions, are established. The presence of Buddhist missionaries in Tibet challenges the indigenous Bon religion. Tibet's King Song Tsan Gampo (r. 627–650) sends the scholar Thonmi Sambhota to Kashmir to collect Indian texts, including Buddhist scriptures. Thonmi Sambhota's translation of Buddhist scriptures into Tibetan stabilizes the language, and Tibetan script develops from the alphabetic Gupta script of the original Sanskrit texts. King Song Tsan Gampo is thus credited with introducing Buddhism into Bhutan, but more likely his two Buddhist wives are responsible. He builds the Buddhist temple of Jo Khang in Lhasa, which will survive, with many modifications, through the 20th century. He also constructs temples at Bumthang and Kyichu in the region called Bhota (present-day Bhutan). **BUDD, TOL**
600s	The *neiguan* (interior meditation) trend in mysticism emerges in Chinese Daoism. A form of silent meditation, it aims to empty the spirit and unify it with the dao. Two important Daoist texts appear, the *Neiguanjing* (*Scripture of Concentration and Meditation*) attributed to Sun Simiao and the *Zuowang lun* (*Essay on Sitting and Forgetting*) of Sima Chengzhen. Sun Simiao (581–682), a physician and alchemist, advocates drug-taking as a method for achieving immortality. Legends about him arise after his death and he is worshiped in temples dedicated to him. Sima Chengzhen

(647–735), the 12th patriarch of the Shangqing school, is a pioneer of what will be known as the interior alchemy method. He adapts Confucian concepts as well as Buddhist meditative practices. **DAO**

600s   Among earliest Jain frescoes are those from this period found in rock-cut temple at Sittannavasal, near Tanjore. **JAIN**

600s   Confucianism is widespread among the Japanese, along with Chinese Daoism and *yin-yang* philosophy harmonizing the two basic forces of nature. All of these stimulate development of Shinto ethical teachings. **TOL**

600s–800s   The Srivijaya Kingdom of Sumatra, centered in Palembang, dominates the Malay Peninsula as well as Sumatra and Java. One of the major schools of Buddhism, Mahayana Buddhism, is practiced. **BUDD**

600–710   During Japan's Asuka period overseas trade intensifies, leading to the introduction of Chinese writing and Buddhism via Korea. Buddhism transforms Japan, creating a motive for the spread of literacy, the building of architecturally impressive temples, and the manufacture of exquisite ritual objects, as well as for changes in dietary habits and funerary practice. As the last stage of the Kofun period, this period takes its name from the Asuka region in southern Nara, which becomes the Yamato dynasty's capital, environs for various palaces, and site of many early Buddhist temples. **BUDD**

600–710   During Japan's Asuka period the status of the sun goddess Amaterasu is raised to a position of political supremacy. Honored as the ancestor of the imperial line, Amaterasu is enshrined at the Grand Shrine of Ise, together with Toyouke, the goddess of food. The era marks the beginning of such Shinto practices as sending the princess to Ise as priestess. Local Shinto divinity worship still includes magical and shamanistic practices. The Shinto priests at Izumo Shrine continue to employ occult practices there. **SHINTO**

600–850   Some Mon people in northern Laos come under the influence of Dvaravati, the strongly Buddhist culture that appears to spread across northern Thailand from the trade routes linking India to Southeast Asia. **SEE c. 500s–800s, BUDD.** **BUDD**

600–1200   During these centuries, when India is largely split apart by struggles among various regional and dynastic states, Jainism and Buddhism are gradually displaced in much of India by Vaishnavism and Saivism, the foundations of orthodox Hinduism, which are spread by *bhaktas,* wandering teachers, seers, and saints from south India who teach and sing their devotional poetry throughout India. During this time Jainism is fairly popular in southern India, particularly in the Karnataka region and to a lesser degree in the Tamil Nadu region; from the latter Jainism is also carried over to the island of Sri Lanka. In northern India most Jains are concentrated in Gujarat, Rajasthan, and parts of Bengal and Orissa. Most all of the kings are adherents of Saiva but some do befriend Jains; this is attested to by the many inscriptions, literary works, temples, and statues.   **JAIN**

603   Japan's imperial regent Prince Shokotu institutes political restructuring by introducing a Chinese-based bureaucratic system of government that consolidates the ideology of the unbroken imperial ancestry, officially beginning in B.C.E. 660 with sun goddess Amaterasu Omikami. This gives divine legitimacy to the imperial lineage.   **SHINTO**

604   The reign of China's Emperor Yang Di (r. 604–618), who assassinates his father, Emperor Wendi, to seize power begins. Like his father, Yang Di uses the scholar/monk Zhi Yi to promote Buddhism as a unifying ideology throughout China. There are only 10 Daoist temples in the capital, Chang'an, as compared with 120 Buddhist religious establishments.   **BUDD**

604   Japan's Prince Shokotu issues the Seventeen Article Constitution, centralizing and codifying the bureaucratic structure of the government and officially retitling the emperor as *Tenno*, or Heavenly Sovereign. The imperial court begins to follow an elaborate calendar of rites derived from Buddhism, Daoism, and Shinto. The Shinto priests conduct rituals based on agricultural symbolism, emphasizing purity, purification, and abstinence rites. They serve the *kami*, the native spirits that are regarded as the divine protectors of the state.   **SHINTO**

607   The Buddhist temple of Horyuji is finished near present-day Nara, Japan; the monastic complex of 45 buildings features the world's oldest authenticated wooden structure and finest surviving example of Chinese T'ang period architecture in a five-story pagoda. In the main hall, bronze statues of Shaka Trinity and Yakushi Niyorai (Buddha of Healing) are attributed to Tori Busshi, Japan's first artist to be known by name (because he signed his works) and the era's foremost sculptor. The monastery's famous frescoes will be destroyed in a fire in 1949.   **BUDD**

610   Muhammad, the founder of Islam, has a practice of retiring to caves to meditate, and in this year he receives his first revelation, thus becoming a prophet. Soon thereafter he begins seeking his first converts to Islam and spreads the message of his revelation that there is only one all-powerful God who will one day judge them. The first converts to Islam are Muhammad's wife, Khadija, his uncle Ali, and his close associate Abu Bakr.   **ISLAM**

612   Mimashi arrives in Japan from the Korean kingdom of Paekche to open a dance school that teaches *gigaku* (skill music). Performers wearing artistically expressive head-covering masks and elaborate costumes portray stock characters from Buddhist and Hindu tradition in this form of ancient dance-drama. Popular until the 17th century, it has come to be performed as mystery plays in Buddhist temples.   **BUDD**

612 | The Visigoths in Spain convert to Christianity, and Jews are given the choice of also converting or leaving the country. **JUD**

613 | Opposition to Muhammad from the ruling elite begins in Mecca. They see him as a political and economic threat and are especially concerned that his new religion of Islam will end the regular and economically profitable pilgrimages by Arabian peoples to Mecca. **ISLAM**

c. 614 | (St.) Maximus the Confessor (580–662) leaves the employ of the Byzantine emperor Heraclius in Constantinople and devotes the rest of his life to the study and development of Christian theology. Although he is executed in 662 after siding with the pope on theological matters, his ideas play a central role in the Ecumenical Council at Constantinople in 681. **ORTHO**

614 | Jews assist the Persians in taking Jerusalem and force the Christians to leave. **CHRIS, JUD**

617 | The Persians return control of Jerusalem to the Christians, and the Jews are driven out. **JUD**

618 | The T'ang dynasty is proclaimed in China. By now Daoism is fully a part of Chinese life. Borrowing from Buddhist organization, Daoists have established temples, male and female monastic orders, holy places, scriptures, and a theology. Daoism flourishes under the T'ang emperors. The T'ang

---

Religion in T'ang Dynasty, China

At this time there had already been traces of the syncretism of the *San Chiao* (Three Religions)—the mixture of Confucian ethics, Daoist merits, and Buddhist reincarnation. The Three Religions school became somewhat popular in Sung and Ming China; it was rejected by most Confucians and Buddhists but received wide support from Daoists. The T'ang dynasty in China created a system of local schools and permitted those wishing a career in upper civil service to take the *chin-shih* examinations, which tested knowledge of the Confucian Classics. The nonhereditary elite that evolved was later known in the West as "mandarins," referring to the dialect of Chinese they used. Confucian texts also became prominent, especially *Chung yung* (*Doctrine of the Mean*) and *I-chuan* (*The Great Commentary of the Classic of Changes*). Although some elements of Buddhism came under attack from some T'ang emperors, Buddhism made a significant contribution, both as an inspiration to artists and as a subject of devotional works of art such as the 97,000 Buddhist images at the Longmen Grottoes in Luoyang. The government allowed publication of a definitive edition of the *Wu Ching* with elaborate commentaries and compilation of the Tang legal code, both examples of resurgent Confucianism, even in a dynasty dominated by Buddhism and Daoism.

emperors' family name is Li, the surname given for Laozi, so they claim Laozi as an ancestor and bestow favor on his followers. The 300 years of this dynasty will see the further consolidation of Daoism and the full integration of Buddhist elements into Daoist ritual and belief. A new canon of Daoist scripture will be developed. **DAO**

618–
626
Gaozu reigns in China as the first emperor of the T'ang dynasty. The 10th patriarch of Shangqing Daoism, Wang Yuanzhi (d. 635), assures him he has received the mandate of heaven, confirming his legitimacy. Gaozu will preside over debates at court among adherents of Confucianism, Buddhism, and Daoism, the three rivals for the allegiance of China's educated elite. **DAO, TOL**

618–
907
The restoration of peace and prosperity in China under the T'ang dynasty leads to a flourishing of arts, letters, and religions. **TOL**

619
When his uncle Abu Talib, who had provided political protection, dies, Muhammad, the founder of Islam, is threatened with physical harm by his enemies in Mecca. He begins looking for converts outside of Mecca. Khadija, the first wife of Muhammad and the first convert to Islam, dies. **ISLAM**

620
A Daoist temple of Laozi is built on holy Mount Longjiao in China. **DAO**

Ka'ba

The Ka'ba is an ancient cubic square shrine located in the holy city of Mecca in Saudi Arabia. It has religious significance to both the pre-Islamic and Islamic periods. During the pre-Islamic or pagan era, it housed the pantheon of deities that flourished in the Hijaz region. At one time many hundreds of deities were worshiped in the region and the Ka'ba was said to have housed some 367. However, during the sixth century only four deities held special importance and were seen as the chief gods of the pantheon. These included *Allah* and the female gods who were believed to be his daughters: the goddesses of power (*al-'Uzzah*) and fate (*Manat*) and the goddess *al-Lat*. The Ka'ba was considered sacred because of its connection with the "black rock" or meteor that fell to earth about 1000 B.C.E. Because it was believed that deities often lived in stones, the black rock acquired iconic status and was eventually embedded into a corner of the Ka'ba. It was only logical, therefore, that over time it became the home of the Arab deities and a place of pilgrimage where the neighboring tribes could come to seek the blessings of the resident deities. With the emergence of Islam, Muhammad incorporated the symbolism of the formerly pagan Ka'ba directly into the new religion in order to ease the transition to Islam by providing a recognizable link to the past.

620	Pilgrims from Medina convert to Islam while at the Ka'ba shrine in Mecca.
	ISLAM

| 620 | In the first Japanese project to record history, the *Kujiki* (*Chronicle of Old Events*) is produced. It includes sections on the early myths and will become an important source for the study of ancient Shinto.   **SHINTO** |

| c. 620– 700 | The Saivite saint Tirujnanasambandhar converts the Pandya king in Madura in southern India from Jainism to the Saiva faith. A tradition claims that Tirujnanasambandhar convinces the newly converted king to persecute and impale 8,000 Jains; although frescoes at the Minaksi temple at Madura depict this event, no historical evidence confirms it.   **JAIN** |

| 622 | Muhammad and his followers in Mecca emigrate to Medina and establish the first Muslim state. This emigration marks the first year of the Muslim, or *hijri*, calendar.   **ISLAM** |

Islam

With over 900 million adherents, Islam is the second-largest religion in the world. Islam began in the Middle East, but within 100 years had spread to Asia and Africa; in the 1990s the nations with the largest Muslim populations are India, Bangladesh, Pakistan, and Indonesia. In Arabic and Muslim the word *Islam* means "he who submits." To Muslims, submission means to the will of God (Allah) as interpreted by Muhammad, the Prophet and founder of Islam. There are three basic beliefs in Islam: First, that Allah revealed his will to Muhammad and that his words, spoken in Arabic, are recorded in the Qur'an. Second, the profession of faith: "There is no god but God, and Muhammad is the messenger of God." Third, the obligation to perform certain duties to ensure that one may enter paradise. These duties are known as the Five Pillars of Islam:

1. The confessional acknowledging that there is only one God.
2. Prayer five times each day.
3. Almsgiving, or the voluntary contribution of money for the poor.
4. Fasting during Ramadan, the ninth month of the Muslim year.
5. The pilgrimage, or *haj*, to Mecca.

The key religious text is the Qur'an. Also of major significance is the *sunna*, a collection of *hadith* (narrations about Muhammad's life), traditions, and sayings assigned to Muhammad. Although there is much unity across Muslim communities regarding basic matters of belief and practice, there is also variation, including that based in interpretations of religious law, that based on the merging of Islam with different cultural traditions (Arab, Turk, Indonesian, Hindu, etc.), and that based on adherence to either the Sunni or Shi'a sects of Islam, with about 85 percent of Muslims being Sunni.

622–623	While living in Medina, Muhammad, the founder of Islam, takes several wives, establishing plural marriage as an acceptable form of marriage for Muslims. **ISLAM**
624	The Gaozu emperor of T'ang China travels to Mount Zhongnan to worship at a temple of Laozi. **DAO**
624	At the Battle of Badr in Arabia, the Muslims win their first significant victory over the rival Meccans, establishing the Islamic community as a political threat in the region. The victory makes Muhammad a popular figure, as it supports his prophecy that the Meccans would suffer for rejecting the word of God. As he gains political control over the Arab tribes and wins converts to Islam, Muhammad drives Jewish tribes out of the region. **ISLAM, JUD**
624–629	China's court astrologer Fu Yi, a nonbeliever, attacks Buddhism as foreign and urges the emperor to suppress it and force Buddhist priests and nuns to return to lay life. In 626 China's Emperor Gaozu limits the numbers of Buddhist and Daoist temples in the capital; each prefecture is allowed one temple per faith. The numbers of priests and nuns are to be reduced. Three months later, after the emperor is removed in a palace coup, the measures are withdrawn. Historians speculate that Buddhist political power may have been behind the coup, in which Gaozu's son ascends the T'ang throne. But in 629 the new emperor, Taizong, orders execution as the penalty for illegal ordination of Buddhist monks; tax evasion is usually the motive for illicit ordinations. **BUDD, DAO, TOL**
625	The Meccans almost succeed in destroying the Muslims of Medina at the Battle of Uhud in Arabia. However, the Muslims survive and remain a threat to Mecca. Muhammad continues his policy of expelling Jewish tribes from Medina. **ISLAM**
626	The emperor Gaozu of T'ang China moves to curb the power and wealth of Buddhist and Daoist religious organizations. The emperor limits the number of Daoist and Buddhist temples and monasteries in the capital; only one Daoist temple is allowed. Many priests and nuns are returned to lay life. The measures are withdrawn later in the year after the emperor is toppled in a palace coup. Buddhist political power may have been behind the coup, in which Gaozu's son ascends the T'ang throne. **BUDD, DAO**
626	Chinese adherents introduce Celestial Masters Daoism into Korea. **DAO**
627	In another attempt to defeat the Muslims, the Meccans are unsuccessful at the Battle of the Ditch in Arabia. The battle is named after a wide ditch dug around Medina by the outnumbered Muslims that rendered the Meccan cavalry useless and enabled the Muslims to resist Meccan attacks. **ISLAM**
628	(St.) Amand (c. 584–679), a French monk and former hermit who later becomes the patron saint of brewers, wine makers, and hotel keepers, is

ordained a bishop in Rome. He spends much of the remainder of his life as a missionary in northern France, Flanders, and Germany, making many converts and founding several monasteries and convents. **CHRIS**

628   Muhammad, the founder of Islam, and the Meccans sign the Treaty of Hudaybiya, in which they agree to end hostilities. **ISLAM**

628   The Byzantine ruler Herculis orders all Jews living within the Byzantine Empire to convert to Christianity. **JUD**

629   Muhammad and his Muslim armies enter Mecca triumphantly with almost no bloodshed. The central shrine (Ka'ba) is stripped of its idols and shrines to other deities in the region are destroyed. The Meccans convert to Islam

Sunni and Shi'a Islam

Sunni and Shi'a Islam are the two major branches of Islam. About 85 percent of Muslims are Sunni Muslims. Sunni is derived from the word *sunna* (tradition) which is an abbreviation for a much longer word meaning "The People of Tradition and the Community." During the early Islamic period, the term initially referred to those (the Orthodox) within the post-Muhammad community who believed it was better to accept a less than an ideal leader than risk the destruction of the community through civil war. Less ideologically oriented than other Islamic sects, Sunnism has no official clergy or formal religious leadership and is generally inclusive and diverse in its outlook in that it does not demand agreement and uniformity in the governance of the community. Rather, one seeks to maintain order and stability and avoid conflict. Moreover, separation from the Sunni community occurs only through consciously promoting political or religious perspectives that violate the conventional views of the Sunni majority. The word *Shi'a* literally means "party" or "faction" and clearly suggests the early Shi'a considered themselves a political party, rather than a purely religious group. Their origins (the Shi'at Ali or Party of Ali) were rooted in the early post-Muhammad leadership struggles in which Ali (Muhammad's cousin and son-in-law) and his closest associates argued that Ali was the true successor to Muhammad and that all future succession should remain within the household of the Prophet. The basis for this belief, they claimed, was in the numerous *hadith* traditions alleging Muhammad's preference for family over other members of the community, as well as traditions that designated Ali as the temporary leader of the community. Despite this, Ali was rejected three times before finally achieving power in 656. After 680 Shi'a political influence waned and more effort was devoted to the development of distinctive and elaborate theological ideas emphasizing the importance of martyrdom and persecution. Ultimately, Shi'ism evolved into three main branches, the Zaydis, the Twelvers, and the Isma'lis, with each establishing their own exclusive permutations of belief.

and join the Muslims in defeating the rival city of Ta'if, making Muhammad
the most powerful leader in Arabia.   ISLAM

629–
645

The Chinese Buddhist monk Xuan Zang (Hsuan Tsang) (602–664) travels
in northern India and Nepal; he reports on the decline of Buddhism and
the many deserted monasteries, but he brings back hundreds of Buddhist
manuscripts to be translated into Chinese. His account of his travels, *Record
of the Western Regions,* will be used as the basis for a comic novel by the

The Spread of Islam

622	Beginning of Islam as a religion in Arabia
630	Mecca is converted to Islam
635	Muslims from Arabia conquer Damascus, Syria
639	Muslims conquer Egypt
640	Muslims conquer Persia
711	Muslims conquer Spain
712	Muslims conquer the Indus Valley in southern Asia
732	Muslim conquest of Europe is halted in southwestern France
751	Muslim forces reach western China
c. 1000	Conversion of peoples in West Africa to Islam begins
1075	Turks defeat the Byzantines and the conquest of the Byzantine Empire begins
1099	European Crusaders capture Jerusalem
1100–1300	Islam spreads to the coastal region of East Africa
1187	Muslims recapture Jerusalem
1220	Mongols from central Asia invade the Middle East
1231	Christian forces begin to push the Muslims out of Spain
1260	Mongols are defeated in Egypt
c. 1280	People in Indonesia and Malaysia are converting to Islam
1345	The Ottoman Empire expands into southern Europe
1492	Muslim rule ends in Spain as they are defeated by Christian forces
1501	Muslims are expelled from Spain
1517	Ottoman Turks conquer Egypt
1526	The Muslim Mughal Empire is established in India
1606	By treaty, the Ottomans retain control of parts of southern Europe
1918	The Ottoman Empire is defeated in World War I and its territory is reduced to Turkey

16th-century Chinese writer Wu Ch'eng-en; in its English translation it is titled *Monkey*. **BUDD**

630   The first Daoist monastery is built on Mount Wudang in northwest Hubei Province in central China. By tradition the birthplace of the war god Xuanwu, it will become an important Daoist holy place. **DAO**

631   The Year of Deputations in Muslim Arabia. Most Arab bedouin tribes (nomadic herders) send delegates to Medina to formally accept Islam as their religion. **ISLAM**

632   After performing the pilgrimage to Mecca (the Farewell Pilgrimage), Muhammad, the Prophet and founder of Islam, dies after a brief illness. The Muslim community divides over the qualifications of a successor. The majority (Sunni Muslims) follow a political leader called the *caliph*. A minority (Shi'a Muslims) prefer an *imam*, a leader who has both political and religious authority. **ISLAM**

632–
634   Abu Bakr (?–634) is elected as Muhammad's successor as leader of the Muslim community in Arabia. Many of the Arab bedouin tribes revolt against the rule of Medina after Muhammad's death and the Campaigns Against Apostasy are fought to keep the community together. The Muslims begin to expand north from Mecca. The first attempts are made to begin writing down the teachings of Muhammad. **ISLAM**

632–
661   This is the period of rule of the first four caliphs of the Muslim community in Arabia known as the *Rashidun*, or righteous caliphs, who set the standards for the rule of the Muslim community according to Sunni Muslims. **ISLAM**

c. 633   Oswald, the King of Northumbria in Britain, chooses to convert to Christianity. Monks from the monastery on Iona assist in the conversion, which is supported as well by his brother Oswin after Oswald's death in 642, thus maintaining Christianity in the region. **CHRIS**

633   By imperial edict in T'ang dynasty China, Buddhists and Daoists must honor their parents; clergy may not accept homage from their parents. **BUDD, DAO**

634–
637   Muslim-Arab armies take Palestine and Syria from the Byzantine empire. **ISLAM**

634–
644   The first caliph (leader) of the Muslim community in Arabia, Abu Bakr, dies after having appointed Umar (?–644) as the second caliph. During his rule, the Muslims begin their conquest of the Near East and North Africa. **ISLAM**

635   Nestorian Christianity, which has spread east from Asia Minor along the trade routes to China, arrives in China during the T'ang dynasty. The reli-

635   gion is accepted by the emperor and survives for nearly two centuries although it draws only a small number of converts.   **CHRIS**

635   As the Muslims begin to expand out of Arabia, they build mosques in towns that they conquer. These mosques are modeled on the basic design suggested by Muhammad and include those at Basra (635), Kufa (637), and Wasit (720) in Iraq and Fustat (641–642) in Egypt.   **ISLAM**

637   An imperial edict gives Daoist monks and nuns preference over Buddhist clergy in court ceremonies in T'ang dynasty China. A second edict attacks Buddhism as a foreign religion and claims it lacks the profundity of native Daoism.   **BUDD, DAO**

637–638   Muslim-Arab forces defeat the Persians in Iraq and take control of Mesopotamia.   **ISLAM**

638   The Muslims conquer Palestine and Jews are permitted to return to Jerusalem. The Muslims also conquer North Africa and the Jews there are involved in resisting Muslim rule. As "peoples of the book" Jews and Christians in lands under Muslim control are permitted to practice their

---

Qur'an

In Arabic the word *Qur'an* means "recitation," or a collection of writings to be recited, and the Qur'an is the scriptural text of Islam. Although the Qur'an occupies a holy place in the Islamic religion as the divine word and presence of Allah, few Muslims refer to these texts simply as the Qur'an. Instead, titles signifying profound respect, such as *Al-Karim* (the Noble) or *Al-Azim* (the Magnificent) are normally used. Within the Qur'an itself, the term *Al-Kitab* (the Book) is used. The text itself is arranged into 114 chapters, or *suras*, that vary in length, from only a few lines to several pages and organized from the longest to the shortest in length, rather than by chronological order of revelation. The *suras* are identified by name, rather than by number, and the names generally reflect a distinctive or unusual word that appears early in the chapter. The *suras* are then subdivided into verses called *ayat* (signs). Finally, 29 chapters begin with seemingly disjointed letters known as the "mysterious letters," which are alleged to possess some form of secret religious meaning. In the early years of Islam, Muslims memorized the Qur'an because no written text existed; there were only scattered writings on fragments of parchment, leaves, and camel bones. The best evidence indicates that an official text or canon was created sometime between 650 and 656 under the leadership of Uthman. Muslims believe that the Qur'an can be written only in Arabic and that all translations lose something of its true meaning.

religions but are subjected to special taxes and periodic repressions, massacres, and exiles over the next centuries.   ISLAM, JUD

638   The Council of Toledo in Spain orders that all Jews in Spain either convert to Christianity or leave. Many convert although the Jewish community survives.

JUD

639–
642   The Muslims from Arabia invade and conquer Egypt and wrest it from Byzantine rule. The Coptic Christians in Egypt, like Jews and Christians in other lands conquered by the Muslims, are given the choice of converting to Islam or paying additional taxes as non-Muslims.   ISLAM

640–
700   Muslim Arabs conquer part of Lebanon. Maronite Christians have long been established in the region, and Islam spreads by conversion and migration, although the country remains predominantly Christian.   ISLAM

641   The Muslim Arabs who have conquered Egypt move south and attack Nubia, a Christian state. Their attack is repulsed and the Muslim invaders are defeated again 10 years later.   ISLAM

642–
650   Most of Sassanian Iran is conquered by the Muslim Arabs.   ISLAM

643   The Muslims continue their conquest of North Africa and conquer Libya.

ISLAM

644   The second Muslim caliph, Umar, is murdered by a Persian slave, and Uthman (?–656) is elected as the third caliph.   ISLAM

644   In Japan Ofube no Oshi of Azuma starts a cult to worship a large green caterpillar. With the arrival of Buddhism, the seventh century is a time of transition and of perceived instability, with a turning away from the old values of Shinto and the establishment of the centralized state. This is fertile ground for the growth of cults. Often sects will combine Shinto and Buddhist elements in a syncretic fashion: En no Gyoja is the legendary leader of the mystical cult of Shugendo whose practitioners, called Yamabushi, prostrate themselves toward mountains such as Mount Hiei or Mount Koya. They also make pilgrimages up the mountains and practice exorcism. The Shugendo leaders will be exiled by the imperial court, and the teachings will remain secret until the 16th century.   SHINTO, TOL

644–
656   Uthman rules the Muslim Empire as the third caliph. During his rule the empire continues to expand, rule is centralized, and efforts begin to produce a definitive version of the Qur'an.   ISLAM

645   The Taika Reform during the reign of Japan's Emperor Kotoku leads to the creation of the Office of Shinto Worship (*Jingikan*). The highest of the eight ministries of government, it begins the amalgamation of indigenous customs

and foreign ritual. The Bureau of Yin and Yang (*Ommoyoryo*) is organized to develop a system of divination to aid political decision-making. Members of the Nakatomi (from which derive the Fujiwara), Imbe, and Urabe clans supervise aspects of Shinto worship, and the Abe and Kamo clans occupy themselves with the *yin-yang* theories of divination.   **SHINTO, TOL**

646   In Japan there is an increase in Buddhist temple construction. Some 483 temples are completed by 710.   **BUDD**

647   The Muslims from Arabia continue their conquest of North Africa and conquer Tunisia.   **ISLAM**

649   (St.) John Climacus (c. 579–649), also called John of Sinai, dies. As the abbot of the monastery of Saint Catherine on Mount Sinai, he organizes the *Ladder of Paradise*, a collection of spiritual writings of early Christian monks that becomes a standard religious text for Orthodox Christians.   **ORTHO**

649–
683   Gaozong reigns in China as the T'ang emperor. He is a generous patron of Daoism. Gaozong has Daoist temples built in every province. At his empress's urging, he will include the *Dao De Jing* among the texts used as a basis for official examinations.   **DAO**

c. 650   Shaiva Siddhanta emerges as a sect of Hindu Shaivism among the Tamil of southern India. It stresses the importance of ritual behavior to achieve salvation.   **HIND**

650–
656   The official version of the Qur'an, the sacred text of Islam, is complied and written.   **ISLAM**

650–
950   Buddhism flourishes in eastern India under Pala patronage. The Pala dynasty founds new universities at Vikramasila and Paharpur and endows the great Buddhist university at Nalanda.   **BUDD**

651   In Korea a royal academy is established in which officials drawn from the aristocracy are exposed to the Confucian Classics. Confucian precepts are gradually seen in the rules of conduct for the *hwarang*, a knightly class instrumental in the Silla unification of Korea in 668.   **CONF**

651   The northeast province of Iran, Khurasan, is conquered by the Muslims from Arabia, and the Sassanid Persians come under Muslim control. The Zoroastrians are forced to convert to Islam or flee. Some migrate along the Silk Road to China, where they establish communities that last into the 10th century.   **ISLAM, SECT**

652   The Muslims in Egypt and the Christians in Nubia to the south enter into a truce agreement following two failed attempts by the Muslims to conquer Nubia. The Nubians' major export to Egypt were African slaves who were used as soldiers by the Muslims. The two states remain trading partners for

some 500 years, with Muslim Arab traders and others settling in Nubia during the period. **ISLAM**

c. 653   The Japanese Buddhist monk Dosho (628–700) founds the Hosso school. Although he learned of his new approach through his studies in China, it is based on the Vijnanavada, or Yogacarin, school founded in India by Vasubandhu. It stresses the quest for achieving pure thought, in part through the practice of meditation and yoga (SEE C. 350, BUDD). **BUDD**

655   The Muslims defeat the Byzantines in the Battle of the Masts off the southern coast of Turkey. As a result, the Muslims become a naval power in the Mediterranean Sea and conquer the island of Cyprus. **ISLAM**

656   The third Muslim caliph, Uthman, is assassinated and Ali (598–661) becomes the fourth caliph. Ali is not a popular choice with all Muslims, and the two factions fight at the Battle of the Carmel in Iraq, with Ali victorious. **ISLAM**

657   In Arabia the rivalry for control of the Muslim Empire is contested at the Battle of Siffin, which leaves Ali in power but with weakened support. **ISLAM**

657   In the aftermath of the Battle of Siffin, the Muslim Kharijite sect emerges. Members of the sect refuse to accept either Ali or Mu'awiya as the leader of Islam and claim that any righteous Muslim can become leader of the community. **ISLAM**

Ali

Ali (598–661) was an early follower of Muhammad and a leader of the community after Muhammad's death. Ali was Muhammad's first cousin and the son of the uncle who raised Muhammad during his formative years following the death of his parents and maternal grandfather. As an adult Ali joined the household of Muhammad and married Fatima, Muhammad's daughter. Ali is considered to be the second convert to Islam and the first male to do so. Considered the closest male companion, a valiant warrior in support of Islam, and Muhammad's chief lieutenant in his absence, many Muslims believed that he would succeed Muhammad as leader of the Islamic community upon the Prophet's death. When this did not occur, the Shi'a religious sect gradually evolved in support of Ali's claims as the successor to Muhammad and in time this exclusive loyalty resulted in a permanent rift between the Sunni and Shi'a sects. Still, the Sunni continued to hold Ali in very high regard, given that many Sufis, most of whom are Sunni, consider Ali to be the first Sufi and believe that their form of Islam derives from him.

658   The Kharijite sect of Muslims is defeated by Ali, the leader of the Muslim community, and survivors flee to the eastern regions of the Muslim world.

ISLAM

660   From this year the emperor Gaozong in T'ang dynasty China shows a growing devotion to Daoism. He gives important imperial court positions to several Daoist adepts.

DAO

660s   The abbot of the Daoist monastery of Louguan, Xi Wencao (d. 688), completes the *Annals of the Sage*, an up-to-its-time history of Daoism. The work, no longer extant, will be a model for other such works during the Song dynasty.

DAO

661   The fourth Muslim caliph, Ali, is assassinated and rule of the Muslim Empire passes to Mu'awiya. The death of Ali marks the end of the period of the rightly guided caliphs in the Muslim Empire and the end of rulers who had a direct tie to Muhammad, the founder of Islam.

ISLAM

Hadith

The term *hadith* refers to a communication or narrative and in Islam means the record of actions or sayings by Muhammad, the Prophet and founder of Islam. Thus the *hadith* constitutes the body of the sacred tradition of Islam. Pre-Islamic Arabs considered it a virtue to follow the traditions of their forefathers. Because such traditions were nonexistent in the Islamic period, *sunna* (new traditions) were required. Given the uniqueness of Muhammad, it was logical that the *sunna* of Muhammad would fulfill that need and that his early companions were the most reliable sources of these actions due to their immediate proximity to the Prophet. Unfortunately, Muhammad's original religious ideas and practices soon became altered to fit the rapidly changing circumstances within the Islamic community, among them the development of more systematic doctrines of duties and beliefs (the Pillars of Faith) and the requirements of expansion. The result was the growth of numerous, often deliberate, forgeries of Muhammad's *sunna* in order to legitimize later actions and beliefs especially in the areas of religious law and obligations, ritual purity, and etiquette. In time the majority of the *hadith* accounts of the Prophet's *sunna* lacked reliability despite their hallowed status throughout Islam. By the early eighth century, Islamic religious scholars grew increasingly concerned over the growing number of *hadith* forgeries and devised elaborate systems to separate truth from fiction. This process continued into the nineth century as religious scholars attempted to create more reliable collections of the *hadith*. Ultimately two—one by Al-Muslim (d. 875) and the other by Al-Bukhari (d. 870)—attained such veracity that many Sunni Muslims rank them just below the Qur'an as sacred texts.

661– 750	The Umayyad dynasty rules the Muslim Empire, with Mu'awiya (?–680) the first ruler. Damascus is established as the capital of the empire that continues to expand into Asia and North Africa, and attacks are made on the Byzantine Empire to the north.　**ISLAM**
663– 664	At the Synod of Whitby in Britain, the king of Northumbria decides that the bishop of Rome rather than Celtic Christian bishops in Britain will be the ultimate arbitrator of religious matters. The decision places British Christianity under the influence of Rome. The synod also approves the use of A.D. (Latin for *anno Domini,* "in the year of our Lord") for marking the years.　**CHRIS**
664	At a Church Synod at Whitby, England, the church leaders decide to ban the practice of Celtic religion and replace it with Christianity. This decision accelerates the assimilation of Celtic peoples into English society.　**CHRIS**
c. 665	Muslims in Iraq construct the first minaret (a tower attached to a mosque from which Muslims are called to worship) adjacent to the mosque in Basra.　**ISLAM**
665	The Muslims in North Africa continue their conquest of the region as they move inland from the Mediterranean coast and conquer territory in the interior of Tunisia.　**ISLAM**
666	Gaozong, the emperor of T'ang China, gives new, more resplendent titles to the Daoist deity Laozi and orders Daoist temples built in every prefecture. He takes part in sacrifice ceremonies on Mount Tai, a Daoist sacred site.　**DAO**
668	In Japan Korean priest Dogyo steals the sacred imperial sword from Atsuta Shrine in Nagoya, where it now rests, to take back to Korea; he is prevented from doing so by a violent storm at sea. This is seen as an example of the divine protective power of Japan's *kami,* or native spirits. The sword had come to Atsuta after Yamato Takeru, son of legendary 12th emperor Keiko (r. 71–130), had taken it, according to tradition, to conquer the "Eastern Barbarians." Atsuta Shrine, the second most important imperial shrine after Ise, supposedly was founded by the hero's consort at the site of his tomb mound.　**SHINTO**
668– 680	Through the work of Theodore of Tarsus (602–690) and synods held in 673 and 680, the Christian Church in Britain is organized, with dioceses established and the archbishop of Canterbury given authority over the entire nation.　**CHRIS**
c. 670	The Chinese Buddhist monk Fa Zang (643–712) systematizes the teachings of what is known as the Hua Yan school of Buddhism. It is based on the *Avatamsaka Sutra,* a large Mahayana text allegedly based on teachings handed down directly from the Buddha; it was translated into Chinese in 402. About this same year (670) the Korean Buddhist monk Uisang, after 20 years of study in China with monks, including Fa Zang, introduces the Hua Yan school of Buddhism into Korea. Hua Yan Buddhism teaches that all

670   earthly phenomena are impure forms of the all-encompassing mind that resolves into the Buddha.   **BUDD**

670   The Muslim conquerors of Tunisia establish the city of Kairwan as the capital of Ifriqiya (Africa). The city becomes a center for trade with peoples in West Africa, with gold and slaves desired by the Muslims. Muslim conquest of Africa halts at this point as the Berbers, the native people of North Africa, resist Muslim expansion. In the following century the Muslim Empire expands to North Africa and then into Spain with the assistance of a Berber Muslim army.   **ISLAM**

671–
695   The Chinese Buddhist pilgrim Ti Jing passes through the Srivijaya Kingdom on Sumatra in 671 on his way to study at the Buddhist university at Nalanda, India. He returns to Sumatra in 685 and spends the next 10 years there working on translations of the Buddhist texts. His diary indicates that both Theravada and Mahayana Buddhism are observed in Sumatra.   **BUDD**

672   Japan's Emperor Temmu (r. 672–686) and his widow, Empress Jito (r. 686–697), while promoting Buddhism, also see to it that the Shinto rites at court are updated and granted parallel status to those of Buddhism. In this era, members of the Nakatomi family's senior branch become the chief imperial court Shinto chaplains and the chief priests at the Grand Shrine of Ise. The family holds these positions until 1872.   **BUDD, SHINTO**

672   Following civil strife over Japan's imperial succession (the Jinshin Disturbance), Emperor Temmu (r. 672–686) occupies the throne. To solidify his power he upgrades the Ise shrine where the ancestral *kami* (native spirits) of the imperial family are worshiped. In this action he emphasizes the ancient role of the emperor as spiritual leader and high priest of Shinto as superior to his role as a patron of Buddhism.   **BUDD, SHINTO**

672–
680   Hostilities continue between the Muslim and Byzantine Empires, on land and sea. Rhodes falls in 672 and Crete in 674 to the Muslims, and there are annual unsuccessful attacks on Constantinople, the capital of the Byzantine Empire.   **ISLAM**

674   The empress Wu of T'ang China (she will reign in her own right from 684 to 704) orders all officials to study the *Dao De Jing*, and it becomes a primary examination text for official examinations. A devout Buddhist, she also manages to revoke the imperial edict giving Daoists precedence at all religious ceremonies.   **BUDD, DAO**

675   Tradition claims that Hui Neng (638–713), a kitchen worker from southern China, wins a poetry competition set up by the dying fifth patriarch of Chan Buddhism, who then appoints Hui Neng his successor. In this version of events, Hui Neng, fearing that he will be attacked by jealous monks, flees south. There he establishes the southern school of Chan Buddhism and becomes the Sixth Patriarch. Meanwhile, the northern school regards Shen

Xiu (600–706) as the Sixth Patriarch. Shen Xiu is responsible for the *sutra* called the *Platform Sutra of the Sixth Patriarch*; in it, he suggests that no one discipline or posture will bring enlightenment. The northern school headed by Shen Xiu emphasizes gradual progress toward enlightenment through the disciplines of meditation, while the southern school allows for a more "sudden" enlightenment. Because the northern school of Chan Buddhism dies out, Hui Neng and his southern school are honored as the true sources of Chan Buddhism in China. SEE C. **500–535,** BUDD.   BUDD

675   The imperial court orders the compilation of the first collected version of Daoist scriptures in T'ang China.   DAO

678   Gaozong, the emperor of China, puts Daoist clergy under control of the Court of Imperial Clan Affairs, a formal acknowledgement of the identification of the T'ang royal house with Laozi. He also declares the *Dao De Jing* a compulsory text for state examinations.   DAO

678   In Japan the Kamo Shrine is built at its present location in Kyoto; its origins go back to the legendary first emperor Jimmu. The Shinto shrine will become powerful in affording protection to the city when the capital is moved to Kyoto in 794. With the endowment of estates and the support of feudal governments, the shrine will accumulate considerable prestige and wealth.   SHINTO

680   The (Third) Council of Constantinople is held. The bishops address the continuing dispute between the Western and Eastern Christian churches over the two natures of Christ and support the two natures doctrine favored by the Western Church. The council also rejects monotheism, the belief that Christ had two natures but one will and officially adopts the cross as the sign of Christianity.   CHRIS

680   Mu'awiya, leader of the Muslim Empire, dies and is succeeded by his son Yazid (?–683) of the Umayyad dynasty. The role of leader is also claimed by Husayn, the son of Ali, the fourth caliph and the grandson of Muhammad, the Prophet and founder of Islam. Husayn and his party are ambushed by Yazid's army at Karbala in Iraq and Husayn is killed. He becomes a martyr for the Shi'a Muslims, who believe that the Muslim community should be ruled by descendants of Ali.   ISLAM

680–
750   In China Buddhist texts are printed from wood blocks.   BUDD

682   *Kukhak,* a royal Confucian college or national academy, is founded in Silla, the southern kingdom under which all Korea was unified during the Silla dynasty (668–935), and a proto-civil service system called *tokso samp'um kwa* is installed. In 750 the name of the academy is changed to *T'aehak.*   CONF

683–692	Following the death of Yazid, the leader of the Umayyad Muslim dynasty, the Muslim Empire is racked by dissension as various individuals and factions compete for power and attempt to overthrow the Umayyad dynasty. Rebellions take place in Mecca, Iraq, and Arabia. **ISLAM**
685–705	The Umayyad caliph Abd al-Malik (?–705) defeats rebellious factions in the Muslim Empire and once again reunites the empire. He makes Arabic the language of its administration, issues his own currency, and begins large building projects. **ISLAM**
686–687	Wilfrid (634–709), a Christian missionary in Britain and later the bishop of York, successfully converts many Saxons in Sussex to Christianity. Their conversion means that Britain is now an almost entirely Christian nation. **CHRIS**
686–697	During the reign of Japan's Empress Jito, the ritualistic practice of razing and rebuilding the Inner Shrine at Ise begins. At first this is done every 20 years, but with the reign of Emperor Go-Mizunoo (r. 1611–1629) it will be done every 21 years. This schedule will not be kept during times of military strife, particularly during the 15th and 16th centuries. **SHINTO**
689	The Visigoths in Spain classify Jews as slaves as part of a general pattern of persecution. **JUD**
690	Frisians in northern Europe in what is now the Netherlands are converted to Christianity by Wilfrid (c. 658–739), a monk from Britain, who is made a bishop in 695. **CHRIS**
691	The empress Wu (r. 690–705) establishes Buddhism as the state religion of T'ang dynasty China, pushing Confucianism and Daoism into secondary roles. **BUDD, CONF, DAO, TOL**
691	The Dome of the Rock in Jerusalem is completed as a pilgrimage site by the Muslim Umayyad dynasty. Muslims believe that it is built on the spot from which Muhammad departed on his night journey to heaven. It is built on the site of the Jewish temple, which had been used as a waste dump when Jerusalem was under Byzantine rule. The Dome of the Rock is built to be more grand than the Christian Church of the Holy Sepulchre also in Jerusalem. The al-Aqsa Mosque is built on the same site but is destroyed in an earthquake in 747 C.E. Jerusalem is now a holy city for Jews, Christians, and Muslims and remains so in the 1990s. **ISLAM**
691	With a Japanese imperial offering at Kehi Shrine in Tsuruga, Fukui Prefecture, this will become one of the largest shrines in the area. It will continue to receive frequent gifts from the court and patronage from warrior families. **SHINTO**
693	China's Empress Wu replaces the *Dao De Jing* as a compulsory text for state examinations with a "classic" of her own compilation called *Rules for*

Officials, a collection of quotations from Confucian and Daoist classics.
CONF, DAO

694　Japan's Empress Jito (r. 686–697) orders copies of Buddhist *Golden Light Sutra* be sent to provinces, to be read at the start of the first month of the year. **BUDD**

698　A Buddhist temple is established near Japan's Ise Shinto shrine. The temple will be dismantled in 772 after Ise is struck by a typhoon, as it is thought that the Shinto divinities are displeased by this effrontery. **BUDD, SHINTO**

c. 700　Kashmir Shaivism, a sect of Hindu Shaivism, emerges in the Kashmir region of northern India. It stresses personal devotion as the route to salvation. **HIND**

c. 700　Muslims from Saudi Arabia and southern India settle in Sri Lanka. They are primarily traders and merchants, and over the centuries their population increases to over one million. **ISLAM**

c. 700　The Christian monk (St.) Andrew of Crete (c. 660–740) is made bishop of Crete. He writes the *Great Canon*, a long poem commenting on the Scriptures that becomes a standard text in Orthodox Christianity. **ORTHO**

c. 700　(St.) John of Damascus (c. 675–c. 749) leaves the employ of the Muslim rulers of Damascus, Syria, and enters the monastery of Mar Sabba in Palestine. As a monk and theologian he writes several texts important to Orthodox Christianity, including *Fount of Wisdom*, *Treatises in Defense of the Holy Icons*, and *Homily on the Transfiguration*. **ORTHO**

c. 700　The *Ginza*, one of the sacred texts of the Mandeans, a Gnostic sect dating to the first century C.E. in the Middle East, is written. The book combines beliefs from Christianity and magic. **SECT**

700　Opportunities in the trades and commerce, coupled with limited opportunities in farming, draw Jews in Arab Muslim regions to the towns and cities, where they become a distinct urban group. About this time Jewish academies (*yeshivah*) in the Muslim world become the center of Jewish religion and cultural life. Major academies develop in Babylonia (which later move to Baghdad) and Jerusalem and compete for influence. Over the next 200 years the Jerusalem academy influences Jews in what is now Israel, Syria, Jordan, and Egypt, while the Babylonian academies influence Jewish communities in the Near East, North Africa, and southern Europe. **JUD**

700s　In India the philosopher Sankara, founder of the Vedanta school of Hinduism, is regarded by some as having been influenced by Buddhism, in particular the Madhyamaka school founded by Nagarjuna **(SEE C. 150, BUDD)**. In any case, it will be such developments within Hinduism that will gradually absorb and virtually eliminate Buddhism in most parts of India. **BUDD, HIND**

700s

700s	In Japan the fusion of Shinto and Buddhism continues. Buddhists posit a parallelism of deities: each Shinto *kami* (native spirit) is seen as a manifestation of a certain Buddhist deity, and most Shinto sanctuaries are provided with an inner sanctuary for Buddhist observances. Numerous Buddhist temples are built near Shinto shrines. **BUDD, SHINTO**
700s	During Japan's Nara period, Buddhism, as the state religion, leads a vigorous campaign of temple-building in the capital and provinces. Nara artistic accomplishments in Buddhist-inspired architecture and statuary (known as Tempyo culture) are matched in the realm of Japanese literature. **BUDD, TOL**
700s	A growing revival of interest in the philosophy of Confucius leads to institution of a required civil service examination for government job candidates throughout China. The examination, based on Confucian precepts, implements the idea that an enduring state must be built on the merit of the advisers to its rulers. **CONF**
700s	The first Muslim settlement in East Africa is established at Shanga in the Lamu Archipelago off the coast of Kenya. The community is occupied for about 300 years, with nine mosques built during that time. It is not known from archaeology whether the occupants were Muslims from Arabia, local peoples converted to Islam, or both. **ISLAM**
700s	Among the few remnants of India's post-Gupta paintings are decorations of the Jain temple at Sittanavasal, near Madras. Their style perpetuates the Ajanta wall paintings of the late Gupta and early Chalukya types, both in drawing and coloring. With their fanciful and intricate drawings of multiple lotus flowers and buds and large leaves, these Jain paintings are not far removed in date or style from the earliest paintings in the Kalisa temple at Ellura. **JAIN**
700–735	Tantric Buddhist missionaries (SEE **500s–600s BUDD, TOL**) Vajrabodhi and Amogavajra visit China from India. From this time into the 11th century, Tantric Buddhism will spread from Bengal into north India, Nepal, Tibet, China, Japan, and Southeast Asia. It greatly influences Hindu and Buddhist ritual and artistic production. During this same period a succession of Japanese delegations to China, one with as many as 500 emissaries, brings Chinese culture—calligraphy, Buddhist and Confucian thought—back to influence Japanese society and sends Chinese culture flowing eastward to Japan. **BUDD, TOL**
700–1000	Shaivism, a major sect of Hinduism, is the dominant form of Hinduism in India as it is supported by many local rulers. Shaivism focuses more on asceticism than do other forms of Hinduism, with yoga a major practice. It comes in a number of regional forms including Pashupata, Lingayat, Kapalika, Kashmir Shaivism, Shaiva Siddhanta, Smarta, and Khanphata. **HIND**

702   Under Japan's Emperor Mommu (r. 697–707), the Taiho Civil Code is promulgated and will remain in force until 757. Based on the Asuka-Kiyomihara Code, the Taiho Code consolidates the Taiho reforms of 701 in its institutionalization of the system of government and laws. With the establishment of the National Cult Department (*Jingi-kwan*), which is considered superior to all other departments of the bureaucracy, the regulation of the activities of Shinto priests spells out the details of court ritual, the cult of all Shinto divinities (not just the national gods but also the worship of clan and communal deities), and the procedures of such practices as the great offering, the propitiation of spirits, divination, and augury. In the state Shinto rites conducted in the palace shrines, the emperor and Nakatomi priests play a central role.   **SHINTO, TOL**

705   Zhongzong reigns as emperor of T'ang China. He reinstates the Daoist *Dao De Jing* as examination material and issues an edict that one Buddhist and one Daoist temple be built in each prefecture.   **BUDD, DAO**

705   Arab Muslim armies moving out of Arabia to the east have expanded the Islamic Empire to the borders of China in central Asia.   **ISLAM**

706   The Great Mosque in Damascus, Syria, is built by the Umayyad dynasty. Although severely damaged by a fire in 1893, it is the only mosque from the Umayyad dynasty that survives into the 20th century in its original form.

      ISLAM

709   Kasuga Shrine is built near Nara on Mount Mikasayama. It is founded by Fujiwara no Fuhito as a clan and national shrine to protect the new capital and is endowed with a large estate throughout Japan and numerous branch shrines. Kasuga is noted for its deer park: deer are seen as sacred messengers. Around 768, Kasuga will be moved nearer to the capital.   **SHINTO**

710   Under the influence of Buddhism, the first permanent capital of Japan is established at Nara. Previously, the capital was moved and the imperial palace rebuilt after the death of each emperor, because of Shinto taboos against death pollution.   **BUDD, SHINTO**

710   Mac Derile, the Pict (Celtic) King of Northumbria in Great Britain, accepts Christianity.   **CHRIS**

710   Zhang Wanfu in China reformulates the Daoist ritual first codified by Lu Xiujing in the fifth century. He also codifies regulations governing the priesthood and monastic life.   **DAO**

710– 794   During the Nara period, the early era of Classical Japan, the groundwork for a synthesized Buddhism and Shinto continues, as Shinto *kami* (native spirits) are denoted as guardians, students, or manifestations of great Buddhas and *bodhisattvas*. Around 750 Shinto tutelary or guardian deities begin to be worshiped in Buddhist temples.   **BUDD, SHINTO**

711   A Chinese court memorial draws attention to how the wealthy men evade their taxes by becoming ordained Buddhist monks and novices. In 714, after an investigation, 30,000 monks and nuns are ordered returned to lay life.   **BUDD**

711   The Arab Muslims from Arabia have now conquered all of North Africa. However, many people in the regions including Berbers, Jews, and Christians resist conversion to Islam. Over the following centuries most Berbers do convert to Islam.   **ISLAM**

711   The Arab Muslims from Arabia defeat the Turks at Khiva in central Asia and take control of the region. Local peoples are forced to convert to Islam and Muslim missionaries are sent to the region to maintain Islam in the newly converted population. In later centuries, when the region is invaded by Mongols and Turks from the east, Islam is firmly established and the invaders convert to Islam.   **ISLAM**

711   In Japan southeast of Kyoto, the Fushimi Inari Shrine is built on Mount Inari. It is dedicated to Inari, Japan's most widely worshiped deity, because of Inari's association with rice cultivation, and to four other divinities.   **SHINTO**

711–713   Arab Muslims from Arabia have pushed as far east as Sind in northwest India and establish Muslim rule over the region. However, this is an isolated outpost of Islam and does not play a role in the Muslim conquest of India that begins in 1030.   **ISLAM**

711–716   Spain (Al-Andalus) is conquered by Muslims from North Africa. Jews are given religious freedom. During Muslim rule into the 14th century the Jews are actively involved in the translation and interpretation of Greek texts for use in the Middle East and Europe.   **ISLAM, JUD**

712   The oldest Japanese book, *Kojiki* (*Record of Ancient Times*), is completed following its commission by Emperor Temmu decades earlier. A compilation of legends, beliefs, and history, its purpose is to confirm the divine origins of the imperial family and of the destiny of the Japanese people. These annals are the main source of the mythology central to Shinto and so become a sacred Shinto text.   **SHINTO**

712–756   The emperor Xuanzong reigns in China in what will be recalled as the Golden Age of the T'ang dynasty. He takes an intelligent interest in poetry, historical works, and religion. A patron of Daoism, Xuanzong retains the *Laozi*, the sacred Dao text, in the curriculum for imperial civil service examinations. The patriarch Li Hangguang (683–769) initiates the emperor into the Shangqing school. Xuanzong and other T'ang emperors are also interested in Daoism for its claim to make elixirs that confer immortality. Consistent with Daoist tenets, Xuanzong gradually withdraws from public affairs, leaving the day-to-day business of government to his ministers and military commanders.   **DAO**

c. 714   Members of the Muslim Kharijite sect, who frequently revolt against Muslim leaders whom they do not accept as the legitimate or deserving leaders of the Muslim community, flee from the east to North Africa where they attract a sizeable following among the Berbers, the indigenous people of North Africa.   **ISLAM**

716   According to Zoroastrian tradition, Zoroastrians fleeing Muslim rule in Persia arrive on the west coast of India. Modern-day scholars believe that they actually arrived in the 10th century. In India they are called Parsis, after Fars, Persia, where they are believed to have migrated from.   **SECT**

717   The Muslim ruler of Babylon places restrictions on Jews and other religious minorities and requires that they wear special clothing to publicly mark their identity as non-Muslims. Restrictions are lessened a few years later and then more restrictions are enacted in 786.   **JUD**

717   Work begins on Japan's Yoro Code, which includes the regulation of Shinto matters. The *Jingiryo* (*Code on Kami of Heaven and Earth*) enumerates directions for Shinto ceremonies, festivals, and administration. Its *Betsushiki* (special regulations) distinguish between heavenly *kami* (those at Ise, Izumo, Sumiyoshi, and so on) and earthly *kami* (native spirits). It also denotes 20 occasions as national holidays. The *Denryo* (*Code on Land Tenure*) grants special privileges to the landholdings of Shinto shrines and Buddhist temples. The Yoro Code will be promulgated in 757.   **SHINTO, TOL**

717–720   Umar II (?–720) is the leader of the Umayyad dynasty that rules the Muslim Empire. The empire has expanded into southern Europe, the Near East, and North Africa and contains many people such as Persians and Berbers who are not Arabs but have converted to Islam. Umar II transforms the empire from an Arab one to a Muslim one by developing a new tax system that taxes all Muslims at the same rate regardless of their ethnic identity, but requires additional taxes from non-Muslims. The tax system lasts for over 1,000 years.   **ISLAM**

720   In Egypt many Coptic Christians have been converting to Islam to avoid the heavy taxes imposed on non-Muslims by the government. The Muslim government is losing much income and requires Coptic converts to continue paying the heavy taxes.   **ISLAM**

720   After Osumi and Hyuga provinces revolt against Japan's Empress Gensho (r. 715–724), prayers at the Hachiman shrine result in the defeat of the enemy by a so-called army of *kami* (native spirits) led by the shrine's Shinto priest.   **SHINTO**

721   Xuanzong, China's emperor, orders the Daoist classic the *Laozi* engraved on tablets in the Longxing monastery in Chang'an.   **DAO**

722	Despite imperial patronage in China, there are only 16 Daoist temples in the T'ang capital of Chang'an, compared to 91 Buddhist places of worship. **BUDD, DAO**
722	(St.) Boniface (Wynfrith of Crediton, c. 680–754), is made bishop of the German frontier by Pope Gregory II. Boniface swears allegiance to Rome and plays a major role in both converting German peoples to Christianity over the 32 years of his reign and in gaining their allegiance to the pope in Rome. **CATH**
724	Christian missionary (St.) Boniface fells the oak of the pagan god Thor at Geismer in the Hesse region of Germany. The act impresses the local people and aids in their conversion to Christianity. **CATH**
726	A dispute develops between the Eastern and Western Christian churches when Byzantine emperor Leo III bans the use of images and pictures in order to placate Christian and Muslim critics. In the west Pope Gregory II refuses to enforce the ban, and Leo III removes territory in southern Italy from papal control. **CHRIS**
726	The emperor Xuanzong orders every Chinese household to keep a copy of the Daoist *Dao De Jing.* **DAO**
726– 843	In the Byzantine Empire, a conflict rages in the Orthodox community over the worship of religious images or icons. Many people view as blasphemy the worship of icons representing saints and other religious figures. These people, called iconoclasts (meaning "icon-breakers"), attack and destroy church icons. They are condemned by many others who love the images of their favorite saints. **ORTHO**
731	The *Ecclesiastical History of the English People* is written by (St.) Bede, the Venerable (c. 673–735). The book becomes a key source of information about early British history and also provides much information about the religious practices of the time. **CHRIS**
732	Showing favoritism to the Daoists, China's government orders every prefecture to establish a temple in honor of Laozi. Within a few years, Emperor Xuanzong will set up special schools in the state university for Daoist studies. At the same time, he is drawn to the new Esoteric Buddhism that takes root during his reign. Doubtless part of the attraction is that it makes use of magical spells and incantations similar to those of Daoism. **BUDD, DAO**
732	Christian forces halt the Muslim advance into Europe via North Africa and Spain at the Battle of Poitiers in southern France. The Umayyad dynasty that rules the Muslim Empire enters a period of decline with expansion halted, income dwindling, and revolts common. **ISLAM**

| 733 | Japan's *fudoki* (provincial compendia of information about local topography, flora, fauna, origins of place names, poetry, customs, and myths) are completed. Apart from the *Izumo fudoki*, most will endure only in fragmentary form. The *fudoki* become supplementary texts for Shinto priests and scholars. **SHINTO** |

| 735 | In Japan the Buddhist priest Gembo (?–746) and scholar and official Kibi no Makibi (695–775) return from study in China. Gembo brings back over 5,000 Buddhist *sutras*; and Makibi, after study of Confucianism, ceremonial rituals, and military science, establishes a school for aspiring government officials. A common understanding of and regard for Confucian principles facilitate diplomatic and other exchanges throughout eastern Asia. **BUDD** |

| 736 | In Japan the Buddhist liturgical chant, *Shomyo*, is introduced and becomes important in the development of Japanese music. **BUDD** |

| 740 | The Kharijite Muslims in Algeria revolt against the Umayyad ruler. **ISLAM** |

| 741 | Japan's Emperor Shomu mandates a provincial Buddhist temple system with a monastery and nunnery for each province, where prayers and readings to protect his realm are to be conducted. In effect, he commits substantial state resources to spread Buddhism. **BUDD, TOL** |

| 741 | The emperor Xuanzong in China orders the establishment of Daoist schools and official examinations on Daoist texts, giving Daoism the status of an authorized teaching. He orders all students to study the *Dao De Jing*. He writes commentaries on the *Dao De Jing* and other Daoist texts. Prominent Daoists take on important roles at court. Xuanzong also promotes efforts to harmonize the Three Teachings—Confucianism, Buddhism, Daoism. **DAO, TOL** |

Pagan

The label *pagan* came into widespread use in Western Europe during the early centuries of Christianity as a name for the indigenous peoples of the region such as the Celts, who were not Christians and who often resisted conversion to Christianity. It was and continues to be used as an insult, as in addition to being non-Christian, pagans were seen as uncultured, coarse, and illiterate. In later centuries, during European colonial expansion into Africa, Asia, and the Americas, it was also sometimes used in reference to native peoples who were not Christians. However, in this context its use was often tempered by the belief that these peoples were worthy of conversion to Christianity. In the 20th century, the term *neo-pagan* has come into use as a self- label for some new religion movements and groups who trace their beliefs and practices to pre-Christian religions in Europe. To adherents of these beliefs, *neo-pagan* is a nonpejorative label.

742– 747	Christian missionary (St.) Boniface unifies the Christian churches of the Frankish Kingdom and establishes Rome as the center of religious authority for the church. In 744 he founds the monastery of Fulda, which becomes the focal point of Christianity in central Germany. **CATH**
742– 798	Khri Song, probably the first true Buddhist king of Tibet, rules. During his reign the Indian Buddhist mystics Santarakshita and Padmasambhava visit Tibet. In 792 Santarakshita arranges for a debate between Chinese and Indian Buddhists; the Indians triumph, and so it is that the Indian strain of Buddhism will prevail in Tibet. Meanwhile, the indigenous Bon religion of Tibetans remains strong, and Santarakshita invites the Indian monk Padmasambhava ("Lotus-born") to contend with the Bon priests. Padmasambhava triumphs and introduces Tantric Buddhism (Vajrayana) into Tibet. He also founds the first Tantric monastic order in Tibet, Nyingma (ancient ones), the so-called Red Hat Buddhist sect. He is traditionally credited as the author of the *Tibetan Book of the Dead*, a sacred text containing the ritual for dying (attributed by modern scholars to Kar-ma Ling-pa in the 15th century), and with the creation of the Tibetan tradition of *terma*, the practice of burying religious texts. **BUDD**
743	On commissioning the construction of the monumental Buddha statue at Todaiji, Japanese emperor Shomu sends a representative to the Grand Shrine at Ise to seek the will of the Shinto sun goddess Amaterasu. She reveals in an oracle that she and the Buddha are two aspects of a single reality. This politically expedient collaboration between Shinto and Buddhism is facilitated by a certain degree of tolerance common to both religions. **BUDD, SHINTO**
743	Official Japanese government permission for the private ownership of undeveloped land for the purpose of rice cultivation benefits those who can afford to clear the land, such as rich farmers and Shinto and Buddhist institutions as well. This will lead to the growth of the feudal landed estates known as *shoen*. **SHINTO**
744	At the Council of Leptinnes, the Christian Church in Europe decides to eradicate pagan beliefs and superstition among the people of Europe. **CHRIS, SPIR**
745	Japan's Usa Hachiman Shinto shrine provides funds for the construction of the Buddhist Todaiji temple and subsequently is named the protector of several Buddhist temples. In 783 the *kami* (native spirit) Hachiman will receive the Buddhist title of *bodhisattva*. **BUDD, SHINTO**
747	The Indian monk Padmasambhava (Bhutanese name *Guru Rimpoche*, "precious teacher") arrives in Bhutan at invitation of a local king. He converts kings of Khempalung and Sindhu and, headquartered in Bumthang, introduces the Nyingmapa ("ancient ones"), or Red Hat, sect of Tibetan Buddhism, a form of Tantric Buddhism. Bhutan becomes a Buddhist kingdom in the eighth century. An independent Himalayan kingdom throughout its recorded history, Bhutan is remarkable for the continuity of its

culture over two and a half thousand years. Neither the Hinduism of neighboring India nor the Islamic influence that permeates so much of central and southern Asia penetrates here (although the Nepalese who will enter Bhutan in later centuries do bring Hinduism with them). **BUDD**

747	The emperor Xuanzong of T'ang dynasty China elevates the *Dao De Jing* to the status of the most important of all canonical works. **DAO**
747– 750	A revolution against the Muslim Umayyad dynasty begins on the edge of the Muslim Empire in the Iranian province of Khurasan. The revolt is called the Abbasid Revolution and is named after the Abbasids, who claim ancestry from an uncle of Muhammad, the founder of Islam. **ISLAM**
748	Some 3,700 scrolls of Daoist scriptures, the first Daoist canon, are compiled in T'ang dynasty China. **DAO**
749	Emperor Shomu (r. 724–749) is the first Japanese ruler to renounce the throne to become a Buddhist monk. Empress Koken (r. 749–758) is enthroned and declares a new era of *Tempyo shoho*, or heavenly peace and victorious Buddhism. **BUDD**
749– 750	The Abbasid Revolution overthrows the Umayyad dynasty as the rulers of the Muslim Empire. The Abbasids come to power by creating a broad coalition that includes Arabs and Persians and Sunni and Shi'a Muslims. **ISLAM**
749– 1258	The Abbasid dynasty rules the Muslim Empire from Iraq. **ISLAM**
c. 750	In the Islamic world two distinct types of mosques emerge. The *masjid* is built as part of a religious complex that also garrisons Muslim troops and houses theological colleges. The *jami* (congregational, Friday, or cathedral mosque) is larger and intended for public worship on Fridays. **ISLAM**
c. 750	In western Europe Rosicrucian beliefs concerning mysticism and spirituality are introduced by the French philosopher Arnaud. **SECT**
750	Native Americans in Alabama build large ceremonial mounds and earthworks at Moundsville, including a sacred path nearly one mile in length. **NATIV**
750– 900	In the southwest China region of Yunnan, the provincial military state of Nan-chao gains some autonomy from the Chinese government and begins to exert its own pressure on its neighbors, including the various peoples in Myanmar. As a Buddhist state Nan-chao also advances the role of Buddhism in Myanmar. **BUDD**
751	The Chinese army and a combined Arab Muslim, Tibetan, and Turk army clash at the Talus River in central Asia. The Chinese are defeated and the

Muslims are now in control of central Asia. This accelerates the conversion of local peoples that began earlier in the century. ISLAM

752   Japan's former emperor Shomu emerges from retirement to dedicate the 53-foot tall Great Buddha, the largest bronze statue in the world, at Todaiji temple in a splendid ceremony attended by other Asian delegations. Exquisite gifts from the event—Persian cut-glass bowls, musical instruments, brocades—survive in the Shoso-in imperial repository in Nara. BUDD

754   Chinese priest Ganjin (688–763) arrives in Japan to teach precepts of Buddhist Ritsu sect and to found, in 759, Toshodaiji as a seminary to retrain, in the spirit of late Nara reform, priests influenced by the decadence of the capital. BUDD

754   (St.) Boniface, who over the past 30 years has converted the Franks to Christianity with allegiance to the church in Rome, is martyred when he and 50 followers are killed by a mob of pagans in the Netherlands. CATH

754   The Franks and the church in Rome forge an alliance and give public recognition to Catholic authority when Pope Stephen II and King Pepin meet and the Franks cede control over Italy to the church. In return, the pope grants the Franks the title "Patricians of the Romans." The Papal States in Italy survive until 1870, when Italy is unified as a nation. CATH

755   The Umayyad (Muslim) dynasty that rules Spain affords Jews much civil, economic, and religious freedom, and other Jews immigrate and settle there. JUD

755–765   In Korea a copy of the *Dharani* scripture found beneath a pagoda at Pulguk Monastery (erected 751) indicates that the art of woodblock printing developed around this time. The process is used to disseminate Buddhist and Confucian materials. BUDD, TOL

756   Muslims from North Africa capture al-Andalus (southern Spain), and Umayyad ruler Abd al-Rahman I (?–788) establishes the Umayyad dynasty there, which retains power until 929. ISLAM

757–787   These years cover the period of Jain philosopher/poet/saint Haribhadra; he is especially known for his works on the practice of yoga. JAIN

758   In Japan Emperor Nakamaro sends officials out to hear the complaints of the peasants and help the poor. He cuts the *zoyo* tax (requiring 60 days of labor per year) in half and commutes interest on debt. In government reforms he encourages filial piety and Confucian behavior. CONF

758   The power of Shinto is seen to preserve the imperial throne against a would-be usurper, the Buddhist priest Dokyo, after Empress Koken (r. 749–758) abdicates. Dokyo cites an oracle from the deity Hachiman supporting his own succession to the throne and then seeks to corrupt and torture the

royal messenger seeking a second oracle from Hachiman, which proves to oppose Dokyo's machinations. In the 19th century, for his heroic service, the royal agent Wake-no Kiyomaro will be made a *kami* (protective spirit) and be enshrined at Kyoto's Go-shrine. **SHINTO**

759   Around this time Japan's earliest poetry anthology *Man'yoshu* (*Collection of Myriad Leaves*) is completed. Among the 4,516 poems are some that reflect naturalistic pre-Buddhist Shinto sensibilities, describe Shinto rites of divination and spells, and mention the Ise shrine. This volume will become a source for later Shinto scholars. **SHINTO**

c. 760   Karaite Judaism begins. It is a reaction to the interpretations of Rabbinic Judaism and stresses the primacy of the Torah. Karaites compete with Rabbinic Jewish leaders and eventually the movement is suppressed, although Karaitism survives as a minority sect. Karaites are now few in number, with most Karaites in the 1990s living in Israel. **JUD**

760   The rulers of the Khazar Empire in southern Russia, by this time in a weakened state, convert to Judaism. The conversion has no long-term impact on either Jews or others in the region. **JUD**

c. 760–860   During the rule of the Shailedra dynasty on Java in Indonesia, Hinduism is adopted as the state religion. **HIND**

762   The city of Baghdad, Iraq, is founded by Muslim Abbasid dynasty ruler al-Mansur. The city is carefully designed and built as a "City of Peace" in a circle. **ISLAM**

762   Manchaeism is adopted as the state religion of the Uighurs in central Asia and remains so until the Uighurs are conquered by the Kirghiz in 840. **SECT**

763–809   During the golden age of Muslim Abbasid rule the center of power shifts to the east. There is great prosperity in the capital city of Baghdad and relative unity in the empire. **ISLAM**

765   Ja'far al-Sadiq, the Muslim Shi'a leader who establishes the basis for Shi'a Islamic law, dies. After his death there is a dispute over succession and Shi'a Muslims split into two main groups: the Imami, or Twelvers, and the Ismali, the latter of which will found the Fatimid dynasty in Egypt. **ISLAM**

765–865   The Buddhist kingdom of Sailendra flourishes in Java until the mid-ninth century, gaining control over both Mataram and Srivijaya kingdoms, the former based in Java, the latter in Sumatra. The Sailendra rulership will extend across western Java, Sumatra, and the Malay Peninsula until the 1190s. Mahayana Buddhism is widely practiced. Borobudur, the Mahayana Buddhist temple complex known for its immense *stupa*, or dome-shaped shrine, is built by Sailendra rulers near Jogakarta in central Java. The temple represents a synthesis of Buddhist belief and indigenous ancestor worship;

its galleries have bas-reliefs depicting events from Mahayana Buddhist tales. Even when the Sanjaya dynasty of Mataram, Java, gains control in the mid–800s and introduces its Saivite Hinduism, it continues to respect Borobudur and other Buddhist shrines. **BUDD, TOL**

766   After a Buddha is enshrined near the Shinto Great Shrine at Ise, disaster seems to occur with some frequency in the imperial household: the divine mirror replica in the palace burns, and the position of the emperor goes into decline. **BUDD, SHINTO**

767   The Muslim legal scholar Abu Hanifah dies in Kufa. Along with his followers Abu Yusuf Yakub and Muhammad Al-Hsan al-Shaybani, he founded one of the four major Sunni Muslim schools of Islamic law. Hanifah law is based on the premise that the Qur'an and *hadith* do not cover all issues or circumstances and therefore allow the influence of local custom, reason, and personal opinion in legal decisions. It is popular in Muslim communities outside the Middle East and in the 20th century is the major school of Muslim law in Iraq, Syria, Turkey, central Asia, China, and southern Asia. **ISLAM**

c. 770–1295   During these centuries, a succession of Khmer kings rule in Cambodia. In addition to extending the state's power, they build a succession of monumental "temple mountains" and shrines in or around the capital cities of Yasodharapura and Angkor. The great temples, the most famous of which is Angkor Wat (completed c. 1150), perform the double function of honoring the Hindu deities and legitimizing their reigns. By the 11th century, some temples and monasteries are also dedicated to Buddhism. **BUDD, HIND**

771–814   Charlemagne is ruler of the Franks in central Europe. During his rule he is frequently at war with the Saxons; eventually he conquers them and in the process converts them to Christianity. **CHRIS**

772   Li Ao (772–841) is born in China and becomes an early proponent of neo-Confucianism. **BUDD**

782   In China *Sangaku*, a form of theatrical entertainment including acrobatics and juggling, loses court patronage, possibly because of the earthiness of some skits. Performers become itinerant players and later associate with Buddhist temples. *Sangaku* is a distant ancestor of *Noh* drama. **BUDD**

784–786   The Great Mosque at Cordova, Spain, is constructed by the Muslim Umayyad ruler in Spain. Because of its size, ornamentation, and mixture of traditional and new architectural techniques, it is considered one of the major architectural achievements of the time. **ISLAM**

785   Tattooing is banned by the Irish Synod of Calcuth because of its associations with Celtic religions. **CHRIS**

| c. 785–
c. 860 | The Catholic monk Paschasius Radbertus lives. He is the first to suggest that the communion wafer and wine are transformed during the Mass into the actual body and blood of Jesus, while still retaining the physical properties of wafer and wine. Taken to its logical conclusion, this idea, known as transubstantiation, means that even the tiniest particle of bread contains the entire essence of Jesus within it. **CATH** |

787   The (Second) Council of Nicaea is held in Turkey. It is the seventh and, according to Orthodox Christians, the last of the ecumenical councils. The council supports the veneration of images of Christ and saints, a practice rejected by Byzantine emperors who control the church in the east. Roman Catholics do not consider it the last council and count 21 ecumenical councils, the last in 1962–1965. **CHRIS**

788   An examination system for the selection of public officials is instituted at the royal academy in the southern Korean kingdom of Silla. This system, like that of the Chinese, is based on knowledge of the Confucian Classics. **CONF**

788–
820   In southern India these are the traditional dates in Hinduism for the life of Sankara, the Hindu philosopher who establishes the doctrine of Advaita Vedanta, which marks a revival of traditional Hinduism, establishes seminaries, and combats the spread of Buddhism. Sankara is the author of the Brahman *Sutras*, commentary on earlier religious texts. **HIND**

789   During the reign of Sankara in southern India, he has 789 loads of the sacred books of the Jains placed on boats to be sunk. But some of the texts are said to have been saved in Nepal and in southern India, and after Sankara's death, Jains seek out all copies of their books and reprint them. **JAIN**

791   The first Buddhist monastery in Tibet, at Samye, in the eastern region, is built. **BUDD**

791   Japanese farmers in Ise, Owari, and Kii provinces are forbidden to sacrifice cows to the *kami* (native spirits) of Shinto shrines. This custom is derived from Chinese practice. **SHINTO**

794–
1185   Japan's Heian period, named after the new capital Heiankyo (Capital of Peace and Tranquility), is regarded as the golden age of Classical Japan. In the milieu of one of the most refined courts ever, a uniquely Japanese literature bursts forth in full glory. With the move to Heiankyo, the Nara Buddhists are left behind, and Buddhism begins to splinter into the esoteric cults of Tendai and Shingon, and the evangelical Jodo (Pure Land) sect. Although large sectors of Shinto come under the influence of Shingon and Tendai Buddhism **(SEE 804 AND 806, BUDD)**, popular Shinto traditions relating to local *kami* (native spirits) and shrines, together with orthodox forms of Shinto, endure and carry on the ancient practices concerned with sacred purity and the offerings to *kami* (native spirits) as before. As the religious foundation of the state, the slow and stylized Shinto rituals at the imperial court focus on the *toshigoi*, or spring prayers, for a good harvest, the *daijo sai*, or harvest festival, which is celebrated by each new emperor as part of his accession ceremony, and the rites at Ise, including the ritual rebuilding of its Grand Shrine every 20 years and the appointment of an imperial princess as its high priestess, a practice that will continue to 1339. BUDD, SHINTO

796   The emperor Dezong (r. 779–805) of T'ang China arranges debates at the imperial court between proponents of the Three Teachings, Confucianism, Buddhism, and Daoism. While heir apparent, Dezong studied at the Daoist "Isles of the Blest" academy west of Chang'an, developing a lifelong interest in alchemy there. DAO, TOL

796   The Monstir military monastery is built by the Muslims in Tunisia to house Muslim troops, and other such buildings are constructed on the edge of the Muslim world in North Africa, Anatolia, and central Asia. ISLAM

796   The Muslim legal scholar Malik ibn Anas dies in Medina. He produces the first compendium of Islamic law and is the founder of the Maliki school of law, one of the four major schools of Sunni Islamic law. Malikites view the Qur'an and the *sunna* as the only sources of Islamic law. In the 20h century the Maliki school of law is followed most often in North Africa and West Africa. ISLAM

797   Charlemagne, the leader of the Franks in central Europe, sends envoys to the leader of the Muslim Abbasid dynasty, Harun al-Rashid, marking the importance of the Muslim Empire. A similar political overture is made in 807. ISLAM

c. 800   The *Tirumurai*, the sacred text of the Shaiva Siddhanta sect of Hindu Shaivism, is written by the Tamil Shaiva poet Manikkavachakar in southern India. HIND

c. 800   Hatha Yoga begins to develop as a full system of mind control separate from earlier yoga traditions in Hindu India. Hatha Yoga is more physically stressful and involves techniques to cleanse the body as well as develop control over the mind. HIND

800   Around this time Buddhist statues regarded as divine images begin to be placed on Japan's Shinto shrine altars, or *kami* (native Shinto spirits) statues are made in the guise of Buddhist priests. Often Buddhist priests supervise Shinto shrines and their festivals. Some Shinto shrines, particularly Ise and Izumo, resist assimilation with Buddhism. BUDD, SHINTO

800   Pope Leo III (c. 750–816) formalizes the growing difference between the Roman and Orthodox churches by crowning Charlemagne (r. 800–814), ruler of the Franks and Lombards, the emperor of Rome, which sets him as an equal power to the Orthodox Byzantine emperor in Constantinople. CATH

800   Giving substance to his developing vision of a Confucian awakening, religious scholar Li Ao composes *Fu-hsing shu*. Opinions are divided on its value; some find it heterodox, others proclaim it among the best Confucian writing ever produced. Li Ao's essay *Returning to Nature* foreshadows features of Sung (960–1279) Confucian thoughts. He quotes the *I Ching* and treats the attainment of enlightenment in ways suggestive of Buddhism and Daoism. By highlighting the importance of equilibrium in the Confucian life, Li brings attention to a conceptually difficult area that occupies greater thinkers for succeeding centuries.   **CONF**

800   In Europe Jewish settlements are established as far north as the Rhine Valley in Germany and France. Jews refer to the region as Ashkenaz, and in later centuries those from central and eastern Europe are labeled Ashkenazi Jews.   **JUD**

800   A multireligious slave trade flourishes in Europe, Africa, and Asia. Christians capture and sell slaves to Jews, who in turn sell them to Muslims in Asia and Africa.   **MISC**

800s   Shangqing Daoist texts arouse great interest among China's literati. Poets and prose writers fill their works with allusions to Shangqing texts and Daoist hagiographies.   **DAO**

800s   Arab Muslims establish a settlement at Munda off the coast of Kenya in East Africa. This is the first settlement built according to Arabian design with some materials imported from Arabia. Later in the century and in the following century, Muslims from Arabia establish settlements at Gezira, Zanibar Island, and Chibuene. These are trading centers where the Arabs trade glass products for ivory, mangrove poles, and possibly slaves.   **ISLAM**

800s   Jain paintings in the Indra Sabha cave at Ellura, India, are a direct continuation of the Gupta tradition; the figures are notable for exaggerations almost like those of the Mannerist style in Renaissance Europe. This cave-temple is carved out of solid rock and includes figures of the early *tirthankaras*, including Mahavira. This is also the period of Jinasena, a teacher/saint in the Digambara sect of Jainism. He is regarded as the principal author (with his disciple Gunabhadra) of the *Mahapurana* (*Great Legend*), a long poem on cosmology; it includes the *Adipurana*, with biographies of the early founders of Jainism. Jinasena is said to have had the full support of King Amoghavarsa I.   **JAIN**

800–835   At Korea's Porim Monastery the monk Toui founds the Mount Kaji sect of the Meditation School (*Son*) of Buddhism. This leads to the establishment of the Nine Mountain Sects of Son.   **BUDD**

800

800–
1000

Hamsavati is a Mon state located on the coast of the Gulf of Martaban in west central Myanmar that is centered on the cities of Pegu and Thaton. Probably through their trading contacts with Sri Lanka and India, the Hamsavati Mon serve to advance the spread of Buddhism into Southeast Asia.   BUDD

802–
1432

In Cambodia during the rule of the Kingdom of Angkor, the Khmer (Cambodian) people are politically unified. The temple complexes, most of which are Hindu but also show some Buddhist influence, play a central role in the kingdom. The temples house priests and teachers and own vast amounts of land and slaves, and wealthy Khmer often give wealth to the temples to ensure prosperity in the next life. The temple complexes contain huge shrines to Hindu and Buddhist gods as well as elaborate tombs for the wealthy and powerful.   CIVIL

804–
805

In Japan during the decadence of Buddhism during the Nara period, the monks Saicho (767–822) and Kukai (774–835) are sent to China to study new forms of Buddhism, including the Tian Tai school. After returning from China in 805, Saicho establishes the Tendai (the Japanese pronunciation of Tian Tai) sect on Mount Hiei. Tendai Buddhism seeks to harmonize all Buddhist teachings and schools by stressing the primacy of the *Lotus Sutra*, an early Indian scripture at the basis of Mahayana Buddhism. Tendai Buddhism also has certain mystical and esoteric aspects. This is the first schism of Japanese Buddhism. In the face of strong opposition, Saicho seeks to start a rigorous 12-year training program for official teachers of Buddhism. After Saicho's death, his temple is renamed Enryakuji; by the 12th century, Enryakuji is immensely wealthy, with 3,000 buildings, vast properties, and an army of warrior monks. Its position is eventually undermined by new sects, in particular the Shingon sect started by Kukai, his fellow visitor to Japan (SEE **806, BUDD**). But although Tendai Buddhism will lose power over the centuries, it will have great influence on the development of Buddhism in Japan.   BUDD

806

A year after Saicho returns from China to Japan and commences the Tendai sect of Buddhism (SEE **804–805, BUDD**), his fellow monk Kukai (774–835) returns. While in China he has studied and become a master of *mikkyo* (secret teachings), a form of Tantric Buddhism developed by Indian sages and known in China as Zhen Yan Buddhism. On his return he starts the Shingon (True Word, or Mantra) sect. The new emperor Saga (r. 806–824) becomes Kukai's friend, student, and patron. In 816 Kukai begins construction of a monastery on Mount Koya; the monastery becomes a base for teaching Shingon and training 50 monks. Shingon practices include meditation on mandalas, repetition of mantras, and use of ritual hand gestures, or mudras. By the 1990s the Shingon sect will have some 12 million followers and 12,000 temples.   BUDD

806

Around this date *Kogoshui* (*Gleanings from Ancient Stories*) is prepared and presented to Japan's Emperor Heizei by Imibe no Hironari. Composed in defense of an old priestly guide, it summarizes ancient Shinto mythology and religion. **SHINTO**

809–
813 The third Muslim civil war of succession is fought between the sons of the Abbasid ruler Harun al-Rashid Amin (?–813) and al-Ma'mun (?–833), with the latter victorious. **ISLAM**

810 The Danes build a wall across the isthmus of Schleswig to prevent the Franks from invading. The wall therefore bars Christianity from the Nordic nations. **CHRIS**

810 The position of Shinto priestess is created at Japan's Kamo shrine in Kyoto. This position will last until 1212. **SHINTO**

814 The Muslim Empire begins to undergo a fundamental change when the future leader al-Mu'tasim (?–842) starts building a private army of Turks instead of trying to win the favor of Arab and Arab-Persian tribesmen. This lays the groundwork for the later emergence of the Turks as the rulers of the Muslim world. **ISLAM**

c. 815 Al-Shafi'i (?–820), who is considered the founder of the Sunni Muslim Shafi'i school of law, begins to reform the Islamic legal system in his book, the *Risala*. The Shafi'i school, one of the four major schools of Sunni Islamic law, views the Qur'an and *hadith* as the sources of Islamic law with allowance made for the use of analogy and consensus. It is followed most often in the Middle East and Southeast Asia in the 20th century. **ISLAM**

816 The Fushimi Inari shrine is moved to its present location at the foot of Mount Inari, southeast of Kyoto, at the petition of Kukai, the founder of the Shingon Buddhist sect, to offer protection to his nearby Shingon temple. The Fuhimi Inari shrine will become the central shrine for some 40,000 Shinto Inari shrines throughout Japan. **BUDD, SHINTO**

816 Louis the Pious, who succeeds his father, Charlemagne, as Holy Roman Emperor, is crowned by Pope Stephen IV at Rheims. The pope emphasizes that the authority of the emperor flows from the church in Rome. **CATH**

817 Under the direction of (St.) Benedict (c. 750–821), the Council of Abbots at Aachen issues the *Capitulare monasticum*, which sets forth rules to govern all aspects of life in Benedictine monasteries. The new rules turn many daily chores over to peasants and leave the monks more time for studying, writing, and prayer. **CATH**

820 An aged Chinese Buddhist monk, Vo Ngon Thong, comes to Vietnam and founds a new sect that adopts his name; he dies in 826 but his sect remains a force in Vietnam until the 13th century. Buddhism in general continues to play a prominent role in Vietnamese society. **BUDD**

820	The emperor Xianzong of T'ang dynasty China is poisoned after ingesting a pill manufactured by a Daoist alchemist. **DAO**
823	Lothar is crowned Emperor of the Holy Roman Empire by Pope Paschal I in Rome. The event establishes Rome as the location for coronations and also symbolizes the authority of the Church in the Holy Roman Empire. **CATH**
823	Legendary Japanese empress Jingu, together with her son Emperor Ojin and his deified wife Hime Okami, are enshrined in the Shinto Usa Hachiman shrine. The added royal prestige raises the Hachiman Shinto shrine to a position second only to the shrine at Ise, as Hachiman is greatly venerated by the imperial family and court. Hachiman is the guardian deity of warriors and a protector of the land. **SHINTO**
826	(St.) Anskar (c. 801–865), a Benedictine monk, begins his missionary activity in Denmark. He later also seeks converts in Sweden and is made archbishop of Hamburg, where he is responsible for missionary activity in Scandinavia. Although many people return to paganism after his death, he establishes Christianity in the region and is made patron saint of Denmark. **CATH**
827	The emperor Wenzong of T'ang dynasty China (r. 827–41) organizes imperial court debates to discuss the Three Teachings: Confucianism, Buddhism, and Daoism. **BUDD, CONF, DAO, TOL**

Witchcraft

Witchcraft refers to a number of religious practices that, despite the common label, have actually varied considerably over time and place in human history. In non-Western cultures that did not traditionally follow major Western religions, witchcraft refers to witchcraft attribution, the belief that some people in the community (usually old, unmarried women) are inherently evil and can cause harm (illness, accidents, death, property destruction) to others by simply wishing it. When disaster fell on such a community, a witch was often blamed and much effort was made to identify and kill the witch. In Christianity witchcraft belief is also tied to the idea of evil but more specifically to Satan or the devil, with the witch, again often a woman, believed to be an agent of the devil. As in non-Western societies, witches were often blamed for societal misfortune in the absence of other explanations and killed. In the 20th century, as part of the spirituality and New Age movements, witchcraft in Europe and the United States has taken on a new meaning. People who identify themselves as witches do not believe that they cause evil but rather that they have a special relationship with the spirit or supernatural world. Their witchcraft is benign and is seen as a form of religious worship.

829	The Synod of Paris rules that witchcraft is to be punished by death. **SPIR**
832	The Franks begin their efforts to spread Christianity into the Nordic nations when Anskar (801–865), a monk from France, is appointed the bishop of Hamburg, a major center of Catholicism in Germany. He is able to establish two churches in Schleswig, but the effort ends with his death in 865. **CATH**
836	Muslim leader al-Mu'tasim founds Samarra as the new capital of the Muslim Abbasid dynasty. **ISLAM**
840–846	China's Emperor Wuzong reigns. His chief minister, Li Deyu, supervises the suppression and even destruction of Buddhist, Daoist, Nestorian, Zoroastrian, and Manichaean temples and monasteries. The power of the Buddhist monasteries is curbed, the wealth of many larger monasteries is confiscated, and 250,000 monks and nuns are forced to return to lay life. Government officials take control of the ordination of monks in an attempt to curb Buddhist growth. Religious persecutions afflict the Christian community; Judaism and Islam are less troubled. A new emperor, Xuanzong, comes to the throne in 846. He relaxes the persecutions, but some curbs remain on Buddhist temple-building and ordination and little confiscated property is restored. **BUDD**
843	The *Synodikon of Orthodoxy* is compiled. It is a collection of blessings that become a part of the worship service on certain holidays in Orthodox churches. Over subsequent centuries it is revised numerous times. **ORTHO**
845	The T'ang emperor Wuzong launches a severe repression of Buddhism in China, partially in reaction to persistent conflict between Buddhists and Daoists. **BUDD, DAO**
845	Nestorian Christianity, which arrived in China in 635, begins to disappear when Nestorian monks are banned as part of general ban on Buddhism by the Daoist emperor. **CHRIS**
846	The emperor Wuzong of T'ang China dies after taking Daoist alchemy pills. The drugs debilitated him for some time before his death, giving him symptoms of depression and mania. **DAO**
846–859	Xuanzong reigns in T'ang China. He lifts the emperor Wuzong's proscriptions on Buddhists and revives debates at court among adherents of Confucianism, Buddhism, and Daoism. He falls into a chronic illness caused by Daoist alchemical elixirs and dies at the comparatively young age of 49. **BUDD, DAO**
847	John Scotus Erigena (810–877), know as John the Scot, emerges as a leading philosopher in the court of Charles the Bald. Erigena becomes the most notable thinker of the Carolingian Renaissance, a brief period of renewed intellectual interest in the early Middle Ages. He argues against the ideas of

transubstantiation and predestination and is convicted of heresy in 855 and 859 but not executed. His ideas about the soul and the nature of the universe influence later Catholic mystics such as Meister Eckehart.　　**CATH**

847–
861

During the reign of Muslim Abbasid dynasty ruler al-Mutawakki, the Great Mosque at Samarra is built. It is the largest mosque in the Muslim world.　　**ISLAM**

c. 850

This is the period of Mahavirachary, the noted Jain-Indian mathematician who lives in Karnataka and writes the *Ganita-sara-samgraha*.　　**JAIN**

850

The Bogomil sect emerges in Bulgaria. It is founded by an Orthodox priest named Theophilus, who takes the name Bogomil, the Bulgarian version of Theophilus. From the 10th to the 15th century the sect attracts numerous adherents in the Balkans and is at times repressed by the Orthodox Church as heresy. In contrast to Orthodoxy, Bogomils have a dualistic view of the universe with a good heaven and an evil earth and therefore reject the rituals of the Orthodox Church. The sect disappears in the 17th century.　　**ORTHO**

850–
859

Mozarabs (Christians in Muslim Spain who adopt an Arab lifestyle) in Cordova launch a series of revolts against Muslim rule as a protest against pressures to assimilate to the Arab-Muslim society.　　**CHRIS**

850–
875

Muslim religious scholars prepare copies of the *hadith*, the actions and sayings of the Prophet Muhammad and his followers, and several become the accepted versions and are considered sacred texts by Muslims.　　**ISLAM**

855

The Muslim legal scholar Ahmad ibn Hanbal dies. He founded the Hanbali school of Islamic law, one of the four major schools of Sunni Islamic law. Hanbali law rests on the Qur'an and *hadith* and rejects analogy, reason, and local custom as sources of law. The law is further developed by followers after his death and is adopted by Muslim rulers in Arabia. In the 20th century it grows in influence in the Muslim world because of its support from Muslim fundamentalism.　　**ISLAM**

858–
879

A schism develops between the Christian churches in Rome and Constantinople, when Emperor Michael III removes Ignatius as the patriarch of Constantinople and replaces him with Photius. Pope Nicholas I in Rome objects to the action, leading to conflict over authority in the Church. As emperors change in Constantinople, Photius is deposed and then restored. Finally, at a council in Constantinople, the matter is resolved with authority still shared by the two churches and friendly relations restored.　　**CHRIS**

859

The Iwashimizu Hachiman shrine, a "branch shrine," is built by Buddhist monk Gyokyo, and the deity of the Usa Hachiman shrine is invited to take up residence there to protect the new capital of Kyoto. The development of branch shrines will become a medieval phenomenon in Japan, and in the 1990s the Usa Hachiman shrine (built in 843) is the central shrine for some

40,000 Hachiman shrines in Japan. The Iwashimizu Hachiman shrine-temple complex will become a major center of Shinto-Buddhist syncretism during the 12th and 13th centuries.   **BUDD, SHINTO**

859–
873
Yizong reigns as emperor of T'ang dynasty China. He dies of poisoning from alchemical elixirs mixed by Daoist magicians.   **DAO**

860
Two documents, the *Pseudo-Dionysian Treatises* and the *Pseudo-Isidorian Decretals*, are put forth by the Catholic Church to support papal claims to authority. These documents provide supposed historical accounts of the power of earlier Catholic churches and set down a church structure. Bishops and monasteries throughout Europe are slow to accept the popes' claim to power and often side with their local kings or emperors in disputes with the pope.   **CATH**

860–
900
The Daoist Celestial Masters movement continues to thrive in China. It plays a key role in expanding interregional commercial and cultural ties. The movement will survive through modern times and remains the most flourishing of existing Daoist movements.   **DAO**

862–
864
Two Eastern Orthodox monks, Cyril (826–869) and Methodius (c. 815–885), convert large numbers of people in Moravia (part of modern day Hungary and Austria) and Russia. Since the Orthodox Church allows services to be

Cyril and Methodius

Cyril (826–869) and Methodius (815–885) were two Greek brothers and missionaries of the Orthodox Church who helped convert Russia and much of eastern Europe to Christianity. Little is known with certainty about their lives. Cyril became a monk in 860 and went to Constantinople, where he was the librarian at the church of Santa Sophia. In 862 the Byzantine emperor dispatched the brothers to Moravia, which had rejected overtures from the Catholic Church, and asked for missionaries who could teach in Slavonic, the native language. Cyril and Methodius, both fluent in Slavonic, converted the Slavs. Cyril translated the gospel and liturgy into Slavonic, and invented an alphabet (the Cyrillic alphabet), which became the written form of Russian and other eastern European languages. The two brothers and the Slavs became the center of a struggle for expansion between the Orthodox and Catholic churches. Despite the Catholic Church's insistence on Latin services, the pope called the brothers to Rome, where Cyril died in 869. Methodius was sanctioned by the pope—who grudgingly accepted his Slavonic liturgy—and returned to Moravia as an archbishop. Yet, opposed by German bishops, Methodius slowly lost papal support and was forbidden by Pope Stephen V from using Slavonic in the church. As a result, Bulgaria, Serbia, and Russia gave their loyalty to the Orthodox Church, which allowed the Slavonic services, while Moravia, Bohemia, Slovakia, Hungary, and Poland embraced Catholicism.

held in the common languages, the two monks translate the Bible and Christian liturgy into Slavonic, which gives them an advantage over Catholic missionaries also working in the region who use Latin texts. **ORTHO**

865–
935

In Korea the Buddhist monk Toson (d. 898) systematizes a theory of geomancy (a form of divination based on features and energy flows in the natural environment) that combines Daoist and Buddhist elements. Wang Kon, the founder of the Koryo dynasty (r. 918–943), later uses Toson's principles to justify the transfer of power on the peninsula away from Kyongju to his native region of Songak. Such calculated use of geomancy becomes a common political strategy in the years of the Koryo dynasty. **BUDD, DAO**

869

When Korean pirates raid Japan's seas and shores, Emperor Seiwa prays at the Iwashimizu Hachiman shrine. Hachiman is believed to protect the nation from foreign foes and to punish rebels and traitors. **SHINTO**

869–
883

A rebellion in Iraq threatens the power of the Abbasid dynasty that rules—sometimes in name only—the Muslim Empire. **ISLAM**

c. 870

The Arab Muslim philosopher al-Kindi dies. During his lifetime and work in Baghdad he writes about leading philosophical and religious issues of the time including creation, immortality, and the philosophical basis of astrology and magic. **ISLAM**

870–
871

Turkish military leaders take control of the Muslim world from the Abbasid dynasty in Samarra. By this time Abbasid power is weakened throughout the empire and many local rulers have more power than do the rulers of the Empire. **ISLAM**

875

The church in Rome continues to exercise authority over the Holy Roman Empire as Pope John VIII chooses Charles the Bald as the new emperor. However, both the church and the empire are weakening as northern and eastern Europe are invaded by the Norse and the Magyars. **CATH**

875

The T'ang dynasty imperial court in China orders the celebration of Daoist ritual to end a drought and epidemic. The authorities often turn to Daoist ceremonies, believed to have exorcising powers, in times of hardship. The emperor himself confers the purple robe, a mark of great distinction, on the Daoist master Du Guangting (850–933), who becomes an influential imperial adviser. **DAO**

876

At the Council of Constantinople, Eastern Catholic bishops condemn the political activities of the pope, again criticize the addition of the *filioque* ("and from the Son") to the Nicene Creed, and seek to end papal claims to rule of the entire Christian world. **CHRIS**

878

Byzantine Emperor Basil I orders all Jews in the empire to convert to Christianity. **JUD**

c. 880–930	The Tamil Hindu poet Nammalvar lives and writes the *Tiruvaymoli*, the most sacred of Vaisnava Hindu texts, which followers view as the equivalent of the ancient *Veda*. The work expresses devotion to the god Vishnu through emotional songs. **HINDU**
885	Ch'oe Ch'iwon (?–857), having passed the T'ang government examinations in China, returns to Korea to take his place in the Silla court as an honored Confucian scholar. He is active in criticizing the rigidity of Silla's *kolp'um* (bone-rank) system, a codification of its levels of aristocracy. He hopes to end anarchic conditions in the provinces but becomes disillusioned. **CONF**
885	Mount Athos, a mountain located on a peninsula in northeast Greece, is officially recognized by the Byzantines as a refuge for Orthodox Christian hermit monks. **ORTHO**
887	Emperor Yozei sends messengers all around Japan to deliver Shinto offerings to 3,132 heavenly and earthly *kami* (protective spirits). **SHINTO**
c. 889–c. 912	In Cambodia, these years mark the reign of Yasovarman I. Yasovarman establishes a new capital, Yasodharapura, at what will become the site of Angkor. During his reign several sanctuaries are built in Angkor, as well as about a hundred focused on the worship of the three main cults of Siva, Vishnu, and the Buddha throughout the realm, each monastery apparently serving as a royal outpost. **BUDD, TOL**
892	The Muslim Abbasid dynasty moves the capital of the Muslim Empire from Samarra back to Baghdad. **ISLAM**
893	(St.) Clement of Ochrid (?–916) is appointed bishop of Macedonia. Along with St. Naum of Ochrid, he plays a leading role in spreading Orthodoxy in the Balkan region of southern Europe and is also instrumental in developing Slavic literature. Under their influence Ochrid becomes a center of Orthodoxy in Europe. **ORTHO**
893–927	During the reign of Simon, Christianity flourishes in Bulgaria, with Greek texts translated into Slavonic to create a Slavonic Christian literature. **ORTHO**
c. 900	A Greek manuscript of this period tells of Barlaam and Josephat, describing them as early Christian missionaries to Asia. (A Persian manuscript of the sixth century C.E. will later be found to recount much the same story.) Because of this account, Josephat will become a Roman Catholic saint in 1583. Modern scholars will establish that "Josephat" is in fact a corruption of the Sanskrit word *bodhisattva*—an individual who postpones attaining *nirvana* to save other humans—and that the life of Josephat is based on that of the Buddha. **BUDD, CHRIS**
900	The scholar Du Guangting revises and reforms Daoist liturgy in China. **DAO**

900	The Yiddish language begins to emerge in Europe as the Hebrew spoken by Jews is combined with the German dialects spoken by neighboring peoples. Over the centuries Yiddish becomes the vernacular language of Jews in central and eastern Europe. **JUD**
900	Nearly 3,000 Japanese Shinto shrines receive financial support from the government. By this time the codification in the *Jogan Gishiki* of the major Shinto rituals relating to the imperial family and its associated clans is completed. **SHINTO**
c. 900–1200	As Hinduism expands during this period, large temples with elaborate carvings and sculptures are built in India, including those at Khajuraho, Bhubaneswar, Tanjore, and Konarak. **HIND**
900s	This is the period of Somadeva Suri, a mendicant monk and teacher in the Digambara sect of Jainism. One of his most famous works is the *Nitivakyamrta* (*Nectar of Aphorisms on Polity*), a collection of aphorisms on politics and proper government; another of his works is *Upasakadhyayana*, a major text for Digambara Jains and the one that prescribes the rules of proper conduct for the Jain laity. During this century several women in Karnataka gain fame for their devotion to and promotion of Jainism. They include Jakkiyabbe, widow of a high government official, who is appointed to take

Yiddish

Yiddish emerged as a distinct language among the Jews of Germany between the 11th and 13th centuries. It was based on the Hebrew and Aramaic already spoken and read by the Jews and the Middle German spoken in the towns of the Rhine Valley. The lexicon was mainly German, but the language was written using the Hebrew alphabet. As Jews spread into eastern Europe, Yiddish went with them. In Russia, Poland, Ukraine, Belarus, and Lithuania, it was modified with new words from Slavic languages added to the German base. By the 18th century Jews were speaking four major regional varieties of Yiddish. In the early 20th century, with the immigration of large numbers of eastern European Jews, Yiddish emerged as a significant cultural form in the United States. In addition to Yiddish newspapers, Yiddish theater, humor, literature, and music attracted both Jewish and non-Jewish audiences. As Jews assimilated, the number who spoke Yiddish decreased. But Yiddish had made its mark in America, and numerous words and phrases found their way into the American English lexicon. Some of these are Yiddish or "Yinglish" words, such as bubbe (sweetie), lox (a kind of smoked salmon), schmuck (loosely translated as "jerk"), chutzpa (nerve or gall), and mensch (an upright man). Since the 1980s Yiddish has enjoyed a revival, with classes taught in speaking Yiddish, the revival of old forms, and the appearance of new forms of Yiddish literature and music.

over her husband's office; Attimabbe, who pays to have Jain texts published and Jain images made; and Pambabbe, who performed penance for 30 years.　　**JAIN**

900s　In Eastern Orthodoxy theologians pay much attention to the question of what happens when humans are faced with the presence of God. In answer to this question, Orthodox mystical theology develops the concept of seeing the divine light of God's presence, exemplified by people like Symean the New Theologian (949–1022), who declares that light is the actual glory and presence of God.　　**ORTHO**

900s–1100s　Buddhism flourishes in Vietnam, as seen in the hundreds of pagodas erected, the many monks, and the great numbers of Buddhist texts.　　**BUDD**

900s–1400s　Jain temple-building reaches its peak during these centuries. At Mount Abu in Rajputana, about 400 miles northeast of Bombay, Jains build several impressive temples, including the Dilwara shrine (900s), and the Tejpal temple (1200s). Other major temple sites include Satrunjaya, Jarsalmer, Ranakpur, and Girnar. Some of these temples are built of sandstone, others of marble; all have interiors carved with intricate details and sometimes translucent thinness; they represent the baroque culmination of the Gujarat style. The numbers and splendor of these temples testify to the wealth of individual Jains, which is largely derived from trade.　　**JAIN**

c. 905　(St.) Naum of Ochrid (830–910), an Orthodox monk, establishes a monastery on Lake Ochrid in Macedonia in the Balkan region of southern Europe. A translator of Christian texts into Slavic for use by the local population, he and other monks at the monastery develop the Cyrillic alphabet that becomes standard in the Balkans, Ukraine, and Russia.　　**ORTHO**

909　Followers of the Muslim Shi'a sect move to North Africa and defeat the local rulers and establish the Fatimid dynasty. The dynasty takes its name from Fatima, the daughter of Muhammad and wife of Ali, to whom all Shi'a leaders trace their ancestry.　　**ISLAM**

910　The Benedictine monastery in Cluny, France, is founded by William of Aquitaine. It is allowed to elect its abbot, or leader, without interference from the state. As a result, it is free from the ties to secular authority that confuse the division of state and church elsewhere in Europe.　　**CATH**

917　An Orthodox Christian patriarch is established in Bulgaria during the rule of Simeon (r. 893–927), who is a supporter of the church. The church is at first centered at Preslav and then moved to Ochrid in 971. Bulgaria is the center of missionary activity in southern Europe. It is where the spread of Orthodoxy to Russia originates.　　**ORTHO**

918– 943	King T'aejo (Wang Kon) reigns in Korea. He adopts a lenient policy toward provincial magnates and appeases the Silla aristocracy by appointing them to high posts in the new government. He issues ten injunctions to serve as the basis of future government. In these injunctions he stresses the importance of national defense, Buddhism, unity among the aristocratic clans, and the strength of local government. **BUDD**
c. 922– 929	(St.) Wenceslas (c. 907–929) is the king of Bohemia and promotes conversion to Christianity. After being murdered by his brother Boleslav he is venerated as a saint and is later made patron saint of Czechoslovakia. **CATH**
923– 973	This is the lifespan of Korea's Great Master Kyunyo, a devout Buddhist. Through his teachings and poems written in the vernacular, he does much to popularize Buddhism. **BUDD**
924– 940	The Athelstan Laws are enacted by the Anglo-Saxons in Britain. For the first time in Britain, witchcraft is punishable by death. **SPIR**
927	This is the preferred date assigned by scholars to the *Engishiki* (*Procedures of the Engi Era*), a 50-volume supplement to a Japanese government legal compilation. The regulations governing Shinto to date cover the duties of the priesthood and the codification of the ritual calendar, as well as 26 *norito* or ancient ritualistic prayers. As the most comprehensive document of Shinto rituals in classic form, the *Engishiki* becomes a sacred text of the Shinto religion. In the register of deities in Books 9 and 10 of this document, a total of 2,861 shrines throughout Japan honoring 3,132 divinities are subdivided into imperial shrines (*kampeisha*), where government officials make annual offerings, and provincial shrines (*kokuheisha*), where provincial governors make offerings. A further category comprises 224 eminent shrines, whose

---

Fatima

The most influential daughter of Muhammad and his wife Khadija, Fatima (c. 605–633) married Muslim leader Ali and became the mother of his grandsons, Hasan and Husayn, who later became early Shi'a Muslim martyrs. Fatima was very close to her father and followed him in death by only several months. This closeness gave rise to a famous Shi'a account that Muhammad is said to have gathered Fatima and her family under his cloak and referred to them as his own family. This event later became a major factor utilized by the Shi'a to legitimize their belief that the descendants of Ali and Fatima were the true leaders of the post-Muhammad Islamic community. In time Fatima became so central to Shi'a Islam that a major Islamic dynasty that ruled in Egypt and eastern northern Africa from 909 to 1171, the Fatimids, claimed descent from her and took her name.

deities are called upon in emergencies. All shrines are ranked and assigned
status according to their popular, historical, and economic importance.

SHINTO

930 Members of the Muslim Qarmatian revolutionary sect take the sacred Black
Stone from the Ka'ba in Mecca. The Black Stone has great ritual significance to
Muslims, who touch it and kiss it when on pilgrimage to Mecca. They return the stone
to the mosque in Kuhah in 951. The Qarmatian movement emerged in ninth-
century Arabia and disappeared during the 12th century.

ISLAM

931 (St.) Odo (c. 879–942), the abbot of the reform monastery of Cluny, continues to develop the monastery as a center of church reform as he negotiates for freedom from state influence and founds similar monasteries
throughout Europe with a focus on spiritual contemplation.

CATH

938 In Japan the Buddhist monk Kuya (903–972) begins preaching Amida
Buddhism in Heiankyo.

BUDD

945 The Shi'a Muslim Buyid dynasty takes control of Baghdad and the Muslim
Empire, although the Abbasid dynasty remains as a figurehead. The new
rulers increase the taxes on Jews, Christians, and Sunni Muslims and restrict
their role in Persian society.

ISLAM, TOL

947 In Japan the Kitano shrine is built near Kyoto on the 44th anniversary of the
death of Sugawara no Michinaze (845–903), a sage and government official
persecuted by the Fujiwara faction. After his death a series of catastrophes
are attributed to his angry spirit. Deified as Tenjin, he becomes the Shinto
patron of poetry and calligraphy, of those suffering injustice, and of students preparing for exams. This is probably the earliest example of the deification of a relative commoner. In 954 the Nagao Tenmangu shrine is built
near the mound regarded as Tenjin's tomb in Kyoto, and eventually a large
number of shrines are dedicated to Tenjin.

SHINTO

950–
1350 Among Christians in Europe, Mary is venerated in poems, psalters, sermons, and songs. Praying to Mary becomes common in 1050 and is the
norm by 1200.

CHRIS

957 Russian princess Olga, who rules in Kiev from 945 to 964, is baptized a
Christian by the patriarch of the Orthodox Church in Constantinople.
However, she fails to convert nobles in Russia and her son Sviatoslav inau-
gurates an anti-Christian agenda when he follows her to the throne. ORTHO

960 In a military coup in China, Zhao Kuangyin deposes the last Zhou emper-
or and proclaims himself first emperor of the Song dynasty (960–1125). He
reigns until 976 as Taizu. The Song era is prosperous: China leads the world
in technical innovation, political theory, and the arts. Though neo-
Confucianism becomes the dominant allegiance of the scholar/official elite,
Daoism flourishes though much of the era, partly because the Song is also

960   a troubled and unstable period, with China threatened (and ultimately split) by waves of invaders from Inner Asia. Daoism is a recourse in difficult times through much of China's history.   **DAO**

960   A fire in Japan's imperial palace damages the replica mirror of the Imperial Regalia. Further fires in 1005 and 1040 will reduce it to precious fragments that will be kept in the *kashikodokoro* of the palace. The original mirror is preserved safely at Ise shrine.   **SHINTO**

961   The new Song imperial court in China prohibits debates among the Three Teachings, Confucianism, Buddhism, and Daoism. Buddhists and Daoists are forbidden to study astronomy and *feng shui*.   **DAO, TOL**

961   The Megisti Lavra, the first Orthodox monastery, is established on Mount Athos in Greece by (St.) Athanasius of Athos (c. 920–1003) with the support of Byzantine emperor Nicephorus Phocas. The 20 monasteries that develop there over the next centuries become a major center of Orthodox scholarship and translation. In the late 20th century the region is home to about 2,000 Orthodox monks. As in the past they come from Greece, Bulgaria, Serbia, Georgia, and Russia.   **ORTHO**

Neo-Confucianism

Neo-Confucianism was a government-supported transformation of Confucianism in China. It developed as an effort by Confucian scholars to combat the growing influence of Buddhism and Daoism and was especially offered as an alternative to the former. It emerged during the Song dynasty (960–1279) and was supported by the rulers of the following Yuan dynasty (1279–1368). A number of Confucian scholars were involved in the development of neo-Confucianism, the most significant being Zhu Xi (Chu Hsi), who organized and edited a great deal of material into a coherent and full system of thought. His work was adopted by the Yuan ruler in 1313 and became the basis of the Chinese civil service exams, which were a prerequisite for government service until 1905. Neo-Confucianism is based on traditional Confucianism and Buddhism and offers a full model of the universe, an explanation for the universe, an emphasis on learning, and various rules to govern social relations. It combines two major schools of thought, the *Li Hsueh* (School of Principle) and the *Hsin Hsueh* (School of Mind). Many academies were established in China to teach neo-Confucianism. Neo-Confucianism also involved a basic revision of the canons of Confucianism with the *Four Books* (*Analects, Menicus, The Great Learning,* and *Doctrine of Mean*) taking precedence over the *Five Classics*. From China neo-Confucianism spread to Korea, where it was interpreted in the Korean cultural context, and then to Japan. In the 20th century neo-Confucianism has declined in importance in all three nations.

| 962 | Otto the Great (r. 936–973), the son of the duke of Saxony, is crowned Emperor of the Holy Roman Empire by Pope John XII in Rome. Otto plays a major role in revitalizing the empire and uses bishops as political officials, although the Church in Rome is weak and no longer enjoys political power. **CATH** |

963 — The division of power in the Holy Roman Empire has now shifted from the Church to the political rulers, and Otto the Great charges Pope John XII with treason and removes him from office. John XIII is replaced by Leo VII, a layman who is required to take a pledge of allegiance to the emperor, a requirement that remains in place for about 100 years. **CATH**

963–
979 — A Vietnamese of rustic background named Dinh Bo Linh, after a series of victories over competing leaders, manages to establish peace across much of northern Vietnam. In 966 he proclaims himself emperor to assert equality with the Chinese, but in fact he has to engage in diplomatic maneuvers to get the Chinese to accept Vietnamese independence. Among his many appointments is that of the Buddhist monk Ngo Chan Luu as "Great Teacher for Correcting and Sustaining Viet." (Ngo Chan Luu's writings are among the oldest extant from Vietnam.) **BUDD**

c. 966 — Roman Catholicism comes to Poland when the ruler Duke Mieszka converts to Roman Catholicism, most likely through the influence of his wife Dobrawa, the sister of Boleslav II, the Christian king of Bohemia. **CATH**

968 — Poznan is established as the center of Roman Catholicism in Poland. **CATH**

969–
973 — After several failures, the Muslim dynasty of Fatimid captures Egypt from the Muslim Abbasid dynasty and establishes the city of Cairo as its capital. **ISLAM**

974 — In Japan a report prepared for Emperor En'yu shows a total of 6,000 Shinto shrines throughout Japan. **SHINTO**

975 — Roman Catholicism begins to spread to Hungary when Prince Geisa converts to Christianity and then attempts—sometimes by violent means—to convert other Hungarians. **CATH**

975 — The bishopric of Prague is established in Czechoslovakia as Roman Catholicism spreads from western to central Europe. **CATH**

976–
1031 — The rule of the Muslims in Spain becomes unstable as rulers come and go and a civil war breaks out among groups attempting to gain control of the region. In 1031 leaders end centralized rule and the territory is broken up into regions, each ruled from a central city. **ISLAM**

977 — The Song emperor of China receives the Daoist Chen Tuan (906–989) at court. He is the first to write specifically on the *neidan*, or interior alchemy, school of Daoism. Interior alchemy is a technique of enlightenment, "a

movement toward interiorization that used alchemical vocabulary," as one scholar describes it. In one aspect a specifically Daoist response to Buddhism, it seeks to achieve a synthesis of the Three Teachings. It features integrated ancient techniques of breathing and alchemy and a systematized use of the trigrams and hexagrams of the *I Ching* (*Book of Change*). The precise date of the school's emergence is not known. The oldest texts are the *Cantongqi* (*Token of Concordance of the Three*), attributed by tradition to the legendary immortal Wei Boyang of the second century. Exact dates and authorship of these texts are unknown, but they are thought to have circulated during the T'ang dynasty (618–907).   DAO, TOL

977–
1040

The Turkish Ghaznavid dynasty is founded in Afghanistan and later extends Muslim rule into India.   ISLAM

c. 980

(St.) Symeon, the New Theologian (949–1022), is appointed abbot of the Orthodox monastery of St. Mamas. A leading theologian and mystic, he stresses the personal experience of God and especially the role of light in that experience. His ideas are repressed by church authorities during his lifetime but are revived by monks in the 14th century.   ORTHO

981

This is the traditional date for completing the colossal statue, 57 feet high, of Gommatesvara, or Bahubali, son of the first *tirthankara* who is worshiped as a god in Karnataka. It is carved in a hill at Sravana Belgola, some 62 miles from Mysore, India. It has been commissioned by Camundaraya, a celebrated Jain general famous for his benevolent ways as well as for his military victories. (Continuing through the 20th century, every 12 years Jains perform a ritual bathing of this statue, a ceremony known as the *mahamastakabhiseka*, attended by thousands of Jains from all over the world.) Jains will erect two other monolithic statues of Gommatesvara at Karkala and Venuru.   JAIN

981–
983

Temples dedicated to the Daoist Taiyi (the Supreme One) are built in Suzhou and Kaifeng in China.   DAO

982

(St.) Adalbert of Prague (c. 956–997), later designated the patron saint of Prussia and Poland, is appointed bishop of Prague. Although he has great trouble converting pagans to Christianity and also with reformers in the Church, he plays a major role in initiating missionary activity in Hungary, Prussia, and Poland.   CATH

985

In Japan the Buddhist monk Genshin (942–1017) completes the religious tract *Ojoyoshu* and spreads Amidism, or Pure Land Buddhism, among the aristocracy.   BUDD

988

Vladimir the Great (r. 980–1015) of Kiev converts to Eastern Orthodoxy, and Russian Orthodoxy begins to develop its own liturgy and as an independent church. The Russian church organization follows that of the Greek Orthodox with a network of metropolitans—bishops with civil authority—

to govern the Church. From 988 until 1240 Kiev is the center of the Russian Church. **ORTHO**

989 A peace movement develops in the Catholic Church, and French bishops at the Council of Charroux call for a ban on war waged against women, children, the poor, and the weak. **CATH**

990s After embracing Orthodoxy the Russian Orthodox Church develops a national character of its own and becomes distinct from both Catholicism and Orthodoxy. Watching from their vantage point in distant Russia, Russians view the religious turmoil in both the East and West as indications of the corruption of Christianity there and believe that their Russian version is changeless and eternal. Russian Orthodoxy emphasizes the Bible, instead of religious belief or the sacraments, as the way to salvation. **ORTHO**

990–1013 The Mosque of al-Hakim is built by the Muslim Fatimid dynasty in Egypt. It is meant primarily for use by the royal family and as a visible sign of their power in the region. **ISLAM**

The Benedictines

Since the fall of the Roman Empire, Benedictine monks and nuns had preserved the learning and art of Western Europe. In the early Middle Ages, Benedictines were the only monks in western Europe. They remained so until the reforms of the 11th century in the Catholic Church. Benedictines were known as Black Monks because of their black robes. They divided their time between prayer and work and lived by a set of rules that ordered every detail of their waking lives. From the 6th to the 12th centuries, Benedictine monks and nuns were some of the most educated and talented people in western Europe. Not surprisingly, Benedictine monks founded schools, libraries, and *scriptoria*, where manuscripts were painstakingly copied to be available to more people. At monastic schools lay people could study theology, the Bible, grammar, rhetoric, argument, mathematics, astronomy, and music; and between 800 and 1000, over 90 percent of educated people had been schooled in these monasteries. The black monks were mainly interested in furthering Christian belief, so they concentrated their teaching on the Latin language, the Bible, and works of the early Church fathers. Benedictine monasteries were self-sufficient communities, yet they became increasingly powerful in local politics, business, farming, and education. By 800 many Benedictine monasteries were wealthy, overseeing huge estates in the same manner as secular lords. Since the monks often ran these estates better than the nobles ran theirs, Benedictine monasteries became models for medieval agriculture, bringing money and jobs to the surrounding areas. Because of their agriculture expertise, the monasteries were given political control over their lands as well and were asked to supply knights to civil rulers, just as secular lords were.

991– 1031	The Muslim Abbasid ruler al-Qadir (?–1031) expands the role of the leader beyond politics and assumes a religious role as defender of Sunni beliefs against the claims of the Shi'a Muslims. **ISLAM**
996– 1021	During the rule of the Muslim Fatimid leader al-Hakim in Egypt, the Jewish and Christian religious minorities are severely persecuted. **ISLAM, TOL**
997– 1022	Zhenzong reigns as emperor of the Song dynasty in China. He claims a Daoist deity among his ancestors. He gives official bureaucratic rank to prominent Daoists. Zhenzong is the protector of the Daoist Wang Jie (980–1020), who produces alchemical gold. **DAO**
997– 1038	During the reign of (St.) Stephen (c. 975–1038), the son of Geisa who had brought Christianity to Hungary, Hungary becomes a Roman Catholic nation. The population is converted, archbishoprics and bishoprics are established, and the Benedictines are given special status. Stephen's reign is followed by a period of pagan revival, but Catholicism survives and Hungary is a Catholic nation by 1100. **CATH**
c. 1000	Contacts between Muslim traders and the ruling families of African kingdoms in sub-Saharan West Africa intensify and set the stage for Islamic conversion by leaders of the communities and traders. About this time the leader of the African kingdom of Goa in northwest Africa converts to Islam, thereby making his kingdom first in sub-Saharan Africa to accept Islam. For several centuries only rulers and traders who are in contact with Muslim traders from North Africa practice Islam, while most people continue to follow indigenous religions. **ISLAM**
c. 1000	A Jewish community is established in Kaifeng, China, by Jews from Persia. Isolated from other Jewish communities, it survives into the early 20th century. A Jewish synagogue is built in Cologne, Germany. The Cochin Jews of India are granted broad civil and political rights by the Hindu rulers. **JUD**
1000	A Roman Catholic Church organization is established in Poland with the leadership based in Gnesen. Poland becomes a major center of Roman Catholicism in eastern Europe. **CATH**
1000	The Toltec Empire centered on its capital city of Tula is at its height in Mexico. The city contains a main pyramid temple and ceremonial ball courts, and the god Quetzalcoatl, the Feathered Serpent, is venerated as the patron of the Toltec Empire. **NATIV**
1000s	Buddhism vanishes across much of northern India; this is due in part to the fact that many Buddhists have been blending their practices and doctrines with those of the Hindu faith. In particular, the newer sects of Hinduism, Vaishnavism, and Saivism have been spread by *bhaktas,* wandering teachers, seers, and saints from south India who teach and sing their devotional poet-

ry throughout India. Some Buddhists now worship goddesses; many also adopt the more mystical beliefs of the Tantric Buddhism. But as Hinduism is the dominant religion in most communities, it gradually reabsorbs the Buddhists. In Sri Lanka Theravada Buddhism has effectively triumphed over Mahayana Buddhism, but elsewhere outside India Mahayana Buddhism is the dominant form. **BUDD, HIND**

1000s The worship of relics—objects, particularly parts of the body, such as bones, hair, or teeth, believed to be fragments of saints or biblical people—is common in Christian Europe, and fake relics are manufactured and sold. These include such relics as the spear that pierced Christ's side, the Holy Grail, the seamless coat that Christ wore, the steps that Jesus climbed to be judged by Pilate, the bones of 11,000 virgins killed by Huns, the horns of Moses, the table from the Lord's Supper, and Christ's foreskin, umbilical cord, and tears. **CATH**

1000s Jainism has flourished in southern India for some centuries but is now fading under the rise of devotional theism; moreover, the sharp boundaries between Jainism and Hinduism are also becoming blurred. In reaction to this various Jain sects and orders split off, one of the most famous being the Digambara order known as Kashtha-sangha. **JAIN**

1000–1100 The Song dynasty in China (960–1279) produces a new social class noted for literary proficiency, social consciousness, and political participation. Representative individuals include Hu Yuan (993–1059), Sun Fu (992–1057), Fan Chung-yen (989–1052), Wang An-shih (1021–1086), Ou-yang Hsiu (1007–1072), Su Shih, pen name of Su Tung-p'o (1036–1101), and Su-ma Kuang (1019–1086). All contribute to a Confucian revival in education, politics, literature, and history. **CONF**

1000s–1100s A religious sect known generally as Cathars spreads in parts of the Mediterranean region; in southern France, where they are strongest, they are known as Albigenses. Although its European adherents began as Christians, Cathar beliefs and practices stem from Manichaeism, a Middle Eastern religion that stresses the conflict between Light (God) and Darkness (Satan), and the Christian Church soon treats the Cathars as heretics. Some historians believe that the Cathars drew their faith from the Balkans, where still earlier the Jains had introduced it. In their stress on asceticism, not eating flesh, regarding life as evil (even to the point of starving oneself to death), the Cathars do seem linked to the Jain faith. **CHRIS, JAIN**

1000–1200 In a second wave of Buddhism, various Tibetan monks reinvigorate Tantric Buddhism by establishing new sects, writing and translating numerous works, and founding monasteries. Tibet draws numerous Buddhist refugees who bring texts from India, where the Muslims are gaining in power. Some Tibetan Buddhists also move into Bhutan, where they establish Tibetan-style religious feudalism: lamas exercise both temporal and spiritual power and rule over estates in western Bhutan. **BUDD**

1000– 1200	Muslim expansion south along the East African coast intensifies, and trading settlements with stone mosques are built in several locations. Muslims trade for gold that is mined by the Shona people of Zimbabwe. ISLAM
1000– 1250	A new artistic genre of miniature painting emerges in India. The paintings illustrate Jain and Buddhist manuscripts from Nepal, Gujarat, and eastern India, as well as Hindu manuscripts from Rajasthan, Delhi, and Jaunpur. They are linear and flat in style and use a limited, bright palette. Among the earliest known examples of Jain miniature paintings are the palm-leaf manuscripts at Nisithacurni, India, which date from the 1000s. JAIN
1000– 1300	In northern India Jainism is thriving only in the states of Rajasthan and Gujarat, although there are some signs of Jainism—temples, inscriptions, epigraphs, etc.—elsewhere in northern India. Particularly in Rajasthan, Jains become prominent in government administration, the military, and trade. In southern India Jainism during this period is almost entirely dominated by the Digambara sect. Even this sect is struggling to maintain itself, with the exception being in Karnataka, as witness epigraphs, inscriptions, and literary and scholarly works produced there. JAIN
1000s– 1300s	The rise of Japanese Shingon Buddhism (SEE 806, BUDD) fosters the development and growth of *Ryobu-shugo* (unification of both sides, or double aspect) Shinto, which, under the idea of *honji suijaku* (original prototype and local manifestation), relates the Buddhist pantheon to indigenous Shinto divinities and attempts a direct connection with traditional Shinto as practiced at Ise. As a modification of Shingon, Ryobu Shinto is a form of syncretism that includes mystical ritualism and occult practices. Ryobu Shinto will come to represent popular syncretism in major cults arising in such classical shrines as Kumano, Hachiman, and Kasuga. Another development is the formation of *Ichijitsu* (One Truth) Shinto, under the influence of Tendai Buddhism (SEE 804–805, BUDD), at Sanno shrine at the foot of Mount Hiei. Ichijitsu Shinto promotes the identification of *kami* (native spirits) and buddhas with each other, as representing similar lines of spiritual force. Tendai Buddhism (SEE 804–805, BUDD) supports as well the Shinto mountain priests who are adherents of Shugendo. BUDD, SHINTO
1000s– 1400s	Period of Nemichandra, a well-known Jain teacher/sage, author of several important works on Jain doctrines. JAIN
c. 1000– 1600	The Polynesian people of Easter Island (Rapa Nui) carve and erect the massive volcanic-stone statues known as *moai*. Although the purpose of the statues is not completely understood in the 1990s, it is likely they had religious significance, possibly representing the ancestors worshiped by the islanders, and were meant to bring rainfall and crops. CIVIL
1008	In China Confucius is honored with the posthumous title "Perfect Sage"; an Imperial Academy petition in 1074 to honor him with the title "Emperor" is rejected by the Board of Rites. CONF

1008	The "Heavenly Book" comes to prominence in China's capital; Daoists build the Zhaoying palace to house it. Later in the year another Heavenly Book appears on sacred Mount Tai. **DAO**
1009	The emperor Zhenzong in Song dynasty China orders Daoist scholars to compile a canon of Daoist scriptures. **DAO**
1009	The oldest surviving Jewish Bible written in Hebrew, called the *Leningrad Manuscript*, is written. **JUD**
1009–1225	As in China, in Vietnam knowledge of Confucianism regulates examinations for the recruitment of the intellectual or mandarin class and is the official ideology. **CONF**
1011	The process of carving woodblocks for Korea's first printing of the Buddhist canon (the Tripitaka) begins. The project is undertaken at the direction of the Hyonjong court in part to petition the Buddha's aid in the struggle against Liao and in part to solidify the authority of the state religion. *Son* (Meditation School) documents are excluded in deference to *Kyo* (Doctrinal School). The process takes 77 years to complete. **BUDD**
1011	Emperor Zhen Zong (Chen Tsung) of the Song dynasty decrees that temples to Confucius are to be built in all district cities. **CONF**
1015	In China Zhang Zhengsui is dubbed the 24th Daoist celestial master or "Daoist pope." Zhang builds the Academy for Transmission of Registers on Mount Longhu in Jiangxi Province, ranked as the 32d Daoist Blessed Spot and the administrative center of Celestial Masters Daoism. **DAO**
1016–1030	During the reign of King Olaf (995–1030), he attempts to convert the people of Norway to Christianity. He is later made the patron saint of Norway, and the Cathedral of Nidaros, where his relics are kept, becomes a major pilgrimage site for Christians in northern Europe. **CATH**
1017	Zhou Dunyi (Chou Tun-i), also called Zhou Lianxi (Chou Lien-Hsi) (1017–1073), is born in Tao-chou, China. He is considered the most important precursor of neo-Confucianism. He combines Daoist ideas of the universe with the concept of an evolutionary process of creation from the *I Ching* (*Book of Changes*): From the Great Ultimate come *yin* (tranquillity) and *yang* (movement); they give rise to the Five Elements (fire, earth, water, metal, and wood), all of which allow emergence of male and female elements, which in turn react to the external environment in terms of good and evil. Zhou's use of the *I Ching* influences Zhu Xi (Chu Hsi) (1130–1200) and other neo-Confucians of the late Sung dynasty, who revere it as a great classic of Confucianism. **CONF**

| c. 1017–1137 | Hindu philosopher Ramanuja lives and plays a major role in developing the Sri Vaisnava sect, Vaisnava Hinduism, in the south Indian state of Tamilnadu. The Sri Vaisnava sect combines beliefs and practices from the Hinduism of northern India, including the worship of Vishnu, with southern Indian traditions such as the worship of personal deities. **HIND** |

1018   The Orthodox patriarch in Bulgaria is repressed by the Byzantine Empire.
        ORTHO

1019   Airlangga (r. 1019–1042) establishes his kingdom over the greater part of
        Java. With its political center at Kediri, it becomes a densely populated agri-
        cultural area and extends influence into Bali. Siva and Buddha are worshiped
        at court and commoners practice a mix of Indian religious influences and
        traditional religion. The arts, adapting Indian themes, flourish. Airlangga
        divides his kingdom in two parts along the Brantas River, forming the
        Kingdoms of Kediri and Janggala for his sons. **BUDD, TOL**

1019   The Daoist canon in 4,565 scrolls is published in China under the supervi-
        sion of the scholar Zhang Junfang (flourished 1008–1029). **DAO**

1022   In Japan the dedication of Hojoji monastery constructed by Fujiwara no
        Michinaga, who has retired to become a Buddhist monk, is a splendid dis-
        play of his wealth and power. **BUDD**

1024   This year sees the emergence of Jain order of Kharatara-gachchha, belong-
        ing to the Svetambara sect; it seeks to restore the mendicant monks. **JAIN**

1028–   The Daoist scholar Zhang Junfang in China finishes his collection of Daoist
1029   scriptures known as the *Yunji qiqan*. **DAO**

1030   The Muslim Ghaznavid dynasty based in Afghanistan makes incursions
        into India and occupies parts of northern India until 1187. **ISLAM**

1033   By imperial edict Daoists are barred from building new temples in Song
        China. **DAO**

1035   Some 6,000 Jews are killed during political unrest in Fez, Morocco. **JUD**

1038   As part of the peace movement in the Catholic Church dating to 989,
        Leagues of Peace are formed in France. Their purpose is to field armies
        against others who have initiated war. The movement, which does mount
        some armies, is short-lived. **CATH**

1038   The Turkish Seljuk dynasty, founded by Tughril Beg (?–1063), rules in Iran
        and Iraq. The Turks come from central Asia and had been converted to
        Islam by the Arab and Persian Muslims and initially serve as soldiers guard-
        ing the frontier. **ISLAM**

c. 1040   The leader of the African kingdom of Takrur in northwest Africa converts to Islam. Most of the population converts as well shortly thereafter leading to rivalries between Muslim religious teachers and traditional religious practitioners. **ISLAM**

1042   Atisa (982–1054), an Indian Buddhist *pandit* (teacher and scholar), arrives in Tibet after traveling to Myanmar and Afghanistan. In Tibet he proceeds to revitalize the declining Buddhist practices. He stresses strict monastic discipline but he also establishes Avalokitsevara, the *bodhisattva* of compassion, at the center of all Tibetan Buddhists' deities. Atisa is regarded as the founder of Kadampa, one of the major sects of Tibetan Buddhism. **BUDD**

1044   Many Jews and Muslims are blamed for riots and are expelled from Constantinople by the Christian rulers. **TOL**

1044–1077   Anawrahta, known as the founder of the First Myanmar Empire, reigns. He supports Theravada Buddhism with the prosperity brought by conquest and by the expansion of agriculture and trade; construction begins on Shwezigon pagoda to house a copy of the sacred Tooth of Buddha relic; the original is in Sri Lanka, the primary source of Buddhism in Myanmar. Subsequent monarchs continue to patronize Theravada Buddhism and engage in large-scale temple building projects. **BUDD**

1049–1057   Naropa (1016–1090) is serving as the abbot of India's famous Buddhist monastic university of Nalanda when in 1057 he has a vision that leads him to resign and set out to seek his spiritual master, Tilopa (988–1069). After 12 years of learning and enduring 12 demanding tests, Naropa achieves enlightenment as a Tantric master. He then passes on his secret knowledge to the Tibetan monk Marpa (1012–1096), who in turn passes on the Tantric tradition to Milarepa (1040–1123). **BUDD**

c. 1050   Ch'oe Ch'ung (984–1068) establishes the Nine Course Academy in Korea for the study of the Confucian Classics and Chinese history. A dozen other schools modeled after this one are founded soon after. These academies are called the *Sibi to*, the Twelve Assemblies. Eventually they eclipse the prestige of the royal Confucian academy *Kukchagam*. **CONF**

1050–1075   The Chinese scholar/priest Zhang Boduan (984–1082) in his *Essay on Understanding Reality* explains the principles of interior alchemy and attempts a synthesis of Daoist, Buddhist, and Confucian thought. "Although there are Three Teachings," Zhang writes, "the Way is ultimately one." A native of Zhejiang, he is regarded as the founder of the Southern school of inner alchemy. **DAO**

c. 1050–1100   These years mark the period of Prabhacandra, the author of *Kathakosa*, a collection of stories, and various philosophical works; he is a member of the Digambara sect of Jains. **JAIN**

1050– 1100	In China the brothers Ch'eng Hao (1032–1085) and Ch'eng I (1033–1107) develop what become two distinct modes of thought in Sung dynasty Confucianism, the learning of the mind and the learning of the principle. Ch'eng Hao defines humanity in terms of mutuality between heaven and mankind, man and man, and man and nature; the *tien-li* (heavenly principle) in all things permits the human mind to purify itself. Ch'eng I, however, stresses *ko-wu* (investigation of things) as part of the extension of knowledge through self-cultivation. **CONF**

Orthodoxy

Orthodoxy (or Eastern Orthodoxy) is one of the three primary branches of Christianity. (Roman Catholicism and Protestantism are the others.) Adherents of Orthodoxy consider themselves to be members of the original Christian Church whose beliefs and practices were established in the seven ecumenical councils that took place between 325 and 787 C.E. Since the earliest days of Christianity, there had been rivalries between communities in the East (Asia Minor) and the West (Rome) that worsened in the fourth century and finally led to a schism in 1054 when the leaders of the churches in Rome and Constantinople excommunicated each other. Although the churches have not reunified, relations have been more cordial since the 1960s. Adherents of Orthodoxy live primarily in southeastern Europe and Russia, with smaller communities in many other nations around the world. Because the eastern European communities were under Muslim (Ottoman Turk) rule from the 15th to the 19th or 20th century, the Russian Orthodox Church developed independently to a large extent. Compared to Roman Catholicism, Orthodoxy is a less formal, more emotional, and more spiritual religion in which the central concern is the relationship between a person's natural state and God's divine state. The Orthodox worship God, Jesus Christ, and the Holy Spirit, with the last considered the source of human redemption. Worship is centered in the local churches, with services led by priests and deacons. Above the local priests are the bishops, who may not be married, although they may be widowers. The major holiday is Easter; Christmas is not celebrated, although the Epiphany on January 6 is a major holiday. The Orthodox view the Bible as a basic religious text but also use their own religious texts, many of which were compiled and preserved by Orthodox monks during the centuries of Muslim rule. The Orthodox reject the primacy of the church in Rome and the authority of the papacy, a major impediment to reunification by the two churches. There are about 220 million adherents of Orthodoxy around the world, with the church divided into 15 autocephalous churches (independent churches that elect their own heads): Constantinople, Alexandria, Antioch, Jerusalem, Russia, Georgia, Serbia, Romania, Bulgaria, Cyprus, Greece, Albania, Poland, Czech and Slovakia, and America, as well as three autonomous churches (Sinai, Finland, and Japan). The ecumenical patriarch, the head of the Church of Constantinople, remains the leader of the church, although his power is much reduced by the absence of a large and active Orthodox community in Turkey.

1050– 1150	During this period relations between the Catholic Church and secular rulers in Europe (the State) undergo a major change. A significant number of clergy in western Europe unite under the bishop of Rome and declare their union a separate political body that is not under the rule of any secular leader. **CATH**
1050– 1200	Throughout the Song dynasty, neo-Confucian thinkers carry on the lineage of the *Dao-hsueh* (Learning of the Dao) from Chou Tun-i (1017–1073) through Shao Yung (1011–1077), Chang Tsai (1020–1077), and the brothers Ch'eng Hao (1032–1085) and Ch'eng I (1033–1107), to the great synthesizer Chu Hsi (1130–1200). They develop a humanist vision integrating self-cultivation with social ethics and moral metaphysics, thus restoring and applying classical Confucian insights to current concerns. **CONF**
1050– 1300	Native Americans of the Anasazi cultural tradition in Arizona, Colorado, and New Mexico build large stone settlements such as Mesa Verde that include underground circular ceremonial chambers called *kivas*. The presence of multiple kivas suggests that the communities are divided into different groups, each with its own kiva. **NATIV**
1054	A permanent schism between what becomes the Roman Catholic and Eastern Orthodox churches begins when several centuries of dispute over papal authority and church doctrine lead Pope Leo IX (1002–1054) and Orthodox patriarch Michael Cerularius to excommunicate each other. **CHRIS**
1055– 1194	The Muslim Seljuk Turks occupy Baghdad with the blessing of the Abbasid ruler, who seeks their help in overthrowing the rival Buyid dynasty. **ISLAM**
1056– 1057	The illuminated *Ostromirovo Gospel*, the oldest Orthodox religious text in Church Slavonic to survive into the 20th century, is copied in Novgorod, Russia. **ORTHO**
1059– 1061	Nicholas I is pope of the Roman Catholic Church. He is the first pope to be elected under a new system of papal elections by a council of cardinals. The new policy reverses the practice going back nearly 100 years wherein the Holy Roman Emperor chooses the pope and other church officials. **CATH**
1060	An examination system for Daoist priests is established in Song dynasty China. **DAO**
1066	Despite two centuries of missionary work by Christians in Scandinavia, many people in the region have not converted, and at about this time there are mass persecutions of Christians, the worst of which occur in Sweden. **CHRIS**
c. 1067	The leader of the West African kingdom of Kanem converts to Islam. Most of the population also converts shortly thereafter, which leads to rivalries between Muslim religious teachers and traditional religious practitioners. **ISLAM**

1068   The Cistercians, a Roman Catholic monastic order, is formed by former Benedictines and named for their home at Cîteaux in Burgundy. The Cistercians seek a more ascetic life than that practiced by the Benedictines.

                                               CATH

1069   The Celtic religion is banned in Scotland by King Malcolm Cannue and replaced with Christianity.   **CHRIS**

c. 1070   The Knights Hospitalers form in Jerusalem. They are one of a number of military orders in Europe that are encouraged by the military culture of northern Europe and the increasing political interests of the Church. Like all monks, these clerical knights vow to live lives of poverty, chastity, and obedience, although a few orders do not require such vows. Their primary purpose is to protect and care for pilgrims, participate in the Crusades, and fight the Muslims in Spain. Other major military orders are the Hospitalers of Saint Thomas of Canterbury formed in Acre about 1191, the Knights of Calatrava formed in the 12th century, the Livonian Knights formed in Germany about 1202, the Knights of Christ formed in Portugal about 1318, the Templars formed about 1119 under French control, and the Teutonic Knights formed as a German order in 1190.   **CATH**

c. 1070   The leader of the West African kingdom of Ghana converts to Islam. For several centuries only the rulers and traders who are in contact with Muslim traders from North Africa practice Islam; most of the population continues to follow indigenous religions.   **ISLAM**

c. 1070   A Muslim dynasty is established at the settlement of Kilwa in southern Tanzania along the coast. The rulers are probably of mixed African and Arab ancestry.   **ISLAM**

c. 1070   The Muslim Almoravids rule in Morocco and then extend their control to the south. A Muslim warrior brotherhood, they maintain loyalty to the Muslim rulers in Baghdad.   **ISLAM**

1070   In Sri Lanka Vijayabahu I of Rohana (r. 1070–1110) expels the Tamil Cholas from their 75-year rule over Rajarata and during a long reign rebuilds Buddhist temples that were destroyed by the Hindu occupiers.   **BUDD**

1070   Jews arrive in the British Isles at the behest of William the Conqueror, a Norman who conquered England at the Battle of Hastings in 1066. There, they serve as finance officials.   **JUD**

1070   A Jewish school is founded in Troyes, France, by Rashi (Rabbi Shlomo Itzhaki, 1040–1105), an influential Jewish philosopher and writer. He provides the first reinterpretation of the *Talmud* dating to the sixth century. By writing the Talmud in Hebrew and in a conversational and flowing style, he makes it available to the common person. His children and grandchildren add commentaries.   **JUD**

1071   The Oghuz peoples, Muslim Turks from central Asia who had formerly founded the Seljuk Empire in Iran and Iraq, have moved into Anatolia and defeat the Byzantines at Manzikert, capturing Byzantine emperor Romanos I. The Seljuk expand their control across the region by subjugating both Christian and pastoral nomads. They capture Jerusalem and the Jewish community there disperses.   **ISLAM, JUD**

1072   Dunfermline Abbey is founded in Scotland by (St.) Margaret of Scotland (c. 1045–1093), the wife of King Macolm III. It becomes the center of Christianity in Scotland and is established as part of Margaret's efforts to renew the Church in Scotland. She also founds other monasteries and churches and in 1673 is made the patron saint of Scotland.   **CATH**

1072   The Camaldolese Roman Catholic monastic order is given Church approval by the pope. The order was started in Italy earlier in the century by St. Romuald (d. 1027) as a secluded offshoot of the Cistercian monastic movement.   **CATH**

1073   Konchok Gyalpo, breaking with Nyingma order, founds Sakya (Gray Earth Monastery). Sakya is the second of the four great orders of Tibetan Buddhism.   **BUDD**

1073–   Gregory VII (1021–1085) is pope of the Roman Catholic Church. He
1085   attempts to increase the political power of the papacy and to place the pope at the center of religious power. Gregory declares that secular rulers have no jurisdiction over the Catholic Church and decrees that only the pope has the power to appoint bishops, convene church councils to determine doctrine, and establish monasteries.   **CATH**

1075   Pope Gregory VII issues his *Dictatis papae* in which he sets forth the supremacy of the pope over political rulers and argues that the pope's authority comes from God, who is the sole judge of the pope's actions. A Church synod supports the pope's position, which is aimed primarily at Holy Roman Emperor Henry IV (r. 1056–1106), who has resisted the new policy and has chosen his own archbishop of Milan in defiance of the pope and has publicly ridiculed the pope. In response the pope excommunicates Henry and his supporters and removes him as the Holy Roman Emperor.   **CATH**

1075–   The Investiture Controversy takes place in Catholic Europe. Popes and sec-
1122   ular rulers struggle over who has the right to appoint religious authorities, including the pope himself.   **CATH**

1076   As the Investiture Controversy continues, a Church council gives Henry IV, the excommunicated and deposed Holy Roman Emperor, until February 1077 to seek absolution from the pope.   **CATH**

1077– 1085	Henry IV, the excommunicated and deposed Holy Roman Emperor, seeks and receives absolution from Pope Gregory VII. However, he is prevented from resuming his rule by political rivals and is excommunicated again when he refuses to let the pope decide the matter. Nonetheless, Henry defeats his rivals, regains the emperorship, and then marches on Rome, forcing the pope to flee. The pope is restored by political supporters, but Rome is burned in the fighting and he dies in exile. **CATH**
1079– 1153	This is the lifespan of Gampopa, a Tibetan monk who learns of the Tantric teachings and practices from Milarepa. Gampopa takes the orally transmitted Tantric teachings and synthesizes them with those of the scholarly Kadimpa sect; in so doing he founds the third major sect of Tibetan Buddhism, Kagyudpa. Gampopa's two major works, which form the bedrock of Tibetan Buddhism, are *The Jewel Ornament of Liberation*, an authoritative introduction to Mahayana Buddhism, and the *Six Teachings of Naropa*, an account of the secret Tantric practices handed down from Naropa. **BUDD**
c. 1080– 1107	In Cambodia Jayavarman VI reigns. Jayavarman VI is probably responsible for the great religious foundations at Phimai (now in Thailand), which honor Hindu and local territorial gods but are particularly influenced in belief by Buddhism. **BUDD**
1081	Violent clerical demonstrations in Japan begin as some 1,000 Buddhist monks from Enryakuji, 200 of them armored and armed, move on the capital. This protest, like subsequent protests—in 1107, 1113, 1139, 1169, and 1177—is spurred by Buddhist sectional rivalries and opposition to court appointments and government weakness in the face of growing domestic disorder. **BUDD**
1081	Japan's Emperor Shirakawa (r. 1072–1086) selects the 22 shrines (*Nijunisha*) to be supported by the imperial family (until the middle of the 15th century). They are divided into three groups: the most prestigious 7 (the Ise, Iwashimizu Hachiman, Kamo, Matsunoo, Hirano, Fushimi Inari, and Kasuga shrines), except for the Fushimi Inari, which is devoted to rice *kami* (native spirits) and has popular support, are directly related to the imperial family; the middle 7 (the Oharano, Omiwa, Isonokami, Oyamato, Hirose, Tatsuta, and Sumiyoshi shrines), except for the Oharano, are ancient shrines of mythic and historic status; and the lower 8 (the Hie, Umenomiya, Yoshida, Hirota, Yasaka, Kitano, Niunokawakami, and Kibune shrines) are associated with major clans, local worship, rain-making rites, or Buddhism. All 22 shrines are situated within or close to the ancient capitals of Nara and Heiankyo (Kyoto). In the modern era the government supports these shrines from 1868 to 1945. **SHINTO**
1084	The Carthusians, a Christian reform order, are established by St. Bruno (c. 1032–1101) at the monastery of La Grand Chartruese to revive the pure roots of monasticism. In the ascetic tradition of Orthodoxy, Carthusians

vow to live in silence, labor, and solitude. Carthusian orders spread from France to other European states and are inspirations to many medieval thinkers, including Bernard of Clairvaux (1090–1153), Peter the Venerable, and William of St. Thierry (c. 1085–c. 1148). **CATH**

1085   The European reconquest of Spain begins when the combined forces of Castile, Leon, and Galicia under the command of Alfonso VI take Toledo, a center of Islamic culture in Spain. Muslims are allowed to remain in the city, which has Muslim, Christian, and Jewish communities. **CHRIS, ISLAM**

1086   The Muslim Almoravids, who rule Morocco, come to the aid of Muslims in Spain and defeat the European Christian forces at Sagrajas and rule Spain from Morocco from 1090 until 1145. **ISLAM**

1087   *Insei*, or "cloister government," begins after Japan's Emperor Shirakawa (r. 1072–1086) abdicates; it remains in effect until 1192 during the Heian era. While reigning emperors head the traditional court and bureaucracy, former emperors (usually emperors' fathers or grandfathers) assert control through their own retinue and administration located in a Buddhist monastery (most emperors abdicate to become Buddhist monks in retirement). In actuality, the *insei* system lasts intermittently in some form until 1840. **BUDD**

c. 1088–1173   Hemachandra, regarded as the greatest teacher of Jainism, is active during this time. He enters the Jain order as a boy and quickly gains a reputation for his learning. The powerful king of the Chaulukya dynasty in Gujarat, Jayasimha (1094–1143), although a Hindu, supports him. **JAIN**

1091   The Daoist Chen Jingyuan receives imperial orders to compile a new *Daozang* (*Treasury of the Dao*), or Daoist scriptural canon, in China. **DAO**

1091   Jewish civil and political rights are restricted in Castile (Spain) by the Christian rulers. **JUD**

1093   The relics of St. Swithin (c. 800–862), who had been the bishop of Winchester, are moved to Winchester Cathedral, which becomes a major pilgrimage site. **CATH**

1093   (St.) Anselm (1033–1109), the Medieval Catholic monk and philosopher, is appointed archbishop of Canterbury. Considered the leading Christian philosopher of his time, he seeks to defend Christian beliefs through the use of logic, in addition to scripture and traditional authorities, as was the previous practice. His most influential writings are *Monologion, Proslogian*, and *Why a Man God?* **CATH**

c. 1095   Attacks are launched on Christians in Palestine by Muslims and Jews. **TOL**

1095   The First Crusade is initiated by Pope Urban II (1044–1099). He calls together knights at Clermont in France and in an emotional message asks them to liberate Jerusalem from Muslim rule. He is also responding to a request from Byzantine emperor Alexius I Comnenus for assistance on repelling the Seljuk Turks.   **CATH**

1096   The European reconquest of Muslim Spain, which began in 1085, continues when the Europeans take Huesca and then Saragossa (1118), Tortosa (1148), and Lerida (1149).   **ISLAM, CHRIS**

1096   During the First Crusade Jewish communities are sacked and burned in the Rhine Valley in Europe and Jews are killed and forced either to convert to Christianity or commit suicide to avoid conversion. The Hungarian forces

---

Crusades

The Crusades were a series of holy wars launched by the Catholic Church in Europe beginning in 1095 and ending in the middle of the 13th century. Although the Crusades were initiated by the Church and many who participated did so because it was the "will of God," the real motivation was often more political than religious. Political purposes included fortifying the Byzantine Empire against Turkish invasions, wresting control of Jerusalem and other areas of the Middle East from the Muslims, demonstrating the political power of the pope over European kings and nobles, and controlling enemies of the church in Europe. The Crusades were launched in 1095 by Pope Urban, who called for a holy war against the Muslims who controlled Jerusalem in an emotional appeal at Clermont, France. That he could convince many people, including nobles, to rally to the cause was an indication of the political power of the Catholic Church in Europe at the time. The initial Crusade, known as the People's Crusade, was poorly organized and ended in defeat and disaster when the Crusaders were destroyed by the Turks at Rum in Asia Minor. The main body of the First Crusade was more successful and by 1099 had established Christian centers in Edessa, Antioch, and Tripoli and had driven the Muslims from Jerusalem, placing it under Christian rule. Success was due more to disorganization among Muslim states than true military superiority of the Crusaders. Participants in the First Crusade were mainly from France; later Crusades saw an increase in the numbers of participants from Germany, Britain, and the Balkans. The last three major Crusades were less successful, with the Second (1147–1149) accomplishing nothing, the Third (1189–1192) failing to retake Jerusalem, which had been captured by the Muslims in 1187, and the Fourth (1202–1204) involving the sack of Constantinople by the Crusaders and resulting in the final break between the Roman and Eastern churches. The later Crusades were mostly aimed at North Africa, and only the Sixth produced any real results, with Jerusalem again in Christian hands from 1229 to 1244. Later Crusades were also aimed at enemies of the church in Europe, including the Albigensian reformers in France and the Holy Roman emperor Frederick II. The Crusades had little lasting political effect. In terms of religion, their primary legacy was continuing animosity between Roman Catholics on the one hand and its enemies during the Crusades—the Muslims, Eastern Orthodox, and Jews—on the other.

refuse to participate in attacks on Jews, and the Crusader attacks on Jews diminish. JUD

1097   After the "People's Crusade" is repelled by the Turks, the main body of European Crusaders arrives in Constantinople and pledges its allegiance to Byzantine emperor Alexius I Comnenus. They begin moving toward Jerusalem and take the Muslim city of Nicaea. CATH

1098   The Cistercians, a Christian reform order, is established in reaction to the lavishness of the Cluny monastery. Cistercians renounced worldly possessions but nonetheless make contributions to the outside world in the important area of farming. Bernard of Clairvaux is the guiding force behind the order's expansion. CATH

1098   The European Crusaders lay siege to the Muslim city of Antioch and take it after four months. They exile the patriarch of the Eastern Church and replace him with a Western (Latin) patriarch, thereby creating conflict between the two churches. CATH

1099   The European Crusaders capture Jerusalem from the Muslims and loot the city, killing or driving off many Jewish and Muslim inhabitants, although the Jewish community survives. The Latin Kingdom of Jerusalem is established with Godfrey of Bouillon as ruler and a papal representative in residence. CATH

c. 1100   The dispersion of Jews across Europe and suffering at the hands of the Crusaders creates a need for a smaller, more accessible *Talmud* that can be read and whose laws can be followed by Jews everywhere. The first attempt to shorten the text and codify it is made by Rabbi Alfasi of Morocco. JUD

c. 1100   As part of the general translation of many ancient Greek works from Greek and Arabic into Latin, many ancient texts on astrology are translated and read by scholars in Europe. During the 12th century at least 20 such works become available in Europe, stimulating an interest in astrology and also reviving debates about the relationship between astrology and Christianity. SPIR

1100   Jews have now spread across Europe and there are now Jewish communities in all major cities and large towns. JUD

1100   Native Americans of the Hohokam cultural tradition in Arizona build settlements and irrigation canals to support agriculture. Among the constructions are ball courts like those built earlier in Mexico that may be used for rituals and ceremonial purposes. NATIV

1100   The Bogomil sect has attracted many followers in the Balkans, and Byzantine emperor Alexius I Comnenus moves to repress it as an enemy of Orthodox Christianity. Bogomil texts are burned, adherents are imprisoned, and the sect's leader, Basil, is executed. The repression is not successful and the sect remains active for another 400 years. **SEE 850, ORTHO.** ORTHO

| 1100s | The Catholic Church weakens its control over marriage, which had been considered a sacrament, when Catholic theologians decide that a couple need only declare verbal consent, without a priest or witness, to have a legal marriage. Although a proper marriage includes a betrothal ceremony, a dowry, and the presence of a priest and witnesses, none of these is required for a valid union. **CATH** |

| 1100s | The most prominent pupil of the Jain teacher Hemachandra is Ramacandra, a poet, dramatist, and critic who belongs to the Svetambara sect. **JAIN** |

| 1100s | In the Orthodox Church a short prayer that brings inner tranquillity to the worshiper, known as the *Jesus Prayer,* becomes popular. By 1200 the prayer is accompanied by breathing and meditation techniques similar to those used in Yoga and Sufism. **ORTHO** |

| 1100s | The leading Shinto shrines of each province in Japan are unofficially ranked in numerical order, and a *soja* (comprehensive shrine) close to the seat of the provincial government is designated. There all the provincial *kami* (native spirits) are worshiped together. **SHINTO** |

| 1100–1125 | The emperor Huizong of the Song dynasty reigns in China. The emperor is deeply interested in Daoism. He writes hymns for collections of Daoist ritual compiled during his reign, builds Daoist temples throughout the |

Sufism

Sufism is an umbrella term denoting a variety of philosophical, social, and literary phenomena within the Islamic world. In the narrow sense Sufism refers to those schools of mystical philosophy and theology that have exerted considerable influence over the development of Islamic politics and society. In a larger context Sufism has been the spiritual force behind pre-modern Islamic verse, the vehicle for expressions of popular piety, the primary social arena for women's religious participation, and a major element in the conversion of many African and Asian peoples to Islam. Sufism originally evolved from an informal seventh century Islamic movement of personal piety that emphasized prayer, asceticism, and withdrawal from society. In fact, many early Sufis frequently lived in caves or simple huts on the edges of cities and wore coarse woolen (*suf* means "wool") garments to demonstrate their religious piety. By doing so they imitated the Qur'anic portrayal of Muhammad's personal simplicity and asceticism as well as his habit of withdrawing to the caves outside Mecca to meditate. Other acts of extreme piety included long hours of prayer, self-mortification, fasting to near starvation, and finally, abject poverty and self-denial. Taken together these actions lead the individual toward the ultimate Sufi goal of a personal spiritual union with Allah: the attainment of spiritual understanding.

empire, establishes Daoist schools, and participates in Daoist ceremonies. He orders a new Daoist canon to be produced, the first to be printed. **DAO**

1100–1300	As trade is expanded down the east coast of Africa, Muslim communities gradually appear and some native peoples are converted to Islam. **ISLAM**

1105   Zhang Jixian in China takes title as the 30th Daoist celestial master. **DAO**

1105   *The Revival of the Religious Sciences* is written by Muslim theologian al-Ghazzai (1058–1111). In this and other works, he stresses the need to return to the principles of early Islam to create a Muslim society and he also supports Sufism, thereby legitimizing it as a form of Islamic devotion. He is considered by many Muslims to be the most important Muslim theologian after Muhammad, the founder of Islam. **ISLAM**

1107   An imperial edict in Song dynasty China gives Daoist priests and nuns precedence over Buddhist monks and nuns. **BUDD, DAO**

1108   The School of St. Victor is established in an Augustinian abbey by the Scholastic philosopher William of Champeaux. The school produces two leading mystics, Hugh (1096–1141) and Richard (?–1173) who seek to reconcile intellectual and mystical experience. **CATH**

1108   The Daoist priest Lin Lingsu (1076–1120) in China receives an imperial order to compile a history and scriptures of Daoism. For some years a great favorite of the emperor, Lin's anti-Buddhist activities will cause him to fall from favor. He will be expelled from court and exiled and will die shortly afterward. **DAO**

1110   China's emperor dispatches Daoist missionaries to Korea. **DAO**

1113   (St.) Bernard of Clairvaux (1090–1153) enters the Cistercian monastic order and in 1115 establishes an abbey at Clairvaux. He is a charismatic leader and able politician and wields much influence with Pope Innocent II. As a result, the Cistercians receive many papal benefits and spread across Europe. **CATH**

1113–1150   During the rule of Suryavarman II of the Kingdom of Angkor, the Angkor Wat temple-tomb complex is built and then is added to by successors. In the 20th century it is the best known example of ancient Cambodian religious architecture. **CIVIL**

1115   In the Christian-ruled regions of Spain, Jews and Muslims are in conflict and the rulers move to reduce friction by granting both groups limited freedoms. **TOL**

1115–1234   The Juchen Chin dynasty rules northern China and despite a lack of knowledge concerning the Confucian rebirth among the Southern Song, continues classical, artistic, literary, and historiographic traditions. **CONF**

1118   The founder of Daoism, Laozi, has his official birthday on the 15th day of the second month designated a "true primordial" festival in China.   **DAO**

1119   William of St. Thierry (1085–1148), the Catholic theologian and mystic, is appointed abbot of St. Thierry near Reims, France. William focuses on God's love and stresses the human experience of God.   **CATH**

1120   *Sic et Non* (*Thus and Otherwise*) is written by philosopher Peter Abelard (1079–1142). The book takes contradictory passages from the Bible and the church fathers and sets them next to logical observation in an effort to force people to create solutions that resolve the contradictions. The book is denounced by influential members of the Catholic Church and soon disappears until it is rediscovered in 1836.   **CATH**

1120   As Jews continue to settle in Europe, Jewish settlements are established as far north and east as the Ukraine.   **JUD**

1122   Peter the Venerable (1092–1156) becomes abbot of the influential Catholic Cluny monastery and retains the position until his death in 1156. In a time of religious change, he balances monastic tradition with the new monastic movements sweeping Europe during his time.   **CATH**

Bernard of Clairvaux

Bernard of Clairvaux was a holy man in an unholy world whose example initiated the reform of monasteries and fanned the religious strivings of the common people. The son of aristocratic Frenchmen, Bernard entered monastic life in 1113 and eventually became abbot of the Cistercian monastery at Clairvaux. Bernard was active politically and wielded major influence in getting Pope Innocent II elected. As a result, the Cistercians received many papal benefits; under Bernard's strong leadership, they expanded and became a powerful force in Europe. Bernard rejected all materialism and worldly pleasures. His theology was very traditional; he bitterly condemned the new ideas of Abelard and the nominalists. He drew his respect and power through his simple faith and example, rather than through any great or revolutionary intellect. He was well versed in the Bible and leaned toward mysticism. According to Bernard, one should love God simply because he is God. Despite an intense and combative personality, he inspired reforms through his insistence that all people at all levels should lead lives of poverty, dedicated to God. His belief in austerity led him to starve himself, eventually precipitating a nervous breakdown. Nonetheless, his strident criticism of all forms of wealth, excess, and pride; his own poverty; and his focus on dignity and morality made him one of Europe's most powerful clerics. Kings, popes, and paupers alike sought him out for advice. So powerful a presence was he, the story goes, that he once excommunicated some flies that buzzed around him while he was preaching, and they promptly died.

1122– 1146	Throughout his reign, Injong in Korea advances the system of education, establishing schools in rural areas and dividing the royal Confucian academy *Kukchagam* into several colleges. Several eminent scholars emerge from the schools he institutes. **CONF**
1125– 1150	Jurchen invaders from the north defeat Chinese forces, occupy north China, and establish the Jin dynasty (1125–1234) as the equal and rival to the Southern Song (1127–1279). A resurgence of Daoism, always a spiritual refuge in difficult times, is a consequence of dislocation and disunion, though northern and southern Daoist movements develop more or less independently. The Quanzhen (or Complete Realization, also known as the Golden Flower) school emerges as an important innovation in Daoist practice during this period. In the Jin state as in Southern Song, government exercises strict control over Daoist institutions. Jin bureaucrats supervise ordinations, examinations, and monastic life. Popular Daoist movements, regarded as heretical, flourish in Jin China. The Celestial Masters school continues to attract a wide following in Southern Song China. **DAO**
1130	The Chan and Pure Land Buddhist sects flourish in the northern China state of Jin, as they do also in the Southern Song region of China. The Jin government strictly regulates religious life. In this year, Jin rules that monks may not be ordained without government authorization. **BUDD**
1130	Zhu Xi (Chu Hsi), whose literary name is Yuan Hui or Chung Hui, with courtesy names Hui An, ch'en Lang, Chi Yen, Hui Weng, Hsun Weng, or Yunku Lao-Jen (1130–1200), interpreter and transmitter of the Confucian way, is born in China. He follows Ch'eng I's school of principle and gives Confucianism a new structure and systematic interpretation that defines Confucianism for the Koreans and Japanese, as well as the Chinese, for centuries to come. It is known as neo-Confucianism in the West but is referred to as *Li Hsueh* (Learning of the Principle) in China. He places together in sequence the *Da Xue* or *Ta Hsueh* (*Great Learning*), the *Lun Yu* (*Analects*), *Meng Zi* or *Meng Tzu* (*Mencius*), and the *Zhong Yong* or *Chung Yung* (*Doctrine of the Mean*), synthesizes and interprets them, and calls them *Si Shu*, the *Four Books*. With the *Five Classics* they become the central texts for education and civil service examinations in China from the 1300s onward. **CONF**
1131	In China the revelations of Hsu Sun, supposed to have lived in the 300s, to Ho Chen-kung inspire the *Ching-ming Chung-hsiao Dao* (*Pure and Luminous Way of Loyalty and Filial Obedience*). As a basis for a syncretistic movement of Daoist origin, this text promotes the Confucian virtues as essential for salvation and inspires a considerable following. **CONF, DAO**
1131	Anti-Song rebels in China capture the Nanchang region of what is in the 1990s Jiangxi Province. A teacher of the Pure Light school of Daoism, He Zhengong, prays for deliverance from the evils of war and receives a revelation from the third century Sichuan saint Xu Sun about rituals for the safety of the people. Xu, it is noted, spent his life in service of others rather than

in pursuit of his own spiritual advancement, a deviation from the inner focus of Daoism. Henceforth, loyalty to the state and deference to parents, elders, and superiors are at the core of the Pure Light school.   **DAO**

1136   (St.) Hildegard of Bingen (c. 1098–1179), the German mystic, becomes prioress of the Benedictine community of Ruperstburg, Germany. A visionary since childhood, she becomes an important early Catholic mystic. Her visions and other works are recorded in *Scivias*, written between 1141 and 1150. **CATH**

1138   The Taiyi (Grand Unity) Daoist sect emerges in Jurchen Jin, north China, and attracts a wide popular following. Among other things, the sect preaches celibacy.   **DAO**

Zhu Xi

Zhu Xi, whose name is synonymous with the revival of Confucian orthodoxy in the late traditional period, was born in 1130 in Fujian Province, China. His father had been an official of the Song imperial government but was forced from office due to his criticisms of the prime minister. This unfortunate event proved to be fateful, because while at home the senior Zhu taught his son the ideas of the outstanding Confucian scholar, Ch'eng I. Zhu Xi continued his studies after his father died but did not devote himself exclusively to Confucian texts. He had an interest in Buddhism and Daoism as well. By the time his passed the civil service examination at the relatively precocious age of 19, he still had not abandoned his studies of non-Confucian ideas. Zhu held a number of official posts, some carrying considerable responsibility, others not. Not surprisingly, it was during the times when he had few official duties that he was at his most productive scholastically. In 1175, at the age of 45, with the assistance of another well-known scholar, he completed his famous *Reflections on Things at Hand*. This book was to serve as a primer of neo-Confucian thought for future generations of scholars all over eastern Asia. By the time Zhu had reached middle age, he had become one of the leading philosophers of the day and carried on extensive dialogues, through correspondence and in person, with other important thinkers. In 1179, when Zhu was appointed prefect of Nankang in present-day Jiangxi, he used his position to revive a local Confucian academy. During the remainder of his life he continued to serve in official posts, sometimes very high-ranking ones. He was an exemplary civil servant who worked hard to alleviate the hardships of the common people, as well as to promote learning among the gentry. Zhu Xi's first love was always his philosophy and his writing. He continued to expound his ideas about neo-Confucianism in such books as *Conversations of Master Chu, Arranged Topically*, and especially in his commentaries on the Confucian classics. It was Zhu who was responsible for establishing the so-called *Four Books*: the *Book of Mencius*, the *Analects*, the *Doctrine of the Mean*, and the *Great Learning*, the core of the Confucian curriculum for students not just in China, but in Korea and Japan as well. In China Zhu Xi's commentaries were declared state orthodoxy in the 14th century and remain so in the modern age. No other scholar since the classical age has been as influential in eastern Asia.

1139 | At the Second Lateran Council, reformers in the Roman Catholic Church ban marriages by clergy and annul all clerical marriages. Although the idea of clerical celibacy dates to the early years of the Church, reformers are motivated in part by a desire to maintain clerical loyalty to the Church and to limit their interaction with lay people. The reforms, however, are sometimes ignored and some clergy continue to father children outside marriage.

CATH

1139 | Lu Chiu-yuan (Lu Hsiang-shan) (1139–1193), contemporary critic of Zhu Xi (Chu Hsi), is born in China. Along with Wang yang-ming (1472–1529), he is known for attacking the rationalist School of Principle in neo-Confucianism propounded by Zhu Xi, calling instead for the study of *hsin* (mind) and the preservation of its original purity. He advocates a return to Mencian idealism through belief that heaven-endowed nobility is the primary basis for self-realization and that the learning of the mind as a quest for self-knowledge provides the basis for any investigation of things. CONF

1140 | Gratian (?–c. 1179) is pope of the Roman Catholic Church. He compiles a collection of decrees and letters by previous popes, called the *Decretum*. These become the basis for a new canon law, used by the Catholic Church until 1904. The *Decretum* includes new decisions of the Second Lateran Council in Rome giving supreme authority to the pope and a more legalistic approach to theology, Christian morality, and the sacraments. CATH

1141– 1173 | Narasimha I reigns in Karnataka, India, and his highest minister and great general Hulla is celebrated as a Jain devotee. Among the several other centers of Jainism Hulla supports, he builds the Jain temple of Caturvimsati Jinalaya at Sravana Belgola. JAIN

1143 | In Gujarat, India, the ruler Jayasimha dies childless and is succeeded by a distant relative, Kumarapal (r. 1143–1173), who seizes the throne by force. Influenced by the Jain scholar Hemachandra, Kumarapal converts to Jainism, which then flourishes in Gujarat. According to Jain legend, Kumarapal becomes so zealous in enforcing the Jain tenet of *ahimsa* (non-killing) that he punishes two merchants because they killed fleas. Hemachandra is a man of great versatility, composing works on philosophy, grammars, dictionaries, a treatise on poetics, and brilliant poetry. The longest of his poems is *Trisastisalakapurusacarita* (*The Deeds of the Sixty-Three Eminent Men*), which tells stories about the original 24 *tirthankaras* and other early figures in Jainism. One section of this work, the *Mahaviracarita* (*The Deeds of Mahavira*), is devoted to the life of Mahavira, the historical founder of Jainism. Hemachandra dies of fasting at the age of 84, and King Kumarapal is said to have died shortly thereafter by the same means. JAIN

1144 | As part of the continuing war between the Muslims and European crusaders, the Muslim Turks capture Edessa from the Christian European Franks. CATH

1144	The first record of the charge of blood libel is recorded in Norwich, England. The blood libel claims that Jews use the blood of Christians in the Passover ritual. The charge is leveled against Jews in European communities over 150 times in the following centuries and continues to be believed in parts of Europe in the 1990s, although it is known to be false. **JUD**
1145	Injong in Korea commissions Confucian scholar Kim Pusik (1075–1151) to compile the *Samguk Sagi* (*Historical Records of the Three Kingdoms*). This is the oldest extant record of Korea's history; it draws heavily from earlier historical records, the *Sogi* and the *Yugi*, later lost. **CONF**
1146	When the Catholic Church in Europe prohibits Christians from lending money, Jews are asked and sometimes required to act as money-lenders. **CATH, JUD**
1147–1149	The Second Crusade is initiated by Pope Eugenius III in retaliation for the Turk recapture of Edessa in 1144. The Crusaders get as far as Damascus and besiege the city, but the siege ends in failure, as does the Crusade. **CATH**
1147–1269	The Muslim Almohads displace the Muslim Almoravids as the rulers of North Africa. The Almohad movement is founded by Muslim reformer Muhammad ibn Tumart (1077–1030) and is a fundamentalist movement that rises in opposition to the spiritual and moral laxness on the part of the Almoravids. The Almohad rulers support scholarship and building projects and convert most of the native Berber peoples of the region to Islam. **ISLAM**
1148	The Albigensians, who openly criticize the Catholic Church, are condemned by the church and again in 1184 and 1215. **SEE 1000s–1100s, CHRIS, JAIN.** **CATH**
1149	The Muslim Almohads in North Africa continue their displacement of the Muslim Almoravids when they take the cities of Seville and Cordova. **ISLAM**
c. 1150	Byzantine emperor Manuel Comnenus and Orthodox monk Michael Glycas debate the merits of astrology. The emperor supports it and relies heavily upon astrological predictions, while Glycas criticizes the practice as anti-Christian and as contrary to belief in the supremacy of God. Although the debate resolves nothing, it does point to the reemergence of astrology, which had gone into decline in the fourth century, and for the next two centuries astrology is again widely discussed. **SPIR**
1150	The Shenxiao school of Daoism (also known as the Divine Empyrean school) gains wide popularity in China. Its founder is Wang Wencheng (1093–1153), who combines inner alchemy with talismans (*fu*) relating to thunder magic, a technique some adepts employ to stimulate the Five Agents (or phases) of the *yin-yang* worldview. **DAO**
1150	The first meeting of Ashkenazic (eastern European Jews) rabbis to discuss Jewish law takes place in France. **JUD**

| 1150 | Muslim rulers in Babylon ease restrictions on Jews. | JUD |

1150   The Muslim Almohads from North Africa wrest control of Muslim Spain from the other Muslims and begin persecutions of the Jews.   **JUD**

1153   On the Maldives Islands the last Buddhist king is converted to Sunni Islam and founds a sultanate (which survives until 1932). He rules as Sultan Muhammad al Adil. Many Buddhist sites are destroyed in the early years of Islamic rule and Buddhism gradually dies out in the Maldives.   **BUDD**

1153–
1186   King Parakrama Bahu I reigns on Sri Lanka; he sponsors many Buddhist buildings in his new capital, Polonnaruwa, and restores others in the earlier Buddhist capital, Anuradhapura. But he abolishes the Abhayagiri and Jetavana monasteries and leaves the Theravada monks of the Mahavihara in control as the sole representatives of Buddhism on Sri Lanka.   **BUDD**

1154   Nicholas Breakspear (c. 1100–1159), the cardinal of Albano, is elected Pope Adrian IV and serves until 1159. Through the 20th century he is the only Englishman to serve as pope.   **CATH**

1156–
1471   The period of the Novgorodian Tradition takes place in the Orthodox Church. During this period the city of Novgorod is independent of Russian control and many elements of Russian Orthodoxy develop including religious texts, architectural form, and iconography.   **ORTHO**

1160–
1173   Rabbi Benjamin of Tudela in Spain travels across the European, Byzantine, and Islamic worlds to survey the Jewish communities. He also gathers information on Jewish communities farther east, in Asia, which he does not visit.   **JUD**

1163   In a coup d'état attempt, Japanese warlord Minomoto no Yoritomo moves the government to Kamakura and there establishes the Tsurugaoka shrine, a branch of the Iwashimizu Hachiman shrine. The spread of the leading Shinto deities throughout Japan is facilitated by branch shrines established by the venerable Inari, Kasuga, Tenjin, Konpira, Munakata, Suwa, and Izumo shrines.   **SHINTO**

1164   Uppsala is made the center of Roman Catholicism in Sweden.   **CATH**

1164   In the *Constitutions of Clarendon*, King Henry II of England seeks to reassert state control over the Church in England and limit papal authority. The archbishop of Canterbury and Henry's friend (St.) Thomas Becket (1118–1170) objects and is forced to flee to France.   **CATH**

1165   Jews in Yemen are forced to convert to Islam by Shi'a Muslims.   **JUD**

1165–1200	The monk Chinul (1158–1210) propagates the teachings of the Chogye sect of Buddhism. The Chogye sect grew out of Uich'on's efforts to fuse the doctrinal (*Kyo*) and meditative (*Son*) schools of Buddhist thought. Unlike Uich'on, however, Chinul places an emphasis on the meditative. This break from the canon did much to foster a uniquely Korean Buddhist tradition. **BUDD**
1165–1200	This is the period of Somaprabha, a Jain author of the didactic poem *Kumarapalapratibodha* (*Arousing of Kumarapala*); its subject is the conversion of King Kumarapal by Hemachandra. **JAIN**
1167–1168	The Quanzhen (or Complete Realization) movement in Daoism emerges in northeastern China. **DAO**
1170	Thomas Becket, the exiled archbishop of Canterbury, returns to England from France and with the support of the pope is prepared to resist efforts by King Henry II to maintain state control over the church. On December 29 he is murdered by four barons in Canterbury Cathedral. The murder causes outrage across Europe and forces Henry to accept the authority of the church. In 1174 Henry does penance at Becket's tomb. **CATH**
1170s	The scholar Qiu Chuji (1148–1227), a Shandong native and a disciple of Wang Zhe, becomes the second patriarch of the Quanzhen school of Daoism in China. **DAO**
1171	Pure Light Daoists in China incorporate into their practice a "ledger of merit and demerit" (this will be a Ming-era convention for monitoring one's spiritual progress; the so-called morality books will serve a similar

Quanzhen (or Complete Realization) Movement

The movement was started by the Daoist Wang Zhe (1112–1170), who took up residence in the mountains of northeastern Shandong province and established five separate congregations of what became known as the Quanzhen (or Complete Realization) movement in China. A native of Shanxi from a family of the landlord class, he failed his civil service examinations and in consequence spent many years in solitary meditation. He was so eccentric that he was sometimes known as "Crazy" Wang. Even so, his movement attracted a broad following and even gained adherents among the social elite. There was a strong syncretic element, a blend of Daoist, Confucian, and Buddhist thought, in the Quanzhen school; Wang himself advocated equal study of all Three Teachings. Ascetic practices, such as fasting, celibacy, and abstention from wine and meat, were prominent features. Purification of the soul and meditation were necessary for one's transformation into a fully realized being able to leave behind the fetters of the world. Self-discipline and self-realization rather than alchemical elixirs and magic spells were the way to salvation.

purpose) on patriotism, loyalty, and support of the state. This is an out-growth of the sage He Zhengong's emphasis on patriotism.   **DAO**

1172   Zhu Xi (Chu Hsi), a neo-Confucian philosopher, completes the *T'ung-chien kang-mu* (*Outline and Digest of the General Mirror*), a condensation of Ssu-ma Kuang's history the *Tzu-chih t'ung-chien* (*Comprehensive Mirror for Aid in Government*), intended to illustrate moral principles in government. It becomes widely used through-out eastern Asia and serves as the basis for the first comprehensive history of China published in Europe, J. A. M. Moyriac de Mailla's *Histoire generale de la Chine* (1777–1785).   **CONF**

1172–   The Muslim Almohads from North Africa displace the Muslim Almoravids
1223   as the rulers of Spain (al-Andalus) and establish their capital at Seville.
                                                                         ISLAM

1173–   The Muslim Ghurid dynasty from Afghanistan begins to conquer northern
1206   India, expanding the territory taken by the Ghaznavids in 1030.   **INDIA**

c. 1175   The Waldenses (Waldensiens or Vaudois) emerge as a Roman Catholic sect in Lyon, France. They are followers of Pierre Valdès (Peter Waldo, d. 1217), who gives up his life as a wealthy merchant to help the poor as a wander-ing preacher. The Waldenses stress spirituality and criticize materialistic Church practices, which leads to their persecution beginning in 1179. **CATH**

1175   The Japanese monk Honen (1133–1212), having finished writing his basic work, the *Senchaku-shu*, begins the preaching that will establish the Jodo (Pure Land) sect of Buddhism as a popular movement in Japan. Followers of this sect worship Amida (or Amitabha) Buddha, the "Buddha of Infinite Radiance," who promises rebirth in paradise if one will constantly chant the *nembutsu*, "homage to Amida Buddha." This is based on the Pure Land school of China (**SEE 402, BUDD**). What makes this sect so attractive to masses of Japanese is that it takes Buddhism out of the hands of the monks and schol-ars and gives it to all willing to perform its simple but pious chanting. **BUDD**

1175   Confucian scholars Zhu Xi and his southern colleague Lu Chiu-yuan con-front each other in a famous meeting at the Goose Lake Temple in China. Lu's challenge to the dominant Chu remains a minority position but later becomes a major intellectual force in Ming China (1368–1644) and Tokugawa Japan (1603–1867). Their debates curiously resemble those that affect Western nominalism during roughly the same period.   **CONF**

1175   Neo-Confucian scholar and teacher Zhu Xi (Chu Hsi) and his friend Lu Tsu-ch'ien (1137–1181) compile passages from the Ch'eng brothers and Chou Tun-i (1017–1073) and Chang Tsai (1020–1077) to form their famous anthology *Chin-ssu Lu* (*Reflections on Things at Hand*). In this year Zhu also holds a widely discussed debate with the philosopher Lu Chiu-yuan (Lu Hsiang-shan), at which neither is seen to prevail. Zhu emphasizes the value of integrity and study including book learning. Lu insists on the exclusive value of inwardness. **CONF**

1175–
1200

With the death of King Kumarapal and the Jain writer Hemachandra, Jainism begins to decline in northern India. During this time, too, in southern India, Basava founds Virasaivism, a popular Hindu/Siva cult in Karnataka and Andhra; also known as Lingayats, this *bhakti* sect flourishes under Chalukya patronage, ousting Jains from the region. But Jainism's core adherents remain loyal: they form solid communities and are often prosperous merchants, taking care of their monks, who in turn take care of their faith. **HIND, JAIN**

1176

The legal doctrine that Jews are the serfs and therefore the property of the rulers of a state first appears in Spain. **JUD**

1176–
1177

At the Battle of Legnano, the forces of the Lombard League in Italy, who are allied with the Roman Catholic Church in Rome, defeat the forces of Holy Roman Emperor Frederick I Barbarossa, who has deposed the pope and attempted to conquer the Lombard states. The defeat and the Treaty of Venice in 1177 enhance the power of the pope over political rulers. **CATH**

1177

Zhu Xi (Chu Hsi) in China completes the enormously influential commentaries on the *Lun Yu* (*Analects*) of Confucius and on *Meng Zi* (*Mencius*). **CONF**

1179

At the Third Lateran Council, the Roman Catholic Church refuses to recognize the Waldenses, a sect in France. At the council severe restrictions are placed on Jews in Europe, and they are required to live in communities or neighborhoods separate from Christians. **SEE C. 1175, CATH.** **CATH, JUD**

1179–
1181

While serving as prefect in Nan-K'ang, Zhu Xi (Chu Hsi) rehabilitates the White Deer Grotto as an academy in what is later Kiangsi Province, China. Founded in the 800s, it flourished in the 900s but had fallen into ruin. Zhu Xi restores it as an intellectual center; its prestige lasts eight centuries and with other academies provides the institutional basis for the neo-Confucian movement. It is a model among schools throughout eastern Asia. **CONF**

1180–
1185

The civil war of Japan's Taira and Minamoto warrior factions, with the Minamoto eventually emerging victorious, will shift political power to the *shogun* government located at Kamakura. The imperial court will remain in Kyoto in a purely symbolic role buttressed by Shinto ritual. The emperor will not regain political power until the Meiji restoration of 1868. **SHINTO**

1180–
1230

Denied an active role in the military regime, a group of Confucian scholars in Korea devote time to producing Korea's first sustained narratives. A notable example is *Kuk son saeng chon* (*Story of Mr. John Barleycorn*) by Yi Kyubo (1168–1241), who also writes *Tongmyong wang p'yon* (*Saga of King Tongmyong*), a verse narrative significant for its patriotic themes. **CONF**

1181– 1218	During the rule of Jayavarman VII of the Kingdom of Angkor, the capital city of Angkor Thom and its Buddhist temple of Bayon is built. Reflecting the influences of both Hinduism and Buddhism in Cambodia, the city itself is designed to represent a Hindu myth and thereby glorify the king. He is evidently a follower of Mahayana Buddhism, which becomes the new state religion, although Hindu cults are still approved. **BUDD, HIND**
1182	Maronite Christians in Lebanon, who from the seventh century have formed a Christian church separate from both the church in Rome and the Orthodox Church, are in contact with the Crusaders from Europe and submit to the authority of the pope in Rome. Over the next centuries their religious practices and beliefs are revised to be in accord with those of Roman Catholicism. **CATH, CHRIS**
1182	Anti-Jewish sentiment grows in Europe; Jews are expelled from France. **JUD**
1184	At the Council of Verone, Pope Lucius III bans the Waldenses, a sect in France, from Roman Catholicism because of unauthorized preaching. The Waldenses respond by organizing a separate religion centered in Provence in southern France. **CATH**
1185	The 14-volume *Mishnah Torah*, an encyclopedic version of the *Talmud*, is written by Moses Maimonides (Rabbi Moses ben Maimon, 1135–1204), the leading Jewish scholar of the Middle Ages. **JUD**
1185	After a series of victories against the Taira clan in Japan's ongoing civil war, the emperor offers thanks to various protective *kami* (native spirits) in the form of tribute, such as swords and an imperial decree conferring a specif-

Moses Maimonides

The single-most important figure in Jewish medieval thought, Moses Maimonides was raised in Cordova, Spain. In 1149 he was forced to flee Spain, going first to Morocco and then to Cairo, Egypt, where he became the leader of the Jewish community. His writings made important contributions to Judaism. In 1168 he finished the *Siraj*, a commentary on the *Mishnah*, and in 1180 finished the *Mishnah Torah*, which organized the Talmudic code into 14 sections by subject, with accompanying commentaries. The *Mishnah Torah* compiled Jewish law as described in the Torah with scholarly teachings and interpretations. In 1190 he wrote the *Guide to the Perplexed* to aid Jews in understanding and reconciling the conflict between faith and reason. The *Guide* incorporated knowledge gained through centuries of Jewish revelation with knowledge from the classical logic of Aristotle. Maimonides was criticized by his contemporaries, who rejected his symbolic interpretation of the Bible. They were especially upset by his questioning God's human appearance and the existence of a physical heaven and hell. His work later influenced the Catholic theologians Albertus Magnus and Thomas Aquinas.

ic rank on all the Great *Kami* in the provinces. The granting of certain ranks or positions to *kami* is a particular form of Shinto offering that indicates the mutual relation between man and *kami* as one of reciprocity. **SHINTO**

1185–
1600

The institution of the *shoen* (feudal estate) in medieval Japan reaches its height in the 12th century, as the owners of combined Shinto shrine and Buddhist temple complexes become large landholders. Within these estates they possess administrative and economic independence from government interference. They exercise taxation, judicial, and police authority over their residents, mainly peasantry. In 1230 the government will ban the establishment of any new *shoen*. **BUDD, SHINTO**

1186

In Cambodia Jayavarman VII dedicates the *Ta Prohm* (Ancestor Temple), which honors his mother in the guise of Prajenaparamita, the goddess of wisdom, conceived metaphorically as the mother of the Buddha. **BUDD**

1187–
1195

The Brahmanic legal system of Sri Lanka's King Nissankamalla (r. 1187–1197) requires for the first time that the monarch be Buddhist. It also institutes hereditary castes in Sri Lanka's ancient occupation-based caste system, under which the *Goyigama*, originally agriculturalists, become Sri Lankan elite. **BUDD**

1189

Zhu Xi (Chu Hsi), synthesizer of neo-Confucian thought, writes a major commentary on *Ta Hsueh* (*Great Learning*), a text on moral government asserting that the emperor's character is the basis for the well-being of the

Saladin

Saladin (1171–1193), or Salah al-Din, was a Kurdish Muslim warrior who began his military career in Damascus during the mid-12th century under the aegis of the Seljuk Turks. After rising through the ranks, he was sent with his uncle to establish Turkish authority in Egypt by deposing the ruling Fatimid dynasty. Their success, however, led them to create their own dynasty in Egypt rather than recognize Seljuk authority, and by 1187 Saladin even incorporated Syria in his domains. With his position now consolidated, Saladin attacked the expanding Crusader states, which had sprung up in Syria and Palestine during earlier European Crusades that sought to reassert Christian control over the Holy Land. The result was a series of major victories over the Crusaders and the reconquest by 1189 of much the lost territory. Saladin then defeated the Third Crusade under Richard the Lion-Hearted between 1189 and 1192 and forced their retreat from Palestine and Syria. Unfortunately, Saladin did not live long enough to enjoy the fruits of his victories, as he died shortly after the Third Crusaders departed. The significance of Saladin's efforts lay not only in the recapture of Jerusalem and the Holy Land, but also in the temporary revitalization of Islam in the region. At the same time, he became a model of the heroic warrior in both Muslim and Christian lore.

realm. He also writes a commentary on *Chung Yung* (*Doctrine of the Mean*). These two texts come to be accepted along with the *Lun Yu* (*Analects*) and the *Meng Zi* (*Mencius*) as the *Four Books* basic to the Confucian curriculum.   CONF

1189–
1192   The Third Crusade is launched by Pope Gregory VIII. Its goal is to retake Jerusalem from the Muslims, who had retaken it from the Christians in 1187. It is led by Holy Roman Emperor Frederick Barbarossa, Richard the Lion-Hearted of Britain, and Philip II of France. The Crusaders take Acre in 1191 but fail to capture Jerusalem. The Crusaders and Muslims agree to a truce, with safety guaranteed for Christian pilgrims to Jerusalem.   CATH

c. 1190   The Muslim sultanate of Shoa, which unites several local tribes, is established by Muslim merchants near Harar in Ethiopia.   ISLAM

1190   Under pressure from Buddhists, the Jin dynasty in north China formally proscribes the Quanzhen school of Daoism. The ban has little or no effect. In fact, as the Jin faces a mounting threat from Inner Asia and instability spreads, Quanzhen Daoism gains an even wider following.   DAO

1190   The Muslims under Saladin retake Jerusalem from the Christians, and they allow Jews to settle there again.   ISLAM, JUD

1191   Eisai (1141–1215), a Japanese Buddhist monk, returns from four years study in China and starts to teach Zen Buddhism in Japan. (*Zen* is the Japanese pronunciation of the Chinese *Chan*: SEE C. 500–535, BUDD). He does not set out to found a new sect but simply preaches that the principles of China's Chan sect underlie true Buddhism; these include not only stressing seated meditation (*zazen*) but also introducing the Buddhist tea ritual.   BUDD

1191   Khmer forces capture the capital of the Cham Kingdom to their east. Also in this year, the Preah Khan (Sacred Sword) temple is dedicated; the shrine contains a carved portrait of Jayavarman's father that shows traits of the Buddha.   BUDD

1191   The Jin dynasty in north China restricts the activities of the popular Taiyi (Grand Unity) and Hunyuan Daoist sects. Daoists are forbidden to communicate with higher-level officials.   DAO

1193   Dusum Chempa (1110–1193), the first head of the Karmapa (Black Hat) sect of Kagyu Buddhism in Tibet, dies. The Karmapas are one of the first orders to identify their head lamas by means of reincarnation.   BUDD

1195   After its destruction in the Gempei War, the Todaiji palace is rebuilt in Nara by the Buddhist Amidist priest Chogen in Daibutsu (Great Buddha) style. Works for its Great Buddha Hall are produced by the family of gifted sculptors in Nara known as the Kei school.   BUDD

1195 *The Guide for the Perplexed* is written by Moses Maimonides. It provides a guide to the philosophical bases of Judaism for many Jews in Europe. **JUD**

1197 The Ghurid Muslims' sack of the great Buddhist university of Nalanda and then of the university of Vikramasila (1203) helps seal the end of Buddhism in India. But the end is not brought about solely by the policies of the Muslims, not even by their destruction of Buddhist monasteries and libraries. Buddhism has been on the decline in India for several centuries, in part because of its gradual assimilation into Hinduism but also because of the growth of popular *bhakti* (devotional) sects, which make the Buddhist monastic institutions appear isolated and expensive, and also because of the decline of royal patronage on which monastic Buddhism depends. By the 1200s most Buddhist monks from northern India are dispersing to Tibet, Nepal, and southern India. **BUDD, ISLAM**

1198–
1216 Innocent III (1160–1216) is pope of the Roman Catholic Church. During his rule the church reaches it maximum control over the political rulers of Europe and is able to remove and select rulers. **CATH**

1199 Eisai, a Japanese Buddhist monk, who started to teach Zen Buddhism in Japan in 1191 moves from the Buddhist monastery at Kyoto and establishes his new Zen-based monastery at Kamakura; there he plants seeds from China on the temple grounds. Eisai teaches the Lin Ji branch of Chan Buddhism. In Japan it becomes known as Rinzai and among its special characteristics is meditation on insoluble riddles (*koans*). In 1202 Eisai is awarded the title of Dai Sojo, the highest religious rank in Japan. As more masters arrive to teach Zen, it spreads to courtiers, samurai, and even to commoners. With its advocacy of meditation and self-discipline as the path to enlightenment, Zen appeals to the warrior class and becomes the favored religion of shogunate. **BUDD**

c. 1200 By the end of the 12th century in Europe, reforms in the Catholic Church and its monasteries create a heightened spirituality among lay people. As a result, many loosely organized groups develop among lay people who do not have the connections or the wealth to enter the monastic life. Some groups are dedicated to doing good works or penance, to honoring saints or the Virgin Mary, or to following a life of poverty and mystical contemplation. **CATH**

c. 1200 The Beguines, a sisterhood of lay women, emerges in Flanders, the Netherlands, and Germany. The Beguines are groups of women who seek a communal life less rigid than that found in monasticism. Beguines do work such as embroidery or sewing, healing the sick, and teaching school. Mechtild of Magdeburg (1210–1280), a Beguine and later member of the Helfta convent, becomes an important voice in medieval mysticism. **CATH**

c. 1200 *Gesta Danorum* (*The Deeds of the Danes*) is written in Denmark by Saxo Grammaticus (?–c. 1220). Presented as a history, it actually recounts tales about Danish heroes and gods and myths. **CIVIL**

c. 1200   The Lingayat or the Virashaiva sect of Shaiva Hinduism emerges in south-
           ern India. It is a popular form of Hinduism in which the local language is
           used in place of Sanskrit and the rigid social hierarchy of Hinduism is soft-
           ened to allow for greater participation by all people. The sect takes its name
           from the *istalinga*, or symbol of Shiva, the Hindu god, which followers wear
           around their necks.   **HIND**

c. 1200   Kabbalah, the Jewish mystical movement, begins in France and spreads to
           Spain. Kabbalists believe that every word, letter, and number in the Bible can
           reveal mysteries. Kabbalah enjoys a revival in the late 20th century, especial-
           ly within Reform Judaism and in association with New Age groups.   **JUD**

c. 1200   The city of Cahokia in southwestern Illinois is the seat of the Native
           American Mississippian culture tradition. At this time it reaches its height
           with about 10,000 inhabitants and over 100 earth mounds with temples or
           homes for the wealthy and powerful on top.   **NATIV**

The Beguines and Beghards

In Flanders, the Netherlands, and Germany, groups of women and men organized
semireligious communities in their search for a communal life less rigid than monasticism. The women, known as Beguines, took no vows, owned property, and joined
and left the community as they pleased. Beguines promised to be celibate while in
the community. Less common than the Beguines, groups of men called Beghards
abstained from owning property as well. Beguine communities helped the sick and
poor while leading lives of contemplation. There were few leaders or rules that the
women followed. New members were taught by older ones and required to live with
others until they had been in the community for six years. Afterward they lived in separate houses, assuming they were at least 30 years old, and gathered as a community
for prayer. Beguines did simple work like embroidery or sewing, healing the sick, and
teaching school, while the Beghards were known for their weaving. Both communities sought the soul's mystical union with God. Mechtild of Magdeburg (1210–1280),
a Beguine and later member of the Helfta convent, became an important voice in
medieval mysticism. The Beguines enjoyed papal support in the early 13th century
and the group expanded accordingly, yet they were targets of suspicion by their neighbors. In addition, they had close ties with Dominican and Franciscan communities,
which exacerbated difficulties with local clergy, since the Beguines were officially
under the rule of the local priest. As a result, these groups were often subject to dis-
criminatory local laws. In 1233 formal laws were passed against the Beguines, and in
the 1300s, the group was banned outright in a decree by the Council of Vienna. Local
rulers were given wide flexibility in enforcing the decree, however, which resulted in
considerable variation in local response. Despite the decree and some resulting
heresy trials, the Beguines ended up often enjoying more legal protection then ever.

1200

1200   In Japan Buddhists and the government join to request suppression of the Pure Land movement, and the shogunate orders the expulsion of all sect priests.   **BUDD**

1200   The Cistercian monastic order that began to expand in 1113 has become the major Catholic order in Europe, with some 525 monasteries across the continent.   **CATH**

1200   Zhu Xi (Chu Hsi), considered the chief Confucian scholar in Song dynasty China, dies. He is known for combining reading, meditation, ritual, exercise, arithmetic, calligraphy, and observation into humanist education.   **CONF**

1200s   In Sri Lanka the *Culavansa* (*Lesser Genealogy*) is compiled. It is a continuation of the *Mahavansa* attributed to the Buddhist monk Dhammakitti and completed by others through the 18th century. Scholars in the 20th century regard these chronicles as an unrivaled source of information about ancient and medieval southern Asian history.   **BUDD**

1200s   By this time Buddhism is firmly entrenched in Tibet as monastic rule. During this century Tibetan translations of the 4,569 works of the Buddhist canon are completed.   **BUDD**

1200s   Scholasticism, a Christian philosophical movement, flourishes in western Europe. The movement seeks to establish a logical foundation for religious revelation. Scholasticism focuses on proving that existing beliefs are true. Scholastics want to know what is truth and reality and how people come to know this reality. They are also concerned with how to balance faith and reason. The work of Scholastic philosophers is set forth in *Summae*, summations of what is known. Two main branches of thinking evolve under Scholasticism. The first is the Platonic/mystical tradition represented by the earlier work of Augustine and embraced by Bernard of Clairvaux and the Franciscans. The second is the intellectual and humanist current of Aristotle as embraced by Abelard, the Dominicans, and Aquinas.   **CATH**

1200s   The papacy's involvement in religious affairs that previously had been the province of bishops and in worldly affairs increases dramatically. Popes like Gregory IX (1227–1241) and Innocent IV (1243–1254) use their power to make the church a wealthy institution. By the century's end papal involvement in politics, finances, and the law begins to erode the public trust in the spiritual authority of the Catholic Church hierarchy.   **CATH**

1200s   This is the period of the major Digambara/Jain dramatist, Hastimalla, who lives in southern India, and also of Asadhara, a major Digambara scholar and poet; it is also the period when the Svetambara/Jain school of *Tapa-gaccha* emerges.   **JAIN**

| 1200–
1235 | In Bhutan Drukpa Kagyupa, a Red Hat order of Tibetan Buddhism, is introduced by Tibetan lama Phajo Drugom Shigpo, one of numerous monks fleeing the domination of the Gelugpa (Yellow Hat) sect in Tibet. Drukpa Kagyu is to become the dominant form of Buddhism and state religion in Bhutan. **BUDD, TOL** |

| 1200–
1600 | Hindu poets who come to be recognized as saints write about and spread the message of Hindu devotionalism throughout north and west India. Their poems are written in the regional languages and encourage the development of regional and local forms of Hinduism. Some of the major poet/saints are Jnamdev, Namdev, Eknath, Tukaram, Tulsidas, Mirabai, Chamar, Chandidas, and Chaiyanya. **HIND** |

| 1201–
1204 | The Fourth Crusade is initiated by Pope Innocent IV with the goal of retaking Jerusalem from the Muslims. The Crusade fails and instead the Crusaders sack Constantinople (the Byzantine capital) in 1203 and place a European, Baldwin I of Flanders, on the throne. The sacking severely weakens the Byzantine Empire, which is already facing assaults by the Turks from the east and creates a deep schism between the Eastern and Western churches that lasts into the 1960s. **CATH** |

| 1204 | In Japan major Buddhist temples unsuccessfully petition the imperial court to ban Honen's teaching of exclusive *nembutsu* (invocation of sacred name of Amida Buddha) as they fear that his doctrines undermine their own position. SEE **1175, BUDD**. **BUDD** |

| 1206–
1526 | The Muslim Delhi sultanates founded by Muslims from Afghanistan rule over northern India. The rulers are either Turks or Afghans who compete for power in the region. By 1335 Muslim rule is extended across almost the entire subcontinent. During this period many Hindus are converted to Islam and there is a mixing of Muslim and Hindu culture producing a society in northern India that reflects both traditions. **ISLAM** |

| 1208–
1229 | Members of the Albigensians, a sect that opposes Roman Catholicism, murder papal representative Peter of Castelnau, and the church initiates the Albigensian Wars to destroy the sect. **CATH** |

| 1209 | Pope Innocent III initiates a Crusade to destroy the Waldenses, a Roman Catholic sect banned by the church in 1184. Although 80 members are burned in 1211, the Crusade fails and the Waldeneses survive in Germany, Spain, and northern Italy. **CATH** |

| 1209 | Hsu Heng (1209–1281), president of the Imperial Academy under Kublai Khan, is born. He introduces Zhu Xi's Confucian teaching to the Mongol court and personally educates sons of the Mongol nobility to become teachers of Confucian classics. **CONF** |

1209– 1224	The Daoist interior alchemist Bo Yuchan (1194–1229), a grand master of the thunder ritual, enjoys a period of wide influence in Southern Song China. Wisdom and enlightenment, he argues, come from the cultivation of human nature and spirit. Bo and his followers are part of what is known as the Southern School of Quanzhen (Complete Realization) Daoism. **DAO**
1210	In an effort to control the teaching of Greek philosophy, a council of bishops in Paris rules that the works of Aristotle may not be taught at the University of Paris. The decision is supported by the pope in 1215 but is never fully enforced. **CATH**
1210– 1234	In Myanmar these years mark the reign of Nadaungmya, last of the kings of the expansionist era during which temple building and lavish patronage of the *sangha*, the monastic community, flourishes. **BUDD**
1212	In China Kamo no Chomei completes his masterpiece the *Hojoki* (*An Account of My Ten Foot Square Hut*). The work describes how he lost his career and fortune to disasters, took Buddhist vows, and retired to a contemplative life of mountain solitude to seek rebirth in the Pure Land of Amida sect of Buddhism. **BUDD**
1212	(St.) Clare of Assisi (1194–1253), a daughter of French nobility, flees her parents' home to join St. Francis at the Porziuncola Chapel. There, she establishes the first Franciscan convent and founds the Second Order of St. Francis, also known as the Poor Clares. She recruits women dedicated to a life of poverty and labor, and the nuns gain a reputation for their work helping the poor and sick. **CATH**
1212	The Brethren and Sisters of the Free Spirit emerge in Augsburg, Germany, and spread along the Rhine River valley. This group is independent of the Catholic Church and is composed of independent mystics. The members believe that humans can achieve perfection and freedom from sin in earthly life. By living in poverty and in total meditation with the Divine, they seek to merge with the spirit of God, a practice at odds with the Catholic Church's teachings of man's separateness from God. **CHRIS**
1212	The Muslim Almohad rulers of Spain are defeated by a Christian force at Las Navas de Tolosa and their rule ends 11 years later as Muslim Spain disintegrates into a number of autonomous Muslim states. **ISLAM**
1213	The spread of Jews across Europe continues and Jews are now living in Switzerland. **JUD**
1213– 1214	In the continuing battle between the popes and political rulers in Europe for political power, Pope Innocent III deposes Otto and replaces him with Frederick II of Sicily as the Holy Roman Emperor. Through the Golden Bull of Eger, Frederick grants the pope much political power over the empire. At the Battle of Bouvines, Frederick defeats Otto and retains power with the

support of the Church. The pope also asserts Church authority in conflicts with King John of England and Philip Augustus of France. **CATH**

1215 The concept of transubstantiation is adopted into church law at the Fourth Lateran Council. For Catholic church-goers in Medieval Europe, the Mass has become a form of miracle during which worshipers experience Christ in their presence. As this reverence increases religious authorities seek to restrict who can be given the wine and wafer and later in the century only the bread is given to commoners. **CATH**

1215 At the Fourth Lateran Council, Pope Innocent III decrees that penance will be enforced by canon (church) law. Excommunication, in which the sinner is cut off from the Church and thus from any hope of salvation, awaits those who refuse to confess or do penance. In this way the Church tightens its control over its congregations. **CATH**

1215 The Fourth Lateran Council places more restrictions on Jews, including the requirement that they wear distinctive clothing or badges to identify them as Jews. Distinctive clothing for Jews in Europe includes special hats and colored circles or Jewish (six-pointed) stars on their cloaks. Prohibitions are also placed on doing business with Jews. **JUD**

1215 In Japan it is reported that the practitioners of Shinto worship some 36,000 different *kami* (native spirits). **SHINTO**

1216 St. Clare beomes abbess of the convent of San Damiano, below the town of Assisi. The Poor Clares, the order she founds in 1212, are accepted by the Catholic Church in 1228. **CATH**

1216 The Dominican order is founded. Both men's and women's branches proliferate in medieval towns and cities, and a few years after its founding the order numbers 60 monasteries. The order's original purpose is to search out nonbelievers and bring them back to the Church. **CATH**

1219 During the Fifth Crusade European Crusaders have some success against the Muslims in North Africa but fail to cross Egypt and take Jerusalem. They also capture the cities of Toulouse and Languedoc in southern France, strongholds of resistance by the heretical Albigensians to the Roman Catholic Church. **CATH**

1219 The Mongol leader Genghis Khan sends an envoy into China to summon the Daoist master Qiu Chuji, the second patriarch of the Quanzhen school, to his court in the Hindu Kush in central Asia. **DAO**

1219 The Serbian Orthodox Church is founded by Archbishop Sava (c. 1175–1233), the son of Stephan Nemanja, the ruler of Serbia. Sava chooses to affiliate his church with the Orthodox Church in Constantinople, rather than with the Catholic Church in Rome. **ORTHO**

1220   *Gukansho* (*Notes on Foolish Views*), an early interpretative history of Japan, is written by Buddhist priest Jien (1155–1225) as partial justification for the Fujiwara regency.   **BUDD**

1220   The Beghards, a brotherhood of laymen and the equivalent of the female Beguines, emerge in the Netherlands, and communities form in Italy, Germany, and France as well. The Beghards do work such as weaving and assisting the poor and sick and abstain from owning property.   **CHRIS**

c. 1220–
1320   During this period the Jain scholar and poet Asadhara writes his major work, the *Dharmamrta*, which deals with the duties of both ascetic monks and lay followers.   **JAIN**

1222   The Daoist Qiu Chuji reaches the mountain court of the Mongol chieftain Genghis Khan. Over a period of several months, Qiu has a series of interviews with Genghis and manages to obtain a grant of immunity for Daoists and special treatment for Daoist clergy in China. His diplomacy is credited with saving 2 million–3 million Chinese lives.   **DAO**

1223   Pope Gregory IX of the Roman Catholic Church assigns the Dominicans the responsibility of converting the remaining Albigensians (many had been killed in the Albigensian Wars earlier in the century) to Catholicism. By the following century the sect has disappeared.   **CATH**

1223   Genghis Khan appoints the Quanzhen patriarch Qiu Chuji supervisor of all Daoist clergy in China.   **DAO**

1224   Shinran (1173–1262), the disciple of Honen, who established the Pure Land sect of Buddhism in Japan **(SEE 1175, BUDD)**, completes the first version of the *Kyogyoshinsho*, marking the beginning of the Jodo Shinshu (True Pure Land) sect of Buddhism. Shinran goes even further than Honen and claims neither morality nor good works play any role in achieving nirvana, that it is achievable only by a total focus on Amida Buddha.   **BUDD**

1224   According to Dao tradition, the Sichuan saint Xu Sun appears at a temple on West Mountain. The appearance leads to a resurgence of the filial piety cult that flourished in the fourth century and the building of new sanctuaries for the cult. Virtually all forms and schools of Daoism are practiced in harmony on West Mountain; there is little evidence of rivalry or conflict among the sects that flourish there. Xu Sun's is a lively cult with a broad popular following. On his birthday, devotees carry torches around their fields to assure a good harvest. They make offerings and prayers to Xu to banish crop-damaging pests. Processions with images of Xu wind through the villages under his protection. A temple ritual exorcises tigers and other dangerous beasts.   **DAO**

1225   The Franciscans are founded by followers of St. Francis of Assisi (1181–1226), who inspires Christians by his dedication to imitating the life of Christ. Franciscans renounce the body and the world to live a life of poverty and humility. Their asceticism spreads rapidly throughout Europe. In their rejection of the world, Franciscans follow the tradition of the wandering holy man that is prevalent in Orthodox lands to the east. Franciscans travel from town to town doing physical work in return for their meals and preaching to peasants and townspeople.   **CATH**

1225–
1400

In Vietnam Tran Thu Do marries his nephew to the Ly emperor's daughter and controls the throne to establish the Tran dynasty. The Tran rulers effect various domestic reforms and projects, but they also spend much of their energies attacking Champa. During the Tran dynasty Confucianism comes to rival Buddhism as a major guiding philosophy of life, at least among upper-class Vietnamese. The Tran dynasty comes to an end in 1400 as the major minister Ho Quy Ly seizes power after intermarrying his family with the Tran.   **BUDD, CONF**

1226

(St.) Antony of Padua (1195–1231) is permitted by Pope Gregory IX to curtail his official duties in Rome and resume his preaching. He attracts many listeners near Padua, Portugal, a phenomenon that develops into a cult after his death in 1231. His shrine is a sacred place associated with miracles, and he is made the patron saint of Portugal and a Doctor of the Church.   **CATH**

Francis of Assisi

Francis of Assisi (1181–1226) was loved by medieval Europeans for his simple, sincere faith, his love of nature, and his lack of pride. By living a Christian life, he inspired reforms within the Church. The son of a wealthy Italian cloth merchant, Francis as a young man threw lavish parties and yearned for adventure and fame. In 1202 Francis joined the military and was imprisoned for a year. A lengthy illness followed his release, during which he grew dissatisfied with his rich lifestyle but didn't know what to replace it with. Slowly he turned to prayer, alienated his family and friends, and befriended the poor. During a pilgrimage to Rome he exchanged clothes with a beggar; upon his return he sold a shipment of his father's cloth and gave away the money, for which he was publicly disowned by his father in front of the bishop of Assisi. Francis responded by taking off all his clothes and giving them to his startled parent. Francis then pursued a life spent ministering to lepers. In 1208 he dedicated his life to poverty and to saving souls. His daily life was one of begging only enough for each day and working only to serve others, rather than to acquire money. Francis soon developed a following, which became the Franciscan order in 1209. Francis's poverty and preaching brought him respect and increasing political influence. His humble life stood in criticism of the Catholic Church's huge wealth and of materialism in general and inspired people to demand church reforms. Francis also won followers among the poor and uneducated because he treated them with the same consideration as he did the wealthy. Indeed, unlike the ascetics, he glorified God's natural creation and is perhaps best remembered for preaching to the birds and wolves.

1227	Buddhist scholar Eisai's student Dogen (1200–1253) brings the Soto sect of Zen Buddhism from China to Japan. The sect is notable for promoting complete equality of the sexes. **BUDD**

1227   Pope Gregory IX excommunicates Emperor Frederick II, who is seen as a threat to church authority in Italy.   **CATH**

1228   The tale of the Wandering Jew appears in the *Flores Historiarum* by Roger of Wendover in England. The image of the Jew as one who is forced to wander for having ignored Christ on his way to the cross becomes a major theme of European anti-Semitism into the 20th century.   **JUD**

1228–1574   The Hafsid dynasty rules in Tunisia. Although its political control is at times weak, the dynasty encourages a revitalization of Islam in the region, aided by the knowledge of Muslims from Spain, Sufi teachers, and religious scholars; building mosques, and opening schools. During Hafsid rule, Sufism emerges as a major force in Tunisian society.   **ISLAM**

1229   During the Sixth Crusade Holy Roman Emperor Frederick II succeeds in taking political control of Jerusalem through negotiations with the Muslims. Although already excommunicated by Pope Gregory IX because of his slowness in mounting the Crusade, Frederick has himself installed as king of Jerusalem. Jerusalem is retaken by the Muslims in 1244.   **CATH**

1229   The Daoist Quanzhen patriarch Li Zhichang in China explains the *Dao De Jing*, the basic text of Daoism, to the Mongol crown prince Mongke, an older brother of Kublai Khan, the future founder of the Yuan dynasty.   **DAO**

1230   Averroism, the philosophy of the Muslim philosopher Ibn Rushd (1126–1198), called Averroes in Europe, gains the attention of Christian and Jewish theologians. Averroism causes much controversy. Ibn Rushd argues for a universal soul, denies individual immortality, and suggests the existence of two separate systems of truth: scientific truth based on logic and religious truth based on revelation. **SEE 1270, CATH.**   **CHRIS**

1230   A new synagogue is built by the Jewish community in Prague, on the site of an older one. In 1998 it is the oldest synagogue in continuous use in Europe.   **JUD**

1230–1255   During the reign of Sunjata, Mali becomes the dominant state in West Africa through the conquest and unification of chiefdoms in the region. Mali becomes the leading Muslim state in West Africa, with Islam brought to Mali through contact with Berbers in North Africa.   **ISLAM**

1231   The Dominicans are put in charge of the Catholic Inquisition. They take over what becomes the Catholic Church's disciplinary arm and become associated with the torture and extermination of nonbelievers. Important Dominicans include Thomas Aquinas (c. 1225–1274), the great theologian, and Albertus Magnus, the philosopher (c. 1200–1280).   **CATH**

1231   The *Reconquista* of southern Spain by Christian Europeans begins. Cordova
        falls in 1236 and Seville in 1248 as Muslim rule declines.   **CHRIS, ISLAM**

1232   Laws issued under Japan's shogun Minamoto Yoritomo are codified as the
        Joei Formulary Laws. The first article covers the upkeep and ceremonies of
        Shinto shrines, and the land tenure regulations continue to afford special
        privileges to Shinto shrine and Buddhist temple landholdings.   **SHINTO**

1232–   In Korea Ch'oe U rejects the Mongol peace proposal and moves the Koryo
1270   court to Kanghwa Island, where it remains severed from contact with its
        ostensible subjects. War with the Mongols continues. While the court
        remains in residence on the well-fortified Kanghwa Island, peasants con-
        tinue to resist the Mongols on the peninsula, often meeting with devastat-
        ing losses. Between c. 1235 and 1250 the court, seeking Buddha's aid in the
        struggle against the Mongols, commissions woodblocks on Kanghwa Island
        for a second Buddhist Tripitaka. This work, commonly known as the *Koryo
        Tripitaka*, takes 16 years to finish, and is recognized as the finest of the east
        Asian editions of the Tripitaka.   **BUDD**

1233   The Statute of Jewry is enacted in Great Britain. It places controls on Jewish
        businesses and commands loyalty to the king.   **JUD**

1233–   Mongols invade China and capture the Jin capital of Kaifeng in the north of
1260   China. They depose the Jin dynasty and threaten the Southern Song
        dynasty. In 1233 they honor Confucius and rebuild his temple in Beijing
        (Peking), a year before their conquest of Juchen.   **CONF**

1235   Robert Grosseteste (1175–1253), the English Catholic theologian and reformer,
        is elected bishop of Lincoln. He seeks to rid the church of corruption by
        removing abbots and priests in his diocese who ignore their religious duties,
        and on a trip to Rome publicly criticizes the church and the pope for the prac-
        tice of appointing wealthy Italians to English posts.   **CATH**

1235   Sufi Muslim Khaja Mu'in Al-Din Chishti dies. During his life he establishes
        the Chishti Sufi order in India, which becomes well known for its unique
        musical performances.   **ISLAM**

1235   The Orthodox patriarchy in Bulgaria, which was repressed by the Byzantine
        Empire in 1018, is restored and retains autonomy until 1393, when it
        comes under rule of the Ottoman Turks and is repressed until 1870. **ORTHO**

1236   The doctrine that Jews are serfs and therefore the property of their rulers is
        extended to the entire Holy Roman Empire by Emperor Frederick II. During
        this time the secular and church rulers compete for the control of the Jews
        and contradictory policies are enacted. Frederick II condemns the blood
        libel as untrue, Pope Gregory IX condemns harsh treatment of the Jews and
        also orders the confiscation of Jewish religious texts, and James I of Aragon
        gives protection to them.   **CATH, JUD**

1236	Mongols and Turks from central Asia, who later come to be called the Golden Horde, conquer parts of Russia and then extend their rule over a large territory in Russia, eastern Europe, and western Asia. Over time, the Mongols and Turks mix with the conquered populations and they convert to Islam. ISLAM
1237	The emerging nomadic Mongol empire, already occupying a large part of northern China, reinstitutes a civil service examination and claims that it is a Confucian state like the Nan Sung, who, however, regard the Mongol Confucianism as spurious. CONF
1239	Ke Da in China receives the title of the 35th Daoist celestial master. DAO
1240	The first public debate concerning Judaism and Christianity takes place when Rabbi Yehiel of Paris defends Judaism against the charges made by Pope Gregory IX in 1236. CATH, JUD
1240	A school for Muslim students from the Kanuri state in west central Africa is founded in Cairo, marking the acceptance of Islam by the rulers of the Kanuri state. ISLAM
1240	With the balance of political power shifting to Russia, the center of the Russian Orthodox Church moves from Kiev to Moscow. ORTHO
1242	(St.) Albertus Magnus (c. 1200–1280), the medieval Catholic theologian, becomes chair of theology at the University of Paris. In his thinking and writings, he seeks to merge Christian tradition with Aristotelian logic, a task later finished by his pupil, Thomas Aquinas. In 1931 he is canonized by Pope Pius XI and also made a Doctor of the Church and the patron saint of the natural sciences, scholars, and students. CATH
1242	As anti-Semitism continues to spread in western Europe, some 20,000 Jewish texts including the Talmud are burned in Paris. JUD
1242–1243	The Seljuk Empire in Anatolia is defeated by the Mongols, who have invaded the region from central Asia. The demise of the Seljuks empowers a number of smaller states in eastern Anatolia. ISLAM
1243	The religious basis of anti-Semitism continues to expand in Europe, when Jews are accused for the first time in Germany of desecrating the Host. JUD
c. 1243–1295	In Cambodia during the reign of Jayavarman VIII, there is some evidence of a resurgence of Hinduism and a number of Buddhist temples are defaced. BUDD, HIND
1244	The *Xuandu Baozang*, a new, more complete Daoist canon in 7,800 scrolls, is compiled in China to replace one destroyed in the Mongol invasion. DAO

1244	The Mevlevi Sufi order is founded by Muslim religious scholar Jalal al-Din Rumi (?–1273) in Turkey. The order stresses dance and music and is known as the Whirling Dervishes in the Western world. **ISLAM**

1249	During the Seventh Crusade European Crusaders have some success against the Muslims in North Africa but fail to cross Egypt and take Jerusalem. **CATH**

1249–1293	This is the lifespan of Liu Yin, the Chinese Confucian hermit scholar. He reportedly refuses Kublai Khan's summons, believing that education is for self-realization. He emphasizes both the learning of the mind and the investigation of things. **CONF**

1249–1333	Lifespan of Wu Chang, contemporary of Liu Yin. He further develops the Confucian learning of the mind, seeking to harmonize the views of Zhu Xi (Chu Hsi) and Lu Chiu-yuan. He reorients Zhu's balanced approach to morality to include Lu's existential emphasis on self-knowledge. This paves the way for a revival of Lu's learning of the mind in the Ming dynasty (1368–1644). **CONF**

c. 1250	By this time in Myanmar, the Buddhist *sangha* (religious community, the organization of monks) is at the center of a cultural "golden age" during which monumental art, scholarly literature, and poetry flourish under generous state patronage. The toll of such patronage on the state's economy contributes to the weakening of the empire, which falls to Mongol invasion, and is followed by two centuries of fragmentation under the warring rulers of the various states. **BUDD**

c. 1250	The Bible, or at least portions of it, are translated into vernacular Italian for the first time. Another two centuries will pass before the entire Bible is translated. **CATH**

c. 1250	Following the translation of astrological texts from Greek and Arabic into Latin in the preceding centuries, astrology as a system of belief gains greater acceptance in Christian Europe, and some leading scholars, such as Roger Bacon, Albertus Magnus, and Thomas Aquinas, accept the validity of astrological predictions. At the same time, astrology is criticized by many leaders of the Church as anti-Christian. **SPIR**

1250	Muslim rule in Spain is nearly over with only Granada still under Muslim rule, although it pays tribute to Castile. Between 1236 and 1250 Spanish and Portuguese forces had taken all other major Muslim centers such as Seville and Cordova from the Muslims. **CATH, ISLAM**

1250s	In a further attempt to control churchgoers, Catholic authorities exclude monks, nuns, and priests, along with the commoners who were excluded earlier, from drinking the wine as part of the Eucharist. **CATH**

| 1250–1265 | Mechtild of Magdeburg (1210–1280), the German mystic, records a series of her visions under the direction of her confessor, called the *Flowing Light of the Godhead*. Her work represents a dialogue between the soul and Jesus, its beloved, described in almost physical terms. **CATH** |

| c. 1250–c. 1350 | Neo-Confucianism is introduced to Japan from China after the death of Zhu Xi (Japanese Shushi) and is combined with Zen Buddhism. **CONF, BUDD** |

| 1250–1517 | The Mamluks (Turks who had been converted to Islam and trained as soldiers) seize power from the Ayyubid dynasty and establish control over Egypt and Syria. **ISLAM** |

| 1251–1252 | The Mongols invade and conquer Tibet (1252). Kublai Khan is converted to Lamaism by the abbot of the Sakya lamasary, who is installed as the first priest/king of Tibet. **MISC** |

| 1253 | This is the traditional date for the founding of Japan's Nichiren Buddhism sect. In 1243 the Japanese Buddhist monk Nichiren (1222–1282) arrives at the Tendai Buddhist center at Mt. Hiei **(SEE 804–805, BUDD).** He studies here for 10 years and comes to decide that the Lotus Sutra, the early Indian Mahayana text, is the foundation of true Buddhism. He sets forth on his ministry, preaching not only that all other forms of Buddhism are false but also that Japan's religious, governmental, and social arrangements are corrupt. **BUDD** |

| 1253 | Jews are the target of economic and religious repression in France and England. **JUD** |

| 1255 | Buddhists step up attacks on Quanzhen Daoism and defeat the Daoists in a doctrinal debate at the Mongol court of Kublai Khan in north China. **BUDD, DAO** |

Mechtild of Magdeburg

Mechtild of Magdeburg came from an aristocratic Saxon family, which she left to join the Beguines, a spiritual community of women where she led a life of prayer and humility. Between 1250 and 1265 she recorded a series of visions under the direction of her confessor, called the *Flowing Light of the Godhead*. With roots in the medieval tradition of courtly love, her work represented a dialogue between the soul and Jesus, its beloved, described in almost physical terms. In 1270 she joined the Helfta convent, where her strong, poetic writing and visions of the Sacred Heart became greatly popular. The visions of St. Gertrude the Great and Mechtild of Magdeburg strongly influenced other nuns at Helfta, including the abbess, Gertrude of Hackenborn, and her sister Mechtild. Mechtild of Hackenborn went on to write the *Book of Special Grace*, in devotion to the Sacred Heart.

1256   *The Picatrix*, a compilation of ancient astrology, magic, and superstition written in Arabic, is translated into Spanish. In the 15th century it is translated into Latin and becomes a source both for those who support magic and astrology and those who condemn it.   **SPIR**

1256–   The Mongol Il-Khanids rule in Iran from their capital of Tabriz. At first
1295   Islam is repressed, but then the Mongol rulers convert to Islam and initiate a cultural and religious revival in the region.   **ISLAM**

1257   Khan Berke (?– 1267), a Mongol who has converted to Islam, becomes the first Muslim ruler of the Golden Horde from central Asia.   **ISLAM**

1257–   Conflict between Daoists and Buddhists in north China escalates into warfare.
1258   Temples and monasteries are destroyed.   **BUDD, DAO**

1258   Kublai Khan in north China convenes a conference of 300 Buddhists, 200 Daoists, and 200 Confucian mediators to debate issues of religious disagreement. Daoists argue that Laozi left China for the western regions and transformed himself into the Buddha, using the coarser Buddhist creed to appeal to the less sophisticated people of India. One of the sources they cite is the third-century scholar Wang Fu's *Laozi Huahujing* (*Conversion of the Barbarians*). Buddhists challenge the authenticity of this text. When the Daoists fail to perform certain magical feats on request, Kublai sides with the Buddhists and judges them to have won the debate. He orders copies of "spurious" Daoist works burned and confiscated property returned to Buddhist owners. More than 230 Daoist monasteries in China are turned over to Buddhists.   **BUDD, DAO**

1258   The rule of the Abbasid dynasty over the Muslim Empire ends when Mongol armies from central Asia led by Hulega take Baghdad and kill all Abbasids they can find.   **ISLAM**

1259   In Italy thousands of people prepare themselves for the end of the world by carrying crosses while marching, singing, and whipping themselves in the streets. They are reacting to a prediction made by Italian Catholic mystic Joachim of Flora (c. 1132–1202) that the current world would end in 1260.
                                                                                                        CATH

1260s   The Mongol Kublai Khan, seeking to establish order in conquered China, cultivates good relations with Confucians, Buddhists, and Daoists. He arranges for a leading master to instruct his son and heir in Daoist mysteries. His court provides funds for the construction of Daoist temples and extends privileges and exemptions to Daoists. Adepts perform sacrifices and ceremonies associated with Daoist cults at Khan's court.   **DAO**

1260–   Following the vigorous evolution of Ryobu (Double Aspect) Shinto in
1333   Japan during the previous half century, the sect's apocryphal scriptures (orally transmitted in secret for some three centuries) are written down as

Tenchi reiki ki (*Notes on the Numinous Energy of Heaven and Earth*). As Ryobu Shinto becomes the dominant form of syncretic Shinto at the height of the medieval era, joint Shinto-Buddhist sanctuaries are set up, to be served by an amalgamated priesthood. **BUDD, SHINTO**

1261

Nichiren, the Japanese Buddhist founder of the Nichiren Buddhism sect, is exiled by the authorities and is exiled again in 1271 to remote regions of Japan, eventually spending the final years of his life with a few followers on the slopes of Mount Fuji and predicting the downfall of a degenerate Japan. The Buddhism that his followers continue stresses the repetition of a chant in praise of the *Lotus Sutra*. Shortly after Nichiren's death, one of his followers, the monk Nikko, forms a sect that is known as Nichiren Shoshu; it claims that Nichiren himself was the Buddha of the present era. Nichiren Shoshu remains a relatively small sect until after World War II, when largely due to the efforts of the Soka Gakkai it becomes the largest Buddhist sect in Japan. **SEE 1930, BUDD.** **BUDD, TOL**

1263

The Urbanists, an offshoot of the Poor Clares Catholic order established in 1215, are given a special dispensation by Pope Urban IV which allows them to own land, while other Poor Clare orders maintain total poverty. **CATH**

Thomas Aquinas

Thomas Aquinas (1225–1274) was a medieval philosopher and theologian whose thinking and writing brought together what had been conflicting ideas about reason and faith. His work brought controversial ideas into conformity with existing beliefs that upheld the structure and authority of both church and society. His ideas enjoyed their highest expression in the *Summa contra Gentiles*, a text for missionaries, and the *Summa Theologica*, which systematized all of Catholic theology. The *Summa Theologica* was controversial when it first appeared but has since become the foundation for modern Catholic theology. Aquinas was born into a family connected to French royalty, and despite family objections he joined the newly established Dominicans in 1244. There he was taught by Albertus Magnus, who introduced him to the ideas of the Greek philosophers. Aquinas soon began writing voluminously on theology and philosophy. Like Aristotle, he claimed that one must use one's senses to discover the natural world, and he applied this to prove the ethical nature of human institutions and the authority of the Church. According to Aquinas, human law reflected natural law, which reflected God's law. Aquinas also insisted that, while reason was indispensable in some areas, much of human understanding still had to be based on faith, and that reason and faith, coming from separate realms, did not contradict each other. Faith, Aquinas said, comes from human will, while reason comes from the intellect. In theology he embraced traditional Catholic ideas, stressing the importance of love and the potential goodness of the world. Human love, he said, was critical to experience the faith that led to salvation. He envisioned God as loving and close, rather than as judgmental or distant.

1263	A dynastic temple is erected in Chung-tu, China. State sacrifices are offered to Confucius by the Mongol court after Kublai's accession and through the efforts of Chinese advisers such as Liu Ping-chung and the great Confucian master Hsu Heng. **CONF**
1263	*Las Sieta Partidas* is enacted in Spain. It provides Jews with more religious liberties than previously but emphasizes the superiority of Christians. **JUD**
1264	Jews fleeing Germany settle in Poland, where they are welcomed by the monarch, who desires their technical and intellectual skills. **JUD**
1265–1273	The *Summa Theologica* is written by philosopher and theologian (St.) Thomas Aquinas (1225–1274). It is the major document of the Scholastic philosophical movement and within 50 years becomes the major statement of theology in the Roman Catholic Church. Aquinas asserts that while some ideas can be proved by reason, others must be accepted as faith, a compromise that continues to be the basis for Catholic theology. **CATH**
1269	A new alphabet is promulgated that is intended to replace the Uighur script in transcribing the Mongolian language. The script is often referred to as the Phags-pa script after its creator, a Buddhist monk employed by Kublai Khan. **BUDD**

Summa Theologica

Thomas Aquinas's *Summa Theologica*, a massive work of 21 volumes, systematized Catholic theology. Precipitating much controversy in Aquinas's time, it today forms the foundation of Catholic theology. *Summa Theologica* defends traditional Catholic teachings using the Bible, the church fathers, and logic. It is divided into three parts. The first concerns the nature of God and God's role in creation, the second deals with man's relationship to God, and the third describes the way to God through Christ. Parts I and II were written between 1265 and 1271, while Part III was written afterwards and remains unfinished. Included in the *Summa* are discussions of psychology, metaphysics, morality, and law. Following Abelard's question-and-answer process, Aquinas set forth a series of 631 questions and then methodically answered them from both affirmative and negative viewpoints. He then countered views that did not support traditional theology. In subject matter he ranged from a 93-page discussion of angels to a catalog of all known plants. Aquinas was later challenged by John Duns Scotus (1264–1308) and William of Ockham (1300–1349). Duns Scotus's highly technical logic made little impact on the force of Aquinas's teachings. (His followers were so little respected that the word *dunce* comes from "Duns.") William of Ockham was the most extreme of the critics and argued that intangibles could not exist. Ockham's razor—his dictum against overly complicating explanations of physical phenomena—became the basis for much of modern science and thought.

c. 1270	The Icelandic work of Eddic poetry, *Codex Regius*, is written. It recounts through a series of poems the exploits of Norse gods and heroes, as well as a history of the world. **CIVIL**
1270	Averroism is condemned by the Roman Catholic Church and again in 1277. It is also attacked by such eminent theologians as Albertus Magnus and Thomas Aquinas. Several Averroism ideas run counter to the teachings of the Church. **CATH**
1270	Mechtild of Magdeburg (1210–1280) joins the Cistercian convent at Helfta, Germany, and St. Gertrude the Great (1256–1302) becomes actively involved in the convent in 1281, having lived there since age five. The two women are spiritual leaders of an intense mystical community focused on the Sacred Heart of Jesus. **CATH**
1270	The Daoist priest Chu Boxiu (c. 1230– c.1287) distributes commentaries on the Daoist classics in China, inlcuding the *Laozi* and the *Zhuangzi*. **DAO**
c. 1270–1600	The Varkari Path sect of Vaisnava Hinduism develops in Maharashta, with a sizable religious literature written in the Marathi language. The sect, which becomes the major Hindu sect in the state, focuses on the worship of Vithoba and pilgrimages to his temple in Pandharpur. **HIND**
c. 1271	In Algeria the Muslim Zayanid dynasty is established at Tlemcen at the northwestern tip of Algeria. The city of Tlemcen is the northern terminus of the Imperial Road, the caravan route to the town of Sijilmas over which

The Helfta Convent

The Cistercian convent at Helfta, Germany, produced some of the most powerful mystical personalities of the 13th century. There Mechtilde of Magdenburg (1210–1280) and St. Gertrude the Great (1256–1302) were spiritual leaders of an intense mystical community focused on the Sacred Heart of Jesus. The Sacred Heart involved devotion to the actual physical heart of Christ, which was seen as his pledge of love to humanity and a connection between the human and divine. St. Gertrude the Great came to Helfta at five years of age but did not fully embrace convent life until she was 25, when she devoted her life to prayer. Drawing on church rituals, she found consuming passion in her mystical experiences. Her contemplation centered on the Sacred Heart and the ecstatic union experienced from it. To her, God bestowed his gifts of revelation on people as a sign of his goodness, and thus her gift was not miraculous but simply a reflection of "feeling the Beloved in herself." Chief amongst her writings are her *Legate of Divine Love* and *Exercises*.

gold and slaves flow from the western Sudan. The Zayanid dynasty rules for 300 years. **ISLAM**

1271   Kublai Khan, in establishing the Yuan dynasty in China, claims the Mandate of Heaven and proclaims himself emperor of China. He adopts a new legal code, incorporating some Mongol customs. The code is comparatively lenient; capital crimes total 135, fewer than half the number in the old Song code. He also restores traditional Confucian court rituals, promotes translation of the Confucian Classics into Mongolian, and makes overtures to Buddhist and Daoist religious groups as well. He reigns until 1294. **BUDD, TOL**

1271–1368   The Mongols conquer China and establish the Yuan dynasty. They support the small Muslim communities in China that are composed mainly of Arab, Persian, and central Asian Muslims who had settled in China as merchants and traders centuries earlier. Under the Mongols contact with Muslim communities elsewhere becomes routine and Muslims are encouraged to settle in China. **ISLAM**

1274   At the Council of Lyon (the First Reunion Council), an attempt is made to reconcile the Roman Catholic and Eastern Orthodox churches, which had broken relations in 1203 after centuries of conflict over doctrine and authority. The effort fails and the schism continues. The council also condemns usury, a practice already banned by the church. **CATH, ORTHO**

1274   Kublai Khan orders the construction of Taiyi (Great Unity) Daoist temples in the two north China capitals. **DAO**

1274   The Mongols invade Japan with a large force of ships and men and are forced to withdraw by a violent storm. The Japanese attribute this good fortune to their *kami*, or protective divinities. **SHINTO**

1274–1308   King Ch'ungyol of Korea becomes the first Koryo ruler to adopt the prefix *ch'ung* meaning loyal (to Yuan), and abandon the suffix *jong* meaning "ancestor." He is also the first ruler to favor the neo-Confucian ideas of China's Zhu Xi (Chu Hsi). He establishes a national academy to foster the study of these ideas and seeks to imbue the ethics of Confucius with a spiritual justification. Thus Buddhism and Confucianism, which had previously exerted a cooperative influence on national policy, are hereafter in conflict. **BUDD, CONF**

1275–1279   Mongol forces cross the Yangzi River, rout the Southern Song army, and complete the conquest and reunification of China under the Yuan dynasty. **DAO, TOL**

1276   Christians in Valencia, Spain, attack Muslims, and the Muslims respond by rioting. The Muslim community is severely punished by the Christian authorities. Although Muslims are permitted to live in Christian Spain,

Christianity is replacing Islam as the basis of society and Muslims are becoming second-class citizens.   **CHRIS, ISLAM**

1276   The Yuan imperial court appoints Zhang Zongyan, the 36th celestial master, supervisor of the Southern school of Daoism in China.   **DAO**

1276   The *Lotus Sutra* is written by Nichiren Shoshu (1222–1282), a Buddhist monk in Japan. He rejects traditional forms of Buddhism and portrays his teachings as the only path to true enlightenment. These teachings are rejected by the Buddhist authorities but lead to the formation of some four dozen Buddhist sects over the following centuries, labeled as Nichiren Shoshu or Soka Gakkai.   **SECT**

c. 1280   The Muslim Ottoman Empire begins to emerge in eastern Anatolia as one of a number of small states that had seized power following the demise of the Seljuk Turks in 1243. The emerging empire is founded by Ertugral (?–c. 1280) and his son Osman, after whom the empire is named.   **ISLAM**

1280–81   Strife between Buddhists and Daoists persists in Yuan dynasty China. Daoist monks set fire to the Changchun temple in the north China city of Dadu and blame the arson on a Buddhist monk. Mongol officials expose

---

Ottoman Millet System

The Ottoman Empire at its height ruled over a large territory that was home to dozens of ethnic and religious groups as well as groups whose allegiance was primarily to their own tribes rather to any religion or ethnic group. The Ottoman rulers and administrators dealt with this diversity by classifying all groups into religious categories, called millets. The four primary millets were the Muslims, Greeks (Orthodox Christians), Armenians (Armenian Christians), and Jews. Ethnic identity was not the basis of classification and each millet was actually ethnically diverse and sometimes religiously diverse as well. The Jewish millet included Sephardic Jews from Spain, Arabic-speaking Jews from Syria, and Greek-speaking Jews. The Armenian millet at times included Copts and Jacobites as well as members of the Armenian Church. The Greek millet included Greeks, Slavs, Albanians, Turks, and Arabs who were followers of Orthodox Christianity. Each millet was allowed to practice its religion, use its own language or languages, and maintain traditional customs so long as they did not conflict with Ottoman rule. However, the system was not one of equality, as the Muslims (Islam being the religion of Ottomans) enjoyed more prestige and power than the other millets and the others were subject to persecution by Ottoman rulers or local administrators. The millet leaders often argued for increased rights for their communities and in the 19th century reforms did lead to more—but not full—equality. The millets were not successful, however, in their quests for political autonomy within the empire.

the plot. Two Daoists are executed, another has his nose and ears cut off, and six others are sent into exile. **BUDD, DAO**

1281   The Dadu temple arson incident gives Kublai Khan a pretext to curb Daoists in Yuan China. Kublai condemns all Daoist works except the *Dao De Jing* and orders them to be burned and the printing blocks smashed. Only fragments of the canon are spared. He also forbids Daoists to sell charms and compels some monks to convert to Buddhism. The moves undercut Daoist political and economic influence; Buddhist wealth, land, and authority correspondingly increase. **BUDD, DAO**

1281   The Mongols again invade Japan, this time with a fleet of some 4,000 ships and some 140,000 warriors. The Japanese fight back fiercely for three months and finally are saved by a typhoon. They attribute their escape from the Mongols to the *kamikazi* (divine winds) of the storm and see this action of the Shinto deities as proof of the heavenly protection of their homeland. As a result, in 1293 the shrine of the sub-*kami* of the wind at Ise will receive the title of *Gu* (Great Shrine) and henceforth be called *Fu-gu* (Geat Shrine of the Wind). This apparently miraculous event will underlie a trend to purify Shinto of Buddhist elements and to regard Shinto as the seat of the more powerful spiritual essence. **BUDD, SHINTO**

1282   The ruler of Sumatra in Indonesia, who is a Hindu, has Muslims among his advisers. This indicates the spread of Islam to Southeast Asia, either by traders, missionaries, or both. **ISLAM**

1285   The Korean Buddhist monk Iryon compiles the *Samguk Yusa* (*Memorabilia of the Three Kingdoms*). Compared to the *Samguk Sagi* (compiled in 1145), Iryon's history puts less emphasis on political events, focusing instead on the daily life and customs of ancient Korea. In China the Buddhist Sangha authorizes restoration of Buddhist temples and monasteries. The monk Yang Lanjianjia ransacks Song imperial tombs to raise money for the work. Yang is said to have taken 1,700 ounces of gold, 6,800 ounces of silver, 111 jade vessels and other valuables from 101 Song tombs. **BUDD**

1285   The Academy of Scholarly Worthies is given the task of supervising Daoist affairs in Yuan China. State-appointed administrators are assigned to all Daoist monasteries. (The Bureau of Tibetan and Buddhist Affairs regulates the Buddhist clergy.) **BUDD, DAO**

1285   The Arab Muslim kingdom of Ifat is established and expands in eastern Ethiopia. It is one of a number of such kingdoms in the region whose advance to the west is halted by the influence of Christianity in the region. **ISLAM**

1285–
1303   A conflict over the power of the state versus that of the Roman Catholic Church develops between King Philip the Fair of France and Pope Boniface VIII (r. 1294–1303). The conflict ends with the French invading the Vatican

and almost capturing the pope, who dies a month later. The church is severely weakened by the conflict and enters a period of decline and weak leadership. CATH

1286 Rinzai Zen master Mugaku Sogen designates as his spiritual heir Mugai Nyodai (1223–1298), the first female Zen priest. She founds and heads the Keiaiji temple and the Niji *gozan* network of over 15 sub-temples. BUDD

1286 Roman Catholic Church reforms place German Dominican nuns under male supervision. Many nuns turn to mysticism as a form of emotional expression, and the deep spirituality of the nuns influences the men who supervise them, including important mystics Meister Eckhart and John Tauler. CATH

1286 Rabbi Moses de Leon (?–1305) in Spain compiles the *Zohar*, which becomes a key text for the Jewish Kabbalah movement. JUD

c. 1290 The Muslim dynasty at Kilwa in Tanzania is conquered and replaced by the Mahdali, devout Muslims from Yemen. The rulers are of mixed African and Arab ancestry while most of the population is composed of native Africans. The dynasty declines and disappears by the end of the 14th century. ISLAM

1290 Li Daochun, author of the Daoist text *Zhonghe ji* and an associate of the southern school of Quanzhen school of interior alchemy, reaches the peak of his influence in China. DAO

1290 Jews are expelled from England and go to France, the Low Countries, and Germany. In Sicily harsh restrictions are placed on the Jews of Naples and by 1293 the community is extinct, all residents either converting to Christianity, fleeing, or being killed. The expulsion of the Jews from these communities and in the next century from France were initiated by the monarchs who sought to centralize political power and viewed the Jews as a population resistant to such control. JUD

1290– European persecutions of Jews is common during the Middle Ages. From
1500 the time of the Crusades, Jews are forbidden to own land, gathered into ghettos to live, prohibited from many occupations, and forced into others such as money lending, which is forbidden to Christians. Jews are also commonly prohibited from bearing arms. Those who survive persecution move to the Netherlands, Turkey, and territories under Ottoman rule. Jews living in Germany flee to Poland. Jewish communities in Turkey flourish. Having lived under persecution by the Byzantines, the Jews welcome the Ottomans as liberators. JUD

1291 Buddhism has enjoyed a resurgence in China and there are now more than 200,000 monks serving 42,318 Buddhist temples in China. BUDD

c. 1292   Muslim traders from Arabia establish Pasai, a major seaport and trading center on the Indonesian island of Sumatra, as the first Muslim state in Southeast Asia.   **ISLAM**

1294   Chengzong, a grandson of Kublai Khan, is enthroned as emperor of the Yuan dynasty. He issues an edict calling for the veneration of Confucius.   **CONF**

1295   In Cambodia Jayavarman VIII is ousted from the throne by Indravarman III, who imposes the Theravada form of Buddhism, which remains the dominant religion until the 1400s. He also puts an abrupt end to the ambitious construction projects of previous centuries and generally seems to reject the extravagant practices of both his Hindu and Mahayana Buddhist predecessors on the throne.   **BUDD**

1295   Ghazan becomes Ilkhan, the leader of the Mongol kingdom based in Persia. He declares Islam the official religion, orders all Buddhist buildings to be destroyed, and exiles all Buddhist monks.   **BUDD, ISLAM**

1296   Liu Yu (1257–1308) redefines the Daoist Pure Light movement in early Yuan dynasty China. It will flourish during the early Ming dynasty in the late 14th century. The Pure Light school looks back to the Six Dynasties-era saint and sage Xu Sun as its founder. The school stresses the Confucian values of loyalty, filiality, and sincerity. People who fail to practice these virtues, it teaches, will suffer illness and disaster. Good deeds will be rewarded and bad deeds punished. The ritual arts are necessary to effect real change of errant ways. The Pure Light school, like neo-Confucianism, seeks to improve the world and aid the common people in times of trouble. Like the neo-Confucians, Pure Light Daoists adopt the Ming era convention of the ledger of merit and demerit. Unlike other Daoist movements, Pure Light addresses itself as much to the educated elite as to the peasant and merchant classes.   **CONF, DAO**

1296   The practice of maintaining records of deceased Jewish community members begins in Nuremberg, Germany. The keeping of these memorial books and remembering the dead during prayer services become regular components of Jewish worship.   **JUD**

1297   Sultan Malik al-Salih, the ruler of a local dynasty on Sumatra in Indonesia, dies. Inscriptions on his tomb indicate that he had converted to Islam. **ISLAM**

c. 1300   Islam has reached the southern islands of the Philippines. It is likely brought there by traders and Sufi missionaries from Indonesia.   **ISLAM**

1300   The Cistercian monastic order, which began to expand in 1113, continues to expand and remains the major Catholic order in Europe, with some 694 monasteries across the continent. This is the high point for the movement, and its membership begins to decline later in the century.   **CATH**

1300	By now at Japan's Ise shrine, Watarai Shinto, also known as Ise Shinto or Geku (Outer Shrine) Shinto, has emerged as the first anti-Buddhist and protonationalist reaction within the main branch of Shinto. Its scholarly priests have completed texts they attribute to semilegendary and divine authors. Titled *Shinto gobusho* (*The Five Books of Shinto*), they are regarded as revealed and sacred scriptures that focus on the symbolic explanation of myths and rituals and emphasize the search for the ultimate primordial divinity. Watarai Shinto was founded and transmitted by the Watarai family, the hereditary priests of the Outer Shrine at Ise. **BUDD, SHINTO**
1300s	The Daoist Quanzhen interior alchemy movement revives in China after a period of stagnation. With the advent of the Ming dynasty, the Quanzhen school and the Celestial Masters school, the oldest Daoist school (dating to the Han dynasty), remain the leading Daoist movements. **DAO**
1300s	The most prominent figure in Jainism in Gujarat, India, is Samarasimha, known as Samara Shah, a merchant who uses his position and prosperity to promote Jainism. **JAIN**
1300–1310	Huang Yuanji (1270–1324), a disciple of the Pure Light sage Liu Yu, edits the *Complete Works on Purity and Illumination, Loyalty, and Filiality*, the definitive compilation of the Pure Light movement in China. He also assimilates the teachings of Taiyi (Great Unity) Daoism into Pure Light practice. **DAO**
c. 1300–1500	The Golden Horde of Mongols and Turks from central Asia disintegrates and a number of distinct ethnic groups emerge. These include the Crimean Tatars, Volga Tatars, Uzbeks, and Kazakhs. **ISLAM**
1300–1500	The religion of the Aztec Empire in Mexico takes shape in the capital city of Tenochtitlán. The religion is based on beliefs and practices of peoples of central Mesoamerica who have come under Aztec dominance and focuses on maintaining harmony in the universe and pleasing the gods. **NATIV**
1300–1600	Almost all of northern India falls under Muslim rule. The Muslims destroy many temples, but at same time various Muslim rulers prove hospitable to individual Hindus and Jains. One of the greatest of these Muslims is the Tughluq sultan, Muhammad bin Tughluq (r. 1325–1351), who gains the throne, historians believe, after murdering his father in a staged "accident." An outstanding general, he greatly extends the Islamic empire based in India. He gains a reputation as a man of broad intellectual sympathies and cultivates Jains along with *yogis* and Hindus at his court. On his death this empire fractures almost immediately, as rebellions (often instigated by Tughluq officials) create independent Islamic kingdoms, divisions that endure for 200 years until Mughal conquests. **ISLAM, JAIN**
1302–1329	During this period Islam reaches Malaysia in Southeast Asia. It is brought there by traders from Arabia. **ISLAM**

1304   The Ming era Chinese emperor Chengzong gives the 38th Daoist celestial master, Zhang Yucai, the title of master Zhengi (orthodox unity) Daoism.

          DAO

1305   The period of the Babylonian Captivity (1305–1378) begins in the Catholic Church when Pope Clement V (1264–1314) moves the papacy to Avignon, France. Why he moves the papacy is unclear; it involves his allegiance to France, his weak and indecisive character, and political instability in Italy. It is called the Babylonian Captivity after the Jewish exile to Babylon.   **CATH**

1306   The nearly 100,000 Jews in France are expelled.   **JUD**

Aztec Religion

The Aztecs were a small group from the southwestern region of North America who migrated into central Mexico, conquered other peoples in the region, and in the 15th and 16th centuries ruled the Aztec Empire from their capital city of Tenochtitlán in the Valley of Mexico. Aztec religion was mostly a mix of religious beliefs and practices drawn from other groups in Mesoamerica. Central to Aztec religion was their ideology of a multilayered world composed of 13 heavens and nine underworlds, with a pantheon of deities occupying these layers. Only select categories of people went to heaven after death. These included the warriors and traveling traders whose work was central to Aztec dominance in the region and victims of sacrifices whose blood fed the sun god. Most other people went to the underworlds. The Aztecs were not the only Mesoamerican people to practice human sacrifice—so too did the Maya and Toltecs, as well as the Inca in the Andes—but they placed greater importance on it and practiced it on a larger scale. The Aztecs believed that they were the people of the sun and that it was their responsibility to feed their sun god, Huitzilopochtli, to keep the universe alive. The food was blood, obtained through bloodletting rituals and animal and human sacrifices. Sacrificial victims were usually men captured from other groups in great numbers. It is estimated that in some years 250,000 people might be sacrificed in one of the many Aztec temples located throughout their empire of some five to six million people. Some scholars also believe that some Aztecs—probably warriors, royalty, and priests—also ate some of the remains of the victims. With the Maya to the southeast, the Aztecs shared a cyclical view of time, with human existence passing through a series of worlds, and they also used calendars to schedule religious and other events. As throughout Mesoamerica, important rituals, including sacrifices, were conducted at grand temples built on mounds, both with elaborate carvings, surrounded by plazas. The role of priest was highly elaborated by the Aztec, with priests enjoying much power and prestige and specializing in the performance of rituals, teaching, divining, advising the rulers, and healing.

1308– 1313	Throughout his reign, King Ch'ungs'on of Korea propagates the Chinese neo-Confucianism of Zhu Xi (Chu Hsi) by means of his own scholarship and authority and the encouragement of others. He provides meeting places for Chinese and Korean scholars and the opportunity for firsthand exposure to Sung dynasty (960–1279) neo-Confucian scholarship, particularly that of Ch'eng I (1033–1107) and Zhu Xi (1130–1200). The result is an array of scholars beginning with An Hyang (1243–1306) and Paek Ijong (flourished 1300), regarded as the introducers of neo-Confucianism to Korea. CONF

1310   The *Golden Haggadah* (*Prayer Book for Passover*) is produced in the Sephardic Jewish community in Barcelona, Spain. It is illuminated and comes to be considered one of the major treasures of Jewish art.   JUD

1311–
1320   During the rule of the emperor Buyantu, one of the most sinicized Mongol rulers, the interpretation and commentaries of the neo-Confucian school are made obligatory. This cements Confucian orthodoxy from the 1300s to the 1800s.   CONF

1312   The Beguines (SEE C. 1200, THE BEGUINES AND BEGHARDS) are banned by the Roman Catholic Church at the Council of Vienna. They have often been at odds with neighbors because of their communal lifestyle and also have become embroiled in Catholic politics because of their ties to the Dominicans and Franciscans. As local rulers are given flexibility in enforcing the decree, the group survives in some places into the next century. The council also again condemns usury and asks that laws that allow usury be removed from the books.   CATH

1313   Henriech Suso (1295–1366), the German mystic, dedicates himself to mysticism and embraces an intense, ascetic, and emotional approach to religion. As director of Dominican nunneries in Germany and as author of *The Little Book of Truth,* he influences those who seek an emotional experience with God.   CHRIS

1315   John Tauler (1300–1361), the German Catholic mystic, becomes a Dominican monk. He is associated with the Friends of God movement, which stresses religious experience over formal religious practice, and through his sermons is an influential figure in the late medieval times.   CATH

1315   The Jews expelled from France in 1306 are permitted to return, although very few do so.   JUD

1317   Following about 75 years of internal political turmoil and conflict with Egypt to the north, the Christian ruler of Nubia is replaced by a Muslim. The population now has a heavy concentration of Muslims and Arabs in the north, including longtime residents and more recent settlers who are fleeing poverty in Egypt.   ISLAM

c. 1320   The Friends of God (*Gottesfreunde*) movement emerges in Germany and Switzerland. Members of the movement, including mystics Meister Eckehart (1260–1327) and his students John Tauler (1300–1361) and Henry Suso (c. 1295–1366), are lay persons and monks who embrace an intense mystical union with God. They believe that the outer trappings of religious expression, such as services and sacraments, are superfluous, an idea that later strongly influences Martin Luther and the Protestant Reformation.   CATH

1320   Watarai Shinto priest Watarai Ieyaki (1256–1351) compiles the *Kuiji jingi hongen*, a compendium regarded as medieval Shinto's essential summation owing to its remarkable level of scholarship. This text marks the beginning of the revival of Shinto in Japan.   SHINTO

1320–
1370   Under the Majapahit reign in Indonesia, the Panataran temple is built near Bitar. Both Buddhism and Shaivite Hinduism are practiced, but the first significant Chinese settlements date from this time and there is evidence of a Muslim presence at court.   BUDD, TOL

c. 1322   Scholar and teacher Buton (1290–1364) completes a history of Buddhism in Tibet. He classifies the Tibetan Buddhist canon into *Kanjur* (*Buddha's Words*) and *Tenjur* (*Commentaries and Treatises*).   BUDD

1322   The Jews who returned to France in 1315 are expelled again.   JUD

1324–
1325   Mansu Musa, the leader of the Mali kingdom in West Africa, shows his devotion to Islam by conducting a pilgrimage through Cairo to Mecca. His pilgrimage makes Arabs aware of the wealth of West Africa and also results in a strengthening of interest in Islam in Mali. Although Islam is embraced by the court, it is practiced by the people alongside indigenous religions.   ISLAM

Meister Eckehart

Meister Eckehart (1260–1327) became a leader in the growing popularity of Rhineland mysticism. To Eckehart, God was so great that human traits could not be applied to him, nor could God be defined except in terms of what he was not. Eckehart's symbolic writings eventually angered the Church, which viewed his teachings as heretical and pantheistic. Eckehart inspired his students John Tauler (c. 1300–1361) and Henry Suso (c. 1295–1366). The three of them are associated with the "Friends of God," a term applied to commoners and monks who embraced an intense mystical union with God. The Friends of God taught the need for the soul's purification and revelation. They also taught that the outer trappings of religious expression, such as services and sacraments, were superfluous, an idea that later strongly influenced Martin Luther and the Reformation. "I" or "mine" became meaningless when the soul was merged with God.

1326   Meister Eckehart (c. 1260–1327), the German reformer and mystic, is accused of heresy by Pope John XXII. Eckehart dies before his case can be resolved. The heresy charges arise from misinterpretation of Eckehart's writings, which argue that God possesses an omnipresence that transcends all human characteristics and therefore is unknowable and can be neither viewed nor understood in human terms.   **CATH**

1326   The Ottoman Empire expands east when it takes the city of Bursa and then moves into Europe with the capture of Gallipoli in 1345.   **ISLAM**

1327   The imperial government of Yuan dynasty China issues an edict requiring the return to lay life of married Daoist priests.   **DAO**

c. 1330   Muslim communities on the eastern coast of Africa such as Kilwa and Mogadishu, which are supported by Muslim trade through the region and east to India, are at their height, with elaborate mosques and schools and Muslim culture dominant.   **ISLAM**

1330–   John Wyclif (Wycliffe) (1330–1384), a British theologian and early Protestant
1384   reformer, lives. During his life he criticizes the extravagances and corruption of the Roman Catholic Church and advocates new ideas, including predestination, the supremacy of the New Testament as the basis of religious authority, and the translation of the Bible into vernacular languages. As he questions the authority of the pope, he is condemned as a heretic. Nonetheless, his ideas lead to the Lollard movement, which is repressed in 1414.   **PROT**

1333   Jews are welcomed in Poland by Casimir the Great, who believes that they will be loyal in his power struggle with the Catholic Church.   **JUD**

The Reformation

The Reformation was a historical movement that extended from the late 14th to the middle of the 17th century, with the key developments taking place during the 16th century. On one hand, it was the logical extension and application of the influences of the secular, urban Renaissance into European religious and philosophic life so that in many ways the Reformation and the Renaissance were little more than two sides of the same coin. At the same time, however, the Reformation was a bitter, intense struggle of competing ideas that sought to define appropriate religious understanding and authority in a changing Europe. In the end, these unrelenting and contradictory pressures fragmented Christianity into a variety of diverse religious expressions and beliefs. It also led to continual wars between Catholics and Protestants, intolerance of religious diversity, and persecution of Protestants by Catholics, Catholics by Protestants, Protestants by other Protestants, and non-Christians (Jews and Muslims) by Christians, all in the name of religious purity.

1334   Japan's Shinto divinities are again believed to intervene when the tide is apparently lowered by sun goddess Amaterasu in Imamura-ga-saki Bay to allow passage by the imperial army so that they may defeat rebel forces and thus bring about the Kenmu Restoration.   **SHINTO, TOL**

1336   Independent Muslim states emerge in India and rule apart from the Delhi sultanates. They are Bengal (1336–1576), Kashmir (1346–1589), Gujarat (1407–1572), Jawnpur (1394–1479), Malwa (1401–1531), and Deccan (1347–1601). In each region the rulers seek Hindu converts to Islam but also react to local or regional customs to forge an accommodation between the Muslim minority and the Hindu majority.   **HIND, ISLAM**

1336–   In southern India the state of Vijayanagar is founded in the context of
1565   increased militarization of Hindu states to compete with northern Islamic sultanates. It takes its name from the capital city, Vijayanagar (city of victory). The Vijayanagar rulers, in addition to supporting indigenous cultural traditions, are also lavish patrons of education, literature, art, music, and architecture, and Jains are involved in many of these activities. Although the rulers of the Vijayanagar empire are Hindu, they generally champion tolerance of all faiths.   **HIND, JAIN**

1338   Kyoto replaces Kamakura as the center of Zen Buddhism. The Ashikaga favor the Rinzai sect, whose *gozan* (five monasteries) monks serve as spiritual advisers to the shogun scribes, diplomats, and tutors. Also adept at economic management, they function as moneylenders and provide revenue to the shogunate in the form of taxation, compulsory "gifts," and purchase of licenses of appointment to abbot and other positions.   **BUDD**

1339   In Kyoto Muso Soseki designs the Saihoji, Japan's first dry garden, as an aid to meditation. A priest, he is the shogun Takauji's spiritual adviser, as well as a pioneer of Zen garden design using rocks and sand to suggest flowing water.   **BUDD**

1339   During Japan's period of the Northern and Southern Courts, scholar and imperial loyalist Kitabatake Chikafusa (1293–1354) begins work on his treatise *Jinno shotoki* (*Chronicle of the Divine Descent of Gods and Sovereigns*). This era of political disruption and strife, when the emperor has no real power, gives rise to this reassertion of the divine descent of the imperial line, the unique superiority of Japan and the power of Shinto. Chikafusa's patriotic Shinto creed will become the model for Shintoists of the following centuries. Other medieval Shinto theologians claim the Shinto *kami* (native spirits) are the original divinities while the buddhas are the secondary ones. Such writings will not be widely known but will be disseminated among the shrine lineages and in the form of memorials at court.   **SHINTO**

c. 1340   In his *Sarvadarsanasamgraha* (*Compendium of All Philosophies*), Hindu philosopher Madhava lists 16 Hindu schools of philosophy. Within the

Hindu *saddarsana* classification system, 6 schools are considered orthodox: Samkyka, Yoga, Mimamsa, Vedanta, Nyayaand, and Vaisesika.   **HIND**

1341   The doctrine that there is a difference in God between divine essence and divine energy is accepted in the Orthodox Church at a council in Constantinople and reaffirmed at councils in 1347 and 1351. The doctrine had been set forth by (St.) Gregory Palamas, a monk and archbishop of Thessalonika in 1347, who in his *The Triads in Defense of the Holy Hesychasts* argues that evidence of the distinction between divine essence and energy can be found in the reported experiences of saints.   **ORTHO**

1343   Pope Clement VI supports the idea that people can avoid punishment for their sins by calling upon the store of merits left on earth by Christ and the saints. This idea is the basis of the sale of indulgences by the Catholic Church which, in effect, allows people to pay for forgiveness.   **CATH**

1343   Jan Van Ruysbroeck (1293–1381), the Catholic priest and mystic, establishes an Augustinian abbey near Brussels, Belgium. He advocates the personal worship of God but within the existing Church structure and influences other mystics who build on his ideas.   **CATH**

1345–
1346   A school of Muslim scholars is established on the island of Sumatra in Indonesia, indicating that Islam is becoming established in the region. **ISLAM**

1346   (St.) Bridget of Sweden (1303–1373), the medieval Catholic mystic, founds the Brigittine order at a monastery in Vadstena, Sweden. Her authority comes from visions she has had since 1341 in which the unrighteous are subject to severe punishments. She is canonized in 1391 and made the patron saint of Sweden.   **CATH**

1347   Oral transmissions of the Sanno Ichijitsu Shinto sect are set down in the text *Keiran juyoshu* (*Compilations of Leaves Gathered in Stormy Seas*), which includes equal parts of Shinto, esoteric Buddhism, Tendai Buddhism, Daoism, and *yin-yang* theory. Ichijitsu Shinto will disappear after the collapse of Japan's shogunate in 1867.   **SHINTO**

1348   Astrology is invoked by scholars in Europe to explain the death and disease spreading across Europe in the Black Death that began in 1347. One explanation offered by scholars at the University of Paris is that the conjunction of Saturn and Jupiter are the cause of the deaths and the conjunction of Mars and Jupiter are responsible for the spread of disease through the air. (Modern scholars now believe it was an epidemic of bubonic and pneumonic plague.)   **SPIR**

1348–
1351   Jews are blamed for the Black Death, which kills about 25 percent of the population of Europe. Proportionally, far fewer Jews die, which in part causes them to be singled out as the spreaders of the disease. In fact, their isolation from the Christian community and their religious rituals that stress

cleanliness are the major factors that reduced their risk. The persecutions are especially severe in Germany, and Jews flee to Poland.   **JUD**

1348–
1385   Islam is established as the official religion in the Hausa chiefdom of Kano by ruler Yaji, who appoints Muslim teachers to positions in his government. Like other rulers in West African states and chiefdoms, he turns to Islam to legitimize his rule and as a source of unity for his community.   **ISLAM**

1349   Bridget of Sweden, the medieval Catholic mystic, settles in Rome and later with another female mystic, Catherine of Siena, helps persuade Pope Gregory XI to return the papacy to Rome.   **CATH**

c. 1350   Principal Confucian scholars in Korea are Yi Saek (1328–1396), Chong Mongju (1337–1392), and Yi Suagin (1346–1392). They succeed in including the *Four Books* and *Five Classics* in the civil service examination and in the curriculum at the Royal College.   **CONF**

c. 1350   At the Kasuga shrine, at Nara, Japan, *Sarugaku no Noh* is performed by priest Kan'ami as a form of *kagura* or sacred dance. He and his son Zeami are said to have invented *Noh* drama, a combination of poetic chant, mime, and slow posture dance. In fact, *Noh* drama draws on classical court literature, folklore, Shintoism, and Buddhism.   **MISC**

1350   A German translation of the Old Testament, the Augsberg Bible, is issued. Between 1389 and 1400 the New Testament is published in German as the

---

Bridget of Sweden

Bridget of Sweden, the daughter of a wealthy landlord, is best known for her startling visions, which she experienced beginning in childhood, and for founding the Brigittine order. After being married at 13 and giving birth to eight children, Bridget made the popular pilgrimage to Santiago de Compestella in Spain in 1341. Her husband died soon afterward, and Bridget retired to a Cistercian monastery, where she experienced such a rush of visions and dreams that she believed she was possessed. The priest to whom she confessed these visions recorded them. Her revelations condemned kings, queens, and noblemen, foretold important meetings between the pope and emperors, and promised God's punishment on the unrighteous. A vision of Mary conceived without sin peripherally involved her in a controversy between followers of Aquinas and John Duns Scotus over the Immaculate Conception. In 1346 she founded a religious order called the Brigittines. Like many late medieval orders, its members took vows of poverty, with the important exception that they were allowed to own as many books as they wished. In 1349, in the midst of the plague epidemic, Bridget traveled to Rome seeking official approval for the new organization. Bridget stayed in Rome for the rest of her life, where she met another mystic, Catherine of Siena. Bridget helped Catherine in persuading Pope Gregory XI to return the papacy to Rome. She is the author of the mystical *Revelations*.

Wenzel Bible. The authorities are opposed to the use of vernacular bibles and they are banned by the emperor in 1369 and the pope in 1375.   **CHRIS**

1350   The Daoist master Zhao Yizhen in China edits the *Qingwei* (*Clarified Tenuity*) scriptures on Pure Light ritual.   **DAO**

1350–   Jain painting, a major school of indigenous Indian painting tradition that
1550   is centered in Gujarat and Rajasthan, reaches its greatest refinement. Recognizable by the angular bodies and protruding eyes of their human figures, these paintings typically illustrate sacred Jain texts, such as the Kalpa sutra or the life of Mahavira. The pictures are as stereotyped as the texts they illustrate; they consist of square panels set into pages of texts—the compositions are borrowed from traditional arrangements in earlier Jain and Buddhist art. These Jain manuscripts are generally characterized by their brilliant, jewel-like color.   **JAIN**

1350–   During the Renaissance in Italy, the Jews enjoy an intellectual and cultural
1550   revival as well, with Hebrew scholarship developing and Jews involved in various intellectual pursuits.   **JUD**

1351   Popular uprisings break out in the region of the Huai River valley and rapidly spread throughout China. One major rebel group, the Red Turbans, grows out of the ardently Buddhist White Lotus Society. Liu Futong rises to prominence as a chief Red Turban leader.   **BUDD**

1353–   In what will become the nation of Laos, Fa Ngum is crowned ruler of the
1373   extended kingdom he calls Lan Xang (Kingdom of the Million Elephants). He has been trained under a Buddhist monk in the court at Angkor, and during the next 20 years, Fa Ngum promotes Theravada Buddhism as the state religion; it will retain this central position in Laos through the 20th century. He sends for his Buddhist master at Angkor, who comes bringing a golden statue of the standing Buddha known as the Prabang. It is placed in a special pagoda in his capital in Muang Sua; this golden statue becomes the palladium of Laos, the sacred symbolic image of national identity and security. In 1563 Muang Sua will be renamed Luang Prabang in honor of the gold Buddha that remains there.   **BUDD, TOL**

1354   The six-pointed star, known as the Shield of David, is first used as a symbol for a Jewish community by the Jews of Prague, Hungary. It is later also similarly used in Vienna (1655) and Amsterdam (1671). The use of the star actually dates to the seventh century B.C.E., during the reign of Solomon.   **JUD**

c. 1360   Time of noted Jain government official and author Mangaraja in the Hoysala Kingdom under the Vijayanagara Empire; his great work is the *Khagendramanidarpana*, a work on medicine that concentrates on poisons.
   JAIN

1360s	Many Daoist temples are destroyed or damaged during the warfare and disruption of the last years of the Yuan dynasty in China. **DAO**
1365	In Indonesia the *Nagarakertagama*, an epic poem and court chronicle composed by Buddhist monk Prapanca in praise of Rajasanagara, celebrates the kingdom of Majapahit. **BUDD**
1367	The Jews are expelled from Hungary. **JUD**
1367	Japan's shogunal regent Hosokawa Yoriyuki facilitates the adoption of ceremonial ritual in the shogunate in order to derive authority from association with the traditional Shinto ritual of the imperial court. **SHINTO**
c. 1368	Islam is by now firmly established on the island of Java in Indonesia. Most of the early converts are members of the ruling class, with Islam filtering down to other Javanese later. **ISLAM**
1368	Zhu Yuanzhang is proclaimed the first emperor of Ming dynasty (1368–1644) in China. He rules as Taizu, the first commoner to reign in 1,500 years. According to legend, Zhu as a child encounters a wandering Daoist monk who predicts he will be a future emperor; he lives at one time in a Buddhist monastery. During his rise to power, he consults Daoist advisers. Zhu tests them when he suspects they are exaggerating their powers. When the Daoist monk known as Crazy Zhou claims he can go a month without food, Zhu locks him up and enforces a 23-day fast; he throws Crazy Zhou into a river after he claims he's unsinkable. **DAO**
1368	King Bukka Raya of the southern Indian state of Vijayanagar declares that the Jains, although a minority, must not be persecuted but must be supported by an annual tax; it is said that this decree gives the Jains in the widespread Vijayanagar Empire relative peace to practice their faith. Other Vijayanagar kings subsidized Jain temples and monks; it is during this period that the 18 Jain temples are built at Mudubidre. During the Vijayanagar Empire, Jainism is not limited to an elite but is taken up by the common people; the trading class who tend to be the most prosperous Jains undoubtedly profit while advancing the Vijayanagar government's interests at the same time they spread Jainism to many cities, centers, and holy places outside the royal capital. **JAIN**
1368–1644	This is the period in China known as the Ming dynasty, during which many achievements were made in literature and the arts. The full-length novel, which existed in the earlier Song and Yuan periods, develops during the Ming. The best known Ming-era work in the West is the 16th-century novel by Wu Ch'eng-en; in its English translation it is titled *Monkey*; it is based on *Record of the Western Regions*, the story of a Buddhist pilgrimage to India during the T'ang dynasty. SEE **629–645, BUDD**. **BUDD**

1368–1644	Under the Ming dynasty the Chinese civil service system reaches its final form. The recruitment examination consists of three stages: the *hsiu-ts'ai* (cultivated talent), held at the local prefecture level; the *chu-jen* (recommended man), given at the prefecture capital, and the *chin-shih*, held at Beijing (Peking). The testing matter is limited to the *Four Books* and *Five Classics* of Confucianism. **CONF**
1368–1644	During the Ming dynasty in China, the rulers employ Muslims as advisers and the Muslim community grows and flourishes. At this time the name *Hui* is first used as a generic label for Muslims in China and includes both Chinese who have converted to Islam and non-Chinese Muslims. The Hui are dispersed throughout China. **ISLAM**

Religion in Early Ming Dynasty China

The Ming dynasty, which lasted from 1368 until 1644, was a prosperous era for China, and the country was entirely free of foreign domination. Literature, the arts, and philosophy flourished. Daoism was rather loosely organized during this era. Various strands of Daoism conflated during the Ming dynasty; consolidation rather than the development of new schools marked the period. Even so, most Ming emperors favored Daoism and gave Daoist masters high honors and titles. Through the masters, Daoism enjoyed great influence on social, political, intellectual, and cultural life throughout the Ming era. The *Daozang*, or Daoist canon, produced during the Ming dynasty remains the standard collection today. Taizu, the first Ming emperor, believed Daoists could influence spirits, and he assigned them responsibility for the music and dance that accompanied the great sacrifices and were regarded as essential to move the spirits. He also chose Daoist priests to provide the incense and silk offerings used in the great sacrifices. A devotee of the war god Xuanwu, he carried out major construction projects on Mount Wudang in what is now Hubei province, the god's traditional birthplace, building eight temples, two monasteries, 36 convents, 39 bridges, and 12 pavilions. Within a few years of his ascension, Taizu moved to closely regulate religion in the empire, with the aim of controlling the size and wealth of religious organizations. He established a Daoist Affairs Academy to oversee Daoist organizations and temples. (A similar bureau regulated Buddhist affairs.) Alarmed by the growing number of ordinations (more than 150,000 Daoist and Buddhist priests and nuns entered religious orders in 1372–1373), the government acted to place restrictions on the clergy. Candidates were required to pass examinations before ordination; those who fail were returned to lay life. Women younger than 40 were barred from the nunnery. By imperial order local temples were consolidated into one official temple for each county. Despite the order, a large number of local temples remained active; many even expanded. The restrictive policies were aimed not so much at mainstream religious organizations as at marginal groups, such as the Buddhist White Lotus and Daoist secret societies that in times of upheaval supplied leadership and organization for popular uprisings. Taizu in fact saw in orthodox Daoist rituals a means of strengthening the throne and legitimizing his rule.

1369	In Laos the Lan Na king Ku Na (r. 1355–1385) invites the Sukhothai Buddhist monk Venerable Sumana to establish the Sri Lankan sect of Theravada Buddhism in Lamphun. Over following centuries Lan Na kings offer patronage to the sect, which becomes a leading religious and cultural influence on the northern Tai people. **BUDD, TOL**
1370	Conversion of the Komi (Zyrians) people of Siberia to Russian Orthodoxy is initiated by Stephan of Perm (c. 1345–1396), a Russian monk born in Siberia. He translates the Bible into the Komi language and also founds a school to train Komi clergy. **ORTHO**
1370s	French theologians such as Nicole Oresme, the bishop of Lisieux, and Peter d'Ailley, the archbishop of Cambrai, write a number of books about astrology. At this time astrology and astronomy are lumped together and the effect of the planets on life on earth is accepted, although some aspects of astrology such as predicting the future are rejected as anti-Christian by some theologians. **SPIR**
1376	Italian Catholic mystic and Dominican nun (St.) Catherine of Siena (1347–1380) travels to Avignon, the seat of the papacy, in an attempt to the end the conflict between her city-state of Florence and the papacy. Her efforts fail but during her life her spiritual letters and prayers give comfort

---

Catherine of Siena

The Dominican nun and Catholic mystic Catherine of Siena played an important and unusual role in 14th century Europe. She was one of very few women of the time who were able to influence both religious and political life. Born in 1347 as Catherine Benincasa in Siena, Italy, she experienced visions as a child and joined the Dominican order at the age of 16. At first she dedicated herself to peaceful meditation and devotion to God and then moved out into the world, where she cared for the poor and did much to promote peace. Although she did not learn to write until adulthood, her letters, prayers, and the *Dialogue*, an important spiritual work, brought her popular acclaim. Catherine lived during a time of great loss of power for the Catholic Church and witnessed both the Avignon papacy and the Great Schism. In 1376 she traveled to Avignon as a spokeswoman for the city-state of Florence, which was at war with the papacy. Although she failed to end the hostilities, she persuaded Pope Gregory XI to return to Rome and end the Avignon papacy. Just as distressing to Catherine was the Great Schism because she viewed the papal power struggle as a major factor in the decline of Church power and influence. In an attempt to mediate the conflict, she traveled to Rome to assist Urban VI, one of the papal contenders. Unfortunately, she died in 1380 before the Schism could be resolved. In 1461 Pope Pius II elevated Catherine of Siena to sainthood for her work in the church.

to many Catholics during a time of much disorder in the Church. In 1461 she is canonized by Pope Pius II and in 1939 she is made a Doctor of the Church and the patron saint of Italy. **CATH**

1378 The Babylonian Captivity of the Catholic Church, which began in 1305, ends when the papacy is returned to Rome from Avignon, France, by Pope Gregory XI (r. 1370–1378). **CATH**

1378– The Great Schism takes place in the Roman Catholic Church, when at times
1417 two popes or three popes are supported by various factions of the church hierarchy. The Schism follows the Babylonian Captivity of 1305–1378, and the two periods mark the low point of church influence in Europe. The Schism begins when different factions support Pope Urban VI in Rome and Pope Clement VII in Avignon, France. **CATH**

1379 The first Ming emperor, Taizu, orders the construction of a Daoist Spirit Music Temple in Nanjing, China, to house young musicians and dancers assigned to court ceremonials and sacrifices. **DAO**

1380 In an effort to end the Great Schism in the Catholic Church (wherein two popes are competing for power), reformists in France offer the conciliar solution in which a council of church leaders can be called to deal with serious matters and whose decisions will be binding on the pope. The solution is controversial and pits those who favor a strong papacy against those who seek to weaken papal authority. **CATH**

1380 To assist the Russians in halting the Tartar advance from the east, (St.) Sergus of Radonezh (c. 1314–1392), an Orthodox monk who had founded a series of monasteries, assists Prince Donskoy of Moscow by sending two monks to the Battle of Kulikovo which the Russians win. For his role in founding monasteries he is renowned as a major figure in Russian Orthodoxy. **ORTHO**

1380– John Wyclif, with the several associates, produces the first English version of
1382 the Bible. Until the early 16th century it is the only version of the Bible in English. **PROT**

1382 China's Emperor Taizu, accused of favoring Buddhist teachings, orders sacrifices for Confucius throughout the empire. He evidently believes that the three Great teachings—Confucianism, Buddhism, Daoism—can be synthesized into one ethical doctrine. Taizu does forbid statues or images of Confucius in Chinese temples. Instead, his spirit-tablet occupies a place of honor behind the central altar, facing south. His tablet is accompanied by those of his four principal disciples, and a place is found in the temples for all the greatest Confucian scholars. Twice a year, in mid-spring and mid-autumn, great feasts are held, with offerings, prayers, solemn music, and dancing. Offerings are also presented twice a month at full moon and new moon. **BUDD, CONF**

| 1383 | Gerhard Groote (1340–1384), who has been influenced by Catholic mystic Jan Van Ruysbroeck, founds a community devoted to the personal worship of God, which then develops into the Brothers and Sisters of the Common Life. This marks the emergence of the *Devotio Moderna* movement, which stresses the worship of God as part of daily life. **CATH** |

1383–
1442
In southern India during this period political influence is exerted by General Irugappa, a Jain general, engineer, and chief minister under several kings of Vijayanagar. **JAIN**

1387
The blood libel (the accusation that Jews kill Christian children to use their blood in the Passover ritual) is revived in England via Geoffrey Chaucer's *Canterbury Tales*. **JUD**

1388
Yi Songgye installs Ch'ang on the throne of Korea, strengthens his position, and soon usurps the throne himself. To prepare for this move he codifies government practices along Confucian lines that Chong Tojon begins at Yi's behest in 1388. The results of these efforts are the *Choson Kyongguk chon* (*Administrative Code of Choson*) and the *Kyongje yukchon* (*Six Codes of Governance*), which become law upon Yi's accession in 1392. **CONF**

1389
The first outstanding Ming dynasty Confucian scholar, Hsueh Hsuan (1389–1464), is born. A follower of Zhu Xi (Chu Hsi), his *Records of Reading* show that he considers the cultivation of mind and nature to be especially important. **CONF**

1389
The Muslim religious scholar Baha Al-Din Naqshband (1317–1389) dies. During his life he establishes the Naqshbandi Sufi order in central Asia. The order spreads to India in the 16th century. Followers believe that people should seek religious goals while simultaneously being productive members of society. The order remains important in the Muslim community in central Asia and the Caucasus and, in the 18th through the 20th centuries, is a major source of resistance to Russian rule. **ISLAM**

1389
The Muslim Ottoman Empire defeats the Serbs at the Battle of Kosovo in Yugoslavia and has now established control of the Balkan region of southern Europe. The event becomes an important symbolic event in Serb and Serbian Orthodox history and is accompanied by the belief that the land will eventually be restored to Serbian control. This belief plays a role between the Serbs and the Albanians who live in the Kosovo region in the late 1990s. **ORTHO, ISLAM**

1389–
1391
Yi Songgye acts on counsel from a group of lower officials faithful to the neo-Confucian ideals of Zhu Xi (Chu Hsi) and institutes sweeping land reforms through the Rank Land law. All land in Korea's Kyonggi region is

reallocated to current and retired government officials according to their rank. All land outside Kyonggi is annexed by the state. **CONF**

1389–
1413

The Muslim Sikander reigns in Kashmir, India. Buddhism has been on the decline in Kashmir ever since the Muslim Shah Mizra assumed the throne in 1339, but Sikander will actively drive out both Hinduism and Buddhism. **BUDD, HIND**

1391

The emperor Taizu in Ming China appoints Zhang Yuchu (1316–1410), the 43d celestial master, to verify the authenticity of Daoist charms and to investigate and suppress heretical priests and sects; Zhang becomes the official guardian of Daoist orthodoxy. **DAO**

1391

Persecution of Jews begins in Spain with the killing of Jews in Castile and Aragon. Attacks on Jews are perpetrated mainly by the poor and the working classes in the cities, and the weak Spanish rulers are unable to protect the Jewish communities. One major result of the persecutions is forced conversion of tens of thousands of Jews to Christianity. Some Jews convert willingly but most do so in order to save their lives. As a group they are labeled *Conversos, Marranos,* "New Christians," or "Crypto-Jews" and many continue to practice Judaism in secret. The conversions continue over the next 50 years and virtually destroy the Jewish community in Spain. **JUD**

1392

Jews are expelled from France. **JUD**

1392–
1910

The founding of the Yi dynasty (1392–1910) in Korea marks not merely a change in power but a massive transformation of society through Confucian values, rituals, and ethics. All its founders are neo-Confucians who seek to create a new order based on moral vision. A leader of this group, Chong Tojon (1342–1398), seeks to discredit Buddhism and articulates the new ideology in the coronation edict he writes for Yi Songgye (r. 1392–1398). Emperor T'aejon (r. 1400 –1418) goes even further; he initiates a severe suppression of Buddhism and in 1406 confiscates all lands held by Buddhist temples. Among all dynasties during this era, in China and elsewhere, the Yi (Choson) in Korea is probably the most thoroughly and consistently Confucian, as evidenced by political behavior, legal practice, veneration of ancestors, school curriculum, and student activism. Neo-Confucianism, with its canon of the *Four Books* and the *Five Classics*, is solidly installed in the Yi state. The ruling class is no longer limited to members of the aristocracy as defined by Silla's bone-rank system or Koryo's hereditary tradition but includes all who pass the Confucian examinations and attain a government position. This new aristocracy is called the *yangban* and includes both military and civil officials. CONF, TOL

1393   *Revelations of Divine Love* is written by English mystic Juliana of Norwich (c. 1342–1413?). The book recounts her visions some 20 years earlier concerning devotion and love. CATH

1393   The Ming China emperor Taizu invites the Pure Light Daoist Liu Yuanran, a rainmaker, to perform Daoist rituals for the imperial family. With imperial patronage, Liu sends his disciples throughout southern China to propagate the Pure Light faith. DAO

1394   The imperial government in Ming China decrees that Daoist priests with wives or lovers may be returned to lay life. DAO

1394   The Italian philosopher Giovanni Pico della Mirandola (1364–1394) publishes his 12-volume *Disputationes adversus astrologian divinatricem*, in which he attacks the use of astrology for divination, a common practice in Italy at the time. The book becomes an important source for later critics of astrology. SPIR

1395   The Ottomans begin taxing their Balkan Christian subjects in southern Europe in human labor for use as slave-troops, known as the *janissaries*, who become the backbone of the Ottoman army. ISLAM

1396   European Christian forces seek to control the Muslim Ottoman expansion into southern Europe but are defeated at Nicopolis and again in 1444 at Varna. CHRIS, ISLAM

1397   At Kyoto, Japan, the *Kinkakuji*, or Golden Pavilion, is completed for the shogun Yoshimitsu. The ultimate in luxury in its days, surrounded by large ponds and set in the deer park of Kitayama estate, this pagoda is evidently not originally dedicated to Buddhism but is part of a villa. In later years the pavilion is converted into a hall of relics when the villa itself is converted into a Buddhist temple, the Rokuonji. The Golden Pavilion is burned in a fire in 1952 but is restored as an exact replica of the original. BUDD

1398   Shinto priests of the Yoshida (originally Urabe) lineage place texts of Japan's ancient classics, the *Kojiki* and *Nihongi*, on their shrine altar and conduct observances of chanted recitation. Thus, generations of these hereditary priests begin to develop their own teachings, which will become known as Yoshida or Yuiitsu (Unique) Shinto and will lead to a national reorganization of the main tradition of Shinto. SHINTO

1399   In Britain the death penalty is instituted for heresy, in reaction to the ideas of reformer John Wyclif and the Lollard movement. CHRIS

1400s	At some point during this period lived Kar-ma Ling-pa, one of Tibet's most revered *Ter-tons*, or "treasure revealers," individuals who revealed mystical texts ascribed to paranormal origin. Modern scholars credit him with writing down the *Bar-do-tho-dol*, widely known in the West as the *Tibetan Book of the Dead*. *Bar-do* refers to the intermediate stage through which Tibetan Buddhists believe a person goes between death and rebirth, and this text is designed to be read as part of the rituals that ease a person's way through this stage. **BUDD**
1400s	Two early Ming dynasty scholars in China, Wu Yu-pi (1391–1469) and Ch'en Hsien-chang (1428–1500), help clarify Confucian education for those who study the Classics, not merely to prepare for civil service examinations but as learning for the body and mind. **CONF**
1400s	The most influential Jain monk of this period in northern India is Somasundara; he builds temples in Gujarat and Rajasthan. Also during this century (1452) a Jain lay person, Lonka Saha, founds a movement or order that is dedicated to denouncing the use of idols and elaborate temples for worship; this movement within Jainism will be revived at various times in ensuing centuries. SEE C. **1650–1740**, JAIN. **JAIN**
1400–1450	This is the period of the great Jain scholar Mallinatha Suri Kolacala, who flourishes at the court of the Vijayanagara king in southern India. **JAIN**
1400–1470	The sect devoted to Hindu god Rama is founded and the first religious writing in Hindi appears. Before this time all religious writings were in Sanskrit, limiting their access to the highly educated. **HIND**
1400s–1800s	Jains develop the craft of wood carving to a great degree, especially in Rajasthan and Gujarat; they carve intricate designs in the architectural elements of their homes and temples. **JAIN**
1402	Expansion of the Ottoman Empire is halted by the Mongols, who invade Anatolia under Timur and defeat the Ottomans. The Ottomans recover and continue to expand into eastern Anatolia and Europe. **ISLAM**
1403–1424	The emperor Taizong, a devout Daoist, reigns in Ming dynasty China. He funds construction of Daoist temples to celebrate the birthdays of members of the royal family. He orders the costly restoration of temples honoring the war god Xuanwu on Mount Wudang. Xuanwu had his origins in folk religion, but through Taizong's devotions a Daoist monastic order and a school known as Wudang Daoism come to be associated with him. **DAO**
1406	The emperor Taizong of Ming dynasty China appoints the Daoist celestial master Zhang Yuchu to prepare a comprehensive edition of Daoist literature. Zhang begins to gather materials from Daoist temples throughout the empire. He includes his own essay, *Ten Standards for Daoists*, in the compilation. In the essay, he emphasizes the importance of morality and integri-

ty in Daoist leadership and declares that Daoist priests and monks should shun the ways of the world. **DAO**

1406–
1428

Claiming their motives are to restore the Tran dynasty to power, the Chinese invade and conquer Vietnam. They require that their orthodoxy be upheld in the schools; women must wear Chinese-style clothing; identification cards must be carried. Chinese Confucianism takes hold alongside the dominating Buddhism. In 1418 Vietnamese landowner Le Loi begins a guerrilla war. In 1426 he defeats the Chinese at Tot Dong. In 1427 the Vietnamese lay siege to the Chinese at the capital Thang Long. In 1428 Le Loi proclaims himself Emperor of Dai Viet and concludes peace with the Ming dynasty. He gains recognition of an independent Vietnam that he and his progeny will rule until 1787. **BUDD, CONF**

1409

First Gelugpa (Yellow Hat) monastery is founded at Ganden, near Lhasa, by religious reformer Tsong Khapa (1357–1419). Gelugpa is the last of the four great orders of Tibetan Buddhism (and destined to become the largest); monasteries are built nearby at Drepung (1416) and Sera (1419). Gelugpas observe strict monastic discipline and institutionalize the practice of identifying religious leaders by recognizing reincarnations of past leaders. **BUDD**

1409

The Great Schism in the Catholic Church that dates to 1378 worsens when the Council of Pisa, which had been convened to unify the papacy, instead picks a new pope, John XXII, thereby leaving the church with three popes. **CATH**

1409

Malacca emerges as the most powerful of the Malay trading states in Southeast Asia and its ruler Iskandar (r. 1390–1413/14) converts to Islam. The state becomes a major center for the development and spread of Islam in Southeast Asia. Islam becomes the state religion after 1446 despite efforts by Hindus and Buddhists to prevent it. **ISLAM**

1412

Jewish immigration from Spain to North Africa and the Middle East increases when Jews are confined to Jewish quarters in Spain. **JUD**

1414

Students from other regions of Southeast Asia are coming to Malacca in Malaysia to study Islam with Muslim scholars as the state continues to emerge as a regional center of Islam. **ISLAM**

1414

Sigismund, the king of Germany, with the pope's approval convenes the Council of Constance to end the Hussite movement led by reformer John Hus (c. 1373–1415). Despite Sigismund's promise to protect Hus, he ultimately condemns Hus, with the rest of the council, for his heretical actions. Sigismund then leads the military campaign against the Hussites. **PROT**

1415

The *Imitation of Christ* is written by Spanish Roman Catholic mystic Thomas à Kempis (1379–1471). The book advocates a spiritual approach to life and stresses Christ's role as a moral compass in everyday life. In the following century it becomes the most popular book in Europe and influences the thinking of many theologians and philosophers.   **CATH**

1415   Reformers in the Catholic Church who seek to end the Great Schism and weaken the authority of the pope propose a conciliar system in which a church council has authority over the pope. The idea is rejected by church authorities.   **CATH**

1415   John Hus, a Bohemian preacher from Prague, is declared a heretic, excommunicated, tried, and finally burned at the stake by the Roman Catholic Church. He had adopted many of John Wyclif's ideas in his attack on church corruption. However, it is another 20 years before the Hussite revolt started by his followers ends.   **CATH, PROT**

1415   In Ethiopia conflict develops between the Christian state in the west and the Muslim states in the east over access to trade routes and Muslim expansion. The Muslim Ifat state and smaller chiefdoms are defeated by the Christians.
                                                                               CHRIS, ISLAM

1415– This is the lifespan of Rennyo, a Japanese monk who is credited with orga
1499   nizing the Shin sect—Shin is a shortened form of its full name, Jodo Shinshu (True Pure Land; **SEE 1224, BUDD**)—into a religious and quasi-military order; as such it will play a major role in feudal Japanese society.
                                                                                  BUDD, TOL

1417   The Great Schism in the Catholic Church, which dates to 1378, ends with the Council of Constance and the election of Pope Martin V as the sole pope in Rome. The council employs a new method of election, with representatives from European nations and the cardinals voting to elect the pope.   **CATH**

1418   In China new Daoist temples are built on holy Mount Wudang in what will become Hubei Province in the 1900s.   **DAO**

1420   The word *palmistry* is first used in English to refer to the practice of divining the future by examining the shape, contours, and lines of the palm.   **SPIR**

1421– The Jews are expelled from cities in Germany and Austria.   **JUD**
1454

1426   The Aztecs defeat the Tepanecs in Mexico and become the rulers of the Valley of Mexico. The Aztec leader Tlacaelel has all written records of rival groups destroyed and an Aztec mythology is created with the Aztec portrayed as the chosen people of the Sun God, Huitzilopochtli, and required to sacrifice prisoners to the Sun God.   **NATIV**

1428   The body of Protestant reformer John Wyclif, who had died in 1384, is disinterred and burned under the directions of the Catholic authorities in order to halt dissension in the Church.   **CATH, PROT**

1429   (St.) Joan of Arc (1412–1431) is placed in command of a French army during the Hundred Years War between France and England. She achieves the position after having received revelations from Saints Michael, Catherine, and Margaret. Her troops are victorious at Orleans and she inspires the French to reverse previous British advances.   **CATH**

1431   Joan of Arc is captured and sold to the English who try her for heresy and sorcery. She is convicted and burned at the stake in Rouen, France, making her both a French and Catholic martyr.   **CATH**

1431   In accord with the conciliar solution to Catholic Church problems during the Great Schism (1378–1417), the Council of Basel is established. The council is opposed by the pope and by 1439 has ceased to function, although it continues to exist in name until 1449.   **CATH**

c. 1432   Islam has spread to Brunei on the northern coast of the island of Borneo in Southeast Asia. Brunei later becomes an Islamic nation.   **ISLAM**

Margery Kempe

Most of what is known about English mystic Margery Kempe (c. 1373–c. 1439) comes from her autobiography, the *Book of Margery Kempe*. Margery Kempe was an unconventional woman in her time and frequently threatened the church authorities with her fearless outspokenness. The daughter of the mayor of Lynn, England, Margery Kempe married an equally prominent man with whom she had 14 children. After an apparent period of mental illness, she experienced visions and then went on a pilgrimage with her husband to Canterbury. In 1413 she made a pilgrimage to Jerusalem, visiting Santiago de Compestella in Spain and Norway and Danzig on the return trip. Kempe's mystical writings, which she dictated, since she could not write, described heaven as a blissful, joyful place. Yet in real life Kempe was an ascetic who rejected worldly pleasures. When she and her husband publicly vowed to be chaste, they were ridiculed by her contemporaries. As a middle-aged woman Kempe traveled about taking people to task for swearing or deceitful actions. Her eccentric behavior and willingness to speak out resulted in accusations of being a heretic. When the archbishop of York threatened her with imprisonment and burning at the stake, she responded that he and all his men would burn in hell for their swearing, after which she was freed. A similar incident shows the circular form of some medieval reasoning. When she was brought before the archbishop of Canterbury—again for voicing her opposition to swearing—clergymen present accused her of harboring the devil because she quoted the scripture in defending herself. Kempe was never convicted during these proceedings and believed that most of the accusations against her were lodged because she was an unconventional woman, rather than because of what she said.

| 1432–1436 | English mystic Margery Kempe (c. 1373–c. 1439) dictates (she is illiterate) the *Book of Margery Kempe*, to clerks. The book describes her visions and pilgrimages and her close relationship with God. The book remains in the 20th century a widely read work. **CATH** |

1433 — The Italian philosopher Marsilio Ficino (1433–1499) is born. He is an early translator of philosophical works from ancient Greek into Latin, including works dealing with astrology. He opposes the use of astrology for divination but supports the uses of astrology in medicine. **SPIR**

c. 1434–1590 — The Counter-Reformation takes place in the Roman Catholic Church. Although church doctrine is not markedly changed, reforms are initiated to end corruption and make Catholicism more available to the common person in an effort to control the spread of Protestant denominations in Europe. A series of popes, among them Paul III (1434–1549), Paul IV (1555–1559), St. Pius V (1566–1572), and Sixtus V (1585–1590), moves to eliminate corruption, educate the clergy, reexamine traditional doctrines and practice, and address many of the challenges raised by the humanists. **CATH**

1438 — Roman Catholic priest and reformer (St.) Bernardino of Siena (1380–1444) becomes a leader of the Franciscan order. He helps popularize the sermon as a religious practice and uses his sermons to preach against sin in Italian society. **CATH**

1438 — The first Jewish quarter (*mellah*) is established for the Jews of Fez, Morocco, by the Muslim rulers. **JUD**

1438–1439 — At the Council of Ferrara-Florence (the Second Reunion Council) an attempt is made to reconcile the Roman Catholic and Eastern Orthodox churches, which had broken relations in 1203 after centuries of conflict over doctrine and authority. The council ends in a general agreement for reconciliation on terms favorable to the church in Rome. The schism continues, however, when the Byzantine emperors are unable to win support for the decisions in Constantinople. Instrumental in the rejection of the agreement is (St.) Mark Eugenicus (c. 1392–1445), the metropolitan of Ephesus, who refuses to endorse it at the council and musters resistance in Constantinople. **CATH, ORTHO**

1439 — Anti-papacy members of the nearly defunct Council of Basel depose Pope Eugenius IV and elect Felix V to replace him. The action has little impact in the Catholic world and Felix V resigns in 1449. He is the last pope elected as an alternative to the pope in Rome. **CATH**

1439 — The Caumukha (four-faced) Jain shrine of Adinatha at Ranpur (or Ranakpur) is built in Jodhpur-Rajasthan, India. It is a gigantic temple, with 29 halls covering 40,000 square feet. **JAIN**

c. 1440   Tarot cards come into use as a tool for divination in Italy. They had formerly been used only for games.   **SPIR**

1440   Italian humanist and scholar Lorenzo Valla (1406–1457) demonstrates that the *Donation of Constantine*, the document that supports Roman Catholic claims of papal authority, is a forgery. Valla carefully studies early Christian documents and through his analysis questions the validity of many beliefs.   **CATH**

1443   The Daoist Changchun temple in Beijing, China's capital, is renamed White Cloud Monastery. The oldest parts of the temple complex date to the mid-700s. White Cloud will become one of the largest and most famous of Daoist sites.   **DAO**

1444   Yingzong, an emperor of Ming dynasty China, (r. 1435–1449), orders the final engraving and printing of the *Daozang*, the Daoist canon. The work is published in 5,305 scrolls.   **DAO**

1444   The Ottomans defeat the coalition of Hungary, Poland, Transylvania, Serbia, Naples, Venice, and Genoa at the Battle of Varna.   **ISLAM**

1447   Yingzong distributes sets of the Daoist canon, the *Daozang*, to Daoist temples throughout Ming China. The printing blocks are stored in Beijing, the capital, so that more copies can be printed when needed.   **DAO**

c. 1450   *Fortalitium Fidei* is written in Spain by Franciscan friar Alfonso de Espina. In it he attacks the *conversos* (Jews who converted to Christianity) for continuing to be Jews in private or in their hearts and condemns them as a threat to Spanish society. The book tends to reflect the view of many church leaders, who doubt the faith of the *conversos*.   **CATH, JUD**

c. 1450   Christian or Biblical humanism emerges in Europe. Humanists, such as the Dutch priest Desiderius Erasmus and Sir Thomas More in England, argue that the moral decay of the church can be reversed through the pursuit of knowledge and faith, and through the study of basic documents of Christianity including the Gospels, Revelations, the letters of St. Paul, and the writings of the early Church fathers, such as Sts. Ambrose, Jerome, and Augustine. They also advocate translating and printing the biblical texts into the European vernacular languages, rather than only in the Church-approved Latin.   **CHRIS**

c. 1450   The rulers of the principalities of Java, Demak, Tuban, Madura, and Surabaya in Indonesia convert to Islam.   **ISLAM**

1450   Around this time, Ichijo Kaneyoshi (1402–1481) seeks the essence of Shinto in his interpretation of Japan's Imperial Regalia: the necklace represents mercy and benevolence, the mirror wisdom, and the sword courage and strength. He sees these virtues as the foundation of imperial rule and of the power of the state. Like Kaneyoshi, many Shinto revivalists of the era come from the class of court nobles who resist the rule of the military shoguns. During the late 1400s nostalgia for the past leads to their study of *wakagu* (classical court literature and ceremony). **SHINTO**

1450–
1459

Several Muslim states are established in Myanmar (Burma). **ISLAM**

1450–
1519

The Aztec engage in the Wars of the Flowers with neighboring peoples. The purpose of the wars is to ostensibly capture prisoners who can be sacrificed to the gods in Aztec rituals. In the Aztec religion "feeding" the sun with human and animal blood is a vital human activity and many captives are needed for this purpose. **NATIV**

1450–
1521

This is the lifespan of Pemalingpa, a greatly revered Buddhist in Bhutan. **BUDD**

1451

Some 50,000 Daoist and Buddhist monks and nuns are ordained in China. **BUDD, DAO**

c. 1452

The printing of the Gutenberg Bible in Germany is started by Johannes Gutenberg (c. 1396–c. 1468) and is completed in 1455 or 1456. It is the first book to be printed by moveable type and revolutionizes European society by making printed materials widely and cheaply available. **MISC**

1453

The Ottoman sultan Mehmet II (?–1481) captures Constantinople (Istanbul), the capital of the Byzantine Empire and the primary city of the

---

Gutenberg Bible

The Gutenberg Bible was the first Bible printed with movable type. Printing by moveable type was invented by German printer Johannes Gutenberg in about 1449. One of the major inventions in human history, it made the mass production of books, pamphlets, letters, and any other written materials easy and quick and thus stimulated education, literacy, and learning across Europe and then around the world. Gutenberg began work on the Bible in 1452 but did not complete the printing until 1455 or 1456 as his six presses were used mainly for shorter documents and texts. Of the 150 produced by Gutenberg, only 8 survive on parchment and 36 on paper. Of these only 21 are complete copies. Gutenberg took printing and the Bible seriously and sought to re-create the beauty of the hand-copied versions of the Middle Ages. His Bible shows careful spacing and proportion, the use of deep black ink, the creative combination of different typefaces, and red and blue as well as black colors. The red and blue, used for initial chapter letters and headings, were added later by artists, as they could not be perfected on the primitive printing presses. The Bibles were bound in two volumes and contain 1,282 pages.

Orthodox Church, and brings the Byzantine (Eastern Roman) Empire to an end, with much of the empire now under Muslim control. Over the next two centuries, peoples in Albania, Bulgaria, Serbia, and Greece are converted to Islam as the Ottomans create a Turkish-Muslim empire. The sultan appoints Gennadius Scholarios of Constantinople (1405–1472) as the patriarch of the Orthodox Church and enters into an agreement with him that governs relations between the Muslim rulers and the Orthodox community until 1923. The agreement organizes all Christians as one people under the control of the Orthodox patriarch in civil matters.   **CHRIS, ISLAM**

1454   In the papal bull *Romanus Pontifex*, Pope Nicholas V awards Portugal, the major European sea exploration nation of the time, the right to settle the west coast of Africa.   **CATH**

1455   Sejo in Korea usurps the throne of the boy king Tanjong. Many scholars find this an unforgivable violation of Confucian principles. Their complaints are met with bloody purges. Conflict between the *yangban* (meritorious elite favored by T'aejo) and the neo-Confucian literati intensifies. Sejo purges the literati.   **CONF**

Sikhism

Sikhism is the most recent of the world's major monotheistic religions. It emerged at the end of the 15th and beginning of the 16th century as an alternative to Hinduism in the Punjab region of northwestern India. Today it is seen by both Sikhs and non-Sikhs as a distinct religion. There are about 20 million Sikhs, with about 90 percent in Punjab State, India, and the remaining in diaspora communities around the world, with the largest populations in Great Britain, the United States, and Canada. As in major religions with a widespread population of adherents, Sikhism includes a variety of beliefs and practices as evidenced by the existence of a number of different sects and movements within the Sikh community. Despite this diversity the core of Sikhism is the Khalsa (Pure) Sikh movement, which by the early 1900s had emerged as the dominant form of Sikh belief and practice in the Punjab. While some non-Khalsa Sikhs are accepted as Sikhs, Khalsa Sikhism is the standard by which alternative forms are judged. Khalsa Sikhs are initiated through a carefully prescribed ritual, enjoy and have a special relationship with God, and must follow a strict code of conduct called the *rahit*. At the core of Sikhism is the desire to cleanse one's soul so as to achieve unity with a god. Cleansing is achieved by resisting the five vices of greed, anger, false pride, lust, and desire for material wealth. In addition, Sikhs attempt to behave in morally correct ways that include being honest, compassionate, and patient. Sikhism was established by the ten gurus, and since the death of the last in 1708, the religion has been carried forth by the *Guru Granth*, the primary religious text, and the *Panth*, the Sikh religious community. Since the 1970s Sikhs in India have been involved in a struggle to create an independent Sikh nation called Khalistan.

1456	The Ottoman Turks capture Athens and convert the Partheneon, which had been a Greek temple and then a shrine to the Virgin Mary, into a mosque. **ISLAM**
1456–1506	The Daoist White Cloud Monastery is rebuilt in Beijing, China's capital. Many of the old buildings in the temple complex remain in use in the 1990s. **DAO**
1459	The legendary sage Zhang Sanfong is canonized in Ming dynasty China. Little is known of his life, including his birth and death dates. He is credited with creating the Taijichuan system, a form of nonaggressive martial arts or physical exercises that makes use of Daoist principles and is frequently practiced in Daoist monasteries. **DAO**
c. 1460	The Kazakhs of central Asia begin to emerge as a distinct people and to form a state separate from the dominant Uzbeks. A distinct Kazakh ethnic identity is in place by the early16th century and its rulers make Islam the state religion. However, most people continue to also practice the indigenous religion, and Islam in Kazakhstan develops as a unique mix of Islam and local beliefs and practices. **ISLAM**
1462–1505	During the reign of Ivan the Great (1440–1505), the pre-Russian state of Muscovy is expanded to the west and east. In 1472 Ivan describes Moscow as the Third Rome, after ancient Rome and Constantinople, and suggests that Moscow will assume the responsibility for the purity of Christianity following the fall of the Byzantine state. He is supported in his opinions by the Russian Orthodox Church. **ORTHO**
1463	The Ottoman Turks defeat the Serbs and all of the Orthodox peoples of eastern Europe, except for those in Russia, are now under Muslim control. **ISLAM, ORTHO**
1463–1499	During the rule of Muhammad Rumfa, the Kano Hausa chiefdom in West Africa becomes a major center for Islam in the region. Rumfa establishes mosques and schools and attracts scholars from North Africa. **ISLAM**
1464–1492	With the Mali Empire in decline in West Africa, the Songhay Empire is established by local leader Sunni Ali and becomes the center for Islam in the region. Contact with Islamic communities is maintained mainly through the trading cities of Timbuktu and Jenne. Although Ali supports Islam officially, it continues to coexist in his empire alongside indigenous religions. **ISLAM**
1466	The Bible is first published in German. **CHRIS**
1467	The Svetambara/Jain school called the Kadavamata is founded; it opposes the claim that monks are purer than ordinary people and instead favors lay followers. **JAIN**

1467– 1477	During Japan's Onin civil war, some Shinto shrines are burned to the ground and many others find it difficult to bring in adequate support. Ise shrine is opened to the public, resulting in the cult of pilgrimages there in order to ensure salvation. During the 1480s religious institutions will find protection under the regional warlords or *daimyo*. **SHINTO**
1469	Guru Nanak (1469–1539), the founder of Sikhism, is born in the Punjab region of northwestern India. During his life he travels in southern Asia and Arabia and is one of a number of men in India who preach new forms of Hinduism. He attracts a small community of followers and establishes the village of Kartarpur. His followers use rooms in their houses for devotional singing, a practice that distinguishes theirs from other Hindu alternative movements of the time. **SIKH**
1471	The Bible is first published in Italian. **CHRIS**
1471	Le Thanh-tong, regarded as the most effective king of Vietnam's Le dynasty (r. 1460–1497), completes the conquest of Champa. He systemizes Vietnamese laws and regulations, centralizes the administration, reorganizes the army, and institutes numerous reforms. The Confucian goal of maintaining order and respect informs his work. A scholar, he promotes learning and literature, including the composition of several histories and anthologies now considered classics. **CONF, TOL**
1471	The Jews, who provide considerable financial support in the form of taxes for the church, are given much freedom in central and northern Italy by the pope. **JUD**
1471– 1721	The period of the Muscovite Tradition in the Russian Orthodox Church begins with the conquest of Novgorod, a center of Orthodoxy, by Peter the Great of Moscow. During the 250 years of the tradition, the Russian Orthodox Church expands, is centered in Moscow, develops a clear organization, and canonizes dozens of Orthodox saints. As the fall of the Byzantine Empire has ended the authority of the patriarch in Constantinople, the Russian Church develops doctrines and practices that differ from other Orthodox churches. **ORTHO**
1472	The Reunion Agreement between the Catholic Church in Rome and the Orthodox Church of 1438–1439, which had never been put into effect by the Orthodox Church, is officially rejected by the patriarch of Constantinople. **CATH, ORTHO**
1472	Wang Yang-ming (1472–1529), widely regarded as the most influential Confucian thinker after Zhu Xi (Chu Hsi), is born in China. He stresses moral education and *liang-chih* (good conscience). He is at one with Lu Chiu-yuan's learning of the mind. He advocates uniting thought and action through willpower and demonstrates throughout his life a combination of meditation, teaching, bureaucratic administration, and military prowess.

He inspires Confucian students to return to the moral idealism of Mencius.

CONF

1472–
1492

In Myanmar this is the reign of the Mon king Dhammazedi, a monk whose effective administration promotes peace and the spread of Theravada Buddhism.

BUDD, TOL

1474

As Islam spreads along the coastal regions of Southeast Asia, the rulers of the principalities of Pahang, Kedah, and Patani in Malaysia and Roken, Siak, Kampar, and Indragiri in Indonesia all convert to Islam.

ISLAM

1476

In China during the Ming dynasty, Buddhism and Daoism are flourishing. One hundred thousand monks are ordained this year; by 1490 there will be 500,000 monks in the empire.

BUDD, DAO

1476–
1534

The Inca Empire rules the Andean region in South America. Political, economic, and religious power are merged by the Inca rulers with major cities serving all three purposes. The rulers develop an ideology, mythology, and rituals that portray them as divinely inspired and deceased rulers as manifestations of the gods. Deceased rulers are mummified and buried in elaborate chambers. The cities contain major temples and associated buildings, with the primary temple devoted to the worship of the sun.

NATIV

1476–
1602

During the rule of Ali B. Dunama (1476–1503), the capital of the Kanuri state in West Africa is established in Bornu and Islam continues to be the religion of the ruling and trading classes.

ISLAM

1477

Ximenes de Cisneros serves as archbishop of Toledo in Spain and during his term, which lasts until his death 40 years later, he works to reform the Catholic Church in Spain. He establishes a seminary at the University of Alcalá and develops a curriculum that combines humanism with Catholicism. The educated Spanish clergy produced by the seminary later become the leaders of the Catholic Counter-Reformation.

CATH

1478

The Inquisition, a tribunal for investigating and punishment, is established by Pope Sixtus IV. Its work focuses mainly on identifying Jewish and Muslim (forced) converts to Christianity who are believed to continue to practice their religions in secret. By 1640 16 permanent tribunals are established.

CATH

1478

The Bible is first published in Catalan, the language of eastern Spain. **CHRIS**

1479–
1531

The Hindu philosopher Vallabha lives and founds the Pusti Marga sect of Vaisnava Hinduism in western India. Followers worship Krishna as a child and assume the role of parent.

HIND

1481

An Inquisition is established in Spain by King Ferdinand and Queen Isabella with the permission of Pope Sixtus IV. The tribunals investigate con-

versos (Jews who converted to Christianity) in Aragon and Castile and many are burned at the stake in public executions. The motivation for the Spanish Inquisition is both religious and political, as the monarchs seek to win the support of wealthy merchants in the cities who see the Jews as economic competitors. **CATH, JUD**

1481 A Daoist priest is given the high title of director of the Court of Imperial Sacrifices under the emperor Xianzong (r. 1465–87) in Ming dynasty China. **DAO**

1484 Pope Innocent VIII condemns witchcraft, initiating a general assault on the practice by the Catholic Church. **CATH, SPIR**

1484 Yoshida Kanetomo (1435–1511), considered the founder of Yoshida Shinto, erects within the precincts of Kyoto's Yoshida shrine the Daigengu (Palace of the Great Origin) shrine. Its architectural elements are based on his interpretation of Shinto, Daoist, and Buddhist symbolism. Kanetomo's is a syncretic view, but he sees Shinto as the origin of all the religions, including Confucianism, Daoism, and Buddhism. He advocates a return to imperial authority by stressing the cult of Amaterasu, systematizes Shinto doctrines, and produces the major text of his school, *Yuiitsu shinto myobo yoshu*, which asserts that the esoteric teachings of Shinto are based on scriptures revealed by various mythological deities and which have been communicated to his family. The Yoshida Shinto aim is to govern Shinto in Japan. Its power over the ordination of priests and the establishment of sanctuaries will span the next centuries. **SHINTO**

1486 Around 200,000 Daoist and Buddhist monks and nuns are ordained in Ming dynasty China. **BUDD, DAO**

1486 The *Malleus Maleficardum*, a guide book to identifying and punishing witches, is published by agents of the Catholic Inquisition in Germany. **CATH, SPIR**

1486 *Oration on the Dignity of Man*, written by Italian Renaissance philosopher Giovanni Pico della Mirandola, is published. Pico argues that humans have control over their destinies and thereby questions the accepted Christian doctrine of predestination. **CHRIS**

1486 Local authorities fund a major expansion of the Pure Light Daoist temple on West Mountain near Nanchang in China's Jiangxi Province. Such projects are often undertaken for political reasons, to solidify local leaders' standing with the common people. **DAO**

1487 The Aztecs sacrifice about 20,000 prisoners when they dedicate the Temple to the Sun and Rain Gods in Tenochtitlán. Human sacrifice is an important component of Aztec religion and is meant to continually feed the sun, which is believed to require human blood to power its movement across the sky each day. **NATIV**

1488	The first Hebrew Bible is printed in Soncino, Italy.	**JUD**

c. 1490	The Ottoman Empire has extended its control in eastern Europe into Romania and the Crimea and comes into conflict with the Russian state.	**ISLAM**

c. 1490	The Digambara/Jain sect called Taranapanth is founded; it condemns the laxity of the Jain monks and the idoltry of the laity.	**JAIN**

c. 1490	Jews introduce the printing press to the Middle East with presses in operation in Salonika and Istanbul. Muslims are opposed to printing on religious grounds; thus the Jewish printers print books in Hebrew.	**JUD**

1492	Christopher Columbus makes the European discovery of the Americas. The Spanish and Portuguese colonization of the Americas that follows involves exploitation of natural resources, settlement, and the religious conversion of native peoples to Roman Catholicism. Priests accompany all expeditions.	**CATH**

1492	Granada, the last Muslim kingdom in Spain (al-Andalus), is conquered by Christian Spaniards. In the same year the Jewish community in Spain is exiled. With Spain now fully in Christian hands, government-sponsored persecution of Muslims begins.	**CHRIS, ISLAM**

1492	The Jews are expelled from Spain. Many go to neighboring Portugal, North Africa, and Turkey, where they are welcomed by the rulers of the Ottoman Empire. In Spain the Jews had developed a new language called Ladino or Judeo-Spanish, which is based on Hebrew, Arabic, and Spanish. They take this new language to the diaspora communities.	**JUD**

1492–1503	Alexander VI (1431–1503) is the Roman Catholic pope. Scholars in the 20th century consider him to have been one of the church's most corrupt popes and, during his reign, he is notorious for his bribery, womanizing, and extravagance. He also conspires with the hated Turks and approves the 1498 execution of Savonarola, one of Catholicism's most influential reformers.	**CATH**

1493	In order to settle the dispute between Portugal and Spain as to which new lands each can colonize, Pope Alexander VI draws a line on the map from the North Pole to the South Pole and awards Spain the right to the lands west of the line and Portugal the lands to the east. In the next year, the line is moved west, giving Portugal the right to Brazil. The pope establishes the line with the requirement that both nations convert peoples in these lands to Christianity.	**CATH**

1493–1528	During the reign of Askiya Muhammad Ture of the Songhay Empire in West Africa, Islam is made the state religion, Muslim religious teachers are afforded much status, and ties are established with Muslims in Mecca. Islam

is now firmly entrenched as the religion of the ruling and trading classes, but most other people continue to practice indigenous religions.   ISLAM

1495   The rulers of Ternate in eastern Indonesia convert to Islam, which is spread from western Indonesia by traders, missionaries, and Muslim teachers.   ISLAM

1495   Jews are expelled from Lithuania. The order is rescinded in 1503.   JUD

1496–
1497   Under pressure from Spain, the Jews are expelled from Portugal.   JUD

1497   In an effort to reform the Catholic Church, lay Catholics establish the Oratory of Divine Love in Genoa, Italy. Members perform good works for others as a means of achieving personal salvation.   CATH

1497–
1498   Vasco da Gama of Portugal sails around Africa into the Indian Ocean and makes the European discovery of the east coast of Africa, thus initiating Europe's struggle for control of the region and its conquest of the Muslim regions of the East African coast. Portugal begins to displace the Arab Muslim rulers of the coastal cities and towns. By 1530 Portugal has taken control of coastal East Africa and the Muslim communities decline.   CHRIS, ISLAM

1498   Dominican preacher and Catholic reformer Girolamo Savonarola (1452–1498) is hanged and his body is then burned at the stake following his conviction for heresy and excommunication in 1495. Savonarola had sought to implement a series of major religious reforms in an attempt to restore the Dominican order to its original spiritual purpose and purity; his fiery protests against the sinfulness and luxury of the wealthy and powerful inspired huge followings and brought him acclaim.   CATH

1498   In Korea Prince Yonsan initiates the *muosahwa*, the Purge of 1498, in which many neo-Confucian intellectuals considered disloyal are executed or exiled.   CONF

1498   The rulers of the Moluccas Islands in eastern Indonesia convert to Islam, which is spread there from western Indonesia by traders, missionaries, and Muslim teachers.   ISLAM

c. 1500   The Theatine order emerges in Rome as an offshoot of the Oratory of Divine Love order founded in Genoa in 1497. The leaders of the order are reformers in the Catholic Church who believe that reforms must begin with the priests who must take vows of poverty, chastity, and obedience. The order also stresses education for priests.   CATH

c. 1500   As Muscovite Rus becomes the center of political power in Russia, a dispute breaks out among leaders of the Orthodox Church. One group, the Possessors, argues that the church should own much property and should be closely aligned with the Russian government. The other group, the non-Possessors, prefers that the church own little property and advocates a separation of church and state. The Possessors are victorious and some non-Possessors are condemned as heretics. The state and church become closely aligned as both expand. ORTHO

1500   The Lu-Wang School of Mind, a second branch of neo-Confucianism in China, remains highly influential, but Zhu Xi's School of Principle continues for centuries to have the greater impact on Chinese thought. CONF

1500   The use of Yiddish as both the daily language and a literary language is widespread in Jewish communities in central and eastern Europe. It begins to decline about 200 years later, as some Jews—for example, those in Germany—begin to use the national languages of the nations where they live. Yiddish survives in eastern Europe and is brought by Jewish immigrants in the late 1800s and early 1900s to other nations. JUD

1500s   Popular Daoism blends into the folk religious tradition of Ming dynasty China and bears a strong resemblance to popular Buddhism as the two borrow liberally from each other. BUDD, DAO

1500s   The followers of Wang Yang-ming in China broaden Confucianism to accommodate a variety of lifestyles. Wang Chi (1498–1583) devotes his long life to building communitarian groups. Li Chih (1527–1602), considered a radical individualist, proposes to reduce all human relationships to friendship. CONF

1500s   Korean neo-Confucian scholars accept the authority of the Chinese Ming dynasty Ch'eng-Chu school but define issues in their own way so as to resist Chinese influence. The scholars Pak Yong (1471–1540), So Kyongdok (1489–1546), and Yi Onjok (1491–1553) reveal the diversity and independence of the Korean school. CONF

1500s   This is the period of the greatest Jain sage of the Vijayanagar period, Vadi Vidyananda, noted for his poetry, scholarly works, religious devotion, and the sheer power of his eloquence in defending Jainism against all other faiths, including Christianity. JAIN

1500–1598   The Muslim Uzbek Shaybanid dynasty, which has ties to the Safavid dynasty in neighboring Iran, rules the Transoxnia region of central Asia. During its reign, several Sufi movements develop in the region and a cultural tradition emerges that displays Iranian and Islamic influences. The dynasty ends and the region divides into a number of chiefdoms when trade declines. ISLAM

1500–1650   During this period a witch craze sweeps across Europe, with people accused of being witches and executed. Both the Catholic and Protestant churches come to believe that witchcraft can have repercussions and move to repress it. Prior to this time witchcraft was generally viewed by the Church as an activity without any lasting effect. SPIR

1500s– 1816	The city of Algiers is the center of the Ottoman Empire in North Africa. A good deal of its wealth comes from privateering in the Mediterranean. **ISLAM**
1501	The Muslims in Christian Spain are given the choice of conversion or expulsion, with the result that many Muslims practice Islam secretly while outwardly pretending to be Christians. **ISLAM**
1501– 1520	During the reign of King Visun in Laos he perpetuates Buddhism by sponsoring an ambitious program of constructing Buddhist buildings in the capital city of Luang Prabang. **BUDD**
1501– 1524	Isma'il (1487–1524) the Muslim Safavid leader, claims to be the Mahdi, the shadow of God on earth, and the divine fire of the hidden Imam, thus beginning the conversion of Iran to Imami Shi'a Islam. He captures the town of Tabriz and establishes Safavid rule over Iran. Iran becomes the only Muslim nation in which Shi'a Muslims are in the majority. **ISLAM**
1501– 1570	This is the lifespan of Yi T'oegye, regarded as the most significant Korean teacher of Confucianism. He interprets and transmits Zhu Xi's teaching. His *Discourse on the Ten Sagely Diagrams*, an aid for educating the king, depicts all major concepts of China's Sung dynasty learning. **CONF**
1501– 1648	The Golden Age for Jews in Poland and Lithuania. The Jews enjoy considerable economic freedom, their population increases tenfold, and the region becomes the center of Jewish cultural life in eastern Europe. **JUD**
c. 1502	The Aztec Calendar Stone containing the carving of the Myth of the Sun is carved by the Aztecs. The stone symbolizes many beliefs of the Aztec religion, including the Four Ages of the universe prior to the current Fifth Age. **NATIV**
1504	A Daoist priest holds the high title of minister of Rites at the court of Emperor Xiaozong (r. 1488–1505) in Ming dynasty China. **DAO**
1504	The Funj Muslim kingdom is established at the conflux of the Blue Nile and White Nile in East Africa when the rulers convert to Islam, which has been brought to the region by Muslim Arabs moving south from Egypt. During the three centuries of the kingdom, the region of northern Nubia becomes increasingly Arab and Muslim with Christianity disappearing from the region in the mid-18th century. **ISLAM**
1504	At a church council in Russia, the Orthodox Church condemns leaders of a movement known as the Judaizing Heresy. Judaizers use only religious texts translated from Hebrew and question basic Orthodox beliefs about Christ and the Messiah. **ORTHO**
1506	*De Rudimentis Hebraicis* (*The Rudiments of Hebrew*), one of the first Hebrew language textbooks, is written by German philosopher and Protestant

reformer Johannes Reuchlin (1455–1522). The Bible must be studied in Hebrew, he argues, because a literal understanding of biblical passages is required to understand the broader theological issues explored in the Bible. This view is at odds with those of the established Church, and he is convicted of heresy. **PROT**

1506–
1544
In reaction to the excessive policies of his predecessor, Prince Yonsan, Chungjong in Korea favors and promotes Confucian scholars, notably Cho Kwangjo (1482–1519). As Cho Kwangjo advances radical reforms, however, resentment grows among the elite. **CONF**

1508
The Gaudiya sect of Vaisnava Hinduism is established in India by the Hindu religious commentator Caitanya (1486–1533). The sect focuses on the worship of Krishna (who is called Lord Jagannatha by Gaudiyas) through pilgrimages to the Puri in Orissa state. The Hare Krishna movement in western nations in the 20th century is a continuation of this tradition. **HIND**

1509
In Praise of Folly is written by leading Renaissance humanist philosopher Desiderius Erasmus (1469–1536). In the book he attacks what he sees as hypocrisy in the Catholic Church. Although Erasmus attacks the church, he does not join the Protestant reform movement that develops in the next decade and he attacks the reformers as well. **PROT**

1511
The first Roman Catholic bishopric in the Americas is established on Santo Domingo in the Caribbean. **CATH**

1511
Debate about the proper treatment of Native Americans by the Spanish settlers begins when Roman Catholic priest Antonio de Montesinos suggests that they are human and have souls. **CATH, NATIV**

1511
The Portuguese conquer Malacca in Southeast Asia and come into conflict with Muslims in the region. Some Muslims move east and spread Islam further into Malaysia, into Indonesia, and then to the Philippines. Major regional centers of Islam are subsequently established at Acheh, Jahore, and Java. **ISLAM**

1511
Theologian Michael Servetus (1511–1553) is born in France. He later writes *Errors of the Trinity* and *Dialogues on the Trinity,* which question traditional Christian beliefs and practices and provide a theological framework for Unitarianism. **SECT**

1512
The Muslim principality of Jahore in Malaysia emerges as a major regional power and competes with Acheh, another Muslim center that emerges in 1521, and the Portuguese for control of Malacca, the major regional trading center. **ISLAM**

1512
The Spanish enact the Laws of Burgos to govern relations with Native Americans. The laws stipulate that colonizers must end harsh treatment of natives and mandate that they be read the *Requerimiento,* which sets forth the

Christian story of creation and requires them to swear allegiance to the church. **NATIV**

1513–
1521

Leo X (1475–1521) is pope of the Roman Catholic Church. He is a supporter of the arts and learning and generously patronizes artists, such as Michelangelo and Raphael, founds the University of Rome, and commissions the construction St. Peter's Basilica as a monument to the power of the papacy. To finance his projects he authorizes the sale of indulgences, an act that sparks the protests of Martin Luther and leads to the Protestant Reformation. **CATH**

1514

In Germany Albert of Brandenburg (1490–1545) popularizes the sale of indulgences in the 16th-century Catholic Church when he uses them to finance his purchase of the position of the archbishop of Mainz from Pope Leo X. He decrees that to achieve complete forgiveness, a sinner has only to confess a sin, repent, and purchase an indulgence, thereby affirming future salvation. It is this practice that eventually outrages Martin Luther and leads to the publication of his *Ninety-five Theses* in 1517, setting off the Protestant Reformation in Europe. **CATH**

1514

The Ottoman Empire defeats the Safavids at the Battle of Chaldiran and takes control of eastern Anatolia and western Iran as well as gaining access to important trade routes. **ISLAM**

1514–
1517

The Complutensian Polyglot Bible (a Bible with the text in more than one language) is written at the University of Complutum in Toledo, Spain. The Old Testament is printed in columns of Hebrew, Latin, and Greek, the New Testament in Greek and Latin. **CATH**

1514–
1580

During this period, the Muslim Ottoman Empire continues to expand as it moves further north into Hungary, east into Iran and southwest across Africa to Morocco. **ISLAM**

1515

Catholic priest Bartolomé de las Casas, who owns land and native slaves on Hispaniola, begins to document Spanish mistreatment of natives as he gathers information for his *Historia de las Indias*. **NATIV**

1516

King Francis I of France and Pope Leo X enter into a concordat that gives the king the authority to appoint bishops and abbots and thereby strengthens state control of the Roman Catholic Church in France. **SEE 1801, CATH.** **CATH**

1516

A Jewish ghetto is established in Venice and later in Rome in 1555. Jews are allowed to leave the ghettos to conduct business but must otherwise stay in them. In towns that are not large enough to support a ghetto, distinct Jewish quarters or streets develop. Ghettos serve the dual purpose of allowing the government to control the Jewish population and also to exploit it by heavily taxing Jews who can be easily identified by their place of residence. **JUD**

1516– 1517	The Ottoman Empire defeats the Mamluks, the Muslim rulers of Egypt and Syria, and also takes control of Muslim sacred places. **ISLAM**
1516– 1542	The Muslims in eastern Ethiopia, who have the support of the Ottoman Empire, and the Christians in western Ethiopia are at war. The Muslims are able to conquer much of southern Ethiopia but suffer a devastating defeat at Lake Tana in the north in 1542, which drives them back to the east. **CHRIS, ISLAM**
1517	At the Lateran Council of the Catholic Church several monks criticize the Church for moral decay, lack of an educated clergy, too much involvement in politics, and too much centralized control. They suggest numerous reforms in clergy education, canon law, and the papacy and advocate regular council meetings. The criticisms and suggestions are ignored by Pope Leo X. **CATH**
1517	The Ottoman Empire begins establishing bases in the Indian Ocean in an attempt to limit Portuguese control and open up trade routes to the Mediterranean Sea. By the middle of the century the Ottomans have estab-

Martin Luther

Protestant reformer Martin Luther (1483–1546) was perhaps the most influential figure during the Protestant Reformation and is the individual credited with setting the movement in motion. Luther was the son of a German copper miner who studied law, was then ordained as an Augustinian monk, and taught at the University of Wittenberg. In 1517 Luther challenged the Church's policy of selling indulgences with the posting of his *Ninety-five Theses* on the door of a church. Luther was swiftly accused of heresy and excommunicated in 1520 by Pope Leo X. To reinforce his stand Luther burned the papal decree in 1521, while at the same time refusing to retract his earlier criticisms. For these new acts of defiance, Luther was banned by Emperor Charles V in 1521 and forced into hiding. Despite these difficulties, Luther's influence in northern Germany remained undiminished. He was protected by the north German princes who sought to increase their autonomy from the Hapsburg emperor, and Luther was able to ignore the ban and return to Wittenberg where he taught and wrote until his death in 1546. During that time, he elaborated on his beliefs that salvation was achieved through faith alone and good deeds were a sign of God's grace, and on his concepts of church and societal reform. Many of these ideas were subsequently published in his major works, *To the Christian Nobility of the German Nation, The Babylonian Captivity of the Church, The Freedom of a Christian,* and *On the Bondage of the Will.*

lished a presence in the region, although major confrontation with the Portuguese has been avoided. **ISLAM**

1517   When word reaches the Aztec rulers that Spanish explorer Hernán Cortés is in the Yucatan region of Mexico, they at first believe that he is the returning god Topiltzin Quetzalcoatl who, according to myth, is expected to return in the Aztec year 1 Reed that corresponds to 1517. **NATIV**

1517   Catholic priest Bartolomé de las Casas, a Spanish settler on Hispaniola, travels to Spain and asks Charles I to halt mistreatment of native peoples in Spanish colonies in the Americas. **NATIV**

1517   Martin Luther, an Augustinian monk and university professor, posts his *Ninety-five Theses* on the door of the Wittenberg Cathedral on the Sunday morning of October 31, 1517. He calls for a formal discussion within the Roman Catholic Church of the statements and propositions he poses in his *Theses*. Most specifically, he questions in his document the moral and spiritual corruption of the clergy, the abuses of church authority, and the sale of indulgences. The Catholic Church condemns his action and his ideas. This event is subsequently identified by historians as the formal start of the Protestant Reformation. **PROT**

1517   Following Martin Luther's posting of his *Ninety-five Theses* and their rejection by the Roman Catholic Church, Lutheranism develops as a Protestant religion and spreads in Europe. Its doctrine is based on Luther's ideas as well as the ideas of other philosophers and theologians, including Erasmus, Johannes Reuchlin, and Jacques Lefevre. It expands rapidly in the next decade, and by 1550 the majority of people in Scandinavia, the Baltic states, northern Poland, and portions of eastern Austria and western Hungary come under its sway. **PROT**

Ninety-five Theses

The *Ninety-five Theses* were a list of 95 statements or theological propositions written by Martin Luther in October 1517 that challenged the popular Catholic practice of selling indulgences. The selling of indulgences was a16th-century practice of the Roman Catholic Church whereby individuals could purchase salvation and forgiveness of sins. Arguing that indulgences did not influence how God punished or forgave a soul after death, Luther stated that true Christians did not need indulgences, since faith alone was all that was required to attain God's forgiveness. Given that, Luther concluded that no theological basis existed for the sale of indulgences. Moreover, he argued, they were deceptive, in that they held out false promises. The publication and distribution of the *Theses* among the people of northern Germany reinforced the growing anti-clericalism toward the Catholic Church and became one of the important catalysts in precipitating the Protestant reform movement.

1518   Philipp Melanchthon (1497–1560), the German Protestant Reformer, becomes a colleague of Protestant Reform leader Martin Luther at the University of Wittenberg. He supports Luther's ideas and calls for Church reform and helps draft the *Augsburg Confession*, which sets forth the principles of Luther's Protestantism.   **PROT**

1519   Responding to the demands of the meritorious elite, Chungjong, the ruler of Korea, launches a purge of the Confucian elite in Korea, including the Confucian scholar Cho Kwangjo, whom he initially supported.   **CONF**

1519   Martin Luther's criticism of the Catholic Church in his *Ninety-five Theses* is debated with Catholic theologian John Eck (1486–1543) in Germany. Eck is a skillful debater and succeeds in blunting much of Luther's criticism and temporarily weakens support for Luther when he is forced to acknowledge that for him "Scripture alone" is the source of authority in religion. A fervent foe of reform, Eck burns Luther's books and later helps draft Luther's excommunication decree from Pope Leo X.   **PROT**

Lutheranism

The Lutheran churches are Protestant churches that trace their beliefs to Martin Luther. From the outset the Bible was the focal point of Lutheran faith and practice. But while Luther believed strongly that its universal accessibility would provide the basis of a Christian community of equal believers, the development of a formal statement of unifying beliefs did not occur until the appearance of the *Augsburg Confession* in 1530. Later, in addition to emphasizing individual authority in place of papal authority, two key doctrines came to form the central core of Lutheran theology. The first was a belief in the attainment of salvation through faith alone that stated one was saved solely through God's grace. Such grace was gained through an abiding personal faith that could be found only in the Bible itself. It could not be gained through good works or special dispensations (indulgences) as the Catholics argued. The second key doctrine was that of consubstantiation, which held that the elements of the Eucharist did not physically change into the Body and Blood of Christ as Catholics believed (transubstantiation). Instead there were two separate entities (not one) that coexisted even though only the elements themselves (bread and wine) were visible. Finally, Lutherans emphasized the importance of preaching. Although this did not represent a theological doctrine, its significance lay in the fact that it served as a means to teach the faithful about the Bible, especially where the laity was still illiterate. In the context, Lutheranism differed little from most of the other Protestant denominations of the 16th century. Lutheranism spread from Germany north to the Nordic nations, Prussia, and Iceland, and then was spread by immigrants out of Europe to North America and by missionaries elsewhere. In the 1990s it is estimated that there are about 75 million Lutherans around the world.

1519–
1521
As the Spanish under Hernán Cortés move across Mexico from Veracruz to Tenochtitlán, they systematically destroy all native religious symbols and replace them with crosses. **NATIV**

1520
Pope Leo X commissions a Catholic Church study of Martin Luther's writings and then issues the papal bull *Exserge Domine,* in which he condemns 41 of Luther's ideas as heresy but stops short of actually excommunicating him. However, the pope does specify which statements are heretical and the bull does little to end the calls for church reform or to lessen support for Luther in Germany. Luther burns the bull and a copy of the canon law. **CATH**

1520
To the Christian Nobility of a German Nation is written by Martin Luther. He argues for basic church reforms, including the abolition of such customs as the papacy, clerical celibacy, monastic orders, pilgrimages, and elaborate religious ceremonies. He also argues that priests are no more holy than lay people and encourages all Christians to become priests to each other. **PROT**

1520s
The Protestant denomination known as Calvinism, or the Reformed Movement, begins to emerge in western Europe as an alternative to the Lutheranism in Germany and adjacent areas and the Anglican Church in England. Calvinism embraces a number of smaller movements, including the Presbyterians, the Puritans, the Huguenots, and the Dutch Reformed churches, and is more liberal than Lutheranism and the Anglican Church. **PROT**

Native Mesoamerican Catholicism

The native peoples of Mexico and Central America were converted to Roman Catholicism by Franciscan and Dominican priests during the period of Spanish conquest and colonization beginning in 1517. The form of Catholicism that resulted there, however, was and remains different from Catholicism elsewhere in the world, since in many communities it incorporates beliefs and practices from the traditional Indian religions with Catholic ones. It is often labeled folk or popular Catholicism. As elsewhere there are parish churches and city cathedrals, a hierarchy of clergy with the local priest playing an important role in community affairs, celebration of Catholic rites and holidays, and a general belief by the Indian peoples that they are Roman Catholic. At the same time, many traditional customs survive or have merged with Catholic customs and are a major element of the belief system. These include the worship of community-specific saints and virgins, pilgrimages, traditional myths and folklore, Indian religious orators, belief in the evil eye, and reliance on traditional religious healers. Although Pentecostal and other forms of Christianity have displaced Roman Catholicism in the region (or at least have competed with it since the 1970s), these traditional customs survive.

1520– 1548	Phothisarat reigns over Lan Xang, one of the kingdoms of Laos, and encourages Buddhism. In 1527 he issues a decree banning the sacrifices to *phi* (local spirits). **BUDD**
1520– 1566	The Ottoman sultan Suleiman the Magnificent (1499–1566) greatly expands his empire and codifies the *Qanun* (*Sultanic Decrees*) on administrative and secular law. **ISLAM**
1521	The *Edict of Worms* is issued by the Catholic Church at the urging of Emperor Charles V. It condemns Martin Luther as a heretic and banishes him from the City of Worms. It is not enforced and Luther later returns to the city. **CATH, PROT**
1521	The Muslims of Acheh in Indonesia defeat the Portuguese (who began their conquest of the region in 1511 at Pidie) and defeat them again at Pasai in 1524. Although Acheh does not become a major regional power and fails to displace Portugal, it does become a major center for Islam in Southeast Asia. **ISLAM**
1521	Dominican monk Martin Bucer (1491–1551) leaves the Dominican order and adopts Protestantism. Not a leader of any specific Protestant movement, he often serves as a mediator between leading reformers such as Martin Luther, John Calvin, and Huldrich Zwingli, as well as between

John Calvin

John Calvin (1509–1564) was the equal to Martin Luther—a religious reformer who had a fundamental and lasting effect on the Protestant movement in the first half of the 16th century. Born in 1509 in Noyon in northern France, Calvin began his education by studying law. As a young man he experienced a profound religious conversion that altered the course of his life. Rejecting what he called the "abyss of filth" resulting from the "superstitions of Popery," he joined the Lutheran movement. Quickly he earned the enmity of French Catholic leaders, who were on guard against Reformers, and was forced to flee to Basel, Switzerland where he spent the next three years. Emerging from his exile in 1536, Calvin astounded the Protestant community with the publication of his *Institutes of the Christian Religion*, through which he set forth the religious principle of predestination. Not only did this tract become the basis of the prevailing teachings of Calvin's theology, but it also became a central statement of Protestant faith. That same year Calvin journeyed to Geneva, Switzerland, where in the company of William Farel he succeeded in building a sizable following. Eventually, the city of Geneva adopted his radical reforms and drafted policies to govern all aspects of city life, including government and education. Forbidding many common pleasures like dancing, Calvin rigidly controlled Geneva and ruthlessly dealt with dissenters, including burning anti-Trinitarian Michael Servetus. Calvin (and Calvinism) thus gained a reputation for intolerance second only to the Catholic Church, despite his many good works that included improving hospitals, sewer systems, and care of the poor.

Protestants and Catholics. Forced to leave Germany by the Catholics, he dies in England. In 1557 his body is disinterred and burned at the orders of the queen, Mary Tudor, a Catholic. **PROT**

1522   Roman Catholic missionaries establish the Church infrastructure in the Antilles Islands in the Caribbean with eight bishoprics. **CATH**

1522   After 12 years of work, Martin Luther completes his translation of the Bible from its earlier Greek and Hebrew versions into German. It is revised several times during his lifetime and again in 1581, 1695, 1883, 1912, 1956, and 1984 and remains the standard edition for Protestants in Germany. **PROT**

1522–   The emperor Shizong reigns in Ming dynasty China. He appears to be antire-
1566   ligious early in his reign, abolishing many religious offices and limiting imperial spending on temples and rituals. He also sponsors persecutions of Buddhists, allowing, for example, 1,300 ounces of gold to be scraped off the surfaces of Buddhist statues. After a near brush with death, however, Shizong becomes interested in the Daoist promise of health and long life through elixirs and sexual practices involving pubescent girls. The Daoist Shao Yuanjie (1459–1539), a Jiangxi native trained in both the Celestial Masters and Shangqing (or Mao Shan) traditions, treats the emperor for his medical problems. Shizong credits Shao with making it possible for him and his empress to conceive and bear a son and heir and rewards him with a mansion, other gifts, and titles. The Daoist magician Tao Zhongwen (1481–1560) is the second leading Daoist adviser of Shizong. His rituals are said to blunt a Mongol threat by taking away the enemy's spears. As a reward, the emperor appoints Tao director of the Central Daoist Registry, the highest Daoist title in the empire. Like other Ming emperors, Shizong sponsors

Suleiman

Suleiman the Magnificent was born in 1495 and served as a governor within the Ottoman Empire prior to assuming the throne in 1520. One of the great Turkish and Muslim conquerors, Suleiman extended the Ottoman Empire and also Islam throughout much of southeastern Europe (the Balkans) from the Straits almost to the gates of Vienna. Included in his conquests were the modern nations of Bulgaria, Romania, the former Yugoslavia, Albania, Greece, and much of Hungary. He even laid siege to Vienna in 1529. But Suleiman's efforts were not confined just to the Balkans. He also campaigned vigorously against the Safavid rulers of Persia as he expanded the Ottoman influence to the east. The result was an enormous expansion of the Ottoman Empire in Europe, North Africa, and along the Mediterranean Sea during the first half of the 16th century. In addition to his military exploits, Suleiman is known as Suleiman the Lawgiver for having issued the Qanun, which codified and clarified the confusing mixture of the *Shari'a* (Islamic law) and imperial decrees that had evolved during the centuries of Ottoman rule.

Daoist rites of purification and renewal at court ceremonies. The rituals are an expression of the court's concern for the welfare of the people. Shizong's own welfare eventually suffers, for he dies of alchemical poisioning. As it turns out, he is the last large-scale imperial patron of Daoism.   **BUDD, DAO**

1523   In *Jesus Christ Was a Jew by Birth*, Protestant reformer Martin Luther argues that Jews can be converted peacefully to Christianity.   **JUD**

1524   The first Spanish Catholic missionaries arrive in Mexico. Many missionaries learn the Nahuatl language of the Aztecs and attempt to use Aztec religious symbols such as the cross and heart to teach Catholicism. The result is a religion that combines elements from both religions, a syncretism that remains a common feature of Christianity in Latin America from then on.   **NATIV**

1524   *On Free Will* is written by Renaissance philosopher Desiderius Erasmus. In the book he attacks the ideas of Protestant reformer Martin Luther. Having earlier (1509) attacked the Catholic Church, he is now under attack from both sides and is forced to leave Basel, although he later returns.   **PROT**

1524–
1525   The Peasants' War takes place in Germany. Rural people across Germany revolt against the nobility over land and farming rights. Many of the peasants are also motivated by Lutheranism as an alternative to the Catholicism of the nobility. The revolt is not supported by Martin Luther and is repressed by the nobles.   **CATH, PROT**

1525   In the Lan Na kingdom within Laos, late in the reign of King Muang Kaeo (r. 1495–1526), the Pali-language chronicle *Jinakalamali* is written to

---

Anabaptism

The Anabaptists were the most radical Protestant sect to emerge in the second half of the 16th century. The Anabaptists opposed the major Protestant movements and thus were persecuted by both Protestants and Catholics. As a result, they often lived in small communal groups and frequently moved from locale to locale in Germany, the Netherlands, Switzerland, and Moravia. What set them apart from other Protestant groups were three doctrines: first, adult baptism (re-baptism), which gave rise to their name and their rejection of infant baptism; and second, separation from the world and its activities. Being a true Christian, they argued, involved constant struggle and preparation for the Second Coming of Christ. This demanded all of one's energies and therefore allowed little time for worldly affairs. (From this core belief arose their pacifism, which often angered the rulers of the nations or states where they lived.) Third was the belief that they represented the only true Christian Church, the persecuted church. Although Anabaptists had little influence on Protestantism and drew few followers, they have survived to modern times as the related though distinct Mennonite, Amish, and Hutterite churches.

memorialize acts of religious merit performed by the king and to celebrate his steady patronage of the Sri Lankan Theravada Buddhist sect.   **BUDD**

1525   The Capuchin order is founded as an offshoot of the Fransicans by Italian monk Matteo da Bascio (1495–1552). The order devotes itself to an austere life and the treatment of the sick.   **CATH**

1525   The first Roman Catholic bishopric in Mexico is established at Tlaxcala; a second one is established at Mexico City in 1526.   **CATH**

1525   Martin Luther responds to Erasmus's criticism of predestination in the previous year in *On the Bondage of the Will*, in which he rejects the idea of free will and stresses the Protestant belief that salvation can be attained through faith alone.   **PROT**

1525   The Swiss Brethren emerge as a distinct sect within the Anabaptist movement in Zurich, Switzerland. They believe in adult rather than infant or child baptism, pacificism, separation of church and state, and allegiance to the community of fellow-believers. They are the basis of the Mennnonite and Amish denominations.   **PROT**

1526   Babur (Zahiruddin Muhammad, 1483–1530), a Mongol who leads the Muslim community in Afghanistan, captures Delhi, suppresses Afghan and Hindu resistance, and establishes the Mughal Empire in southern Asia. He establishes a policy of tolerance toward Hindus, which becomes an important factor in maintaining and spreading the empire.   **ISLAM**

Mughal Empire

The Mughal Empire was the Muslim state that ruled over much of southern Asia from 1526 until 1857. The empire was founded by Babur, a Mongol leader from southern Asia who took advantage of rivalries among Afghan leaders to seize control. The name Mughal comes from Mongol. The empire was greatly expanded by Akbar the Great, who ruled from 1556 until 1605 and who ushered in the Golden Age of the empire. He greatly expanded trade and cultural activities and institutionalized religious tolerance, which made it possible to govern a state whose majority population was Hindu. In addition, there were Sunni and Shi'a Muslims, several Muslim Sufi sects, and Afghans, Turks, Iranians, and central Asians in the government and military. Akbar organized forums at which religious views could be discussed, and near the end of his life sought to develop a new religion called *din ilahi*, which united Hinduism and Islam. The most notable ruler after Akbar was Aurangzeb, who ruled from 1658 to 1707. Although his was a prosperous time, he reversed his predecessor's policy of religious tolerance and began persecuting Hindus, thereby causing the unrest and revolts that marked the beginning of the decline of the empire. From then on there was political pressure from Hindus and Sikhs in India, Afghans in the north, and from the British, who eventually conquered the region, with the last Mughal emperor, Bahadur Shah, forced to leave in 1858.

1526   A new English translation of the New Testament by William Tyndale (c. 1494–1536) is printed in Germany and then distributed in Britain. (Church authorities in England had opposed Tyndale's translation from the Greek, and he had to go elsewhere to find a printer.) The bishop of London acquires and burns many copies and it is condemned by the lord chancellor, Thomas More. For his efforts Tyndale is later labeled "the Father of the English Bible." The Bible is also first published in Dutch this year.   **PROT**

1526   King Gustavus Vasa of Sweden sends missionaries to work among the Sami (Lapps) of the northern Scandinavia. The mission is short-lived and ineffective.   **PROT**

1526–1858   The Mughal dynasty (from the Persian word for Mongol, *Mughal*) gradually dominates much of India. Although Muslims, the Mughals create an elite ruling class, one that is integrated and fully reflective of the rich diversity of India's ethnic and religious groups including Hindus and Jains.   **ISLAM**

1527   A conflict develops between King Henry VIII of England and the papacy in Rome over Henry's wish to divorce his wife Catherine of Aragon, who has failed to produce a male heir to the throne, and to marry Anne Boleyn. The Church refuses to grant a divorce; Henry views the refusal as interfering in

---

Mennonites

The Mennonites are a Christian denomination that emerged from the Anabaptist movement of the 1520s and 1530s in the Netherlands. They subsequently established settlements in Poland and Russia and then in Canada and the United States. Mennonites differed from the Catholic and Reformed churches in Europe over a number of religious matters, including adult baptism, which they strongly advocated (and continue to practice today). They also questioned state and church authority and sought to create communities of believers who lived in independent settlements. For both their religious and political beliefs, they were often persecuted and forced to migrate. Closely related to the Mennonites are the Amish and Hutterites, two other Anabaptist denominations that have survived into the 21st century. The Amish developed as an offshoot of the Mennonite movement while the Hutterites developed independently. Both groups are smaller in number than the Mennonites and followers live mainly in North America. Missionary activities beginning in the 19th century have spread Mennonism and there are now Mennonite settlements in 61 nations. Like most denominations the Mennonites are heterogeneous, and in North America there are 18 Mennonite groups. The largest is the Mennonite Church, with 91,000 members in the United States and Canada. Mennonites number about 800,000, with the largest concentrations in Canada, the United States, Russia, India, and Zaire. Some Mennonites continue to live in Mennonite communities while others live among the general population.

the affairs of state, as he views producing an heir as a political, not a religious, matter. CATH, PROT

1527   Ki Taesung (1527–1572) is born in Korea. His exchange of letters with Yi T'oegye in the famous Four-Seven Debate raises the level of Confucian dialogue to new intellectual heights. The discussion concerns the relationship between the four human feelings that Mencius enumerated—commiseration, shame, modesty, and morality—and seven emotions, such as anger and joy. CONF

1527   The Swiss Brethren, an Anabaptist movement in Switzerland at odds with the Swiss Reformation movement, issues the Brotherly Union declaration later known as the *Schleitheim Articles*. It defines the basic beliefs of the movement: adult baptism, the ban on wrongdoers, communion, separation from evil, leadership by the learned and pious, separation of church and state, and rejection of oath-taking. SECT

1528   Muslim kingdoms along the coast of Java in Indonesia join together and defeat the Kingdom of Majapahit in the interior of the island, resulting in two Muslim kingdoms—Banten and Mataram—that control the island. By the 1670s Mataram takes control of the entire island. ISLAM

1528   To escape conflict between the Hapsburgs and Turks in Europe, Jakob Wiedemann leads a group of Anabaptist pacifists from Moravia to Austerlitz in Czechoslovakia. En route they give up their material possessions and adopt the idea of communal ownership of property, an idea that subsequently defines the denomination as Hutterites and distinguishes it from the other Anabaptist denominations, the Amish and Mennonites. Hutterites see this event as the beginning of their denomination. SECT

1529   At the Diet of Worms, five German territories and 14 cities protest the opposition of the Roman Catholic Church to Lutheran ideas developing in northern Germany. The name *Protestant* is derived from this event. CATH, PROT

1529   Muslims from eastern Ethiopia attack the Christian peoples of the Ethiopian highlands. They destroy villages and churches for the next 14 years until their defeat in 1453, when they withdraw to the east. CHRIS, ISLAM

1529   The Ottomans lay siege to Vienna. Although the siege fails, the Ottomans are able to consolidate their hold on Hungary. The Ottomans also begin to expand across North Africa and the Mediterranean, taking Algiers (1529), Tunis (1535), Tripoli (1551), Bougie (1555), Jerba (1560), Malta (1565), and Cyprus (1570). Attempts by the Hapsburg rulers of Spain to control the Ottoman advance fail. ISLAM

1529   A Roman Catholic mission to Native Americans is established by Franciscan priest Bernardino de Sahagun in Mexico. As part of his work he collects

information from the survivors of the Aztec Empire on Aztec life prior to
Spanish conquest in 1521.   **NATIV**

1530   The Bible is first published in French.   **CHRIS**

1530   As many as 2,200 musicians are employed in the Daoist Spirit Music
            Temple in Beijing, China's capital. They are summoned for elaborate court
            ceremonials.   **DAO**

1530   The *Augsberg Confession* is presented to Holy Roman Emperor Charles V at
            the Diet of Augsberg in Germany. The *Confession* is written by German
            philosopher Philipp Melanchthon for Protestant reformer Martin Luther.
            The document outlines the basic doctrines of Lutheranism and its com-
            plaints with the Catholic Church. Meant as an act of conciliation, the
            Confession is rejected by Charles V and is also criticized by some Protestant
            Reformers as too mild in its calls for reforms.   **PROT**

Protestantism

Protestantism is the generic label for a large number of denominations, sects, and
churches all of which trace their origin to the Reformation in 16th-century Europe. The
origin of the name *Protestant,* is traced to the role of the early European Reformers in
protesting against the policies and practices of the Catholic Church. However, the term
also means "to affirm" and thus also suggests the Reformers' goal of returning to the
traditional practices of Christianity. Although Protestantism is usually classified as a single Christian religion with some 500 million adherents around the world, there is no
single set of beliefs and practices that characterize Protestantism. Rather, there has
always been and there remains considerable variation in belief and practice among the
various Protestant denominations and sects. These denominations include the
Lutherans, Methodists, Baptists, Presbyterians, Anglicans and Episcopalians, the
Reformed Churches, Moravians, Brethren, Congregationalists, Pentecostalists, Church
of Christ, and United Church of Christ. Although these denominations and the numerous sects and churches within each differ in various ways, there is some agreement that
helps to continue to define Protestantism as distinct from Roman Catholicism and the
Orthodox churches. First, all Protestant churches reject five of the seven sacraments of
Catholicism and Orthodoxy and generally accept only baptism and the Lord's Supper.
Second, all Protestant denominations reject the authority of the pope and instead find
authority in the Scriptures, with the Bible (Old and New Testaments) the basic religious
text. Most denominations have also developed additional text that is used in prayer.
Third, worship tends to be simple and generally free of elaborate ritual, although there
is much variation across denominations in how belief is expressed, ranging from quiet
prayer to speaking in tongues to communal singing. Fourth, Protestants strongly
believe in God and his son, Jesus Christ, who looks over the earth.

1530   Protestant Reformers Martin Luther and Huldrich Zwingli attempt to resolve their theological disagreements at a dialogue in Marburg, Germany. They disagree over a number of basic issues including predestination, free will, and the nature of the Eucharist. The dialogue fails to produce agreement, and the Protestant movement fragments into conservative, moderate, and radical denominations.   **PROT**

1530   William Tyndale, "the Father of the English Bible," begins translating the Old Testament, his New Testament having been published in 1526 and then condemned by the Church authorities in England.   **PROT**

1530s   Protestant Reformer John Calvin addresses the issue of predestination and raises its status from a concept that has been discussed by philosophers in ancient Greece to a position in the Protestant theological canon. Calvin argues that salvation is the gift of a benevolent and loving God and that humans cannot determine their spiritual fate. At the same time, individuals can exercise free will in their daily lives, but actions in the temporal world have no impact on the spiritual world and do not influence God's decision to save or damn the individual.   **PROT**

1531   Juan Diego, a recent Indian convert to Roman Catholicism in Mexico, has a vision in which he sees Guadalupe, the Black Virgin Mary, near the Aztec shrine of Tepeyec. She appears as a mestizo (of mixed Indian and Spanish ancestry) and becomes an important personage in Mesoamerican Catholicism, with the Feast of the Virgin of Guadalupe celebrated on December 12.   **CATH**

1531   The Schmalkaldic League is formed by Protestant German nobles as a military alliance to protect their territories from the forces of Holy Roman

Augsberg Confession

The *Augsberg Confession* was one of the first documents of Protestant belief. Drafted for Luther by the German humanist Philipp Melanchthon, it was presented to Emperor Charles V at the Diet (Assembly) of Augsberg (Germany) as an attempt to promote reconciliation with the Catholic Church. As such, Melanchthon made a considerable effort to separate the new Lutheranism from the more radical sects, like the Anabaptists. Although the document gained the support of the north German princes, both Luther and Zwingli criticized it for being too mild, while the emperor condemned it as too radical. The first half of the document described the new Lutheran beliefs. Among the more important were the Church as a community of believers, the rejection of all sacraments not directly referred to by Jesus in the Bible, the conducting of services in the common language, and a belief in the divine presence in the Eucharist. The second half of the *Confession* detailed the abuses by the Catholic Church that Lutherans wanted redressed. Despite its initial controversies, however, the *Confession* established the theological foundations for the new Lutheran Church.

Emperor Charles V, a strong supporter of Roman Catholicism. The alliance ends after being defeated at the Battle of Mühlberg in 1547. **PROT**

1532   Ataw Wallpa Inca (c. 1502–1533) is killed by the Spanish under the direction of Francisco Pizzaro. As the last Inca emperor, to his people his death represents the end of the world and he becomes a major religious figure whose reemergence from the earth at some time in the future will mark the end of Spanish rule and the return of the Inca Empire. **NATIV**

1532   In Switzerland Protestant Reformer William Farel (1489–1565) embarks on an effort to rid the city of Geneva of Roman Catholicism. He leads a movement that expels the bishop, occupies churches and the city cathedral, and destroys religious texts. They then replace the Catholic Mass with services based on the Protestant Bible. In 1536 he joins with Reform leader John Calvin, and although some leading Genevans resist their reforms and even exile them in 1538, they are ultimately successful in converting Geneva into a model Calvinist city. **PROT**

1532   The Waldenses, a former Roman Catholic sect that becomes an independent religion after 1184, join forces with Protestant Reformers in western Europe and become a Protestant denomination. **PROT**

1533   Jakob Hutter (d. 1535), an Austrian hat maker and supporter of the Anabaptist movement, joins the Anabaptist community in Austerlitz and becomes its leader. Hutter is instrumental in attracting new followers and

Huldrich Zwingli

One of the first Protestant reformers, Zwingli (1484–1531) was born into a Swiss peasant family in 1484. As a youth he studied Latin, music, and the classics. Later at the University of Vienna he was exposed to the ideas of leading humanists, such as Erasmus. In response to these humanist influences, Zwingli began to question the teachings and authority of the Catholic Church and accused the church of violating the original biblical teachings. He also attacked such practices as the veneration of saints and relics and the selling of indulgences. Zwingli soon developed widespread support among the Swiss populace and was made a priest in the Zurich cathedral. In 1520 Zwingli initiated a series of reforms in Zurich, including the prohibition of all religious expression not described in the Bible. Despite vigorous protests by Pope Leo X, the Zurich government protected Zwingli and in 1524 adopted his official reform. Zwingli spent the remainder of his life in the cause of the Protestant movement and played a major role in the spread of Protestantism in northern Europe. In the process, Zwingli took a more radical position than did German Reformer Martin Luther on many of the key Protestant doctrines, such as salvation, the strictness of biblical interpretation, and the concept of the Eucharist. In 1531 he died without resolving those differences despite numerous efforts to do so.

in forming the basic communal organization known as Bruderhof that becomes the basis of the Hutterite denomination. **SECT**

1534   The Somaschi order is founded in Venice. It is a reform Roman Catholic order that seeks to reform the church by increasing the spirituality of priests. **CATH**

1534   The Jesuit order begins to form when its founder, Ignatius Loyola, and six friends begin meeting in Paris. **CATH**

1534   The English Parliament passes the Act of Supremacy at the direction of King Henry VIII. The act establishes that the English monarch is the "supreme head" of the Church of England and thereby ends papal religious authority in Britain. The practical effect is the creation of the Anglican Church, a Protestant denomination. **CATH, PROT**

1534– 1535   An Anabaptist faction overthrows the civil and church government in Munster, Germany, in an attempt to create an "ideal" Christian community. Lutherans and Catholics join forces to drive them off. **CATH, PROT**

Church of England

The Church of England, or the Anglican Church, was officially founded by Parliament and King Henry VIII of England through the Act of Supremacy in 1534. The name *Anglican* comes from the Latin *Anglicana ecclesia*, meaning "English Church." The church was established by the king to free it and the monarchy from the control of the church in Rome. It was also influenced by the Protestant Reformation. Its beliefs and practices, which reflect a mix of Catholicism and Protestantism, have changed over the 450 years of the church's existence, and there is also considerable variation among the 37 independent churches around the world that constitute the Anglican Church. Thus, it is impossible to summarize the basic beliefs and practices of the church other than to say that there is a strong ecumenical initiative within and outside the church and a greater concern with religious practice than with theology. Within the church four philosophical strains have coexisted for much of the church's history: first, an evangelical movement to spread the church around the world; second, a Catholic movement to retain the early teaching of the church; third, a liberal movement to use the church as an agent of social change; and fourth, a radical movement to use the church as an agent of major social change to alleviate problems, such as war and poverty. There are about 70 million members of the church organized into 37 autonomous churches. These include, in addition to the Church of England, the Episcopal Church in the U.S.A., the Church of Ireland, the Scottish Episcopal Church, and churches in many other nations around the world. Unity is maintained by regular meetings of church leaders, a Consultative Council, and the Lambeth Conferences.

1534–1549	Paul III (1468–1549) is pope of the Roman Catholic Church. He rules during the time of the Protestant Reformation and plays a leading role in the Catholic Counter-Reformation. He initiates the Council of Trent in 1545 to discuss Church reform, allows discussion of new ideas with the Protestant Reformers, establishes new monastic orders, initiates administrative reform, and revives the Inquisitions. His actions do not halt Protestantism but do stabilize the Catholic Church. **CATH**
1535	(St.) Thomas More (1478–1535), the philosopher and Lord Chancellor of England, is beheaded for refusing to support Henry VIII in his conflict with the Roman Catholic Church. At his execution he proclaims that he is "the king's good servant, but God's first." He is canonized in 1935 and made the patron saint of lawyers. **CATH**
1535	Catholic mystic and reformer (St.) Theresa of Avila (1515–1582) joins the Carmelite religious order. During her life she advocates church reforms and founds 16 organizations for women and 14 for men that strengthen the Spanish Catholic Church at a time when Protestantism is winning converts throughout Europe. For her contributions to the Church, Theresa is canonized in 1622. **CATH**
1535	The Spanish in Mexico order that all pictorial records of Indian life in the city of Texcoco be gathered and destroyed. Nearly all are burned, destroying much information about Aztec religion. **NATIV**

Ignatius Loyola

Ignatius Loyola (1491–1556) was born Don Inigo Lopez de Loyola in 1491 at Azpeitia, Spain, to a Basque noble family. Until he was 30 Loyola lived the life of a soldier and courtier, occupying himself with duels, gambling, and love affairs. However, while bedridden following a battle wound in 1521, he read about the lives of the saints and of Christ. The result was a deep religious conversion, and afterwards, he entered a monastery, where he exchanged clothes with a beggar while living for the next eight months in penance and poverty. In 1523 he made a pilgrimage to Jerusalem, apparently alone and barefoot during part of it. In pursuing his religious activities, Loyola refused an isolated monastic life, instead seeking to bring his spiritual knowledge to others. He therefore educated himself first at Spanish universities and then at the University of Paris, from which he graduated in 1528. In 1534 he founded the religious order that eventually became the Society of Jesus, or Jesuits, who Loyola required to take vows of poverty, educate priests, and spread Christian knowledge instead of fighting heresy. To ensure that Jesuits remained loyal to their spiritual calling, Loyola wrote the *Constitutions of the Order* (which was compiled posthumously) and *Spiritual Exercises*, a training book on developing a spiritual life still used today by Catholic missions.

| 1535 | Jakob Wiedemann and Jakob Hutter, founders of the Hutterite denomination, are executed in Austria as part of the persecution of the Anabaptists by Holy Roman Emperor Ferdinand I. **SECT** |

| 1535–1536 | William Tyndale, "the Father of the English Bible," is captured, imprisoned, and tried in Brussels. Convicted of heresy for his translations of the Bible into English, he is strangled and then burned at the stake. **PROT** |

| 1535–1540 | In his continuing battle with the Roman Catholic Church, Henry VIII of England closes monasteries, executes officials who remain loyal to the church, and confiscates church property. **CATH** |

| 1536 | An Inquisition is established in Portugal. As in Spain in 1481, the purpose is to find and kill *conversos* (Jews who converted to Christianity) who are believed to still practice Judaism in secret. **JUD** |

| 1536 | *Institutes of the Christian Religion* is written by Protestant reformer John Calvin. Revised a number of times until it reaches its final form in 1559, it |

Society of Jesus

Spanish nobleman Ignatius of Loyola (1491–1556) founded the Society of Jesus, or the Order of Jesuits as it is commonly known. Loyola converted to the religious life while recovering from a wound he received in a battle. In 1535 while working in Paris, Loyola and six disciples took vows of poverty and chastity and promised to go as missionaries to Palestine, but the war between Venice and the Turks blocked their passage. Loyola and his friends revised their original promise and began to work in northern Italian cities, where they gathered new recruits and sought direction and approval from Pope Paul III. The Society of Jesus received official approval from the pope in 1540 as an order of Catholic priests dependent on charity. Recruits were carefully selected and thoroughly trained for 15 years. The students cultivated an inner life based on meditation and Loyola's *Spiritual Exercises*. The Jesuits grew rapidly and by 1556 there were over a thousand Jesuits living mostly in Spain, Portugal, and Italy, with a few in France, Germany, the Low Countries, India, Brazil, and Africa. The Society of Jesus was one of main forces in reaction to Protestant Reformation. The Jesuit schools combined Catholic tradition with carefully selected classes, Christian obedience, and a strong sense of competition. As part of their educational philosophy, the Jesuits founded schools and missions all over the world. Francis Xavier (1506–1552) worked in India, Indonesia, and Japan. Matteo Ricci (1552–1610) worked in China and adapted the Bible to Chinese traditions and philosophy. Robert De Nobili (1577–1656) started schools in India. The Jesuits were active missionaries in the Americas and in South America were often in conflict with colonists who sought to exploit the Indians. This caused Pope Clement XIV to revoke their charter in 1773, although it was restored by Pope Pius VII in 1814. The Jesuits reached a peak of 36,000 members in 1964 and numbered about 25,000 in the 1990s.

becomes a basic statement of the Protestant religion and the basis of Calvinism and distinguishes Calvinism from Lutheranism and Anglicanism, the two other major Protestant denominations of the time.   PROT

1536   In Switzerland, the *First Helvetic Confession* is drawn up by Protestant Reformers. It stresses the church ministry and the rule of the state in promoting religion and is an attempt to make Protestantism the state religion of Switzerland.   PROT

1536   In the Netherlands Catholic priest Menno Simons is attracted to the teachings of the Swiss Brethren (SEE 1527, SECT) and becomes the leader of the Anabaptist movement in the Netherlands. His followers, who later emigrate to Russia and then to the Americas, call themselves Mennists or Mennonites.   SECT

1537   Pope Paul III declares the indigenous peoples of the Americas to be worthy of conversion to Christianity.   NATIV

1537   The *Smalcald Articles of Faith* are added to the *Augsberg Confession*. When the *Formula of Concord of 1577* is also added, the theological statement of the Lutheran Church in Germany is complete.   PROT

1537   The Thomas Matthew Bible is published as the first authorized (by the Church of England) Bible in English. It is based on the Tyndale Bible, which had been repressed by church authorities before the break with Rome.   PROT

1539   Although conflict continues between Henry VIII of England and the church in Rome over political and religious authority, Henry has not abandoned Catholicism as a faith and publishes *Six Articles,* which emphasizes adherence to many basic Catholic beliefs and rituals such as Mass, confession, and transubstantiation.   CATH

1539   Construction begins on the Khasseki Khurrem Sultan mosque in Istanbul. It is a large mosque that includes a college, school, and hospital and is the first mosque designed by renowned Ottoman architect Sinan Pasha. The mosque, like others built later, is endowed by Khurren (?–1558), the wife of the Ottoman sultan Suleiman the Magnificent.   ISLAM

1539   Guru Angad (1504–1552) succeeds Guru Nanak, the founder of Sikhism, as the second Sikh Guru and serves until his death in 1552. He works to expand the Sikh community (*Panth*) and is credited with initiating the use of the Gurmukhi script for writing in the Punjabi language.   SIKH

c. 1540   While in prison in Austria as part of persecution of Anabaptists, Peter Riedemann, a cobbler and early follower of the Hutterite denomination, writes his *Rechenschaft*, which becomes and remains the basic statement of the Hutterite denomination.   SECT

1540   The Jesuit order is formally accepted within Roman Catholicism by Pope Paul III in his bull *Regimini militantis*. The order is established to reconvert those who have strayed from the church and to seek new converts from other religions. Over the next 300 years it is the major missionary branch of the Roman Catholic Church.   **CATH**

1540   Mennonites from the Netherlands immigrate to northern Germany and the Vistula Delta region, which is under Polish control, in order to avoid religious persecution.   **SECT**

1540   As part of the witch-hunts in Europe, four women suspected of being witches are burned in Wittenberg, Germany.   **SPIR**

1540s   Spiritualism emerges in western Europe in the context of the Protestant Reformation. Spiritualists focus on the inner self, a personal relationship with God, and mysticism, and they worship individually rather than forming organized churches or congregations. Important spiritualists include Anabaptist Hans Denck, Lutheran Sebastian Franck, Caspar Schwenckfeld, Thomas Muntzer, Nicholas Storch, and Mark Stubner.   **SPIR**

1541   As Spanish control of the Americas spreads, the first Roman Catholic bishoprics in South America are established in Lima and Caracas, with the latter becoming the central church for all of western South America in 1575. **CATH**

1541   The Bible is first translated into Swedish.   **CHRIS**

1541   Muhammad al-Korau dies. During his life, he founds the Muslim Hausa chiefdom of Katsina in West Africa and makes it a center of Islamic scholarship in the region by attracting scholars from North Africa.   **ISLAM**

1541   The *Institutes of the Christian Religion*, the basic statement of Calvinism, is translated into French, which makes it available to educated Christians in Europe and aids in the spread of Calvinist influence in Europe.   **PROT**

1542   Jesuit missionary Francis Xavier (1506–1552), a Basque from Portugal, establishes a mission in Goa and then in southern India. He translates several basic texts, such as the Ten Commandments and the Lord's Prayer, into the local language and makes several thousand converts.   **CATH**

1542   In England witchcraft is legally classified as a felony punishable by death.   **SPIR**

1543   Chu Sebung founds Paegundong Academy, modeled on Zhu Xi's *Bai Lu Dong* in China. Similar schools known as *sowon* begin to appear throughout Korea, all intended to propagate Confucian ideals and serve as a power base for neo-Confucian intellectuals.   **CONF**

1543	The Protestant Reformation causes difficulties for Jews who resist conversion to Christianity when Martin Luther publishes his *About the Jews and Their Lies*. The work is cited by some scholars as marking the beginning of modern anti-Semitism in Europe and represents a shift in Luther's thinking to hostility toward Jews. Previously, he had argued for the peaceful conversion of Jews. **JUD**
1545	Factions struggle for power in Korea following the death of Injong. *Ulsa sahwa*, a fourth and final purge of the neo-Confucian literati, ensues. **CONF**
1545–1563	Pope Paul III convenes the Council of Trent, which meets in three sessions (1545–1547, 1551–1552, 1562–1563) over the 18-year period to revitalize the Roman Catholic Church. It moves to end many of the abuses and corruptions that had crept into church practices and to improve church discipline. Seminaries are created and Sunday schools are opened to teach the Bible to commoners. For the first time, women are provided Catholic education through the Ursulines and the Sisters of Charity. **CATH**
1546	Tao Zhongwen, the influential Daoist adviser to the emperor of Ming China, invites 24,000 of his followers to Beijing to be ordained as priests. **DAO**
1547	The first Roman Catholic bishopric is established in central South America, at Asunción, Paraguay. **CATH**
1547	At a council of the Russian Orthodox Church, saints are canonized and held up as models of Christian behavior and the administrative structure of the Church is streamlined. Similar actions are taken at another council convened in 1549. **ORTHO**
1547	In England Henry VIII is succeeded by his son Edward. Edward is a supporter of the Reformation and appoints Protestant theologians to positions at Oxford and Cambridge. **PROT**
1548	In the *Augsburg Interim*, Holy Roman Emperor Charles V seeks to reconcile Catholics and Protestants in Germany by revising some Catholic practices and applying them to Protestants such as allowing Protestant ministers to marry to make Catholicism more acceptable to Protestants. The compromise is found unacceptable to people on both sides and fails to end the conflict. **CATH**
1548	*Spiritual Exercises* is written by Ignatius Loyola (1491–1556), a Catholic priest and the founder of the Jesuits. The book focuses on overcoming the sinful nature of humanity, and Loyola proposes a four-step process, including personal reform, imitation of Christ, spiritual strengthening, and spiritual transformation. Pope Paul III officially approves its publication so that other Catholic orders can use it as a model of spiritual and moral development. The *Exercises* are still used by Catholic missions in the 20th century. **CATH**

1548– 1572	In what will become the country of Laos, Setthathirat, eldest son of Phothisarat, succeeds his father and unifies the Kingdom of Lan Xang with another kingdom to its west, Lan Na. After three years, however, he loses control over Lan Na. In 1560 Setthathirat moves his capital from Muang Sua south to Vieng Chan (modern Vientiane, Laos); he enshrines the Pra Keo, a green jasper carving of the Buddha, and creates the That Luang, a shrine to house Buddhist relics **(SEE 1778–1779, BUDD)**. **BUDD**
1549	Jesuit missionary Francis Xavier establishes a Roman Catholic mission in Japan, the first Christian mission in the nation. Xavier's experience in Japan over the next two years changes his view of missionary activity and changes the philosophy of Christian missionary activity in general. In the context of Japanese civilization, conversion to Christianity is seen as building on the existing system, rather than rejecting the existing system and replacing it entirely with Christianity. **CATH**
1549	The *Book of Common Prayer* is written by Anglican archbishop Thomas Cranmer in England. It combines Protestant and Catholic beliefs and practices to provide a standard set of practices for the Anglican Church. **PROT**
1550	The Bible is first translated into Danish. **CHRIS**
1550	Charles V of Spain suspends Spanish exploration of the Americas and convenes a meeting of leading theologians at the Council of Fourteen in Valladolid, Spain. The council addresses the questions of whether Native Americans are equal to or inferior to Europeans and whether the Spanish can use force to eradicate native religions and replace them with Christianity. The primary supporter of the inferior/forcible conversion view is Spanish philosopher Juan Ginés de Sepulveda, while Dominican priest and former bishop of Chiapas in Mexico Bartolomé de las Casas argues that Indians are equal—and even superior in some ways—to Europeans. All agree, however, that the Indians must be converted to Christianity. **CHRIS, NATIV**
1550s	The syncretic teachings of the scholar Lin Zhao'en (1517–1598) are influential in late Ming China. Originally a master of the Quanzhen Daoist school, Lin establishes his own movement based on the unity of the Three Teachings and heavily influenced by Daoist practice. Confucian values, he teaches, are the beginning of the Way; he advocates ritual and practical aids to cultivate Confucian virtues. Like the Pure Light school, Lin's Daoism is an example of accommodation with Confucian thought. **CONF, DAO**
c. 1550– c. 1580	Among the Korean Confucians, Yi Hwang (1501–1570), known by his literary name Yi T'oegye, adheres closely to Zhu Xi (Chu Hsi), founding the School of Principle. Yi I (1536–1584), known by his literary name Yulgok, establishes the School of Material Force, holding that the principle in each thing is distinct, determined by its material force. T'oegye's philosophy is developed by the Yongnam school; Yulgok's is developed by the Kiho school; they emerge as political as well as scholarly rivals. **CONF**

| 1550–1600 | Led by the central government, Korean village schools, private academies, and other institutions of learning make the Confucian learning of the principle a political ideology and common creed. **CONF** |

| 1551 | The first Roman Catholic bishopric is established in Brazil, at San Salvador de Bahia. **CATH** |

| 1551 | At the Council of the 100 Chapters of the Russian Orthodox Church held in Moscow, some beliefs and practices associated with the Orthodox Church of the now-defunct Byzantine Empire are revised, creating unique Russian Orthodox forms of worship. The two most significant practices are the chanting of two Alleluias and the use of the two-fingered sign of the cross. **ORTHO** |

| 1552 | The Russians conquer Kazan and then Astrakhan in 1556 and limit Ottoman Empire attempts to expand north into Russian territory. **ISLAM** |

| 1552 | The *Book of Common Prayer*, the standard text for the Anglican Church, is revised by its compiler, Archbishop Thomas Cranmer, to remove all references to Roman Catholicism and to be completely Protestant in nature. It serves as the basis for future editions used in the Anglican Church in Britain and the Episcopal Church in the United States. **PROT** |

Thomas Cranmer

Cranmer was born the son of a village squire in 1489 in Nottinghamshire, England. Following his study at the University of Cambridge, Cranmer remained an obscure Cambridge scholar during much of his early adult life. Finally Cranmer entered the priesthood in 1526 at the rather late age of 37. Ordination brought a measure of success to Cranmer that academic pursuits did not as he quickly became an integral figure in the efforts of Henry VIII to divorce his wife, Catherine of Aragon. He also played a major role in converting England to Protestantism, a process that culminated in 1534 with the passage of the Act of Supremacy by Parliament and the declaration of the English monarch, not the pope, as the head of the English Church. As a reward for his service to the state, Henry VIII appointed Cranmer as the archbishop of Canterbury, the highest religious authority in England. As archbishop, Cranmer sought to institute many changes based on Protestant teachings such as the rejection of papal authority and the removal of Catholic influences. In 1549 he laid the foundation for modern-day Anglicanism by writing the *42 Articles of Religion* and the *Book of Common Prayer*, whose purpose was the elimination of the remaining vestiges of Catholicism from Anglican Church services. However, unlike other Protestant Reformers, Cranmer did believe in the sacredness of the Eucharist and preserved its place as a central event in the service. Cranmer fell from favor when Mary Tudor, a Catholic, ascended the English throne in 1553. He was arrested, imprisoned, and forced to renounce all of the Protestant reforms he had initiated. In ultimate retribution, Cranmer was burned at the stake in 1556.

1552   Guru Amar Das (1479–1574) becomes the third Sikh Guru and holds the position until his death in 1574. Under his direction, the Sikh community begins to emerge as a distinct religious entity in India. Distinct congregations (*sangats*) are formed, communal dining becomes a basic doctrine, festival days are established, and text that will later form the Sikh scripture is recorded.   **SIKH**

1553   Edward, the king of England, dies; his sister, Mary (r. 1553-1558), ascends to the throne. A supporter of Roman Catholicism, she severely represses Protestantism in an attempt to make England a Roman Catholic nation again. During her reign hundreds of Protestants are burned at the stake, Protestant leaders are imprisoned or exiled, Catholic priests are restored, and Catholic doctrine and worship are reintroduced.   **CATH, PROT**

1553   The Bible is first published in Spanish.   **CHRIS**

1553   The *Forty-two Articles of Religion*, written by Archbishop Thomas Cranmer and supported by King Edward of England, are published. It backs many Protestant ideas and is an important document in the movement away from Roman Catholicism and toward the establishment of the Anglican Church in England.   **PROT**

1553–   This is the lifespan of Hirvijaya Suri, leader of the Svetambara/Jain order
1595   known as the Tapagaccha and one of the greatest of all Jain monks and authors. He comes into contact with the Mughal emperor Akbar between 1582 and 1586 and is said to have persuaded Akbar to pass more humane laws. (Some accounts claim he converts Akbar to Jainism, but this is rejected by most historians.)   **JAIN**

Book of Common Prayer

The *Book of Common Prayer* was drafted in 1549 by Archbishop Thomas Cranmer to provide a common set of practices and rituals for Anglicanism. A collection of services drawing upon original Latin rituals, scripture readings, psalms, and prayers, the book fused Catholic tradition with the new Protestant thinking. In writing the work Cranmer attempted to appease both Protestants and Catholics by recognizing some of the former Catholic sacraments (baptism and the Eucharist) while rejecting the rest. In fact, he pleased neither group. As the book was given legal sanction by the English state, penalties were enacted for refusing to use it, but they were not enforced. In 1552 a groundswell of criticism forced Cranmer to revise the book and to remove all Catholic influences. The effect was to make the *Book of Common Prayer* reflect the ceremonies and theology of the Reformed churches and to be completely Protestant in nature. A modern version of the prayer book is still in use by Anglican and Episcopalian congregations.

1554   A Protestant revolt is defeated, and Mary's half-sister and future queen
        Elizabeth I is imprisoned. Mary is also accused of involvement in the exe-
        cution of 300 Protestants and is labeled Bloody Mary as a result. **CATH, PROT**

1554   At a council of the Russian Orthodox Church, various beliefs and practices
        of Protestantism and of the non-Possessors (Russian Orthodox who call for
        a separation of church and state) are condemned.   **ORTHO, PROT**

1554–   With the end of the persecution of Anabaptists in the Hapsburg Empire, the
1592   Hutterites in Moravia and Slovakia attract followers from neighboring
        Germany and Austria and numerous *bruderhofs* (communities) based on the
        communal ownership of property develop. Hutterites refer to these years of
        growth and expansion and peace as the Good Period (1554–1565) and the
        Golden Period (1565–1592).   **SECT**

1555   In Mexico the priesthood and membership in religious orders is restricted
        to men of pure European ancestry, thereby eliminating the opportunity for
        Native Americans converted to Catholicism to become priests.   **CATH**

1555   The Jain tradition of miniature painting, along with Hindu and Islamic tra-
        ditions in India, comes under Persian influence when the Mughal emperor
        Humayum brings master painters of the Persian court, Mir Sayyid Ali and
        Abd al-amad, to Delhi. They train more than a hundred Indian artists and
        establish the Mughal school of painting in India.   **ISLAM, JAIN,**

1555   The Peace of Augsburg treaty is signed by the Lutherans and Catholics in
        Germany. It marks the end of efforts of Charles V to repress Lutheranism
        and recognizes both Lutheranism and Catholicism as religions. It gives
        Protestant princes the right to Protestant Church property and sets forth the
        principle that the religion of the ruler becomes the religion of his state
        (cuius regio, eius religio).   **PROT**

1555   The first edition of *Prophecies* by French physician Michel de Nostredame
        (1503–1566), who is later known as Nostradamus, is published in France. It
        remains in the print in the 1990s and over the centuries has been studied and
        analyzed by spiritualists and others interested in predicting the future.   **SPIR**

1555–   Paul IV (1476–1559) is pope of the Roman Catholic Church. Both as a
1559   cardinal and then pope, he takes a conservative view toward the reforms
        demanded by the Protestant reformers as well as toward their theology and
        seeks to end dissent by harsh means. He institutes the *Index of Forbidden
        Books*, transforms the Inquisition from a tool of political power to one for
        persecution, and seeks to destroy all heretics and unbelievers. He also issues
        a papal bull that places severe restrictions on Jews in areas under church
        control. Jews are required to live in ghettos and to have only minimal con-
        tact with Christians.   **CATH, JUD**

| 1556 | Jesuit monk (St.) Peter Canisius (1521–1597) writes the second of his three *Catechisms*, which remains in print for centuries and becomes a basic source for the renewal of Roman Catholicism in Germany. **CATH** |

| 1556 | Thomas Cranmer, the Protestant Reformer and an important shaper of the Anglican Church in England, is forced to renounce all of the Protestant reforms he had initiated and is then burned at the stake during the reign of Catholic queen Mary Tudor. **CATH, PROT** |

| 1556 | The persecution of Muslims continues in Spain with Muslims prohibited from wearing Muslim- or Arab-style dress, and in 1566 the use of Arabic is prohibited. **ISLAM** |

| 1556–1605 | In India Muslim and Hindu elements begin to merge during this period. One of the most important aspects that results is the adoption of the Hindu caste structure by Muslim society; Muslims are ordered into four hierarchial categories, a practice absent elsewhere in the Islamic world. **HIND, ISLAM** |

| 1556–1605 | In southern Asia the high period of the Muslim Mughal Empire begins with the rule of Akbar (1542–1605). Akbar extends the empire to cover the modern nations of Afghanistan, Pakistan, Bangladesh, the Himalayan states, and the northern half of India. He also continues the policy of religious toleration and appoints Hindus to high government and military posts. Akbar is a man of broad intellectual curiosity; throughout his reign he insists on religious tolerance, promoting a policy of *sulh-I kull* (universal peace). After seven years of talks with Hindus, Jains, Parsis, Buddhists, and Jesuits at his famous religious assembly, *Ibadat Khanah* (House of Worship), he promulgates a new syncretistic faith, *Din-I Ilahi* (Divine Faith). Orthodox Muslims unite in opposition to this heresy, which attracts few adherents and ends with Akbar's reign, although it is claimed that his Mughal successors did show respect for the Jains. **ISLAM** |

| 1557 | Goa, the Portuguese colony in India, is made an archbishopric and becomes the center of the Roman Catholic church in eastern Asia with authority over the churches in Malacca, Cochin, Macao, Cranganore, and Mylapore. **CATH** |

| 1558 | In Scotland Protestant Reformer John Knox (c. 1513–1572), a follower of Reformer John Calvin, writes the *Appellation*, in which he exhorts the Protestant Scottish aristocracy to rebel against Catholic rule. In the next two years Knox is able to organize the Scottish aristocracy and to overthrow the Catholic government. Over the next few years, Knox organizes an independent Scottish Church, which he calls the Kirk. The Kirk is a forerunner of the Presbyterian Church as he seeks to create a structure based on the authority of the ministry and lay persons and develops a Reformed liturgy for the church. **PROT** |

1559   Pope Paul IV and the Council of Trent publish the *Index of Forbidden Books*
        in order to limit the influence of Protestantism. The list includes three-
        fourths of the available books in Europe, including the works of the Dutch
        philosopher Erasmus and all non-Latin Bibles.   CATH

1559   As her first act as queen of England after succeeding her sister Mary in 1558,
        Elizabeth I (1533–1603), the half-sister of Queen Mary, who had persecut-
        ed Protestants, promulgates the Religious Settlement of 1559. On the sur-
        face an attempt to reduce conflict between Catholics and Protestants, the
        settlement actually enforces Protestantism by law, effectively establishing
        the Anglican Church as the Church of England. While persecuting the
        Catholics in England, Elizabeth establishes peaceful relations with France
        and Scotland, secretly helping the Protestants in both of these countries, as
        well as those rebelling against Spanish rule in the Netherlands.   CATH, PROT

1559   In Germany Catholic rulers with the support of the Catholic Church begin
        efforts to repress Protestantism and to revitalize Catholicism. The efforts
        continue in many cities throughout the century and by 1600 the spread of
        Protestantism has been controlled.   CATH, PROT

1559   Protestant Reformer John Calvin founds the Geneva Academy to train
        Protestant ministers. It becomes a major center of Calvinism and the Reformed
        Church and produces many leading ministers in the movement.   PROT

1559–   Pius IV (1499–1565) is pope of the Roman Catholic Church. In reaction to
1565   the Protestant Reformation, he revives the reforms that were initiated by Paul
        III and later halted by Paul IV. He reconvenes the Council of Trent, improves

Presbyterianism

Presbyterianism is a branch of Protestant Christianity. It emerged in the late 16th century in Europe and Scotland as the Reformed and Presbyterian churches following the
reconciliation of the Calvinist and Zwinglian reformers in 1548. Thus, it emerged as
an alternative to the Lutheran Church. The early church stressed an openness to future
reform and a role for lay members in managing the church, leading to the general
practice of church governance by both the ministry and the members. As the
Presbyterian Church spread around the world, numerous churches within the denomination were founded and these churches often split to form separate churches. In the
twentieth century there has been a movement toward reconciliation, and in the United
States, for example, the major Presbyterian churches reunified in 1983 to form the
Presbyterian Church (U.S.A.). Because of the diversity of churches—which arose to
some extent from doctrinal differences along a conservative/traditional versus liber-
al/modernist division—it is impossible to summarize Presbyterian beliefs and practices. However, Presbyterianism in general emphasizes human salvation through Jesus
Christ for those predestined to be saved in order to achieve the glory of God.

the education of the Catholic clergy, and revises the *Index of Forbidden Books* to make it less extreme. Pius IV's tolerance does much to restore credibility to a severely damaged church following the reign of Paul IV. **CATH**

1560 The Spanish-style Inquisition is established in the Portuguese colony of Goa. **CATH**

1560 Since 1529 Franciscan priest Bernardino de Sagahun has gathered volumes of information from natives in the Valley of Mexico about life prior to the Spanish conquest in 1521 and has also documented, from the native point of view, the effect of Spanish colonization. He has organized the material into a series of volumes called *A General History of the Things of New Spain,* which in this year is criticized by the rulers and Catholic hierarchy in Spain as hostile to Spain and Roman Catholicism. **NATIV**

1560 The Geneva Bible, an English Bible prepared by William Whittingham of the English Church in Geneva and dedicated to Queen Elizabeth, is published in England. It becomes the standard Bible in England for over 100 years. **PROT**

1560s The Puritans emerge as a movement in England. They are Protestants who object to the retention of Catholic elements in the Protestantism that has developed in England. They are frequently in conflict with the Anglicans, who maintain some elements of Roman Catholicism, including a priesthood. **PROT**

1560– The Huguenots, a group of French Protestants, emerge in France and form a
1629 substantial minority that includes many families of the French nobility, most notably the Bourbons. The group is at first a mystical sect but then adopts beliefs and practices that place it within the framework of Calvinism. **PROT**

1561 The Bible is first published in Polish. **CHRIS**

1561 *Confession of Faith* is written by Protestant reformer John Knox. The book serves as the basis of Scottish Presbyterianism. **PROT**

1562– Wars take place between the Roman Catholics and Huguenots (Protestants)
1598 in France over Catholic persecution of Huguenots. The wars go on intermittently, with periods of peace brought about by Catholic promises of religious tolerance. **CATH, PROT**

1563 Calvinist theologians in Germany write the *Heidelberg Catechism*, which sets forth the basic doctrine of the church and is used throughout central Europe. It distinguishes the Reformed churches from the Lutheran Church. **PROT**

1563 English law governing witchcraft and spiritualism is made more rigid as all activities that involve the use of evil spirits are made capital crimes. In the this same year, an attack on the witch craze (attacks on people accused of practicing witchcraft) is written by Johann Weyer in Germany. Titled *De Praestigiis Daemonum*, it has little practical effect. **SPIR**

| 1564 | Pope Pius IV revises the *Index of Forbidden Books* first published in 1559 by making it less restrictive and by limiting the number of books listed in it.   CATH |

| 1565 | Augustinian missionaries traveling across the Pacific from the Spanish colony of Mexico arrive in the Philippines and establish the first Christian mission there.   CATH |

| 1565 | The third and final major codification of the Jewish *Talmud* (and the first since the 12th century) is published by Joseph Caro (1488–1575) in Palestine. It is called the *Shulchan Aruch* (prepared table) and provides all Jews with an easy-to-use guide to the laws that govern Jewish life.   JUD |

| 1565–1600 | In India Banarasidas, a layman and poet, leads a reform movement attacking the Jain Digambara sect for its adoption of elaborate rituals over the centuries and for the unresponsiveness of the Digambara monks to criticisms.   JAIN |

| 1566 | A revolt against the rule of Philip I of Spain breaks out in the Netherlands. It is led by nobles who want to control Spanish influence. The precipitating incident is Philip's refusal to ban the Spanish Inquisition in the Netherlands. Catholic churches are pillaged by Protestant Calvinist rebels.   CATH |

| 1566 | Jesuit missionaries seek to convert Native Americans near Spanish settlements in what will become the southeastern United States. Their efforts largely end in failure by 1571.   NATIV |

| 1566 | In Scotland Presbyterians adopt the Second Helvtic Confession as a basic statement of Christian devotion. It expands on the first Confession of 1536 by stressing the central role of the Scriptures and becomes a document of unity in the spread of Protestantism in Europe.   PROT |

| 1566 | Francis David (1510–1579) is appointed bishop of the Calvinist Church in Kolozsvar, Transylvania (then part of Hungary; in the 20th century, part of Romania), and begins preaching a doctrine of unitarianism that rejects the Doctrine of the Trinity and views God as one. This marks the beginning of Unitarianism in Hungary.   SECT |

| 1566 | In an early witch trial in England, one woman accused of witchcraft is hanged.   SPIR |

| 1566–1572 | Pius V (1504–1572) is pope of the Roman Catholic Church. A deeply religious man, he returns a profound spirituality to the papacy and institutes reforms suggested by the Council of Trent. It is during his rule that the Catholic Church begins to recover from centuries of temporal and secular corruption and Protestant competition in Europe.   CATH |

| 1567 | In the Netherlands Philip II of Spain and his Council of Troubles have succeeded in repressing the Protestant Calvinist revolt with an army of 20,000 soldiers. However, the Netherlands is soon in complete anarchy brought on |

by revolution and civil war and marked on both sides by desecrations, confiscations, looting, torture, burnings, and hangings. Philip II sees his mission as unifying all of Europe under his rule with Catholicism as the only religion. **CATH**

1567–
1608
The reign of Sonjo in Korea is marked by rejection of the meritorious elite in favor of the neo-Confucian literati, who return to power following the purges of Sejo and begin to dominate the political process. **CONF**

1568
The Paradesi synagogue is built in Cochin, India, to serve the Jewish community there. **JUD**

1568
Jesuit missionaries are active at the first permanent European settlement in North America founded by the Spanish at St. Augustine, Florida. Jesuits in Cuba found a mission school for Native American children brought there by the Spanish as part of their slave raiding in Florida. **NATIV**

1568
In Britain a revised version of the Geneva Bible (first published in 1560), which removes notes offensive to authorities in the Church of England, is published. Known as the Bishop's Bible, it is placed in all cathedrals but remains second in popularity to the Geneva Bible. **PROT**

1569
Jews are expelled from lands controlled by the Roman Catholic Church in western Europe but in the same year are given broad economic and civil rights in Poland. **JUD**

1569–
1572
The Antwerp Polyglot Bible is written in Belgium. It replaces the Complutensian Polyglot Bible written in Spain in 1514–1517, which has become rare, as only 600 copies were made. **CATH**

1570
A Spanish-style Inquistion is established in Peru and in the following year in Mexico. **CATH**

1570
A commission established by the Roman Catholic Council of Trent issues the *Missale Romnum*, which sets forth detailed instructions for the conduct of the Mass. The new form of the Mass is controlled and rigid and requires the use of Latin. It remains the required form into the 1960s. **CATH**

1570
Spanish explorers have moved up the east coast of the future United States and Jesuit missionaries found a mission to the Powhatan and Piscataway peoples in Maryland. The mission fails when the missionaries are killed by the natives, who are resisting Spanish settlement. **NATIV**

1570
In Poland Protestants declare their devotion to the faith in the *Consensus Sandomir*. **PROT**

1570s
In a campaign to eliminate political and military dominance of Buddhist sects, Japan's Emperor Nobunaga begins a 10-year war against the True Pure

Land sect of Buddhists (SEE **1175, BUDD**). In 1571 he demolishes the Tendai sect's Enryakuji temple, massacring thousands of monks. In 1579, after the Azuchi Disputation between priests of True Pure Land and sects, Nobunaga declares Nichiren Buddhists the losers and orders three leaders executed.

BUDD

1570–
1602

During the rule of Idris b. Ali, Islam becomes more important in the Kanuri state centered in Bornu in West Africa. The state adopts Islamic law as state law, mosques are built, and housing is constructed for Kanuri pilgrims to Mecca. Ngazargamo, the capital city, becomes a center of Islam in West Africa.

ISLAM

1571

Southern European states unite and defeat the Ottoman fleet at the Battle of Lepanto, temporarily halting Ottoman expansion and control of the Mediterranean Sea.

ISLAM

1572

On August 25 the St. Bartholomew's Day Massacre occurs in Paris, France. Thousands of Huguenots (Protestants) are killed by the ruling Catholics after the Catholics have promised their safety. Fighting between the groups spreads across France and lasts for six weeks.

CATH, PROT

1572

In Poland the nobles issue their *Pax Dissidentium* (Peace of the Dissenters), which asks the king to give equal rights to the Protestants and Roman Catholics. The policy is adopted by King Sigismund but reversed by his successors.

CATH, PROT

1572–
1585

Gregory XIII (1502–1585) is pope of the Roman Catholic Church. He continues the reforms of the Council of Trent and his predecessor Pius V and promotes education among the clergy, thereby greatly enhancing the quality of those who serve the church. His rule is sullied by his association with the massacre of Huguenots (French Protestants) in Paris in 1572.

CATH

1574

The leaders of the Kanuri state centered in Bornu in West Africa take what is the first of a series of pilgrimages to Mecca, indicating their commitment to Islam. As in most of West Africa, it is primarily the ruling elite and traders who have converted to Islam while the majority of the population, most of them rural farmers, continues to follow indigenous religions.

ISLAM

1574

Repression of Jews increases in the Muslim world when Ottoman ruler Murad III enforces laws that require Jews to wear distinctive clothing and bans the repair or construction of synagogues. Jews in central Asia are forced to convert to Islam, although many continue to practice Judaism in secret.

JUD

1574

Guru Ram Das (1534–1581) becomes the fourth Sikh guru but holds the position for only seven years, until his death in 1581. The Sikh religion continues to grow as Guru Ram Das establishes the sacred center of Amritsar and appoints leaders to manage the affairs of Sikh congregations.

SIKH

1576   Pope Gregory XIII issues his papal bull *Nuper ad Nos*, in which he notes the absence of priests in the Americas who speak local languages and allows mestizos (persons of mixed Spanish and native ancestry) to become priests. However, the order is ignored and no mestizos or natives become priests until 1794.   **CATH**

1576   As the revolution against Spanish rule continues in the Netherlands, Protestant and Catholic leaders of the provinces unite to drive Spain from the Netherlands.   **CHRIS**

1576   England under Queen Elizabeth formally sides with and begins openly supporting the rebels in the Netherlands, who since 1566 have been seeking to overthrow the Spanish rulers. The conflict in the Netherlands is basically political and economic but also involves tension between Spanish Catholics and local Protestants.   **CHRIS**

1576   The Bengal region of India becomes part of the Muslim Mughal Empire when conquered by Akbar the Great.   **ISLAM**

1576   In Bohemia (in modern-day Hungary) toleration of Protestants ends when Rudolf succeeds his father, Maximilian II, as the Holy Roman Emperor. **PROT**

1577   The poem "Dark Night of the Soul" is written by Spanish Roman Catholic mystic John of the Cross (1542–1591), who is a member of the Carmelite order and an associate of the mystic Teresa of Avila. The poem stresses God's love for mankind and like other Catholic mystical works of the Counter-Reformation allows for the emotional expression of one's relationship to God. Because many Europeans are illiterate, mysticism has much appeal during this time because it permits worship without the need for reading.   **CATH**

1577   The fullest and earliest European description of native life in the Americas, *A General History of the Things of New Spain*, compiled and written in the Valley of Mexico by the Spanish Franciscan priest Bernardino de Sagahun from 1529 on, is nearly destroyed in the Spanish Inquisition. Inquisition officials cite it as a work of heresy and Sagahun is excommunicated. He sends one Spanish-language copy of the 12-volume work to Spain, but it ends up in the library in Florence, Italy, and later is known as the *Florentine Codex*. **SEE 1985, CATH**.   **NATIV**

1578   After his conversion to Buddhism, the Mongol prince Altan Khan bestows the honorific title Dalai Lama ("priest with ocean-like wisdom") on Sonam Gyatso (1543–1588), abbot of Drepung monastery in Tibet. He is thus the first Dalai Lama, but the title is posthumously applied to his predecessors, Gedung Truppa (1391–1474) and Gedung Gyatso (1475–1542), who are henceforth regarded as the first and second Dalai Lamas.   **BUDD**

1578   In Austria King Rudolf and his successor King Ferdinand repress Protestantism, and Roman Catholicism recovers. By 1628 nearly all Austrians are Roman Catholic.   CATH, PROT

1578   Liu Tsung-chou (1578–1645) is born and later becomes a principal critic of leading Chinese Confucian scholar Wang Yang-ming. His *Jen-p'u* (*Human Schemata*) offers a disciplined description of human errors as a corrective to Wang's moral optimism.   CONF

1579   Portuguese Catholic missionaries establish a mission in Macao, the Portuguese trading colony on the coast of China. The Roman Catholic church establishes the bishopric of Manila in the Philippines, under the administration of the archbishopric of Mexico.   CATH

1579   Faustus Socinus (1539–1604) becomes the leader of the Polish Brethren in Cracow. In his writing and preaching he stresses the unity of God, rejects the doctrine of the Trinity, and stresses the humanity and good deeds of Christ. All of these ideas provide a theological framework for Unitarianism.   SECT

c. 1580   The Guarani people in Paraguay revolt against Spanish rule and follow Obera, a native who proclaims that he is the messiah and calls upon his followers to reject Christianity and follow his new religion, which combines elements from Indian religions and Christianity. The movement is suppressed and ends when many followers are massacred.   NATIV

1580   Jesuit missionaries are invited to visit the court of Akbar, the Muslim ruler of the Mughal Empire in India. They fail to convert him to Christianity but are welcomed by the court. Two more Jesuit missions fail in 1591 and 1595.   CATH

1580   Conflict between the Spanish Hapsburg rulers and the Ottoman Empire for control of North Africa and the Mediterranean ends with a truce that leaves each in control of part of the region.   ISLAM

1580   Jews from Portugal settle in Argentina. They are *conversos* who must practice their Judaism in secret.   JUD

1580   In Poland the Jewish Council of Four Lands begins to emerge. It becomes a self-governing organization for Jewish communities in the region that later becomes parts of Poland, Russia, and Lithuania.   JUD

1580   The Ostrog Bible, a Slavic Bible, is published; it is revised the following year. The result of years of work by Orthodox scholars in Lithuania and Poland and based on Hebrew, Latin, Greek, Slavic and other sources, the Bible is considered a work of superior scholarship and becomes the standard source for future Orthodox Bibles.   ORTHO

1580   The Protestant denomination of Congregationalism begins in England when Robert Browne (c. 1550–c. 1633), an Anglican minister supportive of

Puritanism, establishes a church in Norwich without the permission of the Church of England. In this year and the next he continues to preach and establishes churches.   **PROT**

1581   The Ming emperor Shenzong (r. 1573–1620) asks Daoist priests to pray for the birth of a son and heir and sends a delegation to pray at Mount Wudang, a Daoist holy place in Hubei Province in China. An heir appears approximately nine months after the prayers. Buddhists and Daoists both claim credit for the event.   **BUDD, DAO**

1581   Roman Catholic priest and reformer (St.) Charles Borromeo (1538–1584) is made an archbishop. The nephew of Pope Pius IV (r. 1559–1565), he is a leading figure in the Catholic Counter-Reformation. He aids in reviving the Council of Trent and dedicates himself to instituting the clerical reforms set down by the council. In 1610 he is canonized for his work.   **CATH**

1581   The Bible is first published in Slavonic.   **CHRIS**

1581   Robert Browne and several followers who have established Congregational churches as alternatives to the Church of England are forced to flee to Middelburg in the Netherlands to seek religious freedom. Browne has escaped imprisonment by the British monarchy because of his political connections. In the Netherlands Browne writes three treatises on Congregational theology, worship, and church organization that become the basis of the faith.   **PROT**

1581   Upon the death of his father, Guru Arjan (1563–1606) becomes the fifth Sikh guru. His succession marks a new direction in Sikh practice, and the next five gurus are all descendants of Guru Ram Das or of his caste in India. Sikhism continues to expand and draw followers among rural farmers, new Sikh villages are founded, and the sacred center at Amritsar is expanded. Guru Arjan also compiles the first scripture of Sikhism and becomes the first Sikh martyr when he is killed by the Muslim Mughal emperor Jahangir in 1606.   **SIKH**

1582   Pope Gregory XIII revises the Julian calendar (in use since 46 B.C.E.) and replaces it with the Gregorian calendar of 365 days a year and a leap year of 366 days every fourth year.   **CATH**

1582   Matteo Ricci, a Jesuit priest, begins a mission to China, the first major encounter between the two cultural traditions and perhaps the only serious Christian approach to Confucianism. Ricci and his Jesuit successors adopt the dress of local scholar officials, respect Chinese customs, and acknowledge a degree of truth in Confucian doctrine. They allow that "conversion" need not imply alienation from Chinese culture and are prepared to accept ancestor rites.   **CATH, CONF**

1582   Jesuit missionaries bring four Japanese men to Rome to experience the Catholic Church firsthand. Their visit lasts for eight years and they draw the attention of many Europeans.   **CHRIS**

1582   In India the Muslim ruler Akbar promulgates a new syncretistic faith, *Din-I Ilahi* (Divine Faith), the fruit of seven years of talks with Hindus, Jains, Parsis, Buddhists, and Jesuits at his famous religious assembly, *Ibadat Khanah* (House of Worship). Orthodox Muslims unite in opposition to this heresy, which attracts few adherents and ends with the end of Akbar's reign in 1605. A man of broad intellectual curiosity, Akbar insists throughout his reign on religious tolerance, promoting a policy of *sulh-I kull* (universal peace). **TOL**

1583   Robert Browne and several followers return from the Netherlands, where they had fled from England, and seek to establish Congregational churches in Scotland. The effort is opposed by the Scottish Presbyterians and Browne returns to England. Two of Browne's followers are executed for distributing his treatises written in 1581. English Separatism or Congregationalism has evolved from the Protestant sect of Calvinism, but under Browne's leadership, unlike in Calvinism, the Separatists believe in complete freedom of individual church congregations from the control of the state. **PROT**

1583–1598   During the reign of Japan's ruler Hideyoshi, he commissions a number of magnificent buildings—including the great Buddha Hall at Kyoto—and repairs many religious structures. The Great Buddha statue, larger than one in Nara's Todaiji, is twice damaged by earthquakes. **BUDD**

1584   The Bible is first translated into Icelandic and Slovenian. **CHRIS**

1584   Emmanuel College is established at Cambridge University in England and becomes an important center for the training of Puritan clergy. Although active in England for several decades, the Puritans have been unable to convince the government or the established Anglican Church to revise their theology or practices in accord with Puritan beliefs. However, their ideas do spread throughout the general population, primarily through ministers, many of whom are trained at Emmanuel College. **PROT**

1585   In their continuing effort to eradicate native religions and convert natives to Catholicism, the Spanish end the playing of the Mesoamerican ball games in Mexico. The games are played for recreational and religious purposes. **NATIV**

1585   England enters the war between Spain and the Netherlands with English and Dutch sea raiders attacking Spanish ships and Spanish colonies in South America. England is now the major supporter of Protestantism and also a leading challenger of Spanish power. **PROT**

1585–1590   Sixtus V (1521–1590) is pope of the Roman Catholic Church. He continues the reforms of his predecessors and restructures the bureaucracy in Rome into a form that remains in place in the 1990s. **CATH**

1586   In the face of continuing conflict with the monarchy and the Anglican Church, Robert Browne, who established the first Congregational Church in

1580 and then fled to the Netherlands, reunites with the Anglican Church and serves as a minister from 1591 to his death. **PROT**

1586–
1593
Controversies is written by Roman Catholic cardinal and theologian (St.) Robert Bellarmine (1542–1621) in Rome. The work is essentially a defense of the church against Protestantism although it also contains interpretations that displease the pope, including some that question the authority of the pope in nonreligious matters. For that reason he is not canonized until 1930. **CATH**

1587
In Shandong, China, the Buddhist White Lotus sect stages an uprising but it is soon suppressed. **BUDD**

1587
(St.) Aloysius Gonzaga (1568–1591) is ordained a priest in Rome and begins ministering to those suffering from the plague. He catches the disease and dies three years later at the age of 23. As a boy and young man he lived an exemplary life, is canonized in 1726, and is made the patron saint of Catholic youth and Jesuit students in 1926 in recognition of his work with children. **CATH**

1587
Japanese emperor Hideyoshi, who has recently unified Japan after 500 years of decentralized rule, orders that all foreigners, who are primarily Roman Catholics, be expelled. The order is not enforced but establishes a new antiforeigner policy followed by Hideyoshi's successors. **TOL**

1587–
1632
During the rule of Sigismund III over Poland, Protestantism is repressed and through the work of the Jesuits, Roman Catholicism becomes the national religion. Sigismund III is known as the "King of the Jesuits." **CATH, PROT**

1588
Provoked by vandalized Buddhist shrines by converts to Christianity and by Portuguese traders who deal in Japanese slaves, Japan's Emperor Hideyoshi issues more anti-Christian edicts. **BUDD, CHRIS**

1588
The Bible is first translated into Welsh. **CHRIS**

1588
The Spanish Armada is defeated by the English navy off the coast of England. To avoid total defeat the Spanish fleet attempts to return to Spain by following the northern coasts of Scotland and Ireland, a dangerous route for which the Spanish have no charts or pilots. The Spanish lose many of their ships in a great storm off the coast of Scotland, the famous "Protestant Wind." Only half of the "Invincible Armada" makes it back to Spain. This great naval defeat marks a turning point in history, with the Dutch and the English becoming masters of the seas. **PROT**

1588
The Dutch theologian and minister Jacobus Arminius (1560–1609) becomes a minister in Amsterdam. There, and later as a theology professor at the University of Leiden, he advocates the theological position later known as Arminianism. He argues against the strict predestination of Calvinism and suggests instead that salvation or damnation is not fully pre-

destined—that all people can be saved. The idea remains a controversial one in Christianity and is adopted by some later reformers, such as John Wesley, the founder of Methodism. **PROT**

1588–1629 In Iran the Safavid Muslim rulers begin a program of military and administrative reform. They also persecute rival Sufi orders and encourage the conversion of Jews. **ISLAM**

1589 The Russian Orthodox Church gains status as an autocephalous church within Orthodoxy when it breaks with the Greek-dominated church. **ORTHO**

1589 Three women accused of witchcraft are convicted and hanged in England. **SPIR**

1590 The Bible is first translated into Hungarian. **CHRIS**

1590 Jewish *conversos* from Portugal and Brazil immigrate to the northern Netherlands when the region becomes independent of Spain. Although they move in search of religious freedom, they continue to practice Judaism in secret. **JUD**

1590 The Spanish begin explorations from the area of modern-day Mexico City north into what will become New Mexico where they encounter Pueblo peoples living in settled farming communities and practicing religions centered on worship in underground ceremonial chambers called *kivas*. The subsequent Spanish conquest focuses on destroying the native religions and the persecution of Indian religious leaders, as part of their effort to conquer the region. **NATIV**

1591 The Songhay Empire in West Africa is destroyed by invaders from Morocco and the period of Muslim states in West Africa comes to an end. Islam survives, however, in the small chiefdoms that follow the Songhay Empire and gradually spreads among the common people. **ISLAM**

1592 Kandy becomes the royal capital of Sri Lanka. The Tooth Relic of Buddha accompanies the court to the city and the Temple of the Tooth Relic (*Dalada Maligawa*) built to house it becomes Sri Lanka's holiest shrine. **SEE 1998, BUDD.** **BUDD**

1593 Jesuit missionaries open a seminary in Japan to train Japanese for the Catholic priesthood. **CATH**

1594 Japan's supreme warlord Toyotomi Hideyoshi (1536–1598) confiscates and reapportions all Shinto shrine and Buddhist temple properties. In 1595 he issues regulations ordering Shinto shrines and Buddhist temples to devote their energies to scholarship. In this era of widespread political disorder, many regional warlords continue to protect religious institutions. **SHINTO**

1596   Dominican, Franciscan, and Augustinian missionaries have now joined Jesuits in seeking converts in Japan. The group is also now culturally mixed, as it includes Spaniards, Portuguese, and Italians.   **CATH**

1596   The leader of the Orthodox Church in Kiev and many Ukrainian bishops reunite with the Roman Catholic Church and become the Uniate Ukrainian Church.   **CHRIS**

1598   The first *cabildo*, a brotherhood of African slaves, is formed in Cuba. Over the next century centuries many *cabildos* are established and supported by the Roman Catholic Church. They also serve the church as the mechanism through which slaves can be converted to Christianity, although in many *cabildos* traditional African beliefs and practices are maintained, and the organizations serve as mutual aid societies for the slaves.   **AFRICAN**

1598   The Edict of Nantes is decreed by King Henry IV of France. It ends more than 30 years of religious civil war in France between the Catholic majority and a sizable minority of French Protestants known as the Huguenots. The edict grants religious freedom to the Huguenots in return for their allegiance to the French crown. The decree proclaims the following rights for French Protestants: freedom of religious belief, the right of private worship wherever they live, the right to conduct public worship in a number of specific towns and castles, the right to hold public office, and the right to control a number of walled towns and castles for their protection.   **CATH, PROT**

1598   The Spanish conquest and colonization of southwestern North America takes shape with Indian religions repressed and Indians forced to convert to Christianity. Many Indian tribes maintain their religions in secret.   **NATIV**

1598   After the death of Japan's leader Toyotomi Hideyoshi, Yoshida Shinto priests are put in charge of his funeral rites and of his subsequent deification as a great warrior at Toyotomi shrine.   **SHINTO**

1598– 1708   In the late Yi dynasty in Korea, the economy nears collapse following the Imjin War (1592–1598) against the Japanese invaders, and the 1627 and 1636 Manchu invasions further weaken the state. The increasing factionalism of the Confucian literati impedes adoption of needed reforms. The *Sirhak* or Practical Learning school develops, and in 1708 the tax code is revised to remove the burden of debt from the lower classes. Gradually a money economy and vital merchant class develops.   **CONF**

1599   Jesuit educators publish the *Ratio Studiorum*, a manual for education. It provides detailed instructions for the administration of schools, the courses and programs of study, the selection and training of teachers, the techniques of teaching, and the methods of discipline. With the manual's guidance, the Jesuits establish over 400 Jesuit-related colleges by 1626.   **CATH**

1599   At the Synod of Diamper in India, the independence of the Syrian Christian
            Church (Church of the Thomas Christians) ends in India when it is brought
            under the control of the Roman Catholic Church. The Syrian Christians
            resist affiliation with the Catholic Church as they prefer affiliation with the
            Eastern Orthodox Church.   **CHRIS**

1600   By the end of the 16th century, it is clear that the Catholic religious orders
            (Jesuits, Dominicans, and others) have through their example and teach-
            ings reversed the moral and spiritual decline of the 14th and early 15th cen-
            turies. The orders increase in popularity and their memberships increase
            accordingly.   **CATH**

1600   Italian Jesuit missionary Matteo Ricci (1552–1610), operating from the
            Catholic mission at Macao, wins permission to visit the imperial capital in
            Beijing. He wins the favor of the emperor and maintains a mission there for
            10 years until his death.   **CATH**

1600   The British, Dutch, and Danes begin competing with the Spanish and
            Portuguese for control of the Americas. In addition to the political and eco-
            nomic rivalry, rivalries also develop between the Protestant missionaries,
            who are supported by the former three nations, and the Catholic mission-
            aries, who are already active in the Americas and are supported by the lat-
            ter two nations. This rivalry comes to characterize future Chrsitian mission-
            ary activity around the world, with Catholic, Orthodox, Protestant, Seventh-
            Day Adventist, Evangelical, Mormon, and other missionaries often working
            to convert those previously converted by other Christian religions.   **CHRIS**

1600   Indonesian Muslim Sufi teacher Hamza Fansuri dies. During his life he
            founds the Qadri Sufi order in Indonesia, which is an important element of
            Islam in the state of Acheh and plays a major role in spreading and main-
            taining Islam in rural farming communities.   **ISLAM**

1600   Jews from eastern Europe, most of whom had fled there from western
            Europe, begin to settle in Czechoslovakia, marking the beginning of a
            migration back to western Europe. The migration is motivated by new
            repressions in Russia and Poland, such as forced conversion to Eastern
            Orthodoxy and relaxed economic and civil restrictions in the west, which
            are the result of rapid economic growth and expansion.   **JUD**

1600   The British East India Company is chartered to represent British commer-
            cial interests in India. Anglican ministers serve the company's laborers in
            India and also work to convert Indians.   **PROT**

1600s   The Strict Observance movement emerges in the Roman Catholic Church.
            Followers advocate an ascetic lifestyle even including vegetarianism. The
            movement is led by A. de Rance (d. 1700), the abbot of La Trappe, and in
            the 18th century the movement is called the Trappists.   **CATH**

1600s   Jesuit missionaries from the West identify the religious nature (including worship, rituals, and sacrifice) of the belief system based on the teachings of Confucius and coin the Latinized term *Confucianism*. In Chinese, the tradition is called *Rujia (Ju-chia)* or School of the Literati after members of the new *shih* class of educated gentry, who are especially distinguished for scholarship and high moral character.   **CONF**

1600s   With the fall of the Ming dynasty in China (1644), Korean scholars become concerned with orthodoxy as they seek to redefine Korea's role in the Confucian world. The process is seen in the conflict between Song Siyol (1607–1689) and Yun Hyu (1617–1680). Siyol, a follower of Yulgok, wishes to maintain Zhu Xi (Chu Hsi) orthodoxy and the Ch'eng-Chu school. Hyu prefers a wider definition of orthodoxy, as seen in his own commentaries on the *Four Books*.   **CONF**

1600s   Rosicrucian beliefs are revived in Germany, primarily through the publication of the mystical work *Fama Fraternitatis*, whose author is unknown but whom later Rosicrucians believe to be the English philosopher Sir Roger Bacon (1561–1626), who directed the Rosicrucian order in England and Germany.   **SECT**

1601   Eight years after a seminary is opened in Japan, Japanese seminarians are ordained as Roman Catholic priests.   **CATH**

1601   Jesuit missionaries in the Philippines establish a school and then a college in 1611. Their efforts are aimed primarily at lowland Filipinos, and they ignore the tribal peoples of the highlands and the Muslims in the southern islands. Catholic missionary work is very effective in the Philippines, and it becomes the only Roman Catholic nation in Asia and remains so in the 1990s.   **CATH**

1601– 1609   The Italian Jesuit missionary Matteo Ricci (1552–1610), resident in China's capital, Beijing, explains Christianity to Daoist and Buddist adepts. He makes few converts, however, and those mainly among the educated Confucian elite. Ricci's teachings have little influence at lower levels of the social scale.   **CATH**

1602– 1605   Jesuit lay brother Benedict de Goes conducts an overland journey across Muslim central Asia to China. His purpose is to confirm that China is the Cathay known to Europeans, which he does in a letter to missionaries in Beijing.   **CATH**

1603   The Tokugawa shogunate is founded in Edo (later Tokyo) and contact between Shinto and Confucianism is resumed. Scholars try to interpret Shinto from the standpoint of neo-Confucianism, emphasizing the unity of Shinto and Confucian teachings.   **CONF, SHINTO**

1603–1604	The core of the *Adi Granth*, the sacred text of the Sikhs, is compiled by Guru Arjan in India. The text is later called the *Guru Granth*, and is the basic Sikh religious text. **SIKH**
1604	Confucian scholar Hayashi Razan enters the service of Tokugawa Ieyasu, original name Tokugawa Takechiyo (1543–1616), under Toyotomi Hideyoshi, founder of the last shogunate in Japan, the Tokugawa or Edo shogunage (1603–1867). Hayashi Razan establishes a school in Edo. **CONF**
1604	Ku Hsien-ch'eng and K'ao P'an-lung rebuild the Tung-lin Academy, setting the stage for a major reorientation of Confucianism—the rise of Confucian ritualism in the scholarly circle centered in the Lower Yangtze area from the 1600s through the early 19th century. **CONF**
1604	King James I of England (formerly James VI of Scotland) calls a conference to discuss problems resulting from the use of two Bibles—the Bishop's Bible and the Geneva Bible—in the Church of England. The former is preferred by the Church authorities, the latter by the parishioners. He organizes a group of 54 scholars to produce a new Bible based on the Hebrew and Greek versions and other sources, and they begin work in 1606. **PROT**
1604	Scholar Hayashi Razan (1583–1657) becomes an adviser to supreme warlord Tokugawa Ieyasu and founds a school to attempt a synthesis of Shinto and neo-Confucianism. (It is the first school in Japan to make such an attempt.) His writings, which include *Honcho jinja ko* (*Reflections on the Shrines of This Nation*) and *Shinto denju* (*Shinto Transmission*), emphasize the unity of the imperial way and Shinto and of ethical behavior and government as an expression of divinity. The 1600s will see a revival of Shinto in alliance with Confucianism and a continued rejection of Buddhism by many Shinto factions. **SHINTO, CONF**
1604	Continuing a pattern of repression of witchcraft and paganism across Europe, England further restricts activities involving magic and designates them capital crimes. **SPIR**
1605	Italian Jesuit missionary Roberto Nobili (1577–1656) begins his missionary work among the Tamil of South India. His mission, which lasts for 50 years, establishes new approaches in Roman Catholic missionary work. He learns the Tamil language and culture, lives a Tamil Hindu lifestyle, and integrates Hindu and Christian beliefs and practices. Later in his life he also establishes separate missionary efforts for high- and low-caste Hindus. Despite his novel approaches, he actually makes relatively few converts who remain loyal to Roman Catholicism. **CATH**
1605	The *Racovian Catechism* is published in Poland. Its perspective is Unitarian, with God portrayed as a unity, Christian scripture cited as the ultimate authority, and open debate encouraged on theological questions. **SECT**

1606   Gallicanism develops among Roman Catholics in France. Gallicans argue for a weak papacy with little or no control over the Catholic, churches in different nations. Although it is associated with France, Gallicanism is part of a broader trend across Catholic Europe in which Catholic rulers seek to control churches in their states and limit papal authority.   **CATH**

1606   (St.) Rose of Lima (1586–1617) enters a Dominican convent in Lima, Peru, and begins a life devoted to Christ and to helping the unfortunate. For her good deeds she is canonized in 1671 and made patron saint of Peru and later of the entire Western Hemisphere. She is the first person born in the Americas to be canonized.   **CATH**

1606   Through the Treaty of Zsitva Torok, the Ottoman Empire's conquest of Europe is halted. The treaty awards the Ottomans control of Romania, Hungary, and Transylvania but also affirms the control of the Hapsburg Empire elsewhere in Europe. The Ottoman Empire attempts to expand in Europe, and although their power is limited from then on, their efforts do not cease until the failed siege of Vienna in 1683.   **ISLAM**

1606   In England King James I (formerly James VI of Scotland) sets forth the Oath of Allegiance, which makes allegiance to the throne paramount. The oath is supported by the leaders of the Anglican Church but causes difficulty for other Protestants and Catholics whose primary allegiance is to God.   **PROT**

1606   In England John Smyth (?–1612), an Anglican minister, founds the Separatist Congregation at Gainsborough in Nottinghamshire. The church is formed in violation of English law, which recognizes only the Church of England and is the precursor, by three years, of the Baptist denomination also found by Smyth. Members of the church agree to enter personal relationships with God and object to any church hierarchy beyond that of the local church.   **PROT**

1606   Guru Hargobind (1595–1644) succeeds his father and becomes the sixth Sikh guru. During his service, which lasts until his death in 1644, there is considerable conflict with Muslim Mughals who rule northern India, and the role of the guru expands as he is now both the religious leader and the secular leader of the Sikh community in India.   **SIKH**

1607   The *Xu Daozang*, the Continued Daoist Canon, is published in Ming dynasty China under imperial auspices. The editor is Zhang Guozang.   **DAO**

1607   Some Puritans in England, failing to convince the Anglican Church to reform its practices in accord with their beliefs, move to the Netherlands where they believe they can find religious freedom. They are allowed to worship as they please but begin to lose their cultural distinctiveness as their children assimilate into Dutch society.   **PROT**

1607	John Smyth, who initiated the Baptist denomination in England in 1606, flees to the Netherlands with followers to escape prosecution by the English authorities for failure to worship in their Anglican parish church. **PROT**
1607	English settlers affiliated with the Church of England establish the first permanent English settlement in America, in Virginia. Religion is a part of daily life but the church is not dominant in the affairs of the colony. **PROT**
1608	Tukaram (1608–1649), a low-caste grocer, is born. He becomes a major Hindu poet in the Maharstra tradition and composes nearly 5,000 hymns. **HIND**
1608	The French initiate colonization efforts in Canada when explorer Samuel de Champlain founds Quebec. French colonization is based on establishing trading posts for fur and Jesuit missions in or alongside existing native (primarily Huron and Iroquois) villages. **NATIV**
1608	*The Differences of the Churches of Separation* is written by John Smyth, the founder of the Baptist denomination in England. In the book he stresses the teachings of the New Testament as the basis of the faith and calls them *ordinances*, a term that comes into routine use in the Baptist denomination. **PROT**
1609	King Philip III of Spain exiles all Muslims, and they settle in Muslim communities in North Africa, where they contribute to the revitalization of Islamic culture in the region. **ISLAM**
1609	The Baptist denomination of Protestantism is founded in Amsterdam when John Smyth, the Anglican minister who had founded a Separatist church in 1606, rebaptizes himself and several other men. **PROT**
1609	In Bohemia toleration of Protestants is restored when Matthias replaces his brother Rudolf as the Holy Roman Emperor. **PROT**
1609–1610	An English-language version of the Old Testament is published in France for use by Roman Catholics. **CATH**
1610	Jesuit missionaries in Paraguay establish their first mission at Loretto. The mission is a settlement to which Indians are attracted as a way of possibly escaping enslavement by the European colonizers. Subsequent Jesuit missions in the region follow the same plan and are called "reductions." The missions have a central church, living quarters, a school, and fields where the natives work. As the reductions do shelter natives from enslavement, they are criticized and sometimes attacked by Portuguese settlers. **CATH, NATIV**
1610	Huang Tsung-hsi (1610–1695), Confucian student of Liu Tsung-chou (1578–1645), is born in China. He compiles a comprehensive biographical history of Ming dynasty Confucians based on Liu's writings. **CONF**

1611   French Jesuit missionaries are active in eastern Canada and over the century expand their efforts westward among the Algonkians, Huron, Iroquois, and Abnaki.   **CATH, NATIV**

1612   The Oratorians, a community of priests founded by (St.) Philip Neri (d. 1595) in Rome, is approved by Pope Paul V. Unlike in monasteries the priests do not take vows but devote themselves to spiritual growth.   **CATH**

1612   Roman Catholic Jesuit and then Dominican and Augustinian missionaries establish missions in the Portuguese territory of Mozambique in East Africa. As the missionaries are often embroiled in conflicts between the Portuguese and local rulers, they win few converts.   **CATH**

1613   Ku Yen-wu (1613–1682), a critic of Confucian scholar Wang Yang-ming (1472–1529), is born. He studies political institutions, ancient phonology, and classical philology and comes to be famous as the founder and protector of "evidential learning" by the 1700s.   **CONF**

Baptist Churches

The Baptist churches form a Protestant denomination that developed in England and the Netherlands in the early 17th century. The first Baptists were influenced by the Anabaptist Mennonites in the Netherlands and their rejection of infant baptism, and the sacrament of adult baptism (actually, usually in late childhood) by total immersion became a basic element of the church. Other key elements are the sacrament of the Eucharist, the acceptance of the Bible as the ultimate authority, and the independence of each Baptist church, although there are large associations such as the Southern Baptist Convention and the National Baptist Convention, U.S.A. in the United States. Some early Baptists became Mennonites while others founded the first Baptist churches in Britain. In Britain the Baptists were considered to be separatists (from the Church of England) and were persecuted, with some migrating to the British colonies in New England in search of religious freedom. They played a role in establishing religious liberty in Rhode Island and later in having the Bill of Rights amended to the Constitution. Since the late 17th century, the Baptist churches have grown as a primarily American denomination, although through aggressive missionary activity, people around the world have been converted to the Baptist denomination. Of the about 40 million members of Baptist churches around the world, about 75 percent are in the United States. Over the years the Baptists have split into a number of associations in the United States, including those based on race (black and white Baptists) and region (Southern and Northern and National Baptists). Many of the leaders of the so-called Religious Right in the United States, which came to prominence in the 1980s, are Baptists, and the Southern Baptist Convention (the largest association with some 15 million members) has been associated with a conservative religious and social agenda.

1614	In perhaps the first Protestant missionary effort to the Muslims, a Czech language refutation of the Qur'an is published. **PROT**

1614–
1630
Christians in Japan, who are primarily Roman Catholics, including Spanish, Italian, and Portuguese priests and Japanese who have converted in the last 50 years, are persecuted by the Japanese rulers. Nearly all are killed, forced to flee, or forced to reject Christianity. **TOL**

1615
In an effort to convert more Chinese to Roman Catholicism, Pope Paul V gives priests the right to say Mass in Chinese. The decision also results in the translation of Christian literature into Chinese. **CATH**

1615
Roman Catholic Jesuit missionaries from Portugal begin seeking converts in Vietnam. They are expelled in 1625. **CATH**

1615
Mass is celebrated by Roman Catholics for the first time in Canada at the French settlement that becomes the city of Montreal. **CATH**

1615–
1868
The Edo period in Japan is a 250-year era of peace and prosperity under the Tokugawa shoguns. They exclude Westerners and impose social order and stability based on Confucian principles of rigid class stratification and strict moralism affecting nearly all areas of everyday activity. **CONF**

1616
Catholic missionaries are persecuted in China and again in 1622, when they are accused of being enemies of the government. The persecutions are not especially harsh and missionary activity resumes. **CATH**

1616–
1651
Ngawang Namgyal (1594–1651), a Tibetan monk, arrives in Bhutan, in flight from the Dalai Lama. In 1629 he founds his first *dzong* (fortified monastery) at Simthoka. After defeating rival religious leaders, he assumes the title *shabdrung* (the spiritual head of government, sometimes called *dharma raja*). He is Bhutan's first great national figure and will be regarded as the father of the modern nation. In Bhutan's Lamaist theocracy, the monks *(lamas)* are both religious and political leaders. The head of civil government (called *deb raja* or *druk desi*) in a dual system of governance is also generally a monk. Ngawang Namgyal calls his territory *Drukyul* (land of the Thunder Dragon) after his own *Drukpa Kagyupa* Buddhist sect. (Drukyul remains the traditional name of the country; Bhutan is used only in English-language foreign correspondence.) **BUDD**

1617
The unifier of Japan and the founder of the Tokugawa shogunate, Tokugawa Ieyasu (1543–1617), is buried according to Sanno Ichijitsu Shinto ritual. He is enshrined in an elaborate Shinto-Buddhist mausoleum complex at Nikko as the Shinto divinity Tosho Daigongen (the great avatar illuminating the East). **SHINTO**

1618	Yamazaki Ansai (1618–1682) is born in Japan. He receives Zhu Xi's Chinese Confucian thinking as interpreted by Korean Yi T'oegye and recasts native Shintoism in Confucian terms. **CONF, SHINTO**

1618	In Germany Lutheran theologian Johan Valentin Andrea (1586–1654) publishes the story of a man named Christian Rosenkranz who is purported to have founded the Fraternity of the Rose Cross in 1408. The book stirs interest in spiritualism and secret societies and plays a role in the emergence of Rosicrucianism. **SECT**

1619	Kumazawa Banzan (1619–1691), a Confucian samurai/scholar, is born. He exemplifies the diversity and vitality of Japanese Confucianism through his appropriation and interpretation of Wang Yang-ming's dynamic idealism. **CONF**

1619	Wang Fu-chih (1619–1692), one of the most sophisticated and original contributors to Confucian thought, is born. Extensive writings on metaphysics, history, and the classics distinguish him as a thorough critic of Wang Yang-ming in China. **CONF**

1619	British colonists at Jamestown, Virginia, establish a mission school for local Powhatan children. **NATIV**

1620	The Roman Catholic Church in Mexico declares that the use of peyote is the work of the devil and prohibits Christians from using it. Peyote is used by some Native American groups in northern Mexico for ritual purposes. **CATH, NATIV**

1620	In England the Puritans have attracted a large following, centered in the middle class of merchants and professionals but also drawing some followers in the aristocracy. Still, the Puritans are resisted and repressed by the Anglican Church and the teaching of various Puritan beliefs such as predestination is banned at theology schools. **PROT**

1620	The first Puritans (Pilgrims) arrive in North America aboard the *Mayflower* and establish their first colony, Plymouth Plantation, in Massachusetts. Their religion is an important part of daily life in the colony, and dissent is not tolerated. **PROT**

1620	The novel known as *The Romance of the Three Teachings* circulates in late Ming China. Its author is Pan Jingruo. In the novel representatives of the three great religious traditions fail in an assignment to educate the people of Orthodox Village. As a result, 10,000 lost souls are accidentally released from hell. They inhabit the denizens of Orthodox Village, creating havoc. Representatives of the Three Teachings must turn these victims of hell's escapees onto the right path. The Confucian uses logic, while the Buddhists and Daoists rely on ritual and spiritual arts, respectively. The novel illus-

trates the general approach to religion in Ming China—the notion that the three traditions are complementary and lead ultimately to the same goals.   **TOL**

1621   In October the Wampanoag Indians invite the Puritans of Plymouth Plantation, Massachusetts, to join them in their annual harvest ceremony and festival. The celebration becomes the basis for Thanksgiving, which becomes a national holiday in America more than two centuries later.   **NATIV, PROT**

1621–1637   In Laos a period of struggle for the throne of Lan Xang ends with succession of Souligna Vongsa in 1637. During his long reign (until 1694), he will promote Buddhism and the arts, and his reign is regarded as a golden age of Laotian history.   **BUDD**

1622   White Lotus Buddhists revolt in Shandong, China. They block the Grand Canal, capture 50 imperial grain barges and temporarily cut off supplies to Beijing and the Ming forces fighting in the northeast.   **BUDD**

1622   Pope Gregory XV establishes the Sacred Congregation for the Propagation of the Faith as the administrative body to oversee Roman Catholic missions around the world. The body, which is commonly called the *Propaganda*, consists of 13 cardinals, two prelates, and a secretary. Its initial actions center on ending the dominance of Portuguese and Spanish missionaries, bringing the missionary effort under the control of the pope rather than national rulers, and encouraging the training of native priests.   **CATH**

1622   In an effort to hasten the conversion of Hindus to Roman Catholicism, the Roman Catholic Church issues the *Congregation de Propaganda Fide*, which calls for the training of Indians as priests. The training is managed by Jesuits.   **CATH, HIND**

1622   In Persia Jews are forced to convert to Islam, although many continue to practice Judaism in private.   **ISLAM, JUD**

1622   The Dutch East India Company opens a seminary in the Netherlands to train Dutch Reformed ministers to serve the Dutch settlers and to convert natives in the Dutch colonies in Sri Lanka and Indonesia.   **PROT**

1622   Fast days, days of humiliation, and days of thanksgiving become an institution among the Puritans of New England when a day of fasting is followed by rain that breaks a two-month-long drought. Subsequently, fast days are ordered by the church to solve various community problems, such as epidemics, social discord, and crop failures. Days of thanksgiving are also called to give thanks to God for positive developments and events.   **PROT**

1622   In the aftermath of war between the Turks and the Hapsburg Empire and the renewed persecution of the Hutterites, the Hutterites are forced to leave their communities in Monrovia and move to Slovakia, where their numbers decline due to the ravages of the Thirty Years War.   **SECT**

1624   Muslim religious scholar Ahmad Sirhindi dies. During his life he transforms the Naqshbandi Sufi order. He argues that Islam has experienced a period of ethical decline and a messiah must appear to renew the religion. SEE **1389**, ISLAM.   ISLAM

Puritanism

Puritanism was a religious, social, and political movement that developed in Britain in the middle of the 16th century. In a religious sense the early Puritans were Calvinists who sought to serve God by establishing uniform Christian communities on earth. However, Puritanism was not a distinct religion but rather an offshoot of Congregationalism, which itself developed in opposition to the Church of England. Congregationalists stressed the independence and authority of each congregation, hence their name, and were repressed by the state and the Anglican Church. The label *Puritan* was applied to those who opposed the authority of the Anglican Church, even though those so labeled often espoused views that differed greatly from one another. However, Puritans in general were conservative in religious practice in that they stressed a return to the Christianity as set forth in the Bible. They also believed strongly in personal devotion and they opposed public entertainment on the Sabbath, the drinking of alcoholic beverages, gambling, and other vices in general. Despite governmental repression Puritan beliefs spread throughout the middle class, and there was an established cadre of Puritan ministers to preach in Puritan churches. Although Anglicanism remained the official religion, Puritanism was so widespread that it was possible to speak of a "Puritan England." Following the English Civil Wars of 1642–1648, the Puritans under Oliver Cromwell came to power, although they were again repressed when the monarchy was restored in 1660. Because of the repression many Puritans fled ultimately to North America in search of religious freedom and established colonies in Massachusetts, Connecticut, Rhode Island, New York, Virginia, and elsewhere. Known to later historians as the Pilgrims, Puritans, or Congregationalists, they established communities based on their Puritan beliefs, which included a fear of God, a belief that America enjoyed special favor with God, frugality, hard work, avoidance of sin, and simplicity. Just how closely their beliefs corresponded with their actual behavior is not clear. For example, Puritans worked hard, lived simple lives, and prayed a great deal, but the majority of children were born outside of marriage in early American colonies and Puritans were opposed to religious freedom for others. Nonetheless, the Puritans played a major role in shaping early American life, in founding major institutions, such as churches and colleges, and in converting Native Americans to Christianity. Over the centuries Congregational churches became more liberal, and in the 1960s the formal Congregational Church in America disappeared when it united with other churches to become the United Church of Christ, perhaps the most liberal of American Protestant churches.

1624   *De Veritiate* is written by Edward Herbert, the Lord of Cherbury. It is considered by later deists to be the first deist work as it sets forth the five principles of a natural religion. Deism is a philosophical movement in Europe in the 18th and 19th centuries that seeks to explain God and religious events through the use of reason. Deists also reject some aspects of religion, such as a belief in miracles.   **MISC**

1624   Dutch Reformed ministers establish a mission on Taiwan that lasts until the Dutch are driven off the island by the Chinese in 1661.   **PROT**

1625   The Vincentians (Congregation of the Mission) is founded as a religious order and charitable organization in France by (St.) Vincent de Paul (c. 1581–1660). The order gives money and performs services for the poor and is a major missionary organization within Roman Catholicism.   **CATH**

1626   In London the Baptist sect has grown since the first church was founded in 1612 and there are now five churches that unite and call themselves General Baptists. Repressed by the Anglicans and Puritans, they are aligned with Mennonites from the Netherlands as a radical religious community.   **PROT**

1627   Philosopher Hugo Grotius (1583–1645) provides a summary of Christianity in *De Veritate Religionis Christianae* for the use of Dutch sailors journeying to Southeast Asia.   **PROT**

c. 1629   Tommaso Campenella (1568–1639), the leading astrologer of the Italian Renaissance period, writes a textbook on astrology. The book strongly supports the use of astrology for medical purposes but is more careful about advocating astrology for divination.   **SPIR**

1629   With the protection of the Spanish military, Catholic missionaries begin establishing missions among Pueblo groups in New Mexico and Arizona. Churches are built with forced native labor, Pueblo religions are repressed, and some native religious leaders begin to organize resistance to Spanish rule and conversion to Christianity.   **CATH, NATIV**

1629   The Dutch, who began their conquest of the islands of Southeast Asia and their displacement of the Portuguese in 1605, conquer the Muslim state of Acheh, a major Islamic center in the region, and strengthen their control when they take the trading state of Malacca in 1641.   **ISLAM**

1629   The *Confession of Faith* is written by Cyril Lukaris (1572–1638), the patriarch of Constantinople. The book, a harsh break from Orthodoxy, supports many doctrines of Calvinism, and Cyril is criticized by church leaders and killed in 1638.   **ORTHO**

1629   In England King Charles I dismisses Parliament and rules without it. In the absence of a parliament to which it can bring its grievances, some Puritans feel compelled to leave Britain and establish colonies in the Americas, where they can practice their religion without interference from the state and the Church of England. **PROT**

1629–1651 During the last 20 years of his rule over Bhutan, Ngawang Namgyal constructs dozens of *dzongs* (fortified monasteries) in the western valleys of Bhutan; these massive, sloping, stone structures serve both as Buddhist monastic communities and civil administrative centers. His legal code, *Tsa Yig,* is based on Buddhist *dharma* (religious law) and remains in force until the 1960s. **BUDD**

1630 Under the leadership of John Winthrop (1588–1649), a Puritan magistrate, some 1,000 Puritans sail from England to America and establish the Massachusetts Bay Colony. They are followed by tens of thousands of other Puritans over the next few decades who establish other colonies in New England, on Long Island off the coast of Connecticut, and in British Caribbean colonies. The Massachusetts Bay Colony is established as a theocracy in which Puritan principles guide community life and the state and church support one another. There is no church hierarchy and each congregation operates autonomously. The Puritans seek to establish a Christian society and the Native Americans are viewed as the children of the devil. **NATIV, PROT**

1632 King Charles I of England grants Maryland to Cecilius Calvert, the second lord Baltimore, who is a Roman Catholic. Catholics have been persecuted in other British colonies in the Americas, and Calvert grants freedom of religion to all Christians in Maryland. **CATH**

1632 The first edition of the *Relations*—reports of the Jesuit missionaries in French territories in North America—is published in France. Its publication is meant to stimulate settlement of the New World by the French. **CATH**

1632 Peter Mogila (1597–1646), an Orthodox monk and theologian, is appointed leader of the Orthodox Church in Kiev, Ukraine. An influential church leader, he plays a role in containing the spread of Protestantism into eastern Europe but also seeks to strengthen ties to the Catholic Church in Rome, a policy that later church officials look upon with disfavor. **ORTHO**

1632 A school for Sami (Lapps) is established in Lycksela, Sweden, and becomes the center of the Swedish Lutheran missionary effort to the Sami. **PROT**

1632 Presbyterian minister John Eliot (1604–1690) begins missionary work among the Native Americans in Massachusetts. He makes his first converts in 1651, establishes settlements of converted natives, and translates the Bible into the Algonkian language. **NATIV**

1632 Mennonites in the Netherlands issue the *Dordrecht Confession* as a basic statement of Mennonite belief and practice. Although signed by leaders of other Mennonoite communities in Germany and Switzerland, it is never wholly followed by many other communities. **SECT**

1632–
1647

The Taj Mahal is built in Agra, India, by Mughal emperor Shah Jehan for his favorite wife, Mumtaz Mahal, who died in 1631. Upon his death in 1666 he is buried there as well. In the 20th century the complex becomes a primary symbol of India, although the marble exterior is threatened by deterioration due to air pollution. **ISLAM**

1633

The Sisters of Charity is formed in France by (St.) Vincent de Paul and Louise de Marillac. It is the first Catholic religious order for women in which women are not confined. **CATH**

1633

In Italy the Inquisition condemns the astronomer Galileo for his use of science to question the Bible. In 1983 the Catholic Church acknowledges that Galileo was treated unfairly and in 1992 it accepts Galileo's ideas as correct. **CATH**

1633

The Ursulines, a Roman Catholic sisterhood, is founded in France by a Ursuline nun, Mary of the Incarnation. In 1639 they begin missionary work among Native Americans in Montreal, Canada. **CATH**

1633

Jesuit missionaries begin to seek converts among the Huron and other native tribes in French territory in North America. The Jesuits are able to build a number of missions and compile a detailed record of native life (the *Jesuit Relations*), but their efforts end in failure when the region is overrun by the Iroquois. **CATH, NATIV**

1633

The Zuni people of what will become New Mexico revolt against the Spanish rulers and kill two Spanish missionaries. **NATIV**

1633

Courts in New England order that Lecture Days be limited to one afternoon per week so as not to interfere with people's work. Lecture Days are used by the clergy to teach Church doctrine. Lecture Days gradually decline in importance and end in 1845. **PROT**

1633

In India Gurdas Bhalla, a devout Sikh, dies. During his lifetime he writes poetry, which is later published in several collections that become secondary, but important, Sikh religious texts and continue to be recited in Sikh temples to this day. **SIKH**

1634

The Passion Play depicting the life of Jesus Christ is staged for the first time in the town of Oberammergau in the Bavarian Alps in southern Germany. The town residents stage the play and vow to stage it every 10 years thereafter (which they have done to modern times, with few exceptions) as a way of giving thanks for their town being spared from the ravages of the plague that has coincided with fighting between Protestants and Catholics in Europe. **CATH**

1636	Harvard College is founded in Cambridge, Massachusetts, to train Puritan (Congregational) ministers. **PROT**

| 1636 | Minister Roger Williams (c. 1604–1683) of Salem, Massachusetts, criticizes the treatment of the natives by the Puritan Massachusetts Bay Colony and establishes the colony of Rhode Island, where settlers are required to purchase rather than simply take Indian land and where there is a clear separation between church and state. **TOL** |

1637   In order to support its missionary efforts around the world, the Roman Catholic Church appoints vicar apostolics in Japan and interior India. The practice is continued later in mainland Southeast Asia (1659) and China (1660). **CATH**

1637   The Roman Catholic Church ordains its first native priest as a missionary in India. He is Matthew de Castro, a Hindu Brahman from Goa. His role is strongly resisted by the Jesuits in India, who regularly complain about him, and his mission in the interior of India is not especially successful. Because of the commotion it causes in the church, the next native Indian priest is not ordained until 1923. **CATH**

1638   The first "Indian reservation" in the Americas is established by the Puritans for the Quinnipiac people in New Haven, Connecticut. One condition of settlement on the reservation is that the Quinnipiac reject their religion and accept Christianity. **NATIV**

1638   In England the first Particular Baptist Church is founded in London by Separatists. Particular Baptists reject infant baptism and believe in adult baptism by immersion. **PROT**

1638–
1639   In Mongolia leading figures among the Khalkhas accept Zanabazar (1635–1723), the son of Tysheet Khan Gombodorji, as the Bogdo Gegen or *Jebtsundamba Khutuktu* (Living Buddha). This begins a long line of ecclesiastical leaders who assume the same title, the last of whom dies in 1924. This office was the brainchild of Tysheet Khan Gombodorji as part of his drive to unite the Khalkha khanates. The Bogdo Gegen figure would function much like the Dalai Lama of Tibet, concentrating national sentiment on a single religious leader. **BUDD**

1639   In Mongolia the city of Urga (present-day Ulaanbaatar) is founded. The Bogdo Gegen, the Buddhist leader who is trying to assert his authority in much the same way as the Dalai Lama does in Tibet, establishes his residency there. The city grows to be the commercial and artistic center of Mongolia. **BUDD**

1639   Jesuit missionaries in Canada expand their activities westward to seek converts among the Ojibwa and other groups in the Great Lakes region. **CATH, NATIV**

1639   The Ottoman Empire and the Iranians seek to end over 100 years of conflict through the treaty of Qasr Shirin, which gives the Ottomans control of Iraq and Iran control of the Caucasus.   **ISLAM**

1639   Andreas Ehrenpreis (1589–1662) becomes leader of the declining Hutterite communities in Slovakia and compiles the texts of sermons that in the 1990s continue to be read at Hutterite worship services.   **SECT**

1639–
1640   The Bishop's Wars take place between England and Scotland. They are caused by King Charles I's attempt to impose Anglican religious practices on the Scottish Church and end in English defeat.   **PROT**

1640   In Mongolia the Khalkhas and leaders of the Western Mongols meet to forge a stronger union. Despite agreeing to recognize the religious authority of the Bogdo Gegen, the leaders fail to agree on a platform for a united Mongolian state.   **BUDD**

1640   Gushi Khan of the Khoshuts, a subclan of the Mongol Oirats, defeats the king of Tibet, ending secular power in the Buddhist country. The Khoshuts become protectors of the Dalai Lama's authority.   **BUDD**

1640   *Augustinius* is published in France, two years after the death of its author, Cornelius Jansen (1585–1638), the bishop of Ypres. The book becomes the basic document of the Jansenism movement in Roman Catholicism, which is popular in France and spreads to Italy before disappearing by the middle of the 18th century. Jansenists look to the teaching of St. Augustine and believe that a full love of God is required to receive the sacraments. Although they mount an intellectual battle, their ideas are rejected by a series of popes.   **CATH**

1640   The *Brief Catechism* and the *Orthodox Confession* are written by Peter Mogila, the Orthodox metropolitan of Kiev, to counter the pro-Protestant *Confession of Faith* written in 1629 by Cyril Lukaris, the patriarch of Constantinople. The works play a role in the rejection of Lukaris's ideas but are not fully accepted in Orthodoxy as they reflect Roman Catholic influences.   **ORTHO**

1640   The *Whole Booke of Psalmes* by Stephen Daye is printed in the Massachusetts Bay Colony. It is the first book printed in North America.   **PROT**

1640   The Seventh-Day Baptists emerge as the third Baptist group in England. Their belief is marked by the emphasis placed on worship on the Sabbath. Because of the Sabbath-day worship they draw more attention and therefore suffer greater persecution than do the General and Particular Baptists.   **PROT**

1640   In England the Particular Baptists adopt the practice of immersion as the only acceptable form of baptism, and immersion becomes a basic tenet of the Baptist denomination.   **PROT**

1640   In the Massachusetts Bay Colony it has become the accepted practice that Puritans must provide testimony of their personal religious experiences that qualifies them to become members of the Congregational Church.   **PROT**

1640   In England King Charles I reconvenes Parliament after an 11-year recess in order to gain support in the Bishop's Wars with Scotland. Parliament has many Puritan members and is not cooperative with the king, and so instead moves to institute reforms in British society in accord with Puritan beliefs, which leads to the English Civil Wars.   **PROT**

1642   A Jesuit mission is established by French missionaries in Quebec and later becomes the city of Montreal.   **CATH**

1642   The Bible is first published in Finnish.   **CHRIS**

1642   Jews from Amsterdam, who had been openly practicing Judaism for 50 years, settle in Pernambuco, Brazil.   **JUD**

1642   At the Council of Jassy in Moldova, the Orthodox Church rejects the *Confession* of Cyril Lukaris, the patriarch of Constantinople, which reflects Calvinist influences, and accepts the *Confession* of Peter Mogila, the Orthodox metropolitan of Kiev.   **ORTHO**

1642–
1648   The English Civil Wars take place. The opposing forces are King Charles I and Parliament, each fielding armies and the latter forging a crucial alliance with Scotland in 1643. The wars concerned efforts by Parliament to limit the king's power and church reforms, with Parliament supporting Puritan reforms and the king supporting the established Church of England. The wars end with the Parliamentary forces victorious and Charles is beheaded in 1649.   **PROT**

1642–
1720   The Mongols reassert their authority over Tibet. The Mongols do not themselves rule Tibet; instead they invest temporal authority in the Dalai Lama, beginning with the fifth Dalai Lama, Ngawang Lobzang Gyatso (1617–1682). Known in history as "the Great Fifth," he defeats the rival Karmapa sect, creates a monastic administration, and raises the Gelugpa sect to political power **(SEE 1409, BUDD)**. Among his major achievements, the fifth Dalai Lama constructs the Potala Palace in Lhasa; regarded as the residence of the Avalokitesvara, the bodhisattva of compassion, the palace becomes the symbol of the Dalai Lama's spiritual and secular power. Successive Dalai Lamas continue to exercise both spiritual and temporal rule in Tibet; the Dalai Lama will also be recognized as the spiritual leader by Mongolian Buddhists.   **BUDD**

1643–
1647   In Britain Parliament convenes the Westminster Assembly of Divines to end religious conflict and to weaken the authority of the Church of England. The assembly is dominated by Presbyterians from Scotland and members of other Reformed churches in Europe. Over the next several years they produce

a series of creeds that become of the basis of Presbyterianism: *The Form of Presbyterial Church Government* and *The Directory of Public Worship* in 1644 and *The Westminster Confession of Faith, The Larger Catechism,* and *The Shorter Catechism* in 1647. The Presbyterians lose influence after 1648 when those who favor religious tolerance come to power.   **PROT**

1644   Jesuit missionary Adam Von Bell Schall (1592–1666) establishes a second Catholic mission at Macao in China. He forges a strong relationship with the ruling Manchus and is considered one of the most effective Christian missionaries in Asia.   **CATH**

1644   Manchu invaders overthrow the Ming in China and proclaim the Qing dynasty. This last of China's imperial dynasties will survive until 1911. The first 150 years of the Qing are stable and generally prosperous, a golden age of traditional Chinese civilization.   **DAO**

1644   Particular Baptists who are members of seven independent churches in London issue the *Confession of Faith,* which sets forth the principle of cooperation among the independent Baptist churches.   **PROT**

1644   The Massachusetts Bay Colony rejects from membership all Baptists who have been convicted of religious crimes in Britain. At this time, there are numerous laws designed to repress Baptism in Britain.   **PROT**

1644   Guru Hari Rai (1630–1661) becomes the seventh Sikh guru. During his rule, which lasts until his death in 1661, the Sikh community is repressed by the Muslim Mughal rulers, although it survives and perhaps even increases the number of its followers in some rural regions.   **SIKH**

1644   *The Bloudy Tenent of Persecution for Cause of Conscience* is written by Roger Williams (c. 1603–1684), the founder of the Providence Plantations colony in Rhode Island. In the book he argues for religious freedom, which is granted in his colony.   **TOL**

1644   In the United States residents of Rhode Island are granted freedom of worship.   **TOL**

**1644–
1911**   The influence of Confucianism on Chinese society reaches its apex during the Qing dynasty. The Qing emperors transform Confucian teaching into political ideology but undermine the freedom of scholars to transmit the Confucian Way by imposing harsh measures amounting to a literary inquisition.   **CONF**

1645   In southwestern Africa Capuchin missionaries accompanying the Portuguese colonists begin seeking converts. Their efforts are not very effective over the course of the century, as leaders of African societies who convert are often followed by leaders who reject Christianity and support traditional religions.

                    CATH

1645	The Roman Catholic Congregation for the Propagation of the Faith at the Vatican, on the basis of a brief submitted by the Dominicans, condemns the Chinese ceremonies honoring Confucius and family ancestors that the Jesuits were permitting as compatible with Christian beliefs. **CATH, CONF**
1645	Jesuit missionary Eusebio Kino (1645–1711) is born in Austria. As an adult he accompanies Spanish colonists to the southwestern United States and converts thousands of Native Americans to Roman Catholicism. He also helps to introduce cattle ranching to the region. For his work he is known in the Church as the Apostle of Arizona. **CATH, NATIV**
1646	The Westminster *Confession* is drafted by the Westminster Assembly (consisting of English and Scottish Presbyterians) as a sprofession of faith distinct from Anglicanism and Roman Catholicism. The *Confession* draws from Calvinist theology and calls for the literal interpretation of Scripture. It later influences the Congregationalist and Baptist churches. **PROT**
1646–1647	George Fox (1624–c. 1691), the founder of Quakerism (Society of Friends), has a series of religious experiences in England that lead him to begin preaching a form of worship based on inner experience to Separatists (those who oppose the Church of England) in London. **PROT**
1647	*Twelve Questions* is published by John Biddle (1616–1662) in England. A religious reformer and scholar, he questions the Doctrine of the Trinity and spends nearly half his life in prison as punishment for expressing his religious beliefs. He also translates and disseminates early Unitarian writings by others. **SECT**
1647–1648	In response to pressure from Baptists and Presbyterians on Congregational dominance in the British colonies in New England, Congregationalists meet and issue the *Cambridge Platform*, a basic statement of Congregationalist belief that reaffirms the independence of each congregation and the importance of

---

Westminster *Confession*

The Westminster *Confession* was the formal statement of belief by the Presbyterians of England and Scotland in the mid-17th century. Drafted by the Presbyterian-dominated assembly in England at a time when Scottish influence was strong in the English Parliament, the assembly rejected both the power and structure of the Catholic and Anglican churches. As a statement of belief, the *Confession* strongly reflects its Calvinist origins by stating that the purpose of humanity is to praise God and that the biblical texts represented the literal world of God. Although English Presbyterians interpreted the *Confession* somewhat loosely, the Scots viewed it as doctrine. Later the *Confession* also served as a basis for statements of belief in both the Congregationalist and Baptist churches.

---

the saints—members who have provided testimony of their personal religious experience, which makes them eligible for church membership.   PROT

1647–
1648

In Britain Baptists enjoy a brief period free of official persecution that ends when Parliament issues the "Ordinance for Punishing Blasphemies and Heresies."   PROT, TOL

1647–
1680

Under the leadership of Sivaji (1627–1680), Hindus in India revolt against Muslim rule and succeed in establishing the Hindu state of Maratha.   HIND

1648

The first Baptist Church in the Americas is founded in Newport, Rhode Island, by John Clarke, a British lawyer, physician, and theologian. The congregation is established in Rhode Island to avoid persecution in the Massachusetts Bay Colony.   PROT

1648

The Thirty Years War in Europe is ended by a series of treaties called the Peace of Westphalia. The treaties generally give Protestants religious freedom but also establish the primacy of the state over regional or religious bodies.   TOL

1649

In response to Puritan complaints about Roman Catholics, the Catholic-controlled Maryland Assembly enacts the Act Concerning Religion, which grants religious freedom to all Christians in Maryland.   CATH

1649

The Qing court in China confers the title of "Great Perfected" on Zhang Yingjing, the Daoist 52d celestial master.   DAO

1649

The Iroquois of the Great Lakes region are successful in defeating the neighboring Huron in Canada. Huron resistance is weakened by the presence of internal factions resulting from Jesuit missionary activities that divided the Huron into traditionalists, who followed the native religion, and those who accepted Christianity. The missionaries provide weapons and other assistance only to the Christian faction. Three priests are killed by the Iroquois, nearly ending the Jesuit mission to the Huron.   NATIV

1649

The Society for the Propagation of the Gospel in New England is established by an act of Parliament in England. It is the first Protestant missionary society and instrumental in its founding are John Eliot and Thomas Mayhew, British missionaries already active in New England.   PROT

1649–
1658

Following the English Civil Wars, the Puritan Parliament establishes the Commonwealth under the rule of Oliver Cromwell (1599–1658). The period is one of much political and religious turmoil, and while Puritan principles are primary, there is considerable religious freedom for other Protestants and Catholics. After Cromwell's death in 1658, the monarchy is restored with Charles II crowned king.   PROT

c. 1650 The fifth Dalai Lama of Tibet predicts the reincarnation of Panchen Lama Chokyi Gyaltsen (1570–1662), second-highest spiritual authority in Tibet. He thus becomes the first in the reincarnated line of Panchen Lamas. The Chinese emperor grants sovereignty over western Tibet to the second Panchen Lama (1663–1737); he and his successors rule from the Tashilhunpo monastery near Shigatse, western Tibet. **BUDD**

c. 1650 In Japan Yoshikawa Koretaru (1616–1694) and Yamazaki Ansai (1619–1682) are two representative scholars of Confucian Shinto. They add neo-Confucian interpretations to the traditional theories received from Watarai Shinto and Yoshida Shinto, respectively, and each establishes a new school. In both schools the T'ai Chi concept of neo-Confucianism is equated with the first *kami*, or spirits, of the *Nihon shoki*. Yoshikawa emphasizes imperial virtues and national ethics such as loyalty and filial piety. Yamazaki further develops this, advocating both mystic pietism and ardent emperor worship. **CONF, SHINTO**

c. 1650 The Muslims in eastern Ethiopia, who had been defeated by the Christians in 1542, have since then succeeded in converting the Galla and other indigenous peoples to Islam and establish a small Muslim state at Harar. As a major trading center, Harar remains independent for two centuries. **ISLAM**

1650 In response to complaints from missionaries in southwestern Africa that the native peoples are ignorant, the Roman Catholic Church rules that these people may be baptized *in fide ecclesiae*, that is, as though they were small children or others who cannot understand the teachings of the church. **CATH**

1650 In Japan the great pilgrimages begin as the Ise shrine reports the arrival of some 2,500 per day from March to May. Known as *okage mairi* (spontaneous and frenzied events that will occur about 60 years apart) they far surpass the regular pilgrimages usually organized by the confraternities known as *ko*. In 1705 Ise will receive 3.6 million, in 1771 2.7 million, and in 1830 4.6 million. Ise and other major pilgrimage shrines—Kompira, Daizafu, Kumano, Kanda Myojin, and Nezu Gongen—draw visitors by advertising amulets and boons available from deities and by holding elaborate Shinto festivals in concert with large markets. **SHINTO**

1650s A debate develops among Roman Catholic scholars in Rome, Jesuit missionaries in China, and the Chinese emperor. The issue concerns to what extent Confucius and ancestors can be honored and whether those honors should be civil or religious. The Catholic scholars take a restrictive position and in 1704 issue a decree that effectively limits ancestor worship, perhaps the most widespread form of religion in China. The Jesuits prefer a more flexible approach that allows them to coexist with Chinese culture. **CATH**

1650– Xu Shoucheng (?–1692) preaches the Quanzhen doctrine of cultivation of
1690 nature and the life endowment in late Ming and early Qing China. **DAO**

1650– 1696	Muslims from Oman retake the coastal regions of the Persian Gulf from the Portuguese and then push south, driving the Portuguese from coastal East Africa by 1696 and reestablishing Muslim rule in the region. **ISLAM**
c. 1650– 1740	At Surat in west central India, a Svetambara Jain monk named Viraji develops a new sect within Jainism. He bases his views on those of earlier reformers and teaches that true Jainism does not allow idolatry or temple worship. This sect will grow in numbers and extent and become known as Sthanakavasi, "those who dwell in preaching halls"; its name is derived from *sthanakas* buildings, in reference to the austere and unconsecrated buildings where the sect chooses to hold its meetings. SEE **1400s, JAIN**. **JAIN**
c. 1650– c. 1860	In Korean neo-Confucian scholarship, adherents of the School of Principle stress the generative power of principle that T'oegye proposed; Yi Hyonil (1627–1704), Yi Sangjong (1710–1781), Yi Chinsang (1811–1878), and Yi Hangno (1792–1868) give increasing roles to principle; ultimately Hangno identifies it with creative force, divinity, and mind. Adherents of the School of Material Force attribute ever greater function to material force. Their scholars include Song Siyol (1607–1689), Han Wonjin (1682–1750), and Im Songju (1711–1788). Songju even denies the existence of principle in the absence of material force. **CONF**
1651	George Fox, the founder of Quakerism in England, moves his preaching activities from the south to the northwest and is successful in making converts among the Puritans and other Separatists. Since 1647 Fox's preaching has been repressed by the state and Anglican Church and he and followers have been imprisoned on various occasions. **PROT**
1652	Yamaga Soko, original name Yamaga Takasuke, also called Jingozaemon (1622–1685), masterless samurai, military strategist, and Confucian philosopher in Japan, is appointed military instructor to the lord of the great fief of Ako in recognition of his popularity with thousands of disciples. He advocates that Japan learn about Western nations in order to better oppose them. In developing a suitable ethic for the samurai class, he turns to the Chinese Ancient Learning School of Confucianism. **CONF**
1652	*Ill News from New England* is written by Baptist minister John Clarke in Rhode Island (1609–1676). The book is a call for religious freedom, which Clarke hopes will influence the British Parliament to set a policy of toleration for the colonies. **PROT**
1652	Baptists spread their religion from England to Wales in a general English effort to spread the Church of England and other Protestant denominations to Wales. **PROT**
1652	Settlers from the Netherlands establish the Dutch Reformed Church in South Africa. The Church later becomes associated with both apartheid and the anti-apartheid movement in the 20th century. **PROT**

| 1652–1653 | A religious awakening takes place among the people of the Lake District of northwest England. A major catalyst of the awakening is George Fox, the founder of Quakerism, whose preaching, mass rallies, and personal experience approach to religion appeals to the people of the region, who had been ignored by the Anglican Church. The name *Quaker* is applied to the movement as adherents shake physically as a manifestation of their inner experience with God. **PROT** |

| 1653 | Jansenism, which emerged in the Catholic Church in France in 1640, is rejected by Pope Innocent X in his bull *Cum Occasione*. Jansenism is later rejected again following efforts by French Catholics and intellectuals to revive it under Pope Clement XI in 1713. **CATH** |

| 1653 | With the demise of Portuguese control in India, efforts by the Jesuits to convert the Syrian Christians to Roman Catholicism weaken and in this year Syrian Christians reaffirm their ties to the Syrian Orthodox tradition at Mattancherry in southwestern India. They pledge that no outside religious official will have authority over their community and they consecrate a bishop in absentia. The event is known as *Coonan Kurisu Satyam*. **ORTHO** |

Society of Friends

The Society of Friends, or Quakers, as they are commonly known, is a Christian denomination that emerged in the mid-17th century in England in the turmoil of the English Civil Wars. The movement was initiated by George Fox, who preached of a spiritual transformation in which he experienced the "inner light of the living Christ." The notion of the inner light became a basis of the movement, which stressed the individual's personal experience with God through Christ without the need for religious practitioners, sacraments, and other elements of formal religious expression. The name Friends came from John 15:14, in which Jesus states, "You are my friends if you do what I command you." The name *Quakers* has been used since 1650; its origin is unclear. It may have referred to their shaking movements during prayer or may have been first used when Fox ordered a magistrate to tremble at the name of the Lord. Although Quakers was at first considered an insulting name used only by detractors of the new denomination, it is now accepted by Friends. The Quakers were persecuted in England and many fled to the Americas, where the largest number settled in Pennsylvania under the leadership of William Penn. In addition to the inner experience of God, Friends also strongly believe in personal honesty and in treating others with kindness. In accord with these beliefs, Friends have long supported many social causes, including an end to slavery, Indian rights, women's suffrage, peace, prison reform, and health care. In all these causes, they were the first or one of the first religious groups to fight for them and were often criticized and sometimes attacked for their beliefs. There are about 250,000 Friends, with the majority in North America and England but some in virtually every nation, where they are involved in education, health care, and other activities.

1653	Nikon (1605–1681), the Russian Orthodox patriarch of Moscow, institutes reforms that replace traditional Russian Orthodox practices such as the two-fingered sign of the cross with Greek Orthodox ones such as the three-fingered sign of the cross. Some in the church object to the reforms as a threat to Russian Orthodox autonomy and are labeled Old Believers for their adherence to traditional practices. **ORTHO**
1654	The first Jews arrive in the Dutch colony of New Amsterdam (later New York) from Brazil. They are Sephardic Jews who are forced to leave Brazil with other Dutch settlers when the region is taken by the Portuguese. Peter Stuyvesant, the governor of New Amsterdam, opposes the settlement of the Jews there but is overruled by the Dutch West India Company. Although the Jews have much economic freedom, restrictions on civil rights and religious freedom are kept in place. They form their first congregation called *Shearith Israel* (Remnant of Israel) in 1655. **JUD**
1654	The Kiev Metropolitanate of the Orthodox Church in the Ukraine becomes part of the Russian Orthodox Church in Moscow. **ORTHO**
1654	In Britain the first London Yearly Meeting of Quakers takes place. It brings together Quakers from preparative (local), monthly, and general meetings and becomes an annual event from 1668 on. **PROT**
1654	In England the Baptist denomination moves toward unification when the General Baptists hold their first General Assembly in London. The General Assembly founds a missionary branch in 1656, sets forth a confession of faith in 1660, and establishes a permanent administrative organization in 1689 and a pastoral training program in 1700. **PROT**
1654	Henry Dunster (c. 1612–1658), an Anglican minister, is forced to resign as president of Harvard College for his support of "believer's baptism" and his rejection of infant baptism, views at odds with the Puritan leaders of the Massachusetts Bay Colony. **PROT**
1654–1655	Teams of Quakers from the Lake District in northwest England spread out across southern England and Ireland to spread the message of Quakerism. Known to later generations of Quakers as the "First Publishers of Truth" or the "Valiant Sixty," they attract large crowds in some places and are usually tolerated by the Baptists but opposed by the Anglicans and the Puritans. **PROT**
1655	Puritan forces defeat the pro-Catholic forces of the government in Maryland, end religious freedom, and persecute Roman Catholics. Nonetheless, Roman Catholicism survives in Maryland and, with the repression of Catholicism in Britain, it becomes a stronghold of Catholicism in the English-speaking world. **CATH, PROT**
1655	The first Quaker arrives in the colony of Maryland and Quakers subsequently settle in Virginia and North Carolina. **PROT**

1655–
1657
The London Polyglot Bible is prepared by a panel of theologians and scholars. It is meant to combine many earlier editions, chronologies, maps, alphabets, and other materials in one work with the text in Hebrew, Greek, and Latin. As the most complete of the polyglot Bibles, it later becomes an important source for scholars.   PROT

1656
After considering the arguments of the Jesuits, the Roman Catholic Congregation for the Propagation of the Faith in Rome lifts the ban it earlier imposed on Chinese rites. The continuing controversy involves leading universities in Europe, eight popes, and the K'ang-hsi emperor.   CATH, CONF

1656
French Jesuit priests establish a mission among the Onondaga Iroquois in New York. Many Iroquois are resistant to both the French influence and Christianity and two years later another Iroquois nation, the Mohawk, attacks and destroys the mission.   CATH, NATIV

1656
Jewish settlement in England resumes when the Jews are granted religious rights by Oliver Cromwell. The Jewish community on Curaçao founds the Mikveh Israel (Hope of Israel) synagogue.   JUD

1656
Two Quaker missionaries, Mary Fisher and Ann Austin, arrive in New England from Barbados. The Puritans, having already heard of the Quakers and their conversion activities in England, arrest the women, destroy their tracts, and send them back to Barbados. However, Quakers continue to arrive in the colonies and face continual persecution. In the same year Quakers settle in Rhode Island, where in 1657 calls for their persecution by the Puritans are rejected by the government.   PROT

1656–
1657
The Quakers in England split from the Puritans when the Puritans experience difficulties ruling England in the wake of the English Civil Wars and become more conservative and reject the radical religious and social ideas of the Quakers.   PROT

1657
Kaibara Ekiken, original name Atsundou (1638–1714), later considered the father of botany in Japan, leaves the medical profession to study the thought of Chinese neo-Confucian philosopher Zhu Xi (Chu Hsi) under the teachers Yamazaki Ansai and Kinoshita Jun-an. He sets forth Confucian doctrines in simple language that can be understood by Japanese of all classes. He is the first to apply Confucian ethics to women and the Japanese lower classes. Some suggest that his wife, Token, a scholar, calligrapher, and poet, is the real author of his works.   CONF

1657
Five Quakers arrive in New Amsterdam and are persecuted by the local authorities. The persecution ends when the Dutch West India Company orders the Quakers to be left alone.   PROT

1657
Yoshikawa Koretari (1616–1694) effectively becomes head of Yoshida Shinto. He will lean toward neo-Confucianism and sets up the divinity

Kuhinotokotachi no Mikoto as a central figure in the Shinto pantheon. In 1682 he will be appointed head of Shinto affairs for Japan's Tokugawa shogunate. In the same era Deguchi Nobuyoshi (1615–1690), a leading exponent of Watarai Shinto, also regards neo-Confucianism with favor. He will teach Yamazaki Ansai, the founder of Suika Shinto.   **SHINTO**

1658   A Jewish congregation is formed in Newport, Rhode Island. The Jewish community there is composed of Sephardic Jews who settle in Rhode Island because of its religious toleration.   **JUD**

1658   Nikon, the Russian Orthodox patriarch of Moscow, declares a separation of church and state and that he is supreme to the tsar. This view is rejected by the tsar, and Nikon is forced to resign.   **ORTHO**

1658   The *Savoy Declaration*, a basic statement of Congregational belief, is set forth in England. However, the Congregationalists (Puritans) soon fall from power and the declaration later becomes important in Congregational churches in the Americas, where it is accepted by church councils in Massachusetts in 1680 and Connecticut in 1708.   **PROT**

1658–
1707   During the reign of Mughal emperor Aurangzeb (1618–1707), the Mughal Empire is extended south almost to the tip of India. However, his reversal of the long policy of religious tolerance for Hindus and their subsequent persecution causes Hindu resistance and revolts, and by the end of his rule the empire has begun to decline.   **ISLAM**

1659   The Roman Catholic Sacred Congregation for the Propogation of the Faith, which oversees the church's missionary effort, stresses that missionaries should focus on converting non-Europeans to Roman Catholicism and instructs them not to attempt to change the cultures or ways of life of native peoples.   **CATH**

1659   In the Massachusetts Bay Colony, the Puritans continue to repress Quakerism and four Quakers are hanged.   **PROT**

1659–
1661   Quaker religious worship in England experiences a transformation, and in 1659 public revelations and prayer decline as private, silent worship becomes the primary form of worship. In these years the Quakers also make their first Peace Testimony, in which they reject violence and refuse to serve in the military.   **PROT**

1660   Quakers have settled relatively peacefully in Rhode Island and several leading citizens have converted to Quakerism. By the next decade the Quakers have become active in the government, a Quaker is elected governor, and Quakers pass a law legalizing conscientious objection from military service.
                    PROT

1660 | In England the preacher John Bunyan (1628–1688), author of *Pilgrim's Progress* in 1678, is arrested under the Clarendon Code, which restricts religious practice by non-Anglicans and is imprisoned for 12 years. **TOL**

1661 | Indians in Georgia and South Carolina attack Spanish Catholic missions and the missions are abandoned. **CATH, NATIV**

1661 | In an effort to subjugate the Pueblo people of what will become the southwest United States, the Spanish destroy Pueblo ceremonial chambers (*kivas*) and ritual objects. **NATIV**

1661 | The Corporation for Propagating the Gospel in New England publishes the first American edition of the Algonkian-language Bible (New Testament) translated by Puritan missionary John Eliot. The Old Testament translation is published in 1663. **NATIV**

1661 | In England the Quakers state their opposition to war in a declaration to King Charles II that opens with "We utterly deny all outward war and strife and fighting with outward weapons for any end or under any pretense whatever and this is our testimony to the whole world." **PROT**

1661 | In an effort to control Quakerism, the Massachusetts Bay Colony passes a "cart and whip" law dictating that Quakers may be arrested and transported by cart to Rhode Island, being whipped in each village along the way. Nonetheless, Quaker meetings form in several Puritan communities in Massachusetts, Connecticut, and Rhode Island and they are generally tolerated by the Puritans. **PROT, TOL**

1661 | Guru Hari Krishan (1656–1664) becomes the eighth Sikh guru at the age of six upon the death of his father. He rules for only three inconsequential years during which Mughal repression decreases. **SIKH**

1661–1665 | Following the fall of the Puritan government in Britain, Parliament passes a series of laws called the Clarendon Code that makes the Church of England the state religion again but also grants some degree of religious freedom to non-Anglican Protestants such as Baptists and Quakers. However, the activities of non-Anglicans are restricted: they cannot serve in Parliament nor attend universities. **PROT, TOL**

1662 | Following the end of Puritan rule in England and the restoration of the monarchy in 1660, the Act of Uniformity is enacted. It restores the primacy of the Church of England and classifies Congregationalists as nonconformists. Many Congregational ministers are removed from their posts. **PROT**

1662 | Congregationalists in New England meet in Boston and accept the Half-Way Covenant. The Covenant allows grandchildren of church members to be baptized in the church, a practice not available to all community members. A controversial decision, it is not accepted by all churches and is designed primarily to maintain church membership. **PROT**

1662   The Royal Society is founded in London as the first European scientific society. Its early members are all eminent scientists—geographers, astronomers, and mathematicians—but many also study alchemy and believe in astrology. **SPIR**

1663   The Roman Catholic Church establishes the *Société des Missions Étrangères* (Society for Foreign Missions) in Paris as a center for the training of missionaries. Its establishment marks the rise of France and the decline of Spain and Portugal as the headquarters of the Roman Catholic missionary effort. **CATH**

1663   A Baptist Church is established in Swansea, Massachusetts. The church functions smoothly and establishes peaceful relations with the Congregational leaders of the colony. **PROT**

1663   Rhode Island is granted a charter by King Charles II of England. The charter grants religious freedom to residents of the colony. The Baptist minister John Clarke is instrumental in having the charter include the grant of religious freedom. **PROT**

1664   Roman Catholic missionary activity in China is disrupted when missionaries are persecuted and accused of being agents of the Portuguese. The persecutions end in 1667. **CATH**

1664   Guru Tegh Bahadur (1621–1675) becomes the ninth Sikh guru. In 1675 he is executed by the Muslim Mughal ruler Aurangzeb when, according to Sikh tradition, he refuses to convert to Islam. He becomes the second martyr of Sikhism and the second guru to die at the hands of the Mughals, and his death makes the Mughals the greatest enemies of the Sikhs. **ISLAM, SIKH**

1664   When England takes control of New Amsterdam from the Dutch, religious freedom is declared and persecution of the Quakers is curtailed. However, in Britain the Conventicle Act is passed, which makes it a crime to worship in any church other than the Church of England, punishable by imprisonment or deportation. The act curtails the activity of Baptists and Quakers. It is renewed and made more onerous in 1670, when fines are added to the punishments and informants are paid a reward. The act is set aside by the king in 1672 but his decision is overruled by Parliament. **PROT**

1664   The ancient Japanese classic and Shinto sacred text *Kojiki*, kept until this time in manuscript form by the Shinto priesthood, is printed for the first time and becomes available to a wider audience. **SHINTO**

1665   French Jesuit missionaries are active in the American and Canadian Midwest. **CATH, NATIV**

1665   With the British having taken New Amsterdam from the Dutch in the previous year, Jews in New York are granted religious and civil rights.   **JUD**

1665   Messianic fervor sweeps through Jewish communities in Europe and the Middle East when Shabbetai Zevi (1626–1676) of Smyrna is proclaimed the Messiah of the Jews by his followers. The next year he recants before the Ottoman sultan and converts to Islam.   **JUD**

1665   The Syrian Christians, having recently broken free from Jesuit missionary efforts, receive their first Orthodox bishop, further strenghtening their ties to the Orthodox Church.   **ORTHO**

1665   Japan's shogunate issues the *Shosha negi kannushi hatto* law code. The Yoshida lineage, which by this time has assumed the functions of the former Office of Shinto, officially gains jurisdiction over most Shinto shrines and priests. Yoshida duties include the supervision, initiation, and nomination of Shinto priests, as well as playing a major role in setting doctrine, practices, and ethics. By making payments to the Yoshida, provincial shrines and priests are able to advance in rank. The Yoshida administrators will exercise these considerable powers until 1867. Some shrines linked to the imperial house are to be governed by the Shirawaka lineage.   **SHINTO**

1666   Ogyu Sorai (1666–1728), Japanese Confucian scholar, is born. He seeks to discover the original basis for Confucian teaching through philological exactitude.   **CONF**

1666   The first Confucian temple on Taiwan is completed. The Cheng family and their fellow Ming Chinese promote Chinese culture.   **CONF**

1666   The first Lutheran Church in the Americas is established on the island of St. Thomas in the Caribbean, a Dutch colony at the time.   **PROT**

1666–
1667   At the Orthodox Councils of Moscow, the former patriarch of Moscow who had challenged state authority is banished, but his reforms announced in 1653 are accepted and those who criticize them (the Old Believers) are condemned. The Old Believers lack a central organization and divide into a dozen or so small groups outside Moscow, with some groups disappearing, others splintering, and new groups appearing in the next centuries. In the 1990s Old Believers number about five million with groups in Russia, Eastern Europe, Latin America, Australia, and New Zealand.   **ORTHO**

1667   Virginia passes a law that stipulates that conversion to Christianity does not entitle an African slave to freedom. Other colonies pass similar laws.   **AFRICAN**

1667   Scots-Irish immigrants from Ireland have been settling in the Americas and in this year they found a Presbyterian church in Newark, New Jersey. Over the next 25 years other churches are established in New Jersey and in Philadelphia.   **PROT**

1668   The New Testament is translated into the Malay language by Dutch missionaries in Malaysia. It is the first translation of the New Testament into a Southeast Asian language. In 1758 a Malay version is written in Arabic, to appeal to Malay Muslims who read Arabic, the language of Islam.   **PROT**

1668   Around this time, Yamazaki Ansai (1618–1682) founds Suika (grace and protection) Shinto, after training as a Zen monk followed by a shift to neo-Confucianism. He avoids syncretism after his embrace of Shinto and comes to promote loyalty to a superior Japan along with emperor worship. Ansai's Suika Shinto, carried on by Tamaki Masahide, Atobe Yoshiaki, and Yoshimi Yukikazu after his death, will open the way to the National Learning movement and fuel the nationalism leading to the Meiji Restoration. **SEE 1868, SHINTO.**   **SHINTO**

1669   The first African-American, Emmanuel, a freeman, is baptized in the Lutheran Church in the Americas in New York City.   **AFRICAN**

1669   The Orthodox scholar Dositheus (1641–1707) is appointed patriarch of Jerusalem and holds the position until his death in 1707. For most of his term he lives in Moldova in eastern Europe, where he oversees the publication of Orthodox texts and documents. An influential figure in the Church, he helps move Orthodoxy away from Protestant and Roman Catholic influences.   **ORTHO**

Slave Religion

Although scholars have given much attention to the experience of African-Americans in the United States, the religion of African slaves has been largely ignored by historians and others until the last few decades because written documents of the time were thought to be historically insignificant or even nonexistent. Since the 1970s some historians and other scholars have turned to historiographically nontraditional sources of information, such as music, dance, art, folktales, decorations on tombstones, obscure slave legends of family histories, and autobiographies, to provide a portrait of the religion of slaves. Slave religion was an amalgam of African beliefs and practices brought by the slaves to the Americas, new beliefs and practices developed there, and borrowings from Christianity. Among its major forms of expression were dancing, singing, and the telling of stories and tales. Slave religion contained a number of basic themes reflecting the slaves' collectively held ideas about themselves, the world, and their place in it. Slave religion suggests that slaves saw themselves as a chosen people who could appeal to a personal and accessible God (the Judeo-Christian God, defined in slave terms) to escape slavery and achieve salvation. Slave religion also encouraged resistance to white rule, was sometimes the source of slave revolts, and was an important means used by slaves to build and maintain a sense of community.

1670   China's Emperor Kangxi (r. 1669–1722) promulgates the *Sacred Edict*, a compilation of Confucian maxims on morality, manners, and social relations.   **CONF**

1670   Hiacoomes, a Wampanoag on the island of Martha's Vineyard, is ordained a minister by John Eliot and begins preaching to his own people.   **NATIV**

1670   The five churches of the General Six Principle Baptists in Rhode Island hold their first general meeting. It is the first of several such meetings of Baptist churches in various British colonies in North America that help the Baptists form as a distinct and unified denomination.   **PROT**

1671   The first Seventh-Day Baptist church is founded in Newport, Rhode Island. There are now General, Particular, and Seventh-Day Baptist congregations in the British colonies in North America.   **PROT**

1671–
1673   George Fox, the founder of Quakerism in England, visits the American colonies. He establishes the New England Yearly Meeting, which involves meetings of Quakers in Massachusetts, Rhode Island, and Long Island. **PROT**

1671–
1711   To escape persecution in Switzerland, Swiss Mennonites relocate to the Alsace and Palatinate regions of what later become parts of France and Germany.   **SECT**

1672   At the Orthodox Synod of Bethlehem, the church accepts the confession of Dositheus, the patriarch of Jerusalem, a statement more in line with traditional Orthodox belief than the earlier confessions of Cyril Lukaris, the patriarch of Constantinople and Peter Mogila, the metropolitan of Kiev.   **ORTHO**

1673   In the face of persecution and internal dissension, Quaker meetings in Britain begin to change. Their focus on meeting the needs of the individual gives way to an emphasis on meeting the needs of the group. Cohesion is established among meetings by the sharing of minutes and information.   **PROT**

1673–
1677   A Muslim *jihad* (holy war) takes place in Mauritania in West Africa, in which Berbers, who seek a return to traditional Islam and accuse the Arab rulers of being lax in their devotion to Islam, revolt against Arab rule. The Arabs suppress the revolt and become the dominant group in the region.
     ISLAM

1674   The Roman Catholic Church appoints its first Chinese missionary in China, Lo Wen-Tsao (Fray Gregorio López), who is given the title of vicar apostolic of northern China. There is much resistance in China to his work, and his mission lasts only six years, with no successor appointed to replace him. **CATH**

1674   When England takes New Amsterdam from the Netherlands and establishes the colony of New York, religious freedom is granted to Catholics and Protestants.   **CATH, PROT**

1675   *Pia Desideria* is written by the German Lutheran pastor Philipp Jakob Spener (1635–1705). The book initiates the Pietist movement within Protestantism in Europe. Pietism is a movement that stresses good works, Bible study, and a ministry more responsive to the community. Pietism influenced Moravians and John Wesley, who founded the Methodist Church in the next century.   **PROT**

1675   The Quakers lose political power and conscientious objection is again made illegal in Rhode Island when the colony becomes involved in King Philip's War with various Native American tribes.   **PROT**

1675   Guru Gobind Singh (1666–1708) becomes the 10th and last Sikh guru. During his period of service, which ends with his death in 1708, the Sikh Khalsa develops and further conflict with Muslims creates long-lasting enmity between the two groups. A disciple of the guru, Nand Lal Goya (1633–1715) writes poetry that becomes a secondary, though important, Sikh religious text that continues to be recited in Sikh temples.   **SIKH**

1675–
1677   The Rogerenes, a nonconformist sect, are founded in eastern Connecticut by John Rogers, a member of a leading family in the region. The Rogerenes are persecuted for their beliefs, which include separation of church and state, baptism for believers only, no Sabbath worship, and a literal interpretation of the Bible. They disappear after 1818, when the Connecticut Constitution mandates separation of church and state.   **SECT**

1676   Conflict between Russia, Poland, and the Ottoman Empire for control of the Ukraine ends with the Ottomans holding the Black Sea and coastal territory. This marks the farthest expansion north by the Ottomans into Europe.   **ISLAM**

1676   Yemen has long been the scene of attacks by Muslims on Jews, and in this year the Jews are expelled and their property destroyed. They are allowed to return in 1680.   **JUD**

1676   *Apology of the True Christian Theology, Professed and Preached by Those Who Are in Derision Called Quakers* is written by Robert Barclay (1648–1690), a British aristocrat and convert to Quakerism. The book, later known simply as *Barclay's Apology*, sets forth the basic principles of Quakerism and from the 1690s becomes a basic statement of Quaker beliefs used in Quaker communities around the world. It is later translated into numerous other languages.   **PROT**

1676   In Britain the first Meeting for Sufferings is organized by the Quakers. Its purpose is to provide legal assistance to Quakers who are being persecuted, but it evolves into a general organization to meet the needs of Quakers outside the context of the general Yearly Meetings.   **PROT**

1677   British Quaker leaders travel to the Netherlands and Germany to assist in the organization of Quaker communities on the continent. Quaker Meetings (organizations) eventually develop in France, Sweden, Switzerland, Denmark, and Norway as well.   **PROT**

1678   *Critical History of the Old Testament* is written by French priest Richard Simon. It is an attempt to use history to study religion and to bring together faith and reason. The book is condemned by the Church in the Church's general rejection of any writings and thought associated with rationality and science.   **CATH**

1680   After Pueblo religious leaders are arrested and whipped, natives revolt against Spanish rule, kill a dozen Spanish priests, and drive the Spanish from the southwest back into Mexico. The revolt is led by Pope (?–1690), a religious leader of the Taos people who had been punished by the Spanish.   **CATH, NATIV**

1680s–
1690s   Several Westerners, French and British, in writing of the religions they are finding in various Asian lands, describe Buddhism and realize that it seems to be practiced across much of Asia. In 1697 for instance, the French Jesuit Louis Comte states that "all the Indies have been poisoned with this pernicious doctrine," and he realizes that Buddhism is also being practiced in Thailand, central Asia, Japan, and China. For about the next 125 years, the West's knowledge of and attitude toward Buddhism will remain much the same. There is uncertainty about the actual relationship among the various forms of Buddhism practiced throughout Asia, and this ignorance is usually accompanied by Christian antipathy toward all forms of Buddhism as idolatrous heathenism. In particular, many believe that Buddhism is a form of Hinduism, even that the Buddha is a Hindu god, possibly an incarnation of Vishnu.   **BUDD, CHRIS**

1681   King Charles II of England awards a charter for a new colony in the Americas to William Penn (1664–1718), a British aristocrat, a convert to Quakerism, and a friend and adviser of the king.   **PROT**

1681–
1682   At an assembly of the clergy of France convened by King Louis XIV the position of the Gallicans regarding authority in the Catholic Church is set forth. They argue for a weak papacy with no authority over the temporal affairs of Catholic nations, demand a church council, and deny papal infallibility. They are supported by the king, who seeks to weaken papal influence in France. The resulting conflict almost leads to a break between France and the church in Rome but is resolved by compromise in 1689.   **CATH**

1682   The first Jewish synagogue in North America is established by Sephardic Jews in New York City in a rented one-room building.   **JUD**

1682   The first Russian Orthodox missionaries establish a mission to the indigenous peoples of eastern Siberia. Their efforts make few converts and the mission closes in 1733.   **ORTHO**

1682   *Advices and Queries*, a basic text of Quakerism, is published in a form that continues to be used with various modifications through the 20th century.   **PROT**

1682   William Penn, the governor of the new British colony of Pennsylvania, issues his Frame of Government for the colony. The constitution and laws that follow establish freedom of thought and religion, although only those who believe in God and Christ may hold public office. The laws also guarantee trial by jury; restrict many activities disapproved of by the Quakers, such as gambling, drinking toasts for oaths, and card playing; and encourage Quaker courtship and marriage practices. Within two years, Pennsylvania grows to become the major Quaker settlement in the Americas, with about two-thirds of the 5,000 residents Quakers. **PROT, TOL**

1682   A new charter establishes religious freedom in the Massachusetts Bay Colony, effectively ending the Puritan persecution of Quakers, Baptists, and others.   **TOL**

1682   In Pennsylvania religious freedom is given to all residents who acknowledge a belief in one God. **SEE 1701, 1706 TOL**.   **TOL**

1683   The Japan shogunate issues a series of sumptuary laws banning expensive clothing and regulating food, house size, and scale of entertainments. According to Confucian principles, consumption is to be proportional to status.   **CONF**

1683   Francis Makemie (1658–1708), who later is known as the "the father of American Presbyterianism," arrives in Maryland from Ireland. Makemie and other Presbyterians seek converts in the mid-Atlantic states, the upper south, and the Caribbean Islands.   **PROT**

1683   Dutch Mennonites from Germany establish the community of Germantown, Pennsylvania, the first Mennonite community in the Americas.   **SECT**

1684   The Muslim Ottoman Empire, which has been weakened by a loss of trade revenue to European nations and weak internal control of its large empire, begins to lose territory in Europe to the Russians, Hapsburgs, and Venetians.   **ISLAM**

1684   The British reorganize their colonies in New York and New England and place the region under the control of Edmund Andros, an Anglican who seeks to allow Anglican worship, a policy viewed as a threat by the Congregationalists in New England. Control from Britain lessens after 1691, but the Congregational Church no longer has the same level of authority in New England as it once had.   **PROT**

1684   The first Baptist Church is founded in Pennsylvania, where Baptists have been moving from New England, as they have greater religious freedom in the Quaker-controlled colony.   **PROT**

1685   France enacts the *Code Noir*, which requires that all slaves in French colonies in the Caribbean be baptized and instructed in Roman Catholicism.   **AFRICAN**

1685   The Bible is first published in Gaelic (Irish).   **CHRIS**

1685   In England Elizabeth Gaunt (? –1685) is burned at the stake for treason, the last person executed for treason in Britain. A Baptist, her crime had been harboring rebels who had fought against the king.   **PROT**

1685   In France the Edict of Nantes, enacted in 1598 and enforced from 1629 to 1665, which grants Protestants religious freedom, is revoked. Subject to persecution, the Huguenots flee France for other European nations and North America.   **PROT**

1685   Congregationalist minister Cotton Mather (1663–1728) is appointed minister of the Second Congregational Church in Boston, then the most influential Congregational church, and remains in the post until his death in 1728. A devout Puritan, he is the leader of the Congregational community and is the ultimate arbiter on many matters of daily life.   **PROT**

1686   Arai Hakuseki (1657–1725), Japanese statesman and leading Confucian scholar, is named tutor to Tokugawa Ienobu, who becomes shogun (hereditary military dictator) of Japan (r. 1709–1712). Arai grows into his role as a leading architect of government policy through the reign of successor shogun Tokugawa Ietsugu. His works on Japanese geography, philosophy, and history total more than 160 books.   **CONF**

1686   A Jewish community is established in Surat, India, by merchants from the Netherlands.   **JUD**

1688   The Bible is first published in Romanian.   **CHRIS**

1689   The Bible is first published in Latvian.   **CHRIS**

1689   The Conventicle Act passed in Britain in 1664 to restrict the religious activities of non-Anglicans, such as Baptists and Quakers, is repealed. However, other laws such as those that require Quakers to pay extra taxes and others that ban Puritans and Quakers from Parliament and the universities remain in effect until the 19th century.   **PROT, TOL**

1690   The *New England Primer* is published to provide lessons in spelling and the fundamentals of Calvinistic Christianity to schoolchildren in New England, a purpose it serves for 150 years.   **PROT**

1690s A Muslim *jihad* (holy war) develops in the Senegambia region of West Africa. It is led by Muslim scholars, teachers, and students, who succeed in establishing a small Muslim state. **ISLAM**

1691 The colony of New York is placed under the direct control of the British monarch and as a Crown colony, it denies religious freedom to Roman Catholics. **CATH**

1691 An abridged English-language edition of *Confucius Sinarum Philosophus* (*Three Books of Confucius*) titled *The Morals of Confucius* by Reverend Fathers Prospero Intorcetta, Filippo Couplet, and others, is published in London. **CONF**

1692 In China Emperor K'ang-Hsi issues an edict of religious toleration that allows for Roman Catholic missionary activity in China. The edict allows Jesuits, Dominicans, and Franciscan missionaries to operate freely. **CATH**

1692 During the witch trials in Salem, Massachusetts, 19 women are executed as witches. **SPIR**

1692–1694 The Keithan Controversy takes place among Quakers in Pennsylvania. The conflict is set off by Quaker preacher George Keith (1638–1716), who raises issues about the relationship of Quaker devotion to other Christian beliefs, his opposition to slavery, and reforms he calls for in the Quaker community. The controversy also divides the Pennsylvania Quakers along ethnic lines, as most of Keith's supporters are fellow Scots. Keith is censured by the Quakers, but the action fails to heal the rift and most of his followers leave Quakerism and join the Baptists, Anglicans, or Mennonites. **PROT**

1692–1696 The Spanish reconquer the southwest region of the future United States after having been driven south into Mexico by the Pueblo revolt of 1680. Again, the Spanish harshly repress the Pueblo religions. **NATIV**

1693 As part of a conflict among Mennonites (Anabaptists) living in Germany, Jacob Ammann (c. 1656–c. 1712) becomes the leader of one group that grows in size and becomes known as the Amish. Ammann advocates foot washing as a part of religious ritual, communion twice a year, expulsion of members of the community who violate community rules, a dress code, and limited contact with people outside the community. **SECT**

1694 Johannes Kelpius (1673–1708), the leader of the Rosicrucian order in Europe, and several other members travel to America and establish the first American Rosicrucian group in Pennsylvania. Modern Rosicrucian groups in North America trace their ancestry to Kelpius's arrival in America. **SECT**

1696 Yan Yuan (Yen Yuan, literary name Yen Hsi-Chai) (1635–1704), Chinese founder of a pragmatic empirical school of Confucianism opposed to the dominant speculative neo-Confucian philosophy, becomes director of the

Chang-nan Academy. He advocates the views of the early Confucian scholar Mencius. His writings, with those of his most eminent student, Li Kung (1659–1733), become the major works of a new philosophical movement known as the Yen-Li school.   **CONF**

1696   With the Portuguese having been driven from coastal East Africa by Muslim Arabs from Oman, Islam is revived in the region. Many Arabs arrive from the Arabian peninsula and the region again becomes a major Arab trading center.   **ISLAM**

1696   Ebenezer Gay is born (d. 1787) and as minister of the Hingham Church in Massachusetts rejects the Doctrine of the Trinity, an action that leads him to be later hailed as the founder of Unitarianism in America.   **SECT**

1699   Sikh guru Gobind Singh establishes the Khalsa order during the Baisakhi New Year's Day celebration in Anandpur, India. He also develops the Khalsa initiation rite and the Rahit, the code of conduct for members of the Khalsa order. Not all Sikhs join the order, although it becomes the core group within Sikhism. One key requirement of Khalsa membership is the wearing of the "five Ks": uncut hair, comb, iron or steel wristband, sword, and short pants. (All these terms begin with the letter "k" in Hindi.) Men who enter the Khalsa take the surname Singh, meaning lion, and women the surname Kaur, meaning princess.   **SIKH**

c. 1700   The combination of the Protestant Reformation, a growing emphasis on education, the scientific revolution, and the establishment of the science of astronomy as separate from astrology, sends astrology into decline in much of Europe. It does not recover until the late 19th century.   **SPIR**

Unitarianism

Unitarianism began in England and the United States in the late 17th century. In 1998 there were about 240,000 Unitarians worldwide, with about 150,000 in North America, 80,000 in Romania, and 11,000 in Great Britain. Unitarianism has always been associated with the liberal end of the Christian spectrum and remains so in the 1990s. It has no formal creed or sacraments and a flexible policy regarding rites and forms of worship. In the early years of the church it was associated with views in opposition to mainstream Christian belief, most notably the questioning and rejection of the Doctrine of the Trinity. Rather than a formal creed, most Unitarians share a set of core values including beliefs in human dignity, freedom, equality, peace, and truth. Unitarianism has also been associated with many social causes, including the abolition of slavery, women's rights, peace, and the eradication of poverty. Compared with other religions, Unitarianism is open to change, which sometimes involves the incorporation of beliefs or practices from other religions, such as Judaism and Hinduism. As from its beginnings, outsiders continue to debate whether Unitarianism is a form of Christianity or a form of a liberal, secular humanism.

1700	Although the Spanish have reconquered the Pueblo peoples of the Southwest, resistance to Spanish rule and Catholicism continues. In this year the Hopi of Arizona kill all native men in the village of Awatovi and destroy the village because the men allowed Spanish Catholic missionaries to establish a mission and build a church. **CATH, NATIV**
1700	The bases for Confucian thought and learning are widespread in Japan; virtually every educated person is exposed to the *Four Books* by the end of the 1600s. **CONF**
1700	As part of the greater—though not complete—freedoms afforded Jews, the institutions of "Court Jews" and "Port Jews" are established in Europe. Over the next several decades they become common in central Europe and slightly less so in western Europe. Court Jews are Jews who serve the rulers as advisers, diplomats, financiers, or suppliers. Port Jews are Jews who establish shipping or trading companies, primarily on the Mediterranean coast. **JUD**
1700	In Russia Peter the Great initiates the effort to spread Russian Orthodoxy to Siberia when he issues an edict announcing the virtue of such a venture. The peoples of Siberia include Buddhists, Muslims, and adherents of indigenous religions. **ORTHO**
1700	By this time the cult of local Shinto tutelary deities (*ujigami, ubusunagami,* and *chinjugami*) has spread throughout Japan. Related to the formation of villages, this type of *kami* (native spirits) worship ranks the worship of territorial divinities over that of household deities. The larger provincial shrines, usually those linked to a regional warlord, often are controlled by a hereditary priesthood, while in smaller village shrines, rites are conducted by residents who sometimes are organized into parish guilds known as *miyaza.* **SHINTO**
1700s	The Voudou (Voodoo, Vodun) religion develops among poor Africans in Haiti. It is a syncretic religion that combines elements from indigenous African religions and Roman Catholicism. Over the next few centuries the

Five Ks of Sikhism

According to Sikh belief, when Guru Gobind Singh established the Khalsa order in 1699 he also established an initiation and the Rahit, the code of conduct for members of the Khalsa order. One key requirement of Khalsa membership is the wearing of the five Ks: *kes* (uncut hair), *kangha* (comb), *kara* (iron or steel wrist band), *kirpan* (sword), and *kachch* (short pants). Men who enter the Khalsa order are required to wear these five items, as well as the turban. To non-Sikhs this clothing requirement is the most visible sign of Sikhism. It is also a subject of considerable controversy as Sikhs trace the requirement to Guru Gobind Singh, while historians suggest the requirement was added later, a view considered blasphemous by Sikhs.

religion thrives in rural communities but is repressed by the government and the educated elite, who view it as mere magic and superstition. **AFRICAN**

1700s   Korean Confucian scholars entertain diverse ideas. Chong Chedu (1649–1736) receives high honors from King Yongjo (r. 1724–1776) and openly espouses long-suppressed ideas of Wang Yang-ming. The *Sirhak*, or Practical Learning school, flowers with disaffected intellectuals writing on social and economic reform. On the one hand, Yu Hyongwon (1622–1673) and Yi Ik (1681–1763) address land reform and moral rule. On the other, Pak Chiwon (1737–1805), Hong Taeyong (1731–1783), and Pak Chega (b.1750) focus on commerce, science, and technology. Perhaps the greatest Practical Learning scholar is Chong Yagyong (1762–1838), whose work encompasses both sets of concerns.   **CONF**

1700s   The term *Confucianism* is first used in Europe, derived from the Latinized Confucius, referred to as K'ung-tzu or K'ung-fu-tzu (Master K'ung) throughout Chinese history.   **CONF**

African-American Syncretic Religions

Africans imported to the Caribbean and South America as slaves brought with them the religions they had followed in Africa. In the early years of slavery, the colonial administrations gave relatively little attention to converting slaves to Christianity and the native religions survived with new elements added that helped them explain and cope with their new environment. As missionary activity intensified, many slaves reacted by retaining many of their own religious beliefs while also accepting, at least in public, Christian beliefs and practices. Over time the two sets of beliefs were sometimes combined to produce new religions, usually with an African framework and the Christian beliefs and practices interpreted to fit into that framework. Among the major syncretic religions to develop in this way were Vodun (Voudou) in Haiti, Santeria in Cuba, Shango (Xango) in Trinidad and Tobago, and the cluster of Macumba religions, including Umbanda and Candomblé in Brazil. Each of these religions is unique, all are multidenominational, and all differ from Protestantism and Roman Catholicism, but they do share a number of general features. These include a belief in a high god, a pantheon of lesser gods or spirits associated with Christian saints, the use of ceremonies for healing, priests who perform ceremonies, possession trance as a means of communicating with spirits, a belief in patron saints or equivalent concepts, and the use of Christian symbols, such as the cross. At various times the governments of Latin American nations have sought to limit or ban these religions, and since the mid-1880s Vodun especially has often been misrepresented in sensational accounts in the United States as a cult concerned with evil, sacrifice, witchcraft, and sorcery. Since the arrival in the United States of hundreds of thousands of Cubans since 1959, Santeria, like Vodun, has been depicted sensationally by the mainstream media, and as a result both religions are practiced mainly in private.

1700s	The Maria Lionza cults develop among Indians in Venezuela. The cults, which vary from place to place, are based on spirit possession and the veneration of Maria Lionza, a mythical Indian princess. In the 20th century the cults are transformed by elements introduced from Afro-Christian religions in the Caribbean and become popular among poor Indians. **NATIV**
1700–1721	In Russia Tsar Peter the Great initiates a series of reforms designed to westernize and secularize Russian society which, in reference to their effect on Russian Orthodoxy, are called the Spiritual Regulations. He changes the calendar to that used in western Europe, establishes state schools, regulates church schools, revises the Slavic alphabet, and abolishes the Patriarchy of Moscow, replacing it with a council. **ORTHO**
c. 1700–1900	During the Enlightenment in western Europe, Jews are freed from ghettos and are allowed to enter a greater range of occupations, and Jewish culture and intellectual thought develops. The Jewish Enlightenment (*Haskalah*) takes place within the context of the European Enlightenment between about 1720 and 1880. The Jewish Enlightenment is primarily concerned with reviving Jewish intellectual traditions, refining them, and integrating them into emerging intellectual movements in Europe. **JUD**
1701	The Mughals in India attack the Sikhs and lay siege to Anandpur. The siege fails, but a second siege in 1704 involving Muslim forces from Afghanistan and India forces the guru to flee. Two of the guru's sons are killed when they refuse to convert to Islam, and their death leads Sikhs to see all Muslims, not just Mughals in India, as enemies. **ISLAM, SIKH**
1701	The Anglican Society for the Propagation of the Gospel in Foreign Parts is founded by Anglican minister Thomas Bray (1656–1730) in England. The missionaries serve Anglicans in the British colonies in the Americas and later sends missionaries to convert African slaves in the American colonies. The efforts are not very successful, as the slaves resist conversion and many slave holders object to any activity that might lead to freedom for the slaves. The missionaries also seek converts among Native Americans. **PROT**
1701	In Britain the Act of Settlement requires the monarch to be a member of the Church of England and to promise to maintain its status as the official church of the nation. **PROT**
1701	William Penn, a Quaker and the founder of Pennsylvania, issues the Charter of Privileges, which grants freedom of worship to all who believe in one God and restricts to Christians the right to hold public office. **TOL**
1701–1704	As the French in Canada expand their settlements westward, Jesuit missions are established among native peoples such as the Ojibwa, Fox, and Huron in Michigan and Illinois. **NATIV**

1701–1705	Russian Orthodox priests are active in seeking converts among the indigenous peoples (Cheremis, Ostiak, Chuvash, and others) and Muslims of the Middle Volga region of Russia. Although many converts are made, few seriously embrace Christianity; most continue to practice their indigenous religions. **ORTHO**
c. 1702	The *Popul Vuh* (*Book of Council*) of the Maya is discovered in Guatemala and is translated from the Mayan language into Spanish. It contains detailed descriptions of Maya religious beliefs and practices both before and after the Spanish conquest in the 16th century. **NATIV**
1702	In Japan the 47 *ronin* (masterless samurai) defy shogunate law and risk their lives to avenge the death of their lord, following the code of Yamaga Soko (1622–1685), military strategist and Confucian philosopher. This incident becomes famous in Japanese history and brings more attention to Yamaga's

Maya Religion

The religion of the Classic Maya of Mesoamerica, which flourished from 200 to 900 C.E., was a rich mix of beliefs and practices, some adopted from other peoples in Mesoamerica and others mainly of Mayan origin. Central to Maya religion was a cyclical view of the universe, with several worlds inhabited by humans having come into existence and then disappeared before the current world, which began in 3114 B.C.E. and was scheduled to end in 2012 C.E. The Maya believed that their ancestors were humans made from corn flour, a belief consistent with the fact that corn was a staple crop of the Maya. With this cyclical view of the world, months, days, and numerals symbolizing them were considered to be divine, and the Maya borrowed and developed a number of religious, agricultural, and solar calendar systems that they used to order their lives. The Maya were polytheistic, with the gods of the sun and the moon set atop their pantheon, which also included gods of corn, snakes, feathered serpents, darkness, and heaven. Astronomical objects, such as planets and stars were also considered divine objects, and the Maya used astrology to make predictions based on astronomical observations. Maya religious practice centered on the major ceremonial centers, which in many ways resembled such centers elsewhere in Mesoamerica. They usually contained large plazas, pyramids and temples, burial chambers, ball courts for the ancient Mesoamerican ball games, and elaborate stone carvings and stellae. Religious practices included prayers, offerings, dancing, bloodletting, and human sacrifices, all of which were designed to feed the gods and ensure adequate food for the Maya. Religious rituals were carried out by the priests, the most powerful social group in Maya society. The priests were not only religious leaders but also served the rulers as advisers and managers, divined the future, and healed the sick. To what extent this religion influenced the lives of the average Mayan, who often lived in a farming village miles from the ceremonial center, is unclear. But it is likely that religious healers were active in these communities, that images of the divine power of the royalty were used to reinforce their political control, and that witchcraft was quite common.

ideas, including the idea that Japanese civilization is superior to that of China through greater loyalty to its imperial line and to the Confucian conception of duty.   CONF

1702   China's Emperor Kangxi (r. 1669–1722) receives the Sichuan Daoist sage Chen Qingjue and gives him the title "Perfected of Green Profundity," a mark of favor.   DAO

1702   The Russian effort to spread Russian Orthodoxy begins with a mission at Tobolsk that seeks converts among the indigenous peoples of Siberia including the Yakuts and Ostiaks. The mission enjoys limited success but gains more converts after it stabilizes in the early 1800s.   ORTHO

1704   As an outgrowth of the Chinese Rites Controversy in which Matteo Ricci, an Italian Jesuit missionary in China, had tried to attach Roman Catholic understanding to the veneration of Confucius, Pope Clement XI condemns Confucian devotion as incompatible with Christian worship and doctrine. He does so again in 1715, as does Pope Benedict XIV in 1742.   CATH, CONF

1704   As the English attempt to push the Spanish out of North America they destroy Spanish Catholic missions in southern Georgia and Florida, effectively ending Spanish missionary efforts in the east.   NATIV

1704–   The Roman Catholic Church in India and then in China issues orders to
1705   missionaries that require them to ignore existing cultural and religious traditions and to closely follow church policy. Missionaries object to the orders as they disrupt their work, and in China the emperor reacts to what he sees as European intervention in Chinese affairs by placing new restrictions on missionaries.   CATH

1705   A Russian Orthodox mission is established on Kamchatka Peninsula in far eastern Siberia. Early conversion efforts are unsuccessful, but from 1745 to 1748 nearly the entire indigenous population is converted.   ORTHO

1705   The British enact laws that deny Roman Catholics the right to vote or hold office in Pennsylvania. By this time the British have suceeded in repressing Catholicism in its American colonies and religious freedom is not restored until the American Revolution.   TOL

1705–   In Laos the contest for the rule of Lan Xang continues. Setthathirat II
1707   removes the Prabang, the standing Buddha, from Luang Prabang to his capital, Vieng Chan.   BUDD

1706   Dona Béatrice (c. 1682–1706) is executed by the Portuguese in Africa. She had founded the first independent African Christian movement to resist Catholicism, and after her death it became a major point of resistance to Portuguese rule.   AFRICAN

1706   The Manchu emperor orders that the Jesuit practices permitting Chinese Christians to participate in the state cult of Confucianism and ancestor worship be followed.   **CATH, CONF**

1706   The first Presbyterian presbytery is founded in Philadelphia. Its founders declare their intention to hold annual meetings to assist in the work of the Presbyterian Church in America. Francis Makemie, the father of Presbyterianism in America, is the first moderator.   **PROT**

1706   King Frederick IV of Denmark establishes the Royal Danish Mission when he recruits two German priests to open a mission in the Danish colony of Tranquebar in southeast India.   **PROT**

1706   In Pennsylvania religious freedom is taken from Jews, Catholics, and Socinians (Unitarians) due to pressure exerted by the Crown in England.   **TOL**

1707   Mennonites from Switzerland and the Palatine establish their first settlement in eastern Pennsylvania. By the 1750s, some 4,000 Menonnites have settled in the region.   **SECT**

1708   Near death, Sikh guru Gobind Singh announces to the Sikh community that he is the 10th and last of the personal gurus of the Sikh community. He orders that following his death the personal guruship is to be carried forth by the *Guru Granth* (Sikh sacred text) and the *Guru Panth* (the Sikh community).   **SIKH**

1708   In Connecticut residents are granted religious freedom, although all are required to make payments to support the Puritan Church.   **TOL**

1709   German Protestants from the Lower Palatinate region, who had fled to England in 1708 and 1709 to escape religious persecution, are allowed to settle in Ireland, North Carolina, and New York State.   **PROT**

1709   The migration of Swiss Mennonites from the Palatinate regions begins with some going to the Netherlands and Great Britain. As with other immigrants from the region they seek to escape a harsh winter and food shortages.   **SECT**

c. 1710   Korean Confucian scholars Yi Kan (1677–1727) and Han Wonjin (1682–1750) hold at Nak-Ho a debate about the human relationship to the cosmos. Yi claims that individuals share their natures with other things in the universe; Han maintains that the human original nature makes us distinct from other things. The debate generates intense discussion in the scholarly community.   **CONF**

1710   In Russia Peter the Great initiates a new policy designed to convert the Tatar (Muslim) population to Russian Orthodoxy. Muslims are baptized, children are sent to Russian schools, and Russian Orthodox churches are built

1710   in Tatar villages. The policy ends in 1764 as it is disruptive to some Tatar settlements that are vital to Russian trade.   **ISLAM**

1710   Under the leadership of Banda the Brave, a legendary Sikh leader who had led rebellions against the Mughals in India, the Sikhs defeat the Mughals at Sirhind.   **ISLAM, SIKH**

1710   Pietists in Halle, Germany, establish the von Canstein Bible Institution to distribute Bibles to the poor.   **PROT**

1710   Mennonites from Switzerland and southern Germany immigrate to the Americas and establish settlements in Lancaster County, Pennsylvania. The county becomes and remains a major center of both Mennonite and Amish settlement in the world.   **SECT**

1711   *Characteristicism* is written by the British deist Lord Shatesbury. Considered by later deists to be one of the major texts of the movement, it sets forth an argument for the existence of God based on the human relationship with nature.   **MISC**

1711   Several hundred Amish from the German Palatinate region settle in the Netherlands, where they establish a distinct community that lasts for 100 years before it is absorbed by the existing Mennonite community.   **SECT**

1714   The first Lutheran Church is organized in New Jersey and it includes African-Americans as members. Although more African-Americans affiliate with the Baptist and Methodist churches, Lutheran churches continue to attract African-Americans until after the Civil War, when separate white and African-American Lutheran churches develop.   **AFRICAN**

1714   Bartholomew Ziegenbalg, one of the founding missionaries of the Royal Danish Mission to India in 1706, completes his translation of the New Testament into the Tamil language. He dies before he can complete the translation of the Old Testament. Ziegenbalg is an early advocate of making the Bible available to potential converts in their own language; this position later becomes accepted doctrine in Christian missionary activity.   **PROT**

1715   The Roman Catholic Church after several years of discussion rules that missionaries in China may not incorporate Chinese customs and Chinese language into Roman Catholicism. Missionaries had argued in favor of the practice as a means of attracting Chinese converts.   **CATH**

1716   The Presbyterian Church in America has expanded since the 1660s, and there are now four churches. In this year the General Synod is founded to coordinate and assist in the activities of the presbyteries of Long Island, New York; Philadelphia; New Castle; and Snow Hill.   **PROT**

1716	Sikh leader Banda the Brave is captured by the Mughals in India, and when he refuses to convert to Islam, he is executed. Repression of Sikhism continues and for the next decade the Sikhs are forced to flee and live in the forest. **ISLAM, SIKH**
1717	The Ancient Druid order, a pagan group, is founded in England. It survives in London in the 1990s with worship centered on festivals at Stonehenge. **SPIR**
c. 1718	Ogyu Sorai (1666–1728), an influential Confucian scholar and adviser to two shoguns under Emperor Nakamikado, publishes his *Rongocho* (*Commentaries on the Analects*) in Japan. **CONF**
1718	Through the Treaty of Passarowitz and then the Treaty of Belgrade in 1739, the Ottoman Empire is able to halt the loss of territory in Europe to the Russians and Hapsburgs and actually regains some lost territory. **ISLAM**
1718–1731	Spanish Franciscan missionaries establish missions in and around San Antonio, Texas. The first and what later becomes the best known is the Alamo (San Antonio de Valero). **CATH**
1720	Rabbi Elijah ben Solomon Zalman (Elijah Goan) (1720–1797) is born. He becomes the rabbi of Vilna in Lithuania and is a major supporter of traditional Orthodox Judaism and an opponent of Hasidism, a more fundamentalist alternative to Orthodoxy. **JUD**
1720s	Franciscan missionaries establish missions among the Huichol people in northwestern Mexico. The missionaries work to spread Catholicism and to integrate the Huichol into Mexican national life. SEE **1860**, **NATIV**. **NATIV**
1720–1730s	Tensions ease between the Muslim Mughals and the Sikhs in India and Sikhism continues to grow and consolidate as a distinct religion and community during these decades in the Punjab region of India. Important Sikh leaders are Kapur Singh, who becomes leader of the Sikh community in 1733, and Mani Singh, who is martyred when executed by the Muslims in 1738. **SIKH**
1720s–1740s	A religious revival takes place in the British colonies in America. Known at the time as the New School, New Light, or New Side and later called the Great Awakening by historians, it is led by Calvinist minister Jonathan Edwards (1703–1758) in Massachusetts and British Calvinist minister George Whitefield (1714–1770), who makes a number of trips to the American colonies. The revival stresses emotional worship and a personal relationship with Jesus Christ and leads to the strengthening of a number of different forms of Christianity—Baptist, Methodist, and Presbyterian—in the colonies as well as a number of smaller sects, such as Freewill Baptists and Shakerism. **PROT**

1724	Roman Catholic missionary activity in China dwindles when Emperor Yung-cheng orders that missionaries be deported to Macao, although some are allowed to remain in Beijing. By the end of the century, the Roman Catholic presence in China has almost completely vanished. **CATH**
1724	The Chinese emperor Yongzheng bans Christianity in response to Pope Clement XI's rejection in 1704 and 1715 of the Jesuit position accommodating Chinese cultural traditions, such as ancestor rites. **CHRIS, CONF**
1724	The Great Temple of Confucius is built in Qufu (Ch'u-fu or Ku-fow), the town of his birth and death, in eastern China. With an extensive complex of shrines, monuments, and pavilions, it stands inside a walled enclosure that occupies 49 acres. **CONF**
1724–1776	During his reign in Korea, Yongjo adopts the *t'angp'yongch'aek*, the policy of impartiality. It stipulates that official appointments be granted in approximately equal portions to members of each of Choson's principal Confucian factions. **CONF**
1725	While teaching at Oxford University, John Wesley (1703–1791), who later founds Methodism, writes a set of rules for his life stating that it is to be dedicated to God. **PROT**

Great Awakening

The Great Awakening is the name historians use for a religious revival that swept through the British colonies in Canada and the United States from the late 1720s into the early 1740s. It was the American version of the Pietist and Quietism revivals in Europe and the Evangelical revival in Great Britain during the same time period. The Great Awakening was to a large extent a reaction to the stagnation of Protestantism in America. Religion was controlled by a small number of churches and ministers, worship was intellectual and emotionally barren, and there was a general decline in religious interest among the common people. The preaching of Great Awakening leaders, such as George Whitefield from England, and the writings of American minister Jonathan Edwards were very different from traditional sermons and stressed the emotional experience of religion and the personal relationship a Christian could experience with Jesus Christ. The movement had profound and enduring effects on American society. It expanded the Dutch Reformed, Baptist, Presbyterian, and Congregational churches and made America a multidenominational society. It also weakened Harvard College, where there was opposition to the revival, as the center of religious thought, and some historians believe that it helped lay the groundwork for the American Revolution by creating a more democratic society.

1726–
1776

A Muslim *jihad* (holy war) directed at the ruling Jalonke people takes place in the Senegambia region of West Africa. The Muslim victory results in the establishment of the Futa Jallon Muslim state, which in 1881 comes under French control. **ISLAM**

1727

Through the Treaty of Kiachta between Russia and China, the Russians are granted the right to send Russian Orthodox priests to Beijing to serve the small Russian community living there. The priests also seek to convert the Chinese but have very limited success. Irkutsk in eastern Siberia is established as a diocese of the Russian Orthodox Church. **ORTHO**

1727

Presbyterian minister William Tennent, Sr. (1673–1746), opens a school for pastors at his home in Neshaminy, Pennsylvania. The school comes to be known as Log Cabin College in 1735, when a building is constructed. Its major purpose is to train pastors to work in the western regions of the nation. The school closes in 1746 following Tennent's death but is seen by many as the precursor of the College of New Jersey (later Princeton University), which opens in 1746. **PROT**

1727

August Hermann Francke (b.1663) dies. During his lifetime he had been a follower of Philipp Jacob Spencer, the German founder of the Pietism

Jonathan Edwards

The Puritan and Congregationalist minister Jonathan Edwards is considered by many religious scholars to be the most important Christian theologian in North America. Edwards was born the son of a Congregational minister, Timothy Edwards, in East Windsor, Connecticut, in 1703. He graduated from Yale College in 1720 and commenced his ministerial career in 1722–1723 at the Presbyterian Church in New York, followed by several years as a tutor at Yale. He then became minister of the Congregational Church in Northampton, Massachusetts, where he served and produced most of his major theological work until 1750. Doctrinal differences with the congregation then forced him to take up a small church in Stockbridge, Massachusetts, where he served until 1758. He died the same year, shortly after being appointed president of Princeton University. Edwards was a devout Calvinist and therefore believed in salvation by God alone and in some ways took a negative and pessimistic view of the human condition. At the same time, however, he was a reformer who initiated the Great Awakening of the 1740s in the United States through his sermons of 1734 and 1735. Edwards stressed the emotional aspects of religion and especially the feelings of love and devotion that formed the basis of his own belief. He was also a prolific author and many of his writings, such as *Faithful Narrative of the Surprising Work of God*, *Some Thoughts Concerning the Present Revival of Religion in New England*, and *Freedom of the Will*, remain basic statements of early American Protestantism.

movement, and Franke established orphanages and schools in the city of Halle, Germany, that made it the center of Pietism in Europe.   **PROT**

1727   The requirement that residents of Connecticut support the Puritan Church is relaxed as Quakers, Baptists, and Episcopalians are exempted from making payments to the Church.   **TOL**

1728   The first Jewish religious school for children in the Americas is opened by Congregation Shearith Israel in New York City.   **JUD**

1728   In India British Anglican ministers have not proved to be effective missionaries and they are replaced by German missionaries who have not been ordained as Anglican ministers. They prove to be reliable and effective and are used by the Anglican Church until 1861.   **PROT**

1728   Shinto priest Kada Azumamaro (1669–1736) petitions Japan's shogunate to establish a school of national learning (*kokugaku*) after he becomes convinced that only a revival of the true way of the *kami* (native spirits) will protect the nation. This scholarly movement to examine the ancient mythological and classical literary texts has the aim of determining the essence of the Japanese spirit to purify Japanese ideas and institutions of foreign influence. The foundation for the national learning school's ideas and the closely related Fukko (restoration) Shinto was laid by Shingon monk Keichu (1640–1701), who deciphered the orthography of the long neglected eighth-century poetry anthology *Man'yoshu*.   **SHINTO**

1729   The prayer guide *Articles of Faith and Acts of Religion* by Benjamin Franklin is published in Philadelphia. It downplays the importance of religious doctrine and emphasizes the role of reason in religion.   **MISC**

1729   The Presbyterian Synod in the United States promulgates the Adopting Act of 1729. The act is a compromise between those who want ministers to abide by the Westminster *Confession of Faith* and those who take a more liberal view as to the theological doctrine of the church. The Act allows the presbytery to make decisions about the suitability of ministers and also weakens somewhat rigid adherence to the Westminster *Confession*. It also prevents the Presbyterian Church in America from dividing over this issue.   **PROT**

1729   Shingaku, a Japanese popular religion, is established by Ishida Baigan (1685–1744) a clerk in Kyoto. The religion combines elements from Confucianism and Buddhism.   **SECT**

c. 1730   The Zoroastrians, who now live mainly in Iran, Iraq, and India, divide into three sects, Shenshahi, Qadimi, and Fasli. The differences among the sects are not rooted in religious doctrine but rather in how each reckons time, the calendars they use, and the dates of their religious observances.   **SECT**

1730   The Russians have been successful in bringing the Kazakhs in the north and central regions of Kazakhstan under Russian military control. Over the next 100 years they gradually take political control of the region and displace Kazakh pastoral nomads with Russian farmers in the north.   **ISLAM**

1730   The first Jewish synagogue is built in North America by the Sephardic Jewish community in New York City. It later relocates further north on Manhattan.   **JUD**

1730   *Christianity as Old as Creation* is written by British deist Matthew Tolland. It is considered by later deists to be one the most important works of deism.   **MISC**

1730–
1756   French philosopher and author Voltaire (François Arouet), a leading figure of the Enlightenment, is influenced by Jesuit accounts of Confucian morality and love of learning in China.   **CHRIS, CONF**

1731   The Redemptorist order is founded in Italy by (St.) Alfonso Maria de Liguori (1696–1787), a Neapolitan noble and lawyer who had entered the priesthood. The male and female branches of the order are accepted by the Church in 1749 and 1750. Alfonso is canonized in 1839 and made the patron saint of confessors and moral theologians.   **CATH**

1731   In Massachusetts a law is enacted that frees Quakers from having to pay support to the Puritan Church. The exemption is granted a few years later to Baptists and Episcopalians.   **TOL**

1732   The first Moravian mission is established for African slaves in the British colonies on the Caribbean island of St. Thomas. Other missions are established later in Jamaica (1754), Antigua (1756), Barbados (1765), St. Kitts (1774), and Tobago (1790). The missions meet with mixed success, as their efforts are often resisted by white landowners who fear that Christianized slaves are more likely to revolt.   **AFRICAN, PROT**

1732   The Ephrata Colony (The Solitary Brethren of the Community of the Seventh-Day Baptists) is founded by German Pietist leader Johann Conrad Beissel in western Pennsylvania. It is a communal society with religious beliefs and practices centered on mysticism, celibacy, separate religious orders for men and women, and Beissel's claims of divine inspiration. Life in the colony is disrupted by much feuding, and it dissolves in 1770, two years after Beissel's death.   **SECT**

1732   In Georgia religious freedom is granted to all except Roman Catholics.   **TOL**

1733   The *Daozang Jiyao*, a compendium of the Daoist canon, is published in Qing dynasty China.   **DAO**

1733   The first Jewish congregation in the southern United States is founded as Mikveh Israel (Hope of Israel) in Savannah, Georgia.   **JUD**

1733	The Moravians from Germany establish a mission to the Inuit of Greenland that competes with the Lutheran mission established there in 1722. The Moravians, who have been active missionaries since then, mark this as the beginning of their missionary effort. **PROT**
1733	The first Indian Hindu convert to Protestant Christianity, a man named Aaron, is ordained a Protestant minister by the Royal Danish Mission in southeast India. **PROT**
1733– 1760s	The Hutterites in Slovakia, a region now under Roman Catholic Hapsburg influence, are persecuted, their churches closed, their books confiscated, and they are forced to baptize their children as Catholics. **SECT**
1734	In this year Danish missionary Hans Egede and his son Paul establish a Lutheran mission at the village of Christianshaab in Greenland. The senior Egede had begun his efforts in 1722. Paul Egede translates the New Testament into the Inuit language in 1766. **PROT**
1734	The Moravians, a Protestant sect from the Moravia region of Czechoslovakia, attempt to establish a communal society in Savannah, Georgia. **PROT**
1734	The Salzburgers, a German Lutheran sect, are driven out of Germany by the Roman Catholic hierarchy and establish a settlement in Georgia. Their numbers grow to over 1,000, but they are eventually assimilated into mainstream Protestant society in the United States. **PROT**
1734	The Schwenkfelders, a German Protestant sect, are persecuted by Catholics in Germany and establish a settlement in Pennsylvania. There are about 3,000 members of the sect in the United States in the 1990s. **PROT**
1735	The Bible is first published in Lithuanian. **CHRIS**
c. 1736	The Hasidic Jewish movement begins in eastern Europe. Hasidism, an ultra-Orthodox movement, stresses a return to strict traditions, living apart from non-Jewish society, and an emotional expression of one's faith. A number of distinct sects of Hasidim develop, and their adherents are found in the 1990s mainly in the United States, Canada, and Israel. **JUD**
1736	At the Synod of the Presbyterian Church in America, conservatives (the Old Light) in the Church rescind the Adopting Act of 1729 and begin to limit the activities of pastors who preach a more emotional, spiritual form of Presbyterianism. The conservatives' actions are both an attempt to regain control of the church and a reaction to the revivals of the Great Awakening in America. **PROT**
1736	Changes in European views about magic and witchcraft are reflected in the repeal of witchcraft laws in Great Britain. Although such activities are still

illegal, new laws state that witchcraft does not actually exist; that is, people who claim to be witches do not really have supernatural powers, are not agents of the Devil, and so cannot cause harm to others.   **SPIR**

1736–
1796
Qianlong reigns as the fourth emperor of the Qing dynasty China. His 60-year reign is the longest in Chinese history. Qianlong is actively anti-Daoist. He regards the Daoist clergy as parasitical and issues orders restricting Daoist activities. He also strictly regulates the Buddhist clergy.   **BUDD, DAO**

1737
Some Quaker and Mennonite leaders in Pennsylvania form the Friendly Association for Regaining and Preserving the Peace with the Indians by Pacific Measures. The organization is formed because of claims that the natives have lost land to whites through unfair means, but it also seeks to civilize them.   **NATIV, PROT**

1737
Protestant missionary activity begins in Africa when the Moravians establish a mission in South Africa and later in the year one in West Africa.   **PROT**

1737
The first sizable number of Amish from Europe arrive in the Americas and settle in rural communities west of Philadelphia. Some Amish had arrived as early as 1710, but this group is the first that is large enough to establish a local church. Amish immigration to Pennsylvania continues until 1754.   **SECT**

1738
John Wesley, the founder of Methodism, forms a prayer group in London. Wesley has already started developing a theology distinct from that of the Church of England, although he does not intend to start a new denomination. On May 24 Wesley experiences a religious transformation that leads him to adopt what becomes the basic Methodist principle of personal salvation through the grace of God. Methodists in later years date the founding of the denomination to this event and day.   **PROT**

1738
Charles Wesley (1708–1788), the younger brother of John Wesley, the founder of Methodism, undergoes his own conversion experience on May 21 and decides that he must share that experience with others. He devotes himself to the writing of hymns that become widely used in Protestant churches, including "Hark, the Herald-Angels Sing" and "Christ the Lord Is Risen Today."   **PROT**

1738
Evangelical preacher George Whitefield (1714–1770) arrives in Georgia on the first of his seven trips to the United States. An early advocate of Methodism in England, he plays a major role in the religious revival known as the Great Awakening that sweeps across the British colonies in America in the 18th century.   **PROT**

1738
The New Light (liberal) faction of the Presbyterian Church in the United States establishes a new presbytery, the New Brunswick Presbytery in south central New Jersey. This presbytery gives the New Light faction a base of operations outside the control of the Old Light Philadelphia Presbytery.   **PROT**

1738– 1740	*History of the Baptists*, the first history of the Baptist denomination, is written by Thomas Crosby (1683–1751), a schoolteacher in London. **PROT**
1739	The Bible is first published in Estonian. **CHRIS**
1739	John Wesley, the founder of Methodism, agrees to take over from evangelical preacher George Whitefield (1714–1770), in Bristol, England. Wesley adopts Whitefield's highly emotional and effective style and begins to attract followers. Wesley does not intend to create a new denomination, but his work nontheless wins the disapproval of the Church of England and the upper British classes. **PROT**
1740	The New Lights movement is started by British evangelical preacher George Whitefield in New England. The movement stresses personal religious experience and faith in God and draws many adherents from the Congregationalists. It is attacked by mainstream Christian leaders but plays a role in the religious demonstrations that take place as part of the Great Awakening. **PROT**
1740	The *Dasam Granth* is accepted as a basic religious text, although perhaps less important that the *Adi Granth*, by some Sikhs in India. Sikh tradition suggests that the text was compiled by Sikh leader Harimandir Sahib between 1721 and 1734. The *Dasam Granth* contains the *Bachitar Natak*, a religious text that is not considered sacred but is nonetheless important as

---

John Wesley

John Wesley was the founder of the Methodist movement that emerged within the Church of England in the mid-18th century in England. Although Wesley always saw the movement as existing within the Church of England, officials of the church did not accept his teaching. Methodism eventually developed as a separate denomination within Protestant Christianity. Wesley was born in Lincolnshire in 1703, the son of an Anglican pastor. He was educated at Christ Church College at Oxford, ordained an Anglican priest in 1725, and then appointed to a teaching position at Oxford. In 1729 his religious quest began when he and his brother Charles organized groups to explore their religious experience; the brothers journeyed to Georgia in the colonies in 1735 for the same purpose. In May 1738, back in England, both Charles and John reported a personal relationship with Christ and began preaching and organizing groups to enable others to have similar experiences. This event marks the beginning of Methodism as a religion, although the actual church was not organized until several years later. Charles eventually ended his preaching and devoted himself to the writing of hymns. John Wesley continued preaching and organizing and assisted in the spread of the denomination to the United States. He was renowned as a preacher, organizer, and leader and was widely respected during his lifetime and after his death by members of the church. He died in England in 1791.

it recounts Sikh history through tales of the gurus. Other works follow in this tradition into the 20th century, including *Gur Sobha, Gur-bilas Dasvin Patshahi, Prachan Panth Prakash, Nanak Prakash*, and *Tavarikh Guru Khalsa*.

SIKH

1740–
1741

As the conflict between the Old Light (conservative) and New Light (liberal) factions of the Presbyterian Church in America continues, Gilbert Tennent, son of Log Cabin College founder William Tennent, delivers his "The Danger of an Unconverted Ministry" sermon, which is then published and distributed. He attacks the conservative ministry and its resistance to the revival he supports in the church. The Old Light responds in 1741 when the Philadelphia Presbytery issues the *Protestation,* which expels members of the New Brunswick Presbytery from the church. The Philadelphia group takes the name of the Synod of Philadelphia (Old Side Presbyterians) and the New Brunswick group takes the name of Conjunct Presbyteries of New Brunswick and Londonderry (New Side Presbyterians). **PROT**

Methodism

Methodism is a Protestant denomination that was founded in the early 18th century in Britain by John and Charles Wesley and George Whitefield, although Whitefield later left the movement. It emerged as part of the Evangelical Revival. The founders were interested in reforming the Church of England and relied on the Bible as the ultimate source: "A Methodist is one who lives according to the method laid down in the Bible." In addition to reliance on the Bible, the early Methodists were active preachers, and their preaching throughout England did much to attract men and women to the church. Their attempts at reform were not accepted within the church, and Methodism became a distinct denomination and drew a substantial following in Britain and later in the American colonies. As the church expanded in the 19th century, it divided into administratively separate churches in the United States and Britain. In the United States African-American Methodist churches were established early in the century, and in the 1840s the church divided over the issue of slavery. In Great Britain the church divided into various smaller churches, often on the basis of location or belief and practice, although many united as the Methodist Church of Great Britain and Ireland in 1932. A similar reconciliation took place in the United States in 1968 with the establishment of the United Methodist Church. Methodists have been active missionaries, and it is estimated that there are about 60 million Methodists in 100 nations. There are about 14 million in the United States. Methodism lacks a single unifying doctrine or set of practices, as each church has much freedom to interpret the scriptures in accord with its own tradition. Many Methodist churches in the 20th century have been classified within the liberal wing of Protestantism for their frequent support of social causes.

1741– 1762	Russian Orthodox missionary activity among the indigenous peoples of the Middle Volga region intensifies and most are converted to Russian Orthodoxy. Muslims in the region resist conversion. **ORTHO**
1742	Pope Benedict XIV in his bull *Ex quo singulari* supports the policy on missionary activity enacted in China in 1705 and cancels changes in that policy made in the intervening years. **CATH**
1742	A rebellion against Spanish rule in Peru is led by the prophet Juan Santos Atahualpa (c. 1712–c. 1776), who claims to be a descendant of the legendary Inca ruler Ata Wallpa Inca, whose return to earth is believed by Peruvian natives to usher in a period of Inca revival and the end of Spanish rule. The Spanish fail to end the revolt, which is centered in the eastern highland, and when Atahualpa dies sometime between 1755 and 1776, his grave becomes an important regional shrine. **NATIV**
1742	In the United States Lutheran churches begin to be formed by immigrants from Germany in Pennsylvania, New Jersey, and Maryland. **PROT**
1743	Lutherans from the Netherlands establish a church in South America. **PROT**
1744	Pope Benedict XIV in his bull *Ominium Sollictudinum* supports the policy on missionary activity enacted in India in 1704 and cancels changes in that policy made in the intervening years. These actions by the Church from 1704 to 1744 establish the policy that missionary activity will be carefully and fully controlled by the Vatican. **CATH**
1744	In Saudi Arabia the Muslim Wahhabi movement is founded when tribal leaders in the region, Muhammad ibn-Sa'ud and his son 'Abd al-'Aziz, give refuge to the Muslim fundamentalist reformer Muhammad bin 'Abd al-Wahhab (1703–1787) and help spread his message. He preaches against popular reli-

---

George Whitefield

A Calvinist preacher, George Whitefield, was a key figure in both the Great Awakening in the United States and the Evangelical Revival in Britain in the 18th century. Whitefield was born in Gloucester, England, in 1714 and educated at Oxford University, where he was a student of John Wesley, the founder of Methodism, and Wesley's brother Charles. Although he later broke with Wesley over doctrine, they remained friends, and Wesley delivered the sermon at Whitefield's funeral in 1770. Whitefield was a powerful and persuasive preacher who was at his best at the outdoor revivals that attracted large crowds in Britain and on his seven trips to America. In Britain he was closely associated with the Calvinist Methodists and in America with the Presbyterians. He also had a strong social conscience and founded an orphanage in Georgia in 1740 that was supported by donations he collected through his preaching. He died in America and is buried in Newburyport, Massachusetts.

---

gious practices in Arabia and establishes the conservative Wahhabi movement, which attracts many Arab tribes in the region, and creates unity that will eventually lead to the establishment of Saudi Arabia. **ISLAM**

1744   John Wesley, the founder of Methodism, organizes the first conference of Methodists near London, England. The conference creates an organizational structure for the emerging church, although the movement remains within the Church of England. Many Methodists later mark this meeting as the formal beginning of the Methodist denomination. **PROT**

1744   The Izumo Taisha, the largest Shinto shrine hall in Japan, is ritually rebuilt for the final time. The structure has been rebuilt at least 25 times before. **SHINTO**

1745   The Jewish community in Philadelphia founds the *Mikveh Israel* (Hope of Israel) synagogue. **JUD**

1745   In the United States the New York Presbytery joins with the former New Brunswick Presbytery (New Side Presbyterians) and they form the Synod of New York, which stands in opposition to the Old Side Presbyterians in Philadelphia. **PROT**

1745   Charles Wesley writes his first book of hymns, *Hymns on the Lord's Supper*, to be used by Methodists. **PROT**

1746   When a Mughal-Hindu army attacks Sikhs at Kahnuwan in India, many Sikhs are killed in what is known as the Lesser Holocaust (to distinguish from the Greater Holocaust in 1762). **ISLAM, SIKH**

1746   The College of New Jersey is issued a charter by the governor and classes begin in the following year. The College is founded by New Side Presbyterians who support the Great Awakening and is an alternative to Harvard and Yale, both of which are led by theologians who are opposed to the religious revival in the United States. It becomes the center of Presbyterian education in the United States and later becomes Princeton University and Princeton Theological Seminary. **PROT**

1747   In order to take control of northwestern India and Pakistan, the Muslims in Afghanistan begin a series of attacks on Sikh settlements that persist until 1769. In response, the Sikhs organize themselves into semi-autonomous regional armies that follow local leaders but also support the Sikh religion and community. These armies strengthen the Sikh community and further contribute to the emergence of the Sikhs being viewed as a martial group in India. **ISLAM, SIKH**

1747   *A Humble Attempt to Promote Explicit Agreement and Visible Union of God's Peoples in Extraordinary Prayer for the Revival of Religion and the Advancement of Christ's Kingdom on Earth, Pursuant to Scripture Promises, and Prophecies*

Concerning the Last Time is written by Protestant theologian and later president of Princeton University Jonathan Edwards (1703–1758) in the Americas. The book supports the idea of a worldwide missionary attempt to create a spiritual movement that will mark the beginning of a new age. The book remains popular in Protestantism for over a century. **PROT**

1747   The Shakers (United Society of Believers in Christ's Second Appearing) begin to emerge in Manchester, England, when two Quakers, James and Jane Wardely, are influenced by the teaching of the Camisards (French Prophets), who have immigrated to England. The Wardelys' new form of Quakerism includes religious services with dancing, hand waving, and shaking, and participants are called Shaking Quakers. **SECT**

1747   The Abrahamites, a Christian sect that adopts some Jewish beliefs and practices, including celebrating the Sabbbath on Saturday and dietary restrictions, emerges in Bohemia. As they claim to be neither Christians nor Jews, they are persecuted and disappear after 1781. **SECT**

1747   In Sweden Emanuel Swedenborg begins writing about religion, philosophy, and spirituality. His writings are based in part on his dreams, which he began writing down in 1736, and the visions he began to have in 1745. His two best known works are *On the New Jerusalem and Its Heavenly Doctrine* and *The New Christian Religion Containing the Universal Theology of the New Church*. Swedenborg's ideas later influence theologists and philosophers, such as John Wesley, Immanuel Kant, Ralph Waldo Emerson, and W. B. Yeats, and later spiritual movements including Theosophy. **SPIR**

1749   American statesman Benjamin Franklin promulgates his *Proposals Relating to the Education of Youth in Philadelphia*, in which he argues for a "publick religion" based on Protestant Christianity. This is one of the first statements in a continuing debate in the United States that continues through the 20th century about the wisdom of creativity or need to choose a national, public, or civil religion for the entire nation. **TOL**

1749–   The Challoner version of the Rheims-Douai Bible originally translated into
1752   English in France is revised in London by Bishop Challoner for British Catholics. It goes into use in the United States in 1810. **CATH**

c. 1750   Parsis (Zoroastrians) in India move from their communities in Gujarat to Bombay, which becomes home to most Parsis. **SECT**

1750   The Muslim Mughal Empire in southern Asia has been eroded by Hindu revolts in the south and attacks by Afghans in the north, as well as by pressure from the British, and now controls only a small territory around Delhi in India. **ISLAM**

1750   Lithuania becomes the center of Jewish religious scholarship. Jews are granted rights by Frederick II of Prussia.   **JUD**

1751   A mission from Sri Lanka asks the Thai kingdom of Ayudhya for help in restoring Buddhism, now in decline after Portuguese and Dutch rule of Sri Lanka. Ayudhya sends 18 Thai monks to reordain Sri Lankan monks and to found an order of Thai monks in Sri Lanka. It is known as the Siam Nikaya. This request marks Thailand's importance as an international center of Buddhism. It also leads to a major revival of Buddhism in Sri Lanka.   **BUDD**

1751   The Bible is first translated into Portuguese.   **CHRIS**

1751   In accord with their social agenda, Quakers in Pennsylvania found Pennsylvania Hospital to treat the mentally ill.   **PROT**

1753   Rights enjoyed by Jews in Britain are extended to newly arrived Jewish immigrants by Parliament in the so-called Jew Bill. Public opposition causes the bill to be repealed in the same year.   **JUD**

1754   Moravian, Presbyterian, Baptist, and Methodist missionaries begin converting African slaves on Jamaica to their Christian denominations. The missionary efforts eventually result in the conversion of most Afro-Jamaicans but also produce a number of new religions, including Zion Revival and

Shakers

The Shakers are a religious sect within Christianity that began in England but developed in the eastern United States in the late 18th and early 19th centuries. The formal name for the sect is the United Society of Believers in Christ's Second Appearing. Although they lived in harmonious communal societies and were successful farmers and small-scale industrialists, the Shakers were never a large group, having only 18 communities and nearly 5,000 members at their height in the 1830s. Since then their communities have slowly disappeared. In the 1990s there remains only one community, Sabbathday Lake in Maine, with nine members. Although many Shaker beliefs are in accord with Protestantism, they also have a number of unique beliefs and practices. Shakers reject the Doctrine of the Trinity, believe that God has female and male elements, require strict celibacy for their members, and at one time actively sought communication with the dead. Shaker services formerly included ecstatic dancing, the practice for which the group was labeled Shakers or Shaking Quakers by outsiders. Shaker religion and communal life are closely integrated, and the Shakers stress simplicity, humility, efficiency, hard work, and separation of the sexes. Unlike some other communal societies, the Shakers do not reject all worldly goods and have often embraced technological innovations, such as the telephone and electricity, and produce seeds, brooms, ovens, chairs, and other objects for sale to outsiders.

Pocomania, which are based on African religions and Christianity and survive into the 1990s. **AFRICAN, PROT**

1754   The Quakers in Philadelphia condemn slavery in the Epistle of the Philadelphia Yearly Meeting. The Quakers are the first organized religion to condemn slavery, although at this time they do not seek to end the practice, only to stop the slave trade. **PROT**

1755   The issue of Quaker pacificism and nonpayment of taxes levied to support war comes to a head in Pennsylvania due to conflict between the British and French in western Pennsylvania. The issue splits the Quakers and causes them to lose seats in and control of the Pennsylvania Assembly. **PROT**

1755   In Sweden the Bible is translated into the Sami (Lapp) language by Lutheran missionaries. **PROT**

1755   The Hutterite movement is revitalized in Romania when a Hutterite community established there in 1621 attracts new members and new vitality from a group of Carinthian Lutherans who come to the region seeking religious freedom. **SECT**

1758   The first African-American church, the African Baptist Church, is founded on a plantation in Mecklenberg, Virginia. African-American slaves are moved to form their own churches because of discrimination in white churches including prohibitions on African-Americans becoming preachers. **AFRICAN**

1758   John Wesley, the founder of Methodism, on a missionary trip to the Americas, baptizes the first two African-American converts to Methodism. In these early years of Methodism, when the denomination opposes slavery in the Americas, African-Americans are often welcomed into the church and by the 1780s form about 10 percent of the membership. **AFRICAN**

1758   Papoonan, of the indigenous Delaware people, begins preaching a new religion based on Quakerism and Delaware beliefs. Although he gains some followers among natives in Pennsylvania, the new religion is eventually rejected as most of the natives convert to Christianity under the influence of Moravian missionaries. **NATIV, PROT**

1758   The Sandy Creek Association of (Baptist) Churches is formed by Baptist preacher Shubal Stearns (1706–1771), who has moved from Connecticut to North Carolina. The association plays a key role in the spread of Baptist belief in the American South. **PROT**

1758   The Old Side (Philadelphia Synod) and New Side (New York Synod) Presbyterians in the United States reunite and issue the Plan of Union. The plan supports the basic ideas of the Westminster *Confession*, criticizes some revival movements as excessive, and gives the authority to appoint ministers to each presbytery. **PROT**

1758   Ann Lee (1736–1784), who later becomes the leader of the Shakers in the United States, follows her parents and joins the Shaking Quakers in England.
SECT

c. 1760   The Jain Terepantha order is founded in India. It is the last major schism in the Svetambara sect of Jains. It will remain one of the most powerful orders in late-20th-century Jainism.
JAIN

1760   During the Taki slave rebellion on Jamaica, British colonial officials discover the presence of the Myal religion, which had developed among slaves on the island. Based initially on the slaves' African religions, it exists as one unified religion for the slaves. After the rebellion Christian elements are added to the African base, although it continues to exist as an alternative to Christianity.
AFRICAN

1760   When the British defeat the French and take most of Canada, French Jesuit missionary activity is curtailed in North America.
CATH

1760   The Lutheran churches in the United States form the Evangelical Lutheran Ministerium in North America.
PROT

1760s   As a result of deprivations caused by European settlers, several members of the Delaware people emerge as prophets and lead revitalization movements, which in turn lead to resistance to European rule and a new Delaware religion in Ohio. One of the prophets, Neolin (1725–1775), influences the Ottowa leader Pontiac to revolt against white rule. Another

Independent and Native Black Churches

In the middle years of the 18th century, slaves and freed slaves in British colonies in America and the Caribbean began forming their own Christian churches, relatively free of control by whites, at least in their early years. These churches are collectively referred to by historians as Independent or Native churches. Most were either Baptist or Methodist in orientation, as their founders had been members of white Methodist or Baptist churches. Racial discrimination was the primary reason African-Americans established their own churches, as they were allowed only a limited role in white churches and could not become preachers. African-Americans also objected to the support some white churches gave to slavery. As the number of Independent churches and their followers increased in the United States, especially in the south, they became less "independent," as whites feared that they might be the breeding ground for slave revolts or that they might support abolition movements. Thus, they often came under white control in the form of laws that restricted when and where the congregation could meet and even the content of the worship services. Nonetheless, some Independent and Native churches survived and prospered and eventually developed into major black Baptist and Methodist denominations.

prophet, Wangomend (c. 1750–c. 1795), also argues against white rule and preaches a return to the traditional Delaware way of life, but he is rejected after he calls for war in 1775. **NATIV**

1761   The first English-language Jewish prayer book is published in New York. Rabbi Akiva (1761–1837) is born, and as the rabbi of the Psen region of Germany becomes a major humanist force in Judaism, with his stories and proverbs passed on from generation to generation as lessons in Jewish life. **JUD**

1762   Many Sikhs are killed in the Greater Holocaust when they are attacked by an Afghan Muslim army in India. (The Greater Holocaust is so called to distinguish it from the Lesser Holocaust of 1746.) **ISLAM, SIKH**

1762   A congregational constitution is formulated by St. Michael's Lutheran Church in Philadelphia. It provides for independent churches and sets forth a model of church administration that becomes the norm for Lutheran churches in America. **PROT**

1763   The Jewish community in Newport, Rhode Island, builds a synagogue, the oldest in continuous use in North America in the 1990s. **JUD**

1763   Catherine the Great of Russia invites Mennonites from Germany and Prussia to settle in Russia. Mennonites migrate to Russia, which attracts them because of the possibility of religious freedom and the availability of land on which to build Mennonite communities. **SECT**

1764   In a continuation of its efforts dating to 1700 to limit the role of the Russian Orthodox Church, the Russian government confiscates the church's lands and serfs and reduces the level of government financial support. **ORTHO**

1764   The Quakers in the United States, who are concentrated in eastern Pennsylvania, New Jersey, and Maryland, begin moving elsewhere. By 1840 they have established monthly meetings in states along the eastern seaboard from North Carolina to Maine and as far west as Indiana. By 1890 they have established meetings as far west as Nebraska and Kansas. **PROT**

1764   The first Methodist society in the Americas is established by Irish Methodist Robert Strawbridge in Maryland. **PROT**

c. 1765   In China a widely influential group of scholars emerges. Known as the *kaozheng* scholars, their methodology is devoted to facts and to rigorous study. They undertake close textual studies of the Confucian Classics to determine which parts of the canon are the work of Confucius and which parts are later creations. They cast doubt on the works of once-influential Song-era interpreters such as Zhu Xi (**SEE 1130, CONF**). Dai Zhen (1723–1777) is a leading *kaozheng* scholar. In his later work, however, he turns philosophical and speculative about human behavior and the meaning of moral action. **CONF**

1767   Again facing persecution from Catholics, the Hutterites move from Transylvania to Wallachia in eastern Europe.   SECT

1768   The first Jewish synagogue in Canada is founded in Montreal.   JUD

1768   Methodists in New York City begin meeting to conduct services.   PROT

1768   Scottish minister William Witherspoon (1723–1794) is recruited from Scotland and appointed president of the College of New Jersey. An able administrator, he effectively mediates between the competing Old Side and New Side factions in the Presbyterian Church. As an ardent opponent of British rule, he strongly supports the American Revolution.   PROT

1768   In Japan National Learning scholar Kamo no Mabuchi (1697–1769) completes his major work, *Man'yoko*, a study of the eighth-century Japanese poetry anthology *Man'yoshu*. He also turns the attention of National Learning scholar Motoori Norinaga (1730–1801) toward ancient Shinto.   SHINTO

1769   The Spanish seek to colonize California and subjugate the natives by establishing a series of missions along the coast from San Diego north to San Francisco. The first mission is founded by Jesuit Father Juniperro Serra at San Diego in 1769. One activity of the missions is to convert the natives who are brought to live there to Christianity. The missions also garrison troops and function as agricultural centers with the natives used as slave labor. The missions effectively destroy the indigenous cultures of the region, despite frequent native revolts.   CATH, NATIV

1769   Methodists in London agree to send two preachers to the Americas to preach to the small number of Methodists in the British colonies and to others. In October Richard Boardman and Joseph Pilmore arrive in Philadelphia.   PROT

1769   *Body of Divinity*, a basic statement of Baptist theology, is written in London by John Gill, a Baptist pastor and theologian.   PROT

1769   A new revision of the King James Version of the Bible is prepared by Benjamin Blaney of Oxford University. The most thorough revision since the first edition in 1611, it becomes known as the "authorized version" although it is never so designated by the government in Britain.   PROT

1770   The first Methodist mission to slaves in the Caribbean is established on Antigua. The Methodists often employ Africans as preachers and counsel against revolts, thereby winning the support of the white landowners. AFRICAN

1770   A mission to Native Americans is established at Monterey, California.   CATH, NATIV

1770 — Lipan Apache in the United States southwest have borrowed the use of peyote for ritual purposes from native groups in Mexico. It is likely that the later spread of peyote use to Native American groups in Oklahoma is through the Lipan. **NATIV**

1770 — In England the Baptists form their first voluntary association, the Bristol Education Association, to assist in the training of clergy. **PROT**

1770 — Facing persecution by the Muslim Turks, who raid the region for slaves, the Hutterites begin a process of relocation and establishment of communal settlements in Russia that lasts until 1859. **SECT**

1771 — In California missions to Native Americans are established at King City and San Gabriel. A Moravian mission is established among the Labrador Inuit of eastern Canada. **CATH, NATIV**

1771 — Jews are allowed to settle in Sweden. **JUD**

1771 — Two additional Methodist preachers arrive in the British colonies in America from London. One of them, Francis Asbury (1745–1816), becomes the informal leader of the Methodist movement in the United States. **PROT**

1772 — At the Council of Lima, the ban on allowing Native Americans or mestizos to become Roman Catholic priests is officially ended. **CATH, NATIV**

1772 — A mission to Native Americans is established at San Luis Obispo, California. **CATH, NATIV**

1772 — The Moravian Brethren establish a mission to the Delaware peoples in Ohio. **PROT, NATIV**

1772–1773 — Ann Lee, the founder of Shakerism in America, is arrested and imprisoned in Manchester, England, for disturbing the Sabbath by participating in the Shaking Quaker services. While in prison in 1773 she has visions and when released becomes the leader of the Shaking Quakers, at which time she is known to followers as Mother Ann. **SECT**

1773 — Pope Clement XIV formally dissolves the Jesuit order in his *Dominus ac Redemptor*. The property of the order is taken by the Church, its missionary activity is terminated, and Jesuit priests are forced to return from overseas stations to their home nations. The pope's action is motivated mainly by political and economic considerations, as the Jesuits are under attack from colonists in South America because of the Jesuits' role in protecting the natives from enslavement and forced labor, because the Jesuits have often become involved in politics, and because they have amassed much wealth. The action seriously disrupts Catholic missionary activity, especially in South America and India. **CATH**

1773   Tai Chen is appointed by the Ch'ien-lung emperor in China to compile an imperial manuscript library. The result, the massive Complete Library of the Four Treasures, symbolizes the large-scale effort of the Manchu court to account for all important works in the four branches of Confucian learning—the classics, history, philosophy, and literature. The work employs 15,000 copyists over 20 years and involves 36,000 volumes containing comments on about 10,230 titles.   **CONF**

1773   In Arabia the Muslim Wahhabis capture Riyadh and in 1803 take the Muslim holy city of Mecca as they seek to conquer the region and establish the Wahhabi sect of Islam.   **ISLAM**

1773   In Russia Catherine II (the Great) institutes a new policy concerning the Muslim Tatars that ends efforts to convert them to Russian Orthodoxy and allows the revitalization of Muslim culture through the building of schools and mosques and the formation of Muslim organizations. The policy revitalizes Islam in Tatar communities in the Crimea, but it also makes them economically wealthy, thus creating competition with Russian traders and merchants.   **ISLAM**

1773   Mesmerism is developed by Friedrich Anton Mesmer (1733–1815), a physician in Vienna. It is a system of healing based on the belief that the human body, celestial bodies, and the environment influence one another, and the medium of influence is a magnetic energy called animal magnetism. The linking of the human body with the spiritual world and the concept of animal magnetism influence later spiritualists.   **SPIR**

1773   Russian empress Catherine II issues an edict of religious freedom that grants for the first time religious freedom in Russia to religions other than Russian Orthodoxy.   **TOL**

1773–
1775   An early African-American congregation, the Silver Bluff Baptist Church, is founded near Augusta, Georgia.   **AFRICAN**

1774   Russian efforts to wrest territory from the Ottoman Empire continue, and through the Treaty of Kuchuk Kaynarja, the Russians regain access to the Black Sea, which was lost to the Ottomans in 1676.   **ISLAM**

1774   The *Journal* of Quaker leader John Woolman (1720–1772) is published. It sets forth the basic beliefs of Quakerism and covers various other issues, such as slavery, Indian relations, wealth, and pacifism. It becomes basic reading for Quakers and an important record of Quaker life in 18th-century Pennsylvania.   **PROT**

1774   Methodist preacher Joseph Pilmore, who came to the Americas in 1769, has been successful in attracting colonists to Methodism and a number of Methodist societies have formed. When Methodist preachers in the United States hold their first conference, differences with the Methodist Church in

England begin to emerge, although the American group continues to adhere to the decisions made by John Wesley, the founder of Methodism.   **PROT**

1774   The first Unitarian Church is opened in London by Theophilus Lindsey (1723–1808) and Joseph Priestly (1733–1804). In the 1990s it remains the headquarters of British Unitarianism.   **SECT**

1774   In the United States Baptist pastor Isaac Backus (1724–1806) makes an appeal to the Continental Congress for religious liberty and the separation of church and state.   **TOL**

1775   The Kamia people in southern California revolt against Spanish rule and destroy the Catholic mission at San Diego. This is the first major revolt against the Spanish mission system and is followed by several more in other regions of California. None are successful in ending Spanish control.   **CATH, NATIV**

1775   In reaction to missionary activity by Roman Catholics, the Orthodox Church at a synod in Constantinople rules that Roman Catholics and Armenian Christians must be baptized like heretics to be admitted to the Orthodox Church.   **CATH, ORTHO**

1775   Francis Salvador (1747–1776) of South Carolina is the first Jew elected to public office in the United States. He is killed in the American Revolution.   **JUD**

1775   Platon Levshin (1737–1812), who has served Catherine II since 1763 as a court preacher, is appointed metropolitan of the Orthodox Church in Moscow. He writes the first history of the Russian Orthodox Church, reforms the education system, and generally advances the interests of the church.   **ORTHO**

1776   Missions to Native Americans are established at San Juan, Capistrano, and Santa Clara, California.   **CATH, NATIV**

1776   Russian Orthodox missionary Cyril Vasilyevich Suchanov (1741–1814) establishes a mission to the Tungas people of eastern Siberia. He spends the rest of his life ministering to the Tungas and encouraging them to replace their nomadic, herding way of life with a settled life in farming villages.   **ORTHO**

1776   A division takes place among the Quakers in the Americas over what role, if any, they should take in supporting or fighting in the American Revolution. They generally oppose independence, and in Pennsylvania they lose political control when those in favor of independence take control of the assembly.   **PROT**

1776   Ann Lee and several Shaker followers immigrate to the United States from England in 1774 and in 1776 have earned enough money to settle in Niskeyuna (later called Watervliet), New York, near Albany.   **SECT**

1776	During the American Revolution, the Quakers, Mennonites, and Amish refuse to fight in accord with their belief in pacifism and also refuse to take the Oath of Renunciation and Allegiance for religious reasons. Some are jailed and some are threatened with the loss of land and property, but most remain loyal to their religious beliefs. **TOL**
1776	The government of Virginia enacts a Declaration of Rights that gives Baptists, Presbyterians, and other denominations religious freedom but allows the Anglican Church to remain the state church. Although the declaration does not give non-Anglicans full religious freedom, it is an early step in that direction. **TOL**
1776–1777	Muhammad al-Mustafa Saghunughu dies. During his lifetime he serves as a Muslim teacher in West Africa and founds an educational movement that is carried on by his sons and spread throughout West Africa. **ISLAM**
1776–1790	A Muslim *jihad* (holy war) takes place in the Futa Toro region of Senegambia in West Africa. The *jihad* is led by Muslim scholars, teachers, and students and leads to attacks on the Moors to the north and on other non-Muslim or less devout Muslim peoples in the region. The *jihad* ends in defeat in 1790 and centralized Muslim control of the region disintegrates. **ISLAM**
1778	The Freewill Baptist Connexion is organized by Baptist preacher and tailor Benjamin Randall (1749–1808) in New Durham, New Hampshire. The church stresses freedom of worship and plays a role in the revival of religion in New England in the late 18th century. **PROT**
1778	German missionary Christian Friedreich Schwartz (1726–1798), serving the Anglican Church in India, establishes a mission at Tanjore. Before his death he attracts some 2,000 converts and the mission becomes a major center of Anglican missionary activity in India. **PROT**
1778 1779	The Thais seize the thrones of Champassak and Vieng Chan, two of the kingdoms of Laos; after sacking the capital of Vieng Chan, they take the royal family along with the Prabang, the statue of the standing Buddha, and the Pra Keo, the green jasper statue of the Buddha, to Bangkok, Thailand. (The Pra Keo is placed in the Wat Pra Keo, where it remains through the 1990s, a source of resentment to the Laotians.) **BUDD**
1779	The Qajar dynasty comes to power in Iran and rules until 1925. Iran is not a unified state but rather is composed of a number of tribes and tribal federations that are under Qajar influence. During the rule of the Qajar dynasty, Muslim Shi'a scholars gain considerable power, both as advisers to the dynasty and as religious teachers and interpreters to the general population. **ISLAM**

1779   Quakers in Britain found Ackworth boarding school, one of a number of boarding schools founded by Quakers for Quaker and non-Quaker students. The schools stress cooperation and self-reliance.   PROT

1779   The Universalist Church is founded in Gloucester, Massachusetts, by John Murray (1741–1815), a preacher from England. Universalism is closely related to Unitarianism and the two merge in the United States in 1961. The key difference is that early Universalists adhere to a creed and believe in universal salvation, while Unitarians do not.   SECT

1780   Native Baptist churches are founded by Africans in Jamaica and other British colonies in the Caribbean. As British missionary efforts are limited, the Native churches are major religious institutions in the colonies.   AFRICAN

1780   The Sunday school movement begins in England when Robert Raikes, editor of the *Gloucester Journal*, organizes Sunday schools to improve the health, morals, and well-being of poor children.   CHRIS

1780   Lutherans in Germany found the Christendom Society and then merge with the Basel Missionary Society to form a German Lutheran missionary society.   PROT

1780   A division develops among Methodists in the United States over the issue of whether the leaders of local congregations can give the sacraments. Southern Methodists support having local leaders so empowered, while Northerners follow John Wesley and oppose the practice. The breach is healed with the northern view prevailing. In the same year Methodists in the United States also condemn slavery.   PROT

1780s   Christian voluntary societies begin to develop in African-American communities, where they provide educational and social services. By the end of the century such associations are founded Newport, Philadelphia, Charleston, Providence, and Boston.   AFRICAN

1780s   Hinduism comes to the attention of British scholars and then draws the interest of German and American philosophers and linguists as well. In 1784 the *Bhagavad Gita* is translated into English and the academic field of Indology develops with a primary focus on the Sanskrit language.   HIND

1781   The Thais place a vassal king, Chao Nanthasen (r. 1781–1792), on the throne in Vieng Chan, Laos, and allow him to take the Prabang Buddha (the statue of the standing Buddha taken in 1778) back to Laos.   BUDD

1781   Muslim Sufi Ahmad al-Tijani (1737–1815) experiences visions that lead him to found the Tijaniya Sufi order in Morocco. The order spreads across North Africa and to West Africa, where it plays an active role in resisting French rule and also in converting people to Islam.   ISLAM

1781   Muslims revolt in the parts of central Asia under Chinese control. The revolt is defeated, but other revolts, also unsuccessful, break out in the 1820s.   **ISLAM**

1781   In Pennsylvania a small group of Quakers who had supported independence from Britain and been expelled by the majority of Quakers, who opposed independence, found the Society of Free Quakers. The organization attracts small numbers of members in several other states but disappears in the 1830s.   **PROT**

1781   *The Gospel Worthy of All Acceptation* is written by English Baptist pastor and missionary Andrew Fuller (1754–1815). The book helps transforms the Baptist denomination into a more evangelical denomination.   **PROT**

1781   In Austria Emperor Joseph II issues an edict that affords Protestants considerable religious freedom. The Roman Catholic Church remains the national church but Calvinists, Lutherans, and others are now allowed to build small chapels and run schools.   **PROT**

1781   Ann Lee and Shaker followers conduct missionary travels throughout New England that last until September 1783. The trip wins few converts and the Shakers are at various times beaten, arrested, imprisoned, and run out of towns. They are commonly viewed as heretics, witches, and traitors.   **SECT**

1781   The Ancient Order of Druids is founded in London, England, by adherents of neopagan Druid beliefs.   **SPIR**

Druids

Historians do not agree about who the Druids were. Some believe that the Druids were the priests of the Celtic peoples who occupied much of western Europe during the first millenium B.C.E. Others believe that they formed the intellectual class or caste of the Celtic peoples, and while some were priests they also acted as healers, teachers, and advisers. Little is actually known about the religious beliefs and practices of the Druids, as they left no written records and the earliest reports come from ancient Greek and Roman sources whose writers were often hostile to Celtic customs. What is known is that the worship of nature and especially trees was a significant component of Celtic religion and that important people were buried in elaborate tombs. At various times in Western history—during the Renaissance and in the late 19th century, to name only two—there have been revivals of interest in the Druids. The most recent has been in the last half of the 20th century, as the Druids have drawn the attention of New Age, neo-pagan, and witchcraft adherents, although scholars have noted that what is portrayed as Druidism in these movements often has little relation to the actual religion of the Celtic peoples.

1781	French occultists link tarot cards to the ancient Egyptian religion, and the cards come into common use among spiritualists. **SPIR**

1782   A mission to Native Americans is established at Ventura, California. **CATH, NATIV**

1782   Emperor Joseph II, the Holy Roman Emperor, issues his Edict of Tolerance, which eases restrictions on Jews and seeks to involve them more fully in the economic system. **JUD, TOL**

1782   The *Philokalia*, a collection of Orthodox Christian writings compiled by monks at Mount Athos in Greece earlier in the century, is published in Greek. A church Slavonic version is published in Russia in 1793 and the compilation becomes a major text in the Orthodox Church, revised at various times in the 1800s and 1900s. **ORTHO**

1782   The final known legal execution of a witch in Europe takes place in Switzerland. **SPIR**

1783   Baba Dayal (1783–1855) is born and in the following century founds the Nirankari sect of Sikhism in Pakistan. The sect stresses meditation focused on God without external interference. When India is partitioned in 1947, followers of the sect relocate across the border into India. **SIKH**

1783–
1868   Kazakhs in central Asia resist Russian rule and Russian attempts to replace Islam or traditional religions with Russian Orthodoxy. During these years several revolts are launched. All ultimately fail, and the last is repressed in 1868. **ISLAM**

1783–
1896   The Russian policy of allowing Crimean Tatars (Muslims) religious freedom enacted in 1773 has created conflict between Tatars and Russians. Russians begin taking Tatar land and endowments and by 1896 most Tatars have migrated south into territory controlled by the Ottoman Empire. **ISLAM**

1784   John Wesley, the founder of the Methodist denomination, asks the Church of England to ordain preachers to be sent to work in the Americas. Although Wesley sees Methodism as existing within the Church of England, the church does not approve of the movement and Wesley's request is refused. Wesley then ordains Dr. Thomas Coke, the leader of the Methodists in Ireland, and places him in charge of Methodist societies in the Americas. His action effectively separates Methodism from the Church of England. Also during the year Methodists in Britain enact the Deed of Declaration, which authorizes them to select Wesley's successor after his death, another action that creates a breach with the Anglican Church. **PROT**

1784   Methodists in the United States hold the Christmas Conference, in which they set forth Articles of Religion and Church procedures. The conference also condemns slavery, as it had done in 1780, and asks its members to free their slaves. The leaders of Methodism in America, Francis Asbury and

Thomas Coke, set themselves up as bishops, a practice rejected by John Wesley, the founder of Methodism in England. The new church is named the Episcopal Methodist Church in America, indicating ties to both the Anglican and Methodist churches in Britain.   **PROT**

1784   Ann Lee, the founder of Shakerism in America, dies in Watervliet, New York. At the time of her death, the movement is gaining some followers.   **SECT**

1785   The King's Chapel in Boston becomes the first Unitarian church in the United States when the prayer book is revised to omit references to the Trinity.   **SECT**

1785–   There is a revival of Islam and also of centralized political rule in Bukhara
1920   in central Asia during the rule of the Mangit dynasty, one of the successor dynasties to the Shaybanid dynasty, which collapsed in 1598.   **ISLAM**

1786   Archbishops in Germany issue a declaration of partial independence from the papacy in Rome. The declaration is a manifestation of Febronianism in Germany, a movement like the Gallician movement in France dating to the 1680s, which seeks to weaken papal authority in Catholic nations.   **CATH**

1786   A mission to Native Americans is established at Santa Barbara, California.
                                                       CATH, NATIV

1786   The first Sunday school is opened in America, in Hanover, Virginia, by Methodists.   **PROT**

1786   Shaker leader Joseph Meachem creates dual male and female lines of authority in Shaker communities when he appoints a woman to lead the women in the community.   **SECT**

1786   Mennonites from Pennsylvania migrate north and establish the first Mennonite settlement in Ontario, Canada.   **SECT**

1787   After being forced to leave a gallery reserved for white members at St. George's Methodist Episcopal Church in Philadelphia, African-Americans Richard Allen, Absalom Jones, and other members form the Free African Society, the precursor of the African Methodist Episcopal Church founded in 1816.   **AFRICAN**

1787   A mission to natives is established at La Purisima, California.   **CATH, NATIV**

1787   A *jihad* (holy war) led by Muslim Sufis breaks out in the Caucasus region, which is then controlled by Russia and the Ottoman Empire. Leaders of the movement seek a return to traditional Islam, use of Islamic law, and the end of Russian rule. The revolt is defeated but creates lasting hostility between the Muslims in the region and Russians.   **ISLAM**

1787   Frederick William II of Prussia eases restrictions on the Jews of his realm.   **JUD**

1787	The Society for the Abolition of the Slave Trade is founded in Britain. Most of the members are Quakers, the first religious organization to oppose slavery, and they provide most of its financial support. In the United States Quakers take the lead in Pennsylvania in propounding a philosophy of rehabilitation, rather than punishment, for prisoners. **PROT**
1787	In Britain Methodists vote to license Methodist chapels, further separating the denomination from the Church of England. **PROT**
1787	The Shaker movement begins to grow in New York State when several followers of the New Light revival movement from Connecticut join the Shakers. Two settlements are founded, one in Watervliet and a second in nearby New Lebanon. During this time the basic tenets of Shakerism, based on the teachings of Ann Lee, also develop, including a belief in confession, ecstatic worship, communal living, and celibacy. **SECT**
1787	John Leland (1754–1841), a Baptist preacher in Virginia, helps convince James Madison to support the Bill of Rights and the guarantee of religious freedom. **TOL**
1787	In the Northwest Ordinance, the freedom of worship is extended from the original American states to the Northwest Territory. **TOL**
1787–1793	Japanese shogun chief counselor Matsudaira Sadanobu initiates the reactionary Kansei Reforms based on Confucian principles. These include attempts to restrict foreign trade, cancel samurai debt, restore agriculture as the economic basis of the state, and ban unorthodox teachings. He issues severe laws limiting personal expenditures and regulating personal conduct on moral grounds. Overall, this policy proves damaging and leads to famines, uprisings, and urban violence. Sadanobu resigns in 1793. **CONF**
1788	The rulers of the Hausa states in West Africa extend special privileges to the large Muslim population, including an exemption from taxes, the right to wear Muslim dress, and greater freedom to seek converts. **ISLAM**
1788	Joseph Priestly (1733–1804), the scientist and theologian, completes work on his *History of the Corruptions of Christianity*, in which he questions the Virgin Birth and the Divinity of Jesus Christ. It is a major step in the establishment of Unitarianism as a distinct denomination in Great Britain. **SECT**
1788	The Russian government grants a special charter of privileges to the Mennonites that exempts them from military service and grants them religious freedom. In the next year Mennonites establish two settlements in the Ukraine. **SECT**
1789	The first Catholic bishop is elected in the United States. He is John Carroll (1735–1815), a former Jesuit and a priest from Baltimore, Maryland, who

had been a strong supporter of independence and whose cousin had been a signer of the Declaration of Independence.   CATH

1789   The first General Assembly of the Presbyterian Church in the United States of America is held in Philadelphia. It brings together the synods of New York and New Jersey, Philadelphia, Virginia, and the Carolinas.   PROT

1789   The Universal Friends, a communal movement similar to but separate from the Shakers, and founded by Jemima Wilkinson (1752–1819), a Quaker from Rhode Island, is an established sect in the United States with 200 members and settlements in Rhode Island, Connecticut, Pennsylvania, and the main settlement on Seneca Lake in New York State. It disappears after Wilkinson's death in 1819.   SECT

1789   The *Declaration of the Rights of Man* is adopted by the French National Assembly as a preamble to the republic's constitution. Among other rights the document sets forth the freedom of religion and expression and serves as a model for later declarations of human rights.   TOL

1790   The Countess of Huntingdon's Connexion is founded by Selena, countess of Huntingdon in England. It is an organization that brings together a number of small Evangelical Christian churches in England whose members are primarily from the aristocracy.   EVAN

1790   The new rulers of the Hausa states in West Africa are concerned by the influence of the large Muslim population and cancel the special privileges given the community two years earlier. Muslim leaders begin preparing for a revolt as they gather followers from among the Fulbe and Hausa peoples and build an army.   ISLAM

1790   In the United States the first Baptist church west of the Appalachian Mountains is founded in Duck Creek (later Cincinnati), Ohio.   PROT

1790   The expansion of Shakerism accelerates with nine communities begun in Massachusetts, Connecticut, New Hampshire, and Maine between 1790 and 1794, bringing the total number of Shaker communities to 11 in New York and New England.   SECT

1790s   A second religious revival (SEE 1720s–1740s, PROT), known as the Second Great Awakening, takes place in the United States. Although not as widespread as the first in the 1730s and 1740s, it also stresses emotional and personal worship and leads to growth of the Protestant churches in America.   PROT

1790–   During the French Revolution, officials of the Catholic Church are required
1791   to sign an oath of compliance with the Constitution formulated by the National Assembly. The church objects, as they feel it places clergy in the position of having to choose between loyalty to the state or to the church.

Pope Pius VI condemns the oath and forbids clergy from signing it. This leads to a split in France between the Constitutionalists, who sign the oath, and the non-Constitutionalists, who refuse to sign. CATH

1791 St. Mary's, the first Catholic seminary in the United States, is opened by four French Suplician monks in Baltimore, Maryland. The Suplicians (members of the Society of Saint Suplice) play a major role in training clergy and providing financial support for the Catholic Church in America. CATH

1791 Missions to the Native Americans are established at Santa Cruz and Soledad, California. CATH, NATIV

1791 Jews are granted French citizenship as a result of the French Revolution. JUD

1791 The first 10 amendments to the United States Constitution go into effect when the Virginia legislature ratifies the Bill of Rights, meaning that 75 percent of the 13 original colonies have now ratified the document. TOL

1792 The Spanish colonial government in Cuba moves to restrict the *cabildos*, brotherhoods of African slaves who are nominally Roman Catholic but who also allow the continuation of traditional African beliefs. They are viewed as a threat to both the spread of Roman Catholicism and Spanish rule. AFRICAN

1792 Conflict between Russia and the Ottoman Empire ends with the Treaty of Jassy, which recognizes Russian military superiority and places the Crimea and Georgia under Russian control. Although the Ottoman Empire has been losing European territory for over a century, the treaty makes it clear that Christian Europe can now compete with and defeat the Muslim Ottomans. ISLAM

1792 *An Enquiry into the Obligations of Christians to Use Means for the Conversion of the Heathens* is written by British Baptist missionary William Carey (1761–1834). The book questions the prevailing view among many Calvinistic Protestants that missionary work is not needed, as God will eventually convert all people. Later in the year Carey is successful in forming the Baptist Missionary Society, and in 1793 he arrives in India as its first missionary. PROT

1792 Methodists in the United States under the leadership of Thomas Coke and Francis Asbury establish a general conference that will meet every four years to oversee the Methodist Church in the United States. PROT

1792– During the Reign of Terror in France, when presumed enemies of the
1794 Revolution are persecuted, non-Constitutional priests (those who refused to sign a loyalty oath) are exiled or forced into hiding and some are sentenced to death. These years are also marked by an effort to end the influence of Christianity, even including the use of the Gregorian calendar, and many churches are closed. CATH

1793	A Universalist Church is established in London, England, but Universalism disappears in England in the early 20th century. **SECT**

1794   The first South American natives to be ordained as Roman Catholic priests are ordained at Lima, Peru.   **CATH**

1794   The first Russian Orthodox mission to the Aleuts, the indigenous people of the Aleutian islands in the Bering Strait off the coast of Siberia and Alaska, is established by (St.) Herman of Alaska (?–1837). The mission is successful, perhaps because of existing relations between the Aleuts and Russians who had arrived in 1766, and by about 1850 all Aleuts have converted.   **ORTHO**

1795   In France the Reign of Terror comes to an end with order restored and religious freedom guaranteed. Catholicism revives, churches closed during the last three years reopen, and clergy come out of hiding or exile. Nonetheless, the role of the Church is reduced, and civil institutions come to play a greater role in marriage, education, and other matters previously largely controlled by the Church.   **CATH, TOL**

1795   Following the explorations of the South Pacific by Captain Cook, the London Missionary Society decides to send missionaries to the islands of the region, beginning in 1796. Missionaries begin to make converts on New Zealand in 1814, Tahiti in 1819, Hawaii (by American Methodists) in 1820, Tonga in 1830, Samoa in 1830, Fiji in 1835, and the New Hebrides in 1839. The islands have been the subject of regular missionary activity ever since and in addition to the Protestant denominations, Roman Catholics, Jehovah's Witnesses, Evangelical Christians, Mormons, and others have been active there.   **PROT**

1795   With the British having wrested control of South Africa from the Dutch, Protestant missionaries led by the London Missionary Society become active in the region.   **PROT**

1795   *The Age of Reason* is written by pamphleteer Thomas Paine. It attacks Christianity, helps encourage an infidel movement in Great Britain that objects to both Christianity and churches, and draws followers among tradesmen and the working poor.   **PROT**

1796   French forces under Napoleon attack and conquer parts of northern Italy. Napolean enters into the Treaty of Tolentino with the Vatican, which leaves the Vatican in control of the Papal States in Italy.   **CATH**

1796   Russian Orthodox missionaries in the Aleutian Islands have been successful in converting the Aleuts and extend their mission to the Alaska coast, where they begin converting the Pacific Eskimo.   **ORTHO**

1796   In Britain Quakers establish the Retreat as a hospital for the treatment of the mentally ill in York, England.   **PROT**

1796	Methodists in the United States meet at the second General Conference and divide the United States into six territories, with each to hold an annual conference of Methodist churches. **PROT**
1796	Joseph Priestly comes to America to promote Unitarianism and establishes the first permanent church in Philadelphia. **SECT**
1797	Missions to the Native Americans are established at San Fernando, San Jose, San Juan Bautista, and San Miguel, California. **CATH, NATIV**
1797	Jews are given civil rights in the Netherlands, where the first Reform congregation in Europe is founded in Amsterdam. **JUD**
1797	In Ireland the first sign of dissension among the Quakers becomes public when a small group breaks with the movement over matters of belief and practice, including how one experiences the Inner Light, the role of the Bible, and the nature of prayer services. **PROT**
1797	Balak Singh (1797–1862) is born and in the following century is instrumental in founding the Namdhari (Kuka) Sikh sect in southern Asia. Kuka Sikhs use meditation focused on God, are vegetarians, and wear distinctive clothing. They also claim direct descent from the 10 Sikh gurus, a belief that distinguishes their sect from mainstream Sikhism and other Sikh sects. **SIKH**
1797–1800	In violation of the Treaty of Tolentino negotiated in 1796, French forces attack Rome, remove Pope Pius VI to France (he dies en route), and take control of all of Italy after defeating the Austrians at the Battle of Marengo in 1800. **CATH**
1798	The London Missionary Society begins its work in Africa when it sends missionaries to Sierra Leone in West Africa and in the next year to South Africa. **PROT**
1798	In the United States the first Baptist Church manual is written to provide guidance to new churches being founded in the South and West. The manual also sets forth the first general Baptist covenant, although several churches in New England had developed their own covenants earlier. **PROT**
1798	Leading National Learning scholar Motoori Norinaga completes his monumental *Kojikiden*, a 44-volume study of the ancient chronicle *Kojiki*. He sees Japan's history as the unfolding of the will of the *kami* (native spirits) through the divine imperial rule, which has been disturbed by foreign influences such as Buddhism and other religions. **SHINTO**
1798–1802	The preaching of American Quaker Hannah Barnard (1754–1825) in Ireland and England leads to conflict between the New Light Quakers, who take a more rational, liberal view, and the more traditional Quakers. In 1802 she is expelled from her home meeting in Hudson, New York. **PROT**

1799	Sikh leader Ranjit Singh (?–1839) captures Lahore from the Muslims and lays the groundwork for the establishment of a Sikh state in northwestern India. **ISLAM, SIKH**
1799	The Handsome Lake revitalization movement begins among the Seneca of New York when Handsome Lake (1735–1815) has a series of visions that provide messages for the revitalization of Seneca culture following the devastation caused by the American Revolution. Handsome Lake's preaching emphasizes a return to traditional native values and peaceful coexistence with European settlers. **NATIV**
1799	The Russian-American Golikov-Shelikov Company is founded to exploit resources in Alaska. It comes into conflict with Russian Orthodox missionaries, who seek to protect the Aleuts and native Alaskans and to have them made Russian citizens. **ORTHO**
1799	British Baptist missionary William Carey joins with two other missionaries and establishes a mission in the small Danish colony near Calcutta, India. Carey, considered by some later historians to be the founder of the Protestant missionary effort, establishes the basic principles of missionary work: preach the Gospel as often as possible, make the Bible available in the native language, found a local church as quickly as possible, understand the culture of native peoples, and train native missionaries. **PROT**
1799	In Great Britain the Church Missionary Society is formed to support missionary activity in Africa and Asia and later in Canada. **PROT**

Handsome Lake Religion

The Handsome Lake Religion is an American Indian religion that developed in the early 19th century and in the 1990s is practiced by some Iroquois in New York State and Canada, with its headquarters on the Seneca Reservation in Tonawanda, New York. The core of the religion is the "Good Word," the preachings of Seneca prophet Handsome Lake, whose teachings were the basis of the Seneca revival movement in the early 19th century. Key elements of the Good Word that have been carried forth in the Handsome Lake Religion include temperance, harmonious family relations, peace, owning land, living peacefully with whites, and maintaining traditional ceremonies. Handsome Lake's original teachings were modified by his grandson Sosheowa and his nephew Blacksnake, who also incorporated some Christian ideas brought to the Seneca by missionaries. The religion is organized into 10 longhouses or congregations. The major activity is the preaching of the Code of Handsome Lake each fall by men in the longhouses. Some men travel to other Iroquois communities to preach, while others preach only to their own longhouses. In this way they reenact the original preaching of the Code of Handsome Lake in 1803 to the Iroquois communities.

1799

1799–
1807

The lower-caste Buddhist monks of Sri Lanka, finding themselves shut out by the higher-caste monks who have been drawn to the order revived by the Thais (SEE 1751, BUDD), send their own missions to Myanmar over several years; the king of Myanmar and Buddhist monks lend their support to establishing a new school of monks in Sri Lanka known as the Amarapura Nikaya.   **BUDD**

c. 1800

The leader of the Mossi Kingdom in West Africa converts to Islam and makes it the religion of his kingdom. In the 19th century Islam, which had been confined mainly to the ruling and merchant classes in West Africa, spreads to the rural farmers. Instrumental in the spread of Islam are Muslim brotherhoods, who actively proselytize in rural communities.   **ISLAM**

c. 1800

Muslim influence in western Ethiopia, which had previously been controlled by the Christian state, begins to expand as Muslims play a role in the slave, coffee, and wax trade from Africa to the Middle East and Europe. Islam is spread at first by merchants and then by Muslim teachers and Sufi missionaries.   **ISLAM**

c. 1800

As the Muslim religious leaders lose power, Muslim brotherhoods emerge in the northern Sudan. These include the Sammaniya, Khatmiya, and Majdhubiya orders, which become the focal points of local government and also the center of resistance to Egyptian rule, which begins in 1830.   **ISLAM**

c. 1800

A division develops between the Muslim communities in Malaysia and Indonesia. The division at first is between local Muslims and reformers who want Islam in Southeast Asia to more closely follow Islam as it is practiced in the Middle East. In about 1803 the reformers divide into two factions, one of which favors peaceful teaching of traditional Islam and a second that becomes a military movement.   **ISLAM**

1800

As the Roman Catholic population in the United States has increased to about 100,000 from about 35,000 10 years earlier, the diocese of Baltimore is divided, with dioceses added in New York City, Philadelphia, Boston, and Bardstown (later Louisville), Kentucky.   **CATH**

1800

The first Camp Meeting is held by Presbyterians and Methodists in Kentucky. It is the first known Camp Meeting, a form of Evangelical Protestant worship that takes place over a series of days in an outdoor location. Camp Meetings subsequently become popular in the United States and Britain.   **EVAN, PROT**

1800

At the Second Baptist Church in Boston, the first Baptist society in America to support missionary activity is founded.   **PROT**

1800

German immigrants in Maryland form the United Brethren, a sect similar to the Methodists.   **PROT**

1800   In Germany the Moravians found the Institute of Missions to support missionary activities of the Moravians.   **PROT**

1800   *The Anatomy and Physiology of the Nervous System in General and of the Brain in Particular* by Austrian physician Franz Joseph Gall is published in Vienna. The book initiates the practice of phrenology, the identification of character traits through the analysis of contours of the head. An English translation is published in 1935.   **SPIR**

1800s   During this century several European countries—especially Britain and France—assume control of various Asian countries where Buddhism has long played an important role in political affairs, as well as in the religious and cultural life of the people. Whatever else might be said in criticism of these colonial powers, their presence and activities will have the effect in many instances of reinvigorating Buddhism with more scholarly, historical, and rationalistic approaches. Western travelers, adventurers, scholars, colonial administrators, and others, for instance, will uncover whole libraries of forgotten texts; when published in their original languages and in translations, these texts contribute greatly to a renewed respect for Buddhism even among Asians themselves. Meanwhile, the colonial powers give Buddhism another, unanticipated role: in several Asian nations, Buddhism becomes intertwined with nationalistic and independence movements whose supporters will eventually rise up against their foreign masters.   **BUDD**

1800s   Immigration of Chinese to the United States has begun on a noticeable scale by the early 1800s and continues until the Chinese Exclusion Act of 1882. The large numbers of immigrants are fleeing social and political turmoil, famine, and overpopulation in China. After 1848 reports of mountains of gold in California attract many Chinese, but even more come after 1865 to take part in building the transcontinental railroads. The Chinese practice Buddhist and/or Confucian beliefs through calendrical festivals and observances in joss houses, family associations, burials, and grave-tending rituals. The joss houses, derived from the Spanish *Dios* (God) and inspired by the colorfully ornamented Spanish Catholic churches the Chinese find in California, include images of Buddhist gods and/or Confucius.   **BUDD, CONF**

1800s   During the Qing dynasty in China (1644–1911), tensions increase as population pressures, environmental problems, natural disasters, European encroachment, and peasant rebellion combine to threaten the empire's existence. The Qing is a long period of decline for Daoism. Daoist masters are gradually stripped of rank and authority. Popular Daoism and Buddhism flourish in China's villages, however; the villages support a profusion of temple fairs, holidays, and festivals. The authorities tolerate these popular expressions of religion because they present no threat to the formal structure of government. The emperors restore the national civil service examination system based on memorization and analysis of orthodox

Confucian texts and a few approved commentaries (namely Zhu Xi's: SEE **1130, CONF**) on the Confucian canon.   **DAO, CONF**

1801   Richard Allen (1760–1813), one of the founders of St. George's Methodist Episcopal Church in Philadelphia in 1787, publishes two collections of hymns that become the basis for African-American church music throughout the century.   **AFRICAN**

1801   A new concordat replacing the one dating to 1516 is agreed to by Napoleon of France and Pope Pius VII in France. The state retains control of the Catholic Church, as it continues to have the right to appoint bishops, retains property taken from the church during the French Revolution, and financially supports the clergy. This structure lasts until 1905.   **CATH**

1801   Congregationalists and Presbyterians in New England agree to a Plan of Union to coordinate missionary activity in the western United States. The plan allows members of each church to join congregations of the other church in communities large enough to support only one church. The Plan also called for the creation of colleges, including Hamilton College in upstate New York (1812), Western Reserve in Ohio (1826), and Knox in Illinois in (1837).   **PROT**

1801   In Britain Quaker Joseph Lancaster (1778–1838) opens a school to educate poor boys who are not members of the Church of England. This event marks the beginning of an effort that continues for over 100 years to make education widely available in Britain.   **PROT**

1802   (St.) Madeleine Sophie Barat (1779–1865) is appointed superior of the first educational house of the newly formed Society of the Sacred Heart of Jesus in Amiens, France. A strong advocate of education, she goes on to found some 100 houses in 12 nations.   **CATH**

1802   *The Genius of Christianity* is written in France by Vicomte de Chateaubriand. It extols the virtues of Catholicism and influences some intellectuals who had been supporters of the rationality of the French Revolution to embrace religion again.   **CATH**

1802   The first Ashkenazi (Eastern European Jewish) synagogue in North America is established in Philadelphia. It is called *Rodeph Shalom* (Seeker of Peace).   **JUD**

1802   The *Georgia Analytical Repository*, the first Baptist magazine, is published in the United States.   **PROT**

1802   In the United States Boston's Second Baptist Church is instrumental in founding the Massachusetts Baptist Missionary Society, whose primary focus is to seek converts among Europeans who are settling in the American West.   **PROT**

1802   The so-called "new religions" of Japan emerge during the late Tokugawa period (1600–1886) in Japan. During this time the power of local officials weakens, including their control of local Buddhist and Shinto temples and shrines, and new religions emerge in which common people play a major role. Perhaps the first new religion is Nyoraikyo, which is based on Buddhism.   **SECT**

1802–
1819   Vietnamese emperor Gia Long takes an active role in hostilities involving Cambodia, Thailand, and Laos. In 1819 he is succeeded by one of his sons, Minh Mang, who is strongly Confucian and distrusts dealings with the French and other Westerners who increasingly seek influence in Southeast Asia. **CONF**

1803   *Improvements in Education* is written by educational reformer Joseph Lancaster, a British Quaker. The book advocates many reforms to make education available to all boys, including the monitorial system in which older boys tutor younger ones.   **PROT**

1804   A mission to the Native Americans is established at Santa Ines, California.
                                                                              CATH, NATIV

Japanese New Religions

Japanese "new religions" is a general label for new sects, cults, and religions that have emerged in Japan since the early 19th century and have sought to exist apart from the mainstream Shinto religion and traditional, temple-centered Buddhism. They have emerged and grown in two waves, the first during the 19th century and the second after World War II. The main factor behind the emergence of these new religions in the 19th century was the government's repression of Buddhism and support of Shinto as the state religion. Both developments caused charismatic individuals to break with the established religions and found their own sects, some of which attracted hundreds of thousands and in a few cases millions of adherents. A few sects also emerged independent of prior affiliation with Buddhism or Shinto. While the Japanese government chose to classify most of these new religions as sects of Shinto, they can actually be divided into four general groups based on their core theology: those that are essentially revivals of traditional Shinto beliefs, those that focus on ritual purification, those that are based on worship at mountain sites, and those that are faith-healing cults. After World War II a second wave of new religion development swept Japan in reaction to the establishment of religious freedom in the new Japanese constitution and the curtailment of state support for Shinto. Some of the "*new* new religions," as they have been called, originally emerged after World War I, but their memberships expanded rapidly only after 1945. Some of these religions are based on Buddhism and others on traditional religious beliefs such as ancestor worship, and leaders of some have sought to influence Japanese politics and society.

| 1804 | The Bible is first published in Serbo-Croatian. | CHRIS |

1804   In the Hausa states of West Africa, the militant Muslims refuse to leave the region and are attacked by the forces of the state of Gobir. Led by religious scholar Uthman don Fodio (1754–1817), the Muslims withstand the attack. They launch a *jihad* (holy war) against Gobir and other Hausa states.   ISLAM

1804   The first Constitution of the Jews is issued by Tsar Alexander I in Russia. It places economic and civil restrictions on Jews, requires settlement in the Pale of Settlement region, and allows Jews to attend public schools as a means to convert them to Orthodox Christianity.   JUD

1804   The British and Foreign Bible Society is founded as an ecumenical Protestant organization to support the translation of the Bible.   PROT

1804   The London-based Church Missionary Society that represents non-Anglicans in Britain sends missionaries to Sierra Leone in West Africa.   PROT

1805   After gaining independence from France two years earlier, Haiti drafts a constitution that creates a separation of church and state and guarantees religious freedom. The provisions weaken the influence of the Roman Catholic Church, which refuses to recognize the new government, and Roman Catholicism declines in importance on the island. At the same time, Voudou, a syncretic religion based on African religions and Catholicism, attracts more followers.   AFRICAN

1805   The African Baptist Church, later called the Joy Street Church, is founded as an independent African-American church in Boston. Other independent Baptist churches are established in the following years in New York and Philadelphia.   AFRICAN

1805   The Congregation of the Sisters of St. Joseph of Cluny is founded by Anne-Marie Javouhey (1779–1851) and later becomes a major center for Catholic missionary work in Africa. Sisters go as missionaries to Reunion in 1817 and to Senegal in 1819.   CATH

1805   The Ottoman Empire appoints Muhammad Ali the governor of Egypt, and he creates a dynasty free of Ottoman control that lasts until 1952. He achieves and retains power partly by creating a strong central government and military and weakening the power that had traditionally been held by Muslim scholars and local Muslim leaders.   ISLAM

1805   In response to white settlers' attempts to seize land on which Native Americans reside, the Munsee Prophetess in Indiana begins preaching that the natives should keep their land and reject European ways of life. She is especially influential with the Delaware people who moved to the region from the east and changes some ritual of the Delaware religion.   NATIV

| 1805 | The Shawnee Prophet Tenskwatawa (1768–c. 1836) leads a revitalization movement among native groups in the Great Lakes region that calls for a return to traditional ways of life and helps foment resistance to white rule in the region. He is the brother of the Shawnee leader Tecumseh and they work together to resist white domination. **NATIV** |

| 1805 | In an effort to establish Shaker communities in the western United States, Shakers begin a missionary effort to Kentucky (then considered a western region), where they win converts among the New Light Christian revivalists in the region. Although they are persecuted and attacked in places, their efforts are successful throughout the west and between 1806 and 1836 eight Shaker communities are founded in Ohio, Kentucky, Indiana, and western New York. **SECT** |

| 1805 | Clergyman Thomas Belsham (1750–1829) becomes minister of the Unitarian Church in London and influences Unitarian theology by questioning the biblical account of Creation in six days and by suggesting multiple authorship for the Pentateuch, the first five books of the Old Testament. In this same year in the United States, Unitarianism is boosted when Henry Ware (1764–1845), a liberal Christian, is appointed Hollis Professor of Divinity at Harvard College. **SECT** |

| 1805 | The Harmony Society is founded in western Pennsylvania by German religious teacher George Rapp. It is a communal society based on farming and clothing manufacturing, with its religion based on a literal interpretation of the Bible, separation from the Lutheran Church, and Rapp's prophetic leadership. In 1814 the society moves to Indiana and then back to Pennsylvania in 1825. The society folds in 1898 after many of its members defect to splinter groups and it encounters financial problems. **SECT** |

| 1805–1828 | Anuvong (or Chao Anou), king of the region of Laos known as Vieng Chan, leads an invasion of Thailand; he is defeated and flees to Vietnam. The victorious Thai sack the capital city, Vieng Chan, and once again carry off the Prabang Buddha to Bangkok. **BUDD** |

| 1806 | After several years of discussion by government officials and Jewish leaders, Napoleon issues two decrees governing the role and status of Jews in France. Jews are afforded religious freedom but are not allowed to settle in northeast France and are placed under severe economic restrictions. Thirteen regional Jewish councils called consistories are established with responsibility for administering Jewish communities and integrating Jews into French national life. **JUD** |

| 1806 | The Unitarian Fund and a missionary effort to other denominations in Great Britain are established to assist in the spread of Unitarianism. **SECT** |

| 1807 | In Philadelphia African-Americans begin to form Presbyterian churches with the founding of the Presbyterian Evangelical Society and then the First African Presbyterian Church. The church is recognized by the Presbyterian |

presbytery in 1811. Over the next 50 years, churches are established else-where in Pennsylvania and in Maryland, New Jersey, New York, and the District of Columbia.   **AFRICAN, PROT**

1807   The first Protestant missionary, Robert Morrison (1782–1834), begins work in China. Although he translates the Old and New Testaments into Chinese, he makes few converts, as Western activity is controlled by the government. In 1818 he opens a college in Malacca for the Chinese in Malaysia.   **PROT**

1807   In Great Britain the Primitive Methodists, known for their outdoor revival meetings, separate from the Anglican Church.   **PROT**

1808   The *jihad* (holy war) in the Hausa states of West Africa, which began in 1804, ends with the Muslims victorious and the states united under Muslim rule.   **ISLAM**

1808   Methodists in the United States, at their General Conference, establish a plan for a constitution and establish the practice of having delegates attend future General Conferences.   **PROT**

1808   In Britain, the Royal Lancastrian Society is formed to promote educational reform and establish schools on the model formulated by Quaker educational reformer Joseph Lancaster beginning in 1801 and outlined in his 1803 book. The name of the Society is later changed to The British and Foreign School Society.   **PROT**

1808   In the United States Presbyterians organize the Andover Theological Seminary as the first school devoted entirely to training clergy in the United States. Their motivation is to counter the influence of Harvard Divinity School, which is controlled by Unitarians.   **PROT**

1808–   Conflicts continue between Napoleon and Pope Pius VII over control of the
1814   Papal States in Italy, and the pope is taken to France and held as a prisoner for the next six years. He is freed and returns to Rome in 1814 as Napoleon's empire collapses and the Congress of Vienna (1814–1815) reestablishes the pope as the ruler of the Papal States.   **CATH**

1809   The first Catholic women's order in the United States, the Sisters of Charity of St. Joseph, is founded by (St.) Elizabeth Seton (1774–1821), a former Episcopalian and wealthy widow, in Emmitsburg, Maryland, to support St. Joseph's Academy, which she had founded to as a teacher training school. In 1963 she becomes the first person born in North America to be canonized.
                                                                          CATH

1809   Finland comes under Russian control and the number of adherents of Russian Orthodoxy increases, although the majority of Finns remain Lutheran.   **ORTHO**

1809   The British have displaced the Muslim Mughals as the rulers of northern India and Pakistan and they enter into the Treaty of Amritsar with Sikh leader Ranjit Singh. Initially, he controls only the southern Punjab region, but with British support is able to displace other local Sikh leaders and expand the territory under his control. At the same time, the Sikh community remains divided throughout much of the century into a number of religious sects.   **SIKH**

1810   The American Board of Commissioners for Foreign Missions initiates a policy of supporting missionary activity outside of North America. Many board members are Congregationalists from New England.   **PROT**

1810   In Sweden the Lutheran Church begins a period of reform with the development of a new catechism, the founding of the Swedish Bible Society, and later the development of a new church handbook in 1811 and a hymn book in 1819.   **PROT**

1810   In the United States the Cumberland Presbyterian Church is formed by ministers in the west who support church reforms.   **PROT**

1810   The Swedenborg Society is founded in London to publish and disseminate the writings of Emanuel Swedenborg, who wrote about religion and philosophy in Sweden in the previous century (SEE 1747, SPIR). At about the same time, followers of Swedenborg's ideas found the New Church and the Church of the New Jerusalem.   **SPIR**

1811   Tseng Kuo-fan (1811–1872) is born in China. His pragmatic acceptance of the superiority of Western technology casts doubt on the ability of Confucian culture to withstand the overall impact of the West.   **CONF**

1811   Under pressure from the Ottoman Turks to the south, Georgia seeks protection from Russia and is absorbed into the Russian nation. The Georgian Orthodox Church becomes part of the Russian Orthodox Church.   **ORTHO**

1811   In Britain the National Society for Promoting the Education of the Poor in the Principles of the Established Church is formed by Anglican educational reformer Andrew Bell (1753–1832). It competes across the nation with the system established by the Quaker reformer Joseph Lancaster in 1808, often producing two schools in many towns.   **PROT**

1812   Egypt, which is under nominal Ottoman rule, attacks Arabia and takes Mecca and Medina from the ruling Wahhabi sect. By 1818 it has reduced the Wahhabi territory to a small state in the interior.   **ISLAM**

1812   The Pale of Settlement in Russia is firmly established. Jews are forced to live in 25 provinces in western Russia and cannot travel outside the region without official permission. Jews are restricted to certain occupations and most are farmers. The territory within the Pale is located in what are in the 1990s the nations of Russia, Belarus, Ukraine, Poland, and Lithuania. SEE **1915,** JUD. JUD

1812   Fort Ross is built by the Russians about 90 miles north of San Francisco. It is the southernmost settlement established by the Russians moving south from Alaska. The residents are mainly Native Americans who have been converted to Orthodoxy, and the church built with the fort remains in use in the 1990s. NATIV, ORTHO

1812   In Britain Parliament repeals the Five Mile and Conventicle Acts, thereby affording more religious freedom to the non-Conforming (to the Church of England) churches. PROT

1812   The Osgoodite sect is founded by Baptist preacher Jacob Osgood (1777–1844) in New Hampshire. Osgood promotes prophecy, faith healing, and emotional expression during worship. The sect disappears by the close of the century. PROT

1812   The American Board of Commissioners for Foreign Missions (ABCFM) is established in the United States. It is the first missionary society founded in the United States for the purpose of sending missionaries elsewhere in the world. It includes representatives from Congregational, Presbyterian, and Reformed churches, and its first missionaries go to India in this year. PROT

1813   An estimated 100,000 followers of the millenarian Buddhist Eight Trigrams cult rise near Beijing and capture several towns. A rebel force reaches one of the gates of Beijing before being repulsed. The outbreak claims 70,000 lives before it is quelled. BUDD

1813   Primarily through the influence of Congregationalist minister Lyman Beecher, the Connecticut Society for the Reformation of Morals is founded as one of the first temperance societies in the United States. The first such society with a direct base in religion, it represents the growth of interest in religion and related issues in the late 18th and early 19th centuries. Such societies often address themselves to such issues as alcohol and tobacco use, peace, and slavery. MISC

1813   The first Protestant missionary in Burma, Adoniram Judson (1788–1850), an American Baptist, establishes a mission. He has little success in making converts among the Buddhist Burmese but does translate Protestant texts into their language. PROT

1813   The Female Bible Society of Geneva, New York, is founded. It is the first of some 13 such regional women's societies founded in the United States in the early 1800s. PROT

1813   The Scottish Unitarian Association is founded, marking the spread of Unitarianism beyond England and the United States. SECT

1814   Pope Pius VII reestablishes the Jesuit order. Although the order was disbanded in 1773, it had continued to exist—often in secrecy—in Germany, Austria, and Poland. The reestablishment of the Jesuits marks a revival of interest in missionary work by the Roman Catholic Church and is followed by the establishment of new orders and societies.   **CATH**

1814   The Wesleyan Methodists initiate missionary activity in South Asia in Sri Lanka and then expand their activities to India.   **PROT**

1814   The Anglicans assign a bishop to India to aid in their missionary work. He founds Bishop's College in Calcutta to train native missionaries, although it is 100 years before the college becomes successful in this goal.   **PROT**

1814   The Baptist churches in the United States begin to take shape as a unified denomination when representatives meet at the General Missionary Convention of the Baptist Denomination in the United States for Foreign Missions held in Philadelphia.   **PROT**

1814   Lutherans in Denmark found the Danish Bible Society to prepare and distribute materials to support the missionary effort. In 1821 they found the Danish Missionary Society.   **PROT**

1814   Shinto priest Kurozumi Munetada (1780–1850) undergoes a mystical experience of union with the sun goddess Amaterasu. He will start the new religion Kurozumikyo, which emphasizes faith healing. It is based on Shinto but lay persons play a major role as healers. This is the first of a number of new religions and Shinto sects that will be started in Japan during the first half of the 19th century. A second wave of new religions will arise in the 1920s, and a third after 1945.   **SHINTO**

1815   The Roman Catholic Church reestablishes the Society of the Foreign Missions and new missionary societies are founded: Oblates of the Blessed Virgin Mary Immaculate in 1816, the Marists in 1817, the Salesians in 1859, the Scheut Fathers in 1862, the Mill Hill Fathers in 1866, and the White Fathers in 1868.   **CATH**

1815   Large-scale immigration of Irish Roman Catholics to America begins and continues for the next 30 years. Later in the century many German Catholics also immigrate to the United States, and by 1850 the Roman Catholic Church has more adherents than does any Protestant denomination in the United States.   **CATH**

1815   The United Brethren sect in Maryland has attracted a substantial number of followers and formally establishes itself as a Protestant denomination. In terms of doctrine it is much like the Methodist Church, but its structure differs in that less authority is given to bishops and more to local preachers and missionaries.   **PROT**

1815–
1830

Following the Congress of Vienna, Europe is at peace and the monarchs in Germany, France, Britain, and Spain reassert their authority and move to suppress political reform movements. The Roman Catholic Church generally supports the state and represses liberal reform within the church and stresses the authority of the papacy.　　CATH

1816

The African Methodist Episcopal Church (AME) is founded by African-American religious leader Richard Allen in Philadelphia. It grows into one of the major African-American denominations, with over two million members in the 1990s, nearly half in Africa and the Caribbean.　　AFRICAN

1816

The American Colonization Society is established in the United States for the purpose of encouraging and supporting African-American settlements in Africa. Although not a religious movement, the leaders include Protestant clergymen and the movement is influenced in part by religious leaders who seek a compromise between the continuation and abolishment of slavery. In 1822 the society establishes a colony of African-Americans in West Africa, which eventually becomes the nation of Liberia.　　AFRICAN

1816

A Muslim *jihad* (holy war) in West Africa deposes the non-Muslim Bambara rulers and creates the Muslim Masina state with its capital established at Hamdallahi in 1821. The state lasts until 1862 and succeeds in converting many people to Islam.　　ISLAM

1816

The Anglican Church Missionary Society from Britain sends missionaries to work among the Syrian Christians (Thomas Christians) in southwestern India. Although they are not expected to seek converts among the Orthodox Syrian Christians, some do convert, resulting in strained relations between the Syrian Christian Church and the missionary society.　　ORTHO, PROT

1816

The American Bible Society is founded in the United States as a nondenominational organization for the purpose of distributing English-language copies of the Bible and also translating the Bible into Native American languages. It centralizes the efforts of many local and regional societies, and over the years the organization expands its activities until it becomes the leading international distributor of the Bible.　　PROT

1816

The Evangelical Association (also called Albright's People after founder Jacob Albright) is established as a Protestant denomination by German immigrants in Pennsylvania. The group is similar to the Methodists and Lutherans but remains separate partly because members continue to speak German.　　PROT

1816

The second major wave of Amish emigration from Europe to America begins and lasts until 1860. These Amish establish communities in Indiana, Iowa, Ohio, Illinois, New York, Maryland, and Ontario. The emigration occurs in part because of hardships in Europe caused by the Napoleonic Wars and also because of reports of prosperous Amish communities in the United States.　　SECT

1816   The *Complete Dictionary of Astrology* by James Wilson is published in England. Its publication marks the beginning of a revival of European interest in astrology. Astrology had been in disrepute during the two centuries of the Enlightenment, which stressed science, thought, and learning.   **SPIR**

1817   Michel Jean François Ozeray, a Frenchman, publishes *Récherches sur Buddhou*, the first book published in the West dedicated to Buddhism. It does not, however, reach a very large public.   **BUDD**

1817   A mission to the Native Americans is established at San Rafael, California.   **CATH, NATIV**

1817   The American Sunday School Union is founded in Philadelphia as a central headquarters for the many denominational Sunday schools that have opened in the United States since 1786.   **CHRIS**

1817   The Muslims, who had been victorious in the *jihad* (holy war) of 1804–1808, exert control over the Hausa states in West Africa, with centralized rule from the capital of Sokoto and Muslims ruling the local emirates. In several emirates there is resistance to Muslim rule, and it is not until the end of the century that Islam is established throughout the region.   **ISLAM**

1817   A major Muslim *jihad* (holy war) in the Senegambia region of West Africa leads to an effort to create a Muslim state that rules the region. The effort fails when the Muslims are defeated by the French in 1886 but does result in the conversion of the Wolof people, the major ethnic group in modern Senegal, to Islam.   **ISLAM**

1817   The United Foreign Mission Society is established by Presbyterians in New York City with a focus on Native Americans.   **NATIV**

1817   The London Missionary Society sends Congregationalist missionary John Williams to the South Pacific. He plays a major role in setting up missions on many islands   **PROT**

1817   In the United States Quakers found the Friends Tract Association to publish and distribute religious information.   **PROT**

1817   In Britain the Methodist Missionary Society is established to coordinate efforts of Methodist missionaries around the world.   **PROT**

1817   German Pietists escaping persecution emigrate to America and establish a communal society in Zoar, Ohio. The community enjoys some economic success but dissolves in 1898 and the property is divided among the individuals and family members.   **SECT**

1818   Roman Catholic priests establish a mission in the territory administered by the Hudson's Bay Company in Canada.   **CATH, NATIV**

1818   *A jihad* (holy war) takes places in the savannah region of West Africa and Muslims conquer a small region that had been under control of the Bambara ethnic group. The Muslims are unable to bring political stability to the region and in 1862 are replaced by Muslims from the Tukulor ethnic group.   **ISLAM**

1818   Restrictions on Jewish economic activities and settlement in northeastern France that were enacted in 1806 are removed.   **JUD**

1818   In Connecticut the Congregational Church is disestablished, with the government no longer providing financial support. The Congregational Church in New Hampshire is disestablished in the following year and in Massachusetts in 1833. The end of state support means that churches must now raise their own funds and leads to the founding of many voluntary associations to support church activities.   **PROT**

1818   In Britain Quakers for the first time publicly set forth their opposition to capital punishment, a position restated in 1979.   **PROT**

1818   In the United States Lutheran churches centered in the Mid-Atlantic states begin to expand and new churches are established in the south and west in the following decade.   **PROT**

1819   Arthur Schopenhauer (1788–1860), a German philosopher, publishes the first edition of his *Die Welt als Wille und Vorstellung* (*The World as Will and Representation*) and makes sympathetic allusions to Buddhism. This is one of the first and most influential recognitions of Buddhism in the West and is certainly the first by someone not interested in the original texts as such but in the spiritual message of Buddhism. When Schopenhauer publishes his second and greatly expanded edition of his work in 1844, he will have even more to say about Buddhism and his work will reach an even wider public, including the composer Richard Wagner and the philosopher Henri Louis Bergson.   **BUDD**

1819   Priests of the Daoist Celestial Masters school are barred from imperial audiences in Qing dynasty China.   **DAO**

1819   The Kickapoo nation in the United States splits into northern and southern groups. The northern group is led by the prophet Kenekuk (c. 1785–1852), who preaches pacifism, meditation, and peaceful relations with whites. The religious movement disappears following his death in 1852.   **NATIV**

1819   The United States Congress provides funding for programs to "civilize" Native Americans. The money is given to mission groups to help them establish schools for natives.   **NATIV**

1819   Missionary activity in the Russian Orthodox Church is revived when Russian history professor Michael Jakovlevitch Glucharev becomes a monk, changes his name to Makary, and embarks on a missionary trip to the

Kalmuk people of central Asia. The mission is moderately successful and serves as a model for subsequent missionary activity. **ORTHO**

1819　British Protestant missionaries in southern India open a college for the training of native missionaries which is chartered by Denmark in 1827. **PROT**

1819　In the United States the Methodist Episcopal Church establishes the Foreign Mission Board of the Methodist Episcopal Church. It begins its work among Native Americans and in 1933 opens a mission in Liberia in West Africa. **PROT**

1819　William Ellery Channing (1780–1842), leader of the Liberal (Unitarian) Christians in the United States, delivers a sermon titled "Unitarian Christianity" that becomes an important statement of Unitarian thought and belief. **SECT**

1819–1825　A Russian translation of the Church Slavic Bible based on the study of the original Hebrew and Greek texts is completed. The translation is quickly suppressed and then destroyed by the tsar. **ORTHO**

1819–1839　A war breaks out between Muslim reformers (who seek a return to traditional Islam) and the Dutch rulers of Malaysia and Indonesia. Following their defeat, the reform factions seek to unite in 1839 to overthrow the Dutch but are defeated in 1845. **ISLAM**

1820　The African Methodist Episcopal Church (AME) begins its missionary activity in Africa with the founding of an AME church in Liberia. Later in the century, its missionary activities are extended to Sierra Leone and South Africa. **AFRICAN**

1820　The Funj Muslim kingdom, at the conflux of the Blue Nile and White Nile in East Africa, which dates to the early 16th century, falls when it absorbed by Egypt. **ISLAM**

1820　In Lebanon conflict develops between the Maronite Christians, who seek to take control of the government, and the Druze sect. A Druze revolt is repressed in 1825, but there are subsequent conflicts in 1838, 1841–1842, and 1845. **ISLAM**

1820　The Mormon Church (The Church of Jesus Christ of Latter-Day Saints) begins to emerge when Joseph Smith (1805–1844), the son of a farmer in upstate New York and later the Prophet and founder of the church, receives a vision in which he is visited by God and Jesus Christ. They instruct him not to join any existing churches. **MOR**

1820　The Anglican Church establishes a mission to the Native Americans in the territory administered by the Hudson's Bay Company in Canada. **NATIV, PROT**

1820   In the United States the Episcopal Church establishes the Domestic and the Foreign Missionary Society and later begins work in Greece and then Africa. **PROT**

1820   In the United States Methodists at their general conference change the method of selecting presiding elders from appointment by the bishop to election of elders from a list of nominees selected by the bishop. The change is generally accepted but a minority objects and the new plan is not put into effect. The dissent over the motion reveals a split in the Methodist Church between traditionalists and reformers. **PROT**

1820   Protestant missionary efforts among the Jews of Palestine begin with the establishment of a mission by the Anglican Society for Work among the Jews. **PROT**

1820   Congregationalists begin their missionary work on Hawaii. **PROT**

1820s   Late in the decade anti-Catholicism reemerges in the United States. It is motivated in part by increasing Irish Catholic immigration and also by concerns among Protestant ministers over what are seen as criticisms of Protestantism by the pope. **CATH, PROT**

Mormonism

Mormonism, or the Church of Jesus Christ of the Latter-Day Saints, is the largest and most successful of major religions that have developed in the Americas. In the 1990s it had about a million followers worldwide with about five million in the United States and four million elsewhere. Missionary activity is a major component of Mormonism, accounting for the large Mormon population in such places as Africa and South America. Mormonism arose as one of a number of new religious movements as part of the Christian Second Great Awakening in western New England and Upstate New York in the early 19th century. By the middle of the century, it was well established in Utah, where adherents had settled to avoid persecution in the East and Midwest. Mormon religion is based on the Christian Bible and the Book of Mormon, which is an account of the habitation of the New World prior to arrival of Columbus in 1492, which includes a visit by Jesus following his crucifixion. Mormon worship takes place in the home and in temples, with singing, prayer, and blessings especially important. The Mormon community in the United States is highly structured. It is divided into a series of subunits that are overseen by a hierarchy of priests. Personal behavior is controlled to some extent by the church, with marriage and family life supported and such behaviors as smoking, drinking alcoholic beverages, coffee, and tea, and engaging in premarital sex prohibited.

1820s   The Genesis story as recounted in Judeo-Christian Bibles is questioned by geologists in Europe, who argue that the world is much older than claimed in the Old Testament and older than the date of 4004 B.C.E. claimed by Bishop Ussher. **MISC**

1821   A second African Methodist Episcopal Church is founded by African-American religious leader James Varick (c. 1750–1827) in New York City in competition with the church of the same name founded in Philadelphia in 1816. The church is a strong supporter of abolition and many African-American leaders of the abolition movement—among them Sojourner Truth, Harriet Tubman, and Frederick Douglass—are members of the church. **SEE 1848, AFRICAN.** **AFRICAN**

1821   The General Missionary Convention of the Baptist Denomination in the United States of America for Foreign Missions sends two African-American Baptist missionaries to Liberia. **AFRICAN**

1821   After achieving independence from Spain, Peru bans all religions except the state-supported Roman Catholicism. Over the next decades the ban on other religions is relaxed, but Roman Catholicism remains closely linked to the state. **CATH, TOL**

1821   In Prussia King Frederick William III attempts to unify the Lutheran and Calvinist churches. The attempt fails when it is resisted by the Lutherans. **PROT**

1821   Lutherans in Denmark form the Danish Missionary Society to support missionary activity in Greenland and later in India. **PROT**

1821–
1845   During this time B. H. Hodgson serves as Britain's resident-general in Nepal and collects a large number of Sanskrit Buddhist texts that he will bring back and present to libraries in London, Paris, and Calcutta. He also writes articles describing his research into these texts. Later scholars will give much credit to Hodgson's pioneer work in creating an awareness of Buddhism in the West. **BUDD**

1822   With the end of Portuguese rule in Brazil, the influence of the Roman Catholic Church weakens and a number of independent Afro-Brazilian syncretic religions emerge. They combine elements from African religions, Indian religions, and Roman Catholicism, and each is centered in a Brazilian city: Candomblé in Bahia, Xangô in Pernambuco and Alagoas, Casa das Minas in Maranhao, Batuque in Porto Alegre and Belem, and Macumba in Rio de Janerio. These religions draw their followers mainly from the masses of poor, urban Afro-Brazilians. **AFRICAN, NATIV**

1822   To build support for its missionary activities, the Roman Catholic Church begins publishing *Annals of the Association for the Propagation of the Faith: A Periodical Selection from the Letters of Bishops and Missionaries in both the Old World and New, and of All the Documents Relating to the Missions and to the*

Association for the Propagation of the Faith. The reports are expected to create interest in Catholic missionary activities. CATH

1823 The Scottish Missionary Society establishes a mission to African slaves in Jamaica. The work is later taken over by the United Presbyterian Church. AFRICAN

1823 A mission to Native Americans is established at San Francisco. CATH, NATIV

1823 As part of the American government's effort to relocate Native Americans in the East to the west of the Mississippi River, the Jesuits establish a mission school in St. Louis. This school supports other mission efforts in the Plains, which are successful at first but largely disappear during the wars between the Indians and the government in the last half of the 19th century. CATH, NATIV

1823 On September 21 Joseph Smith, the founder of the Mormon Church, is visited by the angel Moroni who tells him of metal plates buried nearby that tell the story of the former people of the Americas who had been visited by Christ. The next day Smith finds the plates buried in a hill on his parents' farm near Palmyra, New York, but is ordered by the angel not to remove them. MOR

1823 A Russian Orthodox mission is established among the Aleuts of the Aleutian Islands by Orthodox priest Ivan Veniaminov (1797–1879). The mission is successful and his activities are later extended to southern Alaska. ORTHO

1824 The first Reform Jewish congregation in the United States is established in Charleston, South Carolina, as the Reform Society of Israelites. The move-

Saint Veniaminov

Orthodox bishop John (or Innocent) Veniaminov was one of the most influential Russian Orthodox clergymen of the 19th century. Born John Popov in Siberia in 1798, he was ordained an Orthodox priest and began an extended missionary journey with his wife and son in Alaska in 1823. In addition to seeking converts among the Aleut people, founding churches, and serving as the bishop from 1840 until 1858, he kept detailed journals in which he recorded much valuable scientific information about the natural environment of Alaska. He was also a strong advocate of indigenous involvement in the Russian Orthodox Church in Alaska, an important consideration in maintaining Orthodoxy in the region after the sale of Alaska to the United States in 1867. When his work in Alaska ended in 1859, he assisted in establishing an Orthodox presence in Japan and in 1868 was appointed the metropolitan of Moscow. Continuing his missionary work from a distance, he founded and led the Imperial Mission Society while leading the Church in Moscow. He died in 1879.

ment ends in 1833 and is not part of the more general Reform Judaism movement in the United States that begins in the 1840s. **JUD**

1824   Sections of the Bible are translated into the Cherokee language and written using the Cherokee syllabary developed by Sequoyah in 1821. **NATIV**

1824   In the Methodist Church in the United States, the disputes that became public in 1820 continue between traditionalists and reformers, and reformers establish Methodist societies to espouse views that are repressed by traditionalists. A major issue is the authority of the bishop, which reformers seek to weaken. **PROT**

1824   In Berlin, Germany, Lutherans form the Berlin Missionary Society to support missionary activities of Lutherans. **PROT**

1824   The Baptist General Tract Society is formed by Baptists in Washington to provide printed material for the Baptist missionary effort. **PROT**

1825   The American Tract Society is founded as an umbrella organization for several dozen moral societies in the United States that are concerned with issues such as slavery, peace, and tobacco and alcohol use. **MISC**

1825   (St.) Seraphim of Sarov (1759–1833), a Russian monk who over the past 35 years has spent time in isolated contemplation and prayer as an ascetic, comes out of isolation and becomes a popular figure among Russian Orthodox who seek his advice and curing powers. He is canonized in 1903 and remains one of the most popular Russian Orthodox saints. **ORTHO**

1825   The British and Foreign Unitarian Association is founded to coordinate Unitarian activities in Great Britain, and the American Unitarian Association is founded in the United States. **SECT**

1825–   Javanese Muslims in Indonesia revolt against Dutch rule. The revolt is pre-
1830   cipitated by Dutch land policies that put new economic burdens on both Javanese landowners and tenants. The revolt also involves a call for a return to traditional Islam by Muslim leaders. **ISLAM**

1825–   The Brethren movement begins in Dublin, Ireland, and in Bristol, Plymouth,
1835   and Barnstable, England. It is started by a number of Christians who object to the rigid practices and structure of the Church of England and also to the very limited role played by lay persons in Church matters. The movement experiences various changes in subsequent years, but by the 1990s numbers nearly 100,000 members, with nearly 1,000 churches in Great Britain, New Zealand, Australia, Canada, and the United States. **PROT**

1826   *Essai sur le Pali* (*An Essay on Pali*) is written by Eugene Burnouf and Christian Lassen. This is a seminal work in studies of Buddhism. Pali is the language in which the Theravada Buddhist texts of Sri Lanka and several other Asian countries were written. Burnouf, a Frenchman, is regarded as the first Western scholar to make a systematic study of Buddhism, and he writes several highly influential books about Buddhism, including *L'Introduction et l'Histoire du Bouddhisme Indien* in 1844.   BUDD

1826   Faced with threats to its empire from the Russians, Greeks, and Egyptians, the Ottoman Empire under Mahmud II (r. 1807–1839) institutes major military, governmental, and religious reforms. The power of the Muslim scholars is limited, much mosque land is placed under government control, and administration is centralized.   ISLAM

1826   Believing that they are following God's will, clergy in Boston found the American Society for the Promotion of Temperance. The society rapidly expands and within a few years has chapters across the nation working to end the drinking of all alcoholic beverages.   MISC

1826   In a process that lasts 20 years, the Spanish government begins to remove the California missions from church control and attempts to establish native settlements on the land. The program is largely a failure, as the land is quickly taken seized by white settlers.   NATIV

1826   In accord with their Plan of Union, the Congregationalist and Presbyterian American Board of Home Missions begins its work in the western United States (New York, Ohio, and Illinois).   PROT

1827   In India Muslim leader Sayyid Ahmad Berelwi (1786–1831) seeks to unify the Pathan tribes of the northwest and launch a revolt against British rule. The revolt fails, but Berelwi's organization survives as the Way of Muhammad movement, which subsequently influences Islam in India. Similar revolts that stress a return to traditional Islam also occur in Bengal in 1833 and 1838.   ISLAM

1827   A Mardi Gras celebration takes place for the first time in Paris. It is linked to Catholicism and develops into a major public and religious celebration in places such as Brazil, New Orleans, and the Caribbean.   MISC

1827   Joseph Smith, the founder of the Mormon Church, takes possession of the gold plates first brought to his attention by the angel Moroni in 1823. Smith begins translating the text on the plates, using the translation keys provided with them. His work is disrupted by curious and suspicious neighbors, and he moves south to Harmony, Pennsylvania.   MOR

1827   The Protestant Church Missionary Society establishes Fourah Bay College in East Africa as an educational institution for native peoples. It becomes one of the most important institutions of its kind in the region for the next 100 years.   PROT

1827   *History and Mystery of Methodist Episcopacy* is written by Methodist reformer Alexander McCaine. He calls for reforms that weaken the authority of the bishop and argues against a powerful bishop, saying the office was never envisioned that way by Methodist founder John Wesley. In the same year reformers, who are being repressed and expelled from churches, found the General Convention of Reformers to present their position to the General Conference scheduled for the next year.   **PROT**

1827–
1828   The Hicksite-Evangelical division takes place among the Quakers in Philadelphia, Ohio, New York, and Baltimore. The Hicksite group is led by Quaker farmer and preacher Elias Hicks (1748–1830) from Long Island. The Hicksite or "Quietest Quakers" stand in opposition to the Evangelical Quakers. The Hicksites take a liberal position on social issues, such as the abolition of slavery, reject an absolute belief in the Bible, and oppose some features of capitalism. They tend to be poor and rural, as opposed to the Evangelicals, who are wealthier and urban.   **PROT**

1828   The Brahmo Samaj (Society for the Worship of One True God) is founded in India by Ram Mohan Roy (1772–1833), a Bengali intellectual. It is an intellectual movement that is intended to both combat the conversion of Hindus to Christianity and reform Hinduism in accord with modern ideas. For the next 90 years it is the major intellectual reform movement in Hinduism and works to raise the status of women, create a Hindu social ethic, reform the educational system, and gain rights for workers. As the

Book of Mormon

The *Book of Mormon* is the sacred text of the Church of Jesus Christ of Latter-day Saints. Mormons consider it equal in importance to the Christian Bible, and it is one of the few basic religious texts produced in the Americas. Mormons believe that the *Book of Mormon* was translated into English from an ancient Egyptian language by Joseph Smith, the founder of Mormonism, in upstate New York in the 1820s. The *Book of Mormon* is both a history and a religious message. As history it recounts the life of the indigenous people of the Americas from 600 B.C.E. to 400 C.E. and includes an account of a visit by Jesus Christ to the region after his death and resurrection. According to the *Book of Mormon*, the New World was first settled by a tribe of ancient Hebrews and Native Americans are their descendants. As a religious work it focus on the issue of good versus evil and especially on the negative influences of wealth and worldly pursuits. It stresses redemption and salvation through devotion to Jesus Christ and a withdrawal from worldly vices. The message of the *Book of Mormon* has special appeal to the people of New York State in the first half of the 19th century as it did not portray wealth as a virtue nor poverty as a sin and also provided for a form of worship free of many of the emotional excesses promulgated by other sects that arose in the region during this same period.

moment draws followers from among highly educated Hindus, its appeal to the average Hindu is limited. **HIND**

1828
At the General Conference of Methodists in the United States, reforms called for by the General Convention of Reformers, such as a weakening of the authority of the bishop, are rejected and reformers who have been expelled are not allowed to return unless they reject their reformist ideas. The actions taken by the conference lead to a split among American Methodists and the reformers establish the Associated Methodist Churches. **PROT**

1828
In Britain Parliament repeals the Test and Corporation Acts, thereby removing legal restraints on the religious freedom of non-Conforming churches. **PROT**

1828
The Basel Mission is established in Ghana. Missionaries work with Dutch traders to develop agricultural enterprises and commerce in the region. **PROT**

1829
Under the leadership of John England, the bishop of Charleston, South Carolina, Catholic bishops initiate a series of regular councils of the Roman Catholic Church in America that meet until 1884. The councils are an important mechanism for forging cooperation among the dioceses in the United States. **CATH**

1829
The custom of *sati* (suttee) is banned by the British in India. *Sati* is the practice of a widow killing herself by burning following the death of her husband. It is confined mainly to upper castes and is not practiced by all widows. Although the practice is outlawed, it continues and even in the late 20th century takes place every few years. **HIND**

1829
Joseph Smith, the founder of the Mormon Church, completes his translation of the gold plates and obtains a copyright for the resulting manuscript, the *Book of Mormon*. He also shows the gold plates to eight men, all of whom attest to having seen and held them. **MOR**

c. 1830
During the reign of Imam Sayyid Sa'id (1804–1856), Arab Muslims from Oman solidify their control over coastal East Africa. Following his death his sons divide the region into Zanzibar and Oman, and Zanzibar becomes a major center for trade into the interior of southern Africa, where slaves and ivory are the most valuable trade goods. **ISLAM**

1830
In India the British begin to institute new policies that weaken the Muslim community. Protestant missionaries are encouraged to seek converts among the Muslims, as well as among the Hindus, English becomes the official language, and secular law replaces Islamic law. **ISLAM**

1830	The French capture Algiers in North Africa and begin to place the Muslim Berbers under their control. **ISLAM**
1830	The Muslim *jihad* (holy war) that began in the Hausa states of West Africa has now spread across northern Nigeria and northern Cameroon. **ISLAM**
1830	Emigration of Jews from Europe (mainly Germany) to the United States begins. This period of emigration lasts until 1861. Jews leave Germany because their civil and religious rights have been restricted since 1815. Jews are, however, given civil rights in Belgium. **JUD**
1830	Hasidism reaches its height of influence in eastern Europe, with many Jews becoming followers of Hasidic rabbis. There is much conflict between Hasidic leaders and leaders of the existing Jewish communities. **JUD**
1830	*Principles of Geology* is written by British geologist Charles Lyell. Publication of the book initiates the debate over evolution versus the biblical version of creation as Lyell attempts to explain geological changes through an examination of natural causes. **MISC**
1830	Joseph Smith, founder of the Mormon Church in America, has 5,000 copies of the *Book of Mormon* printed. Later that year he organizes the Church of Jesus Christ of Latter-Day Saints with six members. **MOR**
1830	Corruption has crept into the Church of England, with many clergy earning considerable amounts of money from wealthy aristocratic patrons or from other employment, such as serving as magistrates and hiring others to perform the ministerial duties. Many also do not live in the parishes they are expected to serve. The Church hierarchy begins instituting reforms, including controls on non-Church incomes for the clergy, a requirment that they live in their parish, and the building of many new churches across Great Britain. **PROT**
1830	The Temperance movement emerges in Britain, when the Seven Men of Preston—who are Methodist lay preachers and ministers—take an oath of abstinence. **PROT**
1830	Alexander Duff (1806–1878) arrives as a missionary of the Church of Scotland in India. He advocates a policy of teaching the Bible in English, a policy in accord with British colonial ambitions of the time. When put into practice the policy leads to the opening of a number of colleges in which Indians are taught in English. **PROT**
1830	In Pennsylvania the government builds the Eastern State Penitentiary with a Quaker as warden and a Quaker approach to imprisonment that stresses rehabilitation over punishment. It becomes a model for prisons built in Ohio and New York. **PROT**

| 1830 | In the United States the Methodist Protestant Church is formed by reformers whose ideas had been rejected at the General Conference of Methodists in 1828. In accord with their proposed reforms, the new church abolishes the office of bishop. **PROT** |

1830s   In response to the immigration of Irish and German Catholics, some Protestants in the United States produce anti-Catholic publications, form anti-Catholic associations, and seek to control Catholic influence in American society. **CATH, PROT**

1830s   The Oxford movement emerges in Great Britain under the leadership of Oxford theologian and writer John Henry Newman (1801–1890). It is an attempt to reform Anglicanism so as to create a single Christian religion in Britain that accommodates Catholics and non-conforming Protestants alike. Newman and some followers convert to Roman Catholicism in 1845. **CATH, PROT**

1830s   The prophet Wobokieshiek (c. 1794–c. 1841) comes to prominence as a political leader during the Black Hawk Wars. Wobokieshiek, a member of the Winnebago people, is a strong opponent of white rule but after the Indian defeat in 1832, he preaches a message that emphasizes proper behavior and cooperation with whites. **NATIV**

1830s   In Britain many of the leaders of the social movement to end the poverty and poor working conditions associated with industrialization come from the ministry of the non-Conforming Protestant churches and especially from the Methodist Church. **PROT**

1830–1843   Kamo Norikiyo (1798–1861), the leader of Kyoto's Kami Kamo shrine, travels to Edo to found Uden (Raven tradition) Shinto based on an allegorical interpretation of the ancient myths. This sect is strongly opposed by the Japanese government, and Norikiyo will be exiled in 1847. **SHINTO**

1830–1850   The Golden Age of Shakerism is marked by a rapid and large increase in the number of adherents of Shakerism: perhaps as many as 6,000 Shakers live in some 19 Shaker communities in the West and New England. The growth is caused in part by social and economic unrest that leads some people to seek security in the largely self-sufficient Shaker communities. **SECT**

1831   Nat Turner's rebellion, led by African-American slave Nat Turner (1800–1831), takes place in Virginia. The rebellion fails but some 60 whites are killed, and Turner is captured and hung in Jerusalem, Virginia. Turner is a deeply religious man who sees an eclipse of the sun as a sign from God to rebel. The rebellion leads to severe controls on slaves but also becomes an important symbol of resistance for African-Americans. **AFRICAN**

1831   The liberal Catholicism movement is taking shape under the leadership of French Catholic priest Felicité de Lamennais (d. 1854) in France. The movement stresses the separation of church and state and a strong papacy. It is criticized both by the rulers and bishops in France as it also advocates open education, freedom of thought, and democracy with universal suffrage. The movement is especially strong in Belgium, where the new constitution reflects these liberal goals and is supported by Belgian Catholics.　　CATH

1831　　A synagogue to serve the Jewish community of Calcutta, India, is built. Jews are given full political rights in Canada.　　JUD

1831　　Joseph Smith and his followers in the Mormon Church move to Kirtland, Ohio, from western New York. In 1932 a second Mormon settlement is established in Hiram, Ohio.　　MOR

1831　　Protestant missionary activity begins in Thailand with the arrival of American Congregational missionaries, followed by the Baptists in 1833 and the Presbyterians in 1840. The missionaries have little success, given the Thais' devout adherence to Buddhism.　　PROT

1831　　The Unitarians in England form a missionary effort to attract followers from among the large number of British who do not affiliate with any church.　　SECT

1831–
1833
The Quakers continue to experience internal divisions as the Wilburite separation takes place in Europe between the Wilburites and the Evangelical Quakers. The Wilburites are led by American farmer and Quaker John Wilbur (1774–1856) from Rhode Island. The Wilburites object to what they see as a too-heavy reliance on the Bible by the Evangelical Quakers and a movement away from worship based on the Inner Light.　　PROT

1831–
1846
Gregory XVI (d. 1846) is pope of the Roman Catholic Church. During his pontificate church missionary activity, which began to reemerge in 1814, expands substantially, with bishoprics and prefectures established in North Africa, East Africa, Japan, and the Pacific Islands.　　CATH

1832　　Pope Gregory XVI rejects the idea of liberal Catholicism in his *Mirari Vos*, in which he rules out any consideration of separation of church and state, freedom of conscience, and freedom of the press.　　CATH

1832　　The Bible is first published in Serbo-Croatian.　　CHRIS

1832　　In an important United States Supreme Court decision in the case of *Worcester v. Georgia*, the court rules that the Cherokee and other nations are legally nations and must be treated as such by the United States and its constituent states. The suit was brought on behalf of the Cherokee by Protestant missionary Samuel Worcester in response to efforts by the state to take Cherokee land. The decision is ignored by the government of Andrew Jackson, which supports the taking of land held by native peoples.　　NATIV

1832	The Lutheran Church is repressed in Russia when the tsar places it under the control of a commission (itself controlled by the government) and ends the independent status of the Lutheran churches in Estonia and Latvia. **PROT**
1832	The American Baptist Home Mission Society is formed to coordinate and support the efforts of Baptist missionaries in North America. Much of the society's effort is aimed at non-English-speaking immigrants from Europe with the goal of making them Americans, as well as converting them to Baptism. **PROT**
1832–1847	The Muslims of northern Algeria revolt against French rule. The Muslim Berber religious and political leader Abd al-Qadir (1808–73) leads a *jihad* (holy war) against the French. Drawing support from the Sufi Qadiriya order, the Muslims establish a state and control two-thirds of the nation by 1839. In 1844 they and their Moroccan allies are defeated by the French at the Battle of Isly, and in 1847 Abd al-Qadir is deported to France and then exiled in Damascus. **ISLAM**
1833	The Society of St. Vincent de Paul is founded as a Roman Catholic lay organization to perform charitable work. **CATH**
1833	The Oxford movement emerges at Oxford University in England when Anglican priest John Henry Newman (1801–1890) begins editing his *Tracts for the Times*, which are published through 1841. The Oxford movement, associated with the high Anglican Church (Anglicans who more closely follow Catholicism), stresses the Roman Catholic basis of the Church and criticizes other Anglicans and other Protestants. It is, in turn, criticized by Protestants. Newman later converts to Catholicism and is made a cardinal in 1879. **CATH, PROT**
1833	The New Hampshire Baptist State Convention issues the New Hampshire Confession of Faith, which establishes the absolute authority of the Bible and baptism as a basis of membership while generally ignoring the issue of organization above the local church level. **PROT**
1833	In response to requests from other Protestant denominations, the British government allows for the expansion of missionary activity in India. Among those who establish missions are the American Congregationalists, American Presbyterians, the Lutherans, the Methodist Episcopal Church, and the Basel Mission (Lutheran and Reformed) from continental Europe. **PROT**
1833	Lutherans in Hamburg, Germany, found the *Rauhes Haus* as a social service agency to detail with the problems of illness, poverty, crime, and homelessness in industrializing cities. **PROT**
1833	William Miller (1782–1849), a farmer from upstate New York who has been studying the Bible for several years in order to determine the date of Christ's Second Coming, gains a license to preach in the Baptist Church.

Miller announces that Christ will return "about 1843" and draws several hundred thousand followers to his new Adventist movement.　**SECT**

1833–
1838
Attempts by Mormons to establish a settlement in Missouri fail when they face hostility from local residents. The settlement of Mormons in Kirtland, Ohio, grows, and again the Mormons are the target of violence by non-Mormons, prompting Joseph Smith and other leaders to flee to Missouri in 1838.　**MOR**

1834
The first organization designed to represent all independent African-American Baptist churches in the United States is founded as the Providence Association in Ohio. Other similar organizations are founded in Illinois, Michigan, and Canada, and they are involved in the abolition movement and the Underground Railroad.　**AFRICAN**

1834
Alexander Csoma de Koros (1784–1842), a Hungarian, had gone to Tibet in 1819 and was among the first Westerners to study the language and read its Buddhist literature. In 1834 he publishes in Calcutta the first authoritative Tibetan grammar and Tibetan-English dictionary, as well as his analysis of the Tibetan Buddhist canon. In 1933 Japanese Buddhists will designate him a *bodhisattva*, an aspirant to Buddhahood, for having "opened the heart of the Western world to an understanding of Buddhism."　**BUDD**

1834
The Spanish Inquisition, which was established in 1478 and put into practice in 1480, is officially ended in Spain.　**CATH**

1834
The Roman Catholic Ursuline convent and school in Charlestown, Massachusetts, is burned by an anti-Catholic mob.　**CATH, PROT**

1834
The Bible is first published in Norwegian.　**CHRIS**

1834
The New York Moral Reform Society is founded as part of the growth of interest in religion and related issues in the late 18th and early 19th centuries. These societies often concern themselves with such issues as alcohol and tobacco use, peace, and slavery.　**MISC**

1834
Russian Orthodox missionary Ivan Veniaminov, who has been successful in making converts in the Aleutian Islands and southern Alaska, writes *A Guide to the Kingdom of Heaven*, a guide to spiritual life that becomes popular in Russia and Germany.　**ORTHO**

1834
A split develops in the Dutch Reformed Church between the traditionalists and moderates. A similar split occurs again in 1886, although the Dutch Reformed Church remains intact.　**PROT**

1834
The Home Mission Society of Baptists in North America launches a major missionary effort among Scandinavian and German immigrants settling in the midwestern United States.　**PROT**

1834– 1840	Missions are established to Native Americans in the northwestern United States, first by the Methodists and then by the Jesuits. **NATIV**
1835	A Muslim *jihad* (holy war) begins in West Africa in the region of Upper Volta, Guinea, and the Ivory Coast, and involves efforts by Muslims to conquer indigenous peoples and convert them to Islam. The Muslim kingdom of Wasulu is established in 1883 but fails to convert all people to Islam. **ISLAM**
1835	In Sweden Lutherans found the Swedish Mission Society, although it does not become active in overseas work until the 1870s. **PROT**
1836	The Mormons send missionaries to South Africa. **MOR**
1836	Lyman Beecher (1775–1863), a Congregationalist minister and president of Lane Seminary in Cincinnati, Ohio, is tried by the Congregationalists for heresy for supporting practices of conservative Presbyterians. Although he is acquitted, the trial points to basic differences that are disrupting the Plan of Union drafted in 1801 between the Congregationalists and Presbyterians in the United States. **PROT**
1836	Several Protestant denominations found the American and Foreign Bible Society to support the publication and distribution of Bibles for use by missionaries. **PROT**
1836– 1886	Hindu mystic Paramahamsa Ramakrishna lives and, having experienced visions over the years, leads a new religious movement in India that views all religions as equally valid. One of his pupils, Swami Vivekananda (1863–1902), goes on to spread a westernized version of Hinduism in the Western world. **HIND**
1837	The Board of Foreign Missions of the Presbyterian Church in the United States of America is established to support missionary activity among Native Americas. **NATIV, PROT**
1837	The Presbyterian Church ends the Plan of Union with the Congregationalist Church in the United States established in 1801. The Plan, established in 1801, had been effective in making many converts to the church in the West but dissolves when Old School (conservative) Presbyterian leaders refuse to modify religious practices that offend Congregationalists. **PROT**
1837– 1838	Mormons establish settlements in Missouri but are again persecuted for their beliefs as they were in Ohio and are attacked by the state militia. They flee to Illinois, although Joseph Smith, the founder of the Mormon Church, and other church leaders are imprisoned. Smith is released in 1839. Nauvoo, Illinois, becomes the center of the church. Mormon missionary efforts outside the United States begin when missionaries are sent to Great Britain. **MOR**

1837– 1838	A schism develops in the Presbyterian Church in the United States between the Old School (conservative) and New School (reformist). Both groups hold their own assemblies and each calls itself the Presbyterian Church in the United States of America. The New School views the break as unneeded, but it is supported by the Old School adherents, who see it as the only means to retain traditional Presbyterian beliefs and practices. **PROT**
1837– 1909	These years cover the lifespan of Chang Chih-tung, the Chinese reformer/scholar. He makes desperate attempts to revivify and save the essence of Confucian learning. **CONF**
1838	With the end of slavery in its colonies in the Americas, the British begin importing Indian contract laborers to work on the sugar plantations. They are primarily Hindus but also include Muslims and Sikhs. They form distinctive ethnic communities, with the caste system less important than in India. Nations with sizable Indian populations are Guyana, Suriname, and Trinidad and Tobago. **HIND**
1838	A Jewish agricultural collective is established in Ulster County, New York. It shortly fails but is the first of many such Jewish colonies established in the East and Midwest throughout the century and into the 20th century. Most fail, and even those that are initially successful are eventually weakened when many young people move to cities in search of education and employment. **JUD**
1838	The Plumstead Peculiars or Peculiar People emerge as a distinct Protestant sect in southern England. They stress faith healing and anointing with oil but draw only a small following and are later absorbed into the Fellowship of Independent Evangelical Churches. **PROT**
1838	In Britain the authority of the Church of England is lessened somewhat when new laws remove the requirement that members of other Protestant churches register the birth of children with the Anglican Church and have their marriages blessed by the church. **PROT**
1838	American scholar and writer Ralph Waldo Emerson (1803–1882) delivers the commencement address at Harvard Divinity School, in which he criticizes what he perceives as stagnation in the American Protestant Church and calls for basic reforms. **PROT**
1838	The Tenrikyo religion begins as an offshoot of Shinto in Japan when Nakayama Miki (1798–1887), the devoutly religious wife of a wealthy landowner, receives revelations about the origins of the universe. Followers base their behavior on her life, which involved reducing herself to a state of poverty and assisting women in childbirth, and receive support from the church. The religion is a messianic and syncretist Shinto sect that combines elements of folk religion and shamanism. **SECT**

1838	The Hamada and Tsuwan domains in western Japan make the performance of Shinto, rather than Buddhist, funerals the official practice. This policy change is influenced by New Learning leader Okuni Takamasa and his disciple Fukuba Bisei (1831–1907), who later will become a high administrator of Shinto affairs in the Meiji government. Before the era of the New Learning movement, the word *Shinto* is not commonly used to describe shrines and *kami* (native spirit) cults. **SHINTO**
1839	In the Ottoman Empire the Noble Rescript of Gülhane declaration gives religious equality to non-Muslims. The declaration is aimed primarily at Christians, whose support the sultan seeks in reforming Ottoman society. **ISLAM, TOL**
1839	American Protestants who are involved in the American and Foreign Bible Society become embroiled in a controversy over which is the authoritative version of the Bible. The Society distributes the King James Version, to which Baptists object, as no Baptists were involved in its initial preparation. **PROT**
1839–1876	In an attempt to halt its decline as a regional power, the Ottoman Empire goes through a period of major societal reform known as the Tanzimat. Laws governing economic, social, and religious matters are substantially revised to create a more modern nation. In terms of religion, the legal and political influence of Islam and Muslim scholars is weakened and equality is afforded to non-Muslims. **ISLAM**
1840	The Roman Catholic population in the United States has increased, and there are now sees under the archbishopric in Baltimore, including Boston, New York, Philadelphia, Bardstown, Charleston, Richmond, Cincinnati, St. Louis, New Orleans, Mobile, Detroit, Vincennes, Dubuque, Nashville, and Natchez. **CATH**
1840	Jesuit missionaries begin establishing a series of missions to the Native Americans who live between the Rockies and the northern Pacific coast. **CATH, NATIV**
1840	The Bible is first translated into modern Greek. **CHRIS**
1840	The Nagarseth order of Jains erect a special shrine at Satrunjaya (near Palitana), Gujarat, long the site of Jain temples. **JAIN**
1840	Russian Orthodox missionary Ivan Veniaminov becomes the bishop of Alaska and in 1848 builds the Cathedral of Saint Michael in Sitka. **ORTHO**
1840	American churches have been active in sending missionaries to Africa to convert Africans to Christianity, and by this year Congregational, Baptist, Presbyterian, Methodist, and Episcopalian missions are established on the continent. **PROT**

1840   Shakerism in the United States begins to decline, and by 1874 the population of the Shaker communities has dropped by nearly 50 percent. The decline is partly a result of urbanization, changing economic conditions that make the agricultural Shaker communities less desirable, and the celibacy rule, which makes it impossible to generate new members from within the movement.   **SECT**

1840   *Lectures on Our Israelitish Origin* by Irish religious theorist John Wilson (?–1871) is published in England. It sets forth the view, which has appeared at times in Britain since the mid-17th century, that the British are the descendants of the 10 lost tribes of Israel. The idea and the movement are known as British-Israelism or Anglo-Israelism.   **SECT**

1840–
1841   The Ottoman Empire is declining in power, and Russia, Britain, and Austria, the leading European powers, enter into an agreement controlling shipping and naval traffic in the Mediterranean. They also allow Muhammad Ali, the Ottoman governor of Egypt, to establish an independent dynasty there. Both actions indicate the weakness of the Ottoman Empire.   **ISLAM**

1840–
1841   The Mormon Church institutes emigrant companies to assist European Mormons in coming to the United States. Until about 1890 emigrants from Europe (especially northern Europe) who had been converted by Mormon missionaries form a sizable percentage of the Mormon population in the United States.   **MOR**

1840s   Muslim Sufism, with a number of sects active, takes root in the Muslim communities of the Caucasus region in Russia. Sufi forms of worship become common in the region, and Sufism becomes the focal pint for resistance to Russian rule.   **ISLAM**

1840–
1850   Reform Judaism, as an alternative to Orthodox Judaism, spreads in Germany and then spreads to and develops in the United States. Cincinnati, Ohio, becomes the center of Reform Judaism, as many German Jews settle there. Reform Judaism stresses the ethical teachings of Judaism, social reform, and the adaptation of ritual to modern life.   **JUD**

1840s–
1850s   A revival of Islam takes place among Muslims in the Banten region of Indonesia. The Muslim reformers stress a return to the traditions of Islam, including pilgrimage to Mecca, and preach that the end of the universe is near. The reform movement is linked to revolts against Dutch rule during this period.   **ISLAM**

c. 1840–
1860   The Slavophile movement takes place in Russia. It is an intellectual movement that begins in reaction to the westernization of Russia and that stresses Russian nationalism and Russian Orthodoxy.   **ORTHO**

1841	Reform Judaism appears in England with the establishment of the West London synagogue. **JUD**
1841	British Protestant missionary David Livingstone (1813–1873) begins his missionary work in Africa with the London Missionary Society in South Africa. He becomes well-known for his explorations and reports on the African environment and peoples and plays a role in stimulating British interest in the commercial exploitation of Africa. **PROT**
1841	The Hopedale communal society is founded by Universalist minister Adin Ballou in Milford, Massachusetts. Although based on Ballou's notion of "practical Christianity" and set forth as a model Christian community, it is more an economic arrangement than a religious movement. It folds in 1886 when the stockholders liquidates their assets. **SECT**
1841	Japan's government confines National Learning scholar Hirata Atutane (1776–1843) to his home domain because of his extremism. As the foremost Fukko (Restoration) Shinto leader, he promotes a fiery ultranationalist and xenophobic resentment against Buddhism. As a scholar, he works on the systematization of ancient Shinto and writes essays on Shinto liturgy. After the Meiji Restoration many of his followers will be appointed to the new government. **SHINTO**

Orthodox, Conservative, and Reform Judaism

In the United States, Israel, Great Britain, Canada, and some other nations, the Jewish community can be subdivided into these three broad categories on the basis of religious practice. Orthodox Jews are the most devout, as they fully or closely adhere to the requirements of Jewish religious observance. For example, they closely adhere to dietary restrictions, abstain from all forms of work on Saturday (the Jewish Sabbath), devoting the day to prayer, and limit the participation of women in religious rites. Conservative Judaism developed as an alternative to both Orthodox and Reform Judaism in the United States. It was an attempt to modify some of these rules to accommodate what some Jews saw as the realities of the modern world. For example, as people sometimes have to travel some distance to attend synagogue services, driving to synagogue is permitted. Conservative Judaism also permits the ordination of women as rabbis. Reform Judaism, which emerged in Germany in the 1800s, differs from the Orthodox and Conservative wings in that even more laxity is applied to traditional rules and also in the emphasis it places on the role of the Jewish religion and community as an agent for social change, not just for Jews but for all peoples. Thus, Reform Jews have been much involved in social issues, such as racism and poverty. At the institutional level, the relations among the three branches of Judaism and their governing rabbinical bodies are sometimes contentious, especially in the United States and Israel.

1841–
1844

Joseph Smith, the founder of the Mormon Church, issues new directives for the church membership. One concerns allowing plural marriage, a decision that creates much conflict with the United States government in subsequent years.   **MOR**

1842

The American Indian Mission Association is established by Baptists in the United States.   **CATH, NATIV**

1842

The first Reform Jewish synagogue in North America, Har Sinai, is founded by German Jewish settlers in Baltimore.   **JUD**

1842

The Treaty of Nanking ends the Opium War between the British and Chinese and allows for the establishment of the British colony of Hong Kong and five British ports. These serve as centers of Protestant missionary activity in China, with virtually all missionary societies in Britain and the United States sending missionaries to China. Much of their activity is in the port cities, and competition between the missionaries hampers their effectiveness.   **PROT**

1842

In Norway laws limiting religious freedom are repealed, and by 1845 religious freedom is established. The Norwegian Missionary Society is formed to support missionary work in southern Africa and Madagascar. In 1901 it absorbs the Norwegian Lutheran China Society, which is formed in 1891.   **PROT**

1842

Members of the Society of True Inspiration move from Marienborn, Germany, to Erie County, New York, where they establish a communal farming community. The Inspirationists developed from the German Pietist movement and believe in the literal interpretation of the Bible, as well as inspiration received from God through visions and dreams.   **PROT**

1843

In Lebanon the Ottoman Empire attempts to end conflict between the Maronite Christians and the Druze minority by establishing two governments—a Maronite government in the north and a Druze government in the south—with a national council representing both groups. The arrangement brings 15 years of peace but ends with war between the Maronites and a Druze-Muslim coalition in 1859 and 1860.   **ISLAM**

1843

The Independent Order of B'nai B'rith is founded as a Jewish fraternal society in New York City.   **JUD**

1843

Priests of the Russian Orthodox Church establish a mission school in Alaska.   **NATIVE, ORTHO**

1843

The Disruption takes place in the Church of Scotland when an Evangelical faction comprising about 40 percent of the church membership leave the church and form the Free Church. The Evangelicals draw their support from the middle class in the cities and the Highland Scots.   **PROT**

1844   In one of the worst outbreaks of anti-Catholicism in the United States, riots involving Nativists, whose agenda is partly anti-Catholic, and Catholics outside Philadelphia leave 13 dead, with two Catholic churches burned and Irish homes destroyed.   **CATH**

1844   *The Vestiges of Creation* is written by British biographer Robert Chambers. The book takes an evolutionary view of human existence and ignores the biblical version of creation, adding to the growing debate between scientists and theologians over evolution.   **MISC**

1844   *Contribution to the Critique of Hegel's "Philosophy of Right,"* an essay by German political theorist Karl Marx (1818–1883), is published. In the essay Marx makes his famous pronouncement: "Religion, the opium of the people." **MISC**

1844   The Mormon Church in Illinois continues to experience much conflict with non-Mormons, and Joseph Smith, the founder of the Mormon Church, and his brother are killed in jail while awaiting trial. Brigham Young (1801–1877), an early follower of Joseph Smith, becomes the new leader of the Church.   **MOR**

1844   In Greece the constitution bans activities designed to convert people from Greek Orthodoxy. The ban is reinforced and then expanded to cover all religions in subsequent constitutions (1952, 1975).   **ORTHO, TOL**

1844   The Laestadian Christian revival movement is started by Lutheran minister Lars Levi Laestadius (1800–1861) in Sweden and then spreads across north-

---

Sojourner Truth

Sojourner Truth was an African-American slave born Isabella Van Wagener in New York State about 1797 who died a free woman in Battle Creek, Michigan, in 1883. Her life points to the importance of religion in the battle by slaves to win their freedom and to end slavery in the United States. Starting in childhood she experienced visions and received messages that she believed came from God. As a young woman she joined the newly established African Methodist Episcopal Church in New York City and devoted herself to street preaching. In 1843 she took the name Sojourner Truth and, answering a call from God "to travel up and down the land," became an itinerant preacher through song and preaching first in New England and later in the Midwest. In 1843 she was exposed to the abolition movement in Massachusetts and added abolition as a basic theme of her preaching. She was also active in the Underground Railroad, helping to move slaves in the South to freedom in the North, and is believed to have assisted over 300 slaves to freedom. To support herself she also dictated her story and sold copies of it as *The Narrative of Sojourner Truth.* In later years, after her move to Michigan in the 1850s, she added women's suffrage and resettlement of former slaves in the North to her list of causes.

ern Scandinavia. The movement stresses emotional worship and a strict moral and ethical code of behavior and in the 1990s has several hundred thousand adherents in the region.   **PROT**

1844   In England the Young Men's Christian Association (YMCA) is founded to provide educational and social services to Christian boys and men.   **PROT**

1844   The Christadelphians, a Protestant group, is founded by physician John Thomas (1805–1871) in Richmond, Virginia. Christadelphians emphasize the millennium when Jesus Christ is to return and create a new world order centered in Jerusalem. Predictions about the date of Christ's return (1865, 1910) do not prove true, thereby limiting its appeal.   **PROT**

1844   For Methodists in the United States, slavery emerges as a divisive issue at the General Conference when the conference supports the suspension of a member from Maryland who has refused to free his slaves. Northerners support the suspension while Southerners vote to overturn the decision. A similar geographical split in voting occurs when the conference votes to suspend a bishop from Georgia who had not freed his slaves, as Georgia law did not allow him to do so.   **PROT**

1844   In Britain the British Anti-State-Church Society is formed by those who seek to end the Church of England's status as the national church. The Society is later renamed the Liberation Society.   **PROT, TOL**

1844   William Miller, the founder the Adventist movement in 1833, who had predicted that Christ would return "about 1843," predicts in February that the Second Coming will take place between March 21, 1843, and March 21, 1844. When the day passes without Christ's return, Miller admits to being in error and the movement loses many followers. Miller then sets October 22, 1844, as the day of Christ's return, and when it fails to take place (the "Great Disappointment"), the Millerite movement dissolves.   **SECT**

1844   The modern Seventh-Day Adventist Church begins to emerge in the wake of the failed Millerite prophecies of the same year. Former Millerite Hiram Edson (1806–1882) in New York State attracts some disillusioned Millerites when he announces that William Miller had erred in predicting Christ's Second Coming and that instead Christ had moved to a new place in heaven to continue his work before his reappearance on earth.   **SECT**

1844   The Baha'i religion begins to emerge when Sayyid Ali Muhammad Shirazi (1819–1850) claims to be the link (the *bab)* between the Muslim community on earth and the hidden Imam (leader) of Islam who Shi'a Muslims believe to be in a state of transubstantiation and who will eventually return to earth. The *Bab*, as he is subsequently known to followers, attracts some followers because he appears at a time of political and religious unrest in Iran and holds forth the promise of better times.   **SECT**

1845	Revolts by Muslims against Dutch rule in the Banten region of Indonesia break out again, the last series of revolts having been suppressed in 1839. The Muslims consider this revolt to be a *jihad* (holy war) and revolt five more times, with the last in 1869. **ISLAM**
1845	In this year slavery becomes a divisive issue in the American South for both the Methodist Church and the Baptist Church. Southern members of these churches form the Methodist Episcopal Church, South and the Southern Baptist Convention, respectively, to represent their interests. **PROT**
1845–1846	Through a series of conferences, rabbis in Germany institute changes in Reform Judaism. These include ending the use of Hebrew as the religious language, terminating various traditional customs, and limiting religious holidays to one day. The more radical suggestion that the Sabbath be moved to Sunday is rejected. In New York Temple Emanuel, which becomes the largest congregation in the United States, is founded. **JUD**

Seventh-Day Adventists

Seventh-Day Adventism is a religion that developed in the United States between 1844 and 1846. It grew out of the failed Millerite movement in New York State, in which William Miller predicted the Second Coming of Christ in 1844. When Miller was proved wrong, the Millerites dissolved and Seventh-Day Adventism was founded by former Millerites Hiram Edson, Joseph Bates, and Ellen Gould Harmon White. Adventists view White as a prophet and believe that her many religious writings are a guide to the word of God in the Bible. Adventists are best known for their observance of the Sabbath from sundown Friday until sundown Saturday. They believe that the day is sacred and that Christ's Second Coming is delayed because Christians do not observe the Sabbath as the seventh day. Adventists also believe that in 1844 Christ moved to the "heavenly sanctuary," where he sits in "investigative judgment" of all human beings. The third major belief of Adventism is that the Second Coming of Christ will occur in the near future and will be in a form observable to human beings. Christ's arrival will mark the start of a 1,000-year period (a millennium), in which the worthy will live in heaven and the devil and fallen angels on earth. At the end of the period, earth and all unworthy humans will be destroyed. In addition to these basic doctrines, Adventists have other beliefs and practices that separate them from other Christian denominations. Many of these pertain to personal behavior: Adventists do not drink alcoholic beverages, coffee, or tea, and do not smoke, and many avoid meat as well. They also prefer a conservative lifestyle and avoid loud forms of entertainment, heavy makeup, and ostentatious jewelry. Since the 1800s the Adventists have conducted missions around the world and, although they have often been the object of persecution, there are now Adventists on all continents and in most nations. There are about 800,000 Seventh-Day Adventists in the United States and 45,000 in Canada, with another 30,000 Adventists who do not believe in the Sabbath as the seventh day.

1845–1846	The Mormon Church continues to experience hostility from non-Mormons, with Mormon buildings burned, Mormons attacked, and political support for their cause disappearing. Many are driven from the settlement at Nauvoo, Illinois. In February 1846 they begin their exodus to the western United States in search of religious freedom. **MOR**

1845–
1853
The leaders of the Iranian Muslim community persecute followers of the *Bab* (the founder of Baha'i), execute some, and in 1850 publicly execute the *Bab* himself. The Babis come close to disappearing as a political and religious movement with virtually all leaders killed or imprisoned and many followers also killed. The Babis and then the Baha'i are persecuted in Muslim nations at various times because they are considered heretics. Muslims do not accept the *Bab* as the 12th Imam. **SECT**

1845–
1856
In the United States the Wilburite-Gurneyite split takes place among the Quakers. The split centers on the rival ideas and preaching of British banker and Quaker Joseph Gurney (1788–1847) and American Quaker John Wilbur, who, preaching in 1831–1833 in Europe, had already precipitated a split among Quakers. Gurney supports the Evangelical position with an emphasis on the use of the Bible and organized prayer, while Wilbur argues for a more traditional approach based on individual worship. **PROT**

1846
The Evangelical Alliance is formed in London by representatives of 50 European and American Protestant churches. The purpose of the organization is to foster cooperation among Protestant denominations, and the Alliance hosts a number of conferences over the next 50 years. **SEE 1908, PROT.** **PROT**

Baha'i

The Baha'i religion, then known as Babism, developed as an alternative to Islam in Iran in 1844. Since then adherents have been seen by Muslims as heretics and have often been persecuted in Muslim nations. Baha'is believe in peace and the unity of humankind and see their purpose as creating a harmonious world in which all people can live together in peace. Knowledge through science, education, equality of the races and sexes, a sharing of wealth, and respect for all people are core values for Baha'is. Although the religion has a distinct body of religious texts and several major religious buildings, it is largely free of institutional trappings, including a formal priesthood, formal conversion requirements and rituals, and a detailed ritual calendar. Nonetheless, followers are expected to express their devotion to Baha'i beliefs through daily worship, usually conducted in members' homes, and fasting during daylight hours on 19 days during the year. Moreover, many members give all their material wealth to the church to support its work. Many members are devoted followers and work to spread the Baha'i message of peace and unity around the world.

1846   In the United States Lutheran churches in the Midwest form the Lutheran Synod of Missouri, Ohio, and Other States. In Wisconsin, Lutheran immigrants from Norway found the Evangelical Lutheran Church in America.   **PROT**

1846   Norwegian immigrants to the United States found the Eielsen Synod, the first Norwegian-American Lutheran organization.   **PROT**

1846   The Seventh-Day Adventist Church, which began to emerge in New York State in 1844, continues to develop when former sea captain and Millerite (the precursors of the Adventists) Joseph Bates (1792–1872) of New Bedford, Massachusetts, writes *The Seventh Day Sabbath, a Perpetual Sign*, in which he argues that the seventh day is the Sabbath day and points to the importance of the Ten Commandments. As a preacher he gains converts across the northern Midwest. In this year Adventism reaches its full doctrinal development through the efforts of Ellen Gould Harmon White (1827–1915) of Maine. Through visions and her identity as a prophet, White confirms the teachings of Bates and of Hiram Edson and thereby brings together the diverse elements that form Seventh-Day Adventism.   **SECT**

1846   Japan's new religion Kurozumikyo becomes a formal organization with the writing of its credo, *Osadamegaki*. The faith-healing sect will begin to turn its emphasis toward emperor worship and semifeudal ethics. In 1876 it will become an official Shinto sect.   **SECT, SHINTO**

1846–
1878   Pius IX (1792–1878) is pope of the Roman Catholic Church. During his pontificate, the Church is split between the liberal and ultramontane movements. The former favors a decentralized church, separation of chuch and state, and basic societal reforms to encourage freedom and progress. The ultramontanes take the opposite view and support a strong papacy, a position also support by Pope Pius IX.   **CATH**

1847   Lionel Rothchild is the first Jew elected to the House of Commons in Britain. However, because of anti-Semitism he is not allowed to be seated until 1858.   **JUD**

1847   The Mormons arrive in the valley of the Great Salt in Utah. Over the next dozen years Mormon settlements are established throughout the state and in neighboring states as Mormons seek land suitable for farming. The first Mormon choir sings in Salt Lake City. It is the predecessor of the larger Mormon Tabernacle Choir, which begins to take its modern form in 1869.   **MOR**

1847   British Presbyterian missionary William Burns (1815–1868) is the first Protestant to attempt systematic missionary work in the interior of China. Although not very successful at attracting converts, he does prove that work in the interior is possible.   **PROT**

1847   Congregational minister Henry Ward Beecher (1813–1887) is appointed minister of Plymouth Congregational Church in Brooklyn, New York, and serves until his death in 1887. Considered to be the most charismatic preacher of the century, he draws large crowds and preaches a liberal theology that is often at odds with the teachings of the other churches. **PROT**

1847	*Christian Nature* is published in the United States by Congregational teacher and journalist Horace Bushell (1802–1876). The book stresses education as a means to salvation and is an early work in the emerging liberal Protestant tradition in the United States. **PROT**
1847	The Worshipers of Shang-ti movement develops in China. It is a syncretic religious movement based on Chinese popular religion and Baptist thought, its adherents having been introduced to Christianity by Baptist missionaries. **SECT**
1848	The African Methodist Episcopal Church of New York City changes it name to the African Methodist Episcopal Zion Church (AME Zion) and by the 1990s has about 1.5 million members. **AFRICAN**
1848	As part of the renewal of missionary activity in the Roman Catholic Church, orders and societies are founded whose focus is Africa. These include the Fathers of the Holy Spirit in 1848, the Lyons Society of African Missions in 1856, the White Sisters in 1857, and the White Fathers in 1868. **CATH**
1848	Pope Pius IX calls on Orthodox Christians to reunite with the Roman Catholic Church. The appeal is rejected by the Orthodox patriarchs of Constantinople, Alexandria, Antioch, and Jerusalem, who issue an enycylical that rejects the authroity of the papacy and calls upon the pope to join the Orthodox Church. The document comes to define Orthodox-Catholic relations into the 1960s. **CATH, ORTHO**
1848	Jews are granted civil rights in Denmark. **JUD**
1848	Jewish emigration from Germany to the United States increases as German democratic reforms fail. **JUD**
1848	The Waldenses, a former Roman Catholic sect dating to the late 1100s which then became an independent religion after 1184 and a Protestant denomination after 1532, are granted religious freedom in Italy. In the 1990s they number about 20,000. **PROT**
1848	The Brethren movement in Great Britain divides into two groups. One group, known as the Independent or Open Brethren, permits Christians from all other denominations to join Brethren churches. The other group, known as Exclusive Brethren, reserves the right to include or exclude other Christians as they choose. Later, the Exclusive churches centralize under one administrative structure while the Open churches remain independent. **PROT**

1848	The Oneida Community is founded near Syracuse, New York, by John Humphrey Noyes (1811–1886). It is a communal society whose economic base rests on the manufacturing of cutlery, clothing, and other goods and whose religion is founded on Noyes's prophetic leadership and a return to biblical Christianity in order to achieve perfection in life. The community engages in group sex and marriage and is often in conflict with the outside world. Due to internal divisions and external pressures, the community dissolves in 1880 and Noyes flees to Canada. **SECT**
1848	An important event in the growth of spiritualism take places in Hydesville, New York, when Kate Fox is reported to have communicated with a spirit who has been awakening the family at night by making noises and moving furniture. The house is visited by others who also communicate with the spirit, thought to be that of a peddler buried under the house years earlier and whose remains are found in 1904. The event is viewed by spiritualists as evidence that supports their belief in direct communication with the spirits of the deceased. **SPIR**
1848– 1853	The Worshipers of Shang-ti movement, which developed in China in the previous year, becomes a political movement and in 1853 attacks the city of Nanking to overthrow the Manchu dynasty, destroy idols, and end the use of opium. Although the revolt enjoys initial success, it is repressed and the movement disintegrates. **SECT**
1849	In Algeria, which is now under French rule, a series of localized revolts begins which lasts for 30 years. The revolts are led by local Muslim teachers who seek to end French rule. **ISLAM**

Spiritualism

In the modern Western world, spiritualism refers to beliefs and customs centered on communication with the dead. Spiritualists believe that the individual personality lives on after death in the form of a force, spirit, ghost, or some other manifestation. Spiritualists also believe that the living can communicate with the dead and devote much effort to making such communication through the use of mediums. A medium is a person who is believed to have an innate ability to communicate with the spirits of the dead. This ability, usually called clairvoyance, is manifested in a variety of ways, including speaking in tongues, going into a possession trance, trance speaking, premonitions, and telepathy. Spiritualists believe that spirits of the dead make their presence known through a large variety of physical signs including movement of objects, making objects disappear, making sounds, discharging electric energy, leaving imprints, and changing the temperature of a room. Spiritualists view spiritualism as a distinct religion in that it explains the relationship between the human and supernatural worlds. At the same time some aspects of spiritualism, such as channeling and soul travel, are claimed by nonspiritualists and especially by some adherents of the New Age.

1849   Roman Catholic priest and leading Irish temperance reformer Theobald Mathew visits the United States, and during his travels through 1851 he persuades over 500,000 Catholics to take pledges of abstinence.   **MISC**

1849   The Mormon Church establishes the Perpetual Emigrating Fund to lend money to Mormons from Europe so that they can immigrate to Utah.   **MOR**

1849   The Leaders of the Mormon Church hold a constitutional convention to form a state they will call Deseret (which means "honey bee" in the *Book of Mormon*) composed of much of the western United States.   **MOR**

1849   Japan's government declares illegal the practices of the Shinto-based Fuji societies, whose members worship and conduct pilgrimages to Mount Fuji.   **SHINTO**

1849   The British take control of the Punjab region in India and the large Sikh population comes under British administration. The British view them as effective warriors and as possible allies against the Hindus and Muslims and begin recruiting Sikhs into the military in the next decades.   **SIKH**

1850   As the debate over liberal Catholicism continues in Europe, Catholic theologians and Church officials in much of Europe are divided into the liberal and the conservative or integrationist factions. They disagree about many basic issues, such as separation of church and state, religious freedom, civil education, and freedom of the press.   **CATH**

1850   With the revival of Roman Catholicism in Britain, bishops are again appointed in England. The growth of Catholicism is resisted by Protestants and leads to riots in 1852 directed at the Church and at the Irish.   **CATH, PROT**

1850   The United States creates the Territory of Utah, encompassing an area much smaller than that desired by the Mormons for their state of Deseret. Mormons and non-Mormons are chosen to govern the territory and conflict soon develops between the two factions.   **MOR**

1850   The Mormon Church founds the University of Deseret in Salt Lake City, Utah. The university later becomes the state-supported University of Utah. Mormon missionaries have been successful in western Europe and are active in nine nations there as well as in India, Hawaii, Chile, South Africa, and the Pacific Islands.   **MOR**

1850   A religious revival movement among the Sokulk people of Washington State is led by the warrior and Catholic Smohalla (c. 1818–1907). Following a near-death experience after being wounded in battle, he experiences visions and preaches that natives must reject white influence and return to their traditional way of life. He also advocates dancing as a way to transform the world. His adherents are called Dreamers and some continue to follow the movement in the 1990s.   **NATIV**

1850   The Greek Orthodox Church becomes an autocephalous church in the Orthodox Church.   ORTHO

1850   With India now under British control, Protestant missionary activity begins, with missionaries from North America and Europe forming missions throughout India. Protestant missionaries remain active in India until about 1900.   PROT

1850   Baptists in New York City who are unhappy with the use of the King James Version of the Bible by the American and Foreign Bible Society form their own Bible society, the American Bible Union, for the purpose of producing a new version of the Bible acceptable to Baptists.   PROT

1850   In Britain the competition between the National (Anglican) and British (non-Conformist) school systems has turned in favor of the National system, which has attracted the wealthier citizens and greater support from the government.   PROT

1850   Around this time in Japan, organizational changes alter the local structure of Shinto. The parish guilds or *miyaza* are being replaced by territorial parish organizations called *ujiko*. Regular priests rarely attend to small parish shrines, where the rites are performed by villagers chosen by lot or rotation to serve at the spring and autumn festivals and others. Those serving first must undergo certain purifications and abstinences.   SHINTO

1850s   A new type of religious music called gospel hymns begins to be sung in African-American churches. It is more melodic than traditional Protestant music and is a forerunner of modern gospel music.   AFRICAN

1850s   The social Catholicism movement develops in Germany, Italy, Belgium, and France as Catholic clergy begin to address the problems of workers that have resulted from industrialization and capitalism. They advocate such reforms as unions, labor laws (including child labor laws), and safety standards. The movement is also critical of socialism, liberalism, and uncontrolled capitalism.   CATH

1851   Henry Venn (1796–1873), secretary of the Anglican Church Missionary Society in England, establishes the policy that missionaries are to be concerned primarily with converting Africans to Christianity and not managing African churches. He encourages missionaries to aid Africans in establishing native congregations and to train native preachers. This policy plays a role in the emergence of independent African churches in Africa and the Caribbean later in the century.   AFRICAN, PROT

1851   The Young Men's Christian Association (YMCA) is founded in Boston, Massachusetts. It expands to become a leading religious, educational, recreational, and social welfare organization in American society.   CHRIS

1851   The Old Mormon Tabernacle is built in Salt Lake City, Utah.   MOR

1851	The Landmarker movement begins among Baptists in the southern United States. The movement is based on the principle that each Baptist church should be independent, following the model of the early Christian churches, and that no central body should have authority over the churches. The most important individual in the movement is Baptist publisher James Robinson Graves (1820–1893) in Tennessee. **PROT**
1851	With the expansion of Protestant missionary activity in 1833, there are now 19 Protestant groups with missionaries in India. However, the missionaries number only 399 and work in a population of some 150 million Hindus, Muslims, Sikhs, and Jains. **PROT**
1851	Although Protestant missionaries have had little success in Burma, they have made many converts among the Karen minority in eastern Burma. **PROT**
1851–1864	The Taiping Rebellion sweeps China, drawing strength from Chinese popular religion with its ghosts, spirits, and admixtures of Daoism, Buddhism, and, in the case of the Taiping leader Hong Xiquan, Christianity. Before it ends an estimated 25 million Chinese and foreigners are killed. **TOL**
1851–1868	Mongkut reigns as king of Thailand (under the name of Rama IV). He has spent some 27 years as a leading Buddhist monk, reforming Buddhist practices and supervising Buddhist education programs. He has studied English and Latin, as well as Western science and mathematics; as king, Mongkut

---

Gospel Music

Gospel music is the major form of religious musical expression in African-American churches. Since the 1940s it has also been a major form of public musical entertainment both for African-American and white audiences. Gospel music emerged as a major form of religious music only in the 1920s, but its origins go back to Africa and then to Protestant hymns and slave songs in the southern United States in the mid-17th century. Over the generations hymns, slave songs, spirituals, and slave banter came together to produce what is now known as gospel music. Gospel music is at its base an emotional expression of thanksgiving, praise, sorrow, and suffering. The melodies, harmonies, and rhythms of gospel are often simple and leave much room for improvisation and creative vocalizing to express the deep feelings embodied in the music and shared by the congregation. Since the 1940s gospel music has spread well beyond African-American churches and is now a common component of worship in some Methodist, Baptist, and Pentecostal churches. Gospel has also influenced other forms of music, including jazz, rock and roll, and rhythm and blues, and many well-known performers, such as Sam Cooke, Mahalia Jackson, Edwin Hawkins, Ray Charles, Stevie Wonder, Aretha Franklin, and James Brown, have either been gospel singers or have incorporated gospel into their music. Since 1961 a Grammy Award has been awarded annually for gospel music.

attempts legal reforms, improves the condition of slaves, and permits women some choice in marriage. He rules with help from hired foreign advisers, including the famous Anna Leonowens, whose accounts of her time as a tutor at the court will become the basis of the Rodgers and Hammerstein musical *The King and I*. **BUDD, TOL**

1852   The Catholic Church under Pope Pius IX sides with the ultramontanes in their conflict with the liberals, prohibits councils by bishops, and encourages clergy to consult directly with the Vatican on Church matters. **CATH**

1852   A Muslim *jihad* (holy war) against lapsed Muslims, non-Muslims, and Europeans led by religious reformer al-Hajj Umar (c. 1794–1864) takes place in the Senegambia region of West Africa. The *jihad* is successful in taking Futa Toro but is halted by the French. **ISLAM**

1852   The Buganda kingdom of East Africa adopts Islam under the leadership of Kabaka Mutesa, who sees Islam as a unifying force that can replace the existing indigenous religions. Islam is brought to the region by Muslim traders from the East Africa coast. **ISLAM**

1852   The New Organization of the Church is formed by Mormons in Illinois who did not move to Utah in 1847. Among its members are the family of Joseph Smith, the founder of the Mormon Church. It later becomes the Reorganized Church of Jesus Christ of Latter-Day Saints (RLDS) and relocates to Independence, Missouri. **SEE 1978, MOR**. **MOR**

1852   In Britain the authority of the Church of England is weakened when Parliament enacts a law that sets aside space in cemeteries for the burial of members of other Protestant denominations. However, it is not until 1880 that ministers from other denominations are allowed to officiate at funerals in the cemeteries. **PROT**

1852   The Congregational Church in the United States formally ends the Plan of Union enacted with the Presbyterian Church in 1801. The Plan had been ended by the Presbyterians in 1837. **PROT**

1852   *Uncle Tom's Cabin* is written by Congregational teacher Harriet Beecher Stowe (1811–1896), the daughter of minister Lyman Beecher. By depicting slaves as human beings, rather than as chattel or beasts, and vividly describing the cruelty of their owners, the book plays a major role in turning Northerners in the United States against slavery. **PROT**

1853   The first Chinese temple in the Americas is built in San Francisco's Chinatown. By 1900 there are 400 such shrines on the West Coast. These syncretistic temples enshrine popular folk deities and include elements of Buddhism, Daoism, and Confucianism. **BUDD, CONF**

1853   Taiping rebels advancing northward from Nanjing under the charismatic leader Hong Xiquan (1814–1864) destroy Confucian, Buddhist, and Daoist temples and monasteries, some a thousand years old. For the most part, Buddhist and Daoist priests and nuns take flight on the approach of the insurgents, for Hong regards them as leaders of competitive ideologies of rebellion. Daoism and Buddhism, he tells his followers, are false teachings of the devil.   **DAO**

1853   The Belokrinits Accord, a group of Russian Old Believers (a heretical sect within Russian Orthodoxy), establish a diocese in Moscow that remains the group's headquarters. With about 800,000 members in the 1990s, they are the largest Old Believer group in existence.   **ORTHO**

1853   Congregational churches in the United States form the American Congregational Union. Although each church remains independent, the formation of a central association is an important step in the emergence of Congregationalism as a distinct denomination.   **PROT**

1853   In the United States the New Hampshire Confession of Faith is published as part of the *Baptist Church Manual*, affording it much influence in Baptist churches.   **PROT**

1853   Baha'u'llah, an early follower of the *Bab* (d. 1892), emerges as the new leader of the Babis in Iran. Over the next few years he is imprisoned by Muslim authorities, writes a number of Baha'i texts, and seeks converts. He is the author of the three primary texts of Baha'i: *Most Holy Book*, the *Book of Certitude*, and the *Book of Covenant*.   **SECT**

1853   The arrival of United States commodore Matthew Perry's warships in Japan, posing the threat of foreign invasion, and the shogun government's vacillating response galvanize activist factions. Government opponents will take up the slogan *Sonno joi* (revere the Emperor, drive out the barbarian), and the National Learning movement will intensify the promotion of its agenda to unify Japan through the common worship of the ancient Shinto deities.   **SHINTO**

1854   The doctrine of Immaculate Conception in Roman Catholicism is made dogma by Pope Pius IX.   **CATH**

1854   The Young Men's Hebrew Association (YMHA) is founded in Baltimore, Maryland, as a community center for Jewish men. After 1965 centers develop in Jewish communities in the South and Midwest with an emphasis on sports and recreation.   **JUD**

1854   In Britain Oxford University allows non-Anglican Protestants to study for the B.A. degree for the first time. Cambridge follows suit in 1856.   **PROT**

1854   In the United States, as Lutheranism continues to spread in the Midwest, the Evangelical Synod of Iowa and Other States is formed.   **PROT**

1854   The Society of True Inspiration relocates from Erie County, New York (where they settled in 1842), to Iowa County, Iowa, where more farm land is available for purchase. They establish farming villages and in 1859 incorporate as the Amana Society.   **PROT**

1855   The Young Women's Christian Association (YWCA) is founded in Great Britain.   **CHRIS**

1855   In Egypt the government seeks to limit the influence of Islamic scholars and local Muslim teachers by giving broad administrative power to a *shaykh* (leader) who follows government policies regarding religion.   **ISLAM**

1855   Muslims who are members of the Tokulor ethnic group in West Africa initiate a *jihad* (holy war) against kingdoms ruled by the non-Muslim Bambara people. They conquer the kingdoms of Kaarta (1855), Segu (1861), and Hamdallahi (1862). They are unable to unify the region, and from 1864 until the French conquer the region in the 1890s, it is racked by internal fighting among Muslims competing for control.   **ISLAM**

1855   Jew's College is founded in London as a seminary to train Orthodox Jewish rabbis and teachers for work in Great Britain and the United States.   **JUD**

1855   American Congregational missionaries establish a mission in Brazil, where they seek converts among Roman Catholic Brazilians. In the next year a similar mission is established by Presbyterians in Colombia. These two missions mark the beginning of missionary efforts by many Protestant denominations among Catholics in Latin America.   **PROT**

1855   Following the arrival of Dutch missionaries, a series of revitalization movements takes place among the peoples of Irian Jaya in Indonesia that continues into the 1940s. Although there are numerous prophets who lead the revitalization cults, they all take similar forms, with worship of the divine being Manseren, ritual dancing to hasten his return to earth, and the hope that his return will bring a better world.   **SECT**

1855   A spiritual movement known as *Spiritisme* is founded by Leon Rivail (1804–1869), a Parisian schoolteacher and translator. Rivail, believing that he has communicated with a Druid named Allan Kardec, changes his name to Allan Kardec, and the movement, now called Kardecism, spreads to Spain. Kardecism draws on beliefs from a number of religions and philosophies and has as its ultimate purpose the fusing of thought and spirituality.   **SPIR**

1856   Wilberforce University in Ohio is founded by Bishop Donald Payne of the African Methodist Episcopal Church. The church is instrumental in founding a number of African-American colleges, including Allen in Columbia, South Carolina (1870), Morris Brown in Atlanta (1881), and Edward Waters in Jacksonville, Florida (1901).   **AFRICAN**

1856   In Egypt during the period of Ottoman rule, the Hamaiouni Line law is enacted, which effectively prohibits Christian denominations from building new churches and from rehabilitating old ones. The law remains in effect in the 1990s and is used to control the spread of the Coptic Christian Church in Egypt.   **CHRIS, TOL**

1856   Muslim intellectuals and landowners in India respond to British rule by initiating policies designed to allow them to live under the British regime. The leader of the movement, Sir Sayyid Ahmad Khan, a government official, in this year founds the National Mohammadan Association and in later years founds other literary and scientific societies meant to expose Indian Muslims to the modern world.   **ISLAM**

1856   In the negotiations that end the Crimean War (1853–1856), the British, French, and Austrians impose the Illustrious Rescript edict of 1856 (*Hat-I Humayan*) on Turkey. The edict moves Turkey toward secularization, as it gives new rights to non-Muslims and weakens the power of Muslims and Christian religious leaders.   **ISLAM**

1856   Muslims in Yunnan Province in China revolt against the weak Qing dynasty and establish a Muslim state that lasts until 1873.   **ISLAM**

1856   Rufus Anderson (1796–1880), corresponding secretary of the American Missionary Board, establishes the "three-self" formula that states missionaries should attempt to develop churches in Africa and elsewhere that will be "self-governing, self-supporting, and self-propagating." This policy remains influential among Protestant missionaries until the 1940s.   **PROT**

1856–   The !Xhosa cattle sacrifice takes place in South Africa. The sacrifice is set off
1857   by a woman named Nongqause (c. 1840–c. 1900), who communicates a dream about a prosperous new age free of European rule that will take place following a massive sacrifice of cattle. Some 15,000 cattle and crops are destroyed, and when the prophecy fails to come true, Nongqause is placed under British protection while her uncle is killed by the !Xhosa. The !Xhosa suffer massive starvation and death.   **AFRICAN**

1857   Bengali Muslim units of the British Indian Army revolt when they are given new cartridges that are believed to be greased with the fat from pigs and cows, which is offensive to both Hindu and Muslim beliefs. The mutiny is the start of the Revolt of 1857 or the Sepoy Rebellion against British rule. The British repress the revolt and place more blame on the Muslims than on the Hindus, although both are involved. Muslims respond by abandoning armed resistance and instead seek accommodation with the British and the Western world while maintaining Islamic traditions.   **HIND, ISLAM**

1857   Persia (Iran), which had lost considerable territory to Russia and Britain earlier in the century, becomes an important economic resource for Russia and Britain. Contact with these European nations leads the Persian government to move toward Westernization and modernization, with economic, administrative, and military reforms instituted, often with British and Russian assistance. The major opponents of modernization are the Muslim scholars who had previously enjoyed much influence but whose activities are now repressed by the government. **ISLAM**

1857   The first Jewish prayer book written for American Jews, the *Minhag America*, is written by Rabbi Isaac Meyer Wise (1814–1900) in Cincinnati.   **JUD**

1857   A period of religious revitalization by the Mormons, combined with ongoing political conflict between Mormons and non-Mormons, creates fear among non-Mormons, and the United States government launches the Utah Expedition, in which troops enter the territory. The short-lived Mormon War involves a series of skirmishes, property burnings, and relocations by Mormons and ultimately the stationing of troops near Salt Lake City.   **MOR**

1857   In India the Revolt of 1857 takes place when Indians revolt against British rule. Some 60 missionaries are killed in the revolt, although antimissionary activity is confined mainly to the north.   **PROT**

1857   *Missionary Travels and Researches in South Africa* by Protestant missionary David Livingstone is published. The book plays a major role in stimulating British interest in the commercial potential of the region.   **PROT**

1857   In South Africa the separatist Nederduitse Gereformeerde Kerk (NGK) Dutch Reformed Church rules that racial segregation can be permitted in the church.   **PROT**

1857   In the United States the New School branch of Presbyterianism condemns slavery, and Southerners withdraw and form the United Synod of the Presbyterian Church in the United States of America. The breach between the two groups deepens in 1861, when the Northerners support the Union and the Southerners form the Presbyterian Church in the Confederated States of America.   **PROT**

1857   The Kuka sect (also known as *Namdhari*), a Sikh revival movement, is founded by Baba Ram Singh, a carpenter in India. The sect emphasizes emotional worship, repetitive rituals, and opposition to British rule in India. In the 1990s the sect has about 500,000 adherents.   **SIKH**

1857   The French spiritual movement known as *Spiritisme*, which began in 1855, emerges in Brazil and in Latin America, where it is called Kardecism. Based on a mix of Christianity, modern science, and mysticism, the movement attracts mainly upper- and middle-class followers in Cuba, Puerto Rico, and Brazil. It later spreads to the lower classes, where it is often combined with Roman Catholicism. It is not a unified movement and contains a number of distinct groups, such as the Umbanda and the Kardecist Spiritualists, who vie for followers and government acceptance.   **SPIR**

1858   (St.) Bernadette (1844–1879), a 14-year-old peasant, experiences 18 visions of a woman identified as the Immaculate Conception over a six-month period near a spring in Lourdes, France. The visions are investigated by the Catholic Church and accepted as authentic, and Lourdes is made a major pilgrimage site for Catholics.   **CATH**

1858   The Society of Missionary Priests of Saint Paul the Apostle, known as the Paulists, is founded in New York City as the first Roman Catholic society for men founded in the United States. **SEE 1866, CATH**.   **CATH**

1858   The Young Women's Christian Association (YWCA) is established in the United States. It expands to become a leading religious, educational, recreational, and social welfare organization in American society.   **CHRIS**

1858   Following the establishment of relations between the United States and Japan in 1854, missionary activity resumes in Japan. Roman Catholic missionaries arrive in 1858 and Protestant missionaries in 1859, with Reformed, Episcopal, Presbyterian, and Baptist missionaries active by 1869.   **CHRIS**

1858   The Baniwa people of northern Brazil participate in a millennial movement led by Venancio Christo in which he predicts the end of the world, to be followed by a prosperous era that followers can bring into being by ritual dancing. The movement fades without making any long-term impact.   **NATIV**

1859   The American College in Rome and other seminaries are established by the Catholic Church. Their purpose is to train clergy who will be loyal to the Vatican.   **CATH**

1859   The Board of Delegates of American Israelites is founded in the United States to speak for American Jews about issues of Jewish interest. It ceases to exist in 1878, when it is replaced by spokesmen for Reform Judaism.   **JUD**

1859   *The Origin of Species by Means of Natural Selection* by Charles Darwin is published and is followed by his *The Descent of Man* in 1871. Both works are based on evolutionary theory, which calls into question the accuracy of the Judeo-Christian version of Genesis.   **MISC**

1859   The Romanian Orthodox Church becomes an autocephalous church in the Orthodox Church.   **ORTHO**

1859   The Second Evangelical Awakening in Britain begins. Over the next several decades it attracts millions of people to the non-Conforming churches (Baptist, Methodist, Congregational) and in Britain also leads to the founding of new churches, such as the Salvation Army.   **PROT**

1859   The Finnish Missionary Society is formed by Lutherans in Finland and supports missionary work in Africa.   **PROT**

1859	Another new Japanese religion arises with the founding of Konkokyo (Golden Light teaching) by farmer Kawate Bunjiro (1814–1883) following a divine revelation. The Shinto-inspired syncretist cult will become an official Shinto sect in 1900 and will begin to spread its activity to China and Korea. Although officially classified as a form of Shinto, it deviates from Shinto in a number of ways, including the emphasis on personal, rather than group, salvation. **SECT, SHINTO**
1859–1860	The First Vatican Council (Vatican I) is convened by Pope Pius IX in Rome. In matters of faith (*Dei Filius*), it supports positions advocated by St. Thomas Aquinas. More controversial is its *Pastor Aeternus,* which, for the time being, settles the conflict between the liberals and ultramontanes by establishing the primacy of the papacy and the doctrine of papal infallibility when he is speaking of matters of faith and morals. **CATH**
1860	Roman Catholicism is reestablished as the official religion of Haiti. It draws most of its followers from the urban elite, while Voudou continues to draw most of its adherents from among rural farmers. **AFRICAN , CATH**
1860	Liberal Catholics have come to power in northern Italy and as part of the political unification of Italy, they attack and take control of the Papal States, leaving the papacy in control only of Rome and its suburbs. **CATH**
1860	The Franciscan missionary effort among the Huichol of northwestern Mexico ends because of political unrest in the region. Many Huichol have resisted assimilation into Mexican society, and in some communities much of the traditional religion based on shamanism survives. **SEE 1950s CATH, NATIV.** **CATH, NATIV**
1860	The New Apostolic Church is founded as an offshoot of the Old Apostolic Church in Germany. It becomes an established Christian church with over two million members in the 1990s. **CHRIS**
1860	Confucian traditionalist Feng Gui-fen (1809–1874) establishes the attitude toward the West that will dominate Chinese thinking until the end of the century. An assistant to Lin Zi-xu, who seized and destroyed British opium in Canton (1839), he coins the term *zi-qiang* (self-strengthening) as the proper attitude of the Chinese toward the Western threat. He recommends establishing translation centers and the study of Western mathematics, physics, chemistry, and medicine but only to supplement Chinese ethics and Confucian teachings, especially in armaments. **CONF**
1860	*Lectures: On Revivals of Religion* is written by American Evangelical preacher Charles Finney (1792–1875). The book instructs Evangelical preachers on how to organize and conduct revival meetings and how to convert people to Christ. Finney stresses the use of emotional appeals, sales techniques, and biblical literalism, a model that continues to be followed in the late 20th century by Evangelical preachers. **EVAN**

1860	The Muslims and French in West Africa agree to a division of territory under their control. The French control Futa Toro while the Muslims are given territory controlled by the Bambara people in the interior. **ISLAM**
1860	The Perkins Professorship of Natural Science in Connection with Revelation is established at the Columbia Theological Seminary. It is the first professorship established in the United States for the study of science and religion. **MISC**
1860	Members of the Seventh-Day Adventists, who have been called Believers in the Second Advent and Sabbath-Keepers after two of their major doctrines, formally take the name Seventh-Day Adventist at a meeting in Battle Creek, Michigan. **SECT**
1860	In Lebanon economic unrest inflames religious antagonisms and the Druze, with Muslim support, attack the Maronite Christians. European nations send naval fleets to support the Maronites and the French send an army into the Mount Lebanon region. **TOL**
1860s	In the shrinking and weakened Muslim Ottoman Empire, a group of intellectual reformers called the Young Ottomans calls for basic changes in Ottoman society that combine Islam, the Turkish language, and accommodation to the modern world. The movement lasts until 1876 when a new Ottoman Sultan (Abd al-Hamid II) initially supports the Young Ottoman agenda and then reverses himself and initiates a return to Islam as the basis of Ottoman society. **ISLAM**
1860s	A basic division emerges in Amish communities in the United States between those who adhere to traditional ways, including not using new technology and limited contact with non-Amish, and those who advocate more contact and limited use of technology. The former are labeled the Old Order Amish, the latter the New Order Amish. **SECT**
1860–1861	The Great Revival takes place among former African slaves in Jamaica, many of whom are followers of the indigenous Myal religion, as well as various denominations of Christianity. The Myal religion is transformed into two new religions, Zion and Pukumina. Zion continues to emphasize Christian beliefs while Pukumina contains more African religious elements, including the control of evil spirits. **AFRICAN**
1861	The "Battle Hymn of the Republic" is written by medical worker Julia Ward Howard in Washington, D.C. Although mainly sung as a patriotic song, it also becomes a part of the hymnal of a number of churches in the United States. **CHRIS**
1861	The English word *analects* is first used by James Legge (1815–1897), pioneer British translator of the Confucian *Lun Yu.* The word originally meant "lit-

erary gleanings"; a more exact translation of *Lun Yu* may be "ethical dialogues," but use of *Analects* becomes a tradition.   **CONF**

1861   The British colonize Lagos in West Africa, an important center of Muslim culture in the region.   **ISLAM**

1861   A Russian Orthodox mission is established in Japan by Nikolai (Ivan Kasatkin, ?–1912), who is later named the archbishop of Tokyo. It was one of the more successful of Christian missions in Japan.   **ORTHO**

1861   Hymns, which were already commonly used in non-Anglican Protestant churches in Great Britain, come into common use in the Anglican Church with the publication of *Hymns Ancient and Modern*.   **PROT**

1861   The Radhasoami Sikh movement begins in India. Later in the century it spawns the Beas Satsang sect, which attracts many Hindu followers in the 1990s but is not accepted as a branch of Sikhism by many other Sikhs. It diverges from mainstream Sikhism in having its own line of gurus and in various religious beliefs and practices, as well as its many Hindu followers.   **SIKH**

1861   To end the fighting between the Maronite Christians, Druze, and Muslims in Lebanon, the Ottoman Empire, under European pressure, establishes a new governmental structure with the president a Christian and the other religious groups represented on a national council.   **TOL**

1862   For both religious and political reasons (local settlers and the federal government both fear Mormon control of the region), the United States Congress bans plural marriage and also revokes Church incorporation, although the law is not yet enforced.   **MOR**

1862   In Japan's new religion Kurozumikyo, the founder's disciple establishes Munetada shrine in Kyoto as a designated site for imperial prayers, as its numbers of believers increase among the nobility. The shrine will become a base of the movement to revere the emperor. After a half century in existence, Kurozumikyo will increase the number of its adherents to some 200,000.   **SECT, SHINTO**

1862–
1874   The Chongxu temple on holy Mount Longhu in China's Guangdong Province is rebuilt.   **DAO**

1863   Thanksgiving Day is proclaimed a national holiday in the United States by President Abraham Lincoln. Although it is a secular holiday, it has a clear religious component, as it is generally understood that thanks are given to God.   **SECT**

1863   Olympia Brown (1835–1926) is ordained a Universalist minister. She is the first woman ordained in any Christian denomination.   **SECT**

| 1863 | The Seventh-Day Adventist Church is formally organized as a denomination at Battle Creek, Michigan. In 1903 they move their headquarters to Washington, D.C. **SECT** |

1864   Robert Childers, an Englishman, leaves Sri Lanka, where he has been working since 1856, for Britain's Ceylon Civil Service, and T. H. Rhys Davids, another Englishman, arrives in Sri Lanka to join that same service. Childers had studied the Pali Buddhist texts and on returning to England continues his studies, eventually publishing the two-volume *Dictionary of the Pali Language* (1872 and 1875). Rhys Davids will leave the Ceylon Civil Service in 1872, return to England, and through his research, translations, lectures, and many publications become one of the pioneering students and promoters of Buddhism in the West. **BUDD**

1864   Pope Pius IX publishes his *Syllabus of Errors*, in which he condemns the liberal movement in the Catholic Church and thereby ends any chance for reforms. The document causes much discussion in the Catholic community, as it seems to condemn modernization and progress and the modern world. **CATH**

1864   Zeng Guofan (Tseng Kuo-fan, canonized name Wen-cheng) (1811–1872), longtime Confucian scholar at the elite Hanlin Academy, suppresses the costly Taiping Rebellion and captures the rebel capital of Nanking, preserving the imperial regime. He earlier serves as vice president of the Boards of Defense, Works, Justice, and Finance. After 1928 conservatives such as the Kuomintang or Nationalist Chinese leaders hail him as a symbol of Confucianism and model of moral cultivation, while revolutionaries criticize him. **CONF**

1864   Muslims from West Africa attack and take control of the inland Muslim state of Masina and rule until 1893, when it comes under French rule. The Muslims in Masina bitterly protest the attack as a war pitting Muslim against Muslim. **ISLAM**

1864   The term *New Age* is used for perhaps the first time in print by Warren Felt Evans in his *The New Age and Its Message*. **SPIR**

1865   Jews are given civil rights in Sweden. **JUD**

1865   The Philosophical Society of Great Britain (the Victoria Institute) is founded to combat the evolutionary theory of Charles Darwin. **MISC**

1865   The Mormon Church sends missionaries to eastern Europe. Their efforts are not especially successful. **MOR**

1865   The Savoy Declaration, a basic statement of Congregational belief set forth in England in 1658 and later adopted by Congregational churches in the Americas, is declared as the basic statement of faith by a council of

1865   American Congregational churches. Although each church is autonomous and so not bound to accept it, most do so.   **PROT**

1865   The Salvation Army is founded when William Booth (1829–1912), a Methodist minister, conducts a tent meeting of his new Christian Mission in London. Booth and his wife, Catherine Mumford Booth (1829–1890), are credited with founding the movement.   **PROT**

1865   Representatives of Congregational churches in the United States meet in Boston and adopt the Burial Hill Declaration, which sets forth the basic doctrine, mission, and structure of the Congregational Church in the United States. Although each church remains independent, the Declaration effectively establishes Congregationalism as a distinct denomination with some centralized control.   **PROT**

1865–1875   In the United States the various Lutheran synods and churches undergo a period of reorganization as smaller groups unite to form new associations. In 1866 associations from Pennsylvania, New York, Ohio, Michigan, Minnesota, Illinois, Iowa, and Canada form the General Council. In 1872 several synods that had associated with the Missouri Synod draw together and form the Synodical Conference. Synods in the South had unified during the Civil War as the Synod of the South.   **PROT**

1866   The Paulists found the Catholic Publication Society, later called the Paulist Press, as a vehicle for seeking converts to Roman Catholicism.   **CATH**

1866   In order to establish European and Christian dominance in Lebanon, the French establish the Syrian Protestant College (later the American University of Beirut) and in 1875 the University of St. Joseph.   **CHRIS**

1866   The curriculum in American Sunday schools begins to be made uniform through the work of religious educator John H. Vincent in New York. In 1870 the *Berean Series* of lessons is published and the *International Series* in 1873.   **CHRIS**

1866   The first Eastern Orthodox church is established in the United States, in New Orleans. Although Orthodox Christians have been in America since the early 1600s, they have remained a small and invisible minority.   **ORTHO**

1866   In New York City the Baptist American Bible Union produces a new version of the Bible acceptable to Baptists. The new version is much like the King James Version they had rejected in 1850, except that it refers to immersion rather than to baptism. It is the only version ever produced by the union.   **PROT**

1866   During the Civil War in the United States, the Methodist Church in the South, which had separated from the Northern church over the issue of slavery in 1845, is devastated. The Northern church enters the region and begins to rebuild the church, although its actions are often resented by the

Southerners. The Northerners establish the Freedmen's Aid and Education Society to assist freed slaves.   PROT

1866   The Women's Commonwealth (also called the Sanctificationists) is founded by Martha McWhirter in Belton, Texas. It is a women's group based on celibacy, the search for a perfect Christian life, and creating financial independence from spouses. The group is successful and by 1899 has about 40 members, including four men, and owns three farms and a hotel. In 1899 they sell the hotel and relocate to Washington, D.C. The group dissolves in the 1930s when the last of the members dies.   SECT

1866   The small Babi group in Iran divides into two. One group, the Azalis, soon disappear. The other group, which follows Baha'u'llah, takes his name and becomes the Baha'i. Later that year Baha'u'llah claims to be the divine presence on earth and is accepted as such by many of his Babi followers.   SECT

1866   Mary Baker Eddy (1821–1910), who later founds the Church of Christ, Scientist (Christian Scientists), severely injures herself in a fall in Lynn, Massachusetts. Ignoring the dire prognosis of her physician, she effects a partial cure by reading of a healing miracle by Christ in the Bible. She calls the healing process Christian Science and over the next three years develops the basic theology for the church.   SECT

Christian Science

Christian Science or the Church of Christ, Scientist is an American Christian religion founded by Mary Baker Eddy in Boston, Massachusetts, in 1879. It is one of only a few Christian religions founded in the United States and the only one whose sole founder was a woman. Christian Science combines Protestant Christianity as reflected in the Bible, metaphysics, and religious healing into a unique religion with beliefs and practices that deviate from other forms of Christianity. The basic text of Christian Science is *Science and Health with Key to the Scriptures* written by Eddy in 1876. The Bible is also used, as are materials prepared by the church's central office in Boston that are used in the Sunday prayer services. In addition to Sunday group and private prayer, there are weekly meetings that focus on healing experiences and two ceremonies a year centered on Christ's meal beside Lake Galilee. Christian Scientists do not celebrate Christmas or Easter and celebrate Christ for his humanity rather than his divinity. Christian Science is a worldwide religion with about 500,000 adherents in some 50 nations. However, its presence is much stronger than its small numbers suggest, with attention brought to the group through its newspaper the *Christian Science Monitor*, which began publication in 1908, and its Christian Science reading rooms in many cities and towns. Christian Science devotees have also gained much media attention for their reluctance to use modern medicine to cure or prevent illness. Following Eddy's example, adherents prefer to use prayer instead. Especially when children are involved, Christian Scientists are sometimes criticized for refusing medical intervention.

1866	The Ku Klux Klan is founded in Pulaski, Tennessee. This, the first of three different organizations to be so called, is primarily a social club but later beomes a vigilante or paramilitary group organized to resist Reconstruction. Its focus gradually shifts to destroying the Republican Party—the party of Lincoln and the Union, and therefore the antislavery party—and keeping newly freed African-American former slaves "in their place." In hopes of achieving these ends, the Klan uses such terrorist tactics as lynching, firebombing houses and businesses, cross burnings, and intimidation. Later, in the 1920s, the Klan's second incarnation appears and this time expands its target to include Catholics, Jews, immigrants, labor unions, and "bolsheviks." The Klan's third incarnation appears in the 1950s, probably spurred by the era's anti-Communist rhetoric and the burgeoning Civil Rights movement. It continues to exist as a white supremacist movement in the 1990s. TOL
1867	The Consolidated American Baptist Missionary Convention is founded in Nashville, Tennessee. It is the first national organization designed to serve all Baptist African-Americans and lasts for 12 years before dissolving into regional organizations. AFRICAN
1867	As a gesture of goodwill, King Mongkut of Thailand allows the Prabang Buddha (SEE 1805–1828, BUDD) to be returned to Luang Prabang, Laos, where it remains in the 1990s. BUDD
1867	The American Protective Association is founded in Iowa. It is an anti-Catholic organization that gains followers and political strength in the Midwest in the 1880s and 1890s in response to economic problems and anti-immigrant sentiments and then declines and folds in 1911. CATH
1867	The Holiness movement among American Protestants begins when some Methodists establish the national Camp Meeting Association for the Promotion of Holiness. The association's main activity is the convening of outdoor camp meetings with preaching and emotional worship. In the 1880s and 1890s the movement dissolves into a number of separate Holiness movements and churches. EVAN
1867	In Ethiopia Menelik II becomes king and rules until 1913. He unifies the Christian and non-Christian communities and moves to absorb the Muslim regions under Christian rule. ISLAM
1867	Deoband College is founded by Muslims in northern India. It offers a reform curriculum that combines the teaching of Islamic law and religion with the modern sciences and philosophy. It attracts students from across South India, who go on to establish some 40 branch campuses, and becomes the focus of modern form of Indian Islam. ISLAM
1867	Jews are granted civil rights in the Austro-Hungarian Empire. JUD
1867	A new Mormon Tabernacle is built in Salt Lake City. MOR

1867   After the United States purchases Alaska from Russia, missionaries become active in Alaska, seeking converts among the Native Americans. Over the next 20 years missions are established by Moravians, Presbyterians, Congregationalists, Roman Catholics, and other denominations.   NATIV

1867   In Britain the first Lambeth Conference, a meeting of Anglican bishops, is held. The conference, which meets periodically from then on, becomes a major mechanism for maintaining unity in the Anglican Church, which has no centralized hierarchy.   PROT

1867   Nakayama Miki, the founder of Japan's new religion Tenrikyo (SEE 1838, SECT, SHINTO), composes the scripture *Mikagura Uta* (*Dancing Psalms*). She will add to this text from 1871 to 1875.   SHINTO, SECT

1867–1879   The Quakers in the United States undergo a number of major transformations, including the increasing use of evangelical forms of prayer and preaching, missionary activities among Native Americans in the midwest, the experience of more dramatic forms of conversion, and the establishment of a pastoral system.   PROT

1867–1901   These years cover the lifespan of Rayacandra Mehta, a jeweler and poet whose life and work inspired the founding of the Jain school known as Kanji Panth. It includes both Svetambara and Digambara beliefs, worships the image of the founder, and recognizes among its canonical texts the *Sriman Rayacandra*, letters written by Rayacandra to various people. There are no monks or nuns in the Kanji Panth school. In the 20th century Mohandas Gandhi, the leader of the Indian independence movement, will give credit to Rayacandra and his school for influencing his ideas on non-violence as a political tactic.   JAIN

1868   Japan's government sets up the Shinto Section (*jingika*), which becomes the Shinto Office (*jingi-jimukyoku*) and then is replaced by the department of Shinto, or department of Divinity (*jingikan*). An April 20 edict separates Shinto and Buddhism, and in May all Buddhist priests associated with Shinto shrines (long a focus of resentment and protest by Shinto priests), along with their statues and artifacts, are ordered removed from the shrines. Some see the Buddhist purge as an occasion for looting and destruction of Buddhist temples. The imperial palace also is cleared of Buddhist influence: its annual rites there are ended and imperial family members who are Buddhist monks are laicized.   BUDD, SHINTO

1868   Militant Japanese nationalists inspired by the Confucian writings of Yamaga Soko (1622–1685) overthrow the Tokugawa Shogunate and restore direct imperial rule. To stabilize rule Emperor Mutsuhito issues the Charter Oath in his name. It seeks to unify the allegiance of all classes and thereby open the way to approved social and political change. The government decrees the separation of Shinto and Buddhism and effectively establishes Shintoism as the state religion. Buddhist priests are to give up vows and leave Shinto shrines to return to laity. At the same time the emperor issues *Gobo no Keiji* (*Five Public Notices*): upholding traditional Confucian values, banning criminal behavior, outlawing Christianity and other sects considered heterodox, prohibiting injury to foreigners, and proscribing travel outside Japan. Except for the ban on injuring foreigners, the notices are mostly ignored.   **BUDD, SHINTO**

1868   The Society of Missionaries of Africa (commonly called the White Fathers for their white cassock and mantle) is founded by Cardinal Lavigerie (1825–1892), the archbishop of Algiers. The society is composed of priests and brothers and plays a major role in Roman Catholic missionary work in Africa and also in speaking against slavery.   **CATH**

1868   In Great Britain, as the role and authority of the Church of England continues to diminish, John Bright becomes the first non-Anglican Protestant elected to Parliament.   **PROT**

1868   The Ringatu Maori religion is established in New Zealand by Te Kooti Rikirangi (c. 1830–1893), a Maori imprisoned by the British. The movement initially stresses the Old Testament mixed with Maori beliefs but develops in the 19th century by adding other Christian elements.   **SECT**

1868   With the Meiji Restoration the imperial house returns to power in Japan and modernizing reform sweeps away the feudal system. The emperor breaks with tradition and, beginning with a visit to Atsuta, starts to visit Shinto shrines in person; previously the emperor sent proxies to shrines with imperial offerings. In 1869 he will pay personal tribute at Ise, which received its last imperial visit in the seventh century. The Ise shrine rites will be coordinated with those in the imperial palace, which is also a religious institution enshrining certain deities. When Emperor Meiji conducts palace rites, the populace is informed of his activity. With the government goal of *saisei itchi* (unity of religious ritual and government administration), a brief golden era begins for Shinto. In the official plan to create a unifying ideology, belief in the emperor's divinity and in the uniqueness of Japan's national polity (*kokutai*) holds a central place.   **SHINTO**

1868– The Fifth Buddhist Council is convened in Myanmar by King Mindon (r.
1871   1853–1887); its major accomplishment is to create a revised edition of the Pali-language Tripitaka, which King Mindon then has engraved on 729 marble slabs. A former Buddhist monk, he promotes a more progressive Buddhism while founding a new, more traditional order of monks, the Schwegon Nikaya.   **BUDD, TOL**

1868– These years mark the lifespan of Vijaya Dharma Suri, a Jain teacher credited
1922   with renewing Jainism.   **JAIN**

| 1868–1972 | The Kuka Sikh sect in India attacks Muslims in the Sikh sacred city of Amritsar. In response the British government executes Sikh rioters and forces the sect leader Baba Ram into exile in Burma. **ISLAM, SIKH** |

1868–
1972
The Kuka Sikh sect in India attacks Muslims in the Sikh sacred city of Amritsar. In response the British government executes Sikh rioters and forces the sect leader Baba Ram into exile in Burma. **ISLAM, SIKH**

1869
In Finland religious freedom is given to Christians who are not Lutherans. **CHRIS, TOL**

1869
The term *agnostic* is first used by the British biologist Thomas H. Huxley, a strong proponent of evolution, to distinguish between those who doubt and those who deny the existence of God. (Huxley's enemies later called him "doubting Thomas," a play on the epithet applied to the apostle who initially questioned the reality of Jesus's resurrection.) **MISC**

1869
Japan's governmental Department of Divinity assumes central control of all Shinto priests and ends the system of licensing priests and shrines by the Yoshida and Shirakawa houses. Hence, some shrine priests are ousted and replaced by people previously uninvolved in shrine affairs, while others are recertified by the local government and are permitted to stay. Hereditary succession to the priesthood will be banned in 1871. An edict dismisses many women employed at shrines as mediums and as performers of sacred dance; they are denied the option of recertification. The Yoshida and Shirakawa are able to retain power over the cults of the tutelary deities of the imperial house. All shrines are officially ranked in a single hierarchy under Ise, with a distinction between the 29 shrines for imperial rites and the prefectural shrines. In August the department of Divinity is granted a position in government higher than that of the Grand Council of State. Internal disagreements divide the Department over Shinto's pastoral role and over whether Shinto is or is not a religion. **SHINTO**

1869
Yasukuni (initially named Shokonsha) shrine is established in Tokyo to memorialize those who have died in battle for Japan since 1853; in June 3,588 fallen soldiers are enshrined. In 1872 the nation's only public military museum will open there. **SHINTO**

1869
Nand Singh (1869–1943) is born in India. He later emerges as one of a number of major Sikh *sants* (pious men who often attract followers) and founds the Nanaksar movement. Most of these movements are accepted by mainstream Sikhs, although they often differ in beliefs and practices, such as attire, austerity requirements, and form of prayer. **SIKH**

1869–
1948
Mohandas Gandhi (1869–1948) lives and during his lifetime becomes the leader of the movement for Indian independence from Britain and an advocate of social justice. His political philosophy is based in Hinduism and rests on the idea that truth, God, and the self are the same. **HIND**

c. 1870
The Hindu Renaissance begins in India. It is an effort to reform Hinduism and Hindu society by combining elements of Western culture with existing Hindu culture and is manifested in the founding of new political parties

and religious groups, the use of the English language in books, magazines, and newspapers, and the imitation of Western literary forms and styles.   **HIND**

1870   The Christian Methodist Episcopal Church is founded by African-Americans in the southern United States. It is an offshoot of the Methodist Episcopal Church, South, the branch of American Methodism that had supported slavery and thus sought to rid itself of African-American members, who themselves sought to be independent of the church.   **AFRICAN**

1870   The United States Congress ends military control of Indian agent posts on Indian reservations and the agency now rests with Christian missionaries who are also put in charge of Native American schools and training programs.   **CHRIS, NATIV**

1870   Muslims from Kilwa, Malindi, and other coastal trading centers in East Africa have been moving into the interior of Africa since the 1820s in search of slaves and ivory. In this year the ruler of the Yao becomes the first ruler of an interior people to convert to Islam. He also accepts Muslim missionaries, who convert other Yao beginning in the 1880s. At about the same time, traders from Zanzibar make Muslim converts in the interior. However, the number of converts is few and Islam coexists with Christianity and indigenous religions.   **ISLAM**

1870   A Muslim reform movement emerges in Bengal. It seeks to replace the existing form of Islam in rural areas that is based on Islam combined with indigenous beliefs and practices with a purer form of Islam taught by Muslim scholars.   **ISLAM**

Zionism

Zionism is a political ideology and movement that developed in the latter part of the 19th century in eastern Europe. It calls for the creation of a Jewish state, which now exists as the State of Israel. The primary motivation for an independent Jewish state was discrimination against and attacks on Jews in Europe. Even though discrimination lessened in western Europe in the 18th and 19th centuries, it reappeared in the late 19th century, leading some Jewish leaders and intellectuals to conclude that Jews would be truly free only in their own nation. Although Zionism is associated with Judaism, it is not an official tenet of Judaism and not all Jews are Zionists. Throughout the 20th century Zionism has been a contentious political issue, as many nations objected to the ideology and questioned the need for a Jewish state. The destruction of the European Jewish community in World War II and the move toward peaceful relations with Arab nations in the 1990s has caused Zionism to fade from prominence as an international issue at the close of the century.

1870   Lithuanian Jews begin discussing the possibility of a Jewish homeland in Palestine. This represents the beginning of the European Zionism movement.   JUD

1870   After nearly 100 years of having their rights expanded and then removed, Jews are given civil rights in Italy and Jewish ghettos are abolished.   JUD

1870   In Great Britain the United Synagogue is established by Parliament to serve the chief rabbi and all congregations associated with him.   JUD

1870   The first Native American Ghost Dance revitalization movement takes place. The leader of the movement is Wovoka (1856-1932), a Northern Paiute in Nevada. To bring a return to the traditional way of life, he preaches that native peoples dance the round dance. A number of Western tribes participate in the dances for several years before the movement ends. NATIV

1870s   The practice of white missionary societies sending African-American representatives to Africa increases dramatically and remains common into the early 20th century. Whites see African-American missionaries as perhaps better able to communicate with Africans, and many African-American missionaries feel a special tie to Africa.   AFRICAN

1870s   As the debate over religion versus science heats up, followers of Charles Darwin, such as Irish scientist John Tyndall and British philosopher Thomas Huxley, conduct lecture tours in the United States to promote evolutionary theory, question the validity of religion, and preach the virtues of atheism. Darwin himself avoids criticizing religion or any specific religion.   MISC

The Ghost Dance

The Ghost Dance was a Native American revitalization movement that began in 1888 and within two years spread across the western United States and Plains with some 35 groups participating in the ritual. The prophet of the Ghost Dance was Wovoka (1856–1932), a Paiute in Nevada who had been trained as a religious healer by his father. Wovoka received revelations and preached the necessity of participation in the Ghost Dance in order to restore the traditional Native American ways of life before the arrival of white settlers. The groups who adopted the Ghost Dance were on the verge of cultural extinction. The herds of bison, which provided meat, hides for clothing and tipis, and bone for tools, had been virtually eradicated by the white settlers. The starving and disorganized tribes had been defeated by United States forces and driven from their lands onto reservations. They began gathering in the hundreds and then the thousands. They danced the round dance during the summer and fall of 1890. The round dance was performed by men and women in a circle. The participants held hands and shuffled side-to-side as they sang in praise of the Great Spirit above and asked for his help. Fearing that it would lead to widespread revolt, the U.S. government repressed the movement.

1870s	The British-Israelite movement grows in Great Britain, with several dozen groups founded. A leader in the movement is Edward Hine (1825–1891), a follower of John Wilson **(SEE 1840, SECT)** who publicizes the idea that Britons are descended from the 10 lost tribes of Israel and works to discredit the idea that Germans, now Britain's major European rival, share a similar descent. Although the movement never has more than 5,000 members, it does enjoy the support of some wealthy British nobles and declines only after the 1920s. **SECT**
1870–1871	A revolt by Muslim farmers in Algeria takes place against French rule. The revolt is the culmination of resistance to French rule that has been building for over 30 years and is precipitated by the French failing to provide adequate aid during a serious drought. The French repress the revolt, seize much of the farmers' lands, and restrict the practice of Islam. **ISLAM**
1870–1884	Japan's government begins the Great Promulgation Campaign to create a state religion, not initially identified as Shinto, known as the Great Teaching to foster public reverence and obedience toward the emperor, the *kami* (native spirits), and the nation. The campaign is carried out by a corps of national evangelists, Shinto and Buddhist priests, along with entertainers, actors, storytellers, ministers of new religions, and ideologues of National Learning. **SHINTO**
1870s–1880s	Western European interest in Jainism is stimulated by the publication in German of translations of Jain texts by such scholars as Johann Georg Buehler, Albrecht Weber, Ernst Leumann, and Hermann Jacobi. By this time, too, Jains are emigrating from India to East Africa and Myanmar, at least partly in the wake of the British colonial rule. **JAIN**
1870–1890	The Baha'i religion begins to expand as adherents in Iran actively seek converts in Iran, India, and Russia. They face continuing persecution by the dominant Shi'a Muslims in Iran but enjoy more freedom in southern Russia. **SECT**
1871	In the western United States, the Cumberland Presbyterian Synod forms the First Synod of the Colored Cumberland Presbyterian Church for its African-American members. In 1873 the members form their own synod, the Negro Cumberland Presbyterian Church. **AFRICAN, PROT**
1871	Under the rule of Prussia, the German states are unified as a single nation. The Prussian government initiates the *kulturkampf,* the persecution of Roman Catholics whose undivided loyalty to Germany is questioned. The persecutions lessen after 1886. **CATH**
1871	The Bible is first translated into Bulgarian. **CHRIS**
1871	In Britain Jews are admitted to the universities for the first time and in Germany, Jews gain full civil rights. **JUD**

1871   In Britain, as the authority of the Church of England continues to weaken, major universities admit students of all Protestant denominations to almost all academic programs, although non-Anglicans are still prohibited from holding teaching positions. The last program, not available until 1918, to open to non-Anglicans is that which leads to a bachelor or doctor of divinity degree.   **PROT**

1871   Japan's government confiscates lands belonging to Shinto shrines and replaces them with some compensation or promises of state support. All Japanese are organized as "parishioners" or *ujiko* of the local Shinto shrines (despite their personal religious beliefs), a designation previously reserved for those of high social status. A plan to use shrine registration (*ujiko shirabe*) as the basis for the national census is implemented; the system will last until 1873. As the new government stabilizes, it begins to turn away from the influence of the Shinto Restoration leaders. The relatively autonomous Department of Divinity is replaced by the Shinto Ministry (*Jingisho*), which comes under the jurisdiction of the Council of State. In 1872 the Ministry will be abolished and replaced by the Department of Religion and Education (*Kyobusho*), which will last until 1877, when the government becomes less aggressive in its religious policy.   **SHINTO**

1871–
1875   With a series of decrees, the government creates the formal structure of State Shinto in Japan: all shrines are to be the sites of national rites, the priests will be appointed by the government, and the shrines will receive support from the state in amounts determined by their official rank. Which rites are to be performed, the wording of the liturgy, and even the ceremonial dress of the priests is stipulated.   **SHINTO**

1872   The Freedmen's Aid and Education Society, established by the Methodists in the United States in 1866, becomes a permanent agency of the Methodist Church. It initially works to convert and assist freed black slaves and then expands its mission to include Native Americans and poor whites. Later, it begins missionary work outside the United States.   **PROT**

1872   The Jehovah's Witnesses are founded in Allegheny, Pennsylvania, by Charles Taze Russell (1852–1916), a businessman who had been attracted to the teachings of William Miller, founder of the Millerites. The name Jehovah's Witnesses is adopted by the group in 1931 and the religion is known by various names over the course of its history, including Dawnites, Russellites, Bible Students, and Rutherfordites. Their name for themselves, Christians, is never accepted by outsiders.   **SECT**

1872   Japan's Office of Propaganda, founded in 1869, is reorganized as the Agency of Spiritual Guidance (*Kyodoshoku*), to which all Shinto priests are appointed, thus making them government officials. By government decree Buddhist priests and nuns are officially permitted again to visit Shinto shrines, including Ise, even during rites and festivals. After their recovery from persecution, Buddhists will begin to advocate freedom of religion.   **SHINTO, TOL**

1872–1950	The Hindu religious teacher Aurobindo Ghose lives, and during his lifetime he develops the Integral Yoga system based on the Hindu Yoga and Tantric traditions. Through his writings the system becomes popular both in India and the Western world and a center is built in Pondicherry, India. **HIND**
c. 1873	The Baha'i book of laws, the *Most Holy Book*, is written by Baha'u'llah, the leader of the sect in Iran. **SECT**
1873	(St.) Therese, a Carmelite nun, dies in Lisieux, France, at the age of 24. Although she has lived a quiet life, her biography, *Histoire d'une âme* (*Story of a Soul*), is published by her sisters, also nuns, after her death. The simplicity of her story makes it a best seller across Europe and leads to her canonization in 1925. **CATH**
1873	*Sacred Songs and Solos*, a collection of revivalist hymns, is compiled by singer and hymn composer Ira D. Sankey (1840–1908) and published in the United States. **CHRIS**

Jehovah's Witnesses

The Jehovah's Witnesses, Christian Science, Mormonism, and Seventh-Day Adventism are the four successful religions that have developed in the United States. To varying degrees, all four rest on the Judeo-Christian tradition, and all four view the Bible as a sacred text. The Jehovah's Witnesses were founded in western Pennsylvania in about 1872 and have developed into a global religion with over two million adherents in almost every nation of the world. Jehovah's Witnesses are avid proselytizers of their message through their literature and door-to-door visits to non-Witnesses. Witnesses believe in the power and authority of the Judeo-Christian God, Jehovah. They interpret the Bible literally and cite passages in support of all religious beliefs and practices. They also believe that the end of the world is near, that the world will be ruled by Satan until then, and that after the world ends the world of heaven will be created on earth. Some people will live on earth, others will receive eternal life, and a small number will rule with Jesus Christ in heaven. To achieve this eternal life, Witnesses follow unique religious practices, such as not observing Sunday as the Sabbath or Christmas or Easter as religious holidays, not taking blood transfusions, and avoiding spirit and image worship. Since the early 20th century, Jehovah's Witnesses have been persecuted in virtually every nation of the world. Witnesses blame much of this persecution on the Roman Catholic Church, which they believe has tried to destroy the movement, often by influencing government officials to ban or restrict Witnesses' missionary activities. While the Catholic Church has at times worked against the Witnesses, governments have often restricted the activities of Jehovah's Witnesses because of concerns about the depth of their loyalty to the state. While most Witnesses can be assumed to follow secular laws, they believe deeply that "We must obey God as ruler rather than men" (Acts 5:29). Most significantly, this has led them to avoid pledging allegiance to any nation and also to take a position of neutrality in times of war.

| 1873 | Confronted with considerable pressure from the emergent Min family and disgruntled Confucian officials, Taewongun resigns as regent in Korea. Korea's previously strict isolationist policy is relaxed. **CONF** |

1873   Confronted with considerable pressure from the emergent Min family and disgruntled Confucian officials, Taewongun resigns as regent in Korea. Korea's previously strict isolationist policy is relaxed. **CONF**

1873   The Union of American Hebrew Congregations (UAHC) is established to serve as a central organization for Reform Jewish congregations in the United States. **JUD**

1873   The Woman's Temperance Crusade is founded in New York State and Ohio, and its members use prayer and the singing of hymns to influence owners of taverns to close their businesses. It also works to end the consumption of alcoholic beverages through educational programs in schools and restrictions on the importation and sale of liquor. **MISC**

1873   Through the missionary efforts of Nikolai I. Kasatkin (1836–1912), the archbishop of Tokyo, a seminary for Orthodox priests is opened in Tokyo and the Church of Japan becomes an autonomous church in the Orthodox Church. **ORTHO**

1873   The Ise Teaching Institute (*Jingukyoin*) is established at Ise as the headquarters for Ise teaching sites throughout Japan for the propagation of the Great Teaching; in 1875 it will become the Ise Shrine Church (*Jingukyokai*). The propagation campaign eventually fails, as it is riddled by internal disagreements and the Shinto bureaucrats who initiated it lose power. **SHINTO**

1873   Sikhs in India form the Singh Babha Society. It brings together conservative and radical Sikhs who had competed for dominance in the Sikh community over the last several decades and exists in part to combat British and Christian influences. **SIKH**

1873   An effort by Mennonites to gain special assistance from Congress in their efforts to settle in the American West is rejected. However, many states assist the Mennonites, and all states where they seek such release relieve them from an obligation to serve in the state militias in accord with the Mennonites' pacifism. **TOL**

1873–1876   In Tunisia the European-controlled government institutes reforms of Muslim practices and law to make them acceptable to Europeans. **ISLAM**

1874   The Bureau of Catholic Indian Missions is established in the United States to assist Catholic missionaries in their new role as managers on Indian reservations. **CATH, NATIV**

1874   The British begin sending Indians to the British colony of Fiji to work on the sugar and coconut plantations. The arrival of the Indians, the majority of whom are Hindus with some Muslims and Sikhs as well, continues until 1920, and they form a large and distinct community separate from the British and native Fijian communities. **HIND**

1874   In Algeria the French rulers institute the *Code de l'indigénat,* which defines many Islamic practices as treason and makes Muslims accused of these crimes subject to imprisonment and loss of property.   ISLAM

1874   Jews are given civil rights in Switzerland.   JUD

1874   The Young Men's Hebrew Association is founded in New York City to provide services to the growing community of Jewish immigrants from eastern Europe.   JUD

1874   The Chautauqua movement is started by Methodist minister John H. Vincent and religious educator Lewis Miller at Lake Chautauqua, New York. Although the teaching of religion—Methodism and many other denominations—is part of the program, the movement rapidly expands into summer programs and camps that offer lectures, concerts, workshops, and so on, on a wide range of topics for adults and children.   MISC

1874   The Public Worship Regulation Act is enacted in Great Britain. It is an effort to control the Anglo-Catholic faction in the Anglican Church that seeks to revive Roman Catholic practices.   PROT

1874   Lutherans in Sweden form the Board of Missions of the Church of Sweden, which supports missionary work in India, southern Africa, and China.   PROT

1874   In Iceland religious freedom is given to Christians who are not Lutherans.   PROT

1874   The British National Association of Spiritualists is founded. Its name is later changed to the Central Association of Spiritualists and then to the London Spiritual Alliance.   SPIR

1874–   The Hutterites in Russia begin immigrating to the United States. They seek
1879   religious freedom and open farm land and establish communities in South Dakota. The Hutterites in the United States divide into three divisions (Schmiedeleut, Dariusleut, and Lehrerleut), each of which forms communal settlements, and the Prairieleut, a group that establishes family farms and does not live communally.   SECT

1874–   About 10,000 Mennonites from Russia settle in the prairie states of the
1880   United States.   SECT

c. 1875   The use of peyote for religious purposes is introduced to the Comanche of the American Southwest by the warrior Quannah Parker (1845–1911). NATIV

1875   A public debate takes place in Sri Lanka between a Buddhist monk and several Christian missionaries. It is the intent of the Christians to convince the people of the presumed superiority of Christianity, but in fact the lone monk makes a strong case for Buddhism. Published reports of the debate will have considerable influence in convincing various Westerners of the value of Buddhism. **BUDD**

1875 James Augustine Healy (1830–1900), a Catholic priest since 1854, is appointed the bishop of Portland, Maine, making him the first African-American bishop in the Roman Catholic Church. **CATH**

1875 The Bible is first translated into Russian. **CHRIS**

1875 The Keswisk Convention begins in Great Britain with the first annual conference held at Broadlands and Brighton. Later conferences are held at Keswick in northwestern England, giving the movement its name. It is a movement within Evangelical Protestantism to create unity among Evangelical churches. The records of the annual meetings are distributed to missionaries around the world toward this end. **EVAN**

1875 The Arya Samaj Hindu (Noble Society) reform movement is founded by Dayananda Sarasvati (1824–1883), a Hindu Brahman and wandering mendicant from the Gujarat state of India. He seeks to promote Hinduism as a monotheistic religion, and the society is active in converting untouchables to Hinduism. The movement is anti-Muslim and anti-Christian. It attracts Hindus and Sikhs and remains active in the 1990s. **HIND**

Evangelicalism

Evangelicism is a movement within Protestant Christianity which, in its modern form, emerged during the Evangelical Revival in the first half of the 18th century in Britain. The Evangelical movement was in part a reaction to the spiritual rigidity of Calvinism and the structural rigidity of the Anglican Church in Britain. It also had strong anti-Catholic sentiments. Early Evangelism was characterized by four primary features: first, a belief that people needed to convert in order to repent and to worship Christ; second, a strong emphasis on preaching and missionizing in order to convert and save others; third, a reliance on the Bible as the ultimate authority; and fourth, a focus on the symbolism of the cross as representing the relationship of human beings to God. Evangelism is not a religion in itself but rather a system of religious belief and practice that was or is present in a number of Christian denominations, including Methodist, Baptist, Congregationalist, and Presbyterian. Over time and in different denominations, Evangelism has taken a variety of forms, and it is no longer possible to speak of Evangelicalism as a single nor a unified movement. In the 19th century, Evangelicals played a major role in the Protestant missionary effort around the world, and in the late 19th and early 20th centuries many adopted a more liberal social philosophy and were involved in the Social Gospel movement to end social problems, such as poverty and inequality. Evangelicals were also involved in the Holiness and Pentecostal movements, although both differ from Evangelicalism.

1875

1875	In Bengal, India, the Muhammadan Anglo Oriental College (later renamed the Muslim University of Aligarh) is established. The college focuses on Islamic culture and follows the British university system. The college is founded to help improve the economic and social status of Muslims in India, who are second-class in comparison to the Hindus, who own most of the local businesses and land. Many Indian Muslim leaders of the early 20th century are educated there. **ISLAM**
1875	Hebrew Union College, a Reform rabbinical school, is founded in Cincinnati. Later, additional campus are established in New York, Los Angeles, and Jerusalem. **JUD**
1875	A Mormon academy (which later becomes Brigham Young University) is founded in Utah. Also in this year, the Mormon Church sends missionaries to Mexico. **MOR**
1875	A new version of the Church Slavic Bible is published in Russian. It becomes the standard edition of the Bible for the Russian Orthodox Church until 1917 and is reissued in 1988 as part of the revival of Orthodoxy in Russia. **ORTHO**
1875	*Science and Health with Key to the Scriptures* is written by Mary Baker Eddy, the founder of Christian Science. The book goes through numerous editions but the basic doctrine set forth by Eddy remains unchanged and the book, together with the Bible, becomes the basic religious text of Christian Science. During this year Eddy also begins conducting prayer services for a small group of followers. **SECT**
1875	The Theosophical Society is founded in New York by intellectuals Helena P. Blavatsky (1831–1891) and Henry Steele Olcutt (1832–1907). The society, which has an influence on the subsequent New Thought and New Age movements, is focused on creating a more peaceful and harmonious world and integrating beliefs from Western and Eastern religions. It also emphasizes the spiritual aspects of the human experience and downplays the importance of rationality and materialism. The movement produces a number of offshoots but eventually fades in importance, although a center remains open in the 1990s in Adyar, India. **SPIR**
1875–1900	The Daoist cult of the third century Sichuan sage Xu Sun (**SEE 300s, DAO**) continues to thrive in late Qing China. A calendar of annual festivals on West Mountain celebrates the life and career of Xu Sun, venerated as the founder of the Pure Light school. **DAO**
1876	The African Methodist Episcopal Zion Church establishes a missionary effort in Africa when it sends missionaries to Liberia. **AFRICAN**
1876	Jews are afforded civil rights in the Ottoman Empire, which is now weakened and on the verge of collapse. **JUD**

1876   The first Ethical Culture Society is founded in New York City. Although not a religious movement, it is founded by and draws many members from the German Jewish community in New York and is seen by some as an alternative to Judaism or religion in general. It also attracts Protestants of German ancestry. Members are primarily individuals who are interested in various social issues and ethical and moral behavior who do not believe that established churches are addressing these matters in ways that benefit society as a whole.   **MISC**

1876   *The Freethinker's Guide* is written by British atheist Charles Bradlaugh. In the book he sets forth a definition of atheism that is widely followed by atheists: "Atheism is without God, it does not assert no God. The atheist does not say that there is no God, but he says, 'I know not what you mean by God. I am without the idea of God.'"   **MISC**

1876   The Society for the Encouragement of Spiritual and Ethical Reasoning is founded as an evangelical movement opposed to Orthodoxy in Russia. At the center of the movement is Colonel V. A. Pashkov, who founds the movement, and British evangelical preacher Lord Radstock (1833–1913), who preaches to certain segments of the Russian aristocracy in 1864, 1875, 1876, and 1878. Followers are called Radstockists or Pashkovists, and the movement ends after Pashkov is exiled in 1884.   **ORTHO**

Theosophical Society

The Theosophical Society was founded in New York City in 1875 by American lawyer Henry Steele Olcott (1832–1907) and Madame Helena Petrovna Blavatsky (1831–1891). Blavatsky was a German-Ukrainian who had been married to a Russian general but left him and traveled in Asia before arriving in America in 1873. Claiming to have been initiated into the mysteries of the occult in Tibet, she gave lectures on Asian religions. The Theosophical Society drew on various religious traditions but particularly Buddhism and Hinduism. The society was divided early on by quarrels, and in 1878 Madame Blavatsky moved to India, settling near Madras and spending her remaining years promoting her version of theosophy. Olcott joined her and in 1880 they visited Sri Lanka, where immediately upon landing they embraced Buddhism at a temple ceremony. In 1882 they established the Adyar Theosophical Society. Olcott devoted himself to promoting Buddhism in Sri Lanka; he also used the Theosophical Society in India to encourage Indians to work for their indigenous traditions and eventual independence from Britain. Olcott also worked to reconcile the Theravada Buddhism of Sri Lanka with the Mahayana Buddhism of Japan. In 1907 British social reformer Annie Besant took over as leader of the society and expanded its membership around the world before her death in 1933. The society remained headquartered in Adyar, India, and Hinduism became somewhat more important than other religious traditions. The society played a major role in bringing Asian religions to the attention of Europeans and Americans.

1876   Danish Protestant missionary Ludwig Inger Nommensen (1834–1918) begins his work among the Batak people of the island of Sumatra in Indonesia. He advocates the acceptance of local customs and sets the framework for the establishment of a Batak Christian church. **PROT**

1876   The Theosophical Society of England is founded. Although similar in goals and philosophy to the American Theosophical Society, it emerges and develops independently. **SPIR**

1876–
1877   In the Balkan region Bosnians revolt against Ottoman rule and the revolt spreads across the Balkans. The conflict ends with the Treaty of San Stefano in 1877, with Bulgaria, Serbia, Romania, and Montenegro gaining their independence. **ISLAM**

1876–
1908   Japan's government officially recognizes 13 independent Shinto sects, which are seen as autonomous religious organizations similar to Buddhism and Christianity. These Shinto sects come under the purview of the Education Ministry while the state Shinto shrines, not technically considered religious organizations, come under the Home Ministry. The independent Shinto sects include three pure Shinto sects, two Confucian sects, two purification sects, three mountain sects, and three faith-healing sects. In order to gain such official recognition, the new religions Tenrikyo (SEE **1838**, SECT, SHINTO) and Konkokyo (SEE **1859**, SECT, SHINTO) prepare doctrines to conform with state Shinto. Ise's Jingukyo, organized in 1872 by Chief Priest Tanaka Yoritsune (1836–1897), becomes the first of these sects. Founded this year are the pure Shinto sect Taishakyo by Senge Takatomi (1848–1918) and the Confucian-Shinto sect Shusei Ha (Strengthening and Consolidating sect) by Nitta Kuniteru (1829–1902). Both are recognized as official Shinto sects. Shinrikyo (Divine Reason teaching), founded in 1880 by Sano Tsunehiko, will become the second pure Shinto sect. Taiseikyo (Great Accomplishment teaching) founded in 1882 by Hirayama Shosai (1815–1890), a form of syncretism influenced by Confucianism, also becomes an independent Shinto sect. A number of these Shinto sects result from the so-called pantheon debate, a doctrinal dispute between the Ise and Izumo shrine priests about which are to be the main dedicated *kami* (native spirits) of Shinto. **SHINTO, TOL**

1877   Anglican missionaries arrive in Uganda and win some converts among the Buganda ruling elite, which also includes Muslims. **ISLAM, PROT**

1877   The United Church of Christ in Japan is founded and unites three independent Presbyterian churches in Japan. Behind the founding of the organization are Japanese Christians who argue that for Christianity to make further inroads in Japan, there must be Japanese control of the churches. **PROT**

1877   In order to make the Christian Mission (Salvation Army) more efficient, it is organized as a quasi-military organization, with members achieving ranks and with founder William Booth in command. **PROT**

1877	Edgar Cayce (1877–1945) is born in Kentucky. During his lifetime he becomes one of the best known clairvoyants in the world. His work is kept alive in a series of books by his son after Cayce's death, and they are a major influence on spiritualists and the New Age movement of the 1960s. **SPIR**
1877–1878	Sufi Muslims in the Caucasus region of Russia revolt against Russian rule. The revolt is defeated but adds to the growing resentment felt by Muslims toward Russians in the region. **ISLAM**
1878	In England the name of the Christian Mission is changed to the Salvation Army. **PROT**
1879	Edwin Arnold, an English poet, publishes a book-length poem, *The Light of Asia*, an editorializing account of Buddha and Buddhism. The phenomenally successful work goes into numerous editions and many translations and sells over a million copies in England and the United States alone. Although scorned by many scholars for its sentimental superficiality and attacked by many Christians for its favorable presentation, Arnold's poem in the end has a greater impact on the introduction of Buddhism to the West than many other scholarly studies have. **BUDD**
1879	Roman Catholic missionaries arrive in Uganda and win some converts among the Buganda ruling elite, which also includes Muslims and Anglicans. **CATH**
1879	The German Worker's Welfare Association is founded in Germany as a labor union. It, like other labor unions in Europe during the 1870s and 1880s, has developed from workers' clubs founded by priests that supported worker rights as part of the Social Catholicism movement. Other Christian labor unions are founded in Belgium, the Netherlands, France, and Italy. **CATH**
1879	The term *anti-Semite* is employed by the German writer and politician William Marr (1818–1904) in the title of his work *League of Anti-Semites*. Although *anti-Semite* comes to be used as a label for haters of Jews, Semites are technically all peoples who speak Semitic languages, including Arabs. **JUD**
1879	Direct conflict threatens between the federal government and the Mormons in Utah when the United States Supreme Court upholds laws banning plural marriage. **MOR**
1879	Charles Taze Russell, founder of the Jehovah's Witnesses, begins publishing a magazine called *Watch Tower and Herald of Christ's Presence* to disseminate his ideas. Publications become a hallmark of the religion; Russell's *Food for Christian Thinking*, published in 1890, and the seven-volume *Studies in the Scriptures* (also called *Millennial Dawn*), published over a series of years, are the most important writings in the early years of the movement. Russell's books are later replaced in importance by the many pamphlets written by Joseph Franklin Rutherford, the second leader of the religion. **SECT**

1879	The first formal meeting of Christian Scientists takes place in Boston, and the Church of Christ, Scientist is established. **SECT**
1879	Radical Sikhs in southern Asia, called Tat Khalsa, leave the Singh Babha Society and form their own group, which advocates a more fundamental form of Sikhism. **SIKH**
1879–1885	During these years, Hermann Oldenburg (1854–1920), a German scholar learned in the early languages of India and the Buddhist and Vedic religions, publishes several books that greatly advance the knowledge of Buddhism in the West. These works include a life of Buddha (published in 1881), as well as translations of Sri Lankan Pali texts. **BUDD**
1879–1950	The Hindu mystic Ramana Maharshi lives and develops a form of Hinduism in Tamilnadu that proves popular with Westerners. Maharshi addresses the question "Who am I?" and he and his pupils help followers answer the question. **HIND**
c. 1880	The Ahmadiya sect of Islam is founded in northwest India by Ghulam Ahmad Qadiyani (c. 1835–1908), a Muslim who at various times claims to be a prophet, the messiah, the Hindu god Krishna, and the reappearance of Muhammad, the Prophet and founder of Islam. The sect is considered heretical by other Muslims and is repressed in neighboring Pakistan and the Middle East. **ISLAM**
1880	The Baptist Mission Convention of the United States of America is established by African-American Baptists to send Baptist missionaries to Africa and also to combat social problems such as alcoholism in the United States. **AFRICAN**

Anti-Semitism

Anti-Semitism is the hatred or dislike of Jews because they are Jews. The origins of and reasons for anti-Semitism are not clearly known and continue to be the subject of scholarly research and debate. Anti-Semitism comes in a number of forms including economic, religious, racial, political, and social. All forms of anti-Semitism are manifested in discrimination against Jews that can range from restrictions on education or employment to confinement in their own neighborhoods, expulsion from a nation, or execution. The Holocaust perpetrated by Nazi Germany from 1938 to 1945 is considered to be the most extreme example of anti-Semitism. From the viewpoint of the relations among religions, anti-Semitism is closely tied to Christianity in Europe. Christian anti-Semitism was based on a trifold belief that Jews killed Christ, that Jews are evil, and that Jews are beyond redemption. In the 20th century these beliefs and the teaching of them have been repudiated by many Christian denominations. Nonetheless, anti-Semitism remains an issue in some nations in the 1990s, especially in Eastern Europe and the Middle East.

1880   In Malaysia the British government allows for considerable freedom of religious expression for Muslims and gives the indigenous Malay officials much authority over religious matters, but not other matters.   **ISLAM**

1880   The period of greatest emigration of Jews from Europe to the Americas and elsewhere begins. It declines after 1914 and ends in 1924, when the United States enacts restrictive immigration laws. The arrival of hundreds of thousands of Jews from Poland, Russia, and Lithuania, as well as central Europe and the Near East, produces a large Jewish population in the United States and Great Britain, with smaller populations in Canada, Mexico, Argentina, Uruguay, France, and South Africa.   **JUD**

1880   The Hebrew Immigrant Aid Society is established in New York City to assist Jews settling in the United States.   **JUD**

1880   The United States government prohibits the Sun Dance, a Native American ceremony popular on reservations in the west. Although the government makes an overt claim that the ban is because dancers inflict wounds on themselves during the dance, the actual covert reason is to destroy traditional native religions and to suppress native resistance to governmental control.   **NATIV**

1880   Unitarian minister and Harvard theology professor Francis Greenwood Peabody (1847–1936) teaches the first course in social ethics at an American seminary. Peabody is an early leader of the Social Gospel movement, which advocates the use of religion as a means to create a more just society.   **PROT**

1880   The Jehovah's Witnesses spread from the United States to Great Britain when they open an office to disseminate religious literature in London.   **SECT**

1880s   The term *Ethiopianism* comes into use in Africa as a label for certain types of indigenous African/Christian churches in South and West Africa. These churches tend to be characterized by an adherence to traditional Christian religion, African nationalism, and the acceptance of some indigenous African customs, such as polygynous marriage. The movement does not involve the nation of Ethiopia. Ethiopia is invoked because of references to it in the Bible and because of its status as an independent African nation.   **AFRICAN**

1880s   In the United States rivalry between Irish Catholics and German Catholics intensifies as the German population increases through immigration, and Irish clergy, who control the Catholic Church in America, argue that the Church should take a more American form and seek greater integration into American life. This approach is rejected by many German leaders who prefer closer links to the Vatican.   **CATH**

1880s   The Modernist or Salafiyya movement develops at al-Azhar University in Cairo. It is led by Muhammad Abduh, a leading Muslim intellectual, and develops in reaction to the Westernization and modernization of Egypt. Abduh stresses a return to the philosophy of early Islam as a model for accepting modern science into the Muslim world. The movement attracts followers among university students in North Africa but does not appeal to the masses. ISLAM

1880s   The Social Gospel movement emerges in American Protestantism. Leaders of the movement, such as minister Walter Rauschenbusch, argue that the role of Christianity is to address social ills such as poverty. The movement conflicts with mainstream Evangelical Protestantism, whose leaders stress the personal relationship of followers with Jesus Christ. The Social Gospel movement fades in the 1930s. PROT

1880–1900   Korea comes under increasing pressure from the major powers, and its Confucian value system also comes under attack. Confucian scholars become conservatives, opposing treaties and modernization. CONF

1881   The *A.M.E. Review* is founded by the African Methodist Evangelical Church in the United States. In the 1990s it is the oldest publication owned by people of African ancestry. AFRICAN

1881   T. H. Rhys Davids, an Englishman who worked in the Ceylon Civil Service, founds the Pali Text Society, which through its publication of many Buddhist texts will promote Buddhism. In 1894 Rhys Davids marries Caroline Augusta Foley, herself a scholar in Pali and Buddhism, who not only collaborates with her husband in a steady stream of publications but also makes an independent reputation as a scholar and interpreter of Buddhism; after his death she continues the work of the Pali Text Society. BUDD

1881   The Muslim Mahdist movement emerges in the Sudan. It is founded by Muhammad Ahmad (1848–1885), a devout Sufi who claims to be al-Mahdi, the Muslim messiah. He calls for the revitalization of traditional Islam in the Sudan, where Islam is for the most part under the control of Sufi brotherhoods, and the end of Egyptian rule. ISLAM

1881   The French—already in control of Algeria since 1830—take control of neighboring Tunisia. Although the Islamic religion is left relatively untouched, new policies are enacted that take land from Muslim communities and establish a European education system. Muslim leaders are divided in support of or opposition to French rule, as the French provide positions for some Muslim scholars in their administration. ISLAM

1881   In the political unrest that follows the assassination of Alexander II of Russia, hundreds of Jewish communities in Russia are attacked, Jewish property destroyed, and Jews beaten and killed. These pogroms and the enactment of restrictive laws governing Jews increase their desire to immigrate to America or elsewhere. Jews in western Europe form organizations to raise money and to help Jews in Russia emigrate. JUD

| 1881 | Methodist churches around the world begin moving toward cooperation and reunification when representatives of various churches at a meeting in London found the Men and Religion Forward Movement. **PROT** |

1881   Methodist churches around the world begin moving toward cooperation and reunification when representatives of various churches at a meeting in London found the Men and Religion Forward Movement. **PROT**

1881   Mary Baker Eddy, the founder of Christian Science, is ordained as the first minister of the church in Boston. **SECT**

1881–
1886   The Salvation Army spreads from England to the United States, Australia, France, Canada, Switzerland, Sweden, India, Sri Lanka, New Zealand, and South Africa. Growth is especially rapid in the United States. **PROT**

1881–
1903   The first *Aliyah* to Palestine takes place. *Aliyah* is a Hebrew word meaning "going up" and in this context refers to immigration to and permanent settlement in Israel. In the modern Jewish settlement history of Palestine there are five periods of *Aliyah*. During this first period, settlers from Russian and Romania establish small farming settlements. SEE **1904–1914,** JUD.
    JUD

1882   In India Hindus who fear that British reforms and modernization are eroding the influence of Hinduism begin forming cattle protection associations that stress traditional Hindu beliefs and practices including the prohibition on eating beef. **HIND**

1882   American industrialist Andrew Carnegie, perhaps the wealthiest man in America, begins formulating a philosophy of religion that moves away from some existing Protestant beliefs and examines the relationship between wealth and religion. In his essay *The Gospel of Wealth*, Carnegie argues that the wealthy have an obligation to encourage initiative in others. **MISC**

1882   The Edmunds Act is enacted by the United States Congress. It prohibits plural marriage and is seen by Mormons as a form of religious repression. The government begins enforcing the anti-polygamy law, seriously disrupting Mormon society, as Mormons are forced to flee federal and state agents who are searching for violators. Over 10,000 Mormons are also disfranchised as polygynists, although such action is ruled unconstitutional by the United States Supreme Court in 1885. **MOR**

1882   The Indian Shaker Church (unrelated to the Shakers of New England origin) emerges in Washington State. It starts through a revelation received by John Slocum (?–c. 1882), of the Salish people, that tells of a religious movement which will bring a revitalization of the traditional Salish culture. The church attracts followers in the northwest and remains active in the 1990s. **NATIV**

1882   In Iran the Muslim government ends the practice of heavily taxing the Zoroastrian religious minority, and they are granted new freedoms. These developments improve Zoroastrian status in Iranian society. In the early

20th century Zoroastrians gain a limited right to representation in the government. **SECT**

1882   The Kotenkokyusho (institute for the study of Japanese documents) is established to gather and study materials concerning the *kokutai* or national polity. In August the Home Affairs Ministry decides that only those who graduate from this institute may be appointed Shinto priests. Shinto shrines and the imperial household contribute to the support of the institute. **SHINTO**

1882   The Society for Psychical Science is founded in London for the purpose of conducting and reporting on scientific studies of spiritual phenomena. **SPIR**

1882   Channeling, a psychic mechanism for receiving communication from spiritual masters of the past, becomes an important component of the New Thought movement in Europe and later the New Age movement with the publication of *Oahspe* by John Ballou Newborough (1828–1891). **SPIR**

1882   The headquarters of the Theosophical Society is moved to Adyar, India, where it remains in the 1990s. A school system based on Buddhist principles is also established in Sri Lanka. **SPIR**

1883   The Student Volunteer movement emerges in the United States. It is a missionary movement led by students from elite colleges in the Northeast that is the major source of missionaries for the rapidly expanding American Christian missionary effort over the next three decades. **CHRIS**

1883   In the Crimea in Russia, Muslim intellectual Ismail Gasprinskii (1851–1914) begins publication of *Tarjuman*, which becomes the primary voice for Muslim interests in the region and advocates the reform of Islam in accord with modernization and Westernization. **ISLAM**

1883   In Algeria the French reorganize the education system to reflect European history and culture. While the system does train some Algerians for service in the French government, it reaches relatively few people and has little impact on most of the Muslim population. **ISLAM**

1883   A number of Reform Jewish rabbis leave the Reform movement when non-kosher (foods Jews are prohibited from eating) foods are served at a religious dinner. The dinner, organized by the Reform Union of Hebrew Congregations in Cincinnati, comes to be called the *Trefa* Banquet, from the Hebrew word *taref,* meaning "not kosher." Three years later, the reform rabbis are involved in founding Conservative Judaism. **JUD**

1883   Congregationalists in the United States adopt the Commission Creed, which sets forth the basic doctrine of the church. It is adopted by most churches. **PROT**

1884   *Cabildos*, organizations of African-Cubans, are banned by the Cuban government following over a century of government actions designed to limit their activities and influence. Although associated with the Roman Catholic Church, *cabildos* are an important means by which African slaves maintained traditional religious beliefs and practices.   **AFRICAN**

1884   The Tembu Church is founded as an independent African Christian Church in South Africa by Nehemiah Tile, an African leader of the local Wesleyan Church. It is the first independent church in South Africa and is meant to present Christian teachings in a way compatible with Tembu culture.   **AFRICAN**

1884   In an effort to prevent the loss of children to other faiths, the Catholic council of bishops in the United States requires that all parishes maintain schools.   **CATH**

1884   The first meeting of the Fribourg Union of Social Catholic Leaders takes place. The group, which discusses the church's role in promoting workers' rights and other social issues in Europe, meets annually until 1891.   **CATH**

1884   At the Conference on Colonial Questions, the major European colonial nations support missionary work in Africa.   **CHRIS**

1884   A Jewish synagogue is established in Nagasaki, Japan.   **JUD**

1884   The Mormon Church makes its first attempt to win converts in the Muslim world when a mission is established in Turkey. It meets with little success; the mission will open and close repeatedly over the next 70 years. Political unrest in the region and Muslim objection to missionary activities account for its lack of success.   **MOR**

1884   With the Canadian Indian Act, the Canadian government begins to ban such ceremonies as the sun dance and potlatch among the Native American tribes of the far west. The government fears that these ceremonies, which bring large numbers of natives together, may be used by native leaders to revolt against government control.   **NATIV**

1884   The Goodwill Department of the Salvation Army opens in London to provide assistance to the poor. In 1930 it becomes the Goodwill League.   **PROT**

1884   The Jehovah's Witnesses, founded in 1872, incorporate in western Pennsylvania as The Zion's Watch Tower Society.   **SECT**

1885   The Indian National Congress political party is founded. A Hindu-dominated political organization, the Congress represents the emerging Hindu middle class. It emerges as the focus of agitation for greater self-rule during the first decades of the following century. The organization does not attract Muslims, who are concerned about calls for self-rule and Hindu dominance; they align themselves with the British instead.   **HIND**

1885   The Muslim Mahdists in the Sudan defeat the Egyptian rulers at Khartoum and begin to centralize the government in order to build a Mahdist Muslim state. They attempt to suppress the Sufi brotherhoods in the rural regions and introduce Islamic reforms in accord with Islam as it is practiced elsewhere in the region.   **ISLAM**

1885   Fearing for their religious freedom, several thousand Mormons, many of them polygymous families, move into northern Mexico from the United States.   **MOR**

1885   Following independence from Ottoman rule, the Romanian Orthodox Church is granted independent status by the Orthodox patriarch in Constantinople (Istanbul).   **ORTHO**

1885   In Britain the Methodist Forward movement establishes missions in east London and Manchester to provide educational and social services to the poor. Other missions are established in central London in 1886, west London in 1887, south London in 1889, and other locations through 1903.   **PROT**

1885   Congregationalist minister Josiah Strong (1847–1916) writes *Our Country: Its Possible Future and Present Crisis* and organizes a meeting of Protestant social reformers in Cincinnati, Ohio. The book becomes popular and makes Strong the leader of the Social Gospel movement in the United States, which calls upon the Christian Church to be an agent of social change to create a better and more just society.   **PROT**

1885   British Protestant missionary James Hudson Taylor (1833–?) founds the China Inland Mission to conduct missionary work in the interior of China. The mission becomes the largest in the world in the early 20th century and develops a number of new approaches, including using missionaries from different Protestant denominations and missionaries with little formal education, establishing the mission headquarters in China, requiring missionaries to adopt Chinese customs, and stressing conversion, rather than education or the establishment of churches.   **PROT**

1885   Following the establishment of relations between the United States and Korea in 1882, Protestant missionary activity begins in Korea with the arrival of Presbyterian and Methodist missionaries.   **PROT**

1885   The Revised Version of the King James Version of the Bible is published in England. It has been revised by a panel of scholars from the Anglican Church and other Protestant denominations who began their work in 1870.   **PROT**

1886   The American National Baptist Convention is organized. It is the first attempt by African-American Baptists to create a single black Baptist denomination.   **AFRICAN**

1886   Mennonites begin seeking converts among African-Americans when they establish a school in North Carolina. Although missionary efforts continue in the late 1990s, African-Americans constitute only about 1 percent, or 3,500, of the United States Mennonite population.   **AFRICAN**

1886   Christian Evangelical preacher Dwight L. Moody (1837–1899) establishes the Moody Bible College in Chicago with a curriculum that emphasizes evangelism, prophecy, and emotional preaching. The college becomes a model for other Evangelical colleges.   **EVAN**

1886   The Muridiya Muslim movement is founded by local religious leader Ahmad Bamba (1850–1927) in Senegal. The movement develops in response to French colonization but does not become involved in armed resistance, instead becoming involved in fusing Islam and local traditions and maintaining Islam during the colonial period and following independence in 1960. Other Muslim movements, such as the Fadiliya, Qadiriya, and Tijaniya, also develop in Senegal.   **ISLAM**

1886   The British in Lagos, Nigeria, establish a school with both a Western and Muslim curriculum. The Muslims find this a threat to their autonomy and establish organizations to serve the Muslim community. By 1960 the Muslims have developed a comprehensive educational system for the Muslim community in West Africa.   **ISLAM**

Dwight Moody

Dwight Lyman Moody was an American Evangelical preacher and the founder of Moody Bible College in Chicago, which became a major teaching center for Pentecostal ministers in the United States. Moody was born in Northfield, Massachusetts, in 1837 and moved to Boston in 1854. He became a member of the Congregational Church in 1856. Although he remained a Congregationalist throughout his life, his religious work was in the evangelical spirit and nondenominational. From Boston he moved to Chicago, where he was successful in the shoe business, but in 1860 he began to devote his time to nursing and missionary work for the YMCA during the Civil War and to teaching Sunday school. After the war he remained committed to the Sunday school movement and organized conferences for teachers in Chicago. He visited England in 1867 and met the organist and musician Ira Sankey; they toured together from 1872 to 1875. The Evangelical tour and their *Sankey and Moody Hymn Book* made them famous, first in England and then in the United States when they toured East Coast cities from 1875 to 1877. Moody preached a fundamentalist message of salvation through a direct relationship with God that was free of emotional displays. Moving to institutionalize his message, he founded religious schools for girls and boys in Northfield in 1879 and 1881 and then returned to Chicago to establish the Moody Bible College in 1886. The College became a major center for training Evangelical fundamentalist preachers and remains so in the 1990s. Moody died in 1899.

1886   The Jewish Theological Seminary of America is established in New York to train Conservative Jewish rabbis. It marks the establishment of Conservative Judaism as an alternative to Reform Judaism in America. In the same year the Eldridge Street Synagogue is founded by eastern European Jewish immigrants on the Lower East Side of Manhattan. As the focus of the large local Jewish community, it becomes an important symbol of Judaism in America.   JUD

1886   German philosopher Friedrich Nietzsche (1844–1900) writes *Beyond Good and Evil*, in which he argues that the traditional God of European Christianity is dead and that Christianity should adopt a new ethos in which it views itself as superior to and more powerful than other religions.   MISC

1886   The New Thought movement, a major forerunner of the New Age movement of the 1960s, emerges when Emma Curtis Hopkins, a former follower of Christian Science founder Mary Baker Eddy, opens the Christian Science Theological Seminary in Chicago. The New Thought movement is eventually composed of a number of separate churches in the United States and Europe. Among their most common themes are healing, family, women taking a major role in church affairs, and a break with conventional Christianity.   SPIR

1887   Paul Carus (1852–1919), a German scholar and philosopher now resident in the United States, is appointed editor of *Open Court*, a Chicago-based journal intended to advance a rational approach to religion and ethics. For the next 30 years, Carus will be an indefatigable promoter of Buddhism, not as a true believer but as someone willing to defend it against the attacks made by many Christians. He published over 50 books and some 950 articles, many of them arguing his view that Buddhism is based not on supernatural revelation but "solely on man's knowledge of the nature of things, upon provable truth." In 1891 Carus will hire as an editor and writer the Japanese scholar Daisetz Suzuki, who will play a similarly important role in promoting Zen Buddhism in the United States. SEE **1927–1933, BUDD**.

                 BUDD

1887   The French colonize Vietnam and prohibit Buddhism, the majority religion, and encourage the spread of Roman Catholicism. French influence is confined mainly to the coastal lowlands and does not reach the highland people in the interior.   BUDD, CATH

1887   With the Indian National Congress seen by Muslims in India as representing Hindu interests, the Muslims form their own political organizations: the Muslim Education Conference in 1887, the Indian Patriotic Association in 1888, and the Upper Indian Muslim Defense Association in 1893.   ISLAM

1887   Hoping to end Mormon polygymous marriage, the United States Congress passes the Edmunds-Tucker Act, which is upheld by the Supreme Court in 1890. Because it advocates polygymy, the Mormon Church is dissolved, much property is taken by the government, individual civil rights of

Mormons are restricted, and management of Mormon organizations is turned over to government officials. The church continues to resist ending polygymy but, facing financial ruin, it adopts the Manifesto, which ends plural marriage. It is adopted by church leaders in 1890 and becomes doctrine in 1908. The majority of Mormons who had previously been polygymous end the practice, although a minority continue the practice. It is estimated that in the 1990s some 40,000 Mormons are members of polygymous families.   MOR

1887   When the United States government effectively bans the teaching of religion in public schools, the Mormon Church begins to develop its own education system.   MOR

1887   At a meeting in Richmond, Indiana, Orthodox Quakers in the United States adopt the Richmond Declaration of Faith, brought to the United States by Quakers from Britain. The Declaration is in accord with Evangelical Christian principles and stresses the authority of the Bible, the centrality of Jesus Christ, and personal atonement. The meeting is not attended by Hicksite and Gurneyite Quakers, who had broken from the main body of Quakers earlier in the century.   PROT

1887   A dispute breaks out among Baptists in Britain about the authority of the Bible. At the center of the dispute is Baptist preacher and publisher Charles H. Spurgeon (1834–1892), who argues for absolute authority of the Bible and the development of a Baptist Creed, views rejected by the Baptist Union but kept alive by Spurgeon through his writings.   PROT

1887   Seventh-Day Adventists begin their missionary activity in Africa by sending missionaries to South Africa.   SECT

1887   The New Thought movement spreads to Great Britain with the publication of *Christian Science Healing* by Frances Lord.   SPIR

1887–   The Hemetic Order of the Golden Dawn is founded as a spiritualist sect in
1888   Great Britain. It draws few followers but gains public attention through the interest expressed by poet W. B. Yeats. An offshoot, the Builders of the Adytum, is founded in the United States in the 1920s.   SPIR

1888   Pope Leo XIII (1810–1903) issues his *Libertas*, in which he accepts some innovations of the modern world and begins the transition of the Catholic Church into the modern age. Although the church continues to reject the liberal agenda, it does recognize the separation of church and state, as well as democracy and other political changes in Europe.   CATH

1888   In Indonesia the Great Insurrection of 1888 takes place, with Muslims revolting against Dutch rule and the Javanese who serve the Dutch. The Muslims seek to end Dutch rule and to create a Muslim state. The revolt is put down by the Dutch.   ISLAM

| 1888 | The first Israeli lodge of the B'nai B'rith, the Jewish fraternal organization, is founded in Jerusalem. JUD |

1888   The first Israeli lodge of the B'nai B'rith, the Jewish fraternal organization, is founded in Jerusalem.   JUD

1888   The Jewish Publication Society of America is founded to publish books in English on Jewish religion, culture, and society.   JUD

1888   The first Young Women's Hebrew Association (YWHA) is established in New York City as a counterpart to the Young Men's Hebrew Association (YMHA).   JUD

1888   The Lambeth Conference of Anglican bishops approves the Lambeth Quadrilateral, which sets forth the four basic principles of the church: the Bible as the basis of faith, the Apostles and the Nicene creeds, baptism and the Eucharist, and the episcopal nature of the church.   PROT

1888   The Jehovah's Witnesses in the United States have been active in sending missionaries abroad and people have been converted in India, China, Africa, the Caribbean, and Turkey.   SECT

1888   The American Order of Druids, a pagan group, is founded in Massachusetts.   SPIR

1888–1889   Wovoka (1856–1932), a Paiute in Nevada, receives revelations about returning Native American society to traditional ways and coexisting with whites. His revelations mark the emergence of the Ghost Dance.   NATIV

1888–1900   The Buganda Kingdom in East Africa is devastated by revolution as four factions, respectively led by Muslims, Protestants, Catholics, and adherents of indigenous religions, vie for control. In 1890 the kingdom comes under British control.   ISLAM

1888–1947   These years cover the lifespan of T'ai-Hsu, a Chinese Buddhist monk and scholar who dedicates his life to promoting and reforming Buddhism in 20th-century China. To this end he teaches others, travels throughout the world, writes numerous books, and founds various associations and institutions. T'ai-Hsu calls for both stricter discipline for monks and a more socially active approach to life by lay Buddhists. This reform movement enjoys modest success but will be suppressed when the Communists take over in 1949.   BUDD

1889   The Alpha Synod, the first African-American Lutheran synod, is formed in North Carolina as an alternative to white Lutheran control of African-American Lutheran churches. The Synod closes in 1891.   AFRICAN

1889   (St.) Frances Xavier Cabrini (1850–1917), later known as Mother Cabrini, arrives in the United States from Italy and establishes an orphanage in New York City. During her life she establishes 66 more hospitals, nursing homes, and schools, the best known of which is Columbus Hospital in New York City, founded in 1892.   CATH

1889   Catholic University is founded in Washington, D.C., as an institution to train Catholic clergy. Its supporters are in the Irish or progressive branch of American Catholicism and it draws criticism from more traditional Catholic leaders.   CATH

1889   In Paris, intellectuals from the Ottoman Empire who have gone into exile following the reversal of reforms found the Ottoman Society for Union and Progress. They come to be known as the Young Turks and argue for a constitutional government in the empire and modernization.   ISLAM

1889   In Egypt Muslim scholar Muhammad Abduh (1849–1905) is appointed as the overseer of Islamic law and serves in the position until 1905. He is an advocate of Islamic reform and modernization and sets forth an agenda that incorporates Islamic traditions based on the Qur'an and the *hadith* with modern science and technology. His reform program influences other Muslim reformers in North Africa and Indonesia.   ISLAM

1889   The Central Conference of American Rabbis is founded as an organization for Reform Jewish rabbis.   JUD

1889   As a consequence of Protestant missionary activity, the Syrian Christian community in southwestern India has divided into a number of Christian sects. Subsequent divisions eventually produce five sects: Romo-Syrian Christians of the Syriac rite, the Malankara Church, the Nestorian Church, the Mar Thoma Syrian Church, and the Anglican Diocese of Central Travancore of the Church of South India.   ORTHO, PROT

1889   *Social Aspects of Christianity* is written by Richard T. Ely (1854–1943), an economics professor at Johns Hopkins University and the founder (in 1885) of the American Economic Association. Ely's work seeks to bring together the emerging Protestant concern about social issues and economic theory to create a better world and is influential in the emerging Social Gospel movement in the United States.   PROT

1889   Despite a guarantee of the freedom of religion, Japan's Meiji constitution consolidates the unity of government and ritual in its promotion of the concept of the divine emperor and of the sacred national entity. State Shinto is not viewed as a religion but as a national civic organization. Two palace shrines are completed: the *Kyuchu sanden*, where the emperor personally performs rites for the imperial ancestors, as well as the rites of the new liturgical calendar, and the *kashikodokoro*, a miniature version of the Ise shrine, which effectively makes the emperor the head of the "real" Ise shrine and hence of all Shinto shrines in Japan.   SHINTO, TOL

| 1889 | In Japan Shinto priests of Kyushu issue a call to other Shinto priests and found a national organization, the Fellowship of Shinto Priests (*Shinkan Doshikai*), to work for the restoration of the Department of Divinity. Their assertion that shrines stand outside the sphere of religion ends their involvement with preaching and funeral rites and strictly confines them to observance of ritual. In 1900 the organization is renamed the National Association of Shinto Priests (*Zenkoku shinshokukai*) and helps to strengthen the privileged position of shrine Shinto as the agent of state rituals and, as thus, superior to sect Shinto. **SHINTO** |

| c. 1890 | A number of new sects develop in the Gabon region of West Africa that combine elements from the traditional African religions of the region and Christianity. Known as Bwiti, the sects continue to develop through the 20th century, with a gradual movement toward Christianity. **AFRICAN** |

| c. 1890 | Large numbers of Indians, mostly Hindus but also Muslims and Sikhs, immigrate to British colonies in East and South Africa. Many initially work building the railroads, and future generations become merchants and low-level government employees. They are most numerous in Kenya, Uganda, and South Africa. **HIND** |

| c. 1890 | Members of the Plains indigenous people placed on reservations in Oklahoma are by this time participating in peyote ceremonies. The ceremonies spread to other tribes and continue in the 1990s as a ritual of the Native American Church. Peyote is a mildly hallucinogenic cactus plant. **SEE 1912, NATIV.** **NATIV** |

| 1890 | The Catholic Cistercian monastic order in Europe formally divides into two groups—the Cistercians of the Strict Observance, who first emerged in the 1600s, and the Cistercians of the Common Observance, who first emerged in 1068. **CATH** |

| 1890 | In Japan an Imperial Rescript on Education is issued. A 315-word text to be read aloud on prescribed occasions, it promotes Confucian virtues to unite a presumptively benevolent ruler and loyal subjects and serves as a means of political indoctrination. **CONF** |

| 1890 | K'ang Yu-wei (1858–1927), Chinese scholar and reformist, opens a school in Canton to teach ideas of historical progress, social equality, world government, and Confucianism as an antidote to moral degeneration and indiscriminate Westernization. **CONF** |

| 1890 | The faith healer and "trance evangelist" Maria Beulah Woodworth-Etter (1844–1924) incorrectly predicts that San Francisco will be destroyed by an earthquake in this year. Nonetheless, her charismatic preaching, coupled with her use of trance, attracts followers who, after 1906, become influential in spreading Pentecostalism in the southern United States. **EVAN** |

| 1890 | Jews are given full civil and political rights in Great Britain. | JUD |

| 1890 | A Hebrew Language Committee is founded in Jerusalem. It later plays a major role in reviving Hebrew as the language of daily life for Jews in Israel by creating new words and rules for pronunciation. Previously, Hebrew had been primarily a religious language. | JUD |

| 1890 | *The Golden Bough*, a 2-volume work written by British comparative social theorist James G. Frazer, is published and later reissued in an expanded 12-volume set. The collection provides a wealth of information about religions around the world, and although it has been widely criticized by anthropologists for containing much inaccurate and misleading information, it remains a major source of information on non-Western religions. | MISC |

| 1890 | The Native American Ghost Dance revitalization movement that began two years earlier spreads to native groups in the west and then to groups in the Plains whose way of life had been virtually destroyed by white settlement and the near-extinction of the bison. SEE 1973, NATIV. | NATIV |

| 1890 | The Wounded Knee massacre occurs on December 29 in South Dakota. In an effort to end the Ghost Dance movement, United States soldiers murder over 300 Native Americans, including many women and children. The massacre at Wounded Knee is the last major engagement of the Indian Wars in the west and also the last massacre of Native Americans on that scale. It also marks the end of the Ghost Dance as a major Native American religious movement. SEE 1973, NATIV. | NATIV |

| 1890 | Lutherans from Finland form the Suomi Synod in the upper U.S. Midwest. In 1898 other Lutherans from Finland found the National Evangelical Lutheran Church. | PROT |

| 1890 | *In Darkest England and the Way Out* by Salvation Army founder William Booth is published. It exposes widespread poverty in England and stimulates interest in social work as a solution to the problem. | PROT |

| 1890 | *The Seat of Authority in Religion* by theologian James Martineau (1805–1900) is published in London. It marks an acceptance of reason rather than faith as the final arbiter of truth in Unitarianism and becomes the key doctrine that separates Unitarianism from other Christian denominations. | SECT |

| 1890 | The *Budget* is established in Ohio as a weekly newspaper serving Amish communities in Ohio, Indiana, and Pennsylvania. It is not owned by the Amish but by outsiders, although contributions come regularly from Amish communities around the country. | SECT |

| 1890 | Mennonites from North America begin their missionary effort among tribal peoples in India. | SECT |

1890   The periodical *Our Race: Its Origins and Destiny* begins a six-year publication run in New Haven, Connecticut. It is edited by C. A. L. Totten, a military instructor affiliated with Yale University, and serves to promulgate the British-Israelite ideology, in which the British and Americans of British descent are believed to be descended from one of the 10 lost tribes of Israel. Primarily through Totten's lectures and publications and visits by Edward Hine, another supporter, the British-Israelite movement gains attention, although not a large following in the United States.   **SECT**

1890   In a reaction against Western ideas, Japan's government publishes the Imperial Rescript on Education, which will become one of the most influential documents issued during the era of state Shinto. As reverently read to students in school, it will become a powerful and symbolic agent of political indoctrination by ritually instilling loyalty to the emperor as a divine entity.   **SHINTO, TOL**

1890s   The Chinese reformer Kang Yuwei (1858–1927), a Guangzhou native of the scholar/official class educated in the Confucian canon, authors the utopian *Book of the Great Harmony*. Daoist and Buddhist influences blend with Western socialism and Confucian ideas of personal virtue and service to society in Kang's utopia.   **BUDD, DAO**

1890s   In Britain and the United States, Quakerism begins to change as beliefs and practices that reflect the influence of Evangelical Christianity begin to give way to more liberal ideas introduced by new members and reflect the rise of science and concerns about social issues, such as poverty.   **PROT**

1891   The Maha Bodhi Society is founded in Sri Lanka by Anagarika Dharmapala (1864–1933), a Buddhist monk. The society holds the first International Buddhist Conference at Bodh Gaya, site of the Buddha's enlightenment. It is dedicated both to restoring and maintaining the Buddhist temple at Bodh Gaya and to promoting Buddhism throughout the world. Dharmapal will travel to the United States on several occasions and his lectures there make a number of converts to Buddhism. In addition to gaining followers throughout the world, the Maha Bodhi Society will play a major role in reviving Buddhism in India.   **BUDD**

1891   Pope Leo XIII issues his *Rerum Novarum*, which encourages the Social Catholicism movement but also condemns socialism and what the church views as the excesses of liberalism. The Social Catholicism movement is a reaction to the Industrial Revolution and especially to the resultant plights of workers, including poverty, child labor, and health problems.   **CATH**

1891   The Asiatic Society of Japan elects George William Knox (1853–1912), a Presbyterian theologian from New York, its vice president in recognition of his outstanding work on making Confucianism better understood through his writings in English.   **CONF**

1891   In West Africa a Muslim mosque and school are established in Freetown, Liberia, to serve the Muslim community that lives alongside the Christian community formed by former slaves from the United States.   **ISLAM**

1891   The composition of the Russian Orthodox community in the United States begins to change as Ruthenians, immigrants from the Carpathian region of central Europe, immigrate to the United States to avoid religious persecution and begin joining established Russian Orthodox congregations. They are later joined by Romanians, Ukrainians, and others who reduce the percentage of ethnic Russians in the Russian Orthodox Church in America to about 50 percent.   **ORTHO**

1891   The first Greek Orthodox Church in the United States is established in New York City. Its founding reflects the growing Greek community in the United States, with immigration continuing into the 1920s. Other Greek churches are founded across the nation but no centralized authority is established until 1930 because of political and other differences dividing the Greek-American population.   **ORTHO**

1891   Tokyo Imperial University historian Kume Kunitake (1839–1931) publishes his view that Shinto is a survival of a primitive cult of heaven. This enrages the Shinto priesthood, who see Shinto as transcending all religions, and he is fired in 1892 by the Education Ministry. This incident virtually ends academic freedom in Japan, as scholars are intimidated into silence until 1945.   **SHINTO**

1892   The Buddhist Text Society is founded in Calcutta; it will promote the discovery, publication, and explication of numerous Buddhist texts. This same year, Sylvain Levi (1863–1935), publishes the first of his many translations of and commentaries on Buddhist texts. He will come to be regarded as one of the greatest Western scholars of Buddhism.   **BUDD**

1892   The French-controlled Algerian government represses Islam. Muslims are denied representation in the National Assembly, they are taxed at a higher rate than non-Muslims, and Islamic schools are closed.   **ISLAM**

1892   As anti-Semitism increases, about 30,000 Jews are expelled from Moscow, Russia.   **JUD**

1892   The Indian Shaker Church in the northwest United States is organized as a religious institution, and in 1910 it incorporates in Washington.   **NATIV**

1892   American sociologist Albion W. Small (1854–1926) establishes the sociology department at the University of Chicago. Small is a strong supporter of the Protestant Social Gospel movement and plays a leading role in encouraging the movement to use sociological research as a tool for studying social issues.   **PROT**

1892

<table>
<tr><td>1892</td><td>The Omotokyo new religion and millennial movement is founded in rural Japan. It attracts followers among the rural poor and is repressed by the government, although it survives with about 200,000 followers in the 1990s.   **SECT**</td></tr>
<tr><td>1892</td><td>At this time in Japan, the Japanese new Shinto-based religions include Omotokyo (Teaching of the Great Origin), founded by Deguchi Nao (1837–1918), and Misogikyo (Purification teaching) of Inouye Masakane (1790–1849), organized by his followers in 1872 and accepted as a Shinto sect in 1894.   **SECT, SHINTO**</td></tr>
<tr><td>1892–
1897</td><td>The first known Jain to spend time in England is Champat Rai Jain, an Indian lawyer who goes there to take his British bar exam. In later years he becomes a well-known author of books promoting Jainism and travels and lectures in Europe.   **JAIN**</td></tr>
<tr><td>1893</td><td>The National Baptist Educational Convention is founded in Washington, D.C., to train African-American Baptists for missionary work in Africa.   **AFRICAN**</td></tr>
<tr><td>1893</td><td>At the World's Parliament of Religions held in Chicago as part of the World's Columbian Exposition, two Buddhist representatives, Anagarika Dharmapala and Soyen Shaku, are influential in transmitting Buddhism to the U.S. The former establishes the Maha Bodhi Societies in America (**SEE 1891, BUDD**) and the latter promotes Zen Buddhism there.   **BUDD**</td></tr>
<tr><td>1893</td><td>Pope Leo XIII isssues his *Providentissimus Dues,* which states that the Bible is infallible and urges Catholic theologians to rely on the earliest teachings of the Church for biblical interpretation. This encyclical is an effort to halt the Modern or Progressive movement among some Catholic theologians, which questions the historical accuracy of the Bible in light of recent scientific discoveries and theories.   **CATH**</td></tr>
<tr><td>1893</td><td>Hindu Swami Vivekananda (1863–1902) from India lectures about Hinduism in the United States and forms the Vedanta Society in 1897. It is influential in introducing Americans to Hinduism and plays a role in the incorporation of Hindu beliefs into the New Age movement in the 20th century.   **HIND**</td></tr>
<tr><td>1893</td><td>Competition between Hindus and Muslims in India for jobs, land, and political influence under the British colonial government leads to riots involving Hindus and Muslims.   **HIND, ISLAM**</td></tr>
<tr><td>1893</td><td>Shri Virchand Raghavji Gandhi (1864–1901), a young Indian Jain lay philosopher and social reformer, represents Jainism at the Parliament of World Religions held in Chicago, Illinois, as part of the World's Columbian Exposition. His presentation effectively introduces Jainism to Americans, and he is so well received that he stays in the United States for two years, lecturing on Jainism in many major cities. While in America he founds the Gandhi Philosophical Society, the School of Oriental Philosophy, and the</td></tr>
</table>

Society for the Education of Women in India. He then goes on to lecture in Europe, makes another trip to the United States (1896–1897), and eventually settles in England, where he wins many converts and founds the Jain Literature Society. He will be widely credited in both the United States and England with having introduced Jainism to these lands. (He is not related to Mahatma Gandhi.)   JAIN

1893   The National Council of Jewish Women is founded as a philanthropic, educational, and cultural organization in the United States.   JUD

1893   The Mormon Tabernacle is opened in Salt Lake City.   MOR

1893   In Pennsylvania Rufus Jones (1863–1948), a Quaker from Maine and an instructor at Haverford College, becomes editor of the Quaker magazine *American Friend*, a position he holds for 20 years. Jones espouses a liberal social philosophy and through his writings and preaching plays a major role in transforming American Quakerism from a religion in accord with Evangelical Christianity to one in the lead of the liberal branch of Protestantism.   PROT

1893   The Waldenses, a Protestant sect from France, establish the settlement of Valdese in North Carolina. The settlement fails as a religious community, but the sect enjoys financial success with wine making, cotton milling, and other enterprises.   SECT

1893   The World's Parliament of Religions meets in Chicago. Convened by liberal Protestants, it brings together representatives from many world and regional religions and is an important event in the New Thought movement.   SPIR

1893   The Anti-Saloon League is founded by Protestant minister H. H. Russell in Ohio. It seeks to ban the sale of alcoholic beverages through the passage of local, county, and state laws and serves as a model for organizations in other states. It declines in influence following Prohibition in the United States and in 1950 it becomes part of the National Temperance League.   TOL

1893–1897   The Canudos millennial movement is active in northeastern Brazil. The movement is a religious revolt against the government by poor people in the region and is led by Antonio Maciel (c. 1842–1897), an ascetic healer and preacher who predicts the end of the world in 1899 and the appearance of a new and better world. The revolt is repressed by the government in 1897 with some 20,000 followers killed in the city of Canudos.   TOL

1894   A Jewish community forms in Rhodesia, Africa, as part of British colonization of the region. In the United States in this year, the Reform Jewish community issues the *Union Prayer Book*, which further modifies traditional Jewish practice.   JUD

1894

1894 The Mormon Church establishes the Genealogical Society of Utah to collect and organize family history information. The church is interested in this information so that Mormons can identify ancestors and arrange for their baptism by proxy. The program eventually compiles the largest collection of family history information in the world and becomes a major center for genealogical research for Mormons and non-Mormons. MOR

1894 African-American Presbyterians form the Afro-American Presbyterian Council to coordinate activities of black Presbyterian churches and to communicate with white Presbyterian churches. PROT

1894 A Baha'i missionary comes to the United States and wins some converts in Chicago. SECT

1894–1895 Japan's main territorial gain from the Sino-Japanese War is the acquisition of Taiwan, which it will rule for the next 50 years. In 1900 Japan establishes an imperial shrine of major grade there to memorialize the Japanese heroes who died in battle during the conquest of Taiwan, along with three *kami* (native spirits) noted for overseeing the Chinese island. Tenrikyo (SEE **1838, SECT, SHINTO**) supports the war by contributing to the cost of shipbuilding and war armaments. As Japan acquires new colonies, hundreds of Shinto shrines are built and the colonial subjects are required to observe their rites; the shrines become symbols of subjugation to the colonized. During wartime and occupation, Shinto priests travel abroad with the troops as military chaplains. SHINTO

1894–1906 Anti-Semitism becomes a public issue in France when army officer Alfred Dreyfus (1859–1935), a Jew, is accused of passing military secrets to the Germans. He is court-martialed and imprisoned on Devil's Island. His family and defenders, who rightly believe him to be innocent of the charges, accuse his accusers of anti-Semitism, and the issue becomes one of public debate. In 1899 he is tried and convicted again but pardoned, and in 1906 the guilty verdict is reversed. Evidence from German records found in 1930 proves his innocence. JUD

1895 The National Baptist Convention, U.S.A. is founded through the unification of three existing African-American organizations, the Baptist Foreign Mission Convention of the U.S.A., the American National Baptist Convention, and the National Baptist Educational Convention of the U.S.A. It becomes the largest African-American church, with nearly eight million members in the 1990s. AFRICAN, PROT

1895 The United States Congress begins to restrict government financial support for missionary schools for Native Americans when it votes to end appropriations for this purpose. While the funding is reduced, the support continues until 1944. CHRIS, NATIV

1895   Evangelical preacher William (Billy) Ashley Sunday (1863–1935) begins preaching at revival meetings in Iowa. Over the next 20 years, Sunday becomes one of the best known and most popular revival preachers in the United States.   **EVAN**

1895   The source of the Old Testament becomes a subject of scholarly inquiry upon publication of H. Sunkel's *Creation and Chaos at the Beginning and End of Time,* which attributes Genesis to the ancient Babylonian text known as *Enuma Elish*. Although this claim is rejected by later scholars, study continues on other possible sources of the Old Testament, including texts from the Sumerian, Babylonian, and Akkadian civilizations in the Near East.   **JUD**

1895   Jews are given full religious and economic rights in Hungary.   **JUD**

1895   The basic beliefs of Protestant fundamentalism are set forth at the Niagara Bible Conference. They are the absolute authority of the Bible, the virgin birth and deity of Jesus Christ, the belief that Jesus died to atone for the sins of humankind, the Resurrection of Jesus, and the expected Second Coming of Jesus.   **PROT**

1895   The World Christian Student Federation is founded by Lutherans in Vadstena, Sweden.   **PROT**

1895   Students at the Christian Science Theological Seminary in Chicago begin founding a number of New Thought denominations, including Divine Science, Unity School of Christianity, Homes of Truth, Church of Truth, and Religious Science.   **SECT**

1895   Until this date, only those who actually died in battle may be deified in Japan's Yasukuni shrine **(SEE 1869, SHINTO)**; now those who died of wounds incurred in battle may also be included. Ceremonies at Yasukuni, attended by the emperor often in military uniform, are a powerful agent for the glorification of death in battle and the glorification of war itself. Yasukuni is the subject of a popular children's board game of the era: the fastest way to win is to land on a "death" square, which takes one to instant deification at Yasukuni.   **SHINTO**

1895–   This is the lifespan of Punyavijaya, a Jain monk noted for promoting
1971   Jainism's message.   **JAIN**

1896   The first of the Temple Beth-El congregations (also called the Church of God and Saints of Christ) is founded by former slave and civil war veteran William S. Crowley (1847–1908) in Lawrence, Kansas. It is an early African-American Jewish denomination that grows and then in the 1990s declines to about 40,000 followers.   **AFRICAN**

1896   Publication begins of the *Jesuit Relations and Allied Documents* edited by historian Reuben Gold Thwaites. The volumes, which eventually number 72 in all, contain the original French or Latin and English translations of the reports, letters, and other documents written by the Jesuit missionaries in North America from 1610 to 1791. They become an important source of information on the indigenous culture of Native Americans.   CATH, NATIV

1896   The breach between the Roman Catholic Church and the church of England (Anglican Church) worsens when Pope Leo XIII condemns Anglican orders.   CATH, PROT

1896   Hindus, Muslims, and Sikhs from India are recruited by the British to build the East African Railroad in the British colonies in East Africa. They eventually move into other professions, with many employed as lower-level officials in the British colonial government, a role that often places them in contact and sometimes conflict with indigenous Africans. Some also acquire some wealth and property.   HIND, ISLAM, SIKH

1896   The Russian government actively encourages and assists in the settlement of Russians and other Slavs, such as Ukrainians and Belorussians, in the central Asian republics, whose populations are mainly Muslim. The Russians are given the best farmland and are favored in government economic plans, and their presence is met with animosity by the Kazakhs and other indigenous central Asian peoples.   ISLAM

1896   After the Mormon Manifesto of 1890 ending plural marriage, normal relations resume with the federal government, and Utah enters the Union as the 45th state.   MOR

1896   In Britain the term *English Free Churches* first comes into use when Congregational, Presbyterian, Baptist, and Methodist churches form the National Free Church Council. Earlier in English history, these churches had been labeled non-Conformists, Dissenters, or Separatists in reference to their relationship with the Church of England.   PROT

1896   In the United States Lutherans from Denmark now living in the Midwest form the United Evangelical Lutheran Church in America. The Church unites groups that had previously formed their own associations.   PROT

1896   Mennonite missionaries from North America begin to seek converts in Africa. Their first mission is in the Cameroons, and in 1912 they expand into Zaire. The Zaire mission is successful, and by the 1970s Zaire ranks fifth among nations in the number of Mennonite residents.   SECT

1896–
1897   Increasing anti-Semitism in Europe energizes the movement for a Jewish homeland. Theodor Herzl (1860–1904) publishes *The Jewish State: An Attempt at a Modern Solution of the Jewish Question*, which argues for a Jewish nation, and in 1897 he convenes the first World Zionist Congress in Basel, Switzerland, which results that same year in the formation of the World Zionist Organization.   JUD

1897   The Church of God in Christ is founded as a Holiness church by African-American Baptist ministers Charles H. Mason and C. P. Jones. They have been excluded from mainstream black churches because of their preaching of the doctrine of sanctification (SEE 1907, AFRICAN).   AFRICAN, EVAN

1897   K'ang Yu-Wei (1858–1927) publishes *Confucius as a Reformer*. His interpretation of Confucian teachings and research on ancient texts energizes later scholars who are reappraising Chinese history. He takes the role of an activist in politics, traveling extensively in Japan, Canada, and Europe, and later calling for the establishment of a reformed Confucian Church.   CONF

1897   Frank Bartleman (1871–1935) becomes active in the Holiness movement in the United States. In 1906 he becomes a follower of William Seymour and the Azusa Street Mission in Los Angeles and through his preaching to Christian churches does much to spread the Pentecostal movement. His 1925 book *How "Pentecost" Came to Los Angeles—How It Was in the Beginning* does much to call attention to the role of the Azusa Street Mission in the emergence of Pentecostalism.   EVAN

1897   The extremist Hindu nationalist movement begins in India when two British health inspectors are killed and Bal G. Tilak, an orthodox Hindu agitator, is imprisoned for the murders.   HIND

1897   The Bund (General Jewish Workers Union) is established in Russia, Poland, and Lithuania and supports Jewish autonomy and rights in eastern Europe.

Holiness Movement

The Holiness movement was a religious revival that occurred in several Protestant denominations in North America and western Europe in the 19th century. Although the movement was most closely associated with the Methodist churches, it also included many denominations, among them Wesleyans, Congregationalists, Pietists, and African-American churches. The basic element of the movement was a personal religious experience called sanctification, the second blessing, or the baptism of the Holy Spirit. In the United States there were three separate Holiness movements in the 19th century. The first was centered in the Northeast and was primarily Methodist. The second emerged in the Midwest and its members were especially involved in social causes, such as the abolition of slavery and women's rights. The third emerged in African-American churches nationwide and emphasized the experience of the Holy Spirit. The Holiness movement was not an organized movement and in fact was characterized by frequent ruptures and the formation of new churches. Nonetheless, it had a long-term influence on Christianity as the precursor of other churches, such as the Salvation Army and the Wesleyan Methodist Church, and the Pentecostal movement, which emerged in 1901 in the United States.

Also in this year, the first museum devoted to Jewish history and culture opens in Vienna, Austria. JUD

1897   The *Jewish Daily Forward*, a Yiddish-language newspaper, begins publication in New York City and draws a large readership among recent Jewish immigrants from Europe. The editor is Abraham Cahan (1860–1951), considered by many to be the leading Jewish intellectual in America in the first half of the 20th century. In the same year, the *Jewish Times*, the first Canadian Jewish newspaper, appears in Canada. JUD

1897   The Rabbi Isaac Elhanan Theological Seminary opens in New York City for Orthodox Jewish rabbis. It maintains its purpose as a seminary but later develops into Yeshiva University, which also provides undergraduate, graduate, and professional education. JUD

1897   In Uganda Anglican missionary Alfred Robert Tucker (1849–1914) attempts to develop a native Anglican Church but fails due to the opposition of other Anglican missionaries to what they fear will be African control. PROT

1897   Charles Taze Russell, founder of the Jehovah's Witnesses, and his wife, Maria, separate and divorce in 1913. She charges him with cruelty and infidelity and the controversy leads some members to become disenchanted with the religion. As a result, the religion loses members. SECT

1897   Jehovah's Witnesses establish their first church in Germany. They are never fully accepted and suffer persecution throughout the 20th century, being banned as a cult in 1998. SECT

1898   The African Baptist Union of West Africa is founded by Mojola Agbebi (1860–1917), a Nigerian who had been involved in founding independent African Baptist and Anglican churches. AFRICAN

1898   The *Action Française*, a political group with close ties to Roman Catholicism, is founded in France. It stresses French nationalism, including the exclusion of Jews, Protestants, and immigrants, and draws many followers among conservative Roman Catholics in France. The group declines when the church bans Roman Catholic membership in 1928 but revives during the German occupation during World War II. CATH

1898   Daoist religious specialists in Shandong, China, train rebel militiamen and enroll women in Red Lantern paramilitary organizations. These forces will participate in the Boxer Rebellion (1898–1900), aimed in part at Christian missions and more generally at Western influence and encroachment. A combined Western expeditionary force will rout the Boxers in 1900 and occupy the imperial capital of Beijing. DAO

1898   In the Fergana Valley of central Asia, Muslims launch a *jihad* (holy war) against the Russians who control the region and whose economic reforms have caused food shortages in the region and disrupted life in general. The revolt is put down and its leaders are executed. **ISLAM**

1898 With the United States victorious in the Spanish-American War, the United States takes control of the Philippines, whose population is mainly Roman Catholic. Missionization is now opened to Protestant missionaries and within a few years nearly all Protestant denominations have sent missionaries to the islands. **PROT**

1898–
1899 In the Sudan the Muslim Mahdist government is defeated by a combined British Egyptian force at the Battle of Omdurman, and in 1899 the British and Egyptians begin joint rule of Sudan, which lasts until 1955. They move to end the influence of the Mahdists and return to the earlier system in which the Muslim community is governed by Muslim scholars. **ISLAM**

1898–
1899 The Baha'i religion spreads with groups established in London and Paris. **SECT**

1898–
1900 During the Boxer Rebellion in China against foreign influence, missionaries and Chinese Christians are persecuted, assaulted, and killed. After the rebellion is crushed, Christian missionary activity resumes. **CHRIS**

1899 The first formal mission for Japanese Buddhists in America is established in California as a branch of the Jodo Shinshu (True Pure Land) sect, founded by Shinran (**SEE 1224, BUDD**). It will eventually grow to become one of the major Buddhist sects in North America. **BUDD**

1899 The Armenian Apostolic Church, the ancient Gregorian Church of Armenia established in 535 C.E., is organized in the United States and becomes the largest Eastern Catholic Church in the nation. The church retains ties to its counterparts in Armenia and Lebanon. **CATH**

1899 In the United States the public debate between the progressives, who favor a more modern and "American" Catholic Church, and the traditionalists is put to rest by Pope Leo XIII, who supports the traditionalists and objects to modernist changes. **CATH**

1899 The Gideon Society, later called Gideons International, is founded by businessmen in the United States to distribute copies of the King James Version of the Christian Bible to the general public. By 1998 the Gideons are active in 172 nations and have placed over 450 million Bibles in hotels, hospitals, schools, and prisons. **CHRIS**

1899 Evangelical Christians begin their missionary activity in Africa when the Disciples of Christ organization sends missionaries to the Congo. In the next two decades other Evangelical churches in the United States also send missionaries to Africa. **EVAN**

1899   German Protestant missionary Christian Keysser (1877–1961) begins his
            work among the Kate people of New Guinea. Keysser is a follower of the
            Volkskirche (People's Church) school of missionary work that advocates the
            creation of churches within their cultural context. Toward this end, he
            intensively studies the Kate and other New Guinea cultures, which are
            described in his 1926 book, *Anutu im Papuagemeinde*.   PROT

1899   The first Hutterite colony in Canada is established by Hutterites from South
            Dakota, but it fails after five years.   SECT

1899   Astrology gets a major boost in the United States when astrologer
            Evangeline Adams (1868?–1932) makes accurate public predictions and
            goes on to have a radio astrology show.   SPIR

c.1900   The Batuque religion emerges among the Afro-Brazilian population in the
            city of Belém, Brazil. It is a syncretic religion that combines elements from
            African religions, South American indigenous religions, and Roman
            Catholicism, and which later also adds elements of spiritualism.   AFRICAN

c.1900   In the Ottoman Empire the Young Ottoman political reformers, who date
            to the 1860s, are replaced by the Young Turk reformers, who argue for a sec-
            ular nation with a constitutional government.   ISLAM

c.1900   The century of Muslim *jihad* (holy war) in West Africa concludes when the
            French and British take control of the region and either depose Muslim
            rulers or place them under their control. Although Muslim rule ends, the
            jihad has resulted in many people in the region converting to Islam, with
            unique forms of Muslim worship emerging in the rural areas, where Islam
            and indigenous religions are often combined. For example, Muslim teach-
            ers and religious leaders are often assigned the role of healer, in accord with
            the traditional practice of using religious ritual to cure illness.   ISLAM

c.1900   The Zoe movement emerges in Greece. It is a movement within Greek
            Orthodoxy that seeks to revive the church by focusing on sacred texts and
            personal behavior. The movement is focused in the activities of a core group
            of followers, including monks, theologians, and lay persons.   ORTHO

1900   The Ecumenical Missionary Conference is held in New York City. It is the
            largest such conference of all time, with over 200,000 people around the
            world attending. The conference demonstrates unity among Christian mis-
            sionaries and also declares as a goal "the evangelization of the world in this
            generation."   CHRIS

1900   More than 250 Daoist temple halls or shrines are in operation at Mount Tai,
            the Daoist holy place in China's Shandong Province.   DAO

1900   The City of Zion is founded north of Chicago, Illinois, by John Alexander
            Dowie (1847–1907). Dowie advocates faith healing and healing through

atonement and discourages followers from seeking medical care. In 1895 he had been convicted of manslaughter for neglecting followers in his care, but the verdict was overruled on appeal. Many early preachers in the Pentecostal movement of the next decade are influenced by his teachings. **EVAN**

1900   The Bethel Bible College is founded by Holiness preacher Charles Parham (1873–1929) in Topeka, Kansas. During the year he lays his hands on one of his students, Agnes Ozman, as a form of "spirit baptism." On New Year's Eve he prays for her and she begins speaking in tongues. The event is interpreted as a sign that she has been baptized with the Holy Spirit. It marks the emergence of the belief that spirit baptism can be observed in outward signs, such as speaking in tongues, a key element of Pentecostalism. **EVAN**

1900   In India young Muslims who seek a more confrontational approach in dealing with the British colonial government form the Urdu Defense Association. Members of the association reject the conciliatory approach advocated by many leaders of the Muslim community in India. **ISLAM**

1900   In Hausaland, in West Africa (the former Hausa states), most of the population has now been converted to Islam, and Hausaland emerges as a major center of Islam in West Africa. **ISLAM**

1900   Zionism develops in Jewish communities in the Arab world with the founding of the first Zionist organization in Morocco. **JUD**

1900   Conservative Judaism emerges in the United States. It advocates the limited modification of traditional rituals to accommodate life in the modern world. **JUD**

1900   In the United States greater cooperation is achieved by the individual members of the Methodist Church when at the General Conference there is agreement that the church should be more involved in social causes and in alleviating suffering. **PROT**

1900   British-Israelism, the idea that the British are descended from one of 10 lost tribes of Israel, is brought to the attention of evangelist Charles Parham, who accepts it and plays a role in popularizing the idea when he later founds the Pentecostal movement in the United States and spreads it to California. **SECT**

1900   The International Council of Unitarian and Other Liberal Religious Thinkers and Workers is founded. In 1961 the name is changed to the International Association for Religious Freedom. Unitarians are active in the association, which promotes religious tolerance, cooperation, and social welfare programs around the world. **SECT**

1900   The last Amish community in Switzerland disappears when it merges with the Swiss Mennonites. **SECT**

1900   Omoto-kyo, a new Japanese millenarian religion is founded by Deguchi Nao (1836–1918), a female shaman, who claims that Deguchi Onisaburo, the husband of her daughter, is the savior. She is openly critical of other religions and government practices and draws a large following.   **SECT**

1900   The Bureau of Shrines (*jinja kyoku*) is established within Japan's Home Ministry, separate from the Bureau of Religions, in hopes of creating a legal standing for the special nonreligious status of Shinto shrines. The Bureau of Shrines regulates Shinto shrines and priests, as well as the construction of shrines in the overseas colonies; it is an agent of indoctrination for state Shinto. This year the total of all shrines reaches its highest point—196,357; after this there will be a steady decrease in their number.   **SHINTO**

1900   Restrictions are placed on modern-day Druids who worship at Stonehenge in southern England. Both the stones and the site itself are being damaged by the worshipers. By the 1990s access to the site is restricted to paved walkways. Modern neo-pagans believe that Stonehenge was a ceremonial site used by the Druids 2,000 years ago.   **SPIR**

1900s   As Buddhism comes to be increasingly better known in the West, numerous writers and poets will allude to Buddhism in their works. Among those in the first half of the century who do so are Rainer Maria Rilke, Hermann Hesse, John Masefield, T. S. Eliot, Edith Sitwell, W. B. Yeats, and Aldous Huxley. In the latter half of the century, Gary Snyder, Alan Ginsberg, and Jack Kerouac, among others, make use of Buddhist imagery. Meanwhile, psychoanalyst Carl Gustav Jung reveals a deep interest in and accommodation of Buddhism in his theories, and philosophers, such as Ludwig Wittgenstein, Karl Jaspers, and Martin Heidegger, admit to having been influenced by Buddhism.   **BUDD**

1900–
1908   Japan's government enacts ordinances that grant the police wide powers of surveillance over religious activities and establish a strict system of bureaucratic control over religious bodies. The Public Peace and Order Police Law prohibits membership in political parties by Shinto and other religious leaders.   **SHINTO**

1900–
1945   State Shintoism, with its emphasis on patriotism and worship of the divine emperor, becomes the ideology of Japanese imperialism, continuing through World War II. To the extent that Confucianism also stresses the worship of ancestors and an orderly, obedient society, it too plays a role in this ideology.   **SHINTO, CONF**

1901   The Pentecostal movement begins in the United States. It derives its earliest members from the conservative factions of Baptist and Holiness churches who look for alternatives to the rationalism and intellectualism of the mainstream Protestant churches. In January the Pentecostal movement continues to grow at the Bethel Bible College in Topeka, Kansas, as students and teacher Charles Parham pray fervently in order to be filled with the Holy Spirit and to display that state by speaking in tongues. Most achieve the goal and begin to preach to others of their experience.   EVAN

1901   An American edition of the Revised Version of the King James Version of the Bible is published in the United States. It follows the British edition published in 1885 but has been rewritten to appeal to an American audience.   PROT

1901   The Social Gospel movement, which advocates a church role in ending social problems, gains support from mainstream Protestant denominations when the Episcopal and Congregational churches look into labor abuse in America. In the next two decades, other denominations, such as the Baptists and Methodists in the north, begin to address social issues, and various Protestant social service organizations are founded.   PROT

1901   Mennonites from North America begin their missionary work in northern China, expanding to southern China in 1911 and then to western China. Mennonite missionary activity in China ends in 1951 when missionaries are forced to end their work by the government.   PROT

Glossolalia

Glossolalia is the technical term for speaking in tongues. Glossolalia is a form of religious behavior in which an individual in a state of religious ecstasy or trance utters words, phrases, or sentences that are not from a language he or she speaks or comprehends. It is commonly assumed that people speaking in tongues are speaking in an actual language that is different from their own language and is a language that they do not know. For example, a speaker of English speaks in Hindi or a speaker of Spanish speaks in Inuit. Actually, research has shown that people who are speaking in tongues do not speak in a language unknown to them or in any language at all. Rather, the sounds or words they make are random utterances that are not part of any language, nor do they form a language of their own. In addition to the words, speaking in tongues also involves other forms of linguistic expression including the use of repetitive sounds, rapid changes in pitch and intensity, and singing or chanting. Glossolalia occurs in many societies around the world and is a widespread, though not especially common, form of religious expression. In all religious contexts glossolalia is a form of emotional worship that indicates a close relationship with a supernatural force (a god or spirit), and in many cultures it is believed that the force is speaking through the individual. Glossolalia is most common and has drawn the most attention in Pentecostal worship in the 20th century. In Pentecostalism speaking in tongues is seen as a holy gift, a visible manifestation of baptism through the Holy Spirit. It was closely associated with the emergence of Pentecostalism in the United States from 1900 to 1906, after which it spread around the world. Since the rise of the New Pentecostalism in the second half of the 20th century it has been a component of worship in some mainstream Protestant and Catholic churches as well.

1901–1902	The Providence Industrial Mission is founded in Malawi by John Chilembwe (c.1860–1915), a Malawi religious leader ordained a minister in the black Baptist Church in the United States. The organization develops a successful education system and becomes a center of resistance to colonial rule by the British. Chilembwe is killed while leading a revolt in 1915 and becomes a national hero. **AFRICAN**
1901–1903	Mormon missionary activity is extended to Africa, Japan, Russia, southern Europe, and Palestine. **MOR**
1901–1906	The 12-volume *Jewish Encyclopedia* is published in the United States. **JUD**

Pentecostalism

Pentecostalism is a Christian denomination that began in 1900–1901 in Kansas and then within 10 or so years had spread around much of the world. Pentecostalists believe that the most important religious act is the direct experience of God. They do not believe that a formal church, denomination, clergy, or set of rules are needed; in fact, they believe that such trappings of organized religion can interfere with the ability to experience God directly. To some extent, Pentecostalism emerged in the United States as an alternative to organized Christian religion. It was also an ecumenical movement in that it attracted people from different denominations and also (at least initially) represented a fusion of white and black southern Christianity. It appealed especially to the poor. The basic religious experience for Pentecostalists is the baptism of the Holy Spirit, which consists of being filled with and overpowered by a force greater than oneself that creates a oneness with God. Pentecostal worship is highly emotional and the baptism of the Holy Spirit is often displayed through "speaking in tongues," dancing, shouting, writhing, and other forms of emotional expression. In addition to speaking in tongues, healing and prophecy are two other "gifts" associated with Pentecostal worship. Early Pentecostalists believed strongly in the independence of each church, but by 1914 the Assemblies of God Church had formed, marking the emergence of Pentecostal Christianity as a denomination, and over the following decades many sects emerged within the movement, as did independent churches. Nonetheless, the number of Pentecostalists remained relatively few until the 1950s, when the New or neo-Pentecostal movement emerged in the United States and then Britain. The New movement differed from Classical Pentecostalism in that to a large extent it took place in mainstream Christian (at first Protestant and then Catholic) churches. It differs also in that many members are upper or middle class, speaking in tongues is not required, there is a focus on being joyful and giving praise, and there is less emphasis on strict morality in personal behavior. Pentecostalism has been the fastest growing Christian denomination in the 1990s, with over 400 million adherents around the world, in hundreds of denominations and tens of thousands of churches. It is a significant presence in every region of the world except the Islamic Middle East and China.

1901–
1907

Pogroms (attacks on Jews and Jewish settlements) take place in Russia, with thousands of Jews killed and their property destroyed. The pogroms spur immigration to the United States. JUD

1902

Pope Leo XIII establishes the Pontifical Bible Commission to support Bible study within the Catholic Church. The commission, whose work is supported by later popes, is charged with studying the Bible in the context of modern scholarship. CATH

1902

In Arabia the Muslim Wahhabi sect, which had been defeated by Egypt in 1818, reasserts itself and takes the city of Riyadh. By the 1930s it has conquered the region and established the modern nation of Saudi Arabia. ISLAM

1902

The Varieties of Religious Experience by Harvard psychologist William James (1842–1910) is published. In this highly influential book, James argues that religion, philosophy, and psychology are interrelated, and he emphasizes the personal experience of religion. MISC

1902

German Protestant missionary Bruno Guttman (1876–1966) begins his work among the Chagga people of East Africa. Guttman is a follower of the *Volkskirche* (People's Church) school of missionary work that advocates creating churches within their cultural context. Toward this end he intensively studies Chagga culture for 18 years and provides a wealth of information for others to study. PROT

1902

A new form of Quakerism emerges in the American Midwest and West. It involves mainly recent converts to Quakerism who espouse a liberal theology and social agenda, conduct meetings based on silent worship, and are active later in the century in the peace, antipoverty, and Civil Rights movements. PROT

1902

Lutherans from Slovakia form the Slovak Evangelical Lutheran Synod in Pennsylvania. PROT

1902

Congregationalist minister and social critic Washington Gladden (1836–1918) writes *Social Salvation*. In this book and others, he questions the role of capitalism in society and advocates religion as a means to end social injustices and to form a more equitable society. Gladden remains a major figure in the American Social Gospel movement until his death in 1918. PROT

1902

The Philippine Independent Church is founded in the Philippines by journalist Isabelo de los Reyes. Early members of the church seek greater Filipino control of the church and thus separate from the Vatican. The church doctrine and ritual are based on an admixture of Roman Catholicism and Protestantism, and the church is aligned with Episcopal and Anglican churches. SECT

1902

Rosicrucianism, which came to America from Europe in 1694 and then essentially disappeared, undergoes a revival when a history of the move-

ment is published in Pennsylvania and the Fraternitatis Rosae Crucis is
founded.   **SECT**

1902   In southern Asia regional and local Sikh organizations unite to name the
chief Khalsa Diwan as the primary spokesman for the Sikh community.
Sanatan Sikhs publish a definitive version of the *Dasam Granth*, the religious text first published in the 1740s. As much of the volume is composed
of Hindu myths, the text is considered of lesser importance by Tat Khalsa
Sikhs, who seek separation from Hinduism.   **SIKH**

1902   In the United States *Outlines of Modern Christianity and Modern Science* is
written by geologist George McCready Price (1870–1963). It is the first
attempt to use science to resolve the creationism/evolution debate in favor
of creationism. Price argues that the world was created recently, in accord

Creationism

In the Judeo-Christian tradition, creationism refers to the belief that the world was
created by God as described in the Book of Genesis. In the United States and Britain
it more specifically refers to a religious and political movement of the 20th century
with roots in earlier centuries, which seeks to replace the teaching of scientific biological evolution in the public schools with creationism. The movement is especially
associated with fundamental and evangelical Christianity. Thus, creationism is one in
a series of conflicts between science and religion that date to the Renaissance.
Although all creationists believe that God created the earth and human beings, there
are a variety of creation theories. Young-earth creationism suggests that the earth was
created in six 24-hour days several thousand years ago. Day-age creationism acknowledges science and conceptualizes the six days of creation as six geological eras. Gap
creationism accepts the six-day genesis but suggests that there were long time periods
between each day. An alternative to these is flood creationism, in which the Noachian
Flood is believed to have mixed the geologic record so that it appears that evolution
took place. Another form of creationism is theistic creationism, in which God is seen
as having created the universe by means of evolution. This theory is rejected by many
creationists who do not believe that creationism and evolution can be reconciled.
The most recent form of creationism is creation science, in which creationism is set
forth as a scientific theory that rivals evolution. Creation scientists argue that evolution is an unproven theory or is wrong. Creationism is rejected as scientific theory by
most scientists. Creationism continues to be an important political issue in the
United States, as creationists, despite losses in court cases, continue their attempts to
limit the teaching of evolution and promote the teaching of creationism. In 1998 1
state (Alabama) cautioned students about the validity of evolution, 9 states advised
teachers to avoid discussing evolution, and in another 25 there were controversies
about the issue.

with Genesis, but that a worldwide environmental catastrophe altered the geological record to make it appear that evolution had taken place.   TOL

1903   *The Negro Church* by African-American social activist and social scientist W. E. B. DuBois (1868–1963) is published. It is the first sociological study of the African-American religion and becomes a model for subsequent research.   AFRICAN

1903   *L'Évangile et L'Église* is written by French priest Alfred Loisy, a leader of the Modernist school of Catholic theologians. The book uses new historical evidence to revise the history of Christianity's emergence, with Jesus portrayed as a prophet who believed he was the Messiah and the emergence of the Catholic Church hierarchy seen as a product of historical events. The book is condemned by the church and placed on the *Index of Forbidden Books*.   CATH

1903   The Bible is translated into Ukrainian for the first time.   CHRIS

1903   The Religious Education Association is founded in the United States to oversee the curriculum and teaching in Sunday schools.   CHRIS

1903   Charles Parham, the Holiness preacher who had initiated the Pentecostal movement in 1901, conducts a three-month revival meeting in Galena, Kansas, and draws thousands of listeners who are attracted to his message of spirit baptism as demonstrated through speaking in tongues.   EVAN

1903   In Senegal the French colonial government begins to restrict Muslim activity, fearing the political influence of Muslim leaders, as the majority of Senegalese are Muslims. In this year schools are required to use the French language, and over the next few years restrictions are placed on Muslim religious teachers, French is made the language of the legal system, and Arabic-language publications are banned.   ISLAM

1903   Jehovah's Witnesses begin their practice of handing out their religious literature door-to-door.   SECT

1903   Kogakukon University for the study of Shinto, under the management of Ise shrine, is made a state institution in Japan. Kokugakuin (the institute for national learning), established in 1890 under the direction of the Kotenkokyusho (the institute for the study of Japanese documents), will later become Kotenkokyusho University.   SHINTO

1903   Sikhs from India immigrate to western Canada and California to seek work in the expanding economy of the region, and in the next four years over 10,000 (mostly men) arrive. In 1908 Canada restricts settlement and in 1913 California does the same, effectively curtailing Sikh immigration until the 1950s.   SIKH

1903–1911	In Egypt a series of laws is passed that limits the role of Muslim scholars and local Muslim teachers, controls Sufi activities, and places the education system under government control. These laws successfully culminate 100 years of efforts to bring the Muslim community under state control. Although the government supports Islam and most Egyptians are Muslims, the authoritarian government sees the Muslim leadership as a rival to centralized rule. **ISLAM**
1904	The Order of Ethiopia Church is established among the !Xhosa people of South Africa by Methodist minister James M. Dwane (1851–1916). At first affiliated with the African Methodist Episcopal Church in America, in 1983 it becomes a semi-autonomous unit of the Anglican Church. **AFRICAN**
1904	Zhang Yuanxi takes office in China as the 62d celestial master. **DAO**
1904	The term *dream time* is first used by anthropologists B. Spencer and F. J. Gillen in *The Northern Tribes of Central Australia* in reference to the belief common among Australian aboriginals that they live in a time of harmony with their ancestors. The origins of the belief are unknown, although it is thought to date back tens of thousands of years. **MISC**
1904	The United States government bans the Sun Dance, an important annual ceremony of the Plains people. The ceremony, which requires group dancing, fasting, and vision quests, is held annually in the spring or early summer at the start of hunting season. The government fears that the resulting large gatherings will be used by native leaders to revolt against government rule. Some Indian nations continue to conduct a less dramatic Sun Dance as part of Fourth of July celebrations in the late 1990s. **SEE 1946, NATIV.** **NATIV**
1904	In the United States representatives from Presbyterian churches begin meeting with the intention of unifying the three main churches: the Presbyterian Church in the United States of America (north), the Presbyterian Church in the United States of America (south), and the Cumberland Presbyterian Church. **PROT**
1904	The first independent Christian seminary, the Tokyo Shingakusha, is founded by Japanese Protestants who seek to establish Japanese control of Christianity in Japan. **PROT**
1904	*The Twentieth Century New Testament* is published in England. It has been prepared by a panel of Protestant scholars and is written in language accessible to children. **PROT**
1904	The Salvation Army has become fully international, with groups established in 49 nations. By the 1990s the Salvation Army nearly doubles the number of missioned nations. **PROT**

1904	The Order of the Cross religious movement is founded in England. The movement spreads to other European nations and North America with adherents strongly opposed to all forms of violence. **SECT**

1904	The Order Templi Orientis, a group that combines the occult with aspects of Buddhism and Freemasonry, is founded in Germany. It later moves to England and survives into the 1990s. **SPIR**

1904–
1905
A replica of the Palitana Jain temple at Gujarat, India, is erected at the St. Louis Exposition in Missouri. Made of teakwood, it is 20 feet square at its base and its central tower is 35 feet high. **JAIN**

1904–
1905
The Protestant Ethic and the Spirit of Capitalism by German sociologist Max Weber (1864–1920) is published. Weber is a major scholar of religion and his research and ideas continue to be influential into the 1990s. He is credited with the idea that Protestantism led to capitalism in Europe, although this is a simplification of his theory. **MISC**

1904–
1905
During the Russo-Japanese War, Japan's General Togo cites the help of *kami* (native spirits) in defeating the Russian navy. Success in this war will widen the boundaries of the Japanese empire and reinforce the nationalist Shinto mythology. Yasukuni shrine will become increasingly prominent as it welcomes more "glorious war dead." Additional military armaments will be put on display there, and the annual festivals, which last for several days, come to include horse racing, sumo wrestling, Noh drama, geisha dancing, and fireworks. By 1929 there will be 124,121 *kami* enshrined there. **SHINTO**

1904–
1907
The Maji-Maji revolt takes place against German rule in Tanzania. The revolt is a religious millenarian movement led by Ngwale Kinjikitile (?–1905), known to his followers as Bokero, who preaches that religious rituals will force the Germans to leave. The revolt is repressed by the Germans, who execute Bokero and kill thousands of others. **AFRICAN**

1904–
1914
The second *Aliyah* to Palestine takes place. During this period more Jews from eastern Europe settle in Palestine and some establish collective settlements known as *kibbutzim*. SEE **1919–1923, JUD. JUD**

1905
In France the Laws of Separation are enacted that end the privileged status enjoyed by the Roman Catholic Church. The laws also end the distinction between recognized religions and nonrecognized religions, although some religions continue to be granted recognized status in a few districts. **CATH, TOL**

1905
Korea becomes a protectorate of Japan. Conservative Confucian scholar Ch'oe Ikhyon (1833–1906), frequently banished for his objection to Korea's domestic and foreign policies, organizes the Righteous Army and fights against Japanese and Korean royal troops. Imprisoned, he dies of starvation rather than accept food from the enemy. **CONF**

| 1905 | State civil service examinations based on Confucian texts are abolished in China in the midst of attempts at modernization. **CONF, TOL** |

1905 — Charles Parham, who initiated the Pentecostal movement in 1901, has been preaching in the Plains states and has drawn thousands of people to the movement. Many of them become evangelists for the movement and preach across the South. Parham also establishes a Bible school in Houston, Texas. One of the students is William Seymour, an African-American Holiness preacher who plays a major role in the development of Pentecostalism in 1906. As Seymour is black and Parham is a segregationist, Seymour is forced to listen to Parham's lectures while sitting in the hallway outside the classroom. **EVAN**

1905 — A group of Muslim reformers known as the Jadids ("new method") emerge among the Muslim Uzbeks in central Asia. They are the counterpart of reformers in Russia who were involved in the 1905 revolution and are repressed by the local Muslim leadership. Muslims from Azerbaijan, Crimea, and Kazan meet secretly to establish the Russian General Muslim Party to represent Muslim interests across Russia. **ISLAM**

1905 — In India the British government divides Bengal into separate provinces, with one province composed mainly of Muslims and the other of Hindus. **ISLAM**

1905 — In Indonesia the Dutch government seeks to control Muslim religious and political movements by placing Muslim education under government control. **ISLAM**

1905 — *The Protocols of the Elders of Zion* are published in Russia. Reputedly a Jewish plan to take control of the world, it is in fact a forgery written in Paris for the Russian government. Even though it is a well-known forgery, the document remains an important element of anti-Semitic propaganda in the 1990s. **SEE 1921, JUD**. **JUD**

1905 — The first Orthodox Christian seminary is opened in the continental United States, in Minneapolis, Minnesota. **ORTHO**

1905 — The Baptist World Alliance is formed to help open lines of communication among various Baptist churches. **PROT**

1905 — The Tat Khalsa Sikhs in southern Asia are successful in having images removed from the region near the Golden Temple as they overcome resistance by less conservative Sikhs. **SIKH**

1905–1906 — The Pentecostal movement is spread from the United States to Norway by Thomas Barratt, an Englishman who has lived in Norway since childhood and has recently experienced the baptism of the Holy Spirit in New York City. In 1916 he founds the Filadelfia Church in Oslo. **EVAN**

1905–
1911
The constitutional crisis takes place in Iran. The crisis is precipitated by almost a century of European contact, modernization, Westernization, and conflict between the secular and Islamic communities. A constitution in 1906 creates a parliamentary government and establishes Islam as the state religion. In 1907 the shah dismisses the parliament and then loses power from 1900 to 1911, when he is restored by the Russian military. **ISLAM**

1906
In the Sudan the African prophet Ngundeng (?–1906) dies. As a prophet he appealed to the Nuer and Dinka people of southern Sudan and encouraged traditional worship and resistance to British rule. After his death, his work is carried on by his son, who is killed by the British. **AFRICAN**

1906
In China the Manchu rulers, in a desperate attempt to salvage their crumbling dynasty, issue an edict to place sacrifices to Confucius on equal footing with those to heaven. It raises the traditional Secondary Sacrifice to Grand Sacrifice and makes Confucius "Assessor of Heaven." **CONF**

1906
The *Daozang Jiyao*, a compendium of the Daoist canon, is reprinted at Erxian temple in Chengdu in China. **DAO**

1906
The Apostolic Faith Gospel Mission in founded on Azusa Street in Los Angeles by Holiness preacher William Seymour. A Pentecostal mission, its worship involves spirit baptism, speaking in tongues, faith healing, testimonies, dancing, and shouting. The church attracts a large and varied following, and over the next several years, the Azusa Street church becomes known around the world. The church building is eventually abandoned and then torn down in 1928. **EVAN, PROT**

1906
The All-India Muslim League is founded to represent Muslim interests in India. In one of its first actions, it supports the partition of the Bengal region into Hindu and Muslim sectors and also proclaims its goal of representing the interests of Muslims in India. The league remains the political voice of Muslim interests in India for the next 50 years. **ISLAM**

1906
The Aliens Bill becomes law in Britain. Passed by Parliament in 1905, it is designed to limit immigration of Russian Jews to Britain. Also in this year the Congress of the United States passes a resolution condemning the Russian pogroms, and American Jews form the American Jewish Committee in response to the persecutions in Russia as an organization to lobby the United States government over issues of concern to the Jewish community. **JUD**

1906
Reform Jewish rabbis issue a statement arguing that the Bible should not be taught in public schools in the United States. **JUD**

1906
The Service Book of the Holy Orthodox Catholic Church is published in the United States and for many years serves as the prayer book for English-speaking Orthodox Christians in North America. **ORTHO**

1906   The Cumberland Presbyterian Church and the Presbyterian Church of the United States of America merge and form the Presbyterian Church U.S.A. **PROT**

1906   The Jehovah's Witnesses extend their missionary activities to Africa when their missionary branch, the Watch Tower movement, establishes a mission center in Rhodesia (Zimbabwe). **SECT**

1906   The Ministry of Home Affairs begins to implement merger plans for Japan's Shinto shrines, of which there are 190,265; of these the majority are small

Azusa Street Mission

The Azusa Street Mission in Los Angeles is seen by many scholars as the birthplace of the Pentecostal movement. Although Pentecostalism emerged in 1900–1901 through the preaching of Charles Parham in Kansas, the Azusa Street Mission was its first permanent church. It became the center of worldwide attention, as Christians from around the world came there to pray and the news media covered events there in much detail. The Azusa Street Mission was founded in 1906 by William Seymour in a former African Methodist Episcopal (AME) Church at 312 Azusa Street in downtown Los Angeles. Seymour was a Holiness preacher who had attended Parham's Bible School in Houston, Texas, in 1905 and was attracted to the practice of spirit baptism of the Holy Spirit as demonstrated through the speaking of tongues. He came to Los Angeles in 1906 to establish a Holiness Church, which became the Azusa Street Mission in April 1906. From 1906 to 1909 the Mission served as a center of Pentecostal worship; Seymour and his followers conducted three services a day, seven days a week. The services centered on baptism of the Holy Spirit and did not involve prayer, singing, or sermons in the usual sense. The services were highly emotional events. Worshipers spoke in tongues, danced, shouted, sang, waved their arms, and fell to the floor in states of religious ecstasy. The services also attracted faith healers, hypnotists, and others and were widely and strongly criticized by some mainstream Christian clergymen. Word of the services and the Pentecostal movement was spread around the world by Seymour's *Apostolic Faith* newspaper and the news media. Worship at the Mission combined elements from African-American churches and southern white churches and thus appealed to a wide range of people, many of whom were poor and felt isolated from mainstream churches. Thus, for a few years religion and social class issues overrode concerns about the segregation of blacks and whites, and the church drew individuals from both groups. It went into decline after 1909, and by 1914 the membership was almost entirely black. The congregation eventually disbanded and the building was torn down in 1928. The role of the Azusa Street Mission was widely ignored by white religious historians and white Pentecostalists themselves into the 1970s, perhaps because Seymour and many of his followers were African-American. It is generally acknowledged in the 1990s that both Seymour and the Mission played an early, central role in the development and spread of Pentecostalism and that most Pentecostal churches around the world can trace their roots to the Azusa Street Mission.

local venues with no rank or assigned clergy. With considerable opposition and confusion, this drastic program will abolish over 83,000 shrines through 1929. The mergers renew the debate over whether or not the shrines are religious. The 1908 Boshin Rescript seeks to reintegrate the shrines more fully into the nation's social and political life.   **SHINTO**

1906   Japan's religious cooperation movement begins with the establishment of the Religionists' Concord Association, consisting of leaders from sect Shinto, Buddhism, and Christianity. In 1912 representatives of these three groups will together vow to support the emperor and to work together to promote national morality.   **SHINTO, TOL**

1906–   In 1906 two Englishmen, R. J. Jackson and J. R. Pain, who as soldiers in
1908   Myanmar had come to appreciate Buddhism, found the Buddhist Society of England. In 1908 Ananda Metteya, an Englishman born Allan Bennett, who became a Buddhist monk in Burma in 1902, comes to England on the invitation of this society (now renamed the Buddhist Society of Great Britain and Ireland) as the head of the first Buddhist mission to the West. This society and its journal, the *Buddhist Review*, will become a major influence in transforming Buddhism in the West from a scholarly study to a religious faith.   **BUDD**

1907   The Church of God in Christ, founded in 1897, is reorganized when one of the founders, Charles H. Mason (1866–1961), is attracted to Pentecostal Christianity and makes speaking in tongues an important component of worship and a requirement for baptism. In the 1990s the church has about four million members in the United States, Africa, and the Caribbean.   **AFRICAN**

1907   The National Primitive Baptist Convention is founded as an umbrella organization for African-American Primitive Baptist churches, which retain autonomy over their own congregations. In the 1990s it has about 1.8 million members.   **AFRICAN**

1907   The Catholic Church in Rome moves to end the Modernist theological movement in the church when it issues the decree *Lamentabili* and the encyclical *Pascendi* that list and attack what it believes are errors in Modernist thinking. Additionally, all clergy are required to take an oath condemning Modernism and committees are set up to review literature for signs of Modernist thinking.   **CATH**

1907   Ch'en Huan-chang (1881–1931), a graduate student at Columbia University, organizes a Confucian Society in New York, then organizes societies in Shanghai (1912), Beijing (1913), and later in Chufu. Within a year, there are 130 such societies.   **CONF**

1907   Pentecostalism spreads from Norway to England. It is centered in the All Saints Church in Monkwearmouth, Sunderland, and draws considerable attention across England after Thomas Barratt of Norway preaches there.

During the same year, Pentecostalism spreads to Chile through the American Methodist minister Thomas Hoover, who after 1910 founds the Methodist Pentecostal Church in Chile.   **EVAN**

1907   In Tunisia reformers known as the Young Tunisians found the *Tunisian* magazine. The Young Tunisians, composed mainly of intellectuals educated in French schools and colleges, advocate the end of French rule, the creation of on Arab-Muslim society, and modernization through selective borrowing from Western society.   **ISLAM**

1907   In the United States the Northern Baptist Convention is founded to coordinate the activities of Baptist churches.   **PROT**

1907   *Christianity and the Social Crisis* is written in the United States by church historian and professor Walter Rauschenbusch (1861–1918), a leader of the Social Gospel movement. It becomes a basic statement of the movement and Rauschenbusch becomes a major figure in the movement, which emphasizes the use of religious faith to create a better world by ending social problems such as poverty.   **PROT**

1907   Japan's Ministry of Home Affairs begins the systematization of Shinto ceremonies, bringing these rituals under uniform government control. Local shrines are forced to abandon their traditional practices and beliefs, as their festivals are transformed into the rites of state Shinto.   **SHINTO**

1907   The term *New Age* is used for the first time in reference to spirituality and inner harmony by Alfred Orage (1873–1934), the editor of the weekly newspaper *New Age*.   **SPIR**

1907   Annie Besant (1847–1933), a British social reformer, becomes president of the Theosophical Society and remains so until her death in 1933. Under her leadership, the movement expands to become worldwide in scope.   **SPIR**

1907   The Rosicrucian Fellowship is founded in Ohio and becomes a major force in the promotion and support of astrology.   **SPIR**

1907   Astrum Argentium (Silver Star), an occult group, is founded by the intellectual Aleister Crowley (1875–1947) in England. It continues to function as a secret society in the 1990s.   **SPIR**

1907–   The Pentecostal movement spreads to Sweden from Norway. Thomas Barratt,
1908   who founded the Norway movement in 1906, assists in its spread to Sweden by preaching there and helping others to experience the baptism of the Holy Spirit. During these years it also spreads to Germany and Switzerland through the efforts of Jonathan Paul of Berlin, who experiences the spirit baptism of the Holy Spirit with Barratt in Norway, and Norwegian preachers who travel to Germany.   **EVAN**

1907– 1908	The Young Turks, who seek basic reforms in the Ottoman Empire, establish the Committee for Union and Progress as a political arm to bring about societal changes. In 1908, with military support, they overthrow the sultan and establish a new government. Although they advocate a constitutional government, they actually rule in an authoritarian manner until 1918 and the defeat of the empire in World War I. **ISLAM**
1907– 1910	The Church of the Nazarene is established in the United States when the Association of Pentecostal Churches in America, the Church of the Nazarene, and the Holiness Church of Christ unite. Basically Methodist in orientation, the church retains some evangelical practices including faith healing and abstinence from tobacco and coffee. In the 1990s it has about 500,000 members. **EVAN**
1908	Adam Clayton Powell Sr. (1865–1953) becomes minister of the Abyssinian Baptist Church in New York City. He plays a key role in making it one of the

---

New Age

New Age is the name given to a social and religious movement that emerged in the United States and Britain in the early 1970s. It is important to note that the New Age is not a religion or even a religious movement in any organized sense. The New Age has no core set of beliefs, religious texts, required rituals, religious specialists, organized leadership, nor a central church. What is common to the movement is a concern with healing, personal growth, and spirituality. The beliefs and practices associated with the New Age are all ones that at least some New Age adherents believe will encourage healing, increased spirituality, or personal growth or transformation. Perhaps the primary source of these beliefs and practices are non-Western religions, such as Buddhism and Hinduism, non-Western cultures such as those of Native Americans, ancient mystical religions, and modern psychology. The list of beliefs and practices that can be considered New Age is extensive and includes, for example, astrology, acupuncture, shiatsu, yoga, chanting, drumming, meditation, nature walks, herbology, *feng shui*, angel worship, tarot readings, vision quests, and a belief in the "power" of crystals. As there is no doctrine and individual freedom is stressed, New Agers are free to choose from among these and dozens of other practices in order to achieve their personal goals. Although the New Age has no formal leaders, there are several prominent New Age teachers or guides whose lectures, workshops, and writings are popular with New Agers. In the 1990s these include Deepak Chopra, Bahgavan Das, Andrew Weil, Marianne Williamson, and Joan Borysenko. The genesis of the movement is unclear. Some experts believe it developed as an offshoot of the counterculture movement of the 1960s and was also influenced by the environmental movement. Others trace its beginnings to the spirituality movement of the late 19th and early 20th centuries, which also looked to non-Western religions for inspiration.

major African-American churches in the nation. It becomes the base for the political career of his son Adam Clayton Powell Jr. (1908–1972), who serves later as the minister of the church and also serves in the U.S. House of Representatives.   AFRICAN

1908   A major religious revival takes place in Malawi. It is led by Elliot Kamwana (c.1890– ?), a supporter of the Church of Scotland whose preaching attracts many Malawans to the church and who in this year founds the Church of the Watchtower. He is deported by the British authorities in 1909 and the new church declines in influence.   AFRICAN

1908   As Pentecostalism draws followers in Britain, Alexander Boddy, the vicar of All Saints Church, where the English movement began, founds an annual meeting for Pentecostalists, keeps records of the meeting, and begins publication of the Pentecostal magazine *Confidence*.   EVAN

1908   In Indonesia non-Muslim Javanese found the *Budi Utomo* (Bold Endeavor) organization to revive the ancient Hindu-Buddhist culture of Java and combat Westernization that has resulted from Dutch rule. In 1917 it breaks with the Dutch government and seeks cultural and political autonomy for the nation.   HIND

1908   The Ahmadiya sect of Islam, founded in northwest India by Ghulam Ahmad Qadiyani in about 1880, splits into two groups upon his death. One group, the Qadis, believes that Qadiyani is a prophet, which constitutes a violation of Muslim belief and causes them to be repressed as heretical. The second group, the Lahore group, views him as a reformer and spreads to Britain and West Africa.   ISLAM

1908   In India the Muslim newspaper *al-Hilal* (the *Crescent*) is published by Muslim journalist Abu al-Kalam Azad (1888–1958). It takes a pan-Islamic position and calls for the unity of Muslims around the world with the ruler of the Ottoman Empire as the leader of the Muslim world.   ISLAM

1908   In South India Congregationalists and Presbyterians form the South India United Church. It is a loose organizational structure that allows each church much leeway in matters of doctrine and ritual.   PROT

1908   In the United States the Federal Council of Churches of Christ in America is founded as a nondenominational Protestant organization to coordinate the activities of Protestant churches.   PROT

1908   The Evangelical Alliance has declined in influence in the United States and becomes the Federal Council of the Churches of Christ in America.   PROT

1908   In the United States the General Conference of the Methodist Church adopts the Methodist Social Creed, which guides Methodist efforts to address social issues. The creed is revised in 1972 to extend the scope of activity to ethnic and religious minorities and to include peace as a goal.   PROT

1908   The Salvation Army extends its efforts to fight poverty by establishing a program for tribal peoples in India.   PROT

1908   The Christian Science Church in Boston begins publication of the *Christian Science Monitor* newspaper.   SECT

1908   Tenrikyo (SEE 1838, SECT, SHINTO) is granted legal and institutional status as one of Japan's 13 official Shinto sects. In 1913 a sub-sect of Tenrikyo will arise with Hommichi, founded in 1913 by Onishi Aijiro (1881–1958). Other new religions include the revivalist Shinto Tokumitsukyo founded by Tokumitsu Kanada (1853–1924) in 1912, and the Tenrikyo-influenced (SEE 1838, SHINTO) Ennokyo, founded by a woman possessed by *kami* (native spirits), Fukada Chiyoko (1887–1925). Although in 1919 Konkokyo (SEE 1859, SECT, SHINTO) will be the first new religion to become established in the mainland United States, Honkyoku Shinto had founded a temple in Hawaii in 1906, followed by Inari Shinto in 1912, and Jinga Shinto in 1913.   SHINTO

1908–
1910   The Pentecostal movement spreads to cities in southern China through the efforts of preachers from the United States, Europe, and Canada. During these years it is also introduced in France and Italy but does not spread widely, as it is opposed by the Roman Catholic Church.   EVAN

1909   A copy of the Cambodian translation of sacred Buddhist writings is deposited at a temple at Angkor Wat. For the next 60 years, Cambodian monarchs frequently visit the site and sponsor religious ceremonies there.

                    BUDD, TOL

1909   In London, England, Zion College becomes a center of Pentecostalism with such leaders as Cecil Polhill and Smith Wigglesworth preaching to followers from around the world who come to hear the Pentecostal message and experience spirit baptism.   EVAN

1909   The Pentecostal movement has spread to India and Korea through the efforts of preachers from the United States and Great Britain. During this year it is also brought to Argentina by Italian immigrants from Chicago. However, it does not spread widely in Argentina until Swedish and Canadian missionaries arrive in 1921.   EVAN

1909   The Hindu Mahasabha political party is founded in northern India. It stands in opposition to the Muslim League, which supports Muslim interests in the region, and advocates efforts to reconvert Indian Muslims to Hinduism and Hindu nationalism. It declines in importance after India gains independence in 1947.   HIND

1909   The Arand Marriage Act is enacted in the Punjab region of southern Asia. It creates a new Sikh marriage rite and ends the use of the Hindu rite by Sikhs. It further separates Sikhism from Hinduism and is a triumph in the Sikh community for the Tat Khalsa Sikhs.   **HIND, SIKH**

1909   In India the British government responds to requests from Muslim leaders for separate elections for Muslim communities by allowing such elections on a limited basis. The decision angers Hindu leaders and increases strain between the Muslims and Hindus.   **ISLAM**

1909   Muslims in India found the Society of Helpers as a pan-Islamic organization to bring together Muslims in Iran, Afghanistan, and Turkey to assist them in expelling the British from India.   **ISLAM**

1909   Tel Aviv is established as a Hebrew-speaking city in Palestine.   **JUD**

1909   Anglican missionary Archibald Lang Fleming (1883–1953) begins his missionary activities among the Inuit of northern Canada. The Anglican effort is successful and eventually the majority of Inuit covert to Anglicanism.   **PROT**

1909   Lawyer and Protestant preacher Cyrus I. Scofield (1843–1921) compiles, edits, and annotates *The Scofield Reference Bible*, which becomes the basic religious text for fundamental Protestants in the United States.   **PROT**

1909   American businessman H. Spencer Lewis travels to France, where he studies Rosicrucianism and is initiated into the Rosicrucian Order in France. **SEE 1915, SECT.**   **SECT**

1909   A Rosicrucian group, the Rosicrucian Fellowship, is founded in Oceanside, California, by Max Heindel, a follower of anthrophosophist Rudolf Steiner and the author of *Mystic Christianity*.   **SECT**

1909   The Jehovah's Witnesses relocate their headquarters to Brooklyn, New York, and change their name to the People's Pulpit Association. Except for one year during World War I, Brooklyn remains its headquarters. The name of the group's magazine is changed from *Zion's Watch Tower and Herald of Christ's Presence* to the *Watch Tower and Herald of Christ's Presence*. The group incorporates in New York as the Watch Tower Bible and Tract Society.   **SECT**

1909   Japanese religion and Shinto officially are separated from each other when the Administration of Shrines in the Bureau of Shrines comes under the Home Ministry, and the Bureau of Religion is transferred from the Home Ministry to the Education Ministry. This separation of state Shinto from religion will be reinforced in the Imperial Ordinance No. 173 of 1913.   **SHINTO, TOL**

c.1910   The practice of snake handling as part of Pentecostal Christian worship begins in Tennessee when Pentecostal preacher George Went Hensley includes the practice in his services. About the same time the drinking of poison is also advocated by some preachers, although it enjoys less popularity than snake handling, which spreads to a small number of Pentecostal churches throughout the southeast and neighboring Midwest states. Both practices are based on Mark 16:15-18: "They shall take up serpents; and if they drink any deadly thing, it shall not hurt them." SEE **1940**, EVAN.   EVAN

1910   Buddhism has been in decline for some centuries when the Chinese National Buddhist Society (*Chung Hua Fu Ciao Tsung Hui*) is founded in this year. It is the most important of several such Buddhist associations founded in China since 1900 both to reform Buddhism and to promote religious liberty in modern China. The new government, however, shuts down this society in 1915 because it is seen as a challenge to its attempts to impose a modern secular state; the new leaders also see the whole Buddhist establishment of monasteries and their lands as potential economic resources.
                                                                      BUDD, TOL

1910   The World Missionary Conference is held in Edinburgh, Scotland. The conference addresses a number of pressing issues for Christian missionary work, including the spread of Islam and concerns that Africa will become an Islamic continent, the need to create unity across all Christian religions and denominations, and the need for a general plan to guide missionary work around the world.   CHRIS

1910   The Pentecostal movement is brought to South Africa by American preachers and attracts black and white South Africans alike. In the same year the movement is spread to São Paulo, Brazil, by preachers from the United States and Sweden and leads to the formation of the Assembly of God and the Christian Congregation of Brazil.   EVAN

1910   Muslim intellectuals in Bukhara in central Asia form the Union of Noble Bukhara as an organization to support Muslim solidarity around the world and to resist Russian rule.   ISLAM

1910   The Sufi Order in the West is founded by Indian Muslim Hazrat Inyat Khan (1882-1927) in London. It seeks to incorporate modern Western culture into Sufism and includes elements taken from Buddhism, Christianity, and spiritualism.   ISLAM, SPIR

1910   Reconstructionist Judaism begins in New York City as a fourth branch of modern Judaism. It rests on the belief that the Jewish religion should reflect the reality that Jews live in a world both Jewish and secular, and that Jewish belief and culture should be flexible and responsive to societal changes.
                                                                      JUD

1910   In Australia several Lutheran organizations unite to form the Evangelical Lutheran Church Union.   PROT

1910   In the United States the Presbyterian Church adopts the five points of belief: inerrancy of the Bible, Christ's virgin birth, his atonement for human sins, his bodily resurrection, and the acceptance of miracles. Over the next several decades there are debates in the church about the acceptance of these five doctrines.   **PROT**

1910   Japan conquers Korea and controls the Protestant missionary activity that had been successful in making converts since the early 1890s. The Japanese government is concerned that the missionaries support Korean nationalism. **PROT**

1910   The Non-Subscribing Presbyterian Church of Ireland is founded as the central organization for non–Anglican and non–Roman Catholic churches in Ireland. Although not Unitarian, it is often aligned politically with the Unitarian Church in Great Britain.   **SECT**

1910   The Pormalin revitalization movement begins among the Batak people of Sumatra in Indonesia and flourishes for about 10 years. It is a reaction to Dutch colonialism and Christian missionary efforts. The movement involves spirit possession, worship of traditional priest/kings, and some Christian practices.   **SECT**

1910   Following the annexation of Korea, which will last until 1945, the Japanese occupation government institutes the cultural policy of compulsory Shinto worship in hopes of making all Koreans loyal subjects of Japan. In 1919 construction begins in Seoul on an imperial shrine of major grade dedicated to the sun goddess Amaterasu and to the Emperor Meiji. By 1936 there will be 51 Korean Shinto shrines, a number of them enshrining Japanese *kami* (native spirits) thought to be involved in the conquest of Korea during ancient times. Koreans are denied their request to have their own national founders enshrined there; the occupation government insists they must worship Japan's imperial divinities.   **SHINTO**

1910   Japan establishes the Karafuto shrine on Sakhalin Island; enshrined there are three *kami* (native spirits) held to be pacifying agents for the northern limits of the Japanese empire and also considered as general guardian divinities for the island.   **SHINTO**

1911   The Nazirite Baptist Church (*AmaNazaretha*) is founded among the Zulu people of South Africa by Isaiah Shembe (1870–1935), who claims to be and is accepted by some followers as the black Messiah. The church combines Christianity and traditional Zulu religion and draws many followers. Shemba is later seen as a threat by the British authorities and is arrested and dies in prison in 1935.   **AFRICAN**

1911   A Buddhist priest, the Eighth Bogdo Gegen, becomes the ruler of a theocratic government of Mongolia, but Russian military advisers are sent from Moscow to create and train a national army.   **BUDD**

1911   Nestorian Christians from the Middle East begin immigrating to the United States to escape persecution by the Muslim Kurds and Turks.   CATH

1911   The Roman Catholic Church approves the founding of the Catholic Foreign Missionary Society of America at Maryknoll, New York. The first Maryknoll missionaries leave for the field (China) in 1918.   CATH

1911   In India the British government reverses its 1905 partition of Bengal into Hindu and Muslim sectors. Muslims had supported the partition, but Hindus strongly objected as they sought to control Muslim autonomy. The decision weakens cooperation between the Muslims and the British government and further strains relations between Muslims and Hindus.
    HIND, ISLAM

1911   A delegation from the Baptist World Alliance visits Russia hoping to convince the tsar to allow Baptists to build churches and a seminary there. The request is refused.   PROT

1911   In the United States the Northern Baptist Convention and the Freewill Baptist Churches unite and form the Northern Baptist Convention, which in 1950 is renamed the American Baptist Convention. Such unions are rare in the Baptist denominations, which favor the independence of churches.   PROT

1911   Missionaries from the United States introduce Protestantism to Vietnam. Over the century it attracts several hundred thousand converts but remains a minority religion in comparison with the number of converts to Buddhism and Roman Catholicism.   PROT

1911   Following the revolution in Iran, followers of Baha'i enjoy more freedom and establish Baha'i schools, centers, and hospitals.   SECT

1911   Japan's Education Ministry orders schoolteachers to take students to local Shinto shrines to pay obeisance on festival days; the rescript especially emphasizes visits to the Yasukuni shrine. In 1928 the shrine visits will be required on a monthly basis, with emphasis on visits to the Ise and Meiji shrines, as well as to Yasukuni.   SHINTO

1911   The first Sikh community is founded in England and is supported by Sikhs in India. However, the British are resistant to Sikh settlement and no other communities are established in Britain until after 1945.   SIKH

1911   In Japan the government requires that all schools have their students attend ceremonies at Shinto shrines as a form of ancestor worship. The requirement is criticized by Christians in Japan as impinging on their religious freedom.   TOL

1911

1911– 1912	The Sarekat Islam nationalist political party is established by Muslims in Indonesia. It is the first nationalist party in Indonesia and is renamed the Partai Sarekat Islam in 1923 and the Partai Sarekat Islam Indonesia in 1929. It is associated with moderate Islam after 1926 and is often in conflict with the colonial Dutch government. A number of splinter parties develop in the 1930s, and by the 1950s the party draws only a small minority of members. **ISLAM**
1912	The Shaker sect, an indigenous movement on the island of St. Vincent in the Caribbean based on a mix of Christianity, African religions, and local customs, is banned by the government. The ban will be lifted in 1965. **AFRICAN**
1912	The Israelites are founded in South Africa by Enoch Mgijima (1858–1928). Viewing himself as an African Jew, he rejects the New Testament and institutes Jewish rituals, such as celebrating the Sabbath on Saturday and observing Passover. The sect is repressed by the British authorities, with some 100 followers killed in a battle in 1921. **AFRICAN**
1912	The Young Christian Workers is founded by Roman Catholics in Brussels, Belgium, to represent the interests of young workers. It becomes a model for similar organizations in other European nations. **CATH**
1912	In Japan the government officials recognize Christianity as one of the religions of Japan and convene the Three Religions Conference, with Buddhism, Shinto, and Christianity represented. The designation of Christianity as one of the three religions in place of Confucianism reflects both the decline of Confucianism and the spread of Christianity in Japan since the 1880s. **CHRIS**
1912	English Protestant missionary Roland Allen (1868–1947) writes *Missionary Methods: St. Paul's or Ours?* It is an influential work that questions the practice of missionaries spending long periods in one place and advocates the method believed to be used by St. Paul of moving from place to place and leaving converts in charge of the local churches. **CHRIS**
1912	The Quanzhen order founds the Central Association of Daoism in Beijing, China's capital. **DAO**
1912	The Pentecostal movement spreads from the United States to Finland. **EVAN**
1912	The Ottoman Empire is driven out of Europe, save for a small area around Istanbul, by a combined force from Serbia, Bulgaria, Montenegro, and Greece. **ISLAM**
1912	The Muhammadiyah social and religious organization is established by politically moderate Muslims in Indonesia. It becomes a major force for social and educational development and is involved in establishing schools, mosques, libraries, and hospitals. **ISLAM**

1912   Hadassah is founded by Jewish women in the United States to provide medical, educational, and philanthropic support to Jews in Palestine.   **JUD**

1912   The Young Israel movement emerges within Orthodox Judaism in the United States. While not calling for major change in religious belief and practice, it institutes changes in dress and behavior to bring Judaism in closer accord with mainstream American customs.   **JUD**

1912   In *The Elementary Forms of Religious Life*, the French sociologist Émile Durkheim (1858–1917) argues that humans divide all elements of the universe into two categories—sacred and profane—and religion concerns matters that are considered sacred. The idea has much influence in later scientific research on religion.   **MISC**

1912   A strong effort by the United States federal government, religious organizations, and others begins to eradicate peyote use among Native Americans. These groups claim that peyote is addictive (it is not) and that it causes physical and mental harm to users. Native Americans see the effort as yet another attempt to interfere with their traditional religions. **SEE 1917, NATIV.**   **NATIV**

1912   The idea of "autonomous" churches is added to Baptist thinking by Baptist pastor E. Y. Mullins (1860–1928) of the influential Southern Baptist Seminary and later president of the Southern Baptist Convention and World Baptist Alliance. The notion of autonomy is basic to the principle that each Baptist church is independent.   **PROT**

1912   Since its founding in 1865, members of the Salvation Army in Britain have often been the victims of insults and assaults on the street. In this year they are given the right of public assembly by the government.   **PROT**

1912   The Anthroposophical Society is founded by philosopher Rudolf Steiner (1861–1925) in Germany. It is based on his philosophical-spiritual system known as Anthroposophy. Followers do not consider it a religion per se, but rather a philosophical and spiritual system that can be used to help individuals reach their highest potential. The movement produces a system of schools (Waldorf schools, which number over 500 around the world), a system of healing (anthroposophical medicine), and principles for living in harmony with the environment.   **SECT**

1912   As the Hutterite colonies in America continue to grow, a new colony is formed in Montana by Hutterites from South Dakota.   **SECT**

1912   Sikhs in California form the Pacific Coast Khalsa Diwan, which represents the Sikh community in the United States, and open a temple in 1913. When Sikh immigration to the United States is effectively ended by the Immigration Act of 1917, the organization plays the major role in preserving the Sikh religion and culture in the United States until 1946, when Sikh immigration to America resumes.   **SIKH**

1912

1912–1913	Muslims in India form the Association of the Servants of the Ka'ba to combat British rule in India and to support the Ottoman Empire. ISLAM
1912–1916	The Contestado Revolt takes place among peasants and laborers in rural Brazil. It is led by José Maria II (?–1913), who claims to be a brother of João Maria, a 19th-century self-described messiah. The revolt is put down by government forces, who kill Maria and then about 3,000 followers in 1914. TOL
1912–1949	With the fall of the Qing dynasty and the advent of the Republican era, China fragments politically. Social change accompanies political upheaval. The anti-Confucian New Culture movement is an intellectual response to this ferment; the movement rejects most forms of traditional Confucian thought. War and revolution convulse China from the late 1920s through the end of the 1940s. The triumph of the Communists in 1949 brings an authoritarian peace and stability to the country. Throughout this tumultuous era, Daoism continues its long decline. CONF, DAO
1913	The Moorish Science Temple is founded by Noble Drew Ali (Timothy Drew, 1886–1929) in Newark, New Jersey. Although it never draws a large following, it is the first African-American religious organization based on Islam, black nationalism, and a rejection of Christianity. AFRICAN
1913	The African Communion is founded by Mojola Agbebi, the founder of the African Baptist Union of West Africa in 1898. The group is meant to unite all independent African churches in West Africa. AFRICAN
1913	A division develops in the Pentecostal movement in the United States when proponents of the "Jesus only" or "oneness" view argue that there is only one figure in the Godhead, a view rejected by other Pentecostalists. EVAN
1913	In India riots break out in Kanpur when Muslims resist a British attempt to build a road through the grounds of a mosque. The riots are a sign of a growing sense of community among Muslims in India and a greater desire to end British rule. The Muslim League passes a resolution calling for eventual self-government for India. Riots take place later in Calcutta (1918), Bombay (1929), and Kanpur (1931). ISLAM
1913	Reform Jewish women in the United States found the National Federation of Temple Sisterhoods to advocate for a greater role for women in Reform congregations. JUD
1913	In the United States the Anti-Defamation League of the B'nai B'rith is founded and becomes a major force for fighting religious intolerance and anti-Semitism and providing information about Jewish life to both Jews and non-Jews. JUD, TOL

| 1913 | At a conference in Kansas City, the Congregationalists adopt the Kansas City Statement, which sets forth a liberal theology and mission for the church and stresses the role of the church in society. It also sets aside older beliefs associated with Calvinism. PROT |

1913 - 1915   The Harris movement takes place among Africans in the Ivory Coast and Ghana. Led by African missionary William Wadé Harris (c.1860–1929), its purpose is to encourage Africans to convert to Christianity. With the involvement of missionaries, many people in the region become Methodists or Roman Catholics, or join new African Christian churches that develop following the decline of the Harris movement. Among these African churches are the Harris Church itself and the Church of the Twelve Apostles. **AFRICAN**

1913– 1915   The Leo Frank affair unfolds in Georgia. Leo Frank, the manager and part owner of a pencil factory in Atlanta, is accused, tried, and convicted of murdering 14-year-old Mary Phagan, an employee of the factory. The evidence against Frank is weak but popular opinion, stirred up by Populist writer and politician Tom Watson, results in a death sentence. In 1915 the sentence is reduced by the governor to life imprisonment. Later that year Frank is taken from jail by a mob and lynched. The Frank affair is considered to be one of the worst acts of anti-Semitism in American history. SEE **1986, JUD.** JUD

1914   The Pentecostal movement in the United States begins to develop as a distinct denomination when the Assemblies of God organization is founded at a meeting of Pentecostalists in Hot Springs, Arkansas. **EVAN**

1914   American Jews form the Joint Distribution Committtee to help Jews in war-torn Europe. In later years the efforts of the organization are focused on assistance to Israel. JUD

1914   The first two Native American organizations centered on the use of peyote as a religious sacrament are founded. The first is the Peyote Society or Union Church Society. The second is the First Born Church of Christ. They are superseded by the Native American Church, which is founded in 1918. **NATIV**

1914   The Sufi Order of the West is founded by Muslim musician Hazrat Inayat Khan (1881–1927) in London. It combines Muslim and Hindu elements and stresses acceptance of all religions. **SECT**

1914   The Christian Ogboni Society is founded by Anglican minister J. A. T. Ogunbiyi, a Yoruba, in Nigeria. Initially a Christian fraternal organization, after 1930 it is opened to people of all religions and the name is accordingly changed to the Reformed Ogboni Fraternity. **SECT**

1914   According to Jehovah's Witnesses belief, this year marks the end of the Gentile time and is the year in which Jesus Christ begins his rule over the nations of the world. **SECT**

| 1914 | Baha'i missionaries begin seeking converts in Japan. | SECT |

1914–
1915
The Pentecostal movement is brought to central Africa by preachers from Great Britain. **EVAN**

1914–
1918
The Ottoman Empire enters World War I as an ally of Germany and Austria. By the end of the war, all that remains of the Ottoman Empire is the territory of modern Turkey, while its former Arab provinces are divided between Britain and France. Lebanon and Syria are under French control, Iraq, Jordan, and Palestine come under British control, Greece is given additional territory in the east and the Aegean Islands, and Armenia becomes an independent nation. **ISLAM**

1914–
1918
Entering World War I on the side of the Allies, Japan is able to seize German possessions in China and the central Pacific, including the Mariana, Caroline, and Marshall Islands, thus increasing the breadth of its growing empire. In Shinto and Buddhist wartime circles, a movement seeking political participation by the clergy succeeds in gaining them eligibility for election.

SHINTO

1914–
1950
This is a period of general decline in the role of the Anglican Church in Great Britain, as both membership and attendance decline markedly (by two-thirds in England). The decline becomes especially severe during and following the Great Depression of the 1930s and continues into the 1950s when the religion revives briefly, only to decline again in the 1960s. **PROT**

1915
A large-scale religious revival takes place among the people of coastal Nigeria. It is led by Garrick Braide (c.1880–1918), who encourages religious practices in line with Anglicanism and is at first supported by Anglican Church officials. However, he also believes Africans should control their own churches and separates from the Anglican Church to form the Christ Army Church. **AFRICAN**

1915
The National Baptist Convention of America forms as an offshoot of the National Baptist Convention of the U.S.A., which was founded in 1895. In the 1990s it has about 2.5 million members. **AFRICAN**

1915
American Protestant missionary Daniel Johnson Fleming (1877–1969) joins the faculty of the Union Theological Seminary. In his teachings and writings, he questions the view commonly held by missionaries that Western culture is superior and encourages the spread of Christianity apart from Western culture. **CHRIS**

1915
The scholar Chen Duxiu (1879–1942) founds the journal *New Youth*, the radical organ of China's New Culture movement. Duxiu and his followers attack the conventional Confucian sociopolitical order and the cultural tradition of the Three Teachings—Confucianism, Buddhism, and Daoism. **DAO, TOL**

1915   In Malaysia the British government institutes a Religious Council. The council has authority over Islam in the nation, collects religious taxes, and, as a major institution for religious reform, is a source of political stability in the nation.   **ISLAM**

1915   The Pale of Settlement dissolves in Russia as Jews flee the German military advance and the Russian government formally abolishes it as a place of Jewish settlement.   **JUD**

1915   H. Spencer Lewis establishes the Rosicrucian Order, AMORC (Ancient and Mystical Order Rosae Crucis) in New York City. The order later moves to San Jose, California, and becomes the largest of a number of Rosicrucian orders in the United States.   **SECT**

1916   In South Africa the village of Ekuphakameni near Durban is established as the holy city of the Nazirite Baptist Church (*AmaNazaretha*) founded among the Zulu people of South Africa by Isaiah Shembe in 1911. After Shembe is buried there in 1935, the city becomes a major shrine and pilgrimage center.   **AFRICAN**

1916   The Pentecostal movement in the United States, which emerged in 1900–1901 and spread after 1906, has divided into three doctrinal groupings: Finished Work or Baptistic, Second Work or Wesleyan, and Oneness or Jesus Only Pentecostalists. The movement has also begun to divide along racial lines, with churches either white or black in membership.   **EVAN**

1916   The Assemblies of God, a Pentecostal church, is established through the joining together of a number of small, independent Pentecostal churches in Arkansas. It becomes the largest white Pentecostal church in the world, with over 1.5 million members in over 100 nations by the 1990s.   **EVAN**

1916   The British take control of Darfur in Africa, and all of Muslim Africa (West, North, and East), except for Liberia and Ethiopia, is now under European (British, French, Italian, Spanish, German, Portuguese, and Belgian) control.   **ISLAM**

1916   The Indian National Congress and the All-India Muslim League in India demand dominion status for India, expansion of voting rights, and the election (rather than the appointment) of 80 percent of the members of the legislative council. Hindu and Muslim leaders conclude the Lucknow pact between their two organizations and agree that the Muslim minority will have separate electorates and more seats in the legislature than are actually required according to their percentage of the population. Majorities, either of Hindu or Muslim legislators, are also granted veto powers.   **HIND, ISLAM**

1916   To maintain a military force in World War I, Britain institutes conscription. As war is in violation of Quaker beliefs, Quakers refuse to serve and many are imprisoned.   **PROT**

1916	Baha'i leader Abdu'l-Baha issues the *Tablets of the Divine Plan*, which calls upon the followers of Baha'i in the United States to work to spread the religion around the world. SECT
1916	The New Thought Alliance is founded and serves as an umbrella organization for the different New Thought denominations that have emerged in Britain and the United States over the last few decades. The New Thought movement emphasizes spirituality over organized religion and is a forerunner of the New Age movement. SPIR
1916–1917	Russia begins drafting Muslims in central Asia for service in World War I. The draft offends the Muslim community because it had previously been exempt from service in the Russian army and also because Muslim participation is confined to noncombat duty. The Muslims launch a *jihad* (holy war) that spreads across central Asia but is interrupted by the Bolshevik Revolution in 1917. ISLAM
1917	The Jordanites, an Afro-Guyanese church, is founded by E. N. Jordan in Guyana, who builds on the missionary work of Joseph MacLaren, the founder of West Evangelist Millennial Pilgrim Church in Guyana in 1895. It is a syncretic church that combines elements from Hinduism, Judaism, Christianity, and African religions. AFRICAN
1917	Following independence, Mexico enacts a constitution with many provisions seeking to limit the power of the Roman Catholic Church, which had been substantial ever since Mexico was colonized by Spain in the 16th century. SEE **1992, TOL.** CATH, TOL
1917	The Interdenominational Foreign Mission Association is founded and serves as an umbrella organization for missionaries unaffiliated with major missionary organizations or societies. A similar association called the Evangelical Foreign Missions Association is founded in 1945. Missionary groups affiliated with these associations include the African Inland Mission, Sudan Interior Mission, Evangelical Mission Alliance, and the Sudan United Mission. CHRIS
1917	As part of the political unrest in southern Asia involving the British rulers, the Hindu majority and the Muslim minority (the Sikhs) in the Punjab demand the right to elect their own representatives and also advocate for the return of all Sikh temples to Sikh control. (Many had been managed by Hindus.) HIND, SIKH
1917	The Sarekat Islam party in Indonesia, which was founded in 1912, calls for a renewal of Islam in Indonesia and demands fundamental political and economic reforms by the Dutch government. ISLAM
1917	The British government issues the Balfour Declaration in support of the creation of a Jewish state in Palestine. In the following year the declaration wins the approval of United States president Woodrow Wilson, although it

is attacked by Arab Palestinians and other Arabs in the Middle East who believe that a large influx of Jews will result in the removal of Palestinians from the territory.   JUD

1917   The Bolshevik Revolution in Russia topples the tsar and the new Communist government bans discrimination against Jews, although the practice of Judaism, like that of other religions, is repressed. The Hebrew language is banned, as is observance of the Sabbath, and the government disrupts the celebration of major Jewish holidays.   JUD

1917   The Jewish Publication Society of America publishes an English-language edition of the King James Old Testament from which it has removed Christian interpretations.   JUD

1917   The Native American Church in Oklahoma advocates the use of peyote, a mild hallucinogen, in its ceremonies, claiming a right to religious freedom. SEE **1918,** NATIV.   NATIV

Native American Church

The Native American Church, with about 250,000 members in the United States, Canada, and Mexico in the 1990s, is the largest indigenous religion in North America. It was founded in 1918 in Oklahoma and has since expanded to include four major organizations: the Native American Church of North America, the Native American Church of Navajoland, the Native American Church of Oklahoma, and the Native American Church of South Dakota. Religious worship in the church centers on the sacramental use of the mildly hallucinogenic peyote plant. Peyote use by Native Americans for religious purposes dates back several thousand years but has been controversial in the 20th century as part of government efforts to control drug use. Structurally, the Native American Church is organized along the lines of mainstream Christian churches and as such is managed by elected officers, is incorporated in many states, and has formal articles of incorporation. Peyote ceremonies are all-night rituals that involve prayer, singing, ingesting peyote, individual contemplation, and personal revelations shared with the group. While in an altered state of consciousness from peyote, participants might have visions in which they communicate with Father Peyote. The ceremonies are held in a circular buildings like tepees where the participants are seated around the edge of the circle facing an altar, with a fire and ritual objects, such as feathers, water, corn, and drums, arranged in their proper places. Ceremonies are led by a Roadman, who is assisted by Chief Drummer, Cederman, who supplies the wood, and the Fire Chief. Different churches have different policies regarding the participation of women and children. In some churches participation in pilgrimages to collect peyote is also a required activity.

1917	In the United States the Hauge Synod, the Norwegian Synod, and the United Church unite to form the Norwegian Lutheran Church in America, which represents 92 percent of Lutherans in the United States. PROT
1917	In the United States Quakers from the Orthodox, Hicksite, and Gurneyite traditions form the American Friends Service Committee to help humanity through peaceful means. PROT
1917	Various Norwegian Lutheran churches and organizations that have been established in the United States since 1847 move toward union when they cooperate in establishing the National Lutheran Commission for Soldiers' and Sailors' Welfare and the related Lutheran Brotherhood. Several churches also form the Norwegian Lutheran Church of North America. In 1946 it changes its name to Evangelical Lutheran Church (SEE **1960**, PROT). PROT
1917	In the Ukraine Mennonites begin to suffer what is to be three years of persecution, first by the German forces who control the region and then, from 1918 through 1920, as a result of the anarchy caused by the Russian Civil War, which follows the Bolshevik Revolution of 1917. SECT
1917	Joseph Franklin Rutherford (1870–1942), chief legal counsel to the Jehovah's Witnesses, succeeds Charles Taze Russell as the religion's leader following Russell's death the previous year. His election and leadership are controversial, and some Witnesses leave the religion or found splinter sects, including the Standfast Movement, the Paul Johnson Movement, the Elijah Voice Movement, and the Eagle Society. Many dissenters claim that Rutherford does not follow Russell's teachings. SECT
1917	In the first constitution of the Soviet Union, all citizens are granted the right to "religious and anti-religious propaganda." TOL
1917–1918	In the context of the Bolshevik Revolution in Russia, Muslims in central Asia declare Turkestan an independent nation and establish a Muslim government. The Bolsheviks renege on their promise of freedom and in 1918 invade Turkestan, remove the Muslim government, and place the region under Bolshevik military control. ISLAM
1917–1920	Muslims in Kazakhstan, the Caucasus, and Azerbaijan seek to create independent nations after the Bolshevik Revolution and the fall of the Russian Empire. Although these nationalist aspirations are supported at first by Bolshevik leaders, they are ultimately rejected and all three regions are incorporated into the Soviet Union. ISLAM
1917–1921	Pogroms in the Ukraine result in the death of over 50,000 Jews. JUD
1918	Independent Christian churches begin to develop in western Nigeria. Most are founded by prophets and stress healing alongside Christian beliefs and

practices. Collectively known as *Aladura*, meaning "praying people" in the Yoruba language, the most successful of these churches are the Cherubim and Seraphim societies founded in 1925 and the Christ Apostolic Church and the Church of the Lord founded in 1930.　　　　　　　　**AFRICAN**

1918　　Under the leadership of Belgian missionary and later Cardinal van Lebbe (d.1940), the Roman Catholic Propaganda initiates a policy of appointing native bishops, and between 1922 and 1939 natives are appointed to that office in China, southern India, Sri Lanka, Japan, Korea, Uganda, and Madagascar.　　　　　　　　　　　　　　　**CATH**

1918　　The United States House of Representatives considers but does not pass a law banning the use of peyote, a drug used as a sacrament by the Native American Church. Some state legislatures do ban peyote use, although state law has only limited authority on Indian reservations.　　　　**NATIV**

1918　　The Native American Church, whose members use peyote as a sacrament, is officially established and incorporated in Oklahoma. It is a pan-tribal Native American religion that draws adherents from many tribes living in the region, including the Comanche, Kiowa, Apache, Cheyenne, and Oto. SEE **1940**, NATIV.　　　　　　　　　　　　　　　**NATIV**

1918　　As the Russian Orthodox Church loses power during the Russian Revolution, Russian control of the Orthodox Church in the United States weakens, and the Romanians organize their own Orthodox Church in America. The Serbs do the same in 1920, the Greeks in 1922, and the Syrians and Ukrainians follow in 1927. The Georgian Orthodox Church, under Russian control since 1811, becomes independent again.　　**ORTHO**

1918　　In the United States the General Council, the General Synod, and the General Synod of the South unite to form the United Lutheran Church in America. Later in the year it joins with the Augustana Synod, the Norwegian Lutheran Church, the Lutheran Free Church, the Joint Synod of Ohio, the Iowa Synod, the Buffalo Synod, the United Danish Church, and the Icelandic Synod to form the National Lutheran Council, with the Suomi Synod joining later.　　　　　　　　　　　　　　**PROT**

1918　　Jehovah's Witnesses begin preaching their doctrine that "millions now living will never die" in accord with their belief that God (Jehovah), through Jesus Christ, began his rule of the nations of the world in 1914.　　**SECT**

1918　　Until the end of the draft in 1976, Mennonites, Amish, and Quakers in the United States whose religious beliefs include pacifism are required to provide two years of alternative service as conscientious objectors in lieu of military service.　　　　　　　　　　　　　　　　　**TOL**

1918　　The Hutterites, who are strict pacifists, are persecuted for their refusal to serve in the military during World War I and some move from South Dakota to Manitoba and Alberta, Canada, and establish settlements. Additional Canadian Hutterite settlements are established in Saskatchewan.   TOL

1918   In Germany the Weimar Republic is established and the new constitution creates a separation of church and state and offers guarantees of religious freedom.   TOL

1918–1919   Joseph Franklin Rutherford, leader of the Jehovah's Witnesses, and seven other leaders of the religion are convicted of violating the United States Espionage Act for refusing to support the United States in World War I. In accord with Witness beliefs, they remain neutral. They are released in 1919 on bail, their convictions are reversed on appeal, and the government drops the case.   TOL

1918–1920   During the civil war following the Bolshevik Revolution in Russia, the Soviet government represses Islam because it is seen as a threat to national unity. Mosques are closed or destroyed, Islamic courts closed, and Muslim religious leaders removed from power. Muslim resistance in central Asia ends the harshest of the repressive acts, such as closing mosques.   ISLAM

1919   Wentworth A. Matthew (1892–1973) founds the Commandment Keepers congregation in Harlem, an African-American Jewish congregation. Four years later he becomes a follower of Arnold J. Ford and they are jointly credited with founding the Black Jews of Harlem denomination, which becomes one of the largest African-American Jewish denominations.   AFRICAN

1919   The Peace Mission is established by Father Divine (1877–1965) in Sayville, New York. The movement attracts African-American and some white followers across the United States over the next three decades. Followers believe that Father Divine is a living manifestation of God. The movement conducts informal church services, provides services to the poor, and runs a chain of employment agencies and hotels. It fades from prominence following Father Divine's death in 1965.   AFRICAN

1919   The Ethiopian Overcoming Holy Church is founded as a Pentecostal African-American Church in Alabama and in the 1990s has over 100,000 members.   AFRICAN, EVAN

1919   Pope Benedict XV issues his *Maximum Illud*. This encyclical reflects the progressive missionary views of the Belgian missionary van Lebbe and calls for the training of native clergy, consideration for the missionized culture, and separation from nationalism.   CATH

1919   Catholic bishops in the United States issue their *Bishop's Program*, which calls for basic social reforms in American society to deal with poverty and social inequality. Representing a new agenda of social action for the church, the *Program* and other similar documents call for worker's rights, a minimum wage, and unemployment and health insurance, all innovative social reforms of the time.   CATH

1919   Efforts to save the core of Confucian learning in China fail with the upsurge of anti-Confucian iconoclasm in the May Fourth Movement, a secular revolutionary movement.   CONF

1919   In Canada the Pentecostal Assemblies of Canada is authorized by the government and in 1921 joins with the larger Assemblies of God Church in the United States.   EVAN

1919   In India the interests of Muslims and Hindus, who have often been in conflict for the past decades, begin to come together as both groups seek to end British rule in India.   HIND, ISLAM

1919   In Algeria the French move to make Algeria part of France and grant voting rights to Muslims who are educated or who serve in the military. Muslims who reject Islam are eligible to become French citizens.   ISLAM

1919   In India the Jami'at al-Ulama-i Hind movement develops as a minority political movement among Muslims. The movement stands in opposition to the much larger Muslim League and supports collaboration with the Hindu Congress Party to end British rule in India while opposing the partition of India into separate Hindu and Muslim sectors. The movement also strongly supports the use of Islamic law in Muslim communities and becomes a major source of Muslim identity for Muslims in India after partition in 1947.   ISLAM

1919   In the United States the World's Christian Fundamentals Association is formed in Philadelphia. Among its early members are Baptists who object to the institutionalization of the Northern and Southern Conventions in the previous two decades and who also object to what they see as liberal ideas in the Church. The organization is active in combating the teaching of evolution in public schools.   PROT

1919   The Vailala Madness cargo cult develops in New Guinea. A reaction by native islanders to white rule, white material wealth, and Christianity, the movement lasts until 1931 and emphasizes the return of ancestors who bring a wealth of white material goods. As part of the movement, many traditional religious practices are abandoned and replaced with practices based on Christianity and practices designed to win the favors of the ancestors.   SECT

1919   The Cao Dai religious movement develops in the Mekong Delta region of Vietnam. It is founded by Ngo Van Chieu, a mystic. Appealing to belief in the supernatural, it draws on Buddhism, Confucianism, Daoism, and Christianity, all mixed with a strain of secularism. Adherents see it as a wide-reaching new religion, and within 20 years it has acquired some 300,000 followers. The movement is also political and is associated with

Vietnamese nationalism and resistance to non-Vietnamese influences on Vietnamese culture. **SECT**

1919   The Jehovah's Witnesses begin publishing the *Golden Age* magazine to bring their views on world issues to the attention of adherents and the general public. **SECT**

1919   The Central Sikh League is established in southern Asia to represent the Sikhs, mainly in their dealings with the British colonial government. **SIKH**

1919   In Germany a new constitution is enacted that creates freedom of religion and separation of church and state. However, the government continues to collect taxes for distribution to the Christian churches and religion continues to be taught in the schools. Administratively, the new arrangement enables churches to form their own governing bodies. **TOL**

1919   The 19th amendment to the United States Constitution, which prohibits the sale of alcoholic beverages, is ratified. It is viewed as a major victory by fundamentalist Christians, who had been active in seeking its ratification. **TOL**

1919–1923   The third *Aliyah* to Palestine takes place. During this period Jews continue to arrive in Palestine and establish farming communities and *kibbutzim*, as well as settling in and expanding cities such as Tel-Aviv, Jaffa, and Haifa. **SEE 1924–1928, JUD.** **JUD**

1919–1924   The Khilafat movement is active in India. It is an attempt by some Indian Muslims to influence the post–World War I peace process and especially to ensure that the Ottoman sultan remains leader of the Islamic world. The movement fails to achieve its goals, with the sultanate abolished but subsequently plays a role in anti-British politics in north India from 1919 to 1922, when it was aligned with the Hindus. **ISLAM**

1920   The practice by white missionary societies of using African-American missionaries in Africa that has been encouraged since the 1870s is curtailed because white colonial governments believe that the missionaries will encourage independence movements. The use of African-American missionaries does not resume until the 1960s. **AFRICAN**

1920   The Bedward movement is founded by Alexander Bedward (1859–1930), a prophet and leader of the Baptist Free Church in Jamaica. The movement has millennial and black nationalist tones, as Bedward preaches that the Bedwardites will rule the world and that white rule will end. Although the movement declines after Bedward is imprisoned in 1921, it serves as a precursor to Rastafarianism. **AFRICAN**

1920   The Foreign Mission Sisters of St. Dominic is established in Maryknoll, New York, alongside the Catholic Foreign Missionary Society of America. The first sisters leave for missionary work in 1921.   **CATH**

1920   Joan of Arc, the French Catholic patriot of the Hundred Years War, is canonized.   **CATH**

1920   The International Federation of Christian Trade Unions is formed in Europe. It draws its membership primarily from Belgium, Switzerland, and the Netherlands but also from Germany, France, and Italy. The interdenominational federation stands in political opposition to the Socialists and Communists and, with the individual unions that make up its membership, is a precursor of the Northern European Christian Democratic political parties that emerge after World War II.   **CHRIS**

1920   Indian Hindu Paramahansa Yogananda (1893–1953) establishes the Hindu-based Self-Realization Fellowship in Boston. He emphasizes the use of yoga and meditation to increase self-awareness.   **HIND, SPIR**

1920   In the Soviet Union the Russians ignore or repress Muslim demands for independence in central Asia and other regions and instead establish Tatar, Crimean, Kazakh, Turkestan, and Azerbaijan Soviet Socialist Republics and two smaller Khiva and Bukhara republics, all of which have large Muslim populations.   **ISLAM**

1920   An English translation of *The Protocols of the Elders of Zion* (**SEE 1921, JUD**), first published in Russia in 1905, is serialized in the *Dearborn Independent*, owned by Henry Ford. In 1927 Ford apologizes for the serial and other anti-Jewish articles in the paper and denies being an anti-Semite.   **JUD**

1920   The *Haganah*, the Jewish military organization, is organized by Jewish settlers in Palestine.   **JUD**

1920   The position of chief rabbi is established in Palestine, with ultimate authority over religious and family matters. The post is actually filled by two rabbis, representing the Ashkenazic (eastern European) and Sephardic (Eastern) Jewish communities, both of which are groups living in Palestine.   **JUD**

1920   In the United States the Presbyterian Church in the United States of America and the Welsh Calvinist Methodist Church unite under the name of the former.   **PROT**

1920   In Switzerland several Protestant denominations and churches unite and form the Federation of Swiss Protestant Churches.   **PROT**

1920   In the United States fundamentalist Christians associated with the World's Christian Fundamental Association begin their effort to combat the teaching of what they consider liberal and modern ideas, including biological evolution, socialism, and non-Christian religions. **PROT**

1920   Mennonites in North America establish the Mennonite Central Committee, which coordinates the social service activities of the Mennonite Church, the General Conference Mennonites, and the Mennonite Brethren. **SECT**

1920   The Meiji shrine in Tokyo is completed after five years of largely volunteer construction by youth groups and by Shinto and Buddhist religious groups. The first Japanese shrine thus built as a national cooperative project, it deifies the Emperor Meiji, who died in 1912, and the empress. The Meiji shrine promotes emperor worship and brings Shinto into new prominence. **SHINTO**

1920   Two new Sikh organizations are established in southern Asia to take control and manage the Sikh temples in the Punjab. **SIKH**

1920   The British College of Psychic Science is founded to conduct scientific studies and issue reports on spiritual events, such as telepathy, prophesy, and mediumship, that spiritualists believe are ignored by mainstream science. **SPIR**

1920s   The migration of Lutheran Afro-Caribbeans to the United States leads to the growth of African-American Lutheran churches and their spread across the nation. **AFRICAN**

Ashkenazic and Sephardic Jews

Ashkenazic and Sephardic Judaism are the two major cultural traditions within Judaism. Each developed independently in the two major population centers of the Jewish Diaspora: Sephardic Judaism on the Iberian peninsula and Ashkenazic Judaism in central and eastern Europe. Both traditions developed primarily during the Middle Ages. Although there are differences between Sephardim and Ashkenazim in religious beliefs and practices, they are relatively minor and each group considers the other to be Jews. The major differences between the two traditions are mainly cultural. Sephardim traditionally spoke Judeo-Spanish (Ladino), a language based on Hebrew and Spanish, while Ashkenazim spoke Yiddish. Today, both languages are used by only a small minority of Jews. After the Sephardim were expelled from Spain in 1492 many went to Arab and Muslim nations in North Africa and the Middle East, where Judeo-Spanish was replaced with Arabic or Judeo-Arabic. In addition to language, there are also significant differences in music, dance, literature, and family names between the two populations. Sephardic Jews were the first to settle in the Americas, although the large influx of Ashkenazim since the middle of the 19th century has made the latter group far more numerous. Neither group is culturally homogeneous and there are important internal variations, for example between Sephardim from Turkey and Morocco and Ashkenazim from Germany and Lithuania.

1920s	The Umbanda Pura religion emerges in Brazil. It is an offshoot of the Macumba religion and the spiritualism associated with French mystic Allan Kardec, although it moves away from both the intellectual emphasis of Kardecism and some Africanized elements of Macumba, such as animal sacrifice. Umbanda's main popularizer is Zélio de Morales (c.1900–?), who claims to have been cured of an illness by a spirit and directed by another spirit to establish the Umbanda religion. The religion combines elements from Roman Catholicism, African religions, and native Brazilian religions and becomes popular in part because of its association with Brazilian nationalism. **AFRICAN**
1920s	Communist Red Guard units in rural China destroy Buddhist and Daoist statues and other religious symbols and burn temples. **BUDD, DAO**
1920s	In Algeria a Muslim reform movement emerges as part of the more general political resistance to French rule. The reform movement opposes the local variant of Islam, which combines Islam with indigenous religious practices, advocates a return to a form of Islam based on the life of Muhammad, the Prophet and founder of Islam, and establishes children's groups and schools to teach Islam. **ISLAM**
1920s	In response to British colonial rule, several Africans in Uganda establish an Orthodox Church. Although resisted at first by the Orthodox Church in Alexandria, Egypt, the Ugandan Church eventually wins acceptance and later expands to include churches centered in Nairobi, Kenya; Kinshasa, Zaire; and the Cameroons. **ORTHO**
1920s	As the Anglican Church loses influence in Great Britain, compulsory chapel attendance is ended at Oxford and Cambridge universities, and several non-Anglican Protestants are appointed to professorships in theology. Such positions are still barred to Catholics and agnostics or atheists. Nonetheless, most faculty members do not attend church and are "methodological atheists." **PROT**
1920–1921	Daoist priests support a series of peasant outbreaks in Sichuan, offering invulnerability potions to rebel forces. **DAO**
1920–1922	In response to Bolshevik control of Muslim Turkestan, the Muslim Basmachi Revolt takes place and the Muslims succeed in taking parts of the countryside and threatening such major cities as Bukhara. The new Soviet government helps to end the revolt by returning confiscated land to Muslim communities, affording Muslim law some offical authority, and supplying food to the region. **ISLAM**
1921	The Church of Jesus Christ on Earth through the Prophet Simon Kimbangu is founded in the Congo (Zaire) by Simon Kimbangu (1889–1951), an oil worker and former Baptist ministerial student. The movement promises an end to Belgian rule, combines Christian and African beliefs, and is involved

in the independence movement. Kimbangu is imprisoned for 30 years and dies in prison. Following independence in 1960, the Church of Jesus Christ on Earth becomes the largest African church in central Africa.   **AFRICAN**

1921   The National Baptist Convention, U.S.A.—the country's largest African-American denomination—publishes *Gospel Pearls*, a collection of hymns, spirituals, and gospel songs that establishes gospel music as an accepted form of music in African-American Baptist churches.   **AFRICAN**

1921   The Pentecostal movement is brought to Indonesia by American missionaries and to Australia by American and British missionaries.   **EVAN**

1921   Revolts break out against British rule in India. Sikhs revolt in the Punjab and Muslims revolt later in the year in Malabar. During the Malabar revolt there are many forced conversions and some Hindus are killed, leading to several years of violent conflict between the two groups.   **HIND**

1921   The *Times* of London publishes a report proving that *The Protocols of the Elders of Zion*, an anti-Semitic tract, is a forgery.   **JUD**

1921   The first Native American religious group centered on peyote use outside Oklahoma is founded as the Peyote Church of Christ in Nebraska.   **NATIV**

1921   In the United States Meletios Metaxakis, the former archbishop of Athens and a recent immigrant to America, seeks to unify the various Orthodox churches and creates the Greek Archdiocese of North and South America. The organization fails to unite adherents of Orthodoxy in the United States.   **ORTHO**

1921   German theologian Karl Barth (1886–1968) becomes a professor at the University of Göttingen. He is a critic of the German *Volkskirche* school of missionary work and instead argues that all Christian theology must be based on the life of Jesus Christ, without regard for cultural context.   **PROT**

1921   The secret religious Society of the Way appears in north China. The names of Confucius, Laozi, and the Buddha and symbols representing Christianity and Islam are inscribed on the altars of the society's temples.   **SECT**

1921   The Church of the Kingdom of God, Philanthropic Assembly, is founded in Switzerland by F. L. Alexander Freytag (1870–1947), the leader of the Jehovah's Witnesses in Switzerland. It is a fundamentalist movement that claims the year 1918 marked the beginning of a new age and that splinters into several groups after 1947.   **SECT**

1921   Japan's persecution of new religions begins when Kyoto police raid Omotokyo headquarters and accuse its leaders of *lese majesté* (its founder's tomb resembles that of the emperor). Honmichi is raided in 1926, 1928, and 1938. The 1928 Peace Preservation Law will be used as a tool for the ongoing investigation and oppression of "heretical" new religions. Government intellectuals see most new sects as reactionary cults practicing such unsophisticated doctrines as faith healing. Regarded officially as little more than superstition, these so-called pseudo-religions will be declared "evil religions" (*jakyo*).   SHINTO, TOL

1921   *The Witch-Cult in Western Europe* by historian Margaret Murray (1863–1963) is published. It, along with her later work, *The God of the Witches* (1931), and Robert Graves's *The White Goddess* (1946), rekindle interest in witchcraft, mythology, and nature-based religions in the last half of the 20th century. These books influence the renewed growth not only of Wicca but of witchcraft and oral traditions as well.   SPIR

1921   The Research Science Bureau is founded in the United States by Presbyterian minister Harry Rimmer (1880–1952) to promote research on creationism for the purpose of proving the scientific validity of creationism. It is an early effort to use science to support creationism as a means of discrediting the biological theory of evolution.   TOL

1922   The first independent African church in Ghana is founded by Jemisimiham Jehu-Appiah (1892–1943). It is the Musama Disco Christo Church (MDCC) or Army of the Cross of Jesus Christ and is an offshoot of the Methodist Church.   AFRICAN

1922   In the Soviet Union the Russian government begins removing Muslim political leaders from power in the Muslim central Asian republics and replacing them with Muslims or non-Muslims who are expected to be loyal to the Soviet government in Moscow. The policy is extended to other Muslim regions of the Soviet Union, and by 1938 all Muslim leaders who had been in power in 1920 have been replaced.   ISLAM

1922   The League of Nations makes Palestine a British mandate and supports the British Balfour Declaration, which calls for the creation of a Jewish state in Palestine.   JUD

1922   A quota on Jewish students is instituted at Harvard College. Jewish quotas become a common practice at elite colleges in the United States.   JUD

1922   Reconstructionist Judaism is established in the United States when Rabbi Mordecai Kaplan (1881–1983) founds the Society for the Advancement of Judaism in New York. The movement has a social welfare and socialist orientation and draws followers among Jewish intellectuals.   JUD

1922   The Society of Jewish Science is founded by Reform Rabbi Morris Lichtenstein (1890–1938) in New York City. It resembles Christian Science and is founded in part to attract Jewish converts to Christian Science back to Judaism.   JUD

1922   A *bat mitzvah* (daughter of commandment) is celebrated for girls for the first time in the United States at a Conservative Jewish congregation in New York. In Orthodox congregations, only boys may celebrate the *bar mitzvah*, with a much-reduced ceremony performed for girls in accord with their limited religious role. In the 1990s boys and girls celebrate the *bar* or *bat mitzvah* in Reform and Conservative congregations, while only boys do so in Orthodox congregations.   JUD

1922   In the Soviet Union repression of Judaism continues with the forced closings of all Jewish elementary and high schools, although some continue to operate in secret.   JUD

1922   *Konfuzianismus und Taoismus* (*The Religion of China: Confucianism and Daoism*) by the German sociologist and political economist Max Weber (1864–1920) is posthumously published. Throughout his works, Weber stresses the concept of "ideal types." Opposing the Marxian view of economic causation, Weber emphasizes the role of religious values, ideologies, and charismatic leaders in shaping societies.   MISC

1922   The Albanian Orthodox Church is granted autocephalous status but remains under the administration of the Orthodox patriarch in Istanbul until 1937.   ORTHO

1922   In the United States the Evangelical Association and the United Evangelical Church unite as the Evangelical Church.   PROT

1922   In Germany 28 Protestant churches across the nation form the Federation of German Evangelical Churches.   PROT

1922   Shakerism has continued to decline in the United States since about 1840. By this year all Shaker communities in the west have dissolved, and only five remain in the east with about 235 members total.   SECT

1922   Shoghi Effendi (1897–1957), a grandson of Baha'u'llah, the founder of the Baha'i religion, becomes the Guardian of the Cause of the Baha'i religion. Under his direction, the religion develops an administrative structure, delineates criteria for membership, and expands to most regions of the world.   SECT

1922   Russian philosopher George I. Gurdjieff (1866?–1949) establishes the Institute for the Harmonious Development of Man in France. Although it closes in 1933, its emphasis on personal growth and transformation becomes an important influence on later programs, such as est (Erhard Seminar Training), encounter groups, and transactional analysis, all parts of the personal growth movement within the New Age movement of the 1960s on.   SPIR

1922	The Fraternity of the Inner Light is founded as an offshoot of the Theosophical Society. **SPIR**

1922–1924	Relations between Hindus and Muslims in northern India, which had been cooperative in the last three years in a united effort to end British rule, are disrupted by factions and riots and Hindu-Muslim cooperation ends. **HIND, ISLAM**

1922–1930s	The Living Church or Renovated Church movement takes place in the Russian Orthodox Church. The movement is a reaction to the Russian Revolution and the rise of Communism and is meant to provide financial support for the church. It involves Orthodox clergy, who take control of church property in Russia and sell items in the United States. They also institute religious changes, including allowing priests to remarry. In the United States, the movement causes much confusion over the ownership of church property and ultimately undermines the authority of American Orthodox bishops. The movement is repressed by Communist officials in Russia in the 1930s and disappears by World War II. **ORTHO**

1923	The Beth B'nai Abraham (House of the Children of Abraham) is founded by Arnold J. Ford (1877–1935) as a congregation for African-American Jews in the Harlem section of New York City. The African-American Jews believe that the ancient Jews were black and follow European Jewish religious practices. Ford is known as Rabbi Ford to his followers. **AFRICAN**

1923	Pentecostal preacher Aimee Semple McPherson (1890–1944) founds the Angelus Temple in Los Angeles. In the same year she also writes *This Is That: Personal Experiences, Sermons, and Writings*. An influential preacher, she plays a leading role in the United States and elsewhere in spreading the religion. **EVAN**

1923	The Pentecostal movement spreads to Austria. **EVAN**

1923	The national Tabligh organization is established in India to coordinate what have been localized efforts by Hindus to reconvert Muslims to Hinduism. The Tabligh movement uses pamphlets that attack Muhammad, the Prophet and founder of Islam, which enrages many Muslims and leads to riots. **HIND**

1923	In the Punjab region of northwestern India, Muslims and Hindus join together to form the National Unionist Party to represent the interest of farmers. The party remains active until Indian independence in 1947 and the partition of India, which creates Pakistan with a mainly Muslim population. **HIND**

1923	The Persatuan Islam movement is founded by Muslims in western Java in Indonesia. It is a religious reform movement that stresses a return to traditional Islam and discourages indigenous religious practices that have been merged with Islam. It also discourages Sufi reforms. **ISLAM**

1923

1923   The B'nai B'rith organization establishes the Hillel Foundation to provide for the religious needs of Jewish students at American colleges.   JUD

1923   *I and Thou* by Jewish philosopher and theologian Martin Buber (1878–1965) is published. In the book Buber attempts to combine ideas from philosophy and religion to explain humanity's place in the universe and discusses the nature of relationships between people.   MISC

1923   In Finland, which gained independence from Russia in 1917, the Finnish Orthodox Church is granted independence by the Orthodox patriarch in Istanbul. Most Orthodox in Finland are ethnic Karelians who live in the east near the border with Russia.   ORTHO

1923   In the United States Baptists from the Northern, Southern, and Canadian Conventions meet in Kansas City, Missouri, to form the Baptist Bible Union to combat modernism and liberalism and to look to the Bible as the ultimate and only authority.   PROT

1923   *Christianity and Liberalism* is written by J. Gresham Machen (1881–1937), a theology professor at Princeton Theological Seminary. He supports the conservative Presbyterian position within the Presbyterian Church U.S.A. and argues that liberalism is a new religion, not a form of Christianity. Machen becomes a leader of the conservative faction in the church.   PROT

1923   In Spain the Spanish Evangelical Church, the Spanish Reformed Church, and the Methodist Church of Ceyana form the Federation of Evangelical Churches in Spain.   PROT

1923   In Eisenach, Germany, Lutherans from around the world hold their first annual conference. In 1929 it comes to be called the Lutheran World Convention and the council plays a role in providing relief to Lutheran communities around the world and in supporting missionary efforts.   PROT

1923   The Cao Dai religion in Vietnam is organized as a single religion with a single leader, although it soon splits into a number of sects, each with its own central place of worship and leadership. Nonetheless, it draws many followers and remains a powerful force in Vietnamese society into the 1970s.   SECT

1923   Beginning this year and through 1927, mass emigration of persecuted Mennonites from Russia to Canada takes place. Some 18,000 Mennonites arrive in Canada, and with the assistance of the existing Mennonite communities, they settle in the western plains provinces.   SECT

1923   As spiritualism continues to grow in popularity, the first International Spiritualist Congress is held in Liege, Belgium, and the American Astrological Society is founded.   SPIR

1923	Following its defeat in World War I, the Ottoman Empire disintegrates and is replaced by the nation of Turkey, whose government moves to create a secular state and end the influence of Islam. Over the next 10 years, education is secularized, Islamic dress banned, religious schools closed, religion put under government administration, and Islamic law replaced by civil laws. **TOL**
1923	In the United States *Hell and the High Schools* is written by Baptist minister T. T. Martin (1862–1939). It is an attack on the teaching of evolution and is one of the first attempts by Baptist and Presbyterian ministers to ban the teaching of evolution in the public schools. **TOL**
1923	The first law in the United States prohibiting the teaching of evolution in public schools is enacted in Oklahoma. Similar laws are later passed in Florida, Tennessee, and Mississippi. **TOL**
1923–1926	Moroccan Muslims in the Spanish-controlled Rif region revolt against Spanish rule and seek to establish an independent state. The revolt is defeated by French and Spanish forces. **ISLAM**
1923–1934	In Afghanistan King Amanullah initiates a Westernization program that includes the use of the solar calendar; the requirement of Western dress; discouraging veiling and seclusion of women; the abolition of slavery and forced labor; and secular education, including education for girls. The reforms are not accepted by all Muslims, and the Khost Rebellion of 1923–1934 breaks out in the region that borders with Pakistan. In the end Islamic law retains its influence. **ISLAM**
1923–1934	The Baha'i religion develops an administrative structure and becomes more established in North America, England, Germany, India, Burma, Iraq, Iran, Australia, and New Zealand. **SECT**
1923–1935	Following the defeat of the Ottoman Empire in World War I, the Republic of Turkey is established and massive reforms begin. These include the substitution of secular law for Islamic law (shari'a), the banning of Sufi orders, the writing of a republican constitution based on popular sovereignty, suppression of religious education in Turkish schools, introduction of a Roman alphabet to replace the traditional Arabic script, the legal upgrading of the position of women, and the requirement that all Turks take European surnames. **ISLAM**
1924	The National Baptist Convention U.S.A., a major African-American denomination in the United States, publishes the *Baptists Standard Hymnal*, which establishes gospel music as a legitimate form of music in African-American Baptist churches. **AFRICAN**
1924	The National Coloured Spiritualist Association of the United States of America is founded to serve American spiritualists of African ancestry. **AFRICAN, SPIR**

1924	Zhang Enfu, the 63d celestial master, takes office as the Daoist pope in China. **DAO**

1924   Zhang Enfu, the 63d celestial master, takes office as the Daoist pope in China. **DAO**

1924   The first church-owned radio station is founded by Pentecostal preacher Aimee Semple McPherson in Los Angeles. **EVAN**

1924   Representatives of Hindu, Muslim, Parsi, Sikh, and Christian communities in India convene a congress at Delhi. They agree to form local committees to prevent religious conflicts. Militant Hindus and Muslims nevertheless continue to agitate for independence and also agitate against one another. **HIND, ISLAM**

1924   In a continuing effort to reorganize the former Russian Empire, the Soviet government establishes the Soviet Republics of Uzbekistan, Kazakhstan, Turkmenistan, and Kyrgizia in central Asia, all of which have majority or large Muslim populations. **ISLAM**

1924   Toba Indian prophet Dionisio Dios Gomez (?–1924) and 50 followers are killed when Argentinian police attack their temple in northern Argentina.

Shari'a (Islamic Law)

The Shari'a is an elaborate and complex system of Islamic religious law that has evolved since the time of Muhammad and is the source of the rules and values governing Muslim life. Derived originally from the Qur'an, the Shari'a is believed to be the collected prescriptions dictated by Allah controlling the universe and all within it. Despite its perceived comprehensive nature, the Shari'a of the early decades of Islamic history soon proved incapable of providing clear rules in an increasingly complex society. Although this was not a difficulty for those initial generations because they still retained the memory of how Muhammad might have responded, ensuing generations encountered growing conflicts over what actually was said. This problem was further exacerbated by continuing expansion into the territory of non-Arab cultures who had not had any contact with Muhammad. By the ninth century, therefore, it became necessary to develop a more systematic legal structure that could provide guidance in a changing world. The result was establishment of the *Usul al-fiqh* (Principles of Jurisprudence), which was a more scientific means for Islamic jurists to balance the Qur'an and the *Sunna* while deriving appropriate laws that could be applied to new situations. Among the *Sunni* jurists, four schools of legal interpretation exist and are differentiated through their emphasis on the written texts (Qur'an and the *hadith*) or the human ability to reason by analogy. The Maliki school of North Africa and the Hanbali school of Saudi Arabia are proponents of the former while the Hanafi school (Turkey, southern Asia, and central Asia) and the Shafi'I school (Middle Eastern Arabs and Indonesia) reflect the latter. Among Shi'a Muslims the Ja'fari school (named for the sixth Imam, Ja'far Al-Sadiq) is the only important source of legal interpretation.

They are part of a revitalization movement initiated by Gomez in hopes of ending white rule and restoring the traditional Toba way of life.   NATIV

1924   In India Protestant ecumenism moves forward when the United Church of Northern India is founded through the uniting of 11 Presbyterian, Anglican, Congregational, and missionary churches.   PROT

1924   In the United States the Reformed Church in the United States and the Hungarian Reformed Church in America unite under the name of the former.   PROT

1924   As part of the continuing debate between conservatives and liberals in the Presbyterian Church U.S.A., 150 clergymen sign a document known as *An Affirmation* that supports the five points of belief adopted in 1910 but also allows for a range of thought and belief within the Church.   PROT

1924   A controversy develops in the United States over the validity of spiritualism when an investigation sponsored by *Scientific American* magazine fails to provide clear conclusions.   SPIR

1924   SUBUD is founded in Indonesia by Muhammad Subuh Sumohadiwidjojo (1901–1987). It is a Hindu-based spiritual sect that focuses on adherents learning to experience their own inner spiritual energy.   SPIR

1924   The *Encyclopaedia of Psychological Astrology* by "Leo" (William Frederick Allen), is published in England. Leo also edits a number of astrology magazines and founds the Modern Astrology Publishing Company.   SPIR

1924   In the Soviet Union the government initiates a new policy designed to eliminate religion as a significant part of life across the nation. Although Russian Orthodoxy is perhaps less subject to restrictions than other religions, new laws enacted over the next six years forbid religious organizations from existing and from owning property. The laws also close churches, mosques, synagogues, and temples, end religious education, and allow for the arrest and imprisonment of religious leaders. The goal is to create a secular nation in which all citizens are loyal to the state.   TOL

1924–
1926   In central Africa the Presbytery of Blantyre, the Presbytery of Livingstonia, and the Presbytery of Mkhoma unite to form the Church of Central Africa, Presbyterian.   PROT

1924–
1928   The fourth *Aliyah* to Palestine takes place. During this period Jewish immigration to Palestine from Europe, North Africa, and the Middle East increases, resulting in the rapid growth of cities and the development of industry. SEE **1933–1939**, JUD.   JUD

1925   The Zion Christian Church is founded by Enginasi Lekganyane (?–c.1948), an African convert to Christianity, in South Africa. It becomes the largest independent South African church, with a major pilgrimage center established at Zion City Moriah. The church combines some Christian themes with some African ones, among them healing rituals, possession, and ritual dancing.   AFRICAN

1925   The Cherubim and Seraphim Society, a faith-healing society, is founded in Nigeria by Christianah Abiodun (1907–?) and Moses Orimolade (c.1879–1933). Both founders were raised as Christians but turned to the use of prayer to heal illness following personal religious experiences.   AFRICAN

1925   (St.) Therese of Lisieux is canonized by Pope Pius XI and her shrine becomes a major pilgrimage site in France. In 1944 she is made joint patron saint of France with Joan of Arc.   CATH

1925   In Japan the autobiographical novel *Across the Death Line*, by Christian evangelist and social reformer Kagawa Toyohiko (1888–1960), is published. In the first half of the 20th century, Kagawa is a leading social reformer in Japan and is involved in helping the poor, forming the Japanese labor movement, and converting Japanese to Christianity.   CHRIS

1925   The Pentecostal movement spreads to Lithuania and Latvia.   EVAN

1925   The Rastriya Sevak Sangh organization is founded in India. It promotes Hindu causes and institutions such as temples and schools as a means of limiting Muslim, Christian, and other non-Hindu influences in Indian society.   HIND

1925   Iran has been in chaos since 1911, and in this year military officer Reza Khan seizes power and establishes the Pahlavi dynasty, which rules until the revolution of 1979. The dynasty unifies the nation, establishes a strong central government, stresses modernization and ties to the Western world, and reduces the power of Muslim scholars.   ISLAM

1925   The Hamalliya Muslim brotherhood is established by Sufi teacher Shaykh Hamallah (1883–1943) in West Africa. The movement, like others that emerge in the region, is apolitical and does not openly resist French rule but does help maintain Islam and is perceived by the French as a threat. The movement declines in importance after the colonies achieve independence from France in 1960.   ISLAM

1925   The city of Fez in Morocco, ignored by the French, who prefer Casablanca, emerges as a center of Islamic reform and resistance to French rule. The reform movement stresses Islamic education, the purging of Islam of indigenous elements, and Islamic law.   ISLAM

1925   The Yiddish Scientific Institute (YIVO) is founded in Vilna, Lithuania, as a center for the study of European Jewish culture. In 1940 the institute is relocated to New York and becomes the YIVO Institute for Jewish Research.   JUD

1925	Mormon missionary activity begins in South America.	**MOR**

1925	In Canada the Presbyterian Church in Canada, the Methodist Church of Canada, the Congregational Churches in Canada, and the Local Union churches unite and form the United Church of Canada.	**PROT**

1925	In the United States the Southern Baptist Convention adopts a statement of Baptist faith and message, which includes the New Hampshire Confession of Faith (first set forth in 1833) with new sections added to it. The Confession of Faith is a basic statement of Baptist fundamentalism, which cites the Bible as the only authority and affords much autonomy to individual congregations.	**PROT**

1925	Reiyukai, a new Japanese religion based on Nichiren Buddhism, is established in Japan. It stresses ancestor worship and is an especially successful new religion in Japan as it avoids control by the government. Following World War II, it both expands its membership and engenders a number of other new religions.	**SECT**

1925	In New Zealand the Ratana Church is founded by Maori farmer Tahupotiki Wuiremu Ratana (1873–1939). Based mainly on Christianity and calling for a rejection of Maori beliefs, the church draws many Maori followers, and some members become political representatives of the Maori in New Zealand. SEE **1941, SECT**.	**SECT**

1925	The first Mennonite World Conference is held in Basel, Switzerland. It becomes an annual event (with interruptions during World War II) and is attended by representatives from Mennonite groups around the world.	**SECT**

1925	In Egypt Baha'is are classified as non-Muslims, a situation that leads to discrimination against the Baha'i in the Muslim nation.	**SECT**

1925	The Sikh Gurdwaras Act is enacted in India by the British. It places Sikh temples under Sikh management and also officially recognizes Sikhism as a distinct religion. The Shiromani Gurdwara Parbandhak Committee, formed in 1920, is charged with managing the temples, a role that affords it much political power in the Sikh community in the Punjab.	**SIKH**

1925	Indian Hindu Paramahansa Yogananda establishes the Hindu-based Self-Realization Fellowship center in Los Angeles, which grows to attract several hundred thousand followers over the next four decades.	**SPIR**

1925	The Boston Society for Psychic Research is founded for the same purpose as the British College founded in 1920.	**SPIR**

1925	In Chile a new constitution is enacted that separates the state and the Roman Catholic Church and establishes religious freedom. Nonetheless,	

the church remains politically active and influential and is perceived as enjoying special privileges not available to other denominations.   TOL

1925   The "Monkey Trial" takes place in Dayton, Tennessee. The defendant is teacher John Thomas Scopes, who is accused by the state of teaching evolution, rather than the biblical account of creation, as required by Tennessee under the newly enacted Butler Act. Scopes is found guilty and fined $100, although the verdict is set aside by the appeals court. The Butler Act is repealed in 1967. The trial embarrasses fundamental Protestants and causes the movement to lose support in the United States.   TOL

1925   In the United States *The Case Against Evolution* is written by Catholic priest and college professor George Barry O'Toole (1886–1944). The book becomes popular among creationists, but it is considered most valuable because it sets forth the Roman Catholic theological opposition to biological evolution.   TOL

1926   The United House of Prayer for All People is founded by Cape Verde Island native Sweet Daddy Grace (1881–1960) in Charlotte, South Carolina. It is a Pentecostal church that stresses speaking in tongues, faith healing, and the divine nature of Sweet Daddy Grace.   AFRICAN

Fundamentalism

Fundamentalism is a term used with great imprecision. Strictly speaking, it refers to a social, political, and religious movement within Protestant Christianity in the United States whose basic features are a personal experience with God, a belief in the infalliblity of the Bible, a conservative social and political agenda, a rejection of science, a belief in traditional Christian beliefs, such as the Virgin Birth, a concern with personal and world salvation, and faith in Christ's return and judgment followed by a millennium. In the United States and Europe, fundamentalism is associated with Pentecostalism, the Religious Right, and fervent missionary activity around the world. Although the core beliefs of fundamentalism date to the Protestant Reformation or earlier, the term did not come into use in the United States until the second decade of the 20th century. After the Scopes Trial in 1925, the movement was discredited and did not recover until after World War II. Since then it has grown rapidly and has increased in members as other Protestant denominations lost members in the 1980s and 1990s. In a more general sense, the term *fundamentalism* is now used to refer to the traditional sector of any religion, and thus one can speak of Islamic fundamentalism or Jewish fundamentalism, although neither shares any religious beliefs with Protestant fundamentalism. The use in reference to other religions relies more on the movement's social and political features and especially to the conservative social agenda and what is seen by some experts as a resistance to modernity.

1926   A new edition of the *Daozang,* the Daoist canon, is published in Shanghai in China.   **DAO**

1926   In the Soviet Union the government bans the use of Arabic and requires that the Latin alphabet be used for all Turkic languages spoken in the republics. As many Muslims in central Asia speak Turkic languages and use the Arabic Qur'an, the policy restricts contact with the outside Muslim world and also makes it more difficult to practice Islam in the Soviet Union.   **ISLAM**

1926   In Korea the Korean Methodist Episcopal Church and the Korean Methodist Episcopal Church, South unite as the Korean Methodist Church.   **PROT**

1926   At its general assembly, the Presbyterian Church U.S.A. approves a report that rejects an earlier (1924) condemnation of liberalism and admits that both conservatism and liberalism can exist in the church.   **PROT**

1926   Bob Jones, Sr., a fundamental Protestant preacher, founds Bob Jones University in Florida. The curriculum stresses Christian fundamental beliefs, and the behavior of students is closely regulated in accord with the fundamentalist rules of personal conduct. In 1947 the university relocates to Greenville, South Carolina.   **PROT**

1926   A new Japanese religion that will later be known as Sekai Kyuseikyo is founded by Okada Mokichi (1882–1955), who views himself as the savior. Although repressed by the government before World War II, it recovers after the war and stresses healing and the preservation of nature.   **SECT**

1926   Tenrikyo (**SEE 1838, SECT**) establishes a foreign language school to prepare missionaries for overseas work; the school eventually will become Japan's Tenri University. Tenrikyo missionaries in China and Korea will be followed in 1927 by missionaries to the West Coast of the United States, and in the 1930s to Brazil.   **SECT, SHINTO**

1926   German authorities begin arresting Jehovah's Witnesses and confiscating their religious texts. Similar actions are taken by the governments of the United States, Romania, Hungary, Italy, and many other nations into the 1930s. Government authorities are concerned about Witnesses' claims that Jehovah began to rule the world in 1914 and also about the refusal of Witnesses to salute the national flag. In many cases the Witnesses win relief from persecution in court cases.   **SECT, TOL**

1926   The French separate the area they call Grand Liban (Great Lebanon) and establish it as a republic. Its constitution requires that power be shared by the major religious groups in the nation. The president is required to be a Maronite Christian, the prime minister a Sunni Muslim, and the president of the National Assembly a Shi'a Muslim.   **TOL**

1927
Pentecostal preacher Aimee Semple McPherson founds the Church of the Foursquare Gospel headquartered in Los Angeles. By the time of her death in 1944, the Church has expanded to include 400 churches, 200 missionaries outside the United States, and the Lighthouse of International Foursquare Evangelical (LIFE) Bible College. **EVAN**

1927
The Tablighi and Tanzim Muslim movements emerge in India and are active into the 1930s. Both movements follow the collapse of Muslim political movements that failed to remove the British rulers and also failed to create a Muslim-Hindu political alliance. The two new movements are basically religious and stress a revival of traditional Islam in India. **ISLAM**

1927
The Future of an Illusion by Austrian psychoanalyst Sigmund Freud (1856–1939) is published. Like his earlier works on religion (*Moses and Monotheism* and *Totem and Taboo*), the book criticizes religion, and Freud argues that religion has outlived its value as a coping mechanism for human beings. **MISC**

1927
A dispute over religious practice divides the Indian Shaker Church into two factions. One remains the Indian Shaker Church, while the other becomes the Indian Full Gospel Church. **NATIV**

1927
In China Baptist, Congregational, Methodist, Presbyterian, Reformed, Brethren, and other independent Protestant churches and missions form the Church of Christ in China and cooperate in missionary activities. **PROT**

1927
In the United States the Southern Baptist Convention becomes more established with the formation of an executive committee and a financial program. The new structure is criticized by some Baptists as a violation of the Baptist principle of independent churches. **PROT**

1927
The American Rosicrucian Order, AMORC relocates from New York City to San Jose, California, where it establishes a permanent American headquarters. **SECT**

1927
In Pennsylvania the Beachy Amish, named after their leader, Moses M. Beachy, separate from the Old Order Amish. The Beachy group allows the use of some modern technology, such as automobiles, and attract other Amish with similar interests. **SECT**

1927
Kishi Itta leaves Omotokyo to found the new religion Meidokai (later Ishinkai), and in 1929 Okano Eizo founds the new Japanese religion Gedatsukai (Salvation Society), or Seiken, with a syncretist doctrine incorporating Shinto ideas. **SECT, SHINTO**

1927–1933
Daisetz Suzuki (1870–1966), a Japanese Buddhist scholar who spends many years in the United States, publishes his three-volume work *Essays in Zen Buddhism*. Through this and later works, along with his lectures in Europe

and America, he plays a major role in spreading Zen Buddhism around the world. **BUDD**

1928 The International Missionary Council (formed in 1921) conference is held in Jerusalem. A key issue discussed is the role of national churches. Led by China, national Protestant churches demand a greater role in the administration of church affairs in their nations and even suggest that foreign missionaries should report to the national churches. **CHRIS**

1928 Sacrifice to Confucius in the Confucian temple in China is banned and thereafter Confucianism ceases to be an official orthodoxy. **CONF**

1928 China's nationalist leader Chiang Kai-shek establishes the Guomindang Central Political Institute in Beijing for political and government administrators; the course of study is nationalist and antiforeign, with a Confucian undercurrent that emphasizes order, harmony, discipline, and hierarchy. **CONF**

1928 In the Soviet Union the government begins to institute policies that restrict the religious freedom of Muslims, most of whom live in the Caucasus region in Russia or in the Soviet republics in central Asia. The new policies, which continue into the mid-1930s, include a ban on the use of Arabic, the language of Islam, begun in 1926; a ban on two basic Muslim practices, the pilgrimage to Mecca and the giving of alms; the closing of mosques and Muslim schools; and the destruction of the Qur'an. In the 1930s Muslim politicians are removed from office and replaced by Russians and Ukrainians. **ISLAM**

1928 In Egypt the Muslim Brotherhood is founded by Muslim teacher Hasan al-Banna (1904–1949). It is a reform movement that seeks to end British rule, remove Western influences from Egyptian society, and revive a form of fundamental Islam based on the Qur'an. A women's organization called the Muslim Sisters is also established to encourage women to lead their lives in accord with Islamic law. The brotherhood draws a large following in Egypt until it is repressed by the government in 1954. **ISLAM**

1928 Repression of Judaism continues in the Soviet Union, with rabbis and itinerant preachers persecuted and synagogues closed by the government. **JUD**

1928 The General Assembly of Unitarian and Free Christian Churches is established in London as the central organization for Unitarianism in Great Britain. **SECT**

1928 Baha'i is repressed by the Communist government in the Soviet Union. **SECT**

1928 The first Mennonite colony in Paraguay is founded by Mennonites from Canada. Subsequently, other colonies in Paraguay are founded by Mennonites from Russia. The Mennonites are fleeing repression in Canada and Russia and are attracted to Paraguay by available farmland and a promise of an exemption from military service. Although the Mennonites number only about

1928

15,000, they become major suppliers of dairy and farm products to the nation and play a role in converting natives to Christianity. **SECT**

1928 In the only popular vote in the United States on the teaching of evolution in the public schools, the people of Oklahoma vote by a two-to-one margin to ban the teaching of evolution. **TOL**

1928 The National Conference of Christians and Jews is founded in the United States. Its purpose is to foster religious tolerance and to end prejudice and discrimination. **TOL**

1929 The African Greek Orthodox Church is founded in Uganda by Reuben Mukasa (1899–1982). Mukasa, who is also called Spartas, models the church on the African Orthodox Church founded by Marcus Garvey in the United States. In 1933 the church affiliates with the Greek Orthodox Church in Alexandria, Egypt, and in 1946 it is accepted by the Greek Orthodox Church. **AFRICAN**

1929 The conflict between the Roman Catholic Church in Rome and the nation of Italy over the political identity of the church is resolved through the Lateran Concordat and Treaty, which creates the Vatican as an independent city-state under the rule of the pope and a commission of cardinals. In addition to the 109 acres within the Vatican, the church also controls 160 acres outside the Vatican. The agreement also gives Roman Catholicism special status in Italy and requires that it be taught in the schools. **CATH**

1929 The Muslim League in India calls for the establishment of Muslim provinces in India, separate elections for Muslims, and guarantees of protection for Islam and Islamic law and traditions. The British initiate some reforms in subsequent years but they fail to satisfy either the Muslims or the Hindus or both. **ISLAM**

1929 In Palestine tensions increase between the Arabs and Jews, and riots break out. The Arabs express concern over the increasing number of Jews settling in Palestine and their perceived dominance in politics and business. **JUD**

1929 The Jewish Museum is founded in New York City by the Conservative Jewish Theological Seminary. **JUD**

1929 *The Mormon Tabernacle Choir Broadcast* begins as the choir's regular Sunday morning radio broadcast. **MOR**

1929 In Scotland the Church of Scotland and the United Free Church of Scotland unite under the name of the former. **PROT**

1929 In the Philippines the Presbyterian Church, the Congregational Churches, and the Church of the United Brethren in Christ unite and form the United Evangelical Church of the Philippines. **PROT**

1929   In the United States, as the conflict between conservatives and liberals continues in the Presbyterian Church U.S.A., conservative theologians withdraw from Princeton Theological Seminary and found the Westminster Seminary in Philadelphia. In 1933 they form their own mission society and in 1936 found the Presbyterian Church of America, which is renamed the Orthodox Presbyterian Church in 1939.   PROT

1929   In the United States an effort is under way by representatives of the Methodist Protestant Church, the Methodist Episcopal Church, and the Methodist Episcopal Church, South to reunify and create a single Methodist Church. A plan is developed that covers organizational issues. The most difficult issue is the question of whether to include black Methodist churches, a policy rejected by the southern churches. A compromise establishes a Central Jurisdiction that will include all African-American churches and therefore exclude them from the regional jurisdictions used for the white churches.   PROT

1929   The New History Society is established in New York as a splinter group of the Baha'i religion.   SECT

1929   Under the new economic and social policies in Russia, Mennonite communities are disbanded and some 14,000 Mennonites flee. Many are killed or imprisoned, with about 6,000 escaping to Germany and then moving on to Canada and South America.   SECT

1929   The laws governing religious freedom in the Soviet Union are changed, with the government given new and broad rights to control religion and religious behavior and the constitution amended to remove the right to "religious propaganda" while continuing to allow "anti-religious propaganda." Affiliation with religious organizations and beliefs is seen by the government as impeding the creation of a unified Soviet nation from a population that is composed of people from over 100 ethnic and religious groups.   TOL

1930   Ras Tafari, his imperial majesty, the emperor of Ethiopia, Haile Selassie I, the king of kings, the lord of lords, and the conquering lion of the tribe of Judah is crowned as king of Ethiopia. He is hailed by some Jamaicans as a "Black God" and Ethiopia is pronounced the "promised land," marking the beginning of the Rastafarian movement.   AFRICAN

1930   The Nation of Islam begins to emerge in Detroit, when Master Fard (also known as Mr. Farrad Mohammad, W. D. Fard, and Mr. Wali Farrad), a street peddler, begins preaching a new religion for African-Americans and establishes a meeting hall called the Temple of Islam. Before his disappearance and assumed death in 1934, he preaches a doctrine of black nationalism and writes the two basic documents for the movement: *The Secret Ritual of the Nation of Islam* and *Teachings for the Lost-Found Nation of Islam in a Mathematical Way.*   AFRICAN

1930

| 1930 | The Church of the Lord, an independent African church that combines traditional African religious practices with Christianity, is founded in Nigeria by Josiah Olunowo Oshitelu (1902–1966), a Nigerian trained as an Anglican teacher. The Church of the Lord spreads to Ghana in 1953, Sierra Leone in 1964, and London, England, in 1964 and becomes one of the major independent churches of West Africa. Much of the church's growth is a result of the work of church leader Emmanuel Adeleke Adejobi (1919–). **AFRICAN** |

| 1930 | In Japan, Tunesaburo Makiguchi and Joei Toda organize a publishing house, the *Soka Kyoiku Gakkai* (Value Creation Education Society), which later becomes the Soka Gakkai new religion. **BUDD** |

| 1930 | The first Zen institute is founded in New York City to promote Zen Buddhism (Chan Buddhism) in the United States, but it is not until the 1950s that Zen Buddhism begins to attract Americans in any numbers. **BUDD** |

| 1930 | While in prison for opposing the British government in India, Mohandas Gandhi (1869–1948) writes *Letters to the Ashram*, and in the next year writes *Experience of Truth*. The works set forth his ideas on religion, which include a central belief that truth is God and God is truth and that truth is also love and inner self. Gandhi suggests that purity, self-control, and nonmaterialism are the means to achieving truth. **HIND** |

Rastafarianism

Rastafarianism is a religion developed by African-Americans on the island of Jamaica in the 1930s. It continues to draw adherents around the world; followers of the movement are known as Rastafarians, Rastas, or Dreadlocks. The dreadlock hairstyle, the sacramental use of marijuana (*ganga*), and reggae music are three Rastafarian cultural forms whose popularity has spread far beyond the movement and outside Jamaica. There are an estimated 100,000 Rastafarians in Jamaica with considerably smaller populations in Great Britain, the United States, Australia, Ethiopia, Canada, New Zealand, South Africa, and Ghana. Rastafarianism has spread primarily as a result of the immigration of Jamaican Rastafarians to other nations, not as a result of Rastafarians attracting converts in other nations. Rastafarianism is a black nationalist movement, as Rastafarians emphasize ties to and an eventual return to Africa, and the movement began in part as a protest against poverty and white rule in Jamaica. Widespread, if superficial, knowledge of Rastafarianism outside the movement is probably due both to the distinctive dreadlocks hairstyle of many Rastafarians and to the increasing popularity of reggae music. Nearly all the early international reggae artists since the 1960s—Bob Marley, for example—were Rastafarians. Reggae lyrics are rich with Rastafarian themes of oppression, revolution, and better times in the future. Within Jamaica and elsewhere it remains an important political as well as religious movement that stresses Afro-Caribbean culture and rejects white European dominance.

1930   In the Soviet Union the government puts severe controls on the establish-
            ment of *waqfs*, income-producing properties given as charity to the Muslim
            community that are important sources of income for mosques and religious
            schools.   ISLAM

1930   Sir Muhammed Iqbal (1876–1938), a Muslim poet and philosopher and
            president of the Muslim League in India, argues for the creation of a
            Muslim state in northwestern India separate from Hindu India. Hindu lead-
            ers want a single state but Muslims, concerned about facing discrimination
            as a religious minority, demand a separate Muslim nation. The state later
            becomes the nation of Pakistan.   ISLAM

1930   Jewish emigration from Europe to South Africa is restricted.   JUD

1930   In the United States the Lutheran Synod of Buffalo, the Evangelical Lutheran
            Synod of Iowa and Other States, and the Evangelical Lutheran Joint Synod of
            Ohio and Other States unite to form the American Lutheran Church.   PROT

1930   In Mexico the Methodist Mexican Episcopal Church and Methodist
            Mexican Episcopal Church, South unite to form the United Methodist
            Church of Mexico.   PROT

Nation of Islam

The Nation of Islam, also commonly called the Black Muslims, is an African-
American religion that developed in the United States beginning in 1930 in Detroit.
The development of the Nation of Islam has been closely associated with four
African-American men: W. D. Fard, Elijah Muhammad, Malcolm X, and Louis
Farrakhan, the current leader. Fard founded the religion, Muhammad expanded it
and developed the basic theology and organizational structure, Malcolm X popular-
ized it, and Farrakhan has maintained traditional beliefs while at the same time
bringing it much public attention. Despite its name, the beliefs and practices of the
Nation differ from Islam as it is practiced elsewhere, and ties to Islam are tenuous,
although some members of the Nation of Islam have sought to strengthen ties to the
international Islamic community. In addition to being a religion, the Nation of Islam
is also a social, political, and economic movement. Elijah Muhammad saw the movement as combating racism and discrimination against African-Americans and strongly encouraged economic self-sufficiency and black pride. The ideology predicts an
imminent conflict between blacks and whites with blacks victorious. Thus, the movement has been associated with the Black Nationalism and Black Separatist movements, and its leaders have been at times at odds with leaders of the Civil Rights
movement, who favor integration. The number of members is unknown but is probably about 500,000, with temples located in most major American cities.

1930   Mennonites from Russia immigrate to Brazil and settle in Santa Catarina,
            where a large German Mennonite community already exists.   SECT

1930   The Baha'i World Union is established in Germany by American and
            German adherents as a splinter Baha'i sect. It is banned by the government
            in 1937 and reestablished in 1948.   SECT

1930   *Der Neue Amerikanische Calendar* (*The New American Almanac*) is published
            in German in Ohio and becomes the basic calendar and directory for Amish
            religious worship.   SECT

1930   The Soka Gakkai religion, which is based on Nichiren Buddhism, is founded
            in Japan. It is formally organized as a religion in 1937, is repressed by the gov-
            ernment during World War II, and emerges again as a popular religion in the
            1950s when it spreads to Europe and the United States. One basic doctrine is
            the pursuit of happiness, including the acquisition of material wealth, and in
            the 1990s it has nearly 20 million adherents worldwide.   SECT

1930   The Anglo-Saxon Federation of America is founded by Maine lawyer
            Howard B. Rand (1899–1991) in Detroit, Michigan. Initially it preaches a
            British-Israelite doctrine, and within a few years chapters are developed in
            a number of cities, among them Philadelphia and Los Angeles. Because
            Rand preaches a message of better times ahead, his group is especially pop-
            ular during the Depression years.   SECT

1930   According to a survey by Japan's Ministry of Education, 414 new religions have
            been organized; the number will reach 1,029 in 1935. Among the new religions
            founded in 1930 is the Shinto-inspired Seicho no Ie (Truth of Life or House of
            Growth) founded by Taniguchi Masaharu (1893–1987).   SECT, SHINTO

1930s   The Baloke or East African Revival takes place among African Christians
            (primarily Anglicans) in Uganda, Kenya, and Tanzania. The movement
            stresses African forms of worship and social organization alongside the
            existing Christian churches, rather than in opposition to them. It is also
            pan-tribal and pan-religion in that it accepts as members people from any
            tribe or religion.   AFRICAN

1930s   The Voudou religion in Haiti is embraced by some intellectuals who claim it
            as the national religion of Haiti, although its adherents are mainly the rural
            poor, with wealthy Haitians being primarily Roman Catholics.   AFRICAN

1930s   The Way of Pervading Unity, a secret religious society, is widespread in
            north China. It blends elements of Confucianism, Daoism, Buddhism,
            Christianity, and Islam, incorporating all their saints, sages, and gods.
            Adherents study the Daoist and Buddhist canons and practice variants of
            Daoist inner alchemy.   DAO

1930s	In Malaysia the Maum Muda Muslim movement becomes politically active. It is a reform movement that is aligned with pan-Islamic movements in other nations and is opposed to British rule. It is repressed by both the government and traditional Muslim leaders. ISLAM
1930s	In Nigeria Muslim brotherhoods, of which the Tijani movement is the largest, develop among the Hausa people and become an important means by which the different ethnic groups in the region express Islam and are linked with one another. ISLAM
1930s	Kanji Swami, originally a Svetambara Jain monk, breaks with his sect and adopts the Digambara Jain doctrines, although he does not accept the Digambara rituals and monks. Kanji Swami's followers will form a major reform movement in late-20th-century Jainism. JAIN
1930s	The John Frum cargo cult develops on Tanna Island in Vanuatu in the Pacific Ocean. The movement focuses on the return of John Frum, whom the islanders believe is a divine figure, the end of white rule, and material wealth for the people of Vanuatu. The movement remains important politically in the 1990s as it is associated with Vanuatu nationalism. SECT
1931	Pope Pius XI issues his *Quadragesimo Anno*, in which he further defines the Social Catholicism movement. He introduces the concept of social justice to the church and argues for limitations on the power of the state and for individual opportunity. CATH
1931	In Afghanistan a new constitution is enacted that is in general accord with Islamic law, reversing policies enacted in 1923 that were designed to make Afghanistan a secular nation. ISLAM
1931	In Ethiopia the new constitution grants Muslims full rights. However, Muslims are a minority in the Christian nation and live mainly in the east, and the government continues with policies that attempt to limit the influence of Islam and end the threat of Muslim separatism. ISLAM
1931	In Algeria the Muslim reform movement that began in the 1920s continues to grow with the founding of the Association of Muslim Ulama of Algeria. In the following year Sufi Muslims found the Association of Ulama. ISLAM
1931	The Cathedral of Christ the Savior, built in Moscow in 1812 to commemorate the Russian defeat of Napoleon, is blown up by the government of Josef Stalin. The cathedral will be rebuilt beginning in the 1990s. ORTHO
1931	In Puerto Rico the Congregational Churches, the Christian Churches, and the Church of the United Brethren in Christ unite and form the United Evangelical Church of Puerto Rico. PROT

1931

1931	In England the Wesleyan Methodist Church, the United Methodist Church, and the Primitive Methodist Church unite and form the Methodist Church. **PROT**
1931	In the United States the General Convention of the Christian Church (located in the south with members who were from the Baptist, Methodist, and Presbyterian denominations) and the Congregational Churches (located mainly in the north) unite and form the Congregational Christian Churches. **PROT**
1931	The first Protestant radio station, known as Heralding Jesus Christ's Blessing, is established in Ecuador by Protestant missionaries. Its broadcasts are meant to aid in missionary work, and over the next 40 years another 60 such radio stations are developed around the world. **PROT**
1931	At its annual convention, the Jehovah's Witnesses officially adopt the term *Jehovah's Witnesses* as the religion's name. **SECT**
1931	The Anglo-Saxon Federation of America begins to attract adherents from the extreme right wing of American politics and also begins to develop an anti-Semitic slant through the influence of Detroit public relations executive William J. Cameron. The merging of these elements plays a role in the subsequent emergence of the Christian Identity movement in the United States. **SECT**
1931	Japan invades Manchuria. Manchuria and part of Outer Mongolia will remain under Japanese control until 1945. A result is that some Shinto shrines will increase in importance as a general is appointed head priest at Yasukuni, and the Hachiman shrines become more influential because of their association with the *kami* (protective spirits) of war. **SHINTO**
1931	The I AM movement is founded in California by Guy Ballard (1878–1939) and Edna Ballard (?–1970). It is a spiritual movement based on personal growth and the use of channeling to draw on the wisdom of masters of the past. By 1938 some one million people are claimed as students in the movement. **SPIR**
1932	The Masowe Apostles and Maranke Apostles begin as apocalyptic Christian movements among Africans in Zimbabwe (Rhodesia). The leaders of the movements are Africans John Masowe (c.1910–1973) and Johane Maranke (1912–1963), an Anglican and Methodist, respectively, who found their movements after undergoing mystical experiences. **AFRICAN**
1932	A group of Catholic students from Sophia University refuse to participate in a service at Yasukuni shrine in Japan, on the grounds of the constitutional guarantee of freedom of religion. This leads the Ministry of Education to declare the shrine a nonreligious institution that aims to instill patriotism

and loyalty. This means that Japanese of all religious affiliations will be required to participate in Shinto shrine rituals. **CATH, SHINTO**

1932   *Moral Man and Immoral Society*, by the American Christian theologian Reinhold Niebuhr (1892–1971), is published. Niebuhr is an influential thinker who writes about social and political issues with the goal of creating a more just world. **CHRIS**

1932   The Chinese Daoist Association is established. **DAO**

1932   In a break from traditional Hindu practice, the British give voting rights to the Untouchable castes. Gandhi condemns the plan to include the Untouchables in communal electorates and vows to "fast until death" in prison. Gandhi ends his fast after making an agreement with the Untouchable leader, B. R. Ambedkar. The compromise, known as the Poona Pact, allows the Untouchables to select a larger number of candidates in their own primary elections, which are to be voted upon by the general electorate. **HIND**

1932   The Kingdom of Saudi Arabia is established with the unification of the four provinces of Hijaz, 'Asir, Najd, and Al-Ahsa. The kingdom is governed in accord with Islamic law as an Islamic state. **ISLAM**

1932   In the United States younger Baptists break with older Baptists and form their own Baptist organizations. In this year the Association of Regular Baptists in the North is formed, followed by the World Baptist Fellowship in 1949 and the Baptist Missionary Association in 1950. These organizations become important in the subsequent growth of the Baptist denomination. **PROT**

1932   The Amana Society in Iowa (**SEE 1854, PROT**), which has enjoyed much economic success as a self-supporting network of farms and villages since the 1850s, is dissolved. Contact with the outside world and economic success has eroded the fundamental Protestant religious base of the community. **PROT**

1932   The Emissaries, an early New Age group that stresses personal growth, love, and community, is founded in Tennessee by Lloyd A. Meeker (1907–1954) and spreads later to Great Britain. **SPIR**

1932   The Evolution Protest Movement is founded in Britain and after 1935 plays an active role in resisting the teaching of biological evolution and in criticizing evolution as a theory rather than established scientific fact. **TOL**

1932–
1933   Rastafarianism, which began in 1930, spreads through Jamaica when three Afro-Jamaicans—Leonard Percivall Howell, Joseph Nathaniel Hibbert, and Henry Archibald Dunkey—began to preach the message of Ethiopia as the promised land and attract small followings. **AFRICAN**

| 1932–1933 | Eight Protestant mission boards in the United States conduct the Laymen's Foreign Missions Inquiry. The report of the inquiry, titled *Rethinking Missions*, is published in 1933 and causes much controversy among missionaries, as it takes an ecumenical position and suggests that Christian missionaries work with the "forces within each [local] religious system." **PROT** |

1933   The Catholic Worker movement and the magazine of the same name are founded by Dorothy Day (1897–1880), a former journalist and recent convert to Roman Catholicism, in the United States. The movement develops services to provide for the hungry, poor, and homeless, and Day is often in conflict with the church hierarchy, which she criticizes for failing to end inequality and tyranny. **CATH**

1933   A partial English translation of the Daoist *Huainanzi* is written. The essays are later translated into French and German. **DAO**

1933   In India independence leader Mohandas Gandhi devotes himself to the cause of the Untouchables, whom he calls *harijans* (children of God). **HIND**

1933   Muslim students at Cambridge University in England publish a pamphlet entitled *Now or Never* in which they demand the partition of India into separate states and assign the name "Pakistan" to the future Muslim nation using an abbreviation of the names of provinces in northwest India (which after 1948 constitute modern-day Pakistan). **ISLAM**

1933   Adolf Hitler, the leader of the National Socialist Party (Nazis), becomes chancellor of Germany. As early as 1922 he had expressed the goal of killing all Jews in Germany. Hitler's rise to power is accompanied by Jewish persecutions. In 1933 prominent Jews are forced to resign their positions and leave Germany, Jewish books are burned, and boycotts are initiated against Jewish businesses. The first new law against Jews bans them from government employment, although Jews in positions considered vital to the government are not immediately dismissed. In the United States the *Christian Science Monitor* holds Jews in Germany partially responsible for these acts, while Protestant theologian Reinhold Niebuhr (1892–1971) attacks anti-Semitism in Germany and Christian acceptance of it. **JUD**

1933   *The Humanist Manifesto* is ratified by leading humanists in the United States. It is often criticized by those on the Religious Right in the 1980s and 1990s in the United States as an antireligious document that promotes secular humanism. **MISC**

1933   In the aftermath of flooding in northern Argentina, some Toba Indians join the millennial movement led by the shaman Notochi. The movement, repressed by the government, centers on a prediction of the end of this world, a new world of prosperity, rejection of Christianity, and ritual dancing. **NATIV**

1933   Joseph Franklin Rutherford, leader of the Jehovah's Witnesses, offers to debate the pope or his representative concerning Catholic criticisms of the Jehovah's Witnesses. The Witnesses claim to be victims of Protestant persecution and especially harsh Roman Catholic persecution, and their proposal is meant to bring public attention to the issue. The pope does not respond.   **SECT**

1933   In Germany the National Socialist (Nazi) government initiates its effort to bring the Christian churches under state control by revoking the constitution of 1919 and terminating freedom of religion.   **TOL**

1933–1935   In Algeria the French attempt to control the expanding Muslim reform movement by controlling mosques and limiting publications in Arabic. The controls are not effective, and in 1935 the Muslim reform movement joins forces with political reform movements to seek an end to French rule.   **ISLAM**

1933–1939   The fifth *Aliyah* to Palestine takes place. Jews continue to immigrate to Palestine from eastern Europe, the Middle East, and North Africa, and the Jewish sectors of Palestine continue to expand and industrialize.   **JUD**

1934   The God's Kingdom Society movement is founded in Nigeria. It provides an alternative to Roman Catholicism, Protestantism, and Islam by drawing upon a number of Christian denominations and Judaism, creating a rigid social hierarchy, and allowing traditional African customs, such as polygymy, to continue. It has several thousand followers centered on the holy site of Salem. The movement is founded by Gideon Meriodore Urhodo (1903–1952), a former Catholic and Jehovah's Witnesss.   **AFRICAN**

1934   The Fraternal Council of Negro Churches is founded. It serves to represent the interest of African-American churches and the concerns of the African-American community in general for 30 years, until its agenda is taken over by the Civil Rights movement.   **AFRICAN**

1934   The Wycliffe Bible Translators is founded in Texas. It is a missionary organization that focuses on translating the Bible into native languages, mainly in Latin America at first but then around the world. It also collects anthropological information on native cultures and helps native people to develop their societies economically. The Summer Institute of Linguistics is also formed as a "scientific organization." At times both organizations are criticized by supporters of indigenous rights for assisting—wittingly or unwittingly—developers and politicians in exploiting indigenous peoples and destroying traditional cultures.   **CHRIS**

1934   The Worldwide Church of God emerges in Oregon when minister Herbert W. Armstrong (1892–1986) begins broadcasting his *World Tomorrow* radio program and publication of the *Plain Truth* magazine. The church expands over the decades and by the 1980s has over five million followers who read its literature and support it with donations.   **CHRIS**

1934   Mohammed Ali Jinnah (1876–1948), a Bombay attorney, becomes leader of the Muslim League and revitalizes it as the major representative of Muslim interests in India.   ISLAM

1934   Muslims in Tanganyika (later Tanzania) in East Africa form the Muslim Association of Tanganyika to represent Muslim interests and create cooperation among Muslim communities in the nation.   ISLAM

1934   In the Soviet Union Josef Stalin establishes the Birobijan, an autonomous Jewish region in Siberia. The region never becomes a home to any significant number of Jews, most of whom continue to live in Russia, Belarus, and the Ukraine.   JUD

1934   Discrimination of Jews in Germany continues, and about 10 percent of the German Jewish population of 500,000 leaves the country.   JUD

1934   John Collier, head of the United States Bureau of Indian Affairs, removes bans on Native American traditional religious practices.   NATIV

1934   In Thailand the Siamese Presbyterian Church, the Chinese Presbyterian Churches in Siam, and the Chinese Baptist Churches in Siam unite and form the Church of Christ in Siam.   PROT

1934   In the United States the Evangelical Synod of North America and the Reformed Churches in the United States unite and form the Evangelical and Reformed Church.   PROT

1934   In Germany leaders of many Lutheran, Reformed, and other churches react to government efforts to bring them under state control by forming the Pastors' Emergency League and then issue a declaration rejecting the government's efforts. However, the Lutheran and Reformed churches fail to unite on all issues and the movement weakens. In 1939 the church leadership is repressed and the church is placed under state control.   PROT

1934   Repression of the Baha'i community begins again in Iran. The Baha'i are viewed by Muslims as heretics.   SECT

1934   Rose-Croix University opens at Rosicrucian Park in San Jose, California, as a center for the study and teaching of Rosicrucian principles.   SECT

1934   Japanese businessman Okada Mokichi (1882–1955) founds a new religion, the messianic syncretist Shinto-based sect Kannonkyo, which later will become Sekai Kyuseikyo.   SECT

1935   Leaders of the Catholic community in the United States issue *Organized Social Justice—An Economic Program for the United States Applying Pius XI's Great Encyclical on Social Life*, which strongly supports workers' rights and unionization.   CATH

1935 The Nuremberg laws are promulgated by the Nazi government in Germany. The laws strip Jews of citizenship, prohibit them from voting, restrict them from public employment, and prohibit their marriage to non-Jews.   JUD

1935 *The Bible: An American Translation* is published in the United States. It is written in American English for use by American Protestants.   PROT

1935 The Omotokyo religion, founded in 1900, is banned by the Japanese government because of its criticism of government policies. When some 500 police attack its headquarters, the buildings are destroyed and its leaders are imprisoned and tortured. It is reestablished after World War II. In 1936 police raid the headquarters of the Hitonomichi new religion and arrest its leaders, resulting in the disbandment of the group. The government will continue the suppression of new religions on the grounds of *lese majesté* when their doctrines seem to contradict official Shinto mythology.   SECT

1935 Joseph Franklin Rutherford, leader of the Jehovah's Witnesses, suggests that all Jehovah's Witnesses tabernacles be called kingdom halls, and since then all have borne signs proclaiming them "Kingdom Hall of Jehovah's Witnesses."   SECT

1935 The Branch Davidian Church is started by Victor Houteff (1886–1955) as an offshoot of the Seventh-Day Adventist Church in Texas.   SECT

1935 The Religion and Science Association is founded in the United States to support scientific research to study creationism and evolution. Although founded as a scientific research society, the leaders are all supporters of creationism and their goal is to marshal evidence in support of creationism and refute evolutionary theory. The organization folds in 1938 after its founders fail to agree on one theory of creation.   TOL

1935– The Mongolian government's policy of religious persecution intensifies. In
1939 1937 and 1938, approximately 2,000 Buddhist monks and abbots are executed; Buddhism is all but eradicated as a public institution.   BUDD, TOL

1936 Elijah Muhammad (1897–1975), the son of a Baptist preacher and an early follower of movement founder W. D. Fard, takes over the leadership of the Nation of Islam and establishes its headquarters at Temple of Islam No. 2 in Chicago.   AFRICAN

1936 In the Soviet Union the Russian-controlled government completes its reorganization of the Muslim peoples of the nation. There are six "Muslim" Socialist Republics (Uzbekistan, Kazakhstan, Azerbaijan, Turkmenistan, Tajikistan, and Kirgizia), eight smaller autonomous republics, and four even smaller autonomous provinces. (Since the Soviets have suppressed religion, the Muslim Socialist Republics are Muslim in name only.)   ISLAM

1936

1936   In Poland anti-Semitism is on the increase, with government support for an informal boycott of Jewish-owned businesses.   JUD

1936   At the General Conference of the Methodist Episcopal Church in the United States, the plan for reunification of the three Methodist churches in the United States, which was developed beginning in 1929, is adopted by the church. The provision creating a separate division for African-American churches is rejected by the African-American delegates but supported by the whites. The plan is also adopted by the Methodist Protestant Church and the Methodist Episcopal Church, South in 1938.   PROT

1936   In Guatemala the Presbyterian Church and the Central American Mission unite and form the Evangelical Church in Guatemala.   PROT

1936   The Vatican orders all Catholics in the Japanese empire to treat Shinto ritual as a "civil affair" and to make obeisance if so ordered. In Korea, where the Shinto shrines number 368 in 1937, Shinto is seen as Japan's agent of political and military control; most Protestants, led by missionaries, remain defiant on this issue and view such obeisance as akin to idolatry. In 1938 Korea's missionary schools will close and after the Westerners leave, Korean Christians will suffer persecution, imprisonment, and death under Shinto rule. The Japanese government will order the placement of portable Shinto shrines in Christian churches.   SHINTO, TOL

1936   The Divine Life Society (later renamed the Divine Light Mission) is founded by Hindu physician Sivananda (1887–1963) in India. It stresses the use of Hatha yoga to achieve the highest sense of spirituality.   SPIR

1936–
1938   In Palestine Muslim and Christian Arabs revolt against British control and Jewish settlement. The revolt is put down and the British establish military rule.   ISLAM

1937   The *Soka Kyoiku Gakkai* (Value Creation Education Society) publishing house, established in Japan in 1930, becomes a religious organization. During World War II, the Soka Gakkai organization (as it is now named) is harassed by the Japanese government for not being sufficiently nationalistic and militaristic. After the war, it gains millions of new members in Japan. It is not a religious sect but seeks to convert everyone to Nichiren Shoshu Buddhism (SEE 1261, BUDD, TOL); it stresses that everyone should seek truth, enlightenment, and a "human revolution" that combines personal "bliss" with a form of humanistic socialism. In practice, however, Soka Gakkai began by appealing mainly to the lower and lower middle classes. It became quite intolerant of all other religions and engaged in aggressive proselytizing, and its strict hierarchy took on a quasi-military character.   BUDD

1937   Pope Pius XI issues his encyclical *Mit Brenender Sorge*, which condemns Nazism and criticizes Nazi assaults on the freedom of the church. The Nazi government responds by tightening repression of Catholicism.   **CATH**

1937   In Ireland the constitution guarantees religious freedom, although it acknowledges that Roman Catholicism occupies a special position as the religion of the majority of the people. This clause is removed by referendum in 1972.   **CATH, TOL**

1937   In India the Hindu Congress Party is victorious and the Muslim League loses power and is effectively excluded from the new government. The loss revitalizes the Muslim League, worsens relations between the Muslims and Hindus, and strengthens the Muslim desire for an independent Muslim state.

    HIND, ISLAM

1937   In response to the Jews fleeing from Germany, South Africa amends its immigration laws to prohibit Jewish immigration.   **JUD**

1937   The British Peel Commission, in an attempt to deal with continuing conflict between Jews and Arabs in Palestine, recommends that the region be divided into Jewish and Arab states. Jews accept the proposal while Arabs reject it.   **JUD**

1937   As part of their effort to combat religious persecution around the world, Baptists in the United States ask the government to look into alleged religious persecution in Romania.   **PROT**

1937   Fundamentalists in the conservative Presbyterian Church of America form their own church, the Bible Presbyterian Church, under the leadership of Carl T. McIntire (1906–).   **PROT**

1937   The Baha'i religion is banned by the Nazi government in Germany.   **SECT**

1937   The last independent Amish church in Europe merges with a Mennonite church, ending the presence of the Amish as a distinct religious community in Europe. Since the 1870s, following immigration to the United States, the Amish have probably never numbered more than 2,000 in Europe.   **SECT**

1937   Beginning in this year a series of annual meetings are held over the next 10 years by members of British-Israelite groups in the United States and Canada. The meetings redefine the movement from one with British roots that was based on the belief that Britons are descendants of one of the 10 lost tribes of Israel to one that is apocalyptic, antigovernment, and anti-Semitic.

    SECT

1937   As Japan begins the Sino-Japanese War (1937–1945), a government emergency order speeds up the establishment and consolidation of overseas Shinto shrines. By 1940 there will be 27 shrines on mainland China in areas conquered by Japan and by 1941, 18 shrines on Taiwan. In November 1938 Japan will announce a "New Order in East Asia," the goal of which is to integrate Japan, Korea, Manchuko, and China into a single political, military, and economic entity. **SHINTO**

1937   Japan's Ministry of Education issues the *Kokutai no hongi* (*Cardinal Principles of the National Polity*) based on Shinto ideals. It rejects "false doctrines of individualism" and views the emperor as "a deity incarnate who rules our country in unison with the august will of the Imperial Ancestors." The treatise is to be used as a school text to disseminate imperial nationalist propaganda. During the 1930s Shinto priests rise to positions of great influence in Japanese government. **SHINTO**

1937–   In Brazil, during the rule of dictator Getúlio Dornelles Vargas from 1937 to
1945   1945, African-based religions are repressed because they are viewed as possible sources of resistance to government rule. **AFRICAN**

1938   The Spiritist Center of Our Lady of Piety is established as the center of the Umbanda religion in Rio de Janeiro, Brazil. **AFRICAN**

1938   The Rissho Koseikai, or Rissho Kosei Kai (RKK), organization is founded in Japan; it is a lay movement of Nichiren Buddhists, emphasizing moral behavior, spirituality, and an end to suffering and conflict over and above traditional Buddhist concepts. By the 1990s it draws adherents throughout Japan. **BUDD**

1938   The International Missionary Conference is held in Madras, India. The conference report acknowledges the existence and worth of non-Christian religions but stresses that a conversion to Christianity requires a break from these traditions. **CHRIS**

1938   In China the Communists initiate a policy of accommodation toward Muslims, of whom the Hui are the largest and most widespread group. Religious freedom is guaranteed, Muslims are granted full rights, and they are expected to be involved in party and government activities. **ISLAM**

1938   Discrimination against Jews continues in Germany and appears in Romania, Finland, and Italy. On November 9–10 *Kristallnacht* takes place. Anti-Jewish riots take place in Germany and Austria, with nearly 200 synagogues burned, Jewish businesses looted, and many Jews arrested. *Kristallnacht* means "Night of the Broken Glass" in German and becomes a day of remembrance for Jews around the world. **JUD**

1938   In France the Union of Reformed Churches of France, the Union of Reformed Evangelical Churches of France, and the Evangelical Methodist Church of France unite and form the Reformed Church of France. **PROT**

1938   In Norway the government grants women the right to be ordained as clergy in the Evangelical Lutheran Church, the state religion.   **PROT**

1938   Following 10 years of government persecution, the Mennonite community in Russia has declined in size, many of its religious leaders have been killed or exiled, and most of its religious institutions closed.   **SECT**

1938   Japan's Ministry of Home Affairs advises the Tenrikyo sect (**SEE 1838, SECT**) to revise its scriptures. Tenrikyo does so, establishing a policy of full support of the government and of participation in the war effort.   **SHINTO**

1938   The American Federation of Astrologers is founded.   **SPIR**

1938   The Society for the Study of Creation, the Deluge, and Related Science (the Deluge Geology Society) is founded to replace the defunct Religion and Science Association. The society is creationist and therefore antievolutionist but limits membership to those who believe that the world was created in six days and that the Noachian Flood was a major cause of later geological change. The society closes in 1948.   **TOL**

1939   In Zaire the Church of the Blacks, modeled on the Church of Jesus Christ on Earth through the Prophet Simon Kimbangu, founded in the Congo (Zaire) by Simon Kimbangu in 1921 and repressed by the Belgian government, is founded by the prophet Simon-Pierre Mpadi (c.1905– ?), who had been trained by and worked for the Salvation Army. Like Kimbangu, Mpadi is imprisoned and is not released until Zaire becomes independent in 1960.   **AFRICAN**

1939   The Apostles Revelation Society is founded in Ghana by C. K. N. Wovenu (1918–), a Ghanaian social reformer. The society becomes active in building schools and hospitals and spreads to the United States and Britain.   **AFRICAN**

1939   The Roman Catholic Church reexamines the question of Chinese rites and authorizes Christian Asians to participate in ceremonies honoring Confucius and to observe ancestral rites.   **CATH, CONF**

1939   Military operations of the Sino-Japanese War (1931–1945) reach the Daoist holy place of Mount Mao; fire destroys most of the temple and shrine buildings there.   **DAO**

1939   In an effort to resolve the conflict in Palestine, Britain issues a White Paper calling for the creation of a Palestinian state and restrictions on Jewish immigration. The British are motivated in part by a desire to win the support of Arabs in the approaching war with Germany. The White Paper is rejected by the League of Nations. Some Jews in Palestine advocate a new approach to the problem that centers on increasing Jewish settlement in

Palestine and refusing to further cooperate with the British. In September, World War II begins with the German invasion of Poland.   ISLAM, JUD

1939   The Mormon Church withdraws its missionaries from Germany due to repression by the Nazi government and the threat of war in Europe.   MOR

1939   In the United States the Methodist Episcopal Church, the Methodist Episcopal Church, South and the Methodist Protestant Church unite and form the Methodist Church.   PROT

1939   In the United States the Southern, Northern, and National Baptists issue the "American Baptist Bill of Rights," which calls for a strict separation of church and state.   PROT, TOL

1939   The Jehovah's Witnesses incorporate in New York as the Watch Tower Bible and Tract Society. They also change the name of their magazine to the *Watchtower Announcing Jehovah's Kingdom* in accord with their belief that Jehovah is the ultimate god ruling the universe. Persecution of the religion begins in the British Commonwealth and lasts until 1945.   SECT

1939   Throughout Japan 117 regional Shinto shrines for the war dead are renamed *Gokoku jinja* (nation-protecting shrines) and are required to serve as local branches of Yasukuni shrine. The Religious Organizations Law is passed, granting the state unlimited power to regulate the activities of all religious groups, to mobilize religion for the war effort, to suppress dissent, and to strengthen the Shinto position. The Bureau of Shrines within the Home Affairs Ministry is raised in rank to the Shrine Board within the same ministry. Sect Shinto, but not shrine Shinto, is included among Japan's religions. The government leases state-owned property free of charge to shrines and temples. The law will go into effect in 1940.   SHINTO

1939–
1945   An increase in anti-Semitism in Europe leads to large-scale migration to Palestine, with over 200,000 Jews mainly from Germany and Poland settling there during this period. Others go to the United States, Great Britian, South Africa, and South America, although many nations restrict or seek to ban settlement by Jews.   JUD

1940   In the United States African-American Methodist churches that have been assigned their own jurisdiction, against their wishes, in the new Methodist Church, hold their first general conference and criticize the church for supporting segregation.   AFRICAN, PROT

1940   Tenzin Gyatso (1935–) is enthroned as the 14th Dalai Lama in Tibet. He will eventually become internationally known and respected for leading the struggle to regain a Tibet independent of China. SEE 1959, BUDD, TOL.   BUDD

1940   The Kentucky legislature passes a law prohibiting the use of reptiles in religious services. The law is aimed at some Evangelicals who practice snake handling and is in response to reports of injuries and deaths resulting from snake bites. In subsequent years many other states in the south and Midwest pass similar laws. SEE **1975, EVAN.**   EVAN

1940   The Assemblies of God of Nigeria, a Pentecostal church, is established by American missionaries.   EVAN

1940   The Muslim League in India formally endorses the creation of a separate Muslim state to be called Pakistan. They ask that regions with Muslim majorities in northwest and northeast India be grouped to form Muslim states.   ISLAM

1940   Persecutions of Jews escalate in all nations occupied by or allied with Germany. In October the Warsaw ghetto is created in Poland and by November 400,000 Jews are confined there. At the same time, the German government continues to allow some Jews to emigrate, a policy that continues into 1941.   JUD

1940   The Navajo Tribal Council bans the use of peyote, a sacrament of the Native American Church, one of a number of religions that have adherents among the Navajo. SEE **1967, NATIV.**   NATIV

1940   The Church of Christ in Japan is formed under pressure by the government as a means of controlling Christians. Following World War II the church regroups and is free of government control.   PROT

1940   The Taizé Community, a Roman Catholic–based commune, is founded by Brother Roger Schutz-Marauche (1915–) in the town of Taizé, France. After World War II it becomes a pilgrimage site and also develops a distinctive chant used in worship that is adopted by other Catholic churches.   SECT

1940   The Jehovah's Witnesses adopt the strategy of disseminating their beliefs publicly by passing out copies of their publications on street corners. SECT

1940   In *Minersville School District v. Gobitis*, the United States Supreme Court overturns lower court decisions and rules that school systems can require children of Jehovah's Witnesses to salute the flag of the United States. The decision leads to verbal and physical assaults on Witnesses who continue to allow their children to refrain from saluting the flag. The Canadian and Australian governments ban the Witnesses, which the Witnesses blame on the influence of Roman Catholic leaders in these nations.   SECT, TOL

1940   According to tradition, this is the 2,600th anniversary of the founding of the Japanese empire. The spectacular celebrations are followed by the building of more Shinto shrines overseas.   SHINTO, TOL

1940s   The Umbanda religion becomes closely associated with Brazilian nationalism and is hailed as the national religion of Brazil in the book *A Genuinely*

Brazilian Religion. Its special appeal is that it combines elements from Europe, Africa, and native Brazilians and therefore represents the three primary cultural heritages in Brazilian society. **AFRICAN**

1940s   The independence of the various Pentecostal denominations and churches begins to erode and some form or join associations. In 1943 the Assemblies of God U.S.A. and the Church of God join the National Association of Evangelicals; in 1948–1949 several groups form the Pentecostal Fellowship of North America, and in 1949 Pentecostal churches begin holding annual Pentecostal World Conferences. **EVAN**

1940s   Wicca (old English for *witch*) emerges as a revival of paganism in Great Britain and then spreads to the United States and continental Europe. **SPIR**

1941   In Haiti the government destroys Voudou temples with the support of the Roman Catholic Church, both of which see Voudou as potential source of resistance to continuing rule by a small group of wealthy landowners and industrialists. **AFRICAN**

1941   The First Congress of the Spiritism of Umbanda is held in Rio de Janeiro, Brazil. At the conference leaders of the religion make an effort to remove African elements, stress the religion's ties to European spiritism, and argue that the origins of Umbanda can be found in such ancient civilizations as Egyptian, Hindu, and Greek. As many leaders of the religion are from the middle class, the efforts to end ties to African religion are viewed by some experts as a racist effort to reduce the role of Afro-Brazilians in Brazilian society. **AFRICAN**

1941   Tens of thousands of Jews are killed in Poland, Romania, Hungary, and Lithuania. In May the "Final Solution" is first mentioned by the Nazis when they ban the emigration of Jews from German-occupied territories. The Final Solution means the killing of all Jews in Europe. In September over 30,000 Jews are killed in 36 hours by Nazis at Babi Yar, a ravine near Kiev in the Ukraine. During the year 1.1 million Jews are killed by the Nazis. **JUD**

1941   In the United States anti-Semitism becomes an issue in the public debate about American involvement in World War II. Some who argue for American isolation and noninvolvement—among them Charles Lindbergh—suggest that Jews are behind the effort to involve America in the war. He and others are accused of anti-Semitism, although Jewish leaders are mainly silent about the issue. **JUD**

1941   The Mormon Church begins missionary activity in Central America. **MOR**

1941   In Japan the Japanese Presbyterian and Reformed Church, the Japan Methodist Church, and the Japan Congregational Churches unite and form the Church of Christ in Japan. **PROT**

1941	The American Council of Christian Churches is founded to represent the interests of fundamental Protestants. **PROT**

1941   In New Zealand the Absolute Established Maori Church of Aotearoa breaks away from the Ratana Church, which it considers to be too involved in New Zealand politics. **SECT**

1941   The American Scientific Affiliation is founded by Evangelical scientists in the United States who are concerned about the absence of Christian ideas in the teaching of science. A creationist group, it devotes much effort over the next two decades to reconciling the notions of creationism and evolution. **TOL**

1941–
1944   Japan enters World War II by carrying out a series of surprise attacks, first on Pearl Harbor in Hawaii and then on the Philippines, Guam, Midway, Hong Kong, and Malaya. By the late spring of 1942, all of the western and central Pacific, including Indonesia and New Guinea, and Southeast Asia, including Indochina, Thailand, and Burma, will be under Japanese control. The battle cry of Japanese soldiers is "We'll meet in Yasukuni!" Shinto ideology, such as the notion of "eight corners of the world under one roof," is used to justify Japan's military aggression: the Japanese are a superior people with the divine and preordained mission of ruling the world. Shinto shrines soon will be established in Singapore, Saigon, Hong Kong, Java, and on Wake Island. In April 1942 the Religious Alliance for Asian Development is formed and the emperor will grant an audience to 40 leaders of religious denominations. In September 1943 the Greater Japan Religious Association for the Protection of the Country During War is established, with the minister of education as its chairman, along with the designation of leaders for wartime religious indoctrination. In 1944, after a series of defeats, Japan will begin to rely increasingly on the suicide missions of *kamikazi* (divine wind) fighter pilots. SEE **1281, BUDD, SHINTO.** **SHINTO**

1941–
1945   In the Soviet Union restrictions on Muslims that date to 1928 are relaxed in an attempt to win their support during World War II. Islam is formally recognized as an official religion by the government, Muslims are permitted to form administrative organizations, a seminary is founded in Tashkent in central Asia, and the closing of mosques slows. **ISLAM**

1942   The African Israel Church Ninevah is founded in Kenya by David Zayako Kivuli (1896–1974), an African evangelist who separates the church from the Canada-based Pentecostal Assemblies of East Africa. The church, which has about 100,000 members in the 1990s, combines Evangelical Christian beliefs and practices with others advocated by Kivuli, including public confession, public processions, and non-Western forms of healing. **AFRICAN**

1942   The Dahima religion is founded in the Ivory Coast by Guigba Dahonon (1892–1951), a poor widow who experiences visions and begins teaching in opposition to the already established Harris churches in the region. Her teachings become the official canon of the church and replace the Bible. She is known to followers as Marie Lalou and is succeeded by other female leaders.

AFRICAN

1942   Roman Catholic priest Charles E. Coughlin (1891–1979) ends publication of his magazine *Social Justice* and ends broadcasts of his radio show, which began in 1925. During the 1930s the show was widely broadcast and Coughlin was known as the "radio priest." However, his controversial political and religious views, anti-Semitic content, attacks on the New Deal, and opposition to American involvement in World War II cause the magazine and program to lose support both within and outside the church.   **CATH**

1942   The New Tribes Mission is founded. Its main focus is on indigenous people in Latin America. At times it is criticized by supporters of indigenous rights for assisting—wittingly or unwittingly—developers and politicians in exploiting indigenous peoples and destroying traditional cultures.   **CHRIS**

1942   *The Screwtape Letters* by British literary scholar C. S. Lewis (1989–1963) is published. The book and other writings by Lewis are in the Christian apologetic tradition and attract many lapsed Christians back to Christianity.   **CHRIS**

1942   The National Association of Evangelicals is established in the United States as an alternative to the American Council of Christian Churches, which is seen by some fundamentalist Christians as too conservative and dogmatic.

EVAN

1942   At the Wannsee Conference the decision to exterminate all Jews, probably made by Nazi leaders earlier, is discussed with leaders of all German government ministries. The mass extermination of Jews in death camps begins in Germany, Poland, and the Ukraine. Some 2.7 million Jews are killed in 1942.   **JUD**

1942   On June 12 Anne Frank, a Jewish schoolgirl in hiding with her family in the Netherlands, begins keeping her diary, which she continues for 26 months until she and her family are captured by the Nazis. Her diary is published in book form shortly after its discovery at the end of the war and becomes an important popular and educational work about the adolescent experience in general and the Jewish experience during the Holocaust.   **JUD**

1942   The British Council of Churches is established to coordinate the activities of the various Protestant denominations in Britain.   **PROT**

1942   In the United States the I AM spiritual and personal growth movement is accused of mail fraud and is prohibited from promoting its activities via the United States postal system.   **SPIR**

1942   In Alberta, Canada, the government bans the sale of land to "enemy aliens, Hutterites, and Doukhobours." The action is motivated in part by resentment of Hutterite pacifism in World War II and also by a desire to conserve land for purchase by other Canadians. **TOL**

1942–
1945

The Japanese defeat the Dutch and rule Indonesia. Although Muslims are under Japanese rule, Muslims gain more power than they had in the past as they serve the Japanese government and are often assigned to leadership roles in rural communities. To a large extent they displace the non-Muslim class of administrators and officials who had served the Dutch. **ISLAM**

1943

Alinestoué (1915–?), the female leader of a religious revival movement in Senegal that stresses traditional beliefs in resistance to French rule, Christianity, and Islam, is arrested by the French government and disappears. **AFRICAN**

1943

The autonomous region of the Kalmyk people in the Soviet Union is abolished and the Kalmyks are forced to leave. They are Buddhists, and the Soviet government claims that they are supporters of Japan in World War II, a charge that cannot be substantiated. **BUDD**

1943

In Lebanon leaders of the nation's Christian and Muslim communities agree to a plan to share political power whereby the president must be a Christian and Christians are to have a 6:5 ratio of representation in the parliament. **CHRIS, ISLAM**

1943

Political leaders in Algeria present France with the Algerian Manifesto. It criticizes French rule and demands an Algerian constitution and full political and legal rights for Muslims. The Manifesto is rejected by the French government in 1944. **ISLAM**

1943

Mass arrests and executions of Jews continue, and Jews confined to ghettos in Poland and Lithuania are killed. The Hungarians, Italians, Danes, Dutch, and Romanians all to varying degrees refuse to assist the Nazis, although some are forced to do so. During the year 500,000 Jews are killed by the Nazis. **JUD**

1943

In Switzerland the National Church of Neuchâtel and the Evangelical Church of Neuchâtel, Independent of the State, unite to form the Reformed Evangelical Church of Neuchâtel. **PROT**

1943

As the German forces withdraw from Russia in World War II, many Mennonites, who speak German and have enjoyed increased freedom during the two years of German occupation, are evacuated to Germany by the German army. Some immigrate to Canada and South America, and at the end of the war in 1945 some are forced to return to Russia. **SECT**

1943

In *Murdock v. Commonwealth of Pennsylvania*, the United States reverses its 1940 decision in *Jones v. City of Opelika* concerning the distribution of religious material by Jehovah's Witnesses and rules that the government cannot place a license tax on the distribution of religious material. The court also reverses its 1940 decision in the *Gobitis* case and rules that the government cannot force individuals to salute the flag or to engage in other similar behavior. In Australia the ban on Jehovah's Witnesses is ended.   SECT, TOL

1943   The term *genocide* is coined by the Polish legal scholar Raphael Lemkin (1901–1959), who has fled to the United States. He uses it to describe the German effort to eradicate all Jews, and it subsequently becomes a generic label for all efforts by one ethnic or religious group to eradicate another. TOL

1943   In the Soviet Union the Communist government abolishes the Ukrainian Catholic Church and turns its property over to the Russian Orthodox Church. SEE **1989**, TOL.   TOL

1944   The African Apostolic Church of John Maranke is founded in southeastern Africa by Johane Maranke (1912–1963), a local Methodist. The church stresses healing, prophecy, and exorcism and attracts tens of thousands of followers in southern Africa.   AFRICAN

1944   The Canadian Council of Churches is formed and serves as an ecumenical body for all major Christian religions and denominations in Canada. CHRIS

1944   Muslim peoples in European sections of the Soviet Union, such as the Meskhetians and Crimean Tatars, are deported to Asiatic Russia on claims by the Soviet government that they are supporters of Nazi Germany. ISLAM

1944   In Uganda the Ugandan Muslim Education Association is founded to create unity among Muslim communities in the nation.   ISLAM

1944   In Sudan the Muslim Mahdist movement, which had been suppressed by the British and Egyptian rulers beginning in 1899 but had retained influence in rural areas, forms the Umma Party. Along with other new Muslim organizations, it becomes a major force for Sudanese independence in 1956.   ISLAM

1944   In Palestine Jewish resistance to British rule and limits on Jewish immigration escalate with attacks on British facilities and personnel.   JUD

1944   In Hungary the Nazis begin to deport hundreds of thousands of Jews to death camps. Thousands of Jews are saved by Swedish diplomat Raoul Wallenberg, who provides them with Swedish identification papers and passports.   JUD

1944   *When?: A Prophetical Novel of the Very Near Future* is published under the pseudonym "H. Ben Judah" by the British Israel Association of Vancouver. It marks the open association of the movement with anti-Semitism and the belief that Jews are the children of the devil, a basic Christian Identity doctrine.   JUD, SECT

516

1944   The Native American Church established in 1918 changes its name to the Native American Church of the United States, indicating membership beyond Oklahoma. SEE **1955**, NATIV.   **NATIV**

1944   In the Philippines churches from a number of Protestant denominations unite and form the Evangelical Church of the Philippines.   **PROT**

1944   The Education Act in Britain requires that schools provide daily religious worship or religious education. By the 1980s the requirement is widely ignored and religious education often focuses on non-Christian religions rather than Anglicanism.   **PROT**

1944   In Albania, despite constitutional guarantees of religious freedom, the Communist government begins to repress religion when it arrests Muslim, Catholic, and Orthodox clergy.   **TOL**

1944–1945   Mass executions of Jews continue. Allied troops liberate concentration camps in Europe and on May 8, World War II ends in Europe. It is estimated that nearly 6 million Jews have died during the war.   **JUD**

1944–1946   The Muslim Kazakh and Uighur peoples in western China revolt against Chinese rule and seek to establish independent republics. The Soviet Union assists the Chinese in ending the revolt and in arranging a settlement in which the Kazakhs and Uighurs remain under Chinese rule but are granted some autonomy.   **ISLAM**

1945   Gospel music is now firmly established as a form of religious music in African-American churches and spreads beyond the churches to become a major form of entertainment in African-American communities. By 1960 it is becoming established as an entertainment form in white communities as well.   **AFRICAN**

1945   The Buddhist Society of London invites one of its founders, Christmas Humphreys, an English judge and lay Buddhist, to compose a summary of Buddhism. Humphreys describes what he calls "The Twelve Principles of Buddhism" and proceeds to convince many Buddhist sects throughout the world to adopt these as a sign of their fundamental unity. Humphreys, through his various writings, is one of the major promoters of Buddhism in the English-speaking world.   **BUDD**

1945   Pope Pius XII begins to reverse the centuries-old trend in the Roman Catholic Church of having a majority of cardinals of Italian ancestry. In this and subsequent years, the College of Cardinals is diversified, with new cardinals appointed from all regions of the world, reflecting the status of Catholicism as a world religion.   **CATH**

| 1945 | In Poland the Roman Catholic Church, to which the majority of Poles adhere, emerges as the main competitor to Communist rule and remains a critic of the government until democracy is achieved in the late 1980s.   CATH |

1945   In India the Indian National Congress renews its demand for independence from Britain and the establishment of a secular nation. The Muslim League continues to campaign for a separate Muslim state.   ISLAM

1945   In Palestine political stability deteriorates as both Jews and Arabs demand a national state and Britain is unable to reach a compromise. Anti-Jewish attacks occur in Arab nations.   JUD

1945   Rabbi Mordecai Kaplan, founder of Reconstructionist Judaism in the United States, is excommunicated by a board of Orthodox rabbis for his failure to follow the tenets of Orthodox Judaism.   JUD

1945   In Zimbabwe (then Rhodesia) the Presbytery of Northeastern Rhodesia, the London Missionary Society, and the Union Church of the Copperbelt unite and form the Church of Central Africa in Rhodesia. In 1951 La Société des Missions Évangéliques de Paris joins as well.   PROT

1945   In Japan prohibitions on religion are relaxed after World War II and many Protestant churches that had joined the Church of Christ in Japan in 1941 become independent.   PROT

1945   The Nag Hammadi Library is discovered at Nag Hammadi along the Nile River in Egypt. It is a collection of 13 texts written in Coptic, which are translations of Greek texts written by Gnostics probably in the second or third century C.E. As the first record of Gnosticism written by adherents, the texts provide new information about the movement, as information came previously only from the writings of Christians who considered the Gnostics to be heretics.   SECT

1945   The Tensho Kotai Jingukyo religion emerges in Japan as a millennial movement, with the founder of the religion, Kitamura Sayo (1900–1967), claiming to be the messiah.   SECT

1945   As World War II reaches its final stage in the Pacific, on July 26 the Allies broadcast a demand for unconditional surrender. Article 10 of the Potsdam Declaration calls for the establishment of freedom of speech, religion, and thought in postwar Japan. Following the atomic bomb explosions over Hiroshima and Nagasaki, Emperor Hirohito decides to end the war unilaterally and announces the surrender of Japan on August 15; the signing of the surrender documents on September 2 initiates the Allied occupation of Japan, which will last until 1952. Under General Douglas MacArthur (1880–1969), the occupation by military and civilian bureaucrats, supported by 500,000 Allied troops, will dismantle Japan's empire and war machine; conduct repatriations, war crimes trials, and purges; and reform the nation's political, economic, and religious structure.   **SHINTO**

1945   On October 4 Japan's occupation rulers issue a directive abolishing restrictions on political, civil, and religious liberties; under this assurance of religious freedom, sect and shrine Shinto are to be protected along with all other religions. In November the emperor travels to the Inner Shrine at Ise to offer to the sun goddess, Amaterasu, the reasons and apologies for Japan's defeat. On December 2 leading members of Shinto's governing bodies are arrested, and on December 12 public funds are denied for the 59th ritual reconstruction of the Ise shrine.   **SHINTO**

1945   On December 15 General Douglas MacArthur, commander of the Allied occupying forces in Japan, issues the Shinto Directive calling for the following: the abolition of the ideology asserting that the emperor and the Japanese people and islands are superior to the rest of the world; the removal of Shinto education from public schools, the revision of textbooks treating Shinto mythology as history, and the cessation of compulsory shrine visits by students; the removal of household shrines (*kamidana*) and all other Shinto symbols from government offices, public schools, and other public buildings, as well as the ending of the appointment of Shinto priests to government positions; and the abolition of government financial support for and visits to Shinto shrines in an official capacity by politicians and public employees. Specifically forbidden are the "use in official writings of the terms 'Greater East Asia War' (*Dai Toa Senso*), 'The Whole World under One Roof' (*Hakko Ichi-u*), and all other terms whose connotation in Japanese is inextricably connected with state Shinto, militarism, and ultranationalism." On March 15, 1946, the Japanese must submit a comprehensive report to the occupying forces on the implementation of the Shinto Directive provisions. The Japanese Diet (parliament) will gradually repeal all laws that were enacted from 1868 to 1940 to assure state Shinto a privileged position, and all shrines will become private religious organizations supported by voluntary donations.   **SHINTO**

1945   On December 23 Shinto ceremonies performed in the imperial palace are transformed into private rituals for the imperial family only. On December 28 the Religious Corporations Ordinance is issued to safeguard, on the basis of the separation of church and state, the religious freedom and property rights of religious organizations; because the establishment of religious organizations is made too easy and supervision is weak, many groups will abuse the ordinance, registering as religious organizations in order to avoid taxes. This will result in a great increase in the registration of new religions until 1951, when it is replaced by the Religious Juridical Persons Law. Founded this year is a new syncretist religion of Shinto origin, Tensho-Kotai-Jingukyo, also known as Odoru-shukyo (Dancing Religion), by Kitamura Sayo (1900–1967), who is known to her followers as Ogamisama (the Goddess). It will spread to Hawaii in 1952, and by 1994 there will be

13 branches there, as well as centers in some 75 countries, including the mainland United States. SHINTO

1945   In India the Sikh Shromani Akali Dal political party sets forth a plan to create a Sikh state in the Punjab region that will be part of India after independence from Britain. Continuing hostility between Sikhs and Muslims makes affiliation with Pakistan unlikely. SIKH

1945   In an effort to create a nation that includes people from hundreds of ethnic groups and religions, the government of Indonesia resists creating an Islamic nation (although the majority of Indonesians are Muslims) and instead develops the ideology of *Pancasila*, which stresses national unity, justice, and inclusiveness. Nonetheless, the constitution adopts many Islamic legal principles as national law, and other religions that are seen as threatening Islam are often repressed in later years. TOL

1946   Francesca Maria Cabrini is canonized by Pope Pius XII as St. Frances Xavier Cabrini. An immigrant from Italy who arrived in the United States in 1889 and founded dozens of hospitals, schools, and orphanages, she became an American citizen in 1907 when her order, the Missionary Sisters of the Sacred Heart, was recognized by the church. She is the first American citizen to be canonized and is made the patron saint of immigrants. CATH

1946   In Britain the New Testament of the Revised Standard Version of the King James Version of the Bible is published and is followed by the Old Testament in 1952. Additional material is added in 1957 and 1977 that makes it useful to Catholics and Orthodox Christians, as well as Protestants. CHRIS

1946   Bossey, an ecumenical Christian institute for study and teaching about Christianity in life, is founded by the World Council of Churches in Geneva, Switzerland. CHRIS

1946   On the island of Balau off the coast of New Guinea, the Balaun Native United Christian Church is founded by Paliau Maloat (1915–), a native constable who had experienced visions of Jesus Christ during World War II. The new religion combines Christianity and millennial beliefs and becomes a religious and political movement that is influential in helping Papua New Guinea become an independent nation. CHRIS

1946   In India the new constituent assembly outlaws the traditional concept of a caste of Untouchables. HIND

1946   The political situation in Palestine continues to deteriorate as the British attempt to control violent Jewish attacks on British personnel and buildings, and attacks by Jewish revolutionary organizations continue. JUD

1946   The Sun Dance, which had been banned by the United States government in 1904, begins a resurgence when a dance is held by the Arapaho people in Wyoming. SEE **1950**, NATIV.   NATIV

1946   In the Netherlands the Dutch Reformed Church and the Reformed Churches in the Netherlands in Restored Connection unite under the name of the former.   PROT

1946   In the United States the Evangelical Church and the Church of the United Brethren in Christ, both of which date to the early 1800s, unite and form the Evangelical United Brethren Church.   PROT

1946   The American Bible Society and 12 Bible societies in Europe form the United Bible Societies to support and coordinate the activities of some 75 Bible societies around the world.   PROT

1946   The Jehovah's Witnesses change the name of the *Golden Age* magazine to *Awake!* in accord with its purpose of alerting people to biblical prophecies coming true on earth.   SECT

1946   A number of Japan's so-called new religions undergo changes this year. After his release from prison, Onishi Anjiro reconstitutes Hommichi, and Hitonomichi Kyodan emerges from wartime suppression as PL (Perfect Liberty) Kyodan. Another new religion this year is Ennokyo, led by Fukada Choji (1908–1976).   SECT

1946   In Japan the new constitution makes a clear separation between religion and state, representing a departure from the 1889 constitution and government policy that often linked government and Shinto. However, the 1946 separation principle is interpreted liberally by the government and the courts, and the government supports and participates in various religious activities, such as the erection of Shinto shrines. On January 1 Japan's Emperor Hirohito delivers a New Year's message renouncing his status as a living god: "The ties between us and our people have always stood upon mutual trust and affection. They do not depend upon mere legends and myths." On January 5 the leaders of Shinto's governing bodies decide to designate Ise as the head shrine of the new Association of Shinto Shrines. Ise is honored thus because of its special history and close connection with the imperial house. On February 2 the Shrine Board is disestablished, the Religious Corporations Ordinance is revised to include shrines, and the new Association of Shinto Shrines (*Jinjahoncho*) officially comes into being on the following day. The association incorporates about 98 percent of the nation's shrines and groups of shrines, numbering some 78,000. Some of the remaining shrines stay independent or come under lesser federations of religious organizations. This restructuring will lead to a decline of the small regional shrines and the increasing prosperity of the larger shrines. While Ise's Kogakukan, Japan's state university for Shinto study, is closed, Tokyo's Kokugakuin is allowed to continue as the nation's sole university where Shinto may be studied. The chair for Shinto learning at Tokyo University is abolished. **SHINTO**

1946 In the Soviet Union the government enacts policies designed to ban religious activity by many religious minorities, including Eastern-Rite Catholics (Uniates), Pentecostal Christians, Jehovah's Witnesses, Russian Old Believers, and nonmainstream branches of Russian Orthodoxy. As such action is in violation of the Soviet constitution, it is carried out in secret. One means of carrying it out is to force some of these groups to merge with other groups that are not banned. For example, Uniates are required to become Russian Orthodox and Pentecostalists to become Baptists. **TOL**

1947 The Celestial Church of Christ is founded as an independent African church in Benin by Samuel Bileou J. Oschoffa (1909–1985). The church begins as a healing cult and then becomes a full-service church and spreads to Nigeria. Oschoffa is renowned as "Papa," and his burial site becomes an important shrine. **AFRICAN**

1947 To escape persecution in Zimbabwe, the Masowe Apostles (**SEE 1932, AFRICAN**) move to South Africa and establish the Apostolic Sabbath Church of God in the slums of Port Elizabeth. It is commonly known as the Basketmaker Church because of its emphasis on teaching technical skills to followers. **SEE 1962, AFRICAN.** **AFRICAN**

1947 Aiyetoro, a utopian Christian community, is founded by African Holy Apostles on the coast of Nigeria. The community establishes a strict code of conduct for members, places a priest-chief in charge, and becomes economically successful as a producer of consumer goods such as soap and clothing and through deep-sea fishing. **AFRICAN**

1947 An Arab bedouin herder accidentally finds ancient documents that come to be called the Dead Sea Scrolls in a cave in Qumran on the northwest coast of the Dead Sea in Israel. Later, additional documents are found in the area, further south, and inland. The hundreds of scrolls and fragments of documents date to the time period between 250 B.C.E.. and 70 C.E..—the latter half of the Second Temple period in Jewish history. The scrolls were written and stored by members of the Essene sect, a divergent group within the Jewish community. The scrolls contain records of daily life, religious texts, and stories and legends, all of which have helped religious scholars fashion a more complete description of Jewish life during this period, as well as contributing to a greater understanding of the emergence of modern Judaism and early Christianity. **CHRIS, JUD**

1947 The Shanghai Municipal Daoist Association is established with the aim of promoting a Daoist revival. The association will disseminate Daoist ideas through a journal titled *Yangshan*. **DAO**

1947   In the United States the Evangelical healer Kathryn Kuhlman (1907–1976) begins preaching that modern-day Christians can perform miracles and can heal the sick. Her healing services attract large audiences of Protestants and Catholics and reflect a reemergence of Pentecostalism.   **EVAN**

1947   The first Pentecostal World Conference is held in Zurich, Switzerland. **EVAN**

1947   The British government divides British India into the two self-governing dominions of India and Pakistan. Pakistan is created by combining contiguous Muslim-majority districts, while the dominion of India constitutes the remainder. The plan is approved by the Muslim League and by the All-India Congress. As a result, there is a mass movement of Hindus, Muslims, and Sikhs who find themselves on the "wrong" side of the new international boundaries; as many as 20 million people eventually relocate and up to 3 million of these are killed in fighting and massacres on both sides of the new border, especially in the Punjab.   **HIND, ISLAM**

1947   The creation of India and Pakistan does not include the princely states, and the state of Jammu and Kashmir, which borders both nations, has a Muslim majority but is ruled by a Hindu maharajah. The rulers of Jammu and Kashmir choose to join India when it is invaded by tribesmen from Pakistan. Indian and Pakistani armed forces are soon engaged in fighting that disrupts the process of partition. After unsuccessful attempts to resolve the issue, the dispute is submitted to the United Nations. The dispute continues, with much killing in the 1990s.   **HIND, ISLAM**

Religion in India

India is one of the more religiously diverse nations in the world. It is also a nation where religion has been both a unifying and divisive force. It is the birthplace of Hinduism, Buddhism, Sikhism, and Jainism and continues to be home to the largest population of Hindus (672 million), Sikhs (17 million), and Jains (3.5 million) of any nation as well as having the fourth-largest Muslim population (96 million). In addition, there are millions of adherents of indigenous tribal religions and nearly 20 million Christians. Further, within each of these major categories of religion there are dozens of denominations, sects, and movements. Religion in India has long been tied to politics, and struggles for power played a role in the emergence of Buddhism, Sikhism, and Jainism as alternatives to Hinduism. During the 18th and 19th centuries much of India was ruled by the Muslim Mughal Empire, with many Hindus converting to Islam during that period. Muslim-Hindu relations, especially in the predominantly Muslim north, have been tense ever since and marked by violence in the late 20th century. In 1998 a pro-Hindu party gained political power running on a platform that views India as a Hindu nation.

1947   In Algeria Muslim rights are expanded by the French-controlled govern-
            ment, including some representation in the National Assembly, the estab-
            lishment of Arabic as the national language, and voting rights for Muslim
            women. These changes do not satisfy Muslim leaders, who seek full rights
            and freedom from French control.   ISLAM

1947   Great Britain announces it will end its mandate over Palestine on May 15,
            1948. Both the Jews and Palestinian Arabs lay claim to the region and
            neighboring Arab nations pledge support for the Palestinians. On
            November 29 the United Nations votes to partition Palestine and thereby
            establish the State of Israel.   JUD

1947   In India the Church of India, Burma, and Ceylon; the South India United
            Church; and the Methodist Church of South India unite and form the
            Church of South India to coordinate church activities, with individual
            churches maintaining control of matters of doctrine and ritual. It is the first
            Protestant church in the world to unify people from different sects and
            includes Anglicans, Methodists, and others.   PROT

1947   Quakers in the United States and Britain are awarded the Nobel Peace Prize in
            recognition of their devotion to peace and the assistance they provide others.
                                                                                  PROT

1947   The Lutheran World Federation is founded by 46 Lutheran churches from
            23 nations in Lund, Sweden. It focuses on developing Lutheran theology
            and supporting missionary and social services around the world.   PROT

1947   On January 16 Japan's new Imperial House Law deletes all specific Shinto
            references to relations between the emperor and the state, particularly those
            regarding coronation ceremonies and the imperial regalia: the Imperial
            House Economy Law passed the same day refers to the imperial regalia as
            "objects of cherished historical value to be handed down with the throne."
            On May 2 a revision of the 1939 law is enacted by which the government
            leases state-owned property rent-free to shrines and temples: the law covers
            how and what land can be transferred or sold to shrines or temples, taking
            past rights into consideration. This law decreases the widespread stealing of
            trees for firewood from shrine and temple precincts.   SHINTO

1947   On May 3 Japan's new constitution takes effect, mandating separation of
            church and state and freedom of religion. The emperor is designated "the
            symbol of the State and of the unity of the people, deriving his position
            from the will of the people." Article 20 states, "No person shall be com-
            pelled to take part in any religious act, celebration, rite, or practice." Article
            89 forbids the use of public property for religious purposes. Thus the Shinto
            mythology of the emperor's divine descent and Shinto's identification with
            the state and the unique spirit of Japan are rejected legally.   SHINTO

1947   After Japanese government financial support to Shinto shrines is cut off on the order of the Shinto Directive, the Association of Shinto Shrines sends representatives to all prefecture shrines to explain ways of coping with this new situation. By now, under the Religious Corporations Ordinance, the registered new religions number 207. Okada Mokichi (considered a living *kami*, or protective spirit) reorganizes the new religion Kannonkyo as Sekai Meshiyakyo (World Messiah Religion); in 1950 it will become Sekai Kyuseikyo (Church of World Messianity), and in 1953 it will spread to the United States. Also known as the Johrei Fellowship, by 1996 it will have over a dozen centers in the United States, as well as in 40 countries, including Brazil, Peru, Mexico, Korea, and Thailand.   **SHINTO**

1947   India is partitioned into the nations of India and Pakistan with the end of British rule. The partition produces much political unrest, religious and ethnic-based violence, and a major population shift along religious lines, with Muslims from India moving to Pakistan and Sikhs and Hindus from Pakistan moving to India. The Sikh population is now concentrated in the Punjab region of northwestern India.   **SIKH**

1947   The Canadian Council of Christians and Jews is founded to foster cooperation between the two religions.   **TOL**

1948   The African Feast cult emerges on the island of Grenada in the Caribbean. It is a syncretic religion based on the Seventh-Day Adventist faith, Shakerism, and magic.   **AFRICAN**

1948   In Romania the Uniate Church (Eastern Rite Catholic Church), to which about 8 percent of the population adheres, is closed down by the government and much of its property given to the Eastern Orthodox Church by the Communist government. The government is opposed to the Uniate Church because of the church's ties to the Western world and to the Vatican. **SEE 1989, CATH.**   **CATH**

1948   Billy Graham (1918–), the best-known American Christian evangelical minister of the 20th century, conducts his first mass crusade when he preaches to an audience in Los Angeles.   **EVAN**

1948   Mohandas Gandhi, who has opposed the partition of Pakistan and worked for Hindu-Muslim friendship, volunteers to travel to Pakistan to seek reconciliation. After his return on January 30, he is assassinated by Nathuram Godse, a Hindu extremist who opposes cooperation with Muslims.   **HIND**

1948   The Svetambara Jain leader Sri Tulasi, head of the Terapantha order, founds the Anuvrata movement in India, a moral revival movement dedicated to purging corruption from individuals and the nation.   **JAIN**

1948   The State of Israel is established. Chaim Weitzman (1874–1952) is elected president by the Assembly, and he asks David Ben-Gurion (1886–1973) to form Israel's first government. War breaks out between Israel and the neighboring Arab nations of Jordan, Syria, and Egypt and involves Palestinians in Israel. A series of truces ends most of the fighting, although the nations remain in a state of war.   JUD

1948   With the establishment of the State of Israel, Jews from many other nations begin a migration to Israel that continues in considerable numbers until 1960. Nearly the entire Jewish populations of Yemen, Aden, Libya, Iraq, Egypt, Syria, Morocco, and Libya move to Israel during this period. Their arrival and settlement alters the composition of the Israeli population, as Jews from the Middle East and Africa (called Oriental Jews) outnumber Jews from Europe, although the latter remain politically and economically dominant.   JUD

1948   In the Philippines the United Evangelical Church of the Philippines, the Philippine Methodist Church, and the Evangelical Church of the Philippines unite and form the United Church of Christ in the Philippines.   PROT

Billy Graham

Billy (William Franklin) Graham is the best known Christian preacher of the 20th century, and if success is counted in numbers of people who hear one's message, the most successful missionary of all time. Graham was born in Charlotte, North Carolina, in 1918, raised in a religious Protestant home, and educated at a series of Christian Bible colleges, graduating from Wheaton College in Illinois in 1942. He was ordained as a Baptist minister in 1939, a year after having decided to devote his life to preaching, an activity that had attracted him since his teenage years. Throughout his career Graham sought to spread one basic message: "Man rebelled against God, and so he separated from God by sin. Christ died, was buried, and he rose again, and men need to repent of their sins and receive Him as their Savior."

It is impossible to say how many people around the world have heard Graham's message, although his success in reaching certainly more than two billion listeners is due in large part to his willingness and ability to communicate in all media possible. From his early days as a revival preacher, congregation minister, and preacher at youth rallies he moved into radio (*The Hour of Decision* broadcast on 1,000 stations at its height in the 1950s), television, books, magazine publishing (*Decision*), a daily advice column ("My Answer"), and most important, his evangelistic crusades, which began in Los Angeles in 1948. While the radio show made him a national figure, the crusades, which often filled huge stadiums, made him a world figure. Over the years they have taken him to many nations, including some resistant to Christianity, such as Japan, Korea, Russia, and India, and have been televised around the world as well. Part of Graham's success has also been his avoidance of politics in the United States and of chauvinistic Americanism in other nations and his ability to avoid identification with the Christian Right. Nonetheless, in the role of unofficial "national minister," he has counseled every president since Harry Truman and was a close friend of Richard Nixon.

| 1948 | In West Germany 27 United, Reformed, and Lutheran churches form the Evangelical Church in Germany. Ten Lutheran churches form the United Evangelical Lutheran Church in Germany but also retain membership in the Evangelical Church in Germany. **PROT** |

1948   The first Quaker Meeting (organization) is established in South Africa. **PROT**

1948   The World Council of Churches is founded. It is an attempt by Christian denominations to end rivalries, foster cooperation, and perhaps one day create a single Christian church. In the 1990s it has over 300 Protestant and Orthodox churches and organizations as members. **PROT**

1948   Baha'i International Community becomes a nongovernmental organization affiliated with the United Nations. **SECT**

1948   The Japanese Diet rescinds the Imperial Rescript of Education at the insistence of occupying authorities, who consider it a powerful propaganda tool for state Shinto and militarism. **SHINTO**

1948   The Universal Declaration of Human Rights is adopted and proclaimed by the General Assembly of the United Nations in Resolution 217 A (III). The right to religious freedom is set forth in Article 18 of the document. **TOL**

1948   The American Declaration of the Rights and Duties of Man is adopted but not made legally binding by the member nations of the Congress of American States. It sets forth the right to religious freedom for all individuals. **TOL**

Article 18 of the Universal Declaration of Human Rights

1. Everyone shall have the right to freedom of thought, conscience, and religion. This right shall include freedom to have or to adopt a religion or belief of his choice, and freedom, either individually or in community with others and in public or private, to manifest his religion or belief in worship, observance, practice, and teaching.

2. No one shall be subject to coercion which would impair his freedom to have or to adopt a religion or belief of his choice.

3. Freedom to manifest one's religion or beliefs may be subject only to such limitations as are prescribed by law and are necessary to protect public safety, order, health, or morals or the fundamental rights and freedoms of others.

4. The States party to the present Covenant undertake to have respect for the liberty of parents and, when applicable, legal guardians to ensure the religious and moral education of their children in conformity with their own convictions.

1948–1950	Godianism (also known as the National Church of Nigeria) is founded by intellectuals in Nigeria. It is a neotraditional religion that rejects Christianity and Islam as appropriate religions for Africans and stresses traditional religions. **AFRICAN**
1949	In an effort to stem the power of Communism in Europe and especially in Italy, Pope Pius XII orders that Catholic Communists must be excommunicted. **CATH**
1949	The triumph of Marxism-Leninism as the official ideology of the People's Republic of China pushes Confucianism into the background. Among other objections to Confucianism, the Communists regard it as too focused on the past. **CONF, TOL**
1949	The 63d patriarch of Celestial Masters Daoism, Zhang Enfu (1904–1969), leaves China for Taiwan. **DAO**
1949	India's constitution establishes the category of Scheduled Tribes and Castes and Other Backward Classes. Groups placed in this category—including many Untouchables and indigenous tribes—are eligible for affirmative action programs designed to increase their role in Indian society. **HIND**

Archbishop Makarios

Orthodox Archbishop Makarios Mouskos III was the religious and political leader of the Greek Orthodox population of Cyprus from the late 1940s until his death in 1977. Makarios was ordained an Orthodox priest in 1946 and while doing graduate work at Boston University was appointed the bishop of Kition. Cyprus was at the time under British rule, and Makarios immediately began organizing the opposition to British rule and strongly supported unification with Greece, a position opposed both by Britain and the Turkish Muslim minority on Cyprus. Both his political and religious roles increased in 1950, when a vote supported his unification policy and he was appointed archbishop. In the mid-1950s he was involved in nonviolent opposition to British rule and perhaps violent opposition as well. After the British deported him to Seychelles off the coast of Africa, he moved to Athens, and then to maintain unity among the Greeks and Turks on the island, he supported independence and in 1958 became the first president of Cyprus. However, he and others in the Greek Orthodox majority continued to support unification with Greece, and by the mid-1960s conflict between the Greeks and Turks required a United Nations peacekeeping force to maintain order and massive population relocations to establish a Turkish sector in the northeast, with Greeks occupying the remainder of the island. Despite the difficulties, Makarios remained popular and was re-elected president in 1968 and 1973. After a brief stay in London to avoid arrest by the Greek military rulers, he returned to Cyprus in 1974 and remained the religious and political leader until his death in 1977.

1949   The United Nations negotiates a cease-fire between India and Pakistan in the fighting over Kashmir. The cease-fire leaves the state of Jammu and Kashmir divided; one-third is allotted to Pakistan and the rest, including the Vale of Kashmir, is under Indian control. Conflict continues with the Muslim majority seeking the end of Indian rule.   **HIND, ISLAM**

1949   In Algeria school segregation ends and French and Algerian children, including Muslim children, are now allowed to attend the same schools. However, as French is the language of instruction, the enrollment of Algerian Muslim children who speak Arabic or Berber languages is effectively limited.   **ISLAM**

1949   The Awami League is founded in Pakistan with an agenda that supports regional rights and secularism and stands in opposition to the ruling Muslim League. **SEE 1970, ISLAM.**   **ISLAM**

1949   In China, after a period of civil war, the Communists under Mao Zedong defeat the nationalists and the People's Republic of China is established. The Communist government suppresses Buddhist, Daoist, and other religious organizations that constitute the majority, while it maintains a policy of accommodation for religious and cultural minorities as it tries to integrate them into national life. This policy initially allows the Muslim minority, concentrated in the west near the Soviet Union, to continue traditional practices and to found a Chinese Islamic Association in 1953 and a seminary in 1955. Later Islam is repressed as well.   **ISLAM**

1949   Israel is admitted to the United Nations. It is the only nation with a Jewish majority population.   **JUD**

1949   In Brazil the Evangelical Church of Rio Grande do Sul, the Lutheran Church in Brazil, the Evangelical Synod of Santa Catarina and Paranà, and the Synod of Central Brazil unite and form The Synodal Federation of Lutheran Churches in Brazil.   **PROT**

1949   In an effort to influence public policy, the American Friends Service Committee founded in 1917 begins publishing position papers. The papers, issued irregularly over the next several decades, deal with disarmament, the Vietnam War, crime, abortion, and other issues.   **PROT**

1949   Mennonites from North America begin their missionary work in Japan. **SECT**

1949   Ananaikyo, a new Shinto-based Japanese sect is founded in Japan. Drawing upon existing Shinto traditions, it stresses a concern with the end of the world and spirit possession.   **SECT**

1949   The Grand Temple is opened in Rosicrucian Park in San Jose, California, for members of the Rosicrucian Order, AMORC. It is a replica of the Great

	Temple of Hathor at Dendera, Egypt, and reflects Rosicrucian beliefs in the ancient Egyptian origin of Rosicrucianism. SECT
1949	In West Germany a new constitution provides for a separation of church and state and guarantees religious freedom but also gives the government authority to grant religions not currently recognized by the government status as religions. TOL
1949	In Albania the government continues an antireligion policy started in 1949 by ending guarantees of religious freedom and requiring all religious leaders to sign a pledge of loyalty to the state. TOL
1949	In Costa Rica a new constitution establishes Roman Catholicism as the state religion while also granting religious freedom to other religions and denominations. TOL
1949	In Hungary the Communist government places religious organizations and religious activity under governmental control, with the opportunity for worship severely curtailed. TOL
1949–1956	In China, under the new Communist government, religious leaders who oppose the government or who seek religious freedom are deported or imprisoned, while those willing to allow government control of religion are allowed to practice their religions. At the same time the government seeks to weaken the role of religion by supporting atheism. TOL
1950	Pope Pius XII establishes as Roman Catholic Church dogma the bodily assumption into heaven of Mary, the Blessed Virgin. This belief has been accepted as true from the earliest days of the Christian Church, and Mary is considered the patron saint of all humans. CATH
1950	Resistance to Western influence in many parts of the world leads to a decrease in Christian missionary activity. In the following decades missionaries in many nations are expelled or denied entry, or their work is restricted. These nations include China, Congo, Cuba, Guinea, Haiti, India, Mozambique, Nigeria, Uganda, and Vietnam. CHRIS
1950	World Vision is founded in the United States as a Christian organization to provide humanitarian assistance and economic and social development support to communities around the world. CHRIS
1950	The Daoist Association of Taiwan is established. DAO
1950	India and Pakistan agree to provide fair treatment to the respective Muslim and Hindu minorities in the nations. HIND, ISLAM
1950	Dutch rule of Indonesia ends and Indonesia becomes an independent nation. Independence is preceded and followed by political and then vio-

lent conflict between political parties that favor a secular nation with ties to the Western world and other parties that favor an Islamic state. The former take political power. **ISLAM**

1950   In Turkey the government weakens its stress on secularization and permits the public worship of Islam, the religion of the majority of Turks. **ISLAM, TOL**

1950   To avoid discrimination Crimean Jews in the Soviet Union claim that they are not Jews by blood but rather through conversion to Judaism by their ancestors centuries earlier. The Soviet officials accept this interpretation and the group is subsequently known as the Krymchaks. **JUD**

1950   The Karaite Jews of Egypt immigrate to Israel. The Karaite settlement in Egypt is some 1,200 years old. **JUD**

1950   The Sun Dance is formally revived by the Sioux, who convene a dance modeled after the traditional sun dances often held before they were banned by the United States government in 1904. **NATIV**

1950   In Madagascar the Norwegian Mission, the Mission of the Evangelical Lutheran Church in America, and the Mission of the Lutheran Free Church in America unite and form the Malagasy Lutheran Church. **PROT**

1950   In the United States the National Council of Churches in Christ in the United States is founded as a nondenominational Protestant organization to coordinate the activities of Protestant churches. It replaces the Federal Council of Churches founded in 1908 and 11 other organizations. **PROT**

1950   The Yali movement develops in New Guinea. It is a cargo cult led by the influential local leader Yali Singina (?-1975), who rejects Christian and European economic development for the island and advocates a return to traditional ways. **SECT**

1950   The Baha'i World Federation is established as a Baha'i splinter sect in Acre, Israel. It is founded by opponents of Shoghi Effendi, the leader of the Baha'i religion. **SECT**

1950   Science fiction writer L. Ron Hubbard (1911–1986) publishes *Dianetics: The Modern Science of Mental Health* and founds the Hubbard Dianetic Research Foundation, a precursor of Scientology. **SECT**

1950   Distracted by the outbreak of the Korean War, Japan's occupation government fails to take action on various incidents opposing the Shinto Directive, such as teachers taking students to visit shrines and village leaders participating in shrine ceremonies in their official role. The Law for the Protection of Cultural Properties covers customs relating to religious faiths, festivals, and "implements, houses, and other objects used therefor." **SHINTO,TOL**

1950   A definitive version of the rules governing Khalsa Sikhism, the *Sikh Rahit Maryada*, is published by the Sikh community in India.   SIKH

1950   The European Convention on Human Rights is adopted by the member nations of the Council of Europe and goes into effect in 1953. It guarantees religious freedom, including the right to change religions. A protocol established in 1953 affords parents the right to educate their children in the religion of their choice.   TOL

1950s   In Jamaica Rastafarian leaders are imprisoned and Rastafarian communities broken up by the government, which fears that the movement might ferment revolts.   AFRICAN

1950s   Afro-Brazilian religious leaders react to the Umbanda religion, which is being publicly presented as devoid of African influence and elements (SEE 1941, AFRICAN), by arguing that it is of African origin and continues to use African elements. They label it "White Umbanda."   AFRICAN

1950s   Communist theoreticians show a degree of sympathy for Daoism, particularly the legendary *Laozi*, as representing opposition to Confucianism and as a radical critique of the social order. In the Communist interpretation the mystical and quietist elements of the *Laozi* are de-emphasized and its supposed author is now seen as a spokesman for the oppressed masses. Some authorities detect Daoist elements in the political ideas of the Communist leader Mao Zedong (1893–1976). He appears to hold quasi-Daoist notions about the ebb and flow of historical change. In practical terms Mao's retirement to the "second line" in the late 1950s suggest the influence of governing principles laid down in the chapter called "The Way of Heaven" in the Daoist *Zhuangzi*: "Emperors and kings do nothing, but the world's work is done."   DAO

1950s   Daoist and Buddhist ideas influence American Beat Generation figures, such as Alan Watts (1915–1973). Watts, the English-born leader of the Zen Buddhist movement in the United States, is the author of *Tao: The Watercourse Way* (1975).   BUDD, DAO

1950s   After earlier mission efforts had ended, Catholic missions are established again among the Huichol people of northwestern Mexico. Although some Huichol resist conversion and traditional religious practices survive in some communities, many Huichol do convert, and Catholicism is practiced with traditional customs in some communities.   NATIV

1950s   Roman Catholic and Evangelical Christian missionaries begin seeking converts among the Mam people of Guatemala. Over the next four decades their efforts are somewhat successful as many Mam convert to Christianity.   NATIV

1950–   Nearly all Kurdish Jews immigrate to Israel from the Kurdistan region in
1951   Iraq, Iran, and Turkey.   JUD

1950–
1953

In October 1950 China invades Tibet with 80,000 troops and annexes Tibet, known in China as Xizang Province. The Dalai Lama is kept as a figurehead and attempts to mediate between the Tibetans and the Chinese. On May 23, 1951, Tibet's integration with China is formalized in a 17-point treaty signed in Beijing. China pledges regional autonomy, and the Dalai Lama accepts the agreement in 1953. Within five months the Chinese army occupies Lhasa, the capital city, and in the years that follow, they kill thousands of Tibetans and subject thousands more to prison, forced labor, and deportation. China resettles millions of ethnic Chinese in Tibet in an effort to destroy Tibetan culture, specifically the Buddhism that dominates Tibetan life.   **BUDD, TOL**

1951

A revival of Buddhism begins in India with several million Indians, most of them Hindu Untouchables, converting to Buddhism over the next 10 years. Those who convert see Buddhism as a means of increasing their social standing. Buddhism, which began in India almost 2,500 years earlier, had virtually disappeared there.   **BUDD**

1951

The International Catholic Migration Commission is established in Geneva, Switzerland, by the Vatican to coordinate the activities of dozens of Catholic humanitarian organizations around the world.   **CATH**

1951

The Campus Crusade for Christ is started in the United States to strengthen Christianity on college campuses.   **CHRIS**

1951

David Du Plessis (1905–1987), a Pentecostal minister from South Africa and an official in the Pentecostal World Congress, first meets with officials of the World Council of Churches and over the next 10 years continues to meet with Council officials, attending the annual conferences of the Council as a delegate from the Pentecostal Churches. He becomes an important link between the Pentecostal Churches and mainstream Christian churches.   **EVAN**

1951

The Christian Crusade (formally named the Christian Echoes National Ministry), an Evangelical, anti-Communist movement, is founded by Evangelical minister Billy James Hargis (1925–) in the United States.   **EVAN**

1951

The Jana Sangh political party is founded in India in opposition to the Congress Party and as an advocate of Hindu nationalism in which India is seen as a Hindu nation.   **HIND**

1951

In Indonesia the government uses troops to suppress a fundamentalist Muslim movement (*Dar ul-Islam*) that is seen as threatening government power, as it calls for the creation of a Islamic state. In the same year the Islamic State University is founded and becomes a major center for the teaching and support of Islam.   **ISLAM**

1951

1951	The Canadian government ends restrictions imposed in 1884 on Native American religious practices. **NATIV**

1951   In the Netherlands the Evangelical Lutheran Church in the Netherlands and the Restored Evangelical Lutheran Church in the Netherlands unite under the name of the former. **PROT**

1951   The new religions of Japan, which have been emerging since 1802, form the Union of New Religious Organizations. The union attempts to field slates of political candidates acceptable to all member religions. **SECT**

1951   Japan's Religious Corporations Ordinance is replaced by the Religious Persons Juridical Law on April 3. It is enacted by the Diet before the occupation ends to guarantee permanent legal capacity in the future to the nation's religious groups, ensuring continued protection of religious freedom and separation of church and state. At the same time the tax loopholes of the earlier law are closed to check the runaway expansion of new religions, of which there now are 720. In August, pensions are reinstated for former Shinto shrine priests. **SHINTO**

1951   In Japan the May funeral of the emperor's mother arouses controversy because certain Shinto rites are celebrated with government participation. Similar controversy occurs with the 1952 installation of Crown Prince Akihito and his 1959 wedding. These ceremonies are seen by some as supporting a reactionary movement by Shinto leaders to revive state Shinto. In September the Ministry of Education permits public officials to participate in funerals and memorial services, which may include certain Shinto rituals, organized by individuals or by private organizations. In October the Ministry allows school visits to Shinto shrines to study national cultural treasures, as long as the students are not forced to participate. **SHINTO**

1951   The Fraudulent Mediums Act in Great Britain makes it legal to practice witchcraft with the provision that it cause no harm. The act enables the Wicca movement to go public. The movement is eclectic in its beliefs and draws upon Celtic and other European pagan beliefs and practices and Freemasonry. The movement subsequently divides into four sects. **SPIR**

1951   *Esoteric Astrology* by Dane Rudhyar is published. It is an early and major work in humanistic astrology. Humanistic or human growth astrology is a component of the New Age movement and involves using astrological predictions to make changes in one's personal life. **SPIR**

1951   The Astara Foundation is founded by Robert Chaney (1913–), a leading American spiritualist, in Santa Monica, California. The foundation combines elements from spiritualism, Theosophy, and Christianity. **SPIR**

1952	The Nation of Islam begins a period of growth and expansion that lasts until 1965. A key figure in the expansion is Malcolm X (1925–1965), who establishes temples in major cities in the United States. **AFRICAN**
1952	Roman Catholic priest Dom Helder Camara (1909–) becomes auxiliary bishop of Rio de Janeiro in Brazil and later Archbishop of Recife. During his career he works to eradicate poverty and also attacks aspects of Brazilian society that he feels cause poverty. **CATH**
1952	The Streams of Power movement, a Pentecostal movement, is founded in the Netherlands and then spreads to the Caribbean and Africa, where it attracts an African following. **EVAN**
1952	*Anne Frank: The Diary of a Young Girl* is published in English and is widely read. **JUD**
1952	Orthodox Jews object to the establishment of Reform Jewish institutions in Israel. Although the majority of Jews in Israel are secular (nonobservant) Jews, tensions between the dominant Orthodox Jews and Conservative and Reform Jews, as well as between non-Orthodox Jews outside of Israel and the Israeli government, become a source of conflict in Israeli life and remain so into the 1990s. **JUD**

Malcolm X

Malcolm X (1925–1965) was one of the most influential leaders of the African-American community in the 20th century. He was born Malcolm Little and was also known by his Muslim name, El-Hajj Malik El-Shabbazz. During his childhood, his father died a violent death and his mother suffered a nervous breakdown. His young adulthood was marked by drug use and crime. Imprisoned from 1946 to 1952, Malcolm Little converted to the Nation of Islam and adopted the letter X as his surname in protest of what he felt was the African-Americans' stolen identity. After his release from prison he joined Elijah Muhammad and became the public spokesman and second in command of the Nation of Islam until his banishment in 1963 for derogatory comments about the recently assassinated President John F. Kennedy. He formed his own organization and was drawn closer to Islam before his own assassination in 1965. Malcom X preached a doctrine of black pride, separatism, and nationalism that attracted young African-Americans and greatly swelled the ranks of the Nation of Islam. His message and rhetoric repelled some African-Americans and whites and created conflict with mainstream civil rights leaders. Since his death his ideas and work have undergone considerable analysis, and many experts now view him as a major figure in creating a strong sense of black identity among African-Americans.

1952   Israel and West Germany enter into an agreement concerning German repa-rations to Jewish victims of the Nazi regime. West Germany agrees to pay $107 million to aid Jews living outside Israel, send $715 million worth of goods to Israel over the next 14 years, and institute a program to provide restitution for property and other losses to Jewish victims or their survivors.   JUD

1952   What comes to be called the "electronic church" or televangelism in the United States begins when Protestant minister Rex Humbard inaugurates his *Cathedral of Tomorrow* television show from Akron, Ohio.   MISC

1952   L. Ron Hubbard forms the Hubbard Association of Scientologists in Phoenix. It is a precursor of the Church of Scientology.   SECT

1952   As the Allied occupation ends, Emperor Hirohito travels to Ise shrine to announce Japan's independence. On October 16 the first great memorial festival since the end of the occupation takes place, as for the first time in seven years the emperor and empress attend ceremonies honoring the war dead at Yasukuni shrine.   SHINTO

1952   The term *channeling* comes into common use among adherents of New Age and spiritual movements. It refers to receiving and communicating the thoughts of spiritual masters of the past, spirits of the dead, or extraterres-trial beings.   SPIR

1952   In Poland the constitution establishes a separation of church and state and freedom of religion.   TOL

1953   In China the government establishes the Chinese Catholic Patriotic Association as the central organization for all Roman Catholics, Catholic churches, and Catholic organizations in China. The government considers the association to have more authority than the Vatican, and priests must follow association policies.   CATH

1953   Muslims in cities in Senegal establish the Muslim Cultural Union, which promotes ties to the Middle East, advocates the use of Arabic, and therefore competes for influence with the rural Sufi Murid brotherhood. As Senegal continues to urbanize throughout the decade and into the 1960s, a split develops between urban Muslims, who favor modernization and an Islamic nation, and rural Muslims associated with brotherhoods, who favor the tra-ditional way of life.   ISLAM

1953   In Iran the Pahlavi dynasty survives a coup and an effort to nationalize the oil industry and establishes an authoritarian regime supported by the mili-tary and the secret police. Protests by Muslim leaders, communists, Arabs, and ethnic minorities are quickly and harshly repressed.   ISLAM`

1953   Israel establishes a commission to develop Hebrew as the national language of Israel. Hebrew has virtually disappeared over the centuries as the daily language of Jews, and many Jews in Israel do not speak it when arriving there. The designation of Hebrew as the national language diffuses conflict over which other language could be the national language.   JUD

1953   In the United States the Conference of Presidents of Major American Jewish Organizations is founded. In the 1990s it serves to coordinate the agendas of 53 national Jewish organizations.   JUD

1953   A Baha'i temple opens in Wilmette, Illinois, and becomes a major center for the Baha'i religion.   SECT

1953   The 59th ritual rebuilding of Japan's Ise shrine takes place, after being rescheduled from 1949 because of difficult postwar conditions. This is the first time it is done without full state support, and it will lead to demands for government aid. The old sacred hall is preserved and taken to Atsuta to replace the shrine destroyed in the war. While visiting Japan United States vice president Richard Nixon refuses to pay respects at Yasukuni Shinto shrine because of the preferential government treatment it receives. The Diet then decides to erect a nondenominational monument to the unknown soldier near Yasukuni. The monument will be unveiled in 1959.   SHINTO

1953–
1954   Nearly the entire Cochin Jew community in India immigrates to Israel. Only a small community of several dozen families remains in India.   JUD

1954   *Obeah*, a traditional form of sorcery used to ward off or cure the effects of evil forces, is banned by the government on St. Lucia in the Caribbean. Many people ignore the ban and continue to practice *obeah* in private.   AFRICAN

1954   The Colored Methodist Church in the United States, founded in 1870, changes its name to the Christian Methodist Episcopal (CME) Church. In the 1990s it has about one million members.   AFRICAN

1954   Billy Graham becomes a major figure in the international Evangelical movement and in Christianity in general when he preaches to an audience numbering in the hundreds of thousands in London, England.   EVAN

1954   The Muslim Brotherhood, founded in 1928, is banned by the Egyptian military government, which fears that it will ferment political dissent. The movement does not end but goes into hiding until it reemerges in 1967. This marks the beginning of a government campaign that lasts into the 1970s to bring Islam under state control. Land owned by Muslim communities is confiscated, Muslim leaders are placed under government administration, Islamic laws are weakened, and the Muslim school curriculum is modernized.   ISLAM

1954   The Mormon Church initiates its Indian Student Placement program, which places Native American children in Mormon homes to provide them with education and convert them to Mormonism.   MOR, NATIV

1954   In China the government establishes the Three-Self Patriotic Movement as an organization to place all Protestant denominations under centralized, government control. With adherence to government policy considered most important, differences among the denominations are minimized.   PROT

1954   In Lancaster County, Pennsylvania, a major Amish center, the Amish end the ban on outside employment for Amish men. Changes in the economy have now made farming less lucrative and some families require external income to support their children in the Amish lifestyle. The men work mainly in local manufacturing plants.   SECT

1954   Sun Myung Moon (1920–), a Korean businessman, founds the Holy Spirit Association for the Unification of World Christianity in South Korea. The church is more commonly known as the Unification Church and followers are called Moonies.   SECT

Unification Church

The Unification Church is a new religion that developed in the 20th century. It was founded in 1954 by the Reverend Sun Myung Moon in Korea as the Holy Spirit Association for the Unification of World Christianity and then moved to the United States in the 1970s after persecution by the Communist government. Moon was born in North Korea in 1920 and his family converted to Christianity when he was 10. On Easter Day in 1936, Moon claims that Jesus visited him and told him that God had selected Moon to carry out the Divinity's work on earth. Over the next nine years, Moon is said to have communicated with major religious personages, such as Buddha, Moses, and even God, and received revelations that formed the basis of Unification Church theology as set forth in *Discourse on the Principle* (published in English as *Divine Principle* in 1973). The basic element of Unification theology is Moon's version of the Fall (the disobedience of Adam and Eve and the appearance of sin): Eve had a spiritual sexual relationship with the devil before she had a physical sexual relationship with Adam. Thus, their children were born with fallen natures, a situation only partly corrected by Christ, who provides only spiritual salvation, as he did not marry before his death. Moon, through his marriage in 1960, provides the means to physical salvation, and followers whom he marries in mass wedding ceremonies can thus be sure that their children will be born without sin. Moon also argues that the messiah will be from Korea and will have been born between 1917 and 1930. Moon and the church have been the subject of investigations and legal action by the governments, religious watch organizations, and the media in the United States and Britain. The church has been attacked for its beliefs, its aggressive methods of recruiting members, its mass wedding ceremonies, the vast wealth of its founder (his holdings are said to include real estate, hotels, and newspapers), and its conservative political ideology. In 1984 Moon was jailed for income tax evasion in the United States. Many civil rights organizations and religious leaders, although they may or may not agree with the church's teachings, have criticized governmental attacks on the church as a violation of religious freedom.

1954   A Japanese fisherman dies from radioactive fallout from a United States hydrogen bomb test at Bikini atoll in the west central Pacific. This leads to the formation of the Japanese Religion and Peace Movement to seek a ban on atomic bombs. The movement is headed by new the religion Omotokyo and will include Konkokyo, Sekai Kyuseikyo, and Tenrikyo, three relatively modern Shinto sects. In the Shibata case members of the Shibata Self Defense Force construct a small Shinto shrine in their camp compound, with labor and funds volunteered by the men, with the permission of their commander. The shrine is then ordered to be removed, as it is held to be in violation of the constitutional separation of church and state: its construction raises questions over the permissibility of religious activities by individuals in government service and on government property. The Association of Shinto Shrines calls this interpretation unreasonable.   **SHINTO**

1954   *Witchcraft Today* by Gerald Gardner (1884–1964) is published in Great Britain and becomes the handbook for the revival of witchcraft, now called Wicca. Gardner takes an eclectic approach and combines information from a number of religions and cultures.   **SPIR**

1954   The United States Congress adds the phrase "under God" to the Pledge of Allegiance, which is commonly recited at public events and in schools. **TOL**

1954   *The Christian View of Science and Scripture* is written by Evangelical theologian Bernard Ramm. It is a major work on creationism and stongly supports a progressive rather than literal or fundamentalist view of creation, in which creation is seen as revealed, not completed, in six days and which allows for contributions from science. It divides the creationist community into two camps—fundamentalists and progressives.   **TOL**

1954–   U Nu, the premier of Myanmar, convokes a Sixth Buddhist Council, but he
1956   is attacked by some Buddhists for trying to assert control over the Buddhist monistic orders.   **BUDD, TOL**

1954–   The Algerian war of independence takes place. It ends with Algeria gaining
1962   its independence from France.   **ISLAM**

1955   Mai Chaza's Church, a Methodist-based new African religion, is founded by Mai Chaza (?–1960), a Manyinka woman in Zimbabwe, when she establishes the holy site of Guita Re Jehovah as a healing center that caters especially to childless women. Other centers are established, a canon written, and rituals developed. The movement declines to only a few thousand followers in the decades after Chaza's death.   **AFRICAN**

1955   *Protestant-Catholic-Jew: An Essay in American Religious Sociology* by American theologian Will Herberg (1901–1977) is published. Herberg argues that each of the three religions in the book title are related variants of a basic "American Way of Life." The book and this central thesis influence much subsequent scholarship on religion in the United States.   **MISC**

1955   The first Mormon Temple in Europe opens in Bern, Switzerland. Later, temples open in London (1958), Sweden (1984), East Germany (1985), and West Germany (1987).   **MOR**

1955   The Native American Church of the United States changes its name to the Native American Church of North America, indicating adherents in the United States, Canada, and Mexico.   **NATIV**

1955   L. Ron Hubbard establishes the Founding Church of Scientology in Washington, D.C.   **SECT**

1955   The Aetherius Society is founded in England by George King (1919–). It is an early New Age movement that combines beliefs and practices from Hinduism, Buddhism, and Christianity with an interest in healing, spirituality, and environmentalism. The unique feature is a belief in and communication with "cosmic masters" from other planets.   **SPIR**

1955   The United States Congress adds the phrase "In God We Trust" to United States currency.   **TOL**

1955–
1956   In India new laws are enacted that are counter to traditional Hindu precepts. Women now have equal rights and may divorce their husbands, and husbands may take only one wife at a time.   **HIND**

1956   The various Kimbangu churches of Zaire, which derive from the first church founded by Simon Kimbangu in 1921, are united under a single administrative structure by Joseph Kuntima Diangienda (1918–1971), the son of Kimbangu.   **AFRICAN**

1956   The Brotherhood of the Cross and Star, an independent African Christian Church, is founded in Nigeria by Olumba Olumba Obu (1918–), a businessman and prayer leader. The church stresses healing and spirituality and develops into a major Christian evangelical organization with an active publication program.   **AFRICAN**

1956   The Methodist Church in the United States ends its policy of segregating black Methodist churches when it amends its constitution to allow churches to affiliate across jurisdictional boundaries.   **AFRICAN, PROT**

1956   In an effort to gain political control of Tibet, the Chinese government seeks to weaken the influence of Tibetan Buddhist leaders and Tibetan Buddhism in general by arresting and killing *lamas* and nuns and destroying temples and monasteries.   **BUDD**

1956   Bhimrao Ambedkar (1893–1956), a leader of the Indian independence movement, a lawyer, India's first minister of law, the "father of the Indian constitution," and spokesman and protector of the Untouchables, presides over a gathering of thousands of Untouchables as they convert to Buddhism.

In 1950 he had announced his conversion to Buddhism in protest against the Hindu caste system. Although Ambedkar dies before the year ends, the movement continues to attract many Untouchables.   BUDD, HIND

1956   The Campus Crusade for Christ, started in the United States in 1951, publishes its pamphlet the *Spiritual Four Laws*, which is eventually translated into more than 200 languages and, with the organization's film on the life of Jesus, becomes the major means of spreading its message around the world.   CHRIS

1956   The French colony of Morocco becomes an independent nation. The new government restores religious authority to Muslim scholars but represses the Sufi movement, as Sufis had been loyal to the French.   ISLAM

1956   The French colony of Tunisia becomes an independent nation. The new government seeks to create a secular, modern state, and Islam is suppressed, with Muslim land taken by the state, religious schools closed, mosques placed under government control, and the celebration of Muslim holidays criticized as counter to the national interest.   ISLAM

1956   In Pakistan the new constitution establishes Pakistan as an Islamic state, with all laws to be reviewed by a board of Muslim scholars.   ISLAM

1956   War breaks out between Israel and Egypt over control of the Sinai region. French and British forces also attack the Egyptians and sunken and damaged ships clog the Suez Canal. The canal reopens in 1957.   JUD

1956   The Orthodox rabbinate in Israel prohibits the practice of Reform Judaism in Israel.   JUD

1956   In the Soviet Union the first Jewish school since the 1920s is legally allowed to operate. It is affiliated with the Jewish synagogue in Moscow. Also during the year the government allows the first Jewish prayer book to be published in the Soviet Union since 1917.   JUD

1956   The concept of Great Tradition/Little Tradition is set forth by anthropologist Robert Redfield in his book *Peasant Society and Culture*. As applied to peasant farmers in Mexico, India, and Southeast Asia, it describes the variation between the major religious traditions, such as Roman Catholicism, Hinduism, and Buddhism, and their manifestations in peasant farming villages.   MISC

1956   The Mormons establishes a church in Chile. By the 1990s there are nearly 500,000 Mormons in Chile.   MOR

1956   In Japan the Association of Shinto Shrines adopts the policy of *Keishin seikatsu no koryo* (general characteristics of a life lived in reverence of the *kami*, or protective spirit), emphasizing the close relationship between shrine Shinto and Japanese life, the Shinto contribution to the nation, and the need for moral regeneration. The association will lead the movement to fly the national flag on public holidays and works for state support for Yasukuni shrine. The Bereaved Society of Japan begins to petition for renewed state support for Yasukuni as well, and conservative Diet members call for the Self Defense Force, the prime minister, and the emperor to attend the spring and fall festivals there. All this is opposed by the Union of New Religions. **SHINTO, TOL**

1956   Dalip Singh Saund, a Sikh in California, is the first American of southern Asian ancestry and the first Sikh to be elected to the United States Congress, as a representative from the Berkeley district. **SIKH**

1956   SUBUD, a spiritual and personal growth movement, is brought from Indonesia to Great Britain and then to the United States, Australia, and Europe. In 1990 it claims over 10,000 adherents. **SPIR**

1956   The newly independent nation of Morocco, in North Africa, establishes itself as an Islamic republic with Islam as the state religion. Other religions are not banned but are subject to various restrictions, including on their right to seek converts. **TOL**

1956–1965   In China the government moves to actively suppress religious expression, with religious leaders arrested, churches, temples, and mosques destroyed, shrines damaged, and books confiscated. The Communist government views religion as an impediment to economic and political development. **TOL**

1957   Voudou gains some degree of acceptance in Haiti under the Duvalier government, which views it as competition to the power of the Roman Catholic Church. **AFRICAN**

1957   The Southern Christian Leadership Conference (SCLC) is founded by African-American civil rights leaders representing Baptist churches and other organizations fighting for civil rights in the American south. **AFRICAN**

1957   The Church of Christ in Africa is founded as an independent African church in Kenya by Abednego Matthew Ajuoga (1925–), a Kenyan Anglican pastor. **AFRICAN**

1957   In China the government allows Roman Catholics to form the Constitutional Catholic Church under the control of the Communist government, not the Vatican. The church is not recognized by the Vatican. **CATH**

1957   The National Daoist Association is established in the People's Republic of China. The association aims to study the history of Daoism, publish journals, and train young Daoist candidates. **DAO**

1957   The British colony of Malaya becomes an independent nation (later renamed Malaysia) and Islam is made the official religion, although religious freedom is guaranteed in the new constitution. **ISLAM**

1957	In China the government ends policies of accommodation to Muslims in response to Muslim calls for more autonomy and complaints about the government. The government relocates Han Chinese to Muslim regions, closes mosques and schools, ends local political autonomy, and in 1958 closes the Chinese Islamic Association that was founded in 1953. **ISLAM**
1957	In Tanganyika (later Tanzania) Muslims form the All-Muslim Nation Union political party as a voice for Muslim interests. It draws only a small following. **ISLAM**
1957	In Malaysia the constitution establishes Islam as the national religion but affords other religious freedom to other religions and does not make Islamic law the law of the state, although certain Islamic laws are applied to Muslims. **ISLAM, TOL**
1957	Sacred sites used by the Umatilla, Nez Perce, Yakima, and other Native Americans of Washington State are destroyed when the area is flooded as part of the construction of the Dalles Dam. **NATIV**
1957	The Presbyterian Church of the United States of America approves the ordination of women as ministers. The southern-based Presbyterian Church in the United States follows suit in 1964. **PROT**
1957	*The Way of Zen* by counterculture icon and philosopher Alan Watts (1915–1973) is published. In this book and *Psychotherapy East and West,* published in 1961, Watts argues that Western culture is too egocentric and confused and can find guidance in Asian religions and philosophy. **SPIR**
1957	The I AM movement begins to gain new adherents when it is granted tax-exempt status as a religion by the United States government. **SPIR**
1957	The New Thought Alliance issues a new set of principles that ignores Christianity and emphasizes the direct link between humans and God and spirituality. **SPIR**
1957	The Geoscience Research Institute is established in California by Seventh-Day Adventists concerned about the absence of biblical teachings in public school science classes. The institute becomes a center for research and publications about creationism. **TOL**
c.1958	The Baha'i religion expands into Latin America, Africa, and southern Asia. **SECT**
1958	St. Clare, who founded the Poor Clare Order in 1215 and was canonized in 1257, is made the patron saint of television. Although she lived long before television, her patronage is based on a miracle in which she is reported to have seen a church service she could not attend due to illness. **CATH**

1958   In Pakistan the 1956 constitution, which created an Islamic state, is revised, and Pakistan is made a republic. The revision brings to the surface an underlying conflict in Pakistan between those who favor a Muslim state and those who prefer a secular state. As nearly the entire population is Muslim, the role of Islam in daily life is not a central issue.   **ISLAM**

1958   Mauritania in West Africa becomes an independent nation with the end of French rule and is established as an Islamic state.   **ISLAM**

1958   As the culmination to talks that began in 1951, the Presbyterian Church of the United States of America and the United Presbyterian Church of the United States merge and form the United Presbyterian Church in the United States of America, the largest Presbyterian Church in the world.   **PROT**

1958   Because of concerns about methods used by the Church of Scientology to attract and retain members and also concerns about whether it is a profit-making business or a religion, the United States government revokes the Church's tax-exempt status. In 1963 it is investigated by the Food and Drug Administration.   **SECT**

1958   In France the revised constitution follows the 1946 constitution in establishing France as a secular nation with freedom of religion for all.   **TOL**

1958–   In Japan more new religions at least partially rooted in Shinto continue to
1960   emerge. *Honbushin* (True Constitution) is followed in 1959 by the syncretist and spiritual healing *Mahikari* (Divine True Light) founded by Okada Kotama (1901–1974); in 1988 there will be 18 American centers, three in Canada and one in Puerto Rico, along with associated centers in 14 other countries. In 1960 Perfect Liberty Kyodan missionaries begin working in the United States and the membership also spreads to Africa and Latin America.   **SHINTO**

1959   The Santeria religion is brought to the United States by immigrants from Cuba who are leaving after the Communist revolution. Although the religion is practiced in private by only a minority of Cubans (the majority are Roman Catholics), it catches the attention of animal rights advocates, the media, and government agencies in New York and Florida, who are concerned about reports of animal sacrifice in Santeria rituals.   **AFRICAN**

1959   The Dalai Lama, the leader of the Buddhist community in Tibet, flees to India, where he accuses the Chinese of genocide. He will eventually be joined by some 100,000 followers who are granted political asylum in India. They establish a government in exile at Dharmsala, 35 miles from the Tibetan border. In 1961 the Dalai Lama appeals to the United Nations to restore Tibetan independence. He will campaign for decades to come for condemnation of Chinese occupation; although he gains great respect and a large following for his person and his message—even winning the Nobel

Peace Prize in 1989—he receives little support from national governments around the world. **BUDD, TOL**

1959   The first Nichiren center for Japanese Buddhists is established in Los Angeles, California. In 1960 the first Nichiren Shoshu organizations in the United States are established in California; this branch of Nichiren Buddhism will grow throughout the United States by attracting many non-Japanese. **BUDD**

1959   Pope John XXIII announces plans to convene an ecumenical council of the Church to unite all Christians of the world. The council, known as Vatican II, meets from 1962 until 1965 and produces basic reforms in the Catholic Church. **CATH**

1959   Pope John XXIII asks that the phrase *"pro perfidis Judaeis"* be deleted from the Roman Catholic Good Friday mass. The phrase means "let us pray for the unbelieving Jews" in Latin and is considered offensive by Jews. **CATH, JUD**

1959   In Afghanistan Prime Minister Daoud invites the wives of his ministers to appear unveiled in public in violation of Islamic law. Muslim religious leaders protest the reform and 50 are jailed for a week until they accept the reform. A number of prominent Afghan women soon abandon both the veil and the practice of *purdah* (isolation) itself. **ISLAM**

Dalai Lama

Dalai Lama is the title given to the leader of Tibetan Buddhists. As both the political and spiritual leader of the community, he is thought of by Westerners as a "God-King," although Tibetans refer to him with terms that mean "Presence" or "Precious Eminence." Each Dalai Lama is believed to be a reincarnation of the Avalokitesvara, the celestial force of compassion. The Dalai Lama is identified during infancy or early childhood by the use of astrology by religious leaders to locate the region of Tibet where the next incarnation of Avalokitesvara is expected to appear and tests that require him to identify religious objects of the previous Dalai Lama. Once identified, the Dalai Lama receives intensive instruction in Buddhist ritual and belief and takes on the role of Dalai Lama at a young age. There have been 14 Dalai Lamas. The first, Dge-'dun-grub-pa held the office from 1391 to 1475. The 14th, Tenzin Gyatso (1935–) was installed in 1940. The first five Dalai Lamas were essentially religious leaders; since then, they have usually been political and religious leaders of the community. In 1959 the Dalai Lama, with over 100,000 followers, fled the Chinese invasion and conquest of Tibet and established himself in exile, in Dharmsala, India. He has since become known around the world as a supporter of independence for Tibet and in 1989 was awarded the Nobel Peace Prize for his use of nonviolent means to reach his goal.

1959   In Malaysia the Pan-Malayan Islamic Party does well in several regional elections and becomes a rival to the ruling United Malay National Organization. Although Malaysia is an Islamic state and Muslims are given preference in employment, housing, and education, the Islamic Party argues for the full establishment of Islamic law as state law and a limited role for the Chinese and Indian Malaysian communities who control most of the economy.   **ISLAM**

1959   The Federation of Reconstructionist Congregations and Fellowships to serve Reconstructionist Jewish organizations is founded in the United States. **JUD**

1959   The Egyptian government seeks to end the practice of female genital mutilation, a practice associated with but not required by Islam, by ruling that only medical doctors can perform the procedure. The government policy is not effective, as lay practitioners continue to perform the operations on girls. **MISC**

1959   The Christian Fellowship Church, a syncretic movement, is founded by native Methodist teacher Silas Eto (1905–) in the Solomon Islands. The church combines elements of Methodism with healing, an emphasis on local economic development, and political self-determination.   **SECT**

1959   The *Book of Shadows* is published as the principal text for the modern Wicca movement in Great Britain.   **SPIR**

c. 1960   In India the Digambara Jain school known as Satya Samaja is founded by Pandit Darabarilala. It emphasizes social and national reforms more than religious elements, is opposed to the caste system, and admits Muslims as members.   **JAIN**

1960   In Jamaica government efforts to control the Rastafarian movement culminate with the arrest of a movement leader, Claudius Henry, his wife, and 12 followers. They are accused of treason against the British Crown. Henry and 2 followers are convicted and sentenced to 10 years in prison, and his son and 3 other Rastafarians are killed in a gunfight with British troops.   **AFRICAN**

1960   Zaire becomes an independent nation with the end of Belgian rule, and the Church of Jesus Christ on Earth through the Prophet Simon Kimbangu founded by Simon Kimbangu is declared the national religion. The religion had been repressed and Kimbangu imprisoned for 30 years by the Belgians. The church grows to some three million members and is the first independent African church to join the World Council of Churches.   **AFRICAN**

1960   In Zaire the idea that a new Christian theology can be developed that fits with indigenous African culture is advanced by Roman Catholic seminarian T. Tshibangu, who later becomes the auxiliary bishop of Zaire. The idea is rejected by African Catholic theologians but becomes widely popular nonetheless.   **AFRICAN**

1960   In Tibet the monastery of the Panchen Lama (the second highest official in Tibetan Buddhism), Tashilhunpo, is sacked by the Chinese; 4,000 monks are killed or sent to labor camps. The seventh Panchen Lama, Chokyi Gyaltsen, denounces China's invasion of Tibet; he is jailed in 1964 for 14 years.   **BUDD, TOL**

1960   *The Council and Reunion* is written by Swiss Roman Catholic theologian Hans Küng (1928–). The book sets forth various ideas for Church reform and many are adopted by the Second Vatican Council (1962–1965). **CATH**

1960   John F. Kennedy, a Roman Catholic, is elected president of the United States, making him the first non-Protestant president. Some believe his election marks the end of discrimination against Catholics in the United States.   **CATH, TOL**

1960   What is called the Modern Charismatic, or New Charismatic, or New Pentecostalism, or neo-Pentecostalism begins in Christianity. The key event takes place at St. Mark's Episcopal Church in Van Nuys, California, when members of the congregation of Dennis Bennett begin speaking in tongues, a key sign of spirit baptism and characteristic of the Pentecostal movement. The speaking in tongues becomes world news when it is reported by the media, and the phenomenon spreads to the Episcopal, Lutheran, and Presbyterian churches. Many members of the church object to the new developments, Bennett resigns, and the bishop of the diocese bans speaking in tongues and related behaviors. Bennett is later in the year offered a small parish in Seattle, and in 1961 many parishioners there also experience spirit baptism.   **EVAN**

1960   The Christian Broadcasting Network (CBN) is founded by Evangelical minister Pat Robertson (1930–). Broadcasts on the station feature Evangelical and politically conservative themes.   **EVAN, PROT**

1960   In Indonesia the teaching of Islam is required at all colleges and universities, extending the teaching of Islam to all levels of the education system, as it is already required in elementary and high schools.   **ISLAM**

1960   The newly independent nation of Mauritania in West Africa establishes itself as an Islamic republic, with Islam as the state religion.   **ISLAM, TOL**

1960   In Israel some rabbis express doubts about whether the Bene Israel (Jews from Bombay, India) are actually Jews. The Bene Israel protest from 1962 through 1964, and the Israel rabbinate accepts them as Jews.   **JUD**

1960   Conservative Jewish rabbis in the United States relax laws governing permitted activities on Saturday to allow the use of electricity and the use of motorized transportation in order to attend synagogue services.   **JUD**

1960	Israel security agents capture Adolf Eichmann, the Nazi officer believed to have overseen the Holocaust, in Argentina and take him to Israel to stand trial. JUD
1960	Japan's security treaty with the United States and President Dwight Eisenhower's planned visit to Japan are opposed by religious groups involved in Japan's peace movement. Omotokyo defends Japan's postwar constitution (which bans war) and collects 7.48 million signatures seeking total world disarmament. In 1964 the second World Religionists' Peace Conference will be held in Tokyo. MISC
1960	The Israelite Mission of the New Covenant begins to attract thousands of followers in Peru. Founded by Ezequiel Ataucuzi Gamonal, it is a syncretic religion combining elements drawn from Judaism, Christianity, and the ancient Inca religion. NATIV
1960	In the United States further unification takes place among Lutheran churches as the American Lutheran Church is formed by the Evangelical Lutheran Church, the American Lutheran Church, and the United Evangelical Lutheran Church. In 1963 the Lutheran Free Church joins. The union also represents a merger of churches of German, Norwegian, and Danish background. The American Lutheran Church has about 3 million members in the 1990s. PROT
1960	Quakers in the United States of all traditions found the Earlham School of religion to provide study in Quakerism. PROT
1960	The Orthodoxy Baha'i is established as a Baha'i splinter sect. SECT
1960	Shakerism has been reduced to two communities—Canterbury, New Hampshire, and Sabbathday Lake, Maine—with a total of 25 members, all of them women. SECT
1960	After the Japanese government proposes the teaching of Shinto in public schools to counter the spread of Communism, the Teachers Union opposes this step based on the separation of church and state. This leads the Association of Shinto Shrines to call for Shinto priests who are employed as teachers to leave the Teachers Union. SHINTO
1960	According to astrologers, the Age of Aquarius dominated by Aquarius (the water-bearer) begins and is to be one of peace and harmony. SPIR
1960s	The Original Hebrew Israelite Nation is founded by Ben Ammi Carter in Chicago. A form of African-American Judaism, it advocates an ancient form of Judaism combined with Middle Eastern customs, vegetarianism, and black nationalism. SEE 1969, AFRICAN. AFRICAN
1960s	The Israeli School of Universal Practical Knowledge emerges in New York City and spreads as an African-American Jewish denomination to other

parts of the nation. Followers believe that they are descendants of the ancient Hebrews, wear distinctive military-style clothing, and preach a message of black nationalism.   **AFRICAN**

1960s   The anti-African movement within the Umbanda religion in Brazil weakens and the African roots of Umbanda are again acknowledged.   **AFRICAN**

1960s   The "quiet revolution" takes place in Quebec, Canada, with the Roman Catholic Church losing its influence in social and political affairs of the province.   **CATH**

1960s   In the United States the Jews for Jesus movement begins and continues into the 1990s. Started by non-Jews who seek to "save" Jews by converting them to Christianity, it also eventually involves Jews who have converted. Many Jews believe that being a "Jew for Jesus" is impossible, as one cannot be both a Jew and accept Jesus Christ as the Savior.   **CHRIS, JUD**

1960s   The Jesus People movement is active in the United States, Great Britain, and other Western nations. Although not an organized movement, adherents stress a personal relationship with Jesus Christ and a literal interpretation of the Bible.   **EVAN**

1960s   Shi'a Muslim scholars in Iraq found the Islamic Mission in opposition to the ruling Ba'th Party and to promote fundamentalist Islam. The movement is small and is easily controlled by the government.   **ISLAM**

1960s   In Iran Muslim religious scholars and Muslim reformers take the lead in opposing the increasing authoritarian rule of the Pahlavi regime. They argue that Muslims have an obligation to act politically to create a society more in accord with Islam.   **ISLAM**

1960s   The Baha'i religion is repressed and followers are persecuted in Muslim nations such as Morocco, Iraq, and Egypt.   **SECT**

1960s   The New Age movement emerges in Great Britain and then the United States. No single event marks the beginning of the movement, but it evidently emerges through contact among individuals from various religious movements and denominations, all of which place much emphasis on spirituality, rejection of mainstream religions, and direct contact with God, as well as other supernatural beings. It also draws followers from the hippie, environmental, and antinuclear movements and incorporates beliefs and practices from Western, Asian, and Native American religions.   **SPIR**

1960–
1964   The government of the Soviet Union conducts a campaign to eliminate religion from Soviet life. The campaign does not succeed, but many religious buildings are seized by the government, religious leaders arrested and imprisoned, worship services disrupted, some religions such as Seventh-

Day Adventist denied representative bodies, and all religions except Baptists prevented from convening national conventions.   TOL

1960s–
1970s

A number of American Roman Catholic priests begin to promote the compatibility of Catholicism and Zen Buddhism through their writings and activities. Among the leaders in this movement are Thomas Merton, a Trappist monk; Dom Aelred Graham, a Benedictine scholar; and Father William Johnston.   BUDD, CATH

1961

The Progressive National Baptist Convention is founded by the Reverend Martin Luther King Jr. and other members who believe that the National Baptists Convention of the U.S.A. should take a more active role in the United States Civil Rights movement. In the 1990s it has about 1.3 million members.   AFRICAN

1961

The publication of *The Black Muslims in America* by religion scholar C. Eric Lincoln establishes Black Muslims as the name for the movement. They had been labeled People of the Temple or Voodoo People and in the 1990s are called the Nation of Islam.   AFRICAN

1961

In Myanmar (called Burma at this time), the government makes Buddhism the state religion and moves to make Burma a Buddhist society, stating "whatever is Burmese is Buddhist and whatever is Buddhist is Burmese." The policy creates friction with ethnic minorities who are Muslims, Christians, and followers of traditional religions.   BUDD, TOL

1961

Following the Cuban Revolution and the establishment of a Communist government under Fidel Castro, Roman Catholicism is repressed, with church schools taken over by the government and priests either forced to leave Cuba or to go into hiding. The Catholic hierarchy, which had been close to the former rulers, no longer enjoys influence in Cuba.   CATH

1961

The International Missionary Council, which was founded in 1921 as an umbrella organization for many Protestant missionary organizations, merges with the World Council of Churches, with the Division of World Mission and Evangelism established to represent missionary interests. CHRIS

1961

The World Council of Churches issues a condemnation of anti-Semitism and asks that Jews not be blamed for the Crucifixion of Jesus Christ.   CHRIS, JUD

1961

The Daoist Association of British Hong Kong is established.   DAO

1961

The first New Pentecostal renewal fellowship, the Blessed Trinity Society, is founded in Van Nuys, California. It plays an important role in distributing information about Pentecostalism to non-Pentecostalists through lectures and its magazine, *Trinity*.   EVAN

1961   Two Chilean Pentecostal denominations join the World Council of Churches. The action is opposed by many Pentecostal churches that believe in the independence of individual churches.   EVAN

1961   Former Nazi officer Adolf Eichmann is tried for crimes against humanity and the Jewish people in Israel. He is convicted and sentenced to death. Israel's actions in kidnapping him from Argentina and trying him for crimes committed in another nation bring criticism as violations of international law by many other nations.   JUD

1961   The poem "Babi Yar" is published by Russian poet Yevgeny Yevtushenko. It becomes a symbol of resistance to Russian anti-Semitism, as it commemorates the massacre of Jews during World War II.   JUD

1961   The United Church of Christ, with some two million members, is formed in the United States. Among its members are former Congregational, General Convention of Christian, German Reformed, and Hungarian Reformed churches. It replaces Congregationalism as a denomination in the United States. Some Congregational churches choose to remain independent, while others form several splinter organizations.   PROT

1961   Several Protestant denominations form the Consultation on Church Union to explore the possible unification of the different denominations. Representatives from Presbyterian, United Church of Christ, Methodist, and Episcopal churches participate in discussions but union does not occur.   PROT

1961   In the United States the Jehovah's Witnesses publish a new version of the Bible, the *New World Translation of the Holy Scriptures*, which reflects their beliefs.   SECT

1961   In the United States the Unitarians and the Universalists join together and form the Unitarian Universalist Association.   SECT

1961   The first Unification Church is established outside South Korea, in Berkeley, California.   SECT

1961   New laws governing religious expression in the Soviet Union mandate prison sentences for those who organize religious activities deemed to be harmful to the state and also for those who attend these activities.   TOL

1961   *The Genesis Flood* is written by Evangelical preacher John C. Whitcomb Jr. (1924–) and engineer Henry M. Morris. It is written in reaction to the progressive creationist book *The Christian View of Science and Scripture* published in 1954 and takes a literal view of creation, arguing that life on earth has gone through three key stages, Creation, the Fall, and the Flood, and using this framework to marshal scientific evidence in support of creationism.   TOL

1962   The African Basketmaker Church is driven from South Africa and relocates to Zambia, Tanzania, Ethiopia, and other East African nations.   **AFRICAN**

1962   Ethiopia annexes Eritrea, the population of which is primarily Muslim. Eritreans revitalize the Eritrean Liberation Front and later form the Eritrean People's Liberation Front to combat Ethiopian rule. Although the Ethiopians are primarily Christians and the Eritreans primarily Muslims, the conflict is not religious in nature and Christian Eritreans join the fight against Ethiopia.   **CHRIS, ISLAM**

Vatican II

Vatican II, or the Second Vatican Council, was a council of the leaders of the Roman Catholic Church convened in Rome by Pope John XXIII in 1962 and concluded by his successor Paul VI in 1965. It was the first general council of the Church since the First Vatican Council of 1869–1870 and is considered to have produced the greatest reforms in the Church since the Council of Trent of 1545 to 1563. The Second Vatican Council met in four three-month sessions over four years and discussed virtually all aspects of Roman Catholicism. A unique feature of the Second Vatican Council was the inclusion of observers from other Christian faiths in accord with John XXIII's wish for ecumenicism. The decisions of the Second Vatican Council were published in 16 documents, of which 5 were seen as setting important new directions for the Church. These major new directions were as follows:

(1) A reform of the liturgy and especially the Mass so that it could be performed in vernacular languages, rather than the traditional Latin, making it available to the average Catholic.

(2) A redefinition of the nature of the Church, from the legal, hierarchical view that dated to the 16th century to one in which the Church was seen as the essence of its members. As part of this new view, authority and hierarchy were seen as less important than cooperation, equality, and service to others.

(3) A redefinition of ecumenicism from the old view that Protestants should become Catholics to a new view in which the Church was to play a role in finding common ground among Christian faiths and in encouraging dialogue and cooperation.

(4) A reconsideration of the history of the Church with allowance made for the historical record and modern methods of historical research.

(5) A new policy regarding the Church's relationship to the world. The Church was now seen as an active participant in the modern world and as a powerful agent for social reform.

These and other reforms brought the Catholic Church into the modern world and to a large extent ended the debates dating to the 18th century over matters such as liberalism, Social Catholicism, and modernity.

1962	The Pentecostal Trinity Society in Van Nuys, California, begins to offer teaching sessions called Christian Advance to non-Pentecostal Christians, which bring the New Pentecostal movement to the attention of people across the nation. **EVAN**
1962	The New Pentecostal movement begins in Great Britain. It is influenced by the movement that started in 1960 in Van Nuys, California, and the *Trinity* magazine of the Blessed Trinity Society in Van Nuys plays a role in the spread of the movement to Britain. As earlier in the century, most British Pentecostalists come from the Anglican Church. **EVAN**
1962	As the New Pentecostal movement spreads in the United States, a small number of students in the Evangelical Inter-Varsity Christian Fellowship begin speaking in tongues, a sign of spirit baptism and a hallmark of Pentecostalism. The movement is interdenominational, and the Yale student group includes Episcopalians, Lutherans, Presbyterians, Methodists, and a Roman Catholic. The movement then spreads to other college campuses, including Princeton, Dartmouth, and Stanford. **EVAN, PROT**
1962	Following Algerian independence from France, most of the Algerian Jewish community leaves and settles mainly in southern France. Their arrival increases the French Jewish population to about 500,000, the largest in Western Europe. **JUD**
1962	Esalen, a center of personal exploration and growth, opens in Big Sur, California, and quickly becomes a model for other centers and programs in the human growth segment of the New Age movement. **SPIR**
1962	In *Engel v. Vitale* the United States Supreme Court bans prayer in the public schools on the grounds that it violates the establishment (of religion) clause of the First Amendment to the United States Constitution. **TOL**
1962	The Indonesian government represses Baha'i organizations, the Divine Life Society, and other small religions and organizations on the grounds that they are a threat to national unity. The Baha'i religion is banned completely in 1972. **TOL**
1962– 1963	In the United States mainstream Protestant churches react negatively to the rise of New Pentecostalism. Church leaders in California and Seattle, where the movement is most active, condemn speaking in tongues. **EVAN**
1963	The All Africa Council of Churches (AACC) is founded as an ecumenical Protestant organization to foster cooperation among churches. It also becomes a major center of institutional support for the emerging effort among churches to create their own African-based theologies. **AFRICAN**
1963	In South Africa the Christian Institute is founded, with white and black members. The institute is closed by the government in 1977, as it is seen as a center

for fermenting opposition to apartheid and the white minority government.

AFRICAN

1963   A religious revival takes place among the Luo people of Kenya. It is led by Gaudencia Aoko (c. 1943–), a Luo Catholic who seeks to create a new, independent African church to be called Maria Legio. The new church does not last, but Aoko's preaching against witchcraft and other practices that harm women leads to increased freedom for Luo women and reforms in the local Catholic Church, which permits more participation by lay members. **AFRICAN**

1963   On May 8, while celebrating the birthday of the Buddha, South Vietnamese Buddhists are fired on and killed by government troops. Buddhists make up some 70 percent of the population of South Vietnam, but they are almost completely dominated by Premier Diem's Catholic supporters. A series of protests by Buddhists ensues, including numerous self-immolations; the first by a Buddhist monk is on June 11. In August government troops attack Buddhist temples and arrest over 1,000 monks and nuns. **BUDD, TOL**

1963   The Commission on World Mission and Evangelism of the World Council of Churches meets in Mexico City. Participants support the expanding view among missionaries that control of churches rests with the local community and national churches rather than with foreign missionary societies, as was the practice in the past. **CHRIS**

1963   The Muslim World League is established in Saudi Arabia to promote Islam and provide assistance to refugees and other people, primarily in the Middle East. **ISLAM**

1963   Pakistan is again made an Islamic republic and the constitution of 1953 is, for the most part, restored, thereby increasing the power of religious leaders to review laws in terms of their adherence to Islamic law. **ISLAM, TOL**

1963   Under the Law of Return in Israel, any Jew who immigrates to Israel immediately becomes a citizen. In a case involving a Catholic monk who had been born a Jew and converted to Catholicism, the Israeli Supreme Court rules that the law applies only to an individual who would be considered a Jew under commonly held definitions of who is a Jew. The monk is not permitted to enter Israel under the Law of Return. This is a departure from the religious definition of Jewish identity, whereby any individual whose mother is Jewish is considered Jewish by birth. **JUD**

1963   *The Secular Meaning of the Gospel: Based on an Analysis of Its Language* by American theologian and university professor Paul Matthews van Buren (1924–1998) is published in the United States. It is a seminal work in the so-called "death of God" liberal theology school of thought that attracts a small group of liberal theologians in the 1960s. The death of God movement rests on the premise that it is impossible to communicate or experience God directly and therefore the focus should be on the actual events in the life of Jesus Christ.   MISC

1963   The Creation Research Society is founded by scientists from a number of Christian denominations to halt the teaching of evolution as an explanation for life on earth and to allow the teaching of creationism in the public schools in the United States. The organization accepts various creationist ideas but restricts membership to Christians.   MISC

1963   A sandstone arch considered sacred by the Navajo, Paiute, and Hopi people is desecrated by rising water levels in Lake Powell when the Glen Canyon Dam is built across the Colorado River.   NATIV

1963   A millenarian movement takes place among the Canela people of Brazil. It is led by the prophet Keekhwei, who has visions while pregnant and encourages the Canela to raid ranches owned by whites and to break tribal rules governing sexual relations. The movement ends in failure when a Canela village is burned and four Canela are killed by whites.   NATIV

1963   The Baha'i religion holds its first international convention in Haifa, Israel, and then celebrates the centennial anniversary of the religion with the Most Great Jubilee in London. The Universal House of Justice, an elected body of nine members, is established as the ruling authority of Baha'i.   SECT

1963   In Russia the Mennonites, whose religious activity is repressed by the government, are accepted into the Baptist Union, as the Baptists are accepted as a registered religion in the Soviet Union.   SECT

1963   On August 15, the anniversary of Japan's World War II surrender, the government sponsors national memorial services attended by the emperor and empress honoring the war dead "as fallen heroes defending the state" at Yasukuni shrine. The rite thereafter becomes an annual state ceremony. The war dead are deified at this Shinto shrine despite their religious affiliation and at times over the opposition of the surviving family. The 1904 practice of conferring decorations on the war dead is reinstituted. All this becomes a means of reviving militarism. The new postwar nationalistic healing religion Shinreikyo founded by Otsuka Kanichi establishes a branch in Hawaii.   SHINTO

1963   In *Abingdon v. Schempp* the United States Supreme Court rules mandatory prayer and Bible recitations in public schools are unconstitutional on the grounds that actions by the government to promote or limit religious expression are both unconstitutional. The court in its decision also rules that the government may not take a hostile view of religion, although it may not promote religion. The case was brought by vocal atheist Madalyn Murray (1919–?).   TOL

1964   *Black Religion: The Negro and Christianity in the United States* is written by African-American intellectual Joseph R. Washington. The book points out the different experiences of African-American and white churches in the United States and stimulates discussion of the nature of African-American Christianity in the United States, an early step in the Black Theology movement that emerges several years later.   **AFRICAN**

1964   Malcolm X, minister of Temple of Islam No. 7 in the Harlem area of New York City, and the second most powerful individual in the Nation of Islam after Elijah Muhammad, leaves the movement to form his own organization more in line with his beliefs in black nationalism and traditional Islam.   **AFRICAN**

1964   At the Second Vatican Council representatives of the Roman Catholic Church speak out against anti-Semitism and ask Catholics not to engage in anti-Jewish teachings.   **CATH, JUD**

1964   The Fountain Trust is founded in Great Britain and becomes the center of the New Pentecostal movement there. It arranges conferences and lectures and publishes the magazine *Renewal*.   **EVAN**

1964   The Visva Hindu Parisad organization is founded in India to support Hindu institutions and to inculcate in Hindus a sense of Hindu nationalism, in which India is seen as a Hindu nation.   **HIND**

1964   In Afghanistan a new constitution establishes Islam as the state religion and establishes secular law but allows Islamic law to be used when no other law exists to decide an issue.   **ISLAM**

1964   Christian theologian and mission doctor Albert Schweitzer (1875–1965), who has for years run a mission hospital in Gabon, is awarded the Nobel Peace Prize.   **MISC**

1964   Protestant missionary Eli Stanley Jones (1884–1973) is awarded the Gandhi Peace Prize. As a missionary in India, he has advocated the formation of an Indian Christian church, supported social reforms, and participated in the independence movement.   **PROT**

1964   The first Quaker Meeting (organization) is established in New Zealand.   **PROT**

1964   A Baha'i temple opens in Frankfurt, West Germany.   **SECT**

1964   Pathway Publishers is founded in Ontario, Canada, and becomes the primary publisher of books, educational materials, and other publications for Amish communities in the United States and Canada.   **SECT**

1964   Japan's major Shinto shrines report their counts of New Year's visitors: the Meiji shrine receives 1,045,000; Osaka's Sumiyoshi shrine 1,092,000;

Aichi's Tokogawa Inari shrine 831,000; Kyoto's Fushimi Inari shrine 800,000; Ise Grand Shrine 788,000; and Atsuta shrine 580,000. The new religion Seicho no Ie creates the *Seicho no Ie Seiji Rengo* (political alliance), which will join with conservative forces to promote direct rule by the emperor and the restoration of state Shinto. The Bereaved Families Association establishes the Board of Inquiry concerning State Support to the Yasukuni Shrine and solicits the views of 24 constitutional, governmental, and religious experts. This public (not religious) group seeking government support for Yasukuni will issue the "Outline of a Yasukuni Law" in October 1964.   SHINTO

1964   The Order of Bards, Oviates, and Druids is founded as a modern pagan association in England.   SPIR

1964   The Chinese government moves to control religion by banning the teaching of religion to those under the age of 18.   TOL

1964   In the United States the Civil Rights Act and future amendments prohibit religious discrimination in housing and employment and require employers to make reasonable efforts to accommodate the religious beliefs and practices of their employees.   TOL

1964   In Israel a law is enacted that provides for the protection of and full access to Jewish, Christian, and Muslim religious places. At times Christians and Muslims complain that less attention is afforded their sites than is given Jewish ones.   TOL

1965   The Reverend Martin Luther King Jr. (1929–1968) of the United States is awarded the Nobel Peace Prize for his leadership of the nonviolent effort to end racial discrimination in the United States.   AFRICAN

1965   Malcolm X, former second in command of the Nation of Islam who left the movement in 1964, is assassinated in the Harlem area of New York. The assassins were never caught but were believed by some of his followers to be members of a rival Nation of Islam faction.   AFRICAN

1965   The Second Vatican Council proclaims the principle of admitting native ceremonies into the liturgy of the Roman Catholic Church whenever feasible.   CATH, CONF

1965   The New Pentecostal movement continues to grow and spread in Great Britain. In this year Dennis Bennett, who initiated the movement in Van Nuys, California, conducts a lecture tour in England, and the Full Gospel Business Men's Fellowship International from the United States holds a two-week convention in London.   EVAN

1965

1965   Evangelical preacher Jim Bakker and his wife, Tammy Faye Bakker, join the Christian Broadcasting Network, and through their Praise the Lord (PTL) Club raise substantial amounts of money for the Evangelical movement.   **EVAN**

1965   Immigration of Jains to Great Britain and North America commences with some intensity. Many Jains have long been living in East Africa, where newly independent African nations—specifically, Uganda, Kenya, and Tanzania—adopt policies to get rid of non-Africans they feel are exercising too much control over their economies. Almost all these Jains in East Africa originally came from the state of Gujarat in India. From now through the 1990s, these East African and other Jains from India itself will continue immigrating to England, Canada, and the United States. (There are virtually no Jains in Caribbean lands or in South America.)   **JAIN**

1965   Anglicans, Methodists, and Presbyterians in Nigeria unite and form the United Church of Nigeria to coordinate church activities, with individual churches maintaining control of matters of doctrine and ritual.   **PROT**

1965   The United States government revises the tax law to excuse self-employed Amish from paying Social Security tax. The revision ends years of conflict, during which the government had at times seized Amish property for non-payment of taxes. The Amish do not believe in Social Security, as they see it as a questioning of God's ability to care for them; even Amish who are entitled to Social Security payments because of work outside the community do not accept the payments.   **SECT**

1965   The Church of Scientology is banned by the Australian government. The ban is lifted by the Australian High Court in 1983 and tax-exempt status is restored in 1984.   **SECT**

1965   In the city of Tsu, Mie Prefecture, Japanese officials use public funds to perform the shrine Shinto ritual of *jichin* (invoking *kami*, or protective spirits, to bless a building site). A legal suit asserting this act to be in violation of the constitutional separation of church and state will be affirmed by a 1971 High Court decision.   **SHINTO**

1965   The Findhorn Community is established in Scotland. The community itself, as well as people associated with it, including David Spangler, Eileen Caddy, and Peter Caddy, are major forces in the emerging New Age movement, as the community is involved in personal growth and change, channeling, Asian religions, living in harmony with the environment, and the creation of a peaceful new world.   **SPIR**

1965   Eckankar is founded by Paul Twitchell (1904–1971) in the United States. It is a spiritual, personal growth movement based in part on Hinduism and Sikhism from India and a belief in soul travel.   **SPIR**

1965   The Association of Cymmry Wicca, a neo-pagan group, is founded in
        Georgia by Rhuddlwm ap Gawr. The group traces its ancestry back over 700
        years to Wales and is a large group with over 15,000 members in the United
        States and Europe.   SPIR

1965   The United States Supreme Court hears *United States v. Seeger*, the first of the
        so-called Draft Law cases, which also include *Welsh v. United States* (1970)
        and *Gillette v. United States* (1971). The cases involve conscientious objec-
        tion to military service. The Court rules that conscientious objectors need
        not be members of a pacifist religion, such as the Quakers or Hutterites,
        because religion is a personal matter and that conscientious objector status
        can be given for nonreligious reasons.   TOL

1965   At the Second Vatican Council representatives of the Roman Catholic
        Church declare that Jews should not be held responsible for the Crucifixion
        of Jesus Christ.   TOL

1966   The African Greek Orthodox Church centered in Uganda separates from the
        Greek Orthodox Church in Egypt, as leaders claim that the central church
        does not adequately support the African Church. In 1972 the African
        Church rejoins the central Greek Orthodox Church and leaders of the
        African churches in Uganda and Kenya are given more authority.   AFRICAN

1966   Haile Selassie, the king of Ethiopia who is revered by Rastafarians, visits
        Jamaica and is greeted by some 100,000 Rastafarians. The end of British rule
        has meant more freedom for Rastafarians on the island.   AFRICAN

1966   Kwanzaa, an African-American holiday lasting seven days, is celebrated for the
        first time on December 26 in Los Angeles, California. The festival is founded
        by Dr. Maulenga Karenga and is celebrated this first time by his family and
        friends. The holiday is meant to celebrate African-American culture and com-
        bines elements from African and African-American life.   AFRICAN

1966   Black Theology emerges as a distinct theology within Christianity and in
        African-American churches with the dissemination of *A Statement by the
        National Committee of Negro Churchmen*, which points to the differences
        between the white and African-American experiences in the Christian Church.
        Over the next four years, the basic question of what is African-American
        Christianity is much discussed in African-American churches.   AFRICAN

1966   With the war raging in both the countryside and cities between March and
        June, South Vietnam continues to be wracked by riots, strikes, and unrest,
        much of it instigated by the Buddhists. By June 22, however, the govern-
        ment has, for the most part, suppressed the revolts.   BUDD, TOL

1966   The *Index of Forbidden Books*, first published by the Roman Catholic Church
        in 1559 and designed to control access to Protestant texts and writings, is
        abolished by Pope Paul VI at the Second Vatican Council.   CATH

1966   In an attempt to modernize the theology and teachings of the Catholic
        Church, Dutch Catholic clergy issue the *New Catechism,* which becomes a
        model for similar revisions in other nations. The document is criticized by
        the Church hierarchy and revised in 1968 to include objections from the
        Vatican as an appendix.   **CATH**

1966   In India the Shiv Sena political party is founded in Bombay to support
        Hinduism in Maharashtra State. Members of the party are responsible for
        attacks on Muslims in the state.   **HIND**

1966   The Hare Krishna movement is founded in the United States by A. C.
        Bhaktivedanta Prabhupada (1896–1977), a Hindu immigrant from India. The
        movement is an offshoot of Hinduism and stresses worship of the Hindu god
        Krishna, a personal relationship between each individual and Krishna, and the
        achievement of a spiritually blissful state on earth. The movement spreads

---

Kwanzaa

Kwanzaa is an African-American holiday that is celebrated from December 26 to
January 1 each year. Kwanzaa was founded as a uniquely African-American holiday in
Los Angeles, California, in 1966 and has since spread to many other African-American
communities. Kwanzaa is more a celebration of African and African-American culture
than a religious holiday and is not tied to any single religious tradition. Nonetheless,
there are religious elements including the religious meanings of the African customs
and beliefs celebrated by Kwanzaa and the temporal association with Christmas. Some
celebrate Kwanzaa as an alternative to Christmas, while others celebrate both. In a general sense, Kwanzaa is based on traditional African harvest festivals, which typically
took place at the end of December. Kwanzaa celebrates seven basic principles through
the use of corresponding symbols of those principles:

Umoja (unity)	mazoa (fruits, nuts, vegetables)
Kujichagulia (self-determination)	mkeke (place mat)
Ujima (collective responsibility)	kinara (candleholder)
Ujamma (cooperation in economics)	vibunzi (ear of corn)
Nia (purpose)	zawadu (gifts)
Kuumba (creativity)	kikombe cha umoja (communal cup of unity)
Imani (faith)	mishumbaa saba (seven candles)

Kwanzaa is celebrated through a mix of community and family activities over its
seven days. It involves the preparation of special dishes and meals, storytelling,
singing, poetry, folktales, and other forms of oral communication. In accord with the
traditions of African and African-American culture, much of the activities takes the
form of oral communication, although written guides to Kwanzaa are available.

rapidly in the United States and then Britain in the 1970s and 1980s, with many followers living in Hare Krishna spiritual communities called ashrams.   HIND

1966   During the Cultural Revolution in China, religion is harshly repressed, with much of the repression aimed at the Hui and other Muslims, Islam being the major minority religion in China. Mosques are closed, copies of the Qur'an confiscated, and religious teachers intimidated. The repression lessens in 1970.   ISLAM

1966   *Signs of the Road*, written by Egyptian Muslim scholar Sayyid Qutb, is published in Egypt. He classifies societies as either Islamic or pagan and advocates the return of Egypt to the Islamic condition. The book influences future generations of Muslim fundamentalists in Egypt.   ISLAM

1966   The *Jain Journal* is begun in Calcutta; it is a quarterly devoted to scholarly articles on Jainism, mostly in English.   JAIN

1966   The Native American Church of Navajoland is established by users of peyote among the Navajo in Arizona. It is separate from the Native American Church of North America.   NATIV

Black Theology

Black Theology refers to new theological directions that developed in black Christian churches beginning in the 1960s. There are two major loci of Black Theology: North American Black Theology and South African Black Theology. The new theological directions that developed in black Christian churches in Africa outside of South Africa beginning at the end of the 19th century are usually called African theology and, because of their stronger emphasis on indigenous African traditions, are not labeled Black Theology. North American Black Theology is a product of slavery, and in South Africa it is a product of apartheid (the absolute separation of the races with the white minority dominant). The Black Theology movement in North America was influenced by the Civil Rights and black power movements that began in the 1950s and 1960s. In South Africa its development was linked to political opposition to apartheid. At its base Black Theology reflects the reality that black Christians have almost always been to various degrees excluded from white Christianity as part of their exclusion from white-dominated society in general. Thus, black theologians seek to interpret the Bible in the context of the continuing experience of oppression and the quest for freedom and justice. In this context God and Christ are seen as sources of liberation, while the Bible is studied for insight into how to end oppression and live harmoniously with one's former white oppressors. In some ways Black Theology resembles Liberation Theology, which emerged at about the same time in Latin America. However, they differ in that the former is concerned with oppression and freedom and the latter is more concerned with poverty and social class conflict.

1966   The American Bible Society publishes a new version of the New Testament, *Good News for Modern Man*, in a style and language accessible to the general public. The Old Testament is added in 1976 and the entire Bible published as the *Good News Bible*.   **PROT**

1966   In the United States and Canada, nearly all Lutherans become members of one body when the Lutheran Council in the United States of America is formed by the American Lutheran Church, the Lutheran Church in America, the Missouri Synod, and the Synod of Evangelical Lutheran Churches.   **PROT**

1966   The Rosicrucian Order opens the Rosicrucian Egyptian Museum at Rosicrucian Park in San Jose, California.   **SECT**

1966   The Amish community in the United States is divided into two major groups, the Old Order and the New Order Amish. While both groups continue to require members to wear traditional simple clothing, live in Amish communities, and use the horse and buggy as their means of transportation, the New Order Amish allow some use of modern technology such as telephones and tractors but not the automobile.   **SECT**

1966   Sun Myung Moon, founder of the Unification Church, writes *Discourse on the Principle* (published in English as *Divine Principle* in 1973), which becomes the core text for the church.   **SECT**

1966   The State of Punjab is created by the Indian government. Sikhs form the majority of the population in the state, with Hindu and Muslim minorities.   **SIKH**

1966   Guru Maraji (1958–) becomes leader of the Elan Vital (Divine Light Mission) in India when his father dies. Efforts to spread the movement to the United States in the 1970s fail, although a small following develops in Great Britain.   **SPIR**

1966   Silva Mind Control, a program for personal and spiritual growth based on meditation, is developed by Mexican-American José Silva in California.   **SPIR**

1966   The repression of religion continues in the Soviet Union with new laws banning Sunday schools and religious discussion groups, and restrictions are placed on the amount of religious instruction parents can give their children.   **TOL**

1966   The United Nations General Assembly adopts the International Covenant on Civil and Political Rights. It becomes effective in 1976 when ratified by 35 nations and strengthens the provisions governing religious freedom set forth in the International Bill of Human Rights.   **TOL**

1966–1967	The Albanian government continues its campaign to ban religion by closing religious institutions, arresting clergy, and confiscating religious property. The program is effective in ending the practice of any religion in Albania. By 1967 the official government policy is one of repression of all religion and the creation of an atheistic state. **TOL**
1966–1969	Six thousand Tibetan monasteries and temples are demolished during the Cultural Revolution in China, their artwork and libraries destroyed, and monks dispersed. Religious activity is banned, as is traditional Tibetan dress. More than a million Tibetans are thought to have been killed during the years of Cultural Revolution in China. **BUDD, TOL**
1966–1976	The Cultural Revolution brings Daoist activity in China to a virtual halt. Temples and shrines are closed; many are destroyed. Red Guards demolish the remaining Daoist religious buildings on sacred Mount Mao in Shandong Province. **DAO**
1966–1976	In China during the Cultural Revolution, the government harshly represses religion by telling people to ignore all religions, forcing religious leaders to publicly reject their religions, and destroying religious buildings (churches, shrines, and mosques), books, and relics. As a result, much religious activity disappears or is conducted in secret. **TOL**
1967	In South Africa the University Christian Movement is founded. It draws black and white members and becomes a center for the discussion of the emerging Black Theology. **AFRICAN**
1967	The Fo Kuang Shen sect of Mahayana Buddhism is established on Taiwan by Chinese who have fled mainland China. **BUDD**
1967	The New Pentecostalism movement begins to attract significant numbers of Roman Catholics in the United States. The first major group of Catholics who experience the baptism of the Holy Spirit are a group of about 30 people in Pittsburgh who attend the Duquesne Weekend, named after Duquesne University, where some meeting participants are faculty members. The group views the experience as making them better Catholics, rather than as replacing Catholicism. The movement then spreads to Notre Dame University and Michigan State University, and in the next few years to Catholic faculty members and students at many other colleges and universities. **EVAN**
1967	The first "charismatic clinics" are held by the Pentecostal minister Ralph Wilkinson at the Melodyland Christian Center in Anaheim, California. The clinics grow in popularity and major Pentecostal leaders are featured as speakers. The clinics serve a variety of purposes, including conflict resolution for congregations with both Pentecostal and non-Pentecostal members, outreach to the Latino and African-American communities, and training of ministers. **EVAN**

1967   Evangelical minister, faith healer, and televangalist Oral Roberts founds Oral Roberts University in Tulsa, Oklahoma, as part of his Oral Roberts Evangelical Association. The university flourishes at first but then experiences financial difficulties, and its assets are sold to other organizations.   EVAN

1967   Egypt is defeated by Israel in the Six-Day War, and with the government humiliated, the Muslim Brotherhood, which had been banned in 1954, reemerges as a political force. It advocates a return to traditional Islam and the end of Western influence.   ISLAM

1967   The Muslim *Muhammadiya* organization in Indonesia founds the *Dewan Da'wah Islamiyah* Indonesia missionary organization to work toward strengthening Islam in the nation to control the efforts of Christian missionaries.   ISLAM

1967   The Six-Day War involving Israel, Egypt, Syria, and Jordan ends with Israel in control of the Sinai, the Golan Heights in Syria, and the West Bank of the Jordan River. The Old City of Jerusalem, annexed by Jordan during the 1948–1949 Arab-Israeli War, is captured by Israel. Jews gain access to the remains (the Eastern Wall) of the Temple, which becomes a site of Jewish pilgrimages.   JUD

1967   The Navajo Tribal Council lifts the ban on peyote use for members of the Native American Church. SEE **1990, NATIV.**   NATIV

1967   In the United States the United Presbyterian Church issues the Confession of 1967, a new and basic statement of church doctrine. The Confession saves some of the traditional doctrine, makes revisions based on liberal reforms of the 20th century, and affords a belief in Christ—a central position in Presbyterian belief—while questioning the inerrancy of the Bible.   PROT

1967   Despite opposition the Japanese government establishes *Kenkoku kinenbi* (National Foundation Day), to be celebrated on February 11th, as a new version of the prewar *Kigensetsu* (Empire Day).   SHINTO

1967   The Ananda Cooperative Village is founded in Nevada City, California, by Swami Kriyananada, a former student of Swami Paramahansa Yogananda. It is a communal society and a spiritual center based on Westernized Hindu and other Asian beliefs and especially the use of meditation yoga to increase one's spirituality.   SPIR

1967   The Lama Foundation is founded in Taos, New Mexico, by intellectuals and artists from New York who want to build a community where people can experience personal and spiritual growth. The foundation stresses yoga, meditation, and Sui dance to achieve these goals.   SPIR

1968   The policy of segregating African-American Methodist churches from white ones in the Methodist Church in the United States, which had been weakened in 1956, is ended completely when the Central Jurisdiction established for African-American churches is abolished.   **AFRICAN, PROT**

1968   Pope Paul VI (1897–1978) issues his encyclical *Humanae Vitae*, in which he states the Church's objection to the use of artificial forms of birth control. The encyclical also deals with the responsibilities of marriage and parenthood. It is widely controversial in the Catholic community, as it is counter to the recommendation of a Church birth control commission and ignores the fact that many Catholics use artificial forms of birth control.   **CATH**

1968   Roman Catholic bishops in Latin America meet at the Conference of Medellín in Colombia; Pope Paul VI is also present. Some bishops at the meeting argue that the Church should take an active role in ending social and economic inequalities in Latin American nations, and the pope's presence suggests Church support for this view and motivates some bishops and priests to support revolutionary movements in the region. The meeting is an important event in the emergence of Liberation Theology in Latin America, which leads to conflicts and confrontations between various

---

Liberation Theology

Liberation Theology is the general name given to a religious movement that developed in Latin America in the late 1960s and provided a new interpretation of Christian theology. In Liberation Theology, theology is seen as a source of liberation from both the poverty and the oppression that have characterized many Latin American societies since European colonization. However, in a departure from traditional views of the role of theology, liberation theologians believe that thought follows action and that a new theology will develop from actions taken to end and reduce poverty and suffering. In addition to being a reaction to poverty and oppression, Liberation Theology has also been informed by the political theology orientation that developed in Germany and Marxist theory. Although the roots of Liberation Theology can be traced to Spanish priests who in the 1500s argued for better treatment of American Indians, the modern manifestation began in the late 1960s and was led by Catholics and Protestants in poor communities. The beginning of the movement is often defined as the publication of *Hacia una teologia de la liberación* (*Towards a Theory of Liberation*) by Peruvian Catholic Gustavo Gutierrez in 1969. It was followed by several other books by Gutierrez and other liberation theologians, such as Methodist minister Jose Miguez Bonino. Liberation Theology has been controversial and was at first criticized by leaders of mainstream churches, most notably the Roman Catholic Church, but has gained greater acceptance since the 1980s. It has been criticized for advocating violence (a charge largely untrue), for suggesting that God "prefers" the poor to the rich, and for merging religion and politics. Liberation policy has spread beyond Latin America and has been adopted as an agenda for ending poverty and oppression in Asia and Africa as well.

1968   authoritarian governments and those priests and bishops who support the poor and oppressed. **CATH**

1968   As the New Pentecostal movement continues to attract small numbers of Catholics, about 150 Pentecostal Catholics hold a conference at Notre Dame University. In 1969 the conference attracts some 450 Pentecostal Catholics, including 30 priests, and in 1970 it attracts some 1,300 people from the United States and Canada. **EVAN**

1968   Hare Krishna is spread from the United States to Great Britain by missionaries from the United States. **HIND**

1968   With the end of French rule and the establishment of an independent government, Algeria embraces a policy of Islamic socialism, which includes the Arabization of Algerian society. The use of Arabic is made mandatory, although many people in government and business continue to use French. The policy is not supported by Berbers, who are not Arabs, and is criticized by some Muslims who want Algeria to be an Islamic society and feel that the reforms are not broad enough. **ISLAM**

1968   In Indonesia, after 20 years of generally successful repression of Muslim political parties and movements, the government allows the formation of the Partai Muslimin Indonesia, although the more radical Muslim reformers are barred from leadership roles. **ISLAM**

1968   A rabbinical college is opened for Reconstructionist Jewish rabbis in Philadelphia. In New York City the Jewish Defense League is founded to protect Jews from anti-Semitic assaults. Many Jewish leaders object to the league and its militant agenda. **JUD**

1968   In the United States the Methodist Church and the Evangelical United Brethren Church merge and form the United Methodist Church. **PROT**

1968   The Unification Church is given official status as a religious organization in Great Britain. **SECT**

1968   The Family (also known as the Children of God), a Christian communal society, is founded by David Berg (1919–1984), known to his followers as Mo, in California. **SECT**

1968   Japan's government sponsors the celebration of the Meiji Centennial, thus encouraging the right-wing movement to restore the imperial state, to excuse its aggressive wars, and to revive state Shinto. **SHINTO**

1968   *Chariots of the Gods* by Swiss writer Erich von Däniken is published in English. It is the first of a large number of books published over the next 10 years that suggest the earth was visited in the distant past by people from other planets or solar systems whose presence influenced later life on earth.

Other books of this type include *The Spaceship of Ezekiel* (1974) by Joseph F. Blumrich; *Jesus Christ: Heir to Astronauts* (1976) by Gerhard R. Steinhauser; and *The Lost Tribes of Outer Space* (1977) by Marc Dem.   **SPIR**

1968   *The Teachings of Don Juan: A Yaqui Way of Knowledge* by anthropology student Carlos Castaneda (c.1925–1998) is published. Although controversial because of questions about the authenticity of its content, the book becomes popular among New Age adherents who value Castaneda's message about other, non-Western, nonscientific paths to knowledge and information about Native American religion. Castaneda writes nine more similarly popular books.   **SPIR**

1968   The United States Supreme Court rules in *Epperson v. Arkansas* that it is unconstitutional for a state to prohibit the teaching of evolution. Although a setback for advocates of creationism, it leads to the development of creation science, in which the Judeo-Christian version of creation is portrayed as a science, and is thereby eligible to be taught in public schools. **SEE 1987, TOL.**   **TOL**

1969   About 1,500 members of the Original Hebrew Israelite Nation living in Liberia immigrate to Israel, where they seek to settle as Jews under the Law of Return, which grants all Jews immediate Israeli citizenship. Their identity as Jews is questioned, and they are not granted citizenship but are allowed to remain in the country indefinitely.   **AFRICAN**

1969   *Black Theology and Black Power* is written by African-American theologian and professor James Cone. It is an early and influential document in the emerging Black Theology movement and stresses the need to consider cultural and historical contexts in asking and answering theological questions.   **AFRICAN**

1969   In the Roman Catholic Church, in reaction to calls from some clergy for a reduction of the power of the pope, a synod of bishops strongly supports papal authority and the pope's right to act as he sees fit.   **CATH**

1969   The Hare Krishna movement garners much international attention when George Harrison of the Beatles records the "Hare Mantra." In this same year Harrison buys a building for the Hare Krishna group in Great Britain, which becomes its headquarters.   **HIND**

1969   The Moro National Liberation Front (MNLF) is founded as a political organization by Muslims on the island of Mindanao in the Philippines in order to win Muslim freedom from rule by the central Filipino government.   **ISLAM**

1969   The Indonesian government establishes a center for training Muslim missionaries. Although the center is meant to help revitalize Islam in Indonesia, it also competes with Muslim-controlled centers and allows for government influence over Islam.   **ISLAM**

1969	In Malaysia riots break out between Chinese and Muslim Malays. Although Malays form the majority of the population and Malaysia is an Islamic state, the Chinese control much of the economy and the wealth of the nation. Throughout the 1960s the pro-Muslim Pan-Malayan Islamic Party has gained supporters, threatening the power-sharing arrangement among the Malays, Chinese, and Indians favored by the government. **ISLAM**
1969	Through the United Nations Security Council, the international community urges Israel to terminate its policy designed to make Jerusalem Israel's capital. Israel rejects the resolution. **JUD**
1969	The Israelite Mission of the New Covenant, a syncretic religion established in Peru in the early 1960s, is recognized by the government as a religion. **NATIV**
1969	Japan's new religion Omotokyo is among the participants at the conference of the World Federation of Religions for Promotion of Peace held in Minobu. **SECT**
1969	Japan's conservative Liberal Democratic Party presents the Yasukuni Shrine Bill to the Diet, to convert the shrine's status to that of a special nonreligious foundation and to place it under the jurisdiction of the prime minister. The numerous opponents of this move, including the left wing, the intelligentsia and academia, led by the Union of New Religions, collect 3,277,405 signatures of those who fear that government administration of Yasukuni would constitute a restoration of state Shinto and would open the door to a revival of Japanese militarism. The bill is presented repeatedly over the next decades and is defeated each time. **SHINTO**
1969	The Inter-American Convention on Human Rights is adopted by representatives of nations in the Americas at a special conference on human rights in Costa Rica. It becomes law in 1978 when ratified by 11 nations. It guarantees religious freedom including the right to change one's religion and to spread one's beliefs. **TOL**
1969	The debate over the teaching of creationism becomes an issue in California, when the Board of Education seeks to establish principles and a curriculum for the teaching of science. The new policy does not allow for the teaching of creation science but reduces the status of evolution to an unproved theory. **TOL**
1970	*Infallible? An Inquiry* is written by Roman Catholic theologian Hans Küng (1928–). A Church reformer, he questions the doctrine of papal infallibility. **CATH**
1970	Dutch Roman Catholic clergy vote to remove celibacy as a requirement for the priesthood and initiate discussions with the church in Rome to revise church doctrine accordingly. **CATH**

1970   French archbishop Marcel Lefebvre, a critic of Vatican II, establishes the St. Pius X fraternity in Switzerland to support his conservative agenda and to combat revisions in Church policy set forth in Vatican II documents. The fraternity attracts some 100,000 Catholic followers around the world. In 1988 Lefebvre is excommunicated after he ordains four bishops.   CATH

1970   In the United States the United Presbyterian Church (U.S.A.) is the first major Protestant denomination to accept the New Pentecostalism when it issues a report asking members to accept new and different Christian experiences. About this time Pentecostalism is also officially recognized by the

Hindu Diaspora

The overwhelming majority of Hindus (about 700 million) live in India, where they constitute about 70 percent of the national population. Since the middle of the 19th century, Hindus have spread across the world, creating one of the largest diasporas, rivaling the African, Chinese, and Jewish diasporas. In the 19th century the emigration of Hindus and Muslims, Sikhs, Jains, and others from India was largely the product of British colonialism. India was a British colony, as were numerous other nations in Asia, Africa, the Caribbean, the Pacific, and Latin America. The British colonists actively encouraged and sometimes forced Indians, the majority of whom were Hindus, to move to these other colonies. In Latin America the British motivation was primarily to replace African slave labor that was no longer available after the end of slavery in the 19th century. Elsewhere, the British imported Indians, many of whom now spoke English, to serve as low-level civil servants in the colonial governments and as merchants and traders, thereby acting as a buffer between the British and the colonized peoples. This colonial policy took its toll after many nations gained independence following World War II, with the Indians, who now saw their diaspora nation as their homeland, in conflict with the formerly colonized native peoples, who saw the Indians as outsiders and agents, ironically, of the colonial regime. In addition, in some nations Indians held key political offices and controlled important segments of the economy. Conflict between Indians and native peoples in Kenya, Uganda, and Fiji caused significant numbers of Indians to flee to other nations, such as Canada, the United States, Australia, and Great Britain. A more recent emigration of Hindus and other Indians has taken place since the 1960s to nations such as Canada and the United States. These immigrants tend to be better-educated than earlier ones and maintain ties to their home communities in India. In Great Britain Hindu immigration increased after India gained independence in 1947. The diaspora nations with the largest Hindu populations are South Africa (about one million), the United States (about 900,000), Malaysia (about 800,000), Great Britain (about 700,000), Mauritius (about 400,000), Trinidad and Tobago (about 350,000), Canada (about 350,000), and Fiji and Guyana (about 300,000 each). Other nations with over 100,000 Hindus each are Kenya, Singapore, and Suriname.

1970   Lutheran Church in America and the Presbyterian Church in the United States and informally accepted by other churches.   **EVAN**

1970   The Awami League wins a majority of seats in the Pakistan legislature but is prevented by supporters of the rival Muslim League from forming a government. The Awami League draws much of its support from East Pakistan (later Bangladesh) and plays a major role in the 1971 civil war that leads to Bangladesh becoming an independent nation.   **ISLAM**

1970   In Iraq the constitution establishes Islam as the state religion, although Shari'a (Islamic law) is not established as civil law and religious freedom is granted to other religions. However, many of these other groups, including Jews, Christians, and Shi'a Muslims, are subject to persecution.   **ISLAM, TOL**

1970   The International Mahavira Mission (IMM) is founded in India by Guruji Sushul Kumar (1926–). It stresses the basic of tenets of Jainism—nonviolence, vegetarianism, and the many-faceted nature of truth—and teaches yoga, breath control, ayurvedic medicine, mantric words of power, and chanting. Its original Indian members spread their message in Europe and North America; the founder visits the United States for first time in 1975. The mission opens centers in Staten Island, New York City, and upstate New York, as well as in Canada, France, and West Germany. The international headquarters remains in New Delhi, India. The IMM remains especially committed to fostering international and interreligious contacts.   **JAIN**

1970   In a series of books, including *Beyond Belief* published in 1970 and *The Broken Covenant* published in 1975, social scientist Robert Bellah discusses the concept of civil religion in the United States. He views civil religion as a set of beliefs, not necessarily religious in origin or expression, that unifies the American people in the absence of an overarching religious belief shared by all. One especially important belief component of civil religion is that the United States has a mission to save the world and to make it a better place.   **MISC**

1970   The United States returns Blue Lake and surrounding land to the Taos people of New Mexico. The Taos consider the lake a sacred pilgrimage site. It had been taken by the government as part of Carson National Forest in the 1800s.   **NATIV**

1970   The American Indian Movement occupies the *Mayflower II* in Plymouth Harbor and declares Thanksgiving Day to be a national day of mourning.   **NATIV**

1970   The first Indian Ecumenical Conference takes place on the Crow Reservation in Montana. Representatives of various religions with Native American adherents, including Roman Catholicism, Protestantism, Baha'i, the Native American Church, and the Handsome Lake religion, meet to discuss problems that face Native American communities, such as poverty, relations with whites, and alcoholism.   **NATIV**

1970   The *Hour of Power* religious television show is founded by Reformed minister Robert Schuller in southern California. By the early 1990s the show is the most popular religious show in the United States and is aired in some 44 nations.   **PROT**

1970   The Tenrikyo religion in Japan ends its affiliation with the Association of Shinto Sects and asks the government to classify it as an "Other Religion" because adherents believe that it is a world religion.   **SECT**

1970   During Japan's elections ties between the political parties, especially the right-wing Liberal Democratic Party (LDP), and religious bodies become stronger. Some religious leaders tell their followers whom to vote for, as Seicho no Ie, Sekai Kyuseikyo, and Perfect Liberty Kyodan support the LDP. During the decade, international criticism of Japan's economic acquisitiveness will increase government attempts to reinstitute the prewar unity of the state and Shinto, as symbolized by the Yasukuni shrine. It covertly provides necessary information on the war dead, which it denies to other religious organizations, to Yasukuni. In a move to legitimate Japan's prewar and World War II–era regimes and to erase its civil rights abuses and Asian atrocities of that era, it will initiate the rewriting of history textbooks used in the public schools.   **SHINTO**

1970   Channeling as a mechanism for communicating with the spiritual masters of the past becomes important in the New Age movement in the United States with the publication of the first volume of *The Seth Material*.   **SPIR**

1970   The National Science Foundation of the United States supports the development of a new social science curriculum for use in the fifth and sixth grades. The curriculum is developed by scholars and teachers and is criticized by fundamental Christian organizations as ignoring religion and giving too much attention to non-Western cultural traditions.   **TOL**

1970   *Biology: A Search for Order in Complexity*, a high school biology text prepared by the Creation Research Society, is published in the United States. The book sets forth creationism as an explanation for the origin of the universe and sells moderately well in its first year but goes out of print after being banned in Indiana.   **TOL**

1970   Fiji becomes an independent nation and conflict develops between the native Fijians and the Asian Indians (Hindus, Muslims, and Sikhs), who form the majority of the population. The native Fijians seek to take political control of the nation, and over the next two years attacks are launched on Hindu temples and Muslim mosques, compelling some Indians to leave, thereby making the Fijians the majority population.   **TOL**

1970s   During the early years of the decade, the Black Theology movement spreads in the United States as it moves from the churches to seminaries and colleges.   **AFRICAN**

1970s

1970s	The Nation of Yahweh (also called the Temple of Love) is founded by Yahweh Ben Yahweh (born Hulon Mitchell, 1935–), a former Pentecostal Christian and Black Muslim. Followers believe that African-Americans are descended from the ancient Israelites, and the group adopts a Black Nationalist and antiwhite ideology. In the 1990s there are followers and congregations across the United States, although Yahweh Ben Yahweh was imprisoned in 1992 for murder and racketeering. **AFRICAN**
1970s	The Nubian Islamic Hebrew Mission (also called Ansaaru Allah Community) emerges as a Black Muslim/Jewish denomination in New York City and draws followers elsewhere in the nation. It rests on the belief that adherents are both Muslims and Jews, as they are descended from Abraham. **AFRICAN**
1970s	America's participation in the war in Vietnam has had the effect among many young people of making them more aware of the teachings of Buddhism. Many young Americans adopt such practices as vegetarianism and pacifism and show a lack of interest in competitive Western society. Among other signs of increasing interaction between the West and East in the United States, Japanese martial arts such as karate begin to be studied; Zen Buddhism and various Indian meditation disciplines are being practiced; the Tibetan *Book of the Dead* and the Chinese *I Ching* gain a new public; young Westerners begin to visit Nepal; and Katmandu, its capital, will become a major tourist destination. **BUDD**
1970s	Evangelical Christians, Seventh-Day Adventists, Jehovah's Witnesses, and others become active in seeking converts among Afro-Caribbeans and Native Americans in the Caribbean and Central America. Most of the people they seek to convert are either Roman Catholic or Protestant; many practice folk versions of Christianity. Over the next three decades, the missionaries are somewhat successful as many people convert, at least nominally. **CHRIS, NATIV**
1970s	The Bharatiya Janata Party emerges in India as a supporter of Indian nationalism and India as a Hindu nation, but it gains few supporters. **HIND**
1970s	In Algeria fundamentalist Muslims promote their agenda of creating an Islamic society by attacking women who do not wear veils, destroying businesses that sell alcoholic beverages, and disrupting the classes of religious teachers with whom they disagree. **ISLAM**
1970s	In the African nations of Senegal, Nigeria, Guinea, and Somalia, all of which have large Muslim populations, Muslims call for the nations to develop Islamic societies, to support Muslim education, and to institute Islamic law. Although Islam is important in these nations, they do not become Islamic societies as political factionalism, membership in different Sufi orders, and ethnic and regional competition interferes with the goal of Muslim unity. **ISLAM**

1970s	In Egypt there is a revival of Islam, which has been under government control from the 1950s. The revival is led by local Muslim teachers and Muslim scholars and is in response to continuing political problems in the Middle East and economic problems in Egypt. The government generally supports the revival of religious elements of Islam. ISLAM
1970s	Early in the decade there is a mass exodus of Jews from the Soviet Union mainly to the United States and Israel. The Jewish population in the Soviet Union declines by about 15 percent. JUD
1970s	Institutional anti-Semitism in the United States declines as quotas on Jewish enrollment in elite colleges end and Jews begin occupying senior management positions in industry and commerce. JUD
1970s	An anticult movement develops in the United States and Europe for the purpose of identifying new cults and sects, providing the public with information about them, and assisting people who are concerned about the well-being of relatives or friends who have joined cults. Some in the movement use "deprogramming" as a technique to end a recruit's allegiance to a cult. SECT
1970s	A Sikh separatist movement develops in the Punjab state in India, with Sikhs first calling for cultural autonomy and some later calling for the establishment of an independent Sikh nation to be called Khalistan. The Sikhs are concerned that their distinct culture and religion will be subverted by the Hindu majority in India. SIKH
1970–1971	Gurdev Chitrabhanu, a highly respected Jain monk, visits Europe, East Africa, and the United States; his lectures gain favorable attention to Jainism. JAIN
1971	Pope Paul VI visits the headquarters of the World Council of Churches in Geneva, Switzerland. As the Church is not a member of the Protestant and Orthodox council, his visit is widely seen as an effort to build ties between the Church and other Christian religions. CATH
1971	Attempts to remove celibacy as a requirement for the Roman Catholic priesthood are ended by the Synod of Bishops, which reaffirms the doctrine. CATH
1971	A group of anthropologists concerned about the destruction of indigenous peoples issues the Declaration of Barbados, which criticizes Christian missionaries for what they see as aiding the exploitation of indigenous peoples in Latin America and demands various rights for indigenous peoples. CHRIS
1971	The Festival of Light (renamed CARE in 1983) is founded as a Christian organization to fight the decline of moral values centering on issues such as abortion, euthanasia, and pornography. CHRIS

1971

1971   The Church of the Lamb of God is founded by Ervil LeBaron (d.1981) as a Mormon group to represent all Mormons who continue to practice polygymy. The group allegedly resorts to murder to get rid of leaders of opposition groups, LeBaron dies in prison, and the group disappears.   **MOR**

1971   The Baha'i Under the Provisions of the Covenant forms as a splinter Baha'i sect.   **SECT**

1971   The Family, founded in 1968 in California and successful in establishing a number of communes in the United States, relocates its headquarters to London. It is an explicitly Christian organization, which follows the Bible and the letters of Mo (the movement's founder). Although successful in founding hundreds of communes, it comes under criticism in a number of nations for allowing sexual freedom and for aggressively recruiting young people. SEE **1995,** SECT.   **SECT**

1971   The Free Children of God organization is founded as an anticult organization in the United States in response to claims that the Family, founded in California in 1968, actively recruits young adults.   **SECT**

1971   The Sikh Dharma of the Western Hemisphere is founded in the United States by Harbhanjan Singh Puri (Yogi Bhajan), an Indian religious teacher. The sect attracts many white American followers, who are labeled "white" Sikhs by some Indian Sikhs. The movement follows many mainstream Sikh beliefs and practices but also emphasizes the practice of yoga, meditation, and the wearing of turbans. Its status in the Sikh community is ambiguous.   **SIKH**

1971   In the Nagoya High Court decision in Japan the court rules that the use of public funds in 1965 to perform a Shinto rite was in violation of the constitutional separation of church and state. This will be overturned by the 1977 Japanese Supreme Court, which views Tsu's rite as secular and hence the use of the funds as constitutional. This finding will greatly encourage the movement to restore state Shinto. In September Shinto ceremonies are held at the conclusion of the Conference on Shinto in Claremont, California. The *kami* (protective spirits) invoked at that rite include those of George Washington and the United States Founding Fathers.   **SHINTO**

1971   The Pagan Front, which later becomes the Pagan Federation, is founded as an international organization to defend paganism. It publishes the magazine *Pagan Dawn*.   **SPIR**

1971   Erhard Seminar Training (est) is developed by Werner Erhard (1935–) in California as a program to help people reach their maximum potential by taking full control of their lives. It becomes a model for other programs within the human growth movement.   **SPIR**

1971   The Emin Society is founded by Raymond Schertenlieb (1924–) in London as a spiritualist movement that draws on beliefs and practices from

Christianity, astrology, and other religions. The movement spreads to North America and Australia.   SPIR

1971   In a case concerning the teaching of religion, the United States Supreme Court in *Lemon v. Kurtzman* establishes guidelines that legislatures must follow in developing laws regarding prayer in schools.   TOL

c. 1972   The New Age movement gains momentum in the United States, as beliefs and practices from Asian religions, such as Buddhism, are integrated with religious movement beliefs from Great Britain into a varied though coherent system of belief. Followers envision a new world characterized by peace and harmony.   SPIR

1972   *Essays in Black Theology* is published in South Africa. The essays in the volume are based on seminars on Black Theology conducted by the University Christian movement in 1971 and are an early statement about Black Theology in South Africa.   AFRICAN

1972   In the United States the Assemblies of God Pentecostal denomination officially accepts the legitimacy of the New Pentecostal movement. However, many traditional Pentecostalists remain skeptical of the New Pentecostalism and criticize its willingness to join with mainstream Christian churches, the relatively relaxed social norms it accepts, and the emphasis on speaking in tongues outside of any doctrinal framework.   EVAN

1972   *Be Here Now* by Baba Ram Dass (1931–) is published. Formerly named Richard Alpert and a professor at Harvard University, Dass experimented with hallucinogenic drugs and personal transformation and studied Hinduism in India. The book, which brings Hindu beliefs to the attention of many Westerners, is viewed by some experts as marking the emergence of the New Age movement.   HIND, SPIR

1972   In Bangladesh (formerly East Pakistan), the new constitution establishes the nation as a secular state and bans political activity by religious groups, an effort to control the influence of Muslim fundamentalists.   ISLAM

1972   President Ferdinand Marcos of the Philippines proclaims martial law in reaction to demands for independence by Muslims who live mainly on the island of Mindanao in the southern Philippines.   ISLAM

1972   In Malaysia the pro-Muslim Pan-Malayan Islamic Party changes it name to the Partai Islam, drops its demand for the institution of Islamic law and other reforms that favor the Muslims, and joins forces with the United Malay National Organization, the dominant party, which favors cooperation among the Malay, Chinese, and Indian communities. Other Islamic movements and parties appear including the *dakwah*, the Malay Muslim Youth League, the Darul Arqam, and the Tabligh.   ISLAM

1972	Sally J. Priesand is ordained as the first Jewish (Reform) woman rabbi in the United States. **JUD**

1972   Sally J. Priesand is ordained as the first Jewish (Reform) woman rabbi in the United States.   JUD

1972   The United States returns Mount Adams, Washington, to the Yakima peoples. The Yakima consider the mountain to be sacred. It had been placed within Gifford Pinchot National Forest some 70 years earlier.   NATIV

1972   The United Methodist Church in the United States sets forth a statement of social principles in which it accepts racial and ethnic diversity and establishes programs to address the needs of ethnic minorities. The statement also accepts homosexuality but does not condone it.   PROT

1972   In the United States several large Presbyterian churches leave the United Presbyterian Church and form the smaller Presbyterian Church in America, which adheres to traditional Presbyterian beliefs and practices. As a conservative branch of Presbyterianism, it draw many adherents in the next two decades.   PROT

1972   In *Wisconsin v. Yoder* the United States Supreme Court rules that Amish children do not have to attend high school. The decision is a victory for the Amish who want to raise their children in Amish communities and see attendance at high schools outside the community as a threat to Amish cultural survival.   SECT

1972   The Servants of the Light is founded by W. E. Butler (1889–1978) in New Jersey. It is a spiritualist group that stresses healing, personal spirituality, and the Kabbalah (Jewish mysticism). With some 2,000 adherents, it is one of the more successful modern spiritual sects.   SPIR

1972   In Uganda Asians, who are mainly Indian Hindus and Pakistani Muslims, are expelled by the government of Idi Amin and their property confiscated. About 75,000 people are forced to leave, and many immigrate to Great Britain and the United States. Several thousand return in the late 1980s. Asians are not forced to leave other East African nations, such as Kenya, although many do so in the 1970s due to discrimination.   TOL

1972   In the United States the National Academy of Sciences and the American Association for the Advancement of Science issue statements objecting to the teaching of religious beliefs as science and to the teaching of creationism as an alternative to biological evolution.   TOL

1972   The Institute for Creation Research is founded in California to study, write about, and speak about creation science. Through the writings of staff members such as Duane Gish (*Evolution: The Fossils Say No!*, 1974), the institute becomes a major proponent of the teaching of creation science as an alternative to biological evolution.   TOL

1973   The Sacred Congregation for the Doctrine of the Faith of the Catholic Church examines and criticizes the writings of Swiss Catholic theologian Hans Küng, which question the doctrine of papal infallibility. The attention given to Küng's ideas is considered by some to be an effort by the Church hierarchy to limit reform and control liberal ideas.   CATH

1973   Golda Meir becomes the first prime minister of Israel to visit the Vatican and meet with the pope.   CATH, JUD

1973   A thaw develops in the relationship between the Roman Catholic Church and the Church of England when a joint commission suggests that there is common ground in various teachings and practices of the churches.   CATH, PROT

1973   In his Easter message Pope Paul VI condemns the fighting in Northern Ireland and labels it Christian fratricide, as it involves Protestants and Catholics.   CATH, PROT

1973   The Bible is first translated into Belorussian.   CHRIS

1973   The Catholic Pentecostal conference at Notre Dame University, which began in 1968, attracts some 22,000 Pentecostal Catholics from 10 nations as more Catholics are attracted to the New Pentecostal movement. In 1974 it continues to grow and 30,000 people attend.   EVAN

1973   In Britain the number of Muslims has increased significantly due to the settlement of people from former British colonies and territories in the Middle East, North Africa, and Asia, and work begins on a large mosque in Regent's Park in London.   ISLAM

1973   In Indonesia the United Development Party is established as a Muslim political party and absorbs smaller, more reformist parties. The United Party supports the government and policies that support Islam as a religion and the religion of most Indonesians but limit Muslim political influence.   ISLAM

1973   In Nigeria the Islamic Council for Nigeria is established to represent Muslim interests. Nigeria has a large Muslim population who live mainly in the north and they campaign for the use of Islamic law and a Muslim education system but are resisted by Christians in the south and other Muslims who prefer a limited role for Islam in Nigerian society.   ISLAM

1973   In Pakistan Islam is the made the state religion. Although Muslims account for 97 percent of the population, since Pakistan became a nation in 1947 there had been debate about the role of Islam in Pakistani society.   ISLAM, TOL

1973   In Leicester, England, the founding of a Jain association that will become known as the Jain Samaj reflects the rising numbers of Jain immigrants in England.   JAIN

1973   Conservative Jews in the United States decide that women may be counted when assembling the 10 adults necessary for certain rituals of worship. Reform Jewish rabbis in the United States declare their opposition to performing mixed marriages but allow each Reform rabbi to make the actual decision for him or herself.   JUD

1973   The Yom Kippur War begins in October when Egypt and Syria attack Israel on the Jewish Day of Atonement. After initial successes by the Egyptian and Syrian forces, Israel drives them back and pushes into the territory of both nations. In 1974 Israel returns much of the territory it captured to Egypt and Syria.   JUD

1973   The Templeton Foundation, founded by British investor Sir John Marks Templeton, issues its first annual Templeton Prize for Progress in Religion. Over the years the award is given to religious figures such as Evangelical preacher Billy Graham, Catholic nun Sister Teresa, and others such as political scientist Michael Novak.   MISC

1973   In order to better train its missionaries, the Mormon Church develops a plan to build a missionary training center in Provo, Utah. The center opens in 1978.   MOR

1973   Wounded Knee II, also known as the Wounded Knee Takeover, takes place between February and May in South Dakota. About 200 Indians take over Sacred Heart Catholic Church, a trading post, and a museum near the mass grave at Wounded Knee on the Pound Ridge Sioux Reservation in South Dakota. SEE **1990**, NATIV.   NATIV

1973   An International Teaching Center of the Baha'i religion is founded.   SECT

1973   The Baha'is Under the Provisions of the Covenant (BUPC) is founded in Montana by expelled Baha'i member Leland Jensen, who attracts some former prisoners as members. It is a prophetic apocalyptic movement in which Jensen makes numerous predictions about catastrophes and the end of the world. SEE **1980**, SECT.   SECT

1973   The Christian widow of a Japanese Self-Defense Force soldier who was accidentally killed refuses to permit his enshrinement in Yamaguchi Prefecture's *Gokuku jinja* (Nation-Protecting Shrine). The prefectural veterans' association has been sponsoring such apotheosis rites since 1964 and carries out this enshrinement over her protests. A lower court will grant her an award in the amount of one million yen, which will be upheld by the appeals court. In 1988 the Japanese supreme court will overturn the decision. The case exposes the close relation between the Shinto shrines and regional public associations.   SHINTO

1973   Japan's emperor and empress make a pilgrimage to Ise and revive *kenji doza*, a Shinto ritual performed on the occasion of the emperor's travels, which has been abolished since the war. This is the year of Ise's 60th ritual rebuilding, and the emperor's third daughter serves as Ise's cult priestess. Another new religion arises with the founding of *Ryugu Kazoku* (Dragon Palace Family) by Fujita Himiko, also known as Mother Otohime, who foresees the coming new age of the goddess.   SHINTO

1973   A survey conducted by the United Nations shows that astrology is popular around the world, with 50 percent of the newspapers in the United States and many Western European nations running daily astrology columns.   SPIR

1973   The Raelian movement is founded in France by French journalist Claude Vorilhon (Rael). It is a New Age, spiritual, personal growth movement whose belief system is based on revelations Rael says he has received from extraterrestrial beings who have visited him on earth.   SPIR

1973   With the end of the "Whites Only" policy in Australia, immigration is opened to people from Asia, and Indian Hindus and Muslims, as well as Southeast Asian Muslims and Buddhists, settle in Australia.   TOL

1973   In *Roe v. Wade* the United States Supreme Court rules that laws restricting abortion during the first six months of pregnancy are unconstitutional. Although the decision does not address religion directly, the ruling is protested by many fundamentalist Protestants and many Roman Catholics, who view abortion as a violation of their religious beliefs.   TOL

1973–   A campaign by China's Communist government attacks Confucius and
1974   Confucian thought as reactionary and praises the first emperor of the Qing dynasty, Shunzhi, long vilified because he was a Manchu. Disgraced officials, such as the former defense minister Lin Biao, are stigmatized as "the Confuciuses of contemporary China."   CONF, TOL

1974   The Dreads of Dominica in the Caribbean, an offshoot of Rastafarianism in Jamaica, are banned by new government laws that restrict the activities of certain types of organizations.   AFRICAN

1974   In France the National Assembly legalizes abortion, despite the opposition of the Catholic Church.   CATH

1974   Lutheran and Roman Catholic theologians in the United States discuss relations between their churches and agree that the papacy occupies a central role in Christianity but that it will need to undergo major reform before it can serve as the central authority for all Christian religions.   CATH, PROT

1974   In Ireland the four main churches (Roman Catholic, Presbyterian, Anglican, and Methodist) hold services for peace to end the fighting in Northern Ireland between Protestants and Catholics.   CATH, PROT

1974   *Theology of Liberation* is written by Peruvian priest Gustavo Guttierrez. It an important and influential statement in the Liberation Theology movement in Latin America in which some Christian clergy argue that the church has a responsibility to work for basic societal changes that will end poverty and inequality.   CHRIS

1974   The Lausanne Congress of World Evangelization is held. The Congress emphasizes the uniqueness of Christianity and notes the importance of social justice but does not advocate a role for missionaries in creating social change.   CHRIS

1974   In China Confucianism is again criticized by the government and Confucius is called the "forefather of all reactionaries."   CONF

1974   In New York City the former Jain monk Gurudev Shree Chitrabhanu founds New Life Now, an organization dedicated to the spiritual illumination of the West; eventually this will become the Jain Meditation International Center. Chitrabhanu had been a well-known and respected Jain monk in his native India, where in 1965 he founded the Divine Knowledge Society in Bombay. In 1971 he abandons the monastic life, marries a disciple, and visits the United States to participate in a conference at Harvard University; he stays in North America to lecture to other Jains, then decides to settle in the United States to advance the Jain message among non-Indians as well as Indians.   JAIN

1974   The Hasidic Jewish Lubavitch movement in the United States begins efforts on college campuses to bring secular Jewish students back into the fold of Orthodox Judaism. Also in this year, the first Reconstructionist Jewish woman rabbi is ordained in the United States.   JUD

1974   Thousands of Falasha (Ethiopian Jews) flee to Sudan and are airlifted over the next 11 years to Israel by the Israeli government.   JUD

1974   Mormon Church leaders call for all young Mormon men to be involved in missionary work, and Mormon missionary activity increases greatly, with missionaries in most parts of the world.   MOR

1974   In Great Britain the House of Commons votes to allow the General Synod of the Church of England to make changes in the prayer book and in forms of worship, so long as they are in accord with basic church doctrine. The vote is contrary to previous policy which upheld the primacy of the *Book of Common Prayer*. Parliament also ends a 300-year ban on a Roman Catholic serving as lord chancellor.   PROT

1974   In South Africa the separatist *Nederduitse Gereformeerde Kerk* (NGK) Dutch Reformed Church issues *Human Relations and the South African Scene in the Light of Scripture*, which offers a religious justification for apartheid.   PROT

1974   Old Order Amish in Pennsylvania begin publishing the weekly paper *Die Botschaft* (the *Message*) as an alternative to the weekly *Budget*, published since 1890 in Ohio. The *Message*, controlled by the Old Order Amish, is more conservative and controls unwanted advertising and the publication of letters from shunned community members who are not allowed to interact with other Amish. **SECT**

1974   The Guru Bawa Fellowship is founded in the United States by Muhaiyaddeen M. R. Bawa, a self-proclaimed Sufi Muslim from Sri Lanka. The movement seeks to create unity among people and with God by continuing the teachings of great religious figures such as Moses, Jesus, and Muhammad. **SECT**

1974   The Citizens Freedom Foundation is founded in the United States as a central organization to coordinate the anticult activities of the many small, local anticult organizations that have emerged in the early 1970s. In 1985 its name is changed to the Cult Awareness Network and it remains active until 1995, when it declares bankruptcy following a lawsuit by Pentecostal Christians. **SECT**

1974   Conservative leaders of Japan's established and new religions will unite to form *Nihon o Mamoru Kai*, an association to defend Japan and to support political reactionaries opposed to the postwar democratic reforms. **SHINTO**

1974   Osho International, a personal and spiritual growth movement, is founded in Poona, India, by Rajneesh (1931–1990), an Indian philosophy professor. **SPIR**

1974   Henry M. Morris, the president of the Creation Research Society in the United States, writes a manual for high school biology teachers called *Scientific Creationism*. Its publication marks the beginning of an effort that continues in the 1990s to teach creation science rather than creationism as an alternative to biological evolution. Creation science makes no reference to the Bible or other religious sources. **TOL**

1975   Elijah Muhammad, the leader of the Nation of Islam in the United States, dies and is replaced by one of his sons, Wallace Deen Muhammad, who revises movement doctrine and refuses to condemn whites, an action that leads to factionalism. **AFRICAN**

1975   Advocates of Liberation Theology in Latin America and Black Theology in the United States begin discussing common ground among the movements. The emphasis on oppression and liberation in the former movement influences the latter. **AFRICAN**

1975   As part of its continuing dialogue on relations with other religions, the Roman Catholic Church issues its *Guidelines and Suggestions for Relations with Judaism*. The document acknowledges that Judaism is a living, evolving religion and asks Catholics to combat anti-Semitism. **CATH, JUD**

1975   Anglican and Roman Catholic theologians in Great Britain discuss relations between their churches and agree that Christianity may benefit from centralized authority in the papacy, but that the papacy would need major reform and that major theological differences exist between the two churches.

CATH, PROT

1975   In an effort to further ecumenicism, Catholic and Protestant theologians write the *Common Catechism*, which sets forth areas of agreement and disagreement among the churches.   CHRIS

1975   In Lebanon civil war breaks out, pitting Maronite Christians against Muslims and Druze, and rightist militants against Palestinian guerrillas and other leftist Arab forces. The conflict lasts until 1990. Among the issues is a Muslim desire for greater representation in the government, which by a 1943 agreement is controlled by the Christians.   CHRIS, ISLAM

1975   The New Pentecostal movement receives official support from the Roman Catholic Church when 10,000 Catholic Pentecostalists from 50 nations meet in Rome and Pope Paul VI indicates support.   EVAN

1975   The Tennessee Supreme Court upholds a state law that bans the handling of snakes and the drinking of poison in the state in a case that is brought by Evangelical Christians who practice snake handling and who bring the case to the court to test its constitutionality. SEE **1976,** EVAN.   EVAN

1975   In Somalia the government that came to power through a military coup in 1966 moves to end the influence of Islam and to create a national state based on socialism. As nearly all Somalis are Muslims, the effort to control Islam is only partially successful.   ISLAM

1975   Libyan leader Mu'aamar Qadhaffi (1938–) begins publishing his *Green Book,* which promulgates his idea that a return to the basics of Islam as set forth in the Qur'an should be the basis of the Libyan state.   ISLAM

1975   The United Nations General Assembly passes Resolution 3379 equating Zionism with racism. SEE **1989,** JUD, TOL.   JUD, TOL

1975   The issue of exorcism comes to public attention in Britain when a man in Yorkshire who had been exorcised is acquitted of killing his wife on grounds of insanity. Following the trial exorcism is banned by the bishop.

PROT, SPIR

1975   In Great Britain the British Humanist Association seeks to substitute teaching about religion for the teaching of religion in the schools.   PROT, TOL

1975   Japan's Liberal Democratic Party (LDP) reveals its Memorial Respect Proposal, a plan to legislate formal visits to Yasukuni shrine by the emperor and prime minister; the plan is supported by many conservative Shinto leaders. On August 15, the anniversary of the World War II surrender, Prime Minister Miki Takeo pays tribute at Yasukuni in the first such postwar visit by a prime minister. Since 1945 nearly all LDP prime ministers have attended Yasukuni's spring and fall festivals. Vigorous debates in the Diet question the details of apparently official visits by the cabinet: whether a public or private car was used, whether the tribute was funded from private or public funds, and whether the shrine registry signature included an official title. **SHINTO**

1975   *The Complete Art of Witchcraft* by Sybyl Leek, a British neopagan witch, is published and becomes a major guide for those interested in neopaganism.
SPIR

1975   *A Course in Miracles*, purported to be communications from Jesus Christ received by psychologist Helen Schucman (?–1981) between 1965 and 1972, becomes a major text for New Age adherents. In the New Age movement, the basic purpose of channeling is altered from communicating with spiritual masters to gain knowledge and insight to a process through which individuals can experience personal emotional and spiritual growth. **SEE 1992, SPIR.**   **SPIR**

1975   The Covenant of the Goddess is founded in California to serve as a national organization for witch groups in the United States, although it fails to gain all independent Wicca and pagan groups as members.   **SPIR**

1975   In the Soviet Union laws dating to 1929 that govern religion are amended, primarily by recognizing the authority of the Council for Religious Affairs to manage all religious issues in the Soviet Union.   **TOL**

1975   In Egypt the Supreme Constitutional Court rules that only Chritianity, Islam, and Judaism are protected by the constitution. This ruling subjects adherents of other religions such as Baha'i to discrimination and repression.   **TOL**

1975   In Vietnam, at the end of the Vietnam War, the Communist government unifies the north and south and represses all expressions of religion. Religion is seen as a hindrance to its ideology.   **TOL**

1975–   *The Turner Diaries*, written by former physics professor William L. Pierce
1978   (although the listed author is Andrew MacDonald), is published in serial form and then as a book in 1978. The book sets forth two major ideas of the Christian Identity movement—resistance to the government and creation of an Aryan nation—and becomes a major text for the movement.
SECT

1975–   The Khmer Rouge, a Communist group, seizes control of Cambodia. Led by
1979   Pol Pot, they proceed immediately to persecute Cambodians of all religions. Buddhists especially are singled out; many of their monasteries are destroyed and some 60,000 Buddhist monks are driven out or simply massacred.
BUDD, TOL

1976   In Bangladesh tribal peoples in southeastern Chittagong Hill Tracts, mostly Buddhists of Tibetan descent, begin a guerrilla campaign against government resettlement of Bengali Muslims in the hill region. Army and Muslim settlers are targeted and 3,500 people killed in a campaign that continues through the late 1990s.   **BUDD, TOL**

1976   The Roman Catholic Church issues a declaration stating again that women may not be ordained as priests. The Church cites Jesus Christ's practice of not involving women in the Church as the reason for its continuing restrictions on women. The limited role afforded women is supported later by Pope Paul II's encyclical *On the Dignity of Women*, which stresses their role as mothers.   **CATH**

1976   The Ecumenical Association of Third World Theologians is founded. The organization brings together Christian theologians from Africa, Asia, and Latin America and becomes an important forum for the idea that Christian theology must reflect the societal context in which it exists. For Third World nations this context includes poverty, oppression, and the quest for freedom.   **CHRIS**

1976   *Liberation of Theology* is written by Uruguayan priest J. L. Segundo. It is an influential book within the Liberation Theology movement in Latin America and provides a model for applying Christian theology to problems of social inequality in Latin America.   **CHRIS**

1976   In an effort to further ecumenicism, the Churches' Unity Commission, composed of Catholics and Protestants, issues *Visible Unity: Ten Propositions*. The propositions are not accepted by all churches, but most agree to continue discussing areas of common interest and agreement.   **CHRIS**

1976   Renewed interest in Confucianism is evident in China following the death of Communist Party chairman Mao Zedong. The impact of foreign capitalism leads to the fading of ideological Marxism and a renewed emphasis on classic Confucian values of discipline, thrift, and task orientation, which harmonizes well with the capitalist sensibility.   **CONF**

1976   The United States Supreme Court refuses to hear an appeal of a case decided by the Tennessee State Supreme Court that upholds a Tennessee law banning snake handling in religious services, a practice engaged in by some Evangelicals in the state.   **EVAN**

1976   In China the repression of Islam that began in 1966 and then lessened in the 1970s ends and Muslims are allowed to reopen mosques and practice Islam. However, in the western regions where there are large numbers of Muslims, they are given only limited political power.   **ISLAM**

1976   The Entebbe rescue takes place in Uganda on July 3 when Israeli commandos rescue Israeli hostages held on a plane hijacked by pro-Palestinian terrorists in June and flown to Entebbe, Uganda.   **JUD**

1976	In Mozambique Jehovah's Witnesses are expelled and forced to flee to Malawi. They are accused by the Mozambique government of being agents of the secret police. **SECT**

1976   The Jehovah's Witnesses are banned in Indonesia as a threat to national unity. **SECT**

1976   Japanese ceremonies honoring the 50th anniversary of Emperor Hirohito's rule are conducted on a grand scale, as the right-wing movement to restore the imperial system reaches a new stage. In Kitakami City, Iwate Prefecture, the Christian minister Watanabe Hironao protests the fact that the ward tax includes funds for the support of the nation-protecting Shinto shrine. **SHINTO**

1976   Sikhs in Great Britain are exempted from the requirement of wearing safety helmets on motorcycles in Great Britain when Parliament passes the Motor-Cycle Crash Helmets (Religious Exemption) Act in response to Sikhs who complain that they cannot wear both the turban required by religious belief and the helmet. The law is used as a basis for exempting Sikhs from wearing other types of special headgear such as construction helmets. **SIKH**

1976   The Fellowship of Isis is founded in Ireland. It is a neopagan movement that stresses both Celtic and ancient Egyptian religious practices and the worship of goddesses. **SPIR**

1976   In Libya a conference of representatives of Islam, Roman Catholicism, and some Orthodox and Protestant churches is held to find common ground and to address issues of mutual concern. The delegates agree on several doctrinal issues but divide over political ones, such as European colonialism, Israel, and Zionism. **TOL**

1976   Conflict breaks out in East Timor, in Southeast Asia, which seeks independence following the end of Portuguese rule and which Indonesia seeks to incorporate as a province. Most East Timorese are Roman Catholics, while Indonesians are mainly Muslims, and the Catholic Church supports independence. **TOL**

1976   In Vietnam the government takes control of all religious colleges and universities, including those run by Catholics and Buddhists. The action is part of the government program to control Vietnamese society following the Vietnam War and the reunification of Vietnam. **TOL**

1977   The Ecumenical Association of African Theologians is founded in Accra, Ghana. It becomes the major institutional center for efforts by Protestants to develop their own African-based Christian theologies. **AFRICAN**

1977   The United States Catholic Bishops issue a public statement apologizing for Catholic mistreatment of Native Americans. **CATH, NATIV**

1977   The Anglican–Roman Catholic Commission recommends that the Anglican Church accept the pope as the head of the Church and also recommends changes in ordination services as steps toward unification of the two churches.   CATH, PROT

1977   In Egypt the first serious conflict in several decades between Coptic Christians and Muslims takes place. The Copts have ordered a four-day protest against the revival of fundamental Islam and attempt to replace secular law with Islamic law.   CHRIS, ISLAM

1977   Official opposition to Confucianism by the Chinese Communist government ends.   CONF

1977   In India the Janata Party, formed by Hindu nationalist Jana Sangh, with other parties opposed to the rule of the Congress Party, defeat the Congress Party in parliamentary elections. However, they fail to form a government, and in 1980 the Congress Party is returned to power.   HIND

1977   In India the Supreme Court rules that the right awarded by the constitution to propagate religion does not give a person the right to convert others to one's own religion. The decision is a victory for Hindus who object to conversion efforts by other religions among the Hindu majority in India.   HIND, TOL

1977   On November 2 and 3 President Anwar al-Sadat visits Israel and addresses the Knesset (Israeli parliament). It is the first visit by the leader of an Arab nation and it is subsequently seen as an early and important step in the resulting peace treaty between Egypt and Israel.   JUD

1977   In the Soviet Union, for the first time since 1917, the government allows prayer books from the United States to be shipped to Jewish congregations in Russia.   JUD

1977   The Mormon Church receives government recognition in Poland.   MOR

1977   *The Sacred Ways of Knowledge: Sources of Life* by Peggy V. Beck and Anna Walters is published. Compiled as part of Navajo Community College's program on Native American healing, it serves as a text on Native American religious and healing beliefs. A new edition is published in 1990.   NATIV

1977   The Coalition for Better Television is founded by Christian fundamentalist Donald Wildmon (1938–) in Mississippi for the purpose of monitoring and influencing the content of television shows so that they contain content suitable for a family audience. In the same year the Focus on the Family organization is founded by psychologist and radio program host James Dobson. The organization embraces conservative Christian values, including opposition to homosexuality and abortion and support for public support of religious schools and school prayer. It remains active in the 1990s in setting the agenda for conservative officials.   PROT

1977   The Synanon Foundation, an organization founded in 1950 and involved in the treatment of alcohol and drug addictions, declares the establishment of the Synanon religion. Its basic doctrines include a belief that unity in the world will be eventually achieved and that individuals should support the Synanon community. **SECT**

1977   The Universal Church of the Kingdom of God is established by Edir Macedo in Brazil as an Evangelical church in opposition to the Roman Catholic Church. The church spreads rapidly throughout South America and becomes wealthy and influential primarily through contributions made by members. **SECT**

1977   Japan's Liberal Democratic Party, in order to consolidate the support of religious organizations, forms a group for the study of religion and politics (*Shukyo seiji kenkyu Kai*); it will be strongly influenced by the new religion Seicho no Ie, which seeks to strengthen the emperor's position. Meanwhile, a Supreme Court verdict declaring that in the 1965 Tsu case a Shinto ritual was secular, rather than religious, leads the government to increase its Yasukuni shrine patronage in the belief that the Tsu decision now permits formal cabinet tributes there. **SHINTO**

1977   In Japan the Supreme Court overturns the 1971 Nagoya High Court decision that banned the use of public funds for Shinto rites. The Supreme Court views Tsu's rite as secular and hence declares the use of the funds as constitutional. This finding will greatly encourage the movement to restore state Shinto. **SHINTO**

1977   In the United States the Church of Scientology, Unification Church, and the Children of God found the Alliance for the Preservation of Religious Liberty. All three groups have been criticized and at times investigated and charged by the government with being profit-making entities rather than religions. **TOL**

1977   In Pakistan, under the rule of General Zia, an Islamization policy is enacted with non-Muslim participation in government limited, Islamic law established as the law of the nation, the education system required to teach Islam, and the press required to support Islam. **TOL**

1977   Following the end of the Cultural Revolution in China, the government embarks on a new policy concerning religion, with religious worship allowed so long as it does not interfere with the goals of the government. In general this means that many people are now able to worship openly, although fears of the harsh repression of religion that had been practiced since 1949 remain. Among the religions benefiting from this new tolerance are Daoism, Christianity, Islam, and Buddhism. **TOL**

1978   Louis Farrakhan (1933–), second in command of the Nation of Islam under Elijah Muhammad before the latter's death in 1975, breaks from the

1978   organization led by Muhammad's son Wallace and reforms the Nation of Islam in accord with Muhammad's beliefs in African-American separatism and nationalism.   **AFRICAN**

1978   The Congress of National Black Churches is established in Washington, D.C., to coordinate the interests of and provide social services for major organized African-American churches.   **AFRICAN**

1978   *Black Theology, Black Power* is written by Allan Aubrey Boesek, a leader of the Dutch Reformed Church in South Africa and a man of mixed black and white ancestry. The book urges blacks to redefine God and Christ in a black context as a means of liberation from white rule.   **AFRICAN**

1978   On August 6 Pope Paul VI dies at age 80 and is succeeded by Pope John Paul, who dies on September 28 of a heart attack. The College of Cardinals then elects Polish Cardinal Karol Jezef Wojtyla (1920–), who takes the name Pope John Paul II. He is the first non-Italian pope since Dutch Pope Adrian VI (r. 1522–1523).   **CATH**

1978   The Shroud of Turin, purported to show the body of Christ, is put on display at the Cathedral of Turin for the first time in 45 years. Although the origin of the shroud and the markings is unclear, it probably dates from the 14th century.   **CHRIS**

1978   The National Daoist Association resumes operation in China, with headquarters at the White Cloud Monastery in Beijing. Between 1978 and 1986 authorities in China return 21 monasteries to Daoist control.   **DAO**

1978   In Iran opposition to the shah grows. Issues include his autocratic rule, repressive use of the secret police (known as SAVAK), rapid Westernization at the expense of Islamic tradition, corruption, and American influence.   **ISLAM**

1978   A television miniseries, *Holocaust*, is broadcast on network television in the United States. Although a fictionalized account, it helps to heighten awareness of the plight of the Jews in Nazi-controlled Europe before and during World War II.   **JUD**

1978   With the overthrow of the shah in Iran and the coming to power of an Islamic government, Iranian Jews immigrate to Israel, Europe, and the United States.   **JUD**

1978   The Mormon Church allows all adult men to become priests. This opens the priesthood to men of African-American ancestry and allows for the expansion of the missionary effort.   **MOR**

1978   Wallace B. Smith, the great-grandson of Joseph Smith, the founder of Mormonism, becomes leader of the Reorganized Church of Jesus Christ of Latter-Day Saints and continues his predecessors' policy of revising church policy to align it with Protestantism and further distance it from the Mormon Church in Utah. **MOR**

1978 The United States Congress enacts the American Indian Religious Freedom Act. The act guarantees Eskimos, Aleuts, Native Americans, and native Hawaiians the right to practice their indigenous religions. **SEE 1988, NATIV.**

NATIV

1978 Archaeologists in Mexico uncover and, over the next five years, study the Mountain of the Serpent, the central Aztec temple of the capital city of Tenochtitlán now under Mexico City. The site provides thousands of ritual objects and examples of monumental religious architecture and points to the central role played by religion in unifying the Aztec Empire in the 15th and 16th centuries. **NATIV**

1978 The New International Version of the New American Standard Bible is published for use by conservative Protestants who question the authenticity of the Revised Standard Version of the King James Version. **PROT**

1978 The General Synod of the Church of England rejects a request that women be allowed to be ordained but recommends that some divorced adherents of the church be allowed to remarry in the church. **PROT**

1978 With the assistance of political consultants, the Christian fundamentalist minister Jerry Falwell (1932–) founds the Moral Majority. It is a social, political, and religious movement that seeks to restore what it perceives as traditional American values in accord with fundamental Christianity. **PROT**

1978 In Guyana 913 members of the People's Temple led by Jim Jones commit mass suicide by drinking poison. The reason for the suicide is unknown, although the cult had recently relocated from San Francisco and is being investigated by United States authorities and journalists for possible mistreatment or coercion of members. **SECT**

1978 In France L. Ron Hubbard and two members of the Church of Scientology are sentenced in absentia to prison and fined for fraud. In 1985 the church's tax-exempt status is removed on grounds that it is a profit-making organization. **SECT**

1978 Herbert W. Armstrong, founder and leader of the Worldwide Church of God, expels his son and expected successor, Garner Ted Armstrong, from the church. Garner Ted goes on to found his own radio, television, and magazine-based church, the Church of God International in Texas. **SECT**

1978 On National Foundation Day Japan's government for the first time encourages popular celebration rites commemorating the origin of the imperial state. In June Hokkaido's Asahikawa City carries out a formal tribute, with the participation of the prefectural governor, the mayor, and Self-Defense

1978	Force company, along with military music, to the local nation-protecting Shinto shrine. **SHINTO**
1978	Controversy erupts in Japan and in Asia as 14 convicted World War II criminals, including Tojo Hideki, are enshrined at Yasukuni as "martyrs of the Showa Era." In 1979 Prime Minister Ohira and several cabinet members make a "private visit" to pay tribute at the shrine. **SHINTO**
1978	The National Christian Action Coalition is founded in the United States. It is a fundamentalist Christian organization that is opposed to taxes and trains members to be more politically active. It closes in 1985 as its agenda has been largely taken over by the Moral Majority. **TOL**
1978	A scholarly conference convenes in Kunming, Yunnan Province, China, to study the long-forbidden subject of comparative religion. Papers are presented on Daoism, Buddhism, Islam, and Christianity. **TOL**
1978	In Sri Lanka the constitution affords special status, including state support, for Buddhism and provides for the freedom of expression of other religions including Hinduism, Christianity, and Islam. **TOL**
1978	In Spain the constitution bans a state religion and establishes freedom of religion. **TOL**
1978	The creationism movement in the United States begins shifting its approach from teaching the biblical version of creation in public schools to one based on teaching creation science as a scientific theory entitled to be taught alongside the theory of biological evolution. This approach is set forth by Yale University law student Wendell R. Bird (1954–). **TOL**
1979	*Toward an African Theology* is written by Ghanaian Anglican theologian John S. Pobee (1937–). The book sets forth the goal of establishing Christian churches in Africa that reflect indigenous African culture and history. **AFRICAN**
1979	The Baptist Ministers Conference of Baltimore, an organization of black Baptist churches, allows women to serve as pastors for the first time. In other black Baptist churches, the official role of women is limited and very few are allowed to serve as pastors. **AFRICAN**
1979	At the Puebla Conference of Latin American Bishops in Mexico, Pope John Paul II addresses the meeting regarding the role of the Church and its priests and bishops in working to end social inequality in the region. He condemns poverty and torture but also speaks of placing limits on Church activity in politics. **CATH**
1979	Pope John Paul II visits Poland and provides symbolic support for the emerging Solidarity movement that opposes Communist rule. He makes two more

visits in future years, and in 1987 provides moral support for the weakening movement that in 1989 nonetheless topples the Communist regime.   CATH

1979   Swiss Roman Catholic theologian Hans Küng is barred from teaching as an official representative of the Church. The Church has been examining his reformist and liberal writings since early in the decade and its ban is seen as an effort to control liberal dissent in the Church.   CATH

1979   Mother Teresa (1910–1997), a Catholic nun who founded the Missions of Charity in India and has devoted her life to working with the poor and sick in India, is awarded the Nobel Peace Prize.   CATH, MISC

1979   In India a bill is introduced designed to limit the freedom of non-Hindus to convert people in India to their religions. The bill is aimed at the activities of Christian missionaries and when Christians object strongly it is withdrawn. Hindus also attempt to assert their influence by attempting to ban the slaughter of cattle across India. Hindus do not east beef, although others in India, including Muslims and Christians, do.   CHRIS, HINDU

1979   In Australia a major religious revival among members of the Aboriginal Christian Uniting Church is led by Aboriginal minister Djiniyini Gondarra (1945–). The revival focuses on combining Christian and Aboriginal beliefs and practices, creating Aboriginal unity, and bringing justice and freedom to Aboriginals in Australia.   CHRIS, TOL

1979   Four hundred Evangelical Christian organizations in the United States form the Evangelical Council for Financial Accountability to establish standards for fund-raising and financial management by Evangelical groups. As the 400 are less than 25 percent of the total number of such groups in the United States, the organization has limited influence.   EVAN

1979   In Iran Shah Reza Pahlavi goes into exile, and after months of political unrest, Ayatollah Ruhollah Khomeini (1900–1989) takes control. Following a national referendum he proclaims Iran an Islamic republic. The Islamic cultural revolution under Khomeini brings a return to strict observance of Muslim beliefs and practices.   ISLAM

1979   In Saudi Arabia Islamic militants who are opposed to government modernization policies and ties to the West seize the Grand Mosque in Mecca, with some 160 people killed.   ISLAM

1979   In Egypt Muslim fundamentalists criticize the Coptic Christians, demand an end to state support for the Copts, and attack Copts and their property. The government responds by both criticizing the Muslims and removing Copts from high-level government positions.   ISLAM

1979   In Iraq a group called the Muslim Warriors is formed by opponents of the Ba'th Party, which rules the nation, and as an advocate for Islamic fundamentalism. The movement is repressed by the government.   **ISLAM**

1979   On March 26 the Israel-Egypt peace treaty is signed by Prime Minister Begin of Israel and President Sadat of Egypt in Washington, D.C. The treaty provides for the withdrawal of Israeli forces from Sinai over a three-year period and for further negotiations concerning autonomy and the future status of Arab residents of the West Bank and the Gaza Strip, territories still under Israeli occupation. Israel withdraws from the Sinai oil fields within a year and from the remainder of Sinai by April 25, 1982. However, the two countries fail to reach agreement on Palestinian autonomy in the West Bank and Gaza, and Israel continues to establish Jewish settlements in the West Bank despite Egyptian protests.   **JUD**

1979   *The Man-Eating Myth* is written by anthropologist William Arens. In the book he questions the belief that there have been in modern times cultures that routinely practiced cannibalism and concludes that no such culture has ever existed. Although other experts question the complete absence of cannibalism for religious reasons, they do revise their thinking and agree that routine cannibalism for religious purposes is extremely rare.   **MISC**

Ayatollah Khomeini

Ayatollah al-Uzma Sayyid Ruhollah Musavi Khomeini was a leading Shi'a Muslim scholar, religious leader, and political leader of the 20th century. He was a leader of the Islamic revolution, which ended the rule of the shah of Iran in 1979, and he led Iran from 1979 until his death in 1989. Because of his opposition to the West, his role in the revolution, and his revitalization of fundamentalist Islam in Iran, he is considered by many Muslims to be one of the major Muslim figures of the 20th century. At the same time he is reviled in the United States and other Western nations. Khomeini was born in western Iran in 1900 and received his religious education and training in the holy city of Qom. As a teacher and religious scholar, he was best known for his work on Islamic mysticism. In 1944 he became involved in politics, calling for a return to Islamic law and openly criticizing the Pahlavi dynasty. In the early 1960s he was arrested, and in 1964 he was forced into an exile that lasted 14 years. By 1978, when the open revolt against the shah began, Khomeini was a widely respected religious and political leader and led the opposition from Iraq. In 1979 he returned to Iran to take over the government from the shah, who had fled two weeks earlier. Once in power he dealt with a number of major crises, including the taking and release of American hostages in 1979–1980, the war with Iraq from 1982 until 1988, the death sentence placed on the novelist Salman Rushdie for blasphemy, and disputes with political rivals. Even after his death in 1989 he remains a major figure in the Muslim world.

1979   In a report by United States government agencies that is required by the American Indian Religious Freedom Act, numerous government programs and policies that interfere with the practice of indigenous religions are noted and administrative reforms recommended.   **NATIV**

1979   The United States Congress enacts the Archaeological Resources Protection Act, which prevents looting of archaeological sites on Indian and government land. Included in the sites now protected are many Native American burial grounds, sacred sites, religious objects, and remains of ceremonial buildings.   **NATIV**

1979   The Medicine Men's Association is incorporated by Navajo religious specialists in Arizona to preserve Navajo religious objects and rituals.   **NATIV**

1979   In *Native American Church of New York v. United States,* the Supreme Court rules against drug use for religious purposes by the New York church, whose

---

Religious Right

The Religious Right or Christian Right is the name given to a number of organizations in the United States that have been at the forefront of a conservative religious, social, and political movement that began in the late 1970s and continues in the late 1990s. Among the major Religious Right organizations are the Moral Majority, the Liberty Council, and the Family Research Council. Although some other religions are represented, nearly all leaders and members of these and other Religious Right organizations are Christians and many are Southern Baptists. The purpose of the movement is to change American government and society by "putting God back in government," in the words of Reverend Pat Robertson, one of the leaders of the movement. The movement espouses a political and social agenda that is in accord with fundamental and evangelical Christianity. Major positions supported by the Religious Right are prayer in schools, a ban on abortion, restricted rights for homosexuals, tuition credits for private schools, less government control of schools, creationism, and policies to encourage the traditional nuclear family structure, with the husband working outside the home and the wife caring for the home and raising the children. The Religious Right has sought to see these policies implemented through public relations campaigns, lobbying of government officials, and supporting local, state, and federal candidates for public office. At times the groups have pursued civil lawsuits. Over the two decades of their existence, Religious Right organizations have changed both their strategies and their message, as by the late 1980s it became clear that they had not achieved the level of influence nor brought about the changes they desired. In the 1990s their rhetoric about morality and traditional Christian values has given way to a more secular approach that stresses individual liberty, freedom, and choice, and efforts have been made through advertisements and grassroots organizations to attract a broader range of members.

1979   members are mainly white and which is not affiliated with any Native American Church that uses peyote as a sacrament.   **NATIV, TOL**

1979   A clear division appears in the Southern Baptist Convention in the United States between the moderate and conservative factions. The Southern Baptist Convention is the largest Protestant denomination in the nation, with about 14 million members. The conservatives support a literal interpretation of the Bible, education in accord with that interpretation, and conservative social policies, such as a ban on abortion and school prayer. The president of the convention is a conservative, while the moderates control the convention bureaucracy.   **PROT**

1979   The Anglican Church in Britain releases an unpublished report prepared in the 1930s called *The Christian Parapsychologist,* which reveals church sympathy for spiritualism as a religious activity. Also this year, in an attempt to maintain Anglican traditions, hundreds of leading Anglicans in Britain call on the church to require use of the *Book of Common Prayer* and the Authorized Version of the Bible, which date to the 16th and 17th centuries. Use of the former has declined and revised versions of the latter have come into common use.   **PROT, SPIR**

1979   The new Islamist government in Iran represses Baha'i and Zoroastrianism and persecutes followers. Baha'i leaders are arrested and executed, property of individual members is confiscated, temples and schools are closed, and even Baha'i burial grounds are destroyed. Repression of Zoroastrians is less severe although they enjoy fewer rights than Muslims and some leave for the United States, Australia, and Britain. The repression continues into the 1990s.   **SECT**

1979   By this year in Japan, there are 82 Shinto sects, with some 5.6 million followers, which have developed from the original 13 sects. New Sect Shinto claims 48 other sects, with 2 million adherents. The previous year saw the emergence of two new religions: Agonshu, rooted in Japanese folk religion and founded by Kiriyama Seiyu; and Sukyo Mahikari, a splinter group of Mahikari, founded by Sekiguchi Sakae. In 1986 Okawa Ryuho will found the syncretist religion Kofuku no kagaku (Institute for Research in Human Happiness).   **SECT, SHINTO**

1979   *The Spiral Dance* is written by Starhawk (Miriam Simos, 1951–), a proponent of witchcraft in the United States. The book sets forth a feminist theology and model of religion that focuses on goddess worship.   **SPIR**

1979   The Religious Roundtable is founded in the United States to train fundamentalist Christians to become more involved in politics. It ceases to function after 1980.   **TOL**

1979   The Christian Voice is started in California. It is a fundamentalist Christian organization that opposes gay rights and issues "moral report cards" on members of Congress. It forms a lobbying branch to lobby Congress on such matters as abortion and governmental support for education. By 1986 the organization is of little importance in the Christian Right.   TOL

1979   The Concerned Women of America is founded in the United States to serve as a counterpoint to the feminist National Organization for Women. Concerned Women is a Religious Right organization.   TOL

1979   In Nigeria the constitution prohibits the establishment of a state religion and guarantees religious freedom. The provisions do not eliminate competition and conflict between Christians and Muslims.   TOL

1979   In Peru the government ends preferential treatment and patronage of the Roman Catholic Church, and in the next year the Roman Catholic Church in Peru becomes an independent organization.   TOL

1979   In Pakistan the Hadood Ordinances revise the penal code by adding provisions from the Shari'a (Islamic law).   TOL

1979–
1990   Vietnam invades Cambodia and drives Pol Pot and his Khmer Rouge into hiding. During the years it dominates Cambodia, Vietnam allows Buddhism to revive among the laity, various monastic orders reestablish themselves, and some monasteries and other Buddhist structures are rebuilt.   BUDD, TOL

1980   As part of the new religious tolerance in China, the Potala Palace in Lhasa, Tibet, the home of the Dalai Lama, who remains in exile in India, is reopened and Buddhists are again allowed to conduct pilgrimages to shrines and sites in Tibet.   BUDD

1980   Oscar Arenulfo Romero (1917–1980), archbishop of San Salvador, is assassinated while saying Mass, and several dozen mourners are killed and hundreds injured days later. The killing is one of dozens of Catholic clergy in El Salvador who are seen by the government as supporting the Sandinista rebels.   CATH

1980   In India the Bharatiya Janata Party is officially founded on a platform that supports Hindu nationalism and is opposed to Westernization of India as supported by the Congress Party.   HIND

1980   During the Iran-Iraq War from 1980 to 1988 the Kuwaiti government loans over $6 billion to Iraq at no interest. Members of Kuwait's large Shi'a Muslim minority support the Iranians, who are primarily Shi's Muslims and are alleged to engage in terrorism against the government.   ISLAM

1980   In China the Chinese Islamic Association begins to function openly again. It was founded in 1953 and banned in 1958.   ISLAM

1980   In Egypt, as part of the revival of Islam, the government sanctions reliance on Islamic law as the basis for new laws.   ISLAM

1980   The *Jain Study Circular*, a quarterly, is begun in United States to keep Jains in North America informed of their faith.   JAIN

1980   Argentinean Roman Catholic Bishop Adolofo Pérez Esquivel, founder of the Peace and Justice Service and critic of the Argentinean government's repression of political opponents, is awarded the Nobel Peace Prize.   MISC

1980   In the Anglican Church *The Alternative Prayer Book* is published and becomes the official prayer book for the church, replacing the *Book of Common Prayer*, although the latter remains in use.   PROT

1980   *Listen America!* is written by Jerry Falwell, the Baptist minister and founder of the Moral Majority. The book sets forth a fundamentalist Christian agenda regarding the family, marriage, homosexuality, abortion, evolution, and other social issues.   PROT

1980   The Baha'is Under the Provisions of the Covenant (BUPC) loses members and credibility when a prophecy of a nuclear catastrophe on April 29 fails to come true after members hide in fallout shelters. Subsequent prophecies by cult leader Leland Jensen over the next 15 years continue to prove false, although the several hundred members of the cult continue to believe that the world will end in the year 2000.   SECT

1980   Activist Shinto devotees celebrate the 90th anniversary of the Emperor Meiji's Imperial Rescript on Education. Those who want to nationalize the Yasukuni shrine organize local groups called *Eirei ni kotaeru kai* ("for the sake of heroic spirits"), to spread the movement to require the emperor and prime minister to worship at Yasukuni as "official acts" rather than as the current "private acts." In December the Legal Bureau of the Lower House of the Diet finds official tribute at Yasukuni to be in violation of the constitutional separation of church and state; this will not deter repeated attempts by the ruling Liberal Democratic Party to force the issue. The Union of New Religions begins withholding campaign contributions from those political candidates who favor state patronage of Shinto.   SHINTO, TOL

1980   The Rune Guild is founded in the United States as a neopagan movement focused on ancient Nordic religions and myths.   SPIR

1980   In China the government establishes the China Christian Council to control the distribution of the Bible.   TOL

1980   In Iran the constitution establishes the Islamic Republic of Iran with Islam the state religion and the shari'a (Islamic law) the law of the land. Although some religious freedom is afforded to Jews, Christians, and Zoroastrians, these groups, along with the Baha'i and Sunni Muslims, are persecuted.   TOL

1980   The scientific journal *Creation/Evolution* begins publication in the United States. It publishes articles by scientists designed to refute the scientific credibility of creation science.   **TOL**

1980   In the Soviet Union religious dissidents from the Baptist, Pentecostal, and Russian Orthodox churches are arrested or exiled to prevent the government from being embarrassed by protests staged during the Olympic Games. **TOL**

1980   In *Stone v. Graham* the United States Supreme Court rules that it is a violation of the First Amendment to the United States Constitution for the Ten Commandments to be posted in public classrooms.   **TOL**

1980s   In central Mexico Evangelical and Pentecostal Christian missionaries are successful in converting some people of indigenious lineage who had formerly been adherents of Roman Catholicism or a mix of Catholicism and traditional native religions.   **CHRIS, NATIV**

1980s   Mount Wudang, the Daoist holy place in northwest Hubei Province in China, is a training center for young Daoists. It is also a tourist attraction. **SEE 630, DAO.**   **DAO**

1980s   The third wave of the Pentecostal movement emerges in the United States. It is characterized by the incorporation of Pentecostal beliefs and practices into mainstream Protestant and Catholic churches but without the members of the churches becoming Pentecostalists.   **EVAN**

1980–
1987   These years are known as the golden age of televangelism in the United States. The most popular television preachers are Robert Schuller, Jimmy Swaggart, Oral Roberts, Rex Humbard, Jerry Falwell, Jim Bakker, Pat Robertson, and James Robison. All are Protestants, and the majority are Evangelicals. Although televangelism remains popular after 1987, it loses viewers and financial support due to scandals involving Bakker and Swaggart.   **PROT**

1981   Robert (Bob) Nesta Marley, the Jamaican reggae musician, dies. Since 1976 he had toured the world performing the reggae music closely associated with Rastafarianism. Through his vastly popular music, he helped to spread knowledge of Rastafarianism far beyond Jamaica to Europe, Asia, and Africa, as well as the Americas.   **AFRICAN**

1981   On May 13 Pope John Paul II is shot in an assassination attempt by Mehmet Ali Agca, a Turkish assassin believed to have been hired by anti-Catholic Bulgarians. The pope is seriously wounded and requires a three-month hospitalization to recover.   **CATH**

1981   In China the Roman Catholic Church appoints an archbishop of Guangdong, the first clergy appointed by the church in Rome since 1956. The appointment is rejected by the Chinese Patriotic Catholic Association, which is recognized by the government as the Catholic Church in China.

CATH, TOL

1981   In China tolerance of Islam continues with several new mosques opened, public prayer allowed during Ramadan, and the Qur'an translated into modern Chinese.   **ISLAM, TOL**

1981   In Bahrain a plot to overthrow the government is discovered. The instigators are said to be members of the Islamic Front for the Liberation of Bahrain, a Shi'a organization based in Iran. Iran has a long-standing claim to Bahrain and continues to support opposition movements in Bahrain.   **ISLAM**

1981   In Egypt President Anwar Sadat is assassinated in Cairo by four Muslim fundamentalists who are members of a radical group within the Muslim Brotherhood. They object to Sadat's peace initiative with Israel, ties to Western nations, and efforts to modernize Egypt. His successor, Muhammad Hosni Mubarak, continues Sadat's policies, imprisons and executes movement leaders, but also seeks to end religious strife by releasing many Islamic fundamentalists from prison.   **ISLAM**

1981   In Indonesia the Indonesian Student Association revises its position regarding the role of Islam in the nation and breaks with the government by suggesting that Islam should be the basis of Indonesian society and not simply a personal religion of the majority of Indonesians.   **ISLAM**

1981   The first North American Jain Conference is held at Berkeley, California. **JAIN**

1981   The Anglican Church in England approves remarriage for divorced members. Remarriage is already allowed in many dioceses outside of Britain. In 1983 the church establishes procedures, including an investigation of the marriage by a bishop and repentance, for remarriage in the church.   **PROT**

1981   The Salvation Army withdraws from the World Council of Churches, claiming that the council supports political movements. In question is financial support given to a group fighting apartheid in South Africa.   **PROT**

1981   In Britain a libel action brought by the Unification Church (Moonies) against the *Daily Mail* for reporting that the church uses mind control over followers and ruins families and that church founder Reverend Sun Myung Moon is wealthy ends in an acquittal for the paper.   **SECT**

1981   The *Etzba Elohim* (Finger of God) cult is founded by poet Rain Shine (born Rina Shomron, 1937–1983) in Israel. The cult stresses the use of marijuana and LSD to achieve mystical experiences and generally escapes government prosecution efforts. It ends with Shine's death in India in 1983.   **SPIR**

1981   Rajneesh moves his Osho International to rural Oregon, where he establishes a large commune and through the labor of followers acquires much wealth. The commune is called the "City of Rajneeshpuram."   SPIR

1981   The Freedom Council is developed by the Reverend Pat Robertson as a grassroots Religious Right organization. It is ineffective in building wide support for its conservative agenda and folds in 1989.   TOL

1981   The African Charter on Human and People's Rights is adopted by the member nations of the Organization of African Unity and goes into force after ratification in 1986. It affords individuals religious freedom.   TOL

1981   In Egypt the government seeks to control widespread opposition to its plan to modernize the nation. Some 1,500 Muslims, Coptic Christians, and other opponents are arrested, and the Coptic pope Shenuda III is stripped of his authority and replaced by a committee of five bishops. Muslim mosques are placed under government administration and Muslim preachers are required to resister with the government.   TOL

1981   The Declaration on the Elimination of All Forms of Intolerance and of Discrimination based on Religion or Belief is adopted by the General Assembly of the United Nations.   TOL

1981   The Universal Islamic Declaration of Human Rights is adopted by Islamic nations. It is similar to the United Nations Declaration of 1948 but is based on Islamic law as found in the Qur'an and *sunna*.   TOL

1981–   In Vietnam the government establishes government-controlled religious
1983   organizations for Buddhism, Catholicism, Protestantism, and other religions.   TOL

1982   A Buddhist Church of Vietnam is founded as the central organization of Buddhism in the nation. Its establishment suggests a weakening of government repression of religion, although other Buddhist churches report that their activities have been curtailed and some monks arrested by the government.   BUDD

1982   In May Pope John Paul II become the first Roman Catholic pope to visit Great Britain. He meets with the queen and the archbishop of Canterbury and calls for unity among all Christians. During the year he also visits Argentina and West Africa and meets with Yasir Arafat, the leader of the Palestine Liberation Organization.   CATH

1982   More than 200 churches, Protestant and Catholic, join the sanctuary movement in the United States. The churches help Salvadorans escape the conflict in their nation and provide them with shelter in the United States. The churches are criticized by the government, which believes they are acting in violation of United States immigration law.   CHRIS, TOL

1982	Billy Graham preaches to a mass audience in Moscow, Russia, as part of his international crusade to convert people to Evangelical Christianity. He conducts another service in Russia in 1984. **EVAN**
1982	In Algeria fundamentalist Muslims mount protests in support of an Islamic state. Protesters are arrested by government forces. **ISLAM**
1982	In Nigeria hundreds are killed in riots in the north that pit Muslim fundamentalists against other Muslims whom they perceive as too accepting of a Westernized version of Islam. **ISLAM**
1982	In Turkey the new constitution guarantees ethnic and religious minorities citizenship and equal rights. **ISLAM, TOL**
1982	Israel launches a military action against Palestinian and Syrian forces in southern Lebanon in order to make Israeli settlements in northern Israel secure from attack. There is opposition to the attack by some Israelis, who stage protest marches. In September Lebanese Christian forces kill hundreds of civilians and Israeli forces fail to stop the massacre. Israel is criti-

The Sanctuary Movement

The sanctuary movement began in the United States in May 1982 when churches began aiding and providing shelter to illegal immigrants from El Salvador and other Central American nations. The immigrants were viewed by the churches as political refugees who were fleeing political repression in their homelands and were likely to be imprisoned or killed if they returned home. This view was not shared by the United States Immigration and Naturalization Service (INS), which viewed the immigrants as illegal aliens who came to the United States to seek employment and were therefore not entitled to political protection. In addition, the sanctuary movement was viewed by the Reagan administration as a political protest against U.S. government policy in the region. By 1985 the movement had come to involve some 200 churches as well as the cities of Berkeley, Chicago, Cambridge, and New York, which also declared themselves as sanctuaries for political refugees from Central America. In that year the INS estimated that between 300,000 and 500,000 illegal El Salvadorans were in the United States and only about 30 percent of those who had been detained and targeted for deportation had actually left the country. In an effort to end the movement, the federal government arrested, tried, and convicted several ministers, priests, and nuns of illegally transporting and sheltering illegal aliens. The convictions had little effect on the movement, as churches continued to serve as sanctuaries. From the viewpoint of the churches, they were engaging in a practice dating to the fourth century C.E., when Christian churches in the Roman Empire began serving as safe havens for those accused of crimes under the belief that it would be a violation of their vows for church officials to turn these people over to the government. Since then churches have been seen as sanctuaries, although their authority has been severely limited by the power of the state.

cized at home and abroad and the government launches an investigation that in 1983 finds several senior officials indirectly responsible.   JUD

1982   The first edition of the *World Christian Encyclopedia* edited by religion scholar David Barrett is published. It is a massive compilation of statistics on Christian and other religions around the world and becomes a standard reference with updated editions published regularly thereafter.   MISC

1982   A Mexican journalist steals the *Tonalamatl Aubin*, an Aztec religious manuscript, from the National Library of France in Paris and brings it back to Mexico. Although the two governments argue over its ownership, it remains in the National Library in Mexico City.   NATIV

1982   The World Alliance of Reformed Churches issues a statement condemning apartheid. Several separatist churches in South Africa reject the statement.   PROT

1982   The white branch of the South African Dutch Reformed Church, which supports apartheid, is expelled from the World Reformed Alliance and apartheid is declared a heresy.   PROT

1982   On July 2 the Reverend Sun Myung Moon of the Unification Church conducts a mass marriage ceremony in which he marries 2,075 couples in New York City. Two weeks later Moon is convicted of income tax evasion in the United States and then serves 13 months in prison. Moon and his church have been under attack from individuals, organizations, and government agencies in Britain and the United States. Critics charge that followers are brainwashed, that they do not identify themselves with the church when collecting money, and that too much church money is invested in business enterprises. The government action is criticized by leaders of other religions and denominations who view it as an assault on the freedom of religion.   SECT, TOL

1982   In Japan seven prefectures make donations from public funds to Yasukuni shrine and to prefectural nation-protecting shrines, leading to civil suits by opposing citizens and religious leaders. Also in this year China, Taiwan, and Korea vigorously protest textbook revisions that minimize Japanese aggression of the 1930s and 1940s; despite a government promise to correct this problem, similar incidents will occur in 1986 and 1988.   SHINTO

1982   The Sikhs in Punjab, India, launch a violent movement for independence from India. The revolt is crushed by Indian troops.   SIKH

1982   President Ronald Reagan announces his support for an amendment to the Constitution calling for prayer in public schools.   TOL

1982   In China a new constitution drafted this year is similar to constitutions enacted in 1954, 1975, and 1978; it provides for a general freedom of belief but states that freedom is secondary to the four basic principles of the constitution, which support the creation of a socialist nation.   TOL

1982   In Turkey the constitution provides for religious freedom and prohibits the criticism of any religion. These measures relax the general prohibition on religion that began in 1924 when the government began to create a secular state.
                                                                                  TOL

1983   In acknowledgment of the 500th anniversary of Protestant reformer Martin Luther's birth, Pope John Paul II publicly praises Luther. Also during the year he acknowledges that the Church was wrong to condemn Galileo as a heretic in the 17th century. Both actions are seen as efforts by the Church to open itself to the non-Catholic world.   CATH

1983   In Ireland, a predominately Roman Catholic nation, voters support a referendum to make abortion illegal in the constitution. The ban is supported by Catholics but criticized by Protestants and Jews.   CATH, TOL

1983   The Daoist White Cloud Monastery reopens in Beijing, China's capital city, after restoration. The monastery becomes a popular tourist destination. DAO

1983   Hindu mobs in the state of Assam, India, attack Muslims from Bangladesh and West Bengal, killing at least 3,000 persons.   HIND, ISLAM

1983   The Chinese government relaxes its controls on the practice of Islam, the religion of over 10 million people mainly in western China, and the Institute of Islamic Theology is reopened in Beijing and copies of the Qur'an distributed.   ISLAM

1983   Al-Azhar University in Cairo, Egypt, celebrates 1,000 years of existence as the center for Muslim religious education and as the oldest continuously operating school in the world.   ISLAM

1983   The Sudanese government, which came to power through a military coup in 1969, begins to embrace Islamic fundamentalism and tensions escalate between Muslims in the north and non-Muslim African peoples in the south.
                                                                                  ISLAM

1983   The Conservative Jewish Theological Seminary permits women to be ordained as rabbis. Women may now be ordained as Conservative, Reform, and Reconstructionist rabbis but not as Orthodox rabbis. SEE 1984, JUD.   JUD

1983   Jewish and Lutheran leaders meet in Sweden, and Lutheran leaders reject Martin Luther's attacks on Judaism in the 16th century and speak out against anti-Semitism.   JUD, PROT

1983   The Mormon Church opens a temple in Mexico City.   MOR

1983   In the United States the two major Presbyterian churches, the Presbyterian Church U.S. and the Presbyterian Church U.S.A., merge after 14 years of discussion and form the Presbyterian Church (U.S.A.).   **PROT**

1983   In Morocco the practice of the Baha'i religion is restricted to private worship.   **SECT**

1983   In Britain the Sikhs, who form a small but visible minority, are classified as an ethnic group and are therefore deemed entitled to protection in accord with the Race Relations Act. The classification determines that the Sikhs share a unique history and independent status that makes them more than followers of a religion.   **SIKH**

1983   *The Hidden Dangers of the Rainbow: The New Age Movement and the Coming of Age of Barbarism* by Constance Cumbey and *Peace, Prosperity, and the Coming Holocaust: The New Age Movement in Prophecy* by Dave Hunt are published. Both are critiques of the New Age movement from a Christian Evangelical perspective.   **SPIR**

1983   Bob Jones University, a fundamentalist Christian university in Greenville, South Carolina, loses its tax-exempt status as a religious organization in a Supreme Court ruling in *Bob Jones v. United States*. The case centers on the university policy that prohibits dating between white and African-American students, a policy that violates civil rights laws.   **TOL**

1984   The leader of the Nation of Islam in the United States, Louis Farrakhan, attacks Judaism as a "gutter religion." When some mainstream African-American leaders refuse to publicly attack Farrakhan, a rift develops in Jewish–African-American relations.   **AFRICAN, JUD**

1984   The Bharatiya Janata Party in India draws more followers and wins two seats in the legislative elections.   **HIND**

1984   The Sikh desire for independence leads to widespread violence by Sikh separatist militants in Punjab. The Indian government imposes direct rule in Punjab. In an effort to end the Sikh separatist movement, the Indian army attacks militants at the Golden Temple in Amritsar, causing much damage and desecrating the site. In retaliation Indian prime minister Indira Gandhi is assassinated by Sikh bodyguards in October, setting off widespread Hindu-Sikh riots in the Punjab and Delhi, with almost 3,000 Sikhs killed in revenge for the assassination. The Sikhs claim the killings were organized and planned by Congress Party officials. The fighting initiates a decade of violence involving Sikh separatists and the Indian army.   **HIND, SIKH**

1984   In Algeria, in response to demands by Muslim fundamentalists, the government opens an Islamic university in Constantine and adopts a new family code more in line with Islamic law that reduces the rights of women.   **ISLAM**

1984   The Communist government in Bulgaria, in an effort to end ethnic conflict and to assimilate Muslim Turks into Bulgarian society, limits Islamic worship and closes many mosques. The Turks protest these and other restrictions, and after the end of Communist rule in 1989 religious liberties are restored. ISLAM

1984   Conservative Jewish rabbis who do not support the 1983 decision to allow women to be ordained form their own Conservative organization, the Union for Traditional Conservative Judaism. SEE **1990, JUD.**   JUD

1984   The nine-part television documentary *Heritage: Civilization of the Jews* airs in the United States on the Public Broadcasting Service.   JUD

1984   Desmond Tutu (1931–), the Anglican archbishop of Cape Town, South Africa, is awarded the Nobel Prize for Peace in recognition of his opposition to apartheid.   MISC, PROT

1984   The Mormon Church opens a temple in Guatemala City.   MOR

1984   Continuing its move toward Protestantism, the Reorganized Church of Jesus Christ of Latter-Day Saints moves to begin ordaining women as priests, a practice not permitted by the Mormon Church in Utah.   MOR

1984   In Britain controversial Anglican minister David Jenkins, who has questioned traditional views of the virginity of Mary and the Resurrection, is appointed bishop of Durham. Three days after the consecration, the church where he was ordained is struck by lightning, an act his critics view as God's comment on the proceeding.   PROT

1984   A Baha'i temple is built in Western Samoa.   SECT

1984   The World Sikh Organization is founded by Sikhs in the United States to support the separatist Sikh movement in India.   SIKH

1984   The American Coalition for Traditional Values is organized as a Christian Right organization to support the reelection campaign of President Ronald Reagan. With Reagan reelected, the organization folds in 1986.   TOL

1984   The United States Congress passes the Equal Access Act, which allows students to hold prayer groups in public schools and public colleges and universities. Critics view the law as a violation of the constitutional principle of separation of church and state. SEE **1990, TOL.**   TOL

1984   In the United States the National Academy of Sciences supplies public schools with copies of its *Science and Creationism: A View from the National Academy of Sciences*. The booklet urges the teaching of science and stresses the value of science to the nation. It is an attempt to control the effort by creationists to require schools to teach creation science.   TOL

1984   In Malaysia leaders of non-Muslim religions establish the Malaysian Consultative Council of Buddhism, Christianity, Hinduism, and Sikhism to addresses discrimination against non-Muslims.   TOL

1984   In Norway the constitution establishes the Evangelical Lutheran religion as the state religion, provides freedom of religion to other religions, and promises state support for established religious organizations.   TOL

1985   The best and earliest European description of Native American life, the *Florentine Codex or A General History of the Things of New Spain*, compiled and written in the Valley of Mexico by Spanish Franciscan priest Bernardino de Sagahun in the 16th century, is translated by scholars from Spanish into English. One copy of the book escaped destruction by the Spanish Inquisition in 1577, when it was hidden in a library in Florence, Italy.   CATH

1985   In a continuation of its ecumenical effort, the Roman Catholic Church issues *The Common Bond: Christians and Jews; Notes for Preaching and Teaching*, which asks Catholics not to ignore Jews, the Holocaust, and Israel.   CATH, JUD

1985   In Egypt Coptic pope Shenuda III, who was stripped of his authority in 1981, is allowed to resume his duties, although the Copts in Egypt continue to be excluded from many activities of national life including representation in the government.   CHRIS

1985   The United States government places on trial 12 individuals, including a nun, two priests, and two ministers, involved in the sanctuary movement. The movement, which began in 1982, involves helping Salvadorans escape the violence in the their nation and housing them in the United States in violation of immigration laws. Eight of the accused are convicted in the trial in Arizona.   CHRIS, TOL

1985   Conflict continues in northwestern India between Hindus and Sikhs when the secretary of the Congress Party secretary is shot, allegedly by Sikhs, and in retaliation Hindus attack Sikhs in the sacred city of Amritsar.   HIND, SIKH

1985   In Egypt, in an effort to appease Muslim fundamentalists, the government repeals laws governing divorce and child custody that are at odds with Shari'a (Islamic law).   ISLAM

1985   The second edition of *The Call of the Minaret* by Anglican theologian Kenneth (A. K.) Cragg (1913–) is published. Cragg brings many elements of Islam to the attention of the Christian world, including Muhammad's influence and the worship of the same God as in Christianity, although his basic purpose is to assist in the conversion of Muslims to Christianity.   ISLAM, PROT

1985   The *Jain Digest*, a quarterly, is begun in North America by Bhuvanendra Kumar.   JAIN

1985   The Jewish Publication Society of America publishes a new edition of the Old Testament that omits Christian interpretations and is based instead on the interpretations of Jewish theologians and scholars. It replaces the 1917 edition.   **JUD**

1985   Amy Eilberg is the first woman ordained as a Conservative Jewish rabbi in the United States.   **JUD**

1985   Two people are killed by car bombs in Salt Lake City, Utah. Police investigations suggest that the deaths are related to an attempt to sell early Mormon documents related to Joseph Smith, the founder of Mormonism.   **MOR**

1985   Several Protestant ministers lead protests in the United States against apartheid in South Africa. They lead congregants in picketing South African missions and criticize companies that do business with South Africa. They act in support of Protestant leaders in South Africa who oppose apartheid.   **PROT**

1985   The Main World Shrine of the Mahikari new religion in Japan is the locale of a major autumn celebration attended by government officials. Mahikari emerged after World War II and has become a major new religion, combining elements from Buddhism, Shinto, and ancestor worship and emphasizing healing through the use of spiritual energy.   **SECT**

1985   In Denmark the courts rule that the Church of Scientology is a profit-making organization and therefore must pay taxes. In the following year church leaders of the European and African offices located in Copenhagen are expelled from Denmark.   **SECT**

1985   Japan's Prime Minister Nakasone Yasuhiro and his cabinet pay the government's first official postwar tribute at Yasukuni shrine on the anniversary of the surrender. This raises a storm of protest from Japan's former colonies in Asia, which see Yasukuni as a symbol of Japan's aggression, militarism, and glorification of war. Nakasone is shocked by the international outcry, which is led by China, and will suspend all future official tributes, as will the succeeding government.   **SHINTO**

1985   The Osho International commune known as the "City of Rajneeshpuram" in Oregon has been involved in a series of conflicts with local residents, state and federal government agencies, and critics who complain about its treatment of residents, failure to pay taxes, and the community's perceived wealth. Rajneesh, the founder of the community, is arrested, fined, and deported.   **SPIR**

1985   The Covenant of Unitarian Universalist Pagans is founded and reflects the role of the Unitarian Church in providing leadership training for modern witches, most of whom are women.   **SPIR**

1985   In *Wallace v. Jaffree* the United States Supreme Court rules that laws allowing schoolchildren a moment of silence for voluntary prayer are unconstitutional. **TOL**

1985   In Canada the Canadian Human Rights Act prohibits religious discrimination. **TOL**

1985   In Ireland a law is enacted that permits the sale of contraceptives. The sale of contraceptives had been banned or controlled since 1935 in accord with the wishes of the majority Roman Catholic population. **TOL**

1985–1986   An important goal of Pope John Paul II is to continue the work of Vatican II (1962–1965) in creating ties to other Christian religions and non-Christian religions. Toward this end, he makes dozens of trips around the world and in 1985 prays with a rabbi in a Jewish synagogue in Rome, speaks to Muslims in Morocco, and prays with adherents of traditional religions in Togo. In 1986 he visits India and speaks to a large gathering of Hindus, Muslims, Sikhs, Buddhists, Jains, and Parsees (Zoroastrians). In 1985 he also convenes a Synod of Bishops to discuss ways to implement Vatican II. **CATH**

1986   Black Lutheran leaders issue "A Harare Message," in which they emphasize the unique identity of the Black Lutheran Church and its place in the Lutheran denomination. **AFRICAN**

1986   In the *Kairos Document* South African black theologians answer basic questions about the nature of Christianity in black South Africa and address the issue of theological sources for reconciliation between blacks and whites. **AFRICAN**

1986   Roman Catholic priest Charles E. Curran is removed from the faculty of Catholic University in Washington, D.C., by the Vatican for his teachings about homosexuality, contraception, and other matters that are counter to Church doctrine, and Archbishop Raymond Hubthausen of Seattle has his authority reduced for failing to follow conservative directives from Rome. These actions are followed by others over the next 13 years designed to control liberal dissent in the Church. The Vatican issues its "Instruction on Christian Freedom and Liberation," in which it rejects Communism and provides partial support for Liberation Theology. **CATH**

1986   Pope John Paul II organizes a day of prayer for world peace and prays at Assisi with representatives of a dozen other major religions. **CATH**

1986   Pope John Paul II becomes the first pope to enter a synagogue when he visits the Central Synagogue in Rome. **CATH, JUD**

1986   In India a new law is enacted in accord with Islamic law that exempts Muslim men from having to pay alimony to their divorced wives. The law is criticized by Hindus as giving unfair rights to Muslims and leads to an upsurge of anti-Muslim activity and Hindu nationalism.   **HIND, ISLAM**

1986   There is a resurgence of Islam as a political movement in nations with large Muslim populations. The movement is centered in the Organization of the Islamic Conference, which represents 46 nations and seeks to protect Muslim cultural, religious, and political rights.   **ISLAM**

1986   Orthodox Jews in the United States call a conference on the question of "Will There Be One Jewish People by the Year 2000?" The conference addresses conflict and divisions in the American Jewish community that concern the interpretation of religious matters in the Orthodox, Conservative, and Reform Jewish communities, differences on social issues, such as the role of women and homosexuals in Judaism, and differences over religious authority in Israel.   **JUD**

1986   The State of Georgia formally pardons Leo Frank who, as a victim of anti-Semitism in the United States, was wrongly convicted of murder and lynched in 1915.   **JUD**

1986   After much debate the Israeli government agrees to allow Brigham Young University, based in Utah, to build its Jerusalem Center for Near Eastern Studies in Jerusalem. The institute is affiliated with the Mormon Church, and some Jews in Israel have opposed its construction on the belief that it would be used as a center to proselytize among Jews.   **JUD, MOR**

1986   The Smithsonian Institution agrees to return skeletal remains of Native Americans that are in its collections to Native American tribes. To obtain the skeletal material, a tribe must prove that the deceased was a biological or cultural ancestor of the tribe.   **NATIV**

1986   The American Lutheran Church, the Association of Evangelical Lutheran Churches, and the Lutheran Church in America each approve a plan to merge the three bodies to form the Evangelical Lutheran Church in America with 5.3 million members, subject to ratification by church members in 1987.   **PROT**

1986   Eva Burrows (1930–) of Australia is elected general commissioner of the Salvation Army. She is only the second woman to hold the position, the first being Evangeline Booth, the daughter of Army founder William Booth. **PROT**

1986   In the United States bishops of the United Methodist Church take a stand against violence and war when they strongly reject the holding or use of nuclear weapons and vote to remove *Onward Christian Soldiers* and the *Battle Hymn of the Republic* from the standard hymnal. The latter decision is reversed after church members object.   **PROT**

1986   A Baha'i temple is built in New Delhi, India.   **SECT**

1986 In Greece the constitution establishes the Eastern Orthodox Church of Greece as the "prevailing religion" (about 98 percent of Greeks are Greek Orthodox) with limited religious freedom granted to other religions. **TOL**

1986 The new Soviet policy of *glasnost* (openness) leads to a lessening of restrictions on worship and the organization of public worship in the Soviet Union. **TOL**

1986 In reaction to a booklet supporting the teaching of science and evolution issued in 1984 by the National Academy of Sciences, the American Scientific Affiliation issues *Teaching Science in a Climate of Controversy: A View from the American Scientific Affiliation*, which encourages the teaching of religion alongside science in public schools. **TOL**

1987 The first public Santeria Church in the United States is opened by immigrants from Cuba in Hialeah, Florida. Two years later the town passes a law banning animal sacrifice that is directed at the church. **AFRICAN**

1987 Buddhist groups in the United States found the American Buddhist Congress to represent their shared interests and to represent the 3.5 million Buddhists in the nation. The organization applies for representation on the board of the World Fellowship of Buddhists. **BUDD**

1987 Throughout his pontificate Pope John Paul II has strongly supported devotion to Marianism or the Blessed Virgin, and in this year he issues his encyclical *Mater Redemptoris* urging all Christians to worship the Virgin Mary. He also meets with Lutherans in Germany and acknowledges the role of the Reformation in revitalizing the Church. In a continuation of his travels to encourage ecumenicism, he travels to the United States and addresses an audience composed of members of some 24 denominations. **CATH**

1987 Pope John Paul II meets with Austrian president Kurt Waldheim, who is charged with involvement in Nazi war crimes against Jews and Orthodox Serbs during World War II. The meeting damages Catholic and Jewish relations, but later in the year the pope visits Miami, Florida, and meets with Jewish leaders there, announces support for Israel as the Jewish homeland, and condemns anti-Semitism. **CATH, JUD**

1987 The National Council of Churches in the United States installs the Reverend Patricia McClung of the Presbyterian Church as its first woman president. It also installs Leonid Kishkovsky as president-elect, the first Orthodox member to be designated president. **CHRIS**

1987 Leaders of Protestant and Catholic churches in the northwest United States apologize for mistreatment of Native Americans. **CHRIS, NATIV**

1987 A conference of scholars is held to discuss Confucianism in Qufu, China, the birthplace of Confucius. It is the first such conference since the 1960s and suggests a revival of acceptance of Confucianism by the Chinese government.

CONF, TOL

1987   A military coup overthrows the elected government of Fiji and places indigenous Fijians in control. The population of Fiji is over 50 percent Indian, the
majority of whom are Hindus brought to Fiji by the British between 1874
and 1920. Many Indians leave the islands after the coup.   HIND

1987   Reflecting tension between Saudi Arabia and Iran, Iranian Muslim pilgrims
riot during the annual pilgrimage to Mecca in an attempt to destabilize the
Saudi royal family. The incident embarrasses the rulers of Saudi Arabia in
the Islamic world and some 400 people are killed.   ISLAM

1987   In Egypt the Muslim Brotherhood, although banned by the government,
becomes the major opposition in the People's Assembly. Its candidates have
been elected as members of the Socialist Labor Party. The Muslim
Brotherhood presses its agenda for the adoption of Shari'a (Islamic law) as
the law of the nation. The government arrests and imprisons members of
Muslim fundamentalist groups in an effort to control the movement. ISLAM

1987   An exodus of Jews from the Soviet Union begins and continues into the
1990s. The Jews immigrate mainly to Israel and the United States.   JUD

1987   The Presbyterian Church in the United States calls for an end to hostility
toward Jews. The United Church of Christ affords full recognition to
Judaism as a religion equal to Christianity and asks forgiveness for mistreatment of Jews in the past.   JUD, PROT

1987   The 16-volume *Encyclopedia of Religions*, edited by religion scholar Mircea
Eliade, is published and becomes the standard general reference work on
religion.   MISC

1987   In Salt Lake City, Utah, Mark Hoffman pleads guilty to car bombings that
killed two people in 1985 and to fraud in connection with his attempt to
sell forged documents to the Mormon Church that raised doubts about the
authenticity of Mormon Church founder Joseph Smith's actions in the early
1800s.   MOR

1987   Pope John Paul II speaks to Native Americans in the United States and
Canada during visits to the two nations.   NATIV

1987   A site sacred to the Kootenai people in the northwest United States is saved
from destruction when plans for the hydroelectric development of the river
are rejected by the federal government.   NATIV

1987   The Evangelical Lutheran Church in America is founded with 5.3 million
members when members of the American Lutheran Church, the
Association of Evangelical Lutheran Churches, and the Lutheran Church in

America approve a plan to merge the three bodies. It is the fourth largest Protestant denomination in the United States.   PROT

1987   The Southern Baptist Convention, the largest Protestant denomination in the United States, issues a statement urging affiliates to adopt fundamentalist interpretations of the Bible. The statement reflects the continuing influence of the conservative faction and loss of influence by the moderates in the Convention.   PROT

1987   Chizuo Matsumoto (1955–), a Japanese who has spent much of his life studying Asian religions, changes his name to Shoko Asahara and founds the Aum Shinrikyo movement in Japan. It is an apocalyptic movement based on Japanese Buddhism with beliefs and practices added from Tibetan Buddhism and Hinduism. Before its demise (SEE 1995, SECT) it attracts over 50,000 adherents in Japan and Russia.   SECT

1987   The Wiccan Church of Canada is founded.   SPIR

1987   The New Age movement gains much attention when a film version of *Out on a Limb* by actress Shirley MacLaine appears. In the book and film she recounts her contacts with the spirit world.   SPIR

1987   In two court decisions, *McLean v. Arkansas* by the Federal District Court and *Edwards v. Aguillard* by the United States Supreme Court, laws in Arkansas and Louisiana requiring the teaching of creationism alongside evolution are ruled to be a form of religious advocacy and are therefore ruled unconstitutional under the First Amendment. The decisions represent a setback for advocates of creationism and creation science.   TOL

1987   In the Philippines the new constitution creates an absolute separation of church and state and guarantees religious freedom for all, including the freedom to have no beliefs at all.   TOL

1987   The American Freedom Coalition is founded as an offshoot of the Christian Voice in the United States. Although it is not very effective, it is organized as a grassroots group to campaign for issues of concern to the Christian Right. TOL

1987   In the United States a Supreme Court decision extends the Civil Rights Act of 1966 to cover discrimination based on ancestry or ethnic identity. The case before the Court concerns desecration of a Jewish synagogue in Maryland.   TOL

1987–
1989   The Religious Right political movement in the United States experiences a loss of support and financial contributions in the wake of a number of scandals involving well-known Evangelical preachers. Jim Bakker, leader of the Praise the Lord (PTL) Club and television show, is involved in a sex scandal and cover-up with an employee and is convicted and imprisoned for defrauding contributors. Jimmy Swaggart, another television evangelist, is

1987

also involved in a sex scandal. In an effort to make Evangelical organizations more accountable to their financial supporters, various organizations such as the National Religious Broadcasters establish guidelines for financial reporting, and the issue is discussed in a hearing convened by the House of Representatives in 1987. **EVAN**

1988   In Tibet 18 Buddhist monks are killed in anti-Chinese riots at the Jokhang Temple in Lhasa. **BUDD**

1988   The largest Buddhist temple in the Americas is built by the Tainwan Fo Kuang Shen sect of Mahayana Buddhism in Hacienda Heights, California. The complex covers 14 acres and includes 11,000 statues of Buddha. **BUDD**

1988   In Sri Lanka violence breaks out between the majority Buddhist Sinhalese and the minority Hindu Tamils. Buddhist pilgrims at the Anuradhapura are killed and a Hindu temple is burned in retalition. **BUDD, HIND**

1988   A schism develops in the Roman Catholic Church when French archbishop Marcel Lefebvre, who had formed a separate Church organization in 1970 in reaction to the reforms of Vatican II (1962–1965), is excommunicated for having ordained four bishops. In this year the Church also announces that radiocarbon testing shows that the Shroud of Turin dates only to the Middle Ages and thus cannot be the shroud worn by Christ. **CATH**

1988   With the political situation in Lebanon still unstable, two governments are formed: a Muslim one in West Beirut and a Christian one in East Beirut. **CHRIS, ISLAM**

1988   In the United States controversy develops over the film *The Last Temptation of Christ* when some Christian groups complain about depictions of Christ, including his trusting of Judas and his relationship with Mary Magdalene. **CHRIS, TOL**

1988   At a final session of the first international conference of Nobel Prize winners in Paris, the 75 participants, including 52 scientists, issue 16 conclusions after deliberating four days on the theme "Facing the 21st Century." Their chief conclusion: "If mankind is to survive, it must go back 25 centuries to tap the wisdom of Confucius." **CONF**

1988   Following the death of more than 700 people in an August 21 earthquake in Nepal, Hindus hold a massive Gaj Yatra ceremony to honor the dead. **HIND**

1988   In Egypt the writer Naguib Mahfouz wins the Nobel Prize for Literature. His work is criticized by Islamic fundamentalists in Egypt as blasphemous, and when he later criticizes the *fatwa* (death sentence) imposed on the Indian writer Salman Rushdie by the Iranian leader Ayatollah Khomeini, he receives death threats. In 1994 he is stabbed but survives the attack. **ISLAM**

1988   In Bangladesh the constitution is amended, making Islam the state religion. Opposition parties protest the decision and a general strike paralyzes the capital city, Dhaka.   **ISLAM**

1988   In the United States Conservative Jews issue their first statement of principles, which calls for moderation and accommodation between the traditional and the modern worlds.   **JUD**

1988   George Patrick Lee, a Native American who serves in the leadership of the Mormon Church, is excommunicated for criticizing the Indian Student Placement Program.   **MOR, NATIV**

1988   The Oregon Supreme Court rules that the use of peyote, a mildly hallucinogenic drug, by members of the Native American Church is a religious activity protected by the First Amendment to the United States Constitution. **SEE 1990, NATIV.**   **NATIV**

1988   The United States Supreme Court rules that the American Indian Religious Freedom Act of 1978 was essentially a statement of government policy and thereby renders much of the act unenforceable.   **NATIV**

1988   Native Americans are active in recovering and burying remains of deceased ancestors held in government and private collections. Such ceremonies are conducted by tribes in Kentucky, North Dakota, Minnesota, and Maryland.   **NATIV**

1988   In the United States the Supreme Court refuses to block road construction in California that will involve paving over land considered sacred by Native Americans. The Court reasons that not every issue of religious entitlement can be used to stop government action.   **NATIV, TOL**

1988   In Britain, at a conference of all the churches that constitute the Anglican Church, an attempt is made to resolve the continuing dispute over the ordination of women as bishops when it is decided that each church can make its own ruling on the matter.   **PROT**

1988   In the United States a number of Protestant denominations, including the United Methodist Church and the Evangelical Lutheran Church in America, continue to condemn or restrict the role of homosexuals in the church. In Canada the General Council of the United Churches of Canada accept homosexuals as seminary students. A number of denominations, including the Southern Baptist Convention, the United Methodist Church, and the Episcopal Church, pass resolutions objecting to abortion.   **PROT, TOL**

1988   In Spain government agents raid the international convention of Scientologists and arrest church leaders, including Heber Janetch, the church leader in Spain, and charge some with fraud and other crimes. The cases remain unresolved in 1999 as they work their way slowly through the legal system.   SECT

1988   Japan's Supreme Court decision on the 1973 Self-Defense Force apotheosis case deems inapplicable the lower court rulings upholding separation of church and state and, in effect, finds no standing for the concept of "religious human rights." Yasukuni and the prefectural nation-protecting shrines may continue to memorialize anyone they choose, and the government is essentially free to patronize Yasukuni.   SHINTO

1988   The first of what becomes the annual Vaisakhi Day parade to commemorate the establishment of Khalsa Sikhism in India takes place in New York City, where there is a large Sikh community.   SIKH

1988   *Vibrational Medicine: New Choices for Healing Ourselves* by Richard Gerber is published in the United States. It popularizes the idea, accepted within the New Age movement, that good health involves balancing the energy "forces" within the body both with one another and with "forces" outside the body in the environment.   SPIR

1988   In Connecticut a New Age tarot card reader is acquitted of charges that she violated the municipal ban on fortune-telling for money. The woman claims that she is exercising her New Age religious beliefs, an argument evidently accepted by the jury.   SPIR

1988   In the United States the Supreme Court rules that federal funds can be used to support programs in churches that advise teenagers against abortion and pregnancy outside of marriage on the grounds that those programs do not promote religion.   TOL

1988   In Brazil the new constitution creates a separation of church and state, reflecting the reality that the Roman Catholic Church is no longer dominant in national life, as many Brazilians adhere to numerous Protestant denominations, religions of African-American origin, and other faiths.   TOL

1988   In Great Britain the Education Reform Act requires that religious education in public schools reflect the Christian nature of British society and that prayers be Christian ones.   TOL

1988   In Bangladesh the parliament establishes Islam as the state religion and guarantees religious freedom for other religions. About 87 percent of the population is Muslim; the remainder are primarily Hindu and they demonstrate against the action.   TOL

1989   The Imani Temple African-American Catholic Congregation is founded in Washington, D.C., by former Roman Catholic priest George Stallings. A critic of the Catholic Church and what he perceives as its failure to properly minister to the African-American community, he had left the priesthood to form the Imani Church. It draws a following of few thousand but is hindered by financial problems. **AFRICAN**

1989   The Dalai Lama (1935–), the highest-ranking official in Tibetan Buddhism, is awarded the Nobel Prize for Peace for his leadership of the nonviolent protest against Communist Chinese control of Tibet and repression of Buddhism. The Dalai Lama went into exile in 1959 and has lived in northern India since then. **BUDD**

1989   The Panchen Lama, the second-highest-ranking official in Tibetan Buddhism, dies in Tibet at the age of 50. As the Dalai Lama fled the nation in opposition to Communist Chinese control in 1959, the Panchen Lama has been the highest Tibetan Buddhist official in Tibet and has been accused by Tibetan exiles of being a puppet of the Communist government for allowing the destruction of most monasteries and the repression of Buddhism. **BUDD**

1989   In a reaction to what they perceive as Pope John Paul II's attempt to control liberal dissent in the Catholic Church, hundreds of Catholic theologians from eight nations issue a statement criticizing the pope's conservative policies. The National Conference of Bishops in the United States rejects a Vatican report that supports a limited role for bishops' councils. Both actions are part of the debate in the Church between conservatives, who support a strong papacy, and liberals, who call for revisions in some Church practices and more autonomy for national churches. **CATH**

1989   In Romania, following the overthrow of the Communist government, the ban on the Uniate Church dating to 1948 is lifted. However, local discrimination against church members continues in some places and the issue of the return of Uniate Church property, which had been given to the Eastern Orthodox Church, remains unresolved. **CATH**

1989   The fall of Communist governments in Eastern Europe opens these nations to Christian missionaries. Many Protestant missionaries, as well as Mormons, Jehovah's Witnesses, Seventh-Day Adventists, and others, become active in the region. **CHRIS**

1989   In Jordan support for fundamentalist Islam grows, and those who support transforming Jordan into an Islamic state win the most seats in the parliamentary elections. They want Shari'a (Islamic law) to replace secular law. **ISLAM**

1989   In central Asia Muslims in the Soviet republics replace Muslim community leaders appointed by Soviet authorities with leaders who they believe better represent the Muslims of the region and are more devout adherents of Islam. Similar actions follow in Muslim communities in the Caucasus region, Russia, and Siberia. **ISLAM**

Chinese Popular Religion

Chinese voluntary religions, such as Daoism, Buddhism, and state religion, or Confucianism, which function specifically for religious purposes, were never powerful or popular enough to displace communal religion, consisting of beliefs that are integrated into all aspects of common life. As they share the people's spiritual loyalties, voluntary and communal religions have successfully fused. The Buddhist vision of hell and the afterlife, for example, is commonly accepted among all Chinese, while the common people adhere to Confucian morality. The Daoist pantheon is fused with that of communal religion, and Daoist priests are the ritual specialists of choice for both the common people and the state. But the Chinese people, the vast majority of whom live in small rural villages, always remained faithful to their local gods. China's vastness and many regional variations make giving an accurate account of the general characteristics of the communal religion extremely difficult. To the common people, the natural world was animated by a great number of unseen forces and beings who, according to popular religion, assist in protecting the local community's social and economic interests. Certain divinities were held primarily responsible for maintaining order in the unseen world, just as certain authority figures were charged with ensuring the smooth functioning of the material world. The gods were believed to operate through a centralized bureaucratic government patterned after the imperial government of traditional China and were considered subject to the authority of the Chinese people, or at least existed in a relationship of mutual obligation. In any Chinese village or city were many temples, large and small, that housed gods who were believed to possess special powers to protect against natural disaster, cure illnesses, assist women in childbirth, or save sailors at sea. Legends may or may not exist to explain how a god's powers had been acquired, and popular religion often deified real historical personalities, including cultural heroes, such as those who had distinguished themselves by moral strength or military prowess. This usually occurred on a local level, but in some cases a figure's popularity might spread to other areas or become a national phenomenon.

The Chinese family, a center of ritual activity since ancient times, changed significantly as Confucianism seeped slowly down from the nobility to the common people. Although ancestor worship appeared very early in China, the formal and ideological aspects of such rituals as funerals, weddings, and posthumous rites became steadily more imbued with Confucianism. The Chinese have traditionally held the belief that human destiny is not determined by behavior but through the help of superhuman agencies who assist in protecting and bringing prosperity. The closest, most obvious place to look for such assistance was among the family's ancestors. Although they had proceded to a different level of existence and had special needs, they were still regarded as part of the family, with as strong an interest in family affairs as when they had lived. Rituals performed for the ancestors were aimed at making their postmortal existence as comfortable as possible while assisting their passage through the otherworldly purgatories, where divine authorities judged their past conduct. On household altars were tablets bearing the ancestors' names, along with offerings of food and drink. On special occasions elaborate rites were enacted before the altars, at the graveside, or at a temple. Paper money was burned in the belief that it would be transformed and conveyed to those in the afterlife. In addition to ancestors, other spiritual presences in the Chinese household are believed to inhabit strategic locations.

1989   A novel called *The Satanic Verses* is written by Indian-born British Muslim author Salman Rushdie and published in Britain. Many Muslims consider portions of it blasphemous to Islam, and Ayatollah Khomeini, the ruler of Iran, issues a *fatwa* (a legal ruling) calling for Rushdie's death. Rushdie goes into hiding in Britain. The ruling is lifted by the Iranian government in 1998.

                                      ISLAM

1989   In Bulgaria the government seeks to control the Turkish Muslim minority of about one million people and to assimilate them into the Orthodox nation by banning various Muslim practices and attempting to force Turks to take Bulgarian names.   **ISLAM, ORTHO**

1989   Ultra-Orthodox Israelis attack a group of Jewish women praying at the Western Wall in Jerusalem. The Ultra-Orthodox believe in a limited religious role for women, which does not permit them to pray in public.   **JUD**

1989   The United Nations General Assembly revokes its 1975 resolution that equates Zionism with racism by a vote of 111 to 25 with 13 abstentions.

                                      JUD, TOL

1989   A school for the training of rabbis and teachers opens in Russia for the first time since 1917, and a national conference of Soviet Jewish organizations meets for the first time since the Russian Revolution.   **JUD**

1989   Native Americans are active in recovering and burying remains of deceased ancestors and sacred objects held in government and private collections. Such ceremonies are conducted by tribes in Nebraska, California, and New York.

                                      NATIV

1989   Conservatives in the Episcopal Church in the United States break from the main church body and form the Episcopal Synod of America. The new group establishes its own hierarchy of priests and bishops but claims that it remains within the main church.   **PROT**

1989   The American Association of University Professors (AAUP) censures several Baptist seminaries for their newly enacted policies of requiring faculty to teach in accord with Southern Baptist Convention principles and therefore denying them intellectual freedom.   **PROT**

1989   The United Church of Christ in the United States, one of the most liberal of Protestant denominations, supports an "economic bill of rights" that calls for a base income for all Americans. Another liberal denomination, the Christian Church (Disciples of Christ), elects a Roman Catholic priest to its board, the first such action by a Protestant denomination in the United States.   **PROT**

1989   Barbara Harris (1930–), a former public relations executive who has worked her way up through the ranks of the Episcopal Church, is appointed the first female bishop in the church when she becomes the assistant bishop for Massachusetts.   PROT

1989   The Aum Shinrikyo movement is officially recognized as a religion by the government of Japan and is given tax-exempt status. **SEE 1995, SECT.**   SECT

1989   Restrictions are eased or ended on Jehovah's Witnesses in nations in Eastern Europe and Africa and missionary activity intensifies in these regions. SECT

1989   Japan's longest reigning emperor in history, Hirohito, dies and is succeeded by his son Akihito, who will be enthroned in 1990 in a splendid ceremony incorporating traditional Shinto ritual.   SHINTO

1989   Hoblick, a British pagan organization for homosexuals and lesbians, is founded.   SPIR

1989   *Quantum Healing: Exploring the Frontiers of Mind/Body Medicine* by Depak Chopra, a physician and New Age teacher, is published. It popularizes the idea that there is a link between the physical, mental, and spiritual states and that healing requires a consideration of all three. These ideas are widely accepted in the New Age and alternative medicine movements.   SPIR

1989   The Moral Majority **(SEE 1979, RELIGIOUS RIGHT)** is dissolved by its founder, Jerry Falwell, when financial contributions decline and its influence on the political process in the United States seems to be weakening.   TOL

1989   The Family Research Council is formed by followers of the Christian Right in the United States to lobby for policies that it feels will encourage the stability of the traditional nuclear family. With the demise of other Christian Right organizations, it is the largest and best-funded organization in the 1990s.   TOL

1989   The Christian Coalition is formed by fundamentalist Christian leaders and conservative politicians to influence the political process in the United States.   TOL

1989   In Algeria a constitution is enacted that makes Islam the state religion but also guarantees religious freedom to followers of other religions.   TOL

1989   In Sudan a successful coup is staged by Islamic fundamentalists, who begin enacting a policy of establishing the Shari'a (Islamic religious law) as the law of the nation and begin persecuting non-Muslims including Roman Catholics and Coptic Christians.   TOL

1989   In Lebanon the 15-year civil war among Christians, Muslims, and Druze is ended by the Taif agreement, which gives more power to the Muslim majority. Although the president will be a Christian, the prime minister, the most powerful government official, will be a Sunni Muslim, the Speaker of parliament a Shi'a Muslim, and Muslims will have 50 percent of the parliament seats.   TOL

1989   In France the *hijab* case brings the matter of religious rights for religious minorities to public discussion. The case concerns three Muslim girls who are expelled from public school for wearing veils in accord with Islamic practice. The case leads to a number of administrative and judicial rulings, which in 1994 result in local school authorities being given the power to determine whether religious symbols can be worn in school.   TOL

1989   The Soviet government restores the Ukrainian Catholic Church, which had been banned in 1943. Three priests of the Russian Orthodox Church are elected to the Congress of Peoples' Deputies. In a speech in Italy, Soviet leader Mikhail Gorbachev notes the positive influence of religion in Soviet society. All three of these developments mark the continuing relaxation of restrictions on religion in the Soviet Union.   TOL

1989–
1990   In Hungary the new democratic government eases restrictions on religion that had been in place under the Communist government since 1949, with people now free to practice their religions and religion playing a part in politics.   TOL

1990   The Dalai Lama, the highest-ranking official of Tibetan Buddhism, who has lived in exile in India since 1959, declares that 1990–1991 is dedicated to preserving traditional Tibetan culture, which is threatened by Chinese rule and the settlement of large numbers of Han Chinese in Tibet. The Dalai Lama's autobiography *Freedom in Exile* is published in the United States, where Tibetan Buddhism has strong support.   BUDD

1990   In Laos there is a revival of Buddhism, which had been repressed during the 15 years of Communist rule.   BUDD

1990   In Mongolia there is a revival of Buddhism, which had been repressed with most monasteries closed during the 70 years of Communist rule that ends in 1990. In 1990 and 1991 over 100 monasteries are reopened.   BUDD

1990   A major survey finds that 95 percent of the Japanese population is affiliated with Shinto through Shinto organizations and local shrine rituals, but their "belief rating" is about 3 to 4 percent. Many Japanese practice both Shinto and Buddhism. The total of 80,000 registered shrines in Japan does not include wayside or unattended shrines.   BUDD, SHINTO

1990   With the departure of the Vietnamese occupiers of Cambodia, Premier Hun Sen declares that Buddhism is the state religion of Cambodia.   BUDD, TOL

1990   The Passion Play staged in Oberammergau in southern Germany since 1634 begins to undergo revisions that lessen what some have called anti-Semitism, wherein Jews are depicted as causing and being insensitive to Christ's Crucifixion.   CATH, JUD

1990   With the end of Communist rule in Eastern Europe and the easing of restrictions on religion, the Vatican moves to strengthen the Roman Catholic Church in the region. Diplomatic ties are established with Czechoslovakia, Romania, and Hungary, and discussions begin with the Russian Orthodox Church over control of religious property in what will soon become the former Soviet Union.   **CATH, ORTHO**

1990   Several Christian denominations address the role of women in their churches. The Christian Reform Church in the United States moves to allow women to hold all church offices, and the Anglican Church in Ireland appoints the first two female Anglican ministers in Europe. The Seventh-Day Adventists persist in disallowing women to serve as clergy, although the idea is supported by some Adventists in the United States.   **CHRIS, PROT**

1990   Fighting between Muslims and Indian Hindu soldiers takes place in the Kashmir region of India. The Muslims seek reunification with Pakistan as India and Pakistan dispute ownership of the province, which is rich in natural resources.   **HIND, ISLAM**

1990   Conflict in northwestern India continues between Hindus and Sikhs. In the worst incident, 34 Hindus are killed during a religious celebration in the Punjab and Hindus retaliate by raiding Sikh villages, with 16 people killed.   **HIND, SIKH**

1990   In Saudi Arabia over 1,000 Muslim pilgrims are suffocated in a tunnel at the Grand Mosque in Mecca when overcrowding leads to panic. As more and more Muslims make pilgrimages to Mecca, crowd control has become a logistical problem for the government.   **ISLAM**

1990   During the Gulf War Saudi Arabia alters its traditional policy to permit stationing non-Muslim foreign troops on its soil. Troops from the United States and other nations are required to moderate their dress and public behavior so as not to insult Saudi morality. The move is criticized by senior Saudi religious scholars.   **ISLAM**

1990   In Algeria a new political party, the Islamic Salvation Front (*Front Islamique du Salut-FIS*), is victorious in local and parliamentary elections. However, the existing government refuses to leave office as it objects to the FIS's agenda of creating an Islamic state.   **ISLAM**

1990   In the former Soviet Union, Muslims form the Islamic Renaissance Party to help revive Islam in the former Soviet republics. It is one of many such parties that emerge at this time but is broader in its representation than others, as its members come from the central Asian republics, the Caucasus, Russia, and Siberia.   **ISLAM**

1990   The Central Conference of American Rabbis, which represents Reform Jewish rabbis in the United States, votes to allow homosexuals to become rabbis. Conservative and Orthodox seminaries do not accept homosexuals as rabbinical students. JUD

1990   The Union for Traditional Conservative Judaism opens its own seminary, which does not allow women to be ordained as rabbis. The organization changes its name this year to the Union for Traditional Judaism. JUD

1990   In two signs of increasing assimilation by Jews into American society, the Yiddish-language newspaper *Forward* begins publishing a weekly English edition, and a study shows that 29 percent of Jews in America have non-Jewish husbands or wives. The study raises concern that many children in these marriages will not be raised as Jews. JUD

1990   The B'nai Noah (Children of Noah) movement coalesces as an international Jewish movement with the establishment of the Union of the Vineyard of the Children of Noah at the annual conference of the Children of Noah in Texas. The movement began in the 1970s and is based on the seven Noachian commandments (prohibitions on idolatry, blasphemy, sexual sins, murder, theft, and eating the limb of a living animal and the requirement to establish courts). It draws followers from both Judaism and Christianity and in the 1980s and 1990s draws the support of a few Hasidic and Orthodox rabbis. JUD

1990   In France the Gayssot Law is passed. It prohibits the publication of literature denying the Holocaust. JUD

1990   Leaders of the Mormon Church end the practice of collecting additional payments beyond the required tithes from members to support local congregations. This is one of a number of financial reforms instituted since the early 1980s that recognize the wealth of the Mormon Church and reduce the contributions of individual members. The church also reforms some policies regarding women and ends the requirement that women pledge obedience to their husbands, although the ban on women serving as priests remains in place. MOR

1990   The Reorganized Church of Jesus Christ of Latter-Day Saints continues to reform its policies and by this time is much like mainstream Protestantism in the United States as it has little in common with the Mormon Church in Utah. The Reorganized Church numbers about 240,000 members, compared with over eight million members in the Utah-based Mormon Church. MOR

1990   In *Employment Division v. Smith* the United States Supreme Court rules that the free exercise clause of the First Amendment to the Constitution does not provide protection from religion-neutral application of criminal law. The case involves a Native American in Oregon who was fired from his job for using peyote for religious purposes and was then denied unemployment compensation. This ruling reinforces a similar ruling in 1988 and allows local law enforcement officers to prosecute members of the Native

American Church for using peyote, a mild hallucinogen, which church adherents consider to be a sacrament. SEE **1991, NATIV; 1993,** TOL. NATIV

1990   The Mohawk people in Quebec protest plans to build a golf course on an ancient native burial ground. NATIV

1990   The United States Congress passes the Native American Graves Protection and Repatriation Act. The act protects burial grounds and graves and also requires all organizations supported by federal funding to inventory Native American materials in their collections and to return to native tribes all skeletal material and artifacts of cultural significance. NATIV

1990   The Zuni Pueblo of New Mexico recover 34 wooden war god statues from private and public collections and set them in the desert so that they may return to nature. NATIV

1990   The percentage of Native American children attending mission schools has declined to an all-time low of 3 percent. Most now attend public schools. NATIV

1990   On December 29 about 400 people gather at the mass grave in Wounded Knee, South Dakota, to mark the centennial of the Wounded Knee massacre. For Native Americans the massacre remains a vivid reminder of white oppression and native resistance. NATIV

1990   In Russia, in the atmosphere of new religious freedom, conflict develops between the Russian Orthodox Church and the Russian Orthodox Church in Exile (Free Russian Orthodox Church) over matters of doctrine, political influence, and control of church property. The Russian Orthodox Church grants administrative independence to the Orthodox churches in the Ukraine and Belarus. ORTHO

1990   A break develops in the Southern Baptist Convention in the United States when moderates who have lost power to the conservatives convene their own meeting and discuss separation from the parent body. PROT

1990   The World Alliance of Reformed Churches issues the Rustenburg Declaration, in which it expresses guilt for its part in apartheid and offers a plan to pay restitution to its victims in South Africa. PROT

1990   In the United States the National Council of Churches objects to celebrations planned for the 500th anniversary of Columbus's exploration of America on the grounds that his voyage led to the conquest of the native peoples of the Americas. PROT, TOL

1990   In the United States two Christian Scientists are convicted of manslaughter after their son dies. They refused to provide medical treatment, instead relying on Christian Science prayer. SECT

1990	Following nearly a decade of efforts to take control of the Branch Davidian Church, David Koresh (1959–1993) establishes a commune with several dozen followers in Waco, Texas. SECT
1990	In Egypt the government bans the Baha'i religion, which has about 10,000 adherents in the nation, and confiscates all Baha'i assets. SECT
1990	The Dragon Environmental Network is founded as an organization that combines paganism with environmentalism in London. SPIR
1990	In *Board of Education of Westside Community School District v. Mergens,* the United States Supreme Court rules that it is constitutional to allow religious groups access to public facilities. TOL
1990	The United States Supreme Court rules that the State of New York cannot force Rastafarian prisoners to cut their dreadlocks to conform to prison rules. TOL
1990	In the Russian Federation the Law on Freedom of Conscience is adopted. It provides for religious freedom and ends the restrictions on religion that were in place during the Communist era in the Soviet Union. However, the law is criticized by those who fear the growth of "foreign" religions in Russia and is amended in 1993 to control the activities of Pentecostal and other religious organizations. The government also abolishes the Council for Religious Affairs, which had regulated religion in the Soviet Union. In some republics it is replaced by other agencies or offices that continue to administer religious matters. TOL
1990s	In China Daoism has divided into two major schools, ritual and interior alchemy. DAO
1990s	The "Next Church" movement develops in the United States. Next churches are large, nondenominational Protestant churches with memberships numbering more than 2,000 and some with memberships over 10,000. The buildings are secular in appearance and many religious rituals are eliminated from worship services. The churches are aggressive in recruiting members and provide a wide range of services including sport leagues and educational courses and lectures. The largest Next churches are located in the southwest. PROT
1990s	Throughout the decade there is continually expanding interest in angels in the United States. They first attract the interest of New Age adherents, and surveys show that by the middle of the decade over 50 percent of Americans believe in angels and their ability to influence the lives of earthly persons. Workshops, books, movies, and television shows about angels are all extremely popular. SPIR

1990s	Chinese living in communities scattered throughout the world, when they have not converted to another major religion, tend to maintain a mixture of beliefs and practices that incorporate elements of Buddhism, Daoism, and Confucianism. **TOL**
1990–1991	In Poland the Roman Catholic Church works with the government to require religious education in the schools. In response to complaints public religious education is limited in 1993 but not banned. **TOL**
1991	In what will soon become the former Soviet Union, the Roman Catholic Church establishes two dioceses in Belarus and appoints administrators of Catholic churches in Russian cities. **CATH**
1991	In the United States the Promise Keepers, a Christian men's organization, is founded in Colorado by Bill McCartney, a former football coach at the University of Colorado. The organization seeks to promote a Christian lifestyle among men and places an emphasis on men acting responsibly, especially toward their wives and children. The organization is criticized by some women's groups for supporting a male-dominated family ideology. **CHRIS**

Buddhism in the 1990s

There are about 326 million Buddhists in the world, with the overwhelming majority (322 million) in Asia. Although Buddhism thrives in many parts of the world, in its homeland, India, it is distinctly a minority faith; it survives there only in small communities, mostly in the northeast in the states of Jammu, Kashmir, Himachal, and Sikkim. It also survives in former Indian territories that are now the independent kingdoms of Nepal and Bhutan and the independent nation of Bangladesh; much of the Buddhism in these lands, however, is derived from Tibetan Buddhism or has been brought into this region by immigrants from Myanmar since the 1700s. Since the 1960s in particular, over 100,000 Tibetan refugees from Chinese Communism have brought Buddhism back to northern India. Mahayana Buddhism thrives in Japan, Korea, Vietnam, and Taiwan. Theravada Buddhism dominates in Sri Lanka, Myanmar, Cambodia, Thailand, and Laos. In China and Mongolia, where Communist governments have for decades worked to stamp out all religions, there are only pockets of Buddhism, mostly of the Mahayana variety. In Indonesia Buddhism survives only on Bali and eastern Java, where Theravada Buddhism is practiced. Asian immigrants to otherwise non-Buddhist societies—in Asia itself (the Philippines), Hawaii, and the West—have carried Buddhism with them, although many Chinese, Japanese, and Koreans tend to observe a mixture of Buddhism, Daoism, Confucianism, Shintoism, and other indigenous faiths and folklore. Meanwhile, Buddhism is increasingly being adopted by Westerners, ranging from those who actually become monks to those who simply adopt Zen or other Buddhist practices alongside their other faiths and practices.

1991   In an effort to promote Hindu-Muslim tolerance, the film *Henna* is released in India. It is a love story that stars an Indian Hindu male lead and a Pakistani Muslim female lead and is marketed with the slogan "God made land, man made borders."   **HIND, ISLAM**

1991   In Brunei the government stresses *Melayu Islam Beraja* as a state ideology, resulting in the promulgation of traditional Islamic values. The sale of alcohol and the public celebration of Christmas are banned.   **ISLAM**

1991   In post-Soviet Russia, Ukraine, and Poland, anti-Semitism increases as Jews are blamed for the economic problems of these nations. In Poland this is labeled "anti-Semitism without Jews," as Jews in Poland number less than 10,000 and most are elderly.   **JUD**

1991   In New York City hostility between the Hasidic (ultra-Orthodox) Jewish community and African-American community turns violent with riots and protests. The violence is precipitated by the death of an African-American boy after he is hit by a car driven by a Hasidic Jew. This incident is followed by the murder of a Hasidic man. Leaders of the Hasidic community and others accuse Mayor David Dinkins, who is African-American, of favoring the African-American community and not protecting the Hasidic community adequately.   **JUD**

1991   In the United States the Nation of Islam issues a report called *The Secret Relationship Between Blacks and Jews* that holds Jews responsible for the Atlantic slave trade. The report is criticized by many scholars as inaccurate.   **JUD**

Daoism in China in the 1990s

Contemporary Daoism in China is divided into two major schools, ritual and interior alchemy. The ritualist Celestial Masters dominate popular Daoism. They operate on Taiwan and on the mainland, where possible. Celestial Masters preside over local festivals, funerals, and religious observances and function as both exorcists and healers. The masters of interior alchemy, generally belonging to the Quanzhen school, carry on the literary and contemplative traditions of Daoism. Monasteries on Taiwan offer an austere life, with praying, chanting of texts, and collecting herbs. Some mainland monasteries, shut down or abandoned after 1949, are being reoccupied. There is a revival of Daoist activity in Hong Kong (which reverted to Chinese sovereignty in 1997), Singapore, and Malaysia. Neverthless, some scholarly authorities regard Daoism as a dying religion. Daoists operate 600 temples, with 6,000 priests and nuns, in a country with a population of more than 1 billion. By contrast, Buddhism has 9,500 temples and 170,000 priests and nuns.

1991

1991	Skeletal remains from the Smithsonian Institution are returned to the Aleuts of the Kodiak Islands in Alaska, who bury them in accord with their Russian Orthodox religion. **NATIV**
1991	The State of Oregon passes a law that leagalizes the religious use of peyote by American Indians. **NATIV**
1991	A major issue addressed by several Protestant denominations is their policies concerning sexuality. In the United States the Presbyterian Church U.S.A., Episcopal Church, American Baptist Churches, the Southern Baptist Convention, and the Disciples of Christ all condemn homosexuality, ban homosexuals from the ministry, or refuse to liberalize their policies concerning homosexuality. **PROT**
1991	The schism in the Southern Baptist Convention between conservatives, who control the organization, and moderates deepens when the latter group holds its own annual meeting and elects its own leadership, although it does not withdraw from the Convention. The overwhelming majority of Baptists in the United States and their churches remain within the Convention. **PROT**
1991	One of the two surviving members of the Shaker community in Canterbury, New Hampshire, dies, and the community ceases to function as a Shaker community. This leaves only Sabbathday Lake, Maine, as an extant Shaker community, with nine members. While the Shaker religion and communities have almost completely disappeared, their ways of life remain an important component of American culture. Several Shaker communities have been reconstructed as historical and cultural sites, and Shaker productions, such as furniture, are among the most prized antique and folk art finds. **SECT**
1991	In India the Places of Worship Act is enacted, which protects shrines, churches, mosques, and temples that were places of worship when India achieved independence in 1947. The act is meant to diffuse conflict between Hindus and Muslims over thousands of mosques, which Hindus claim were built centuries ago on sites previously occupied by Hindu temples. **TOL**
1991	*Darwin on Trial* by University of California law professor Phillip E. Johnson is published. The book offers a creationist argument against science and evolution and argues that supernatural factors should be considered in explaining natural phenomena. **TOL**
1991	With the breakup of the Soviet Union and the creation of 15 independent nations that form the Commonwealth of Independent States, centralized control of religion ends and each state is now free to establish its own policies. **TOL**

| 1991 | In Cuba restrictions on religious worship are eased by the Communist government that had instituted a policy of atheism in 1961 and non-atheists are allowed to join the Communist Party. **TOL** |

1991– 1996   In Algeria the Islamic Salvation Front, which seeks to establish an Islamic state, is victorious in elections for the National Assembly. The government resigns and the military takes control, arresting Islamic Salvation Front leaders and banning the party; protesters respond by launching terrorist attacks on civilian and government targets that take some 30,000 lives by the end of 1995. **ISLAM**

1992   In the Dominican Republic the Fourth General Conference of Latin American Bishops is held in Santo Domingo. These bishops are more conservative than those who controlled the Puebla Conference in 1979 (who supported Liberation Theology) and their conference supports more traditional approaches to social issues, such as personal devotion over more radical approaches, such as basic societal change. Commentators see the shift as reflecting the pope's conservative approach to Church involvement in politics and social issues and as an effort to limit the Liberation Theology movement. **CATH**

1992   In Ireland in the *X* case the High Court rules that a mother may travel to another nation to have a legal abortion if there is a grave threat to the life of the mother. The decision weakens the Irish constitutional ban on abortion and causes much controversy among the majority Roman Catholic population in Ireland. **CATH**

1992   Hindu nationalists in northern India destroy the Muslim Babri Masjid mosque at Ayodhya, the culmination of years of antagonism between Muslims and Hidus. The Hindus claim that the mosque is built on the spot where Rama, the incarnation of the Hindu God, Vishnu, was born. The destruction of the mosque is followed by attacks on Muslims, the sacking of other mosques, and the rape of Muslim women. **HIND, ISLAM**

1992   Tensions between Muslims and Christians in Indonesia erupt in violence and many churches and mosques are vandalized. President Suharto urges religious tolerance. **ISLAM**

1992   With the end of the war with the Soviet Union and the final withdrawal of Soviet forces, the Afghanistan government collapses, the Seven Party Alliance of Islamic groups based in Pakistan proclaims the Islamic State of Afghanistan, and Islam is reestablished as the state religion. **ISLAM**

1992   In Egypt the Muslim Brotherhood, a group that calls for societal reforms in accord with Islamic beliefs and which stresses nonviolent change, is denied status as a political party by the courts. **ISLAM**

1992   In Tajikistan the Islamic Renaissance Party leads a successful political campaign to remove the president of the republic from office and create an Islamic state.   ISLAM

1992   In Algeria the government cancels the elections when it becomes clear that the Islamic Salvation Front, which wants to transform Algeria from a secular to an Islamic nation, will be victorious. The action is followed by violence that continues into 1998 with over 60,000 Algerians killed.   ISLAM

1992   Following the dissolution of the Soviet Union, Jews in a number of former Soviet republics, among them Russia, Belarus, and Ukraine, begin to revitalize Jewish culture by forming Jewish organizations.   JUD

1992   Anti-Semitism emerges as an issue in United States politics when Republican presidential hopeful Patrick J. Buchanan is accused by some of being anti-Semitic, and David Duke, a former leader of the anti-Semitic Ku Klux Klan, seeks the Republican nomination for senator from Louisiana.   JUD

1992   Surveys indicate that over 50 percent of Jews in the United States marry non-Jews and only about 25 percent of their children are raised as Jews. Reform and Conservative Jewish organizations discuss ways that such families can be made part of their congregations.   JUD

1992   The last museum in the United States that displays Native American skeletal remains, the Dickson Mounds Museum in Illinois, closes.   NATIV

1992   A number of Protestant denominations act to increase the role of women in the church. The General Synod of the Church of England (Anglican Church) approves the ordination of women as ministers, a practice already permitted in many other Anglican churches, including those in Australia and South Africa and in the Episcopal Church in the United States. The Lutheran Church in Germany and the Evangelical Lutheran Church in America both appoint their first female bishops. However, the Christian Reformed Church refuses to allow women to be ordained.   PROT

1992   The trend of the last several years continues in Protestant denominations in the United States as they reconsider their policies concerning homosexuality. In general, they continue to view homosexuality as inconsistent with Christian teachings. The Presbyterian Church denies a ministry to a lesbian, the Southern Baptist Convention expels two congregations that approve of homosexuality, and the National Council of Churches refuses to admit a church whose membership is openly homosexual.   PROT

1992   The Family Research Council is founded in the United States by Gary Bauer, a former adviser to former President Ronald Reagan. The organization supports a conservative political agenda, including opposition to homosexuality and abortion and support for public religious education and school prayer. It draws many supporters from the Religious Right.   PROT

1992	The Council of Churches for Britain and Ireland refuses to allow Unitarian churches to become members, reflecting the opinion of some that Unitarianism is not a Christian denomination. **SECT**
1992	The Falun Gong (Buddhist Law) spiritual sect is founded in China by Li Hongzhi, a teacher of controlled breathing and meditation. It is one of a number of sects that advocate the use of ancient and previously repressed techniques to maintain health. In 1993 it is accepted into the China Qigong Science Association but is expelled in 1996 when its claims about curing illness are questioned by scientists. In 1997 Li moves to New York but continues to direct the sect, which stages several large demonstrations in 1999 in China. It appeals mainly to retired people and middle-aged women and therefore the government is careful not to harshly repress it. **SECT**
1992	In Iran a member of the Baha'i religion is arrested and executed for seeking to convert Muslims to Baha'i. **SECT**
1992	The Sikh separatist movement in Punjab, India, is largely repressed by the Indian government when many movement leaders are killed or captured by the Indian military, which is stationed in large numbers in the Punjab. **SIKH**
1992	*A Return to Love* by author and New Age leader Marianne Williamson is published. It is Williamson's personal statement about human spiritual and emotional growth and is based on the widely influential book *A Course in Miracles* that was published in 1975. The book is a best-seller, and Williamson becomes a major figure in the human growth movement within the New Age movement. **SPIR**
1992	In a decision bearing on the separation of church and state, the United States Supreme Court rules that prayers mentioning God or quoting from the Bible may not be given at public-school graduations. **TOL**
1992	The official policy of atheism is dropped by the Cuban government and open expression of religion is tolerated. The two major religions in Cuba are Roman Catholicism and Santeria, although there are also Baptists, Presbyterians, and a small community of Jews. **TOL**
1992	In Mexico the 1917 constitution is revised and new laws are enacted that remove some earlier restrictions on religion that had been aimed at the Roman Catholic Church. The new laws give religious organizations legal standing, allow religious schools, and make it possible for religious organizations to own property. **TOL**
1992	In Cuba the 1992 constitution grants religious freedom to all. Nonetheless, religious organizations and activities are monitored and controlled by the government. **TOL**

1992	A two-hour television special is shown on the CBS network that takes a creation science viewpoint and purports to provide scientific evidence for the Great Flood of the Judeo-Christian Bible and evidence that humans and dinosaurs inhabited the earth at the same time. **TOL**
1992	In Vietnam the new constitution grants greater freedom of religion, but religious activity is still largely controlled by the government. **TOL**
1993	In Australia Roman Catholics form the Ordination of Catholic Women to lobby for increased participation, including ordination as priests, for women in the church. **CATH**
1993	In his continuing travels Pope John Paul II prays in Denver, Colorado, with some 375,000 Catholic youths at World Youth Day and later in the year meets outside Rome with the chief Ashkenazi rabbi of Israel. In the United States the bishops form a committee to address the issue of sexual abuse by Catholic clergy. Several cases in which clergy have been charged with the sexual abuse of boys have become public and have embarassed the Church. **CATH, JUD**
1993	The Bharatiya Janata Party, which was founded in the 1970s, has now become a major political party in India and occupies 119 of 553 legislative seats. It calls for India's return to Hindu control and advocates renaming it Hindustan, its ancient Sanskrit name. Two bombs kill six people and wound a dozen others at a Hindu festival in Sri Lanka. The bombings are attributed to rival Hindu factions. **HIND**
1993	In India violence continues between Hindus and Muslims with over 600 people killed in terrorist bombings in Bombay and Calcutta. **HIND**
1993	The conflict in Kashmir continues with fighting between Indian troops and Muslim separatists. Indian troops kill 40 Muslims and surround the Hazratbal mosque, where other protesters have hidden. The mosque is considered the holiest place in Kashmir by Muslims. **ISLAM**
1993	The second-largest mosque in the world, the Hassan II Mosque, is opened in Casablanca, Morocco. The only larger mosque is the Haram al-Sharif in Mecca. **ISLAM**
1993	In Turkey those who favor a secular society with ties to Europe and those who favor an Islamic society with ties to the Muslim world continue to clash when 37 people are killed in an attack by Muslim fundamentalists on a meeting of writers and intellectuals. **ISLAM**
1993	On September 13 a peace agreement is signed in Washington, D.C., between the Israeli government and the Palestine Liberation Organization (PLO). The agreement was difficult to achieve, with meetings and subsequent negotiations producing few results, until, under a Labor government, Israeli and Palestinian representatives meet secretly in Oslo, Norway, to

work out a peace agreement. The agreement, signed in Washington, D.C., by Prime Minister Yitzak Rabin and PLO chairman Yasir Arafat, involves mutual recognition and the transfer of authority in Gaza and Jericho to interim Palestinian rule, with the final status of a Palestinian entity to be resolved in five years.   ISLAM, JUD

1993   At Monroeville (near Pittsburgh), Pennsylvania, the seventh annual convention of the Federation of Jain Associations in North America takes place for three days. Five thousand people attend, including many from India and other overseas locations. The conference organizers claim there are some 50,000 Jains now in North America.   JAIN

1993   The Jewish Reconstructionist Rabbinical Association approves the performance of marriage ceremonies for same-sex couples.   JUD

1993   On April 22 the United States Holocaust Memorial Museum, in development since 1980, opens in Washington, D.C.   JUD

1993   In the United States the Anti-Defamation League (ADL) of B'nai B'rith is criticized by some in the Religious Right, the media, and civil libertarians for its involvement in collecting information about groups it considers to be "domestic terrorist groups" and for sharing that information with government law enforcement agencies. The controversy ends with the ADL denying any wrongdoing and the government deciding that the acts criticized are not crimes.   JUD

1993   In the Mormon Church in the United States, controversy continues over the role and status of women in the church, with some reformers continuing to call for women to be allowed to serve as priests, a reform rejected by the church hierarchy.   MOR

1993   In Chile the constitution is revised to guarantee cultural and religious freedom to native peoples. The new laws also protect ancient religious sites.   NATIV

1993   In Ukraine the end of the Soviet Union has meant new religious freedom and three Ukrainian churches vie for the status of the national church. They are the Ukrainian Catholic Church, which is strongest in the west, the Ukrainian Orthodox Church, which is strongest in the east, and the newly formed Independent United Ukrainian Orthodox Church.   ORTHO

1993   The issue of the ordination of women continues to draw mixed responses from Protestant denominations. Several leading Anglicans leave the Church of England over its decision to ordain women, and the Presbyterian Church in the United States objects to ordination. However, the Christian Reformed Church votes to allow congregations to decide the matter, and a woman is ordained as the Episcopal bishop of Vermont.   PROT

| 1993 | Three member churches of the Consultation on Christian Union in the United States (the Disciples of Christ, United Church of Christ, and the Presbyterian Church) agree to allow members of one church to celebrate communion in other member churches. **PROT** |

| 1993 | In Minneapolis a jury awards $9 million in damages to the father of a boy who died while receiving Christian Science treatment. The boy's mother, stepfather, and members of the church are held liable. It is the first time that adherents have been held liable for damages due to Christian Science treatment. **SECT** |

| 1993 | In the United States the Internal Revenue Service grants the Church of Scientology tax-exempt status, ending several decades of what the church claims is government repression. **SECT** |

| 1993 | The Committee for the Salvation of Youth is formed in the Soviet Union by parents concerned about the influence of the Japanese Aum Shinrikyo cult on their children. The Committee later turns its attention to other religious groups, such as the Baptists and Jehovah's Witnesses. **SECT, TOL** |

| 1993 | The United States Supreme Court rules that laws that ban animal sacrifice for religious purposes are unconstitutional, as they discriminate against the free exercise of religion. The decision is especially relevant for the Santeria religion, as it requires the sacrifice of animals such as chickens and goats, which are eaten after their ritual use. **TOL** |

| 1993 | The United States Congress, in reaction to the 1990 *Employment Division v. Smith* Supreme Court ruling, passes the Religious Freedom Restoration Act, which requires government agencies to provide a compelling reason for restricting any form of religious practice. **TOL** |

| 1993 | When the United States Bureau of Alcohol, Tobacco, and Firearms attempts to arrest Branch Davidian leader David Koresh for illegally selling guns, a 51-day siege of the Davidian compound results. The siege ends with an assault on the compound, a fire that destroys it, and over 80 people killed. **TOL** |

| 1993 | In Albania, following the end of Communist rule in 1990, the government enacts a Charter of Rights that grants religious freedom, ending Albania's status as the only officially atheist state in the world. **TOL** |

| 1993 | In the *Kokkinakis* case the European Court of Human Rights rules that Greece's prosecution of a Jehovah's Witness for proselytizing is not in accord with the freedom of religion guaranteed by the European Convention on Human Rights. The court does not, however, rule on the legitimacy of Greek laws banning proselytizing in general. **TOL** |

| 1993 | In Poland the government and the Vatican enter into an agreement that stipulates that the Polish state and the Roman Catholic Church shall be |

"autonomous and independent." The agreement is controversial, as it ends the separation of church and state called for in the constitution and gives privileged status to Roman Catholicism. The agreement is not ratified by the Polish parliament.   TOL

1993   In Vietnam Buddhists hoping to end governmental control of religion engage in hunger strikes, self-immolation, and a mass protest in Hue that is repressed by the government.   TOL

1994   In response to liberal reformers who call for a consideration of the ordination of women as priests in the Roman Catholic Church, Pope John Paul II issues an apostolic letter that continues the practice of forbidding women to be ordained as priests. Later this year the Church issues its *Catechism of the Catholic Church* in English. It is the first full collection of the Church's doctrines since 1965. Pope John Paul II also writes *Crossing the Threshold of Hope*, which sets forth his views about the role of the Church in modern society, and it becomes a best-seller.   CATH

1994   In the United States the Southern Baptist Convention and leaders of the Roman Catholic community agree to cooperate in combating pornography, abortion, and other social issues and also agree to refrain from seeking converts from one another.   CATH, PROT

1994   In Australia the National Council of Churches in Australia is formed to represent the interests of Protestants and Catholics in the nation.   CHRIS

1994   The Anti-Defamation League of the B'nai B'rith publishes *The Religious Right: The Assault on Tolerance and Pluralism in America*, in which it accuses some in the Religious Right and the Christian Coalition of exacerbating ethnic and religious divisions in American society. The conclusion is attacked by leaders of the Religious Right, and in 1995 Jewish and Christian fundamentalist leaders meet to discuss their differences.   CHRIS, JUD

1994   In Iran Muslim women from 15 nations compete in the first Islamic Women's Games. The games are organized in accord with Islamic law, which requires that women keep their bodies covered in the presence of men to whom they are not related by blood or marriage. Men are banned from events in which the women compete in sports attire.   ISLAM

1994   Taslima Nasrin, a Bangladeshi feminist writer, is charged in court with offending the Muslim faith and is threatened with death by Islamic militants. She goes into exile in Sweden.   ISLAM

1994   In Afghanistan the fundamentalist Islamic Taliban (Seminarians) movement develops in Afghan refugee camps in the Pakistan city of Peshawar and the area around the Khyber Pass. Students at Islamic seminaries take control of five Afghan provinces.   ISLAM

1994	In Saudi Arabia King Saud Fahd establishes the Supreme Council of Islamic Affairs to advise the king on religious and governmental matters. The council is headed by the king's brother, Prince Sultan. The council is viewed by outsiders as an effort by the king to weaken the influence of the Ulema Council, which is composed of Islamic fundamentalists. **ISLAM**

| 1994 | In Egypt violence by Muslim fundamentalists seeking to create an Islamic state intensifies with attacks on Coptic Christians and tourists, in an apparent effort to destabilize the economy. The government responds by arresting and imprisoning leaders of the movement. The government also limits the activities of Islamic investment companies, which provide a source of income for Muslims. **ISLAM** |

| 1994 | Throughout the year violence continues between Indian troops and Muslims in Kashmir with over 2,000 people killed. **ISLAM, HIND** |

| 1994 | In February an Israeli kills 29 Arab Muslims who are praying at the mosque at the Cave of the Patriarchs in Jerusalem. **ISLAM, JUD** |

| 1994 | Palestinian self-rule goes into effect. After a delay of several months, Israeli forces are withdrawn and Palestinian self-rule is established on the West Bank. **ISLAM, JUD** |

| 1994 | Stephen Spielberg's film *Schindler's List* is released in United States movie theaters. It is a fictionalized account of how one German man saved hundreds of Jews in Europe during the Holocaust and also graphically depicts the plight of the Jews during the Holocaust. It is also shown widely in Germany. **JUD** |

| 1994 | Relations between the African-American and Jewish communities continue to deteriorate in the United States when representatives of Jewish organizations accuse leaders of the Nation of Islam of making derogatory statements about Jews. **JUD** |

| 1994 | A Hasidic (ultra-Orthodox) Jewish community in New York State is involved in a case regarding separation of state and church that comes before the United States Supreme Court. The community had convinced the state to establish a separate school district for its handicapped children. The court finds such schools unconstitutional. **JUD, TOL** |

| 1994 | Ezra Taft Benson, the former United States secretary of agriculture and the current president of the Mormon Church, dies. He is replaced by Howard W. Hunter, who dies after serving just over one year and is replaced by Gordon W. Hinckley in 1995. **MOR** |

| 1994 | The Church of England ordains 32 women as priests, ending a ban on women serving as priests that has been in place for 460 years. **PROT** |

| 1994 | The role of the Sikh religious court *Akal Takht* in controlling Sikh life comes into conflict among Sikh religious scholars when a Sikh scholar at the University of Michigan is charged with and convicted of blasphemy for questions about the divine origin of early Sikh texts. **SIKH** |

| 1994 | In Trinidad and Tobago the government revises the calendar of national holidays to limit the number of Christian holidays and to include an additional one for the Indian community but refuses to add one for the African-American Orisha religion. **TOL** |

| 1995 | At its annual meeting and while celebrating its 150th anniversary, the Southern Baptist Convention in the United States apologizes to African-Americans "for condoning and/or permitting systematic individual racism in our lifetime." The apology is considered to be far too late by some African-American Baptist organizations. **AFRICAN, PROT** |

| 1995 | The conflict over control of Buddhism in Tibet between the Chinese government and the Dalai Lama in exile in India continues when the Dalai Lama selects six-year-old Gedhun Choeklyi Nyima as 11th Panchen Lama, Tibetan Buddhism's second-highest office. His choice is rejected by the Chinese government, which arrests the boy and installs its own candidate, Gyaincain Norbu. The incident causes an international outcry. **BUDD** |

| 1995 | The Congregation for the Doctrine of Faith, the central Roman Catholic Church body that issues opinions on Church doctrine, supports the pope's 1994 letter denying women the right to become priests by ruling that his teaching on the matter is infallible. **CATH** |

| 1995 | The largest prayer meeting in history takes place in San Juan, Puerto Rico, when the American Evangelical preacher Billy Graham conducts a service that is televised by satellite to some one billion people around the world. **EVAN** |

| 1995 | The Christian novel *Left Behind* by Tim LaHaye and Jerry B. Jenkins is published by the Christian-oriented Tyndale House Publishers in the United States. It is the first in a series of books published over the next few years that comes to be called the Left Behind series that sells well in Christian bookstores, as well as to a general market. The novels are based on Evangelical Christian interpretations of the Bible and tell millenarian tales of escape to a Christian heaven during a period of catastrophe on earth. **EVAN** |

| 1995 | The Swaminarayan Hindu sect in London constructs the largest Hindu temple in the world in north London. **HIND** |

| 1995 | In India the cabinet agrees to change the name of Bombay to Mumbai, its Hindu name. The decision is supported by the ruling Hindu Shiv Party in Maharashtra State. **HIND** |

1995   In Egypt attacks on tourists by Muslim fundamentalists continue and the government continues its repression of Islamic fundamentalists. It arrests and imprisons 54 leaders of the Muslim Brotherhood, a moderate group that seeks to change society through nonviolent means.   ISLAM

1995   Fundamentalist Islam loses its appeal in Jordan and the Islamic Action Front suffers a number of defeats in local elections.   ISLAM

1995   In Turkey riots involving Muslims who seek a return to Islamic rule leave 30 people dead.   ISLAM

1995   In Turkey the Welfare Party, considered by many to represent the interests of Islamic fundamentalism, but which also advocates reforms to assist the poor, wins the general election for seats in the legislature. It forms a coalition government with a small secular party but is prevented by the existing secular government, backed by the military, from taking power.   ISLAM

1995   The Organization of the Islamic Conference declares that it will no longer support the United Nations arms embargo on Bosnian and Serb forces in Bosnia as it claims that the United Nations peacekeeping forces have been unable to maintain the safety of Bosnian Muslims. Before this decision, some Islamic nations have been providing financial support for the Bosnians, but after the decision it increases, and volunteers from several Islamic nations, including Egypt, Iran, and the Sudan, go to Bosnia to assist the Bosnian Muslims.   ISLAM

1995   The sheik of Al-Azhar, the senior Islamic official in Egypt, defends the practice of performing operations to mutilate the genitals of girls. Although not required by Islam, the practice is common in some Islamic societies in the Middle East and Africa. The practice is highly controversial, with supporters viewing it as a marker of ethnic identity, and critics viewing it as a means to control women.   ISLAM

1995   On September 28 Prime Minister Yitzak Rabin of Israel and Palestine Liberation Organization chairman Yasir Arafat sign an interim peace agreement in a White House ceremony in Washington, D.C. The agreement augments the 1993 agreement by extending home rule to Palestinians living on the West Bank. In November, Rabin is assassinated by a right-wing Jewish law student who objects to giving land to Palestinians.   ISLAM, JUD

1995   Madalyn Murray O'Hair, founder of American Atheists, Inc., her son, and her granddaughter disappear from their home in San Antonio, Texas, along with $500,000 in gold coins from the organization's account. In 1999 two men, one a former employee of the organization, were under investigation for involvement in the disappearance. Although no bodies have been found, law officers assume that O'Hair and her relatives were murdered.   MISC

1995   Several Protestant denominations that have allowed women to be ordained in recent years move to support that policy in the face of internal criticism. They include the Lutheran World Federation, the World Alliance of Reformed Churches, and Episcopal Church in the United States.   PROT

1995   The International Council of Unitarians and Universalists is established to coordinate activities of Unitarian and Universal churches in 20 nations.   SECT

1995   On March 20 in Japan, a nerve gas attack in three Tokyo subway lines leaves 12 people dead and over 5,000 injured. The new religion Aum Shinrikyo and its leader, Shoko Asahara, are blamed for the attack. The movement's offices are raided, incriminating nerve gas confiscated, and members of Shoko Asahara are arrested despite their claims of innocence. Authorities believe the attack and at least one earlier attack in 1994 are motivated by a desire to create a major catastrophe in accord with the apocalyptic beliefs of the movement.   SECT

1955   The Universal Church of the Kingdom of God, a major Evangelical denomination in Brazil, is the subject of an investigation by the Brazilian government that charges that the church is guilty of tax fraud and is involved in drug trafficking.   SECT

1995   In Great Britain the High Court refuses to remove a young man from a commune run by the Family even though his grandmother claims he has been mistreated. The court rules that charges of sexual misconduct, overly aggressive recruiting techniques, and secrecy no longer accurately describe the movement.   SECT

1995   Two managers of the "City of Rajneeshpuram" commune in Oregon are arrested, convicted, and sentenced to five-year prison terms for plotting to kill an Oregon official. This marks the end of the movement in the United States, although a community continues in Poona, India.   SPIR

1995   Murayama Tomiichi, Japan's first Socialist leader since 1948, issues a "heartfelt apology" on the 50th anniversary of the end of World War II. This will help to defuse problems with China, South Korea, and the Philippines. The Sarin nerve gas attack by the Aum Shinrikyo cult in the Tokyo subway will lead to the amendment passed this year of the 1951 law governing religious corporations: greater control is to be exerted over cults. This move is opposed by some as an attack on religious freedom.   TOL

1995   The Soka Gakkai movement, which traces its ancestry to a Buddhist movement in the 13th century, becomes controversial in Japan because of its support for the minority Shinshinto Party.   TOL

1995   In Japan the government enacts the Religious Corporation Revision Act, which gives the government greater power to investigate and collect information about religious groups. The act is criticized by some as interfering with the freedom of religious expression in Japan. TOL

1995 In Ireland a referendum removes the ban on divorce from the constitution. TOL

1995 The Christian Coalition in the United States issues its *Contract with the American Family*, with a political agenda that appeals to conservative politicians. The agenda emphasizes religion and restrictions on secular humanism. TOL

1995 Representatives from 40 denominations and religions meet in Manila, the Philippines, to discuss the issue of pornography. The meeting concludes that pornography is a major social problem that causes the decay of society. TOL

1995 In *Rosenberg v. Rector & Visitors of University of Virginia*, the United States Supreme Court rules that state universities are required to support the free speech of students expressing religious beliefs. TOL

1995 In the United States the Internal Revenue Service for the first time revokes the tax-exempt status of a church when it does so for the Church of Pierce Creek in Conklin, New York. The church had engaged in prohibited political activity when it placed advertisements in newspapers urging people not to vote for Bill Clinton for president. TOL

1995–1996 In Afghanistan the fundamentalist Islamic Taliban regime takes control of much of the nation. The Taliban end armed conflict in much of the nation and also rule in accord with their fundamental Islamic beliefs. Restrictions are placed on women, Islamic worship is made compulsory, and crimes are severely punished. ISLAM

1995–1996 Dozens of African-American Christian churches as well as fewer numbers of white churches, Muslim mosques, and Jewish synagogues are burned in the rural south. African-American leaders charge that the church burnings are the work of racists. A government investigation fails to support the charge although some Ku Klux Klan members are charged with several of the arsons. AFRICAN, TOL

1996 Archaeologists discover what they believe is the birthplace of the Buddha in Lumbini, Nepal, just north of the Indian border. Later in the year the British Museum acquires ancient Buddhist texts written on bark in the first and second centuries B.C.E. The texts relate to the spread of Buddhism into central Asia. BUDD

1996 Pope John Paul II continues his world travels and visits a number of Latin American nations, where he calls for peace in the region, then meets with

Cuban Communist leader Fidel Castro in Rome, suggesting a thaw in relations between Cuba and the Church. **CATH**

1996 The Roman Catholic Church asks for forgiveness for its role in the Argentinean "dirty war" of 1976 to 1983, when the military dictatorship repressed, tortured, and killed political opponents, at times with the assistance or acquiescence of the Roman Catholic Church. **CATH**

1996 In the United States 40 leaders of Roman Catholic and Evangelical organizations call on Congress to investigate and enact laws to control the persecution of Christians in other nations. **CHRIS, TOL**

1996 In India the secular Congress Party loses the parliamentary election to Hindu Nationalists. The Bharatiya Janata Party, which promotes an agenda of Hindu nationalism and is the largest vote getter among the parties contesting the election, begins to form a coalition government. **HIND**

1996 The first McDonald's fast-food restaurant opens in Delhi, India. In accord with the Hindu prohibition on the eating of beef, no beef is served. "Hamburgers" are made from lamb. **HIND**

1996 In the United States 10 children of Hare Krishna members in the 1970s and 1980s charge that they and other children were often emotionally, physically, and sexually abused while living at Krishna-run boarding schools in the United States. The schools were staffed by Krishna members who often had little training or experience in child care. **HIND**

1996 In Turkey the Welfare Party, which advocates a greater role for Islamic law in the government and supports the poor and workers, comes to power when it forms a coalition with the True Path Party. **ISLAM**

1996 In the United States the growth of the Islamic community is recognized when representatives are invited to the White House to mark the end of Ramadan, the Muslim holy month. **ISLAM**

1996 The Palestine National Council votes to delete the clause in its charter that calls for the destruction of Israel. **ISLAM, JUD**

1996 Israel opens a tunnel near a sacred Muslim site in Jerusalem. The action leads to Arab protests and several days of rioting as well as fighting between Israeli soldiers and Palestinian police. **ISLAM, JUD**

1996 An international controversy develops over the issue of how the Swiss government and Swiss banks handled money and other wealth deposited there by the Nazis during World War II. At the core of the issue is the handling of money and wealth taken from Jews and money deposited there by Jews who died in the Holocaust. **JUD**

1996   The conflict between Orthodox and Reform Judaism in the United States worsens when the leader of a major Reform organization criticizes Orthodox leaders for being rigid and unwilling to react to the realities of modern life. At the same time Reform Judaism is criticized by some within the movement for moving toward exclusionary policies when it adopts a policy stating that children raised in another religion must be excluded from Reform religious schools.   **JUD**

1996   The Southern Baptist Convention establishes a missionary effort to the Jews. The action is condemned by many leading Jewish organizations.   **JUD, PROT**

1996   Several Protestant denominations continue to address the issue of sexuality. The United Methodist Church in the United States rejects a call by some members to allow homosexuals to serve as ministers, and the Presbyterian Church U.S.A. rules that all church officials must confine sexual activity to the marital relationship.   **PROT**

1996   In Sweden a movement toward separation of the state and church begins when children with one Lutheran parent are no longer considered at birth to be Lutherans.   **PROT**

1996   In the United States the missionary agencies of the United Church of Christ and the Disciples of Christ are combined to form the Common Global Ministries Board.   **PROT**

1996   In the United States the federal welfare system is reformed by President Clinton, with the level of federal support reduced. It is expected that private charities will become more involved in aiding the poor, and toward that end the new welfare law permits the government to give funds to religious organizations for that purpose.   **TOL**

1996   In South Africa the new constitution establishes South Africa as a secular nation and drops language of earlier constitutions, which implied that South Africa was a Christian nation.   **TOL**

1997   A schism develops in the Tibetan Buddhist community in exile in India. It centers on the followers of a Buddhist monk, Cheme Tsering, who attracts some 20,000 followers who claim authority from a monk named Dorje Shugden. Although the Dalai Lama remains in control, three of his close followers are murdered, with the Shugden sect suspected.   **BUDD**

1997   The Roman Catholic Church excommunicates Sri Lankan priest Tissa Balasuriya for questioning the authority of the pope. He is reinstated after signing a profession of faith, the basic listing of Catholic beliefs adopted by the Church in 1989. The excommunication is seen by outsiders as an effort by the pope to control liberal dissent.   **CATH**

| 1997 | In the continuing debate in the Roman Catholic Church over the ordination of women, the Catholic Theological Society of America asks the Vatican to study the matter further. **CATH** |

| 1997 | Conflict develops between the Eastern and Russian Orthodox churches and the Roman Catholic Church over charges by the former that the latter is seeking to convert Orthodox Christians in Eastern Europe to Roman Catholicism. **CATH, ORTHO** |

| 1997 | In the United States the Promise Keepers hold a mass rally attended by hundreds of thousands of people (almost entirely men) in Washington, D.C. The group has become controversial; it is praised by some for requiring that men act responsibly toward their wives and children but has also been criticized by the National Organization for Women for setting forth what it views as an agenda that subordinates women to men. The rally is the high point of the movement in 1997 and it loses members and influence in 1998. **CHRIS** |

| 1997 | All-female Muslim popular singing groups called Nasyid groups become popular in Malaysia. The women wear traditional Islamic clothing combined with western adornments, such as red lipstick and platform shoes. They seek to provide a role model for young women that stresses devotion to Islam. **ISLAM** |

| 1997 | Conflict, including riots and beatings, breaks out in western China between non-Muslims and members of the Muslim Uighur ethnic minority, who seek to emphasize their ethnic identity. **ISLAM** |

| 1997 | The national Yiddish Book Center is established in Amherst, Massachusetts, as a repository for and research center on Yiddish literature. **JUD** |

| 1997 | New York City Mayor Rudolph Giuliani criticizes former mayor David Dinkins for his handling of the conflict between Hasidic Jews and African-Americans in Brooklyn in 1991. Giuliani apologizes to the Hasidic community and agrees to pay them $1.1 million to settle a lawsuit they filed against the city. Dinkins and leaders of the African-American community accuse Giuliani of pandering to the politically powerful Hasidic community. **JUD** |

| 1997 | In the largest mass suicide in the United States, 39 members of the Heaven's Gate cult in California kill themselves, evidently believing that after death their souls will be free to travel in a spaceship in a path following the Hale-Bopp comet, visible in the sky at this time. **MISC** |

| 1997 | A number of books that claim to reveal secret coded messages in the Old Testament of the Bible are published in the United States. The most popular is *The Bible Code* by Michael Drossin, which claims that the Old Testament contains hidden information about such modern events as the Watergate scandal and the Oklahoma City bombing. The claims of the |

book are rejected by Israeli mathematician Eliyahu Rips, whose work Drossin claims is the basis of the book. **MISC**

1997   To celebrate the Mormon migration to Utah that occurred from 1847 to 1869, some 300 people re-trace the journey through the Big Mountain Pass in Utah. **MOR**

1997   Ecumenicism is advanced among Protestant denominations in the United States when the Evangelical Lutheran Church in America agrees to share communion with the Presbyterian Church, the Reformed Church in America, and the United Church of Christ. **PROT**

1997   Ecumenicism is advanced among Protestant churches in Wales when five churches agree to appoint one bishop for all the churches in 2000. The churches are the Church of Wales, the Presbyterian Church of Wales, the Methodist Church, the United Reformed Church, and the Covenanted Churches of the Baptist Union of Great Britain. **PROT**

1997   In the United States the Southern Baptist Convention, the largest denomination in the nation, votes to boycott the Walt Disney Company because, it alleges, the company supports a homosexual lifestyle by extending employee benefits to gay partners of employees. The boycott does not appear to affect the media conglomerate's profits. **PROT**

1997   In a landmark case Japan's Supreme Court rules that government donations to Shinto shrines are illegal under the constitutional separation of church and state. The defendants, former Ehime Prefecture officials, argue the donations provide moral support to bereaved families and are a form of social courtesy rather than government support of religion. Despite repeated efforts during the postwar years by conservatives to revive a form of state Shinto sect, and shrine Shinto undergo decline after the withdrawal of government and compulsory parishioner financial support. Some Shinto groups start commercial enterprises such as wedding halls. The new religions, many of which appeal to women, attract large numbers of adherents. **SHINTO, TOL**

1997   There is a revival of witchcraft accusations amid the economic and political turmoil in Russia, and one woman accused of witchcraft is killed. **SPIR**

1998   Henry J. Lyons, the president of the National Baptist Convention, U.S.A., the largest African-American church and the third-largest church in the United States, is indicted by the federal government on 56 counts of fraud, extortion, and tax evasion. Two other church managers are also indicted. Lyons is accused of using his role in the church to extort payments from businesses seeking access to the African-American Baptist community and embezzling $250,000 given to the organization by the Anti-Defamation League to rebuild African-American churches destroyed by arson. **AFRICAN**

| 1998 | In Tibet Chinese government authorities ask 49 Buddhist monks over the age of 60 to retire. The action is seen by the Dalai Lama, the exiled leader of the Tibetan Buddhist community in India, as an effort by the government to eradicate Buddhism. **BUDD** |

1998   The sacred Temple of the Tooth Relic at Kandy, Sri Lanka's holiest Buddhist shrine and a UNESCO World Heritage Site, is bombed by the Tamil Tigers, the rebel group. In Taiwan, thousands of Buddhists attend ceremonies on April 20, greeting the arrival of what is regarded as a holy tooth that once belonged to Buddha. **SEE 1592, BUDD.**   **BUDD**

1998   On April 26 Monsignor Juan Geraldi, auxiliary archbishop in Guatemala, is murdered two days after delivering a 1,400-page report detailing human rights violations that took place during the civil war from 1960 to 1996. He was one of the most prominent of the Catholic clergy who worked for human rights in Latin America.   **CATH**

1998   In May the People's Republic of China releases Roman Catholic bishop Zeng Jingmu from prison six months early. He was imprisoned for refusing to acknowledge the authority of the Chinese Patriotic Catholic Association over the Vatican in various church matters. The Chinese government does not recognize the authority of the Vatican, nor does it have diplomatic relations with it.   **CATH**

1998   In the latest effort to control liberal dissent in the Roman Catholic Church, Pope John Paul II, in June, makes changes in canon law that include in the profession of faith a number of teachings and decisions of the pope. He does not specify the issues, but they concern matters such as the ordination of women, euthanasia, and protests by priests and teachers at Catholic colleges.   **CATH**

1998   Pope John Paul II beatifies (the step before sainthood) Alojzije Cardinal Stepinac, the archbishop of Zagreb, as a martyr to "the atrocities of the Communist system." Stepinac had been imprisoned by the Communist government in Yugoslavia as a Nazi sympathizer after World War II and died in 1960. The beatification causes controversy in the Balkans and beyond, as Stepinac is revered by Catholic Croats but is criticized by Orthodox Serbs and Jews as a Nazi sympathizer who allowed the persecution of Serbs and Jews before he turned against the Nazis in 1943.   **CATH**

1998   Pope John Paul II cannonizes Edith Stein (1891–1942), a German Jewish philosopher who converted to Roman Catholicism in 1922 and became a Carmelite nun in 1933 when forced to give up her teaching position because of her Jewish ancestry. Stein was deported to the Auschwitz concentration camp and killed there in 1942. She is perhaps the first person of Jewish ancestry since the early Apostles and martyrs of the Christian Church to be made a saint. Although the pope acknowledges that she was killed because of her Jewish ancestry and also acknowledges the Holocaust, the canonization is criticized by some Jewish groups who see it as inappropriate as she was killed because she was of Jewish ancestry, not because she was Catholic.   CATH, JUD

1998   A peace agreement is reached in Northern Ireland that is expected to end the fighting between the primarily Roman Catholic population that has sought independence from Great Britain and unification with Ireland and the mainly Protestant population that has sought to remain part of Great Britain. The agreement affords Northern Ireland much independence, with internal government, administrative links to Ireland, and continuing ties to Great Britain.   CATH, PROT, TOL

1998   In India attacks by Hindus on Catholics and Protestants, including the destruction of churches and the raping of nuns, escalate. The attacks are especially frequent in Gujarat State, which is the base of the *Vishwa Hindu Parishad* (World Hindu Council), one of the most pro-Hindu, anti-West movements in India.   CHRIS, HIND

1998   In November Christians in Jakarta, Indonesia, are attacked by mobs of Javanese Muslims who destroy 11 churches, kill 18 people, and injure dozens of others. Attacks are aimed mainly at Christians from the island of Ambon who had immigrated to Java. The attacks are believed to be motivated mainly by economic problems. Additional attacks take place in 1999. They are believed by experts to be the result of economic problems in Indonesia, with Christians blamed for the problems by the Muslim majority.   CHRIS, ISLAM

1998   An estimated 30 Daoist priests are in residence on Mount Mao, a holy spot of Daoism in China's Shandong Province.   DAO

1998   In its journal the International Society of Krishna Consciousness (Iskcon, the Hare Krishna movement) admits and details cases of emotional, sexual, and physical abuse of children in Hare Krishna boarding schools during the 1970s and 1980s, which were first made public by former students in 1996.   HIND

1998   The Hare Krishna movement has become an international movement and many United States adherents are immigrants from India. Krishna centers are established in India and Eastern Europe as well as in the United States and Western Europe. (In the 1970s and 1980s the movement was confined mainly to the United States and Western Europe.) The movement has also changed from one in which many adherents live in spiritual communities called ashrams to one in which most adherents live among the general population.   HIND

1998   A Hare Krishna temple opens in New Delhi, India. It has nine robotic models of gods that recite passages from Hindu religious texts.   HIND

1998   In Afghanistan resistance to rule by the fundamentalist Taliban Party in the north is crushed and effectively ends with a Taliban victory.   ISLAM

1998   In Iran the government lifts the *fatwa* (death threat) placed on British author Salman Rushdie by the Ayatollah Khomeini in 1989. The death threat was issued because passages in Rushdie's novel *The Satanic Verses* were considered blasphemous to Islam. Since 1989 Rushdie has lived in hiding in Britain. The British government responds by reestablishing diplomatic relations with Iran and Rushdie comes out of hiding.   ISLAM

1998   During the annual Ramadan pilgrimage to Mecca, Saudi Arabia, 138 Muslims are trampled to death. About two million pilgrims have made the journey this year, and their numbers are expected to increase in future years and to continue to pose an administrative problem for the Saudi government.   ISLAM

1998   Iran's harsh rules governing personal conduct, which are in accord with a strict interpretation of Islamic law, are relaxed after the election of the reformist religious leader Mohammad Khatami, in 1997.   ISLAM

1998   In Israel a controversy develops over the content of a television series on the history of Israel aired as part of Israel's 50th-anniversary celebration. The controversy centers on segments describing the founding of Israel and conflict with Palestinians and Arabs in Israel, which call into question the accuracy of the traditional Israeli view that the settlers developed a thriving nation in a place where no one lived and that the settlers were always the victims of and never the perpetrators of attacks on Palestinians and other Arabs. It suggests that some Arabs and Palestinians were treated harshly or killed. The series also raises the question of the second-class status afforded Middle Eastern Jews by the European Jews in Israel.   JUD

1998   In May a Jewish synagogue in Moscow is bombed and damaged. Jews in Russia cite the incident as another in a continuing series of attacks on the Russian Jewish community by those in Russia who support Russian nationalism and want all non-Russians removed from Russian society. The attack is condemned by the Russian government and the Russian Orthodox Church.   JUD

1998   Three Swiss banks offer to pay $600 million to settle claims of Jewish Holocaust victims and their survivors who claim that wealth stolen from Jews in Germany was kept in Swiss banks. The settlement offer is rejected by leaders of major Jewish organizations in the United States, who find the amount inadequate.   JUD

1998   American rabbi Arthur Scheier sanctifies the Ohel Rachel Synagogue, which, along with five other synagogues, had served the small Iraqi Jewish community in Shanghai, China, in the 1800s, and some 20,000 Jews who immigrated to China during World War II fled here. The Jewish community left China after World War II and after the 1949 Communist rise to power. Jews hope that the synagogue, which had been a warehouse, will be reopened to serve the small community of non-Chinese Jews who live in Shanghai. JUD

1998   Two Swiss banks and Jewish organizations reach an agreement in which banks will pay $1.2 billion to survivors of the Holocaust or their descendants as compensation for money kept in Swiss bank accounts during and after World War II. The agreement does not involve the Swiss National Bank, which held most of the wealth, and is accepted by only a small plurality of the Swiss people. JUD

1998   An Islamic school funded by the government opens in Great Britain. There are also 7,000 Christian and 24 Jewish government-funded schools in the nation. They are required to teach the national curriculum but are also allowed to teach their own religions. ISLAM, TOL

1998   Popular religion has become increasingly important among farmers in China. Ancestor worship, fortune telling, worship at local temples, *feng shui*, and other traditional religious practices are now common in villages, towns, and cities in southern, western, and northern China. Such practices had been repressed during the Cultural Revolution but have become increasingly more common since the early 1980s. MISC

1998   The Public Broadcasting System in the United States airs the documentary *Faith and Reason*, which examines the relationship between science and religion, a topic that has become of increasing interest to both some scientists and theologians during the decade. MISC

1998   Several dozen Jewish, Protestant, and Greek Orthodox religious organizations in the United States campaign publicly for government approval of the Kyoto Protocol. The protocol asks economically developed nations to reduce the emission of heat-trapping gases so as to control global warming. MISC

1998   In March a group of Huichol Native Americans in northern Mexico is arrested by the military for possession of peyote, which the Huichol obtained during their pilgrimage to their sacred land of Wirikuta in San Luis Potosi State. Human rights activists criticize the arrest, stating it is a violation of the Huichol's religious right to practice their traditional religion. NATIV, TOL

1998   The General Assembly of the Presbyterian Church (U.S.A.), with 2.6 million members, passes an advisory resolution asking its members to give up any handguns and assault weapons in their possession and work to make society safer for children. PROT

1998   The Southern Baptist Convention in the United States amends its Statement of Baptist Faith and Message by declaring that the husband is the head of the family and that a wife should submit to his leadership. The statement is criticized by leaders of other less conservative Protestant organizations.

PROT

1998   The Northern Province of the Moravian Church in America appoints the Reverend Kay Ward as the first Moravian woman bishop.   **PROT**

1998   In Germany a report commissioned by the parliament concludes that Scientology is not a religion but a political movement with profit-making motives. The report allows the government to continue monitoring the organization, which had been previously accused by government officials of being totalitarian and of brainwashing its members.   **SECT**

1998   In July two Amish men, aged 23 and 24 who, in accord with Amish custom had been living outside their native Amish community in Pennsylvania in order to experience life in the outside world, are indicted for possession of drugs and are accused by federal authorities of being members of a drug distribution ring. They are the first Amish to be arrested for drug use, and the incident is viewed by some as a sign that the Amish are becoming more involved in the outside world, while others view it as normal experimentation by young men and not typical of Amish behavior in general.   **SECT**

1998   In Iran the government closes down an underground university run by members of the Baha'i religion. The university was started in 1987 after the government banned Baha'i from attending government-run universities. During the year, in a continuing repression of Baha'i, three Baha'i are arrested on charges of proselytizing and one is executed.   **SECT**

1998   Fourteen members of the Concerned Christians millennial cult are deported by Israel back to Denver, Colorado, where the members had lived before moving to Israel earlier in the year. The Israeli government claims that the group had planned to commit mass suicide as a means of ensuring the return of Christ in the year 2000.   **SECT**

1998   In San Francisco the Salvation Army gives up city funding and cuts its staff as it refuses to cooperate with a new law requiring publicly funded organizations to provide benefits to same-sex or unmarried partners of employees. Salvation Army officials view the law as inconsistent with their religious beliefs, which stress the sanctity of the nuclear family.   **TOL**

1998   The Wisconsin Supreme Court rules that it is constitutional and does not represent a violation of the principle of separation of state and church for parents to use school vouchers supported by tax money to pay tuition at religious schools. The United States Supreme Court refuses to hear the case on appeal and other states are thereby encouraged to enact similar legislation.   **TOL**

1998   The United States Congress passes and President Clinton signs a bill designed to withhold aid and support from nations that persecute religious minorities. The bill is aimed at such nations as China, Pakistan, Sudan, and Indonesia and is a reaction to complaints about persecution of Christians in these nations. Opponents claim that the bill will not end religious persecution and instead will cause harm to the peoples of these and other nations. The bill is supported by the Christian Coalition and some other religious organizations and opposed by many human rights organizations.

TOL

1999   Henry J. Lyons, head of the National Baptist Convention, U.S.A., the largest African-American church, is convicted on state (Florida) charges of racketeering and grand theft and then pleads guilty to related federal charges. He resigns his position with the church, is sentenced to five years in prison, and is required to repay the $5.2 million in funds that he was convicted of misusing.

AFRICAN

1999   A new and much larger and modern Ebenezer Baptist Church is consecrated in Atlanta, Georgia, across the street from the original church where civil rights leader the Reverend Martin Luther King Jr. delivered his first and final sermons.

AFRICAN

1999   A dispute breaks out in the Turkish parliament between secularists and those who favor an Islamic state when Merve Kavakci, a new member, wears a head scarf to the opening session. Although she argues that she is expressing only her personal views by wearing the scarf, secularists refuse to let her take the oath of office. In Turkey wearing the head scarf suggests to some support of an Islamic nation, a position opposed by the secularists. **ISLAM**

1999   There are an estimated 3,500,000 Jains in India, most in western India. Many pursue careers in banking and commerce. The Svetambaras, who make up the majority of Jains in India, reside mainly in Gujarat and Rajasthan (respectively west-central and northwest India); the Digambaras are found mostly in the Deccan region and southern India, especially in the city of Mysore. Although there have been countless schisms and schools and orders within Jainism—each emphasizing different aspects of the scriptures, cosmology, practices, diet, etc.—all retain the fundamental teachings. Some estimates claim there are as many as 75,000 Jains in North America. In the United States, the Jains are concentrated in and around a number of cities: New York City, Boston, Chicago, Cleveland, Pittsburgh, Atlanta, San Francisco, and several other California cities. In Canada most Jains are in the Province of Ontario. The Jains build temples in many of these centers or share temples with other Indian religious faiths (Hindu, Sikh, etc.). **JAIN**

1999   In the United States the Central Conference of American Rabbis, the rabbinical organization of Reform Judaism, adopts the "Statement of Principles." The statement reverses the trend in American Reform Judaism, dating to 1885, of rejecting traditional Jewish ritual and instead affirms the importance of traditional ritual including the use of Hebrew and the following of Jewish dietary laws. It also weakens previous support for intermarriage.   **JUD**

1999   A dispute develops on the Navajo reservation in Arizona over the maintenance of a zoo. Some Navajo argue that the zoo should be closed as it violates traditional religious beliefs about the reverence for animals, while others argue that the zoo should be kept open as Navajo children like to visit it.   **NATIV**

1999   On March 26 a jury of 13 Methodist ministers suspends United Methodist Church minister Greg Dill of Chicago for officiating at a marriage ceremony of two gay men. The issue is a contentious one in the church, and another minister was acquitted in March 1998, while similar charges were brought against 69 ministers who co-officiated at a gay wedding in California in 1999.   **PROT**

1999   In the United States, for the first time an openly homosexual man is allowed to serve on the board of a Presbyterian church. In a judicial ruling the Presbyterian Church U.S.A. allows Wayne Osborne to serve on the board of the First Presbyterian Church of Stamford, Connecticut.   **PROT**

1999   The first international Sikh convention is held in New Jersey and attracts 6,000 Sikhs. It is held on April 4 to coincide with the 330th anniversary of the Khalsa movement within Sikhism.   **SIKH**

1999   A legal battle emerges in New York over the distribution of the assets of Frederick P. Lenz III, which are estimated at $18 million. Lenz, who committed suicide in 1998, had been a well-known New Age figure who called himself Rama and was widely known as the Yuppie Guru. The dispute centers on ambiguities in the will about whether the estate should go to the National Audobon Society or be used to set up a foundation to continue his work.   **SPIR**

1999   A survey conducted by the National Center for Science Education in the United States shows that in a majority of states there is controversy about teaching evolution in the public schools or discussion of evolution is avoided. In one state (Alabama) a disclaimer is placed in textbooks that mention evolution.   **TOL**

1999   In Russia prosecutors in Moscow charge Jehovah's Witnesses with violating the new law on religion because they have been breaking the ban on seeking converts. Behind the prosecution is the Orthodox Church and the Committee for the Salvation of Youth, both of which seek to limit the influence of non-Orthodox religions in Russia. In the post-Soviet 1990s the Baptists and Jehovah's Witnesses have been especially active in taking converts from the Orthodox Church.   **TOL**

2000   The Nation of Islam, with the cooperation of the Unification Church, organizes the Million Family March in Washington, D.C., in October. The purpose of the march is to strengthen the family and emphasize morality.   **AFRICAN**

2000   On October 28–29 the annual Interfaith Call for Universal Freedom and Freedom of Worship in Tibet takes place. It involves some 70,000 individuals (up from 8,000 in 1999) who offer special prayers and rituals in a number of religions (Judaism, Roman Catholicism, Anglicism, Buddhism, Hiduism, and Islam, among others) in support of religious freedom for Tibetan Buddhists.   **BUDD, TOL**

2000   Encuento 2000 is held in the United States to mark ethnic diversity among American Roman Catholics. Previous encuentos in 1972, 1977, and 1985 focused on Latino Catholics. This one also gives attention to Asian and African-American Catholics.   **CATH**

2000   Jewish and Catholic Holocaust scholars ask the Vatican to open its archives so that a full study can be made of the response of the Vatican and Pope Pius XII to the Holocaust.   **CATH, JUD**

2000   The Potomac Adventist Book and Health Food Store opens in Silver Spring, Maryland. With over 40,000 square feet of floor space, it is thought to be the largest Christian book store in the world. The typical Christian book store in the United States has about 10,000 square feet of floor space. **CHRIS**

2000   In Egypt the court rules that attendants on Egypt Air can refuse to serve alcoholic beverages, as the consumption of alcohol is banned by Islamic law.   **ISLAM**

2000   In several nations in Central Asia, governments seek to repress Muslim fundamentalism. Although the majority of the population is Muslim, fundamentalism is seen as a threat by governments.   **ISLAM**

2000   During the presidential campaign in the United States, religion becomes an important issue, as both Al Gore and George W. Bush cite the importance of religion in their lives, and vice-presidential candidate Joseph Leiberman talks openly of the importance of faith. Leiberman is the first Jewish vice-presidential candidate on a major party ticket.   **JUD, PROT**

2000   The Central Conference of Rabbis in the United States, which represents Reform Jewish rabbis, votes to approve gay marriages. It is the largest religious organization in the United States to approve of gay marriage. **JUD, TOL**

2000   In the United States there is a resurgence of interest in religion among scholars. The resurgence is attributed to a greater role of religion in general in American life, foundation support for research on religion, and the growing religious diversity in the United States.   **MISC**

2000   The Templeton Prize for Progress in Religion is awarded to Freeman Dyson, a Princeton University mathematician and physicist, for his efforts to combine religion and science to benefit humanity. The award comes as a surprise to many, including experts on religion, since Dyson is not personally religious.   **MISC**

2000   Former United States President Jimmy Carter ends his membership in the Southern Baptist Convention, citing differences between its increasingly conservative approach and his personal religious values.   **PROT**

2000   In June the Presbyterian Church of America votes to allow women to speak at conferences but continues the ban on women speaking from the pulpit. The Church is small, with about 220,000 members.   **PROT**

2000   In China, government repression of the Falun Gong sect continues, with mass demonstrations by adherents and government arrests, detention, and imprisonment of sect leaders. The government describes the movement as an "evil cult."   **SECT, TOL**

2000   In *Tangipahoa Parish Board of Education* v. *Freiler*, the U.S. Supreme Court upholds a lower court ruling which disallows disclaimers mentioning the biblical version of the creation in the teaching of evolution.   **TOL**

2000   In *Adler* v. *Duval County School Board*, the U.S. Supreme Court reverses a lower court ruling that had allowed student-led prayer at a high school graduation.   **TOL**

Bibliography

Adams, Charles J., ed. *A Reader's Guide to the Great Religions*. 2nd ed. New York: Free Press, 1977.

Ahlstrom, Sydney E. *A Religious History of the American People*. New Haven, CT: Yale University Press, 1972.

Almond, Philip C. *The British Discovery of Buddhism*. Cambridge: Cambridge University Press, 1988.

Anderson, Edward F. *Peyote: The Divine Cactus*. Tucson, AZ: University of Arizona Press, 1996.

Anderson, John. *Religion, State and Politics in the Soviet Union and Successor States*. Cambridge: Cambridge University Press, 1994.

Atiya, Aziz S. *A History of Eastern Christianity*. New York: Methuen and Co., 1968; Millwood, NJ: Kraus Reprint, 1980.

Backman, Milton V., Jr. *Christian Churches of America: Origins and Beliefs*. Rev. ed. New York: Charles Scribner's Sons, 1983.

Bainton, Roland H. *Christendom: A Short History of Christianity and Its Impact on Western Civilization*. New York: Harper, 1964.

Balmer, Randall and John R. Fitzmier. *The Presbyterians*. Westport, CT: Greenwood Press, 1993.

Banks, Marcus. *Organizing Jainism in India and England*. Oxford: Clarendon Press, 1992.

Bapat, P.V., ed. *2500 Years of Buddhism*. Delhi: Publications Division, Ministry of Information and Broadcasting, Government of India, 1956.

Barbour, Hugh and J. William Frost. *The Quakers*. Westport, CT: Greenwood Press, 1988.

Barbour, Ian G. *Religion and Science: Historical and Contemporary Issues*. San Francisco: HarperSanFrancisco, 1997.

Barkun, Michael. *Religion and the Racist Right: The Origins of the Christian Identity Movement*. Rev. ed. Chapel Hill, NC: University of North Carolina Press, 1997.

Barnavi, Eli. *A Historical Atlas of the Jewish People from the Time of the Patriarchs to the Present*. New York: Alfred A. Knopf, 1992.

Barrett, David C. *Sects, Cults and Alternative Religions*. London: Blanford, 1996.

Barrier, N. Gerald and Van Dusenberry, eds. *The Sikh Disapora*. New Delhi: Chanakya, 1990.

Bibliography

Beit-Hallahmi, Benjamin. *The Illustrated Encyclopedia of Active New Religions, Sects, and Cults.* New York: Rosen Publishing Group, 1993.

Benz, Ernest. *The Eastern Orthodox Church: Its Thought and Life.* Trans. Winston, Richard and Clara Winston. New York: Anchord Books, 1963.

Bergendoff, Conrad *The Church of the Lutheran Reformation: A Historical Survey of Lutheranism.* St. Louis, MO: Concordia Publishing House, 1988.

Bokenkamp, Stephen R. *Early Daoist Scriptures.* Berkeley, CA: University of California Press, 1997.

Bokenkotter, Thomas. *A Concise History of the Catholic Church.* Rev. and exp. ed. New York: Doubleday, 1990.

Borchert, Bruno. *Mysticism: Its History and Challenge.* York Beach, ME: Samuel Weiser, Inc., 1993.

Bourdeaux, Michael. *Religious Minorities in the Soviet Union.* 3rd ed. London: Minority Rights Group, 1977.

Bowker, John. *The Oxford Dictionary of World Religions.* Oxford: Oxford University Press, 1997.

Boyle, Kevin and Juliet Sheen, eds. *Freedom of Religion and Belief: A World Report.* London: Routledge, 1997.

Brackney, William Henry. *The Baptists.* Westport, CT: Greenwood Press, 1988.

Brandon, George. *Santería from Africa to the New World: The Dead Sell Memories.* Bloomington, IN: Indiana University Press, 1993.

Bredero, Adrian H. *Christendom and Christianity in the Middle Ages: The Relations Between Religion, Church, and Society.* Grand Rapids, MI: William B. Erdmans, 1994.

Brosse, Jacques. *Religious Leaders.* Edinburgh: Chambers, 1988.

Brown, Diana DeG. *Umbanda: Religion and Politics in Urban Brazil.* Ann Arbor, MI: UMI Research Press, 1986.

Bunson, Matthew E. *Encyclopedia of the Middle Ages.* New York: Facts on File, 1995.

Cameron, Euan. *The European Reformation.* Oxford: Oxford University Press, 1991.

Campbell, Bruce F. *Ancient Wisdom Revised: A History of the Theosophical Movement.* Berkeley: University of California Press, 1980.

Carrasco, David. *Religions of Mesoamerica.* New York: HarperCollins, 1990.

Carrasco, Pedro. *Tarascan Folk Religion.* New Orleans, LA: Tulane University, Middle American Research Institute, 1952.

Chadwick, Nora. *The Celts.* Hammondsworth, England: Penguin, 1970.

Chan, Wing-tsit. *Religious Trends in Modern China.* New York: Columbia University Press, 1953.

Chatterjee, Asim Kumar. *A Comprehensive History of Jainism.* 2 vols. Calcutta: Firma KLM Private Limited, 1978 and 1984.

Chevannes, Barry. *Rastafari: Roots and Ideology.* New York: Syracuse University Press, 1994.

Chryssides, George. *The Elements of Unitarianism.* Shaftesbury, England: Element, 1998.

Cohen-Sherbok, Lavina. *A History of Jewish Civilization.* Edison, NJ: Chartwell Books, 1997.

Confucius. *The Analects of Confucius (Lun Yu): A Literal Translation.* New York: Oxford University Press, 1997.

Clarke, Peter B. and Jeffrey Somers. *Japanese New Religions in the West.* Folkestone, England: Japan Library/Curzon Press, 1994.

Conze, Edward. *A Short History of Buddhism.* London: George Allen & Unwin, 1980.

Cousins, Peter. *The Brethren.* Oxford: Religious Education Press, 1982.

Creemers, Wilhelmus H. M. *Shrine Shinto After World War II.* Leiden, the Netherlands: E. J. Brill, 1968.

Crim, Keith. *Abingdon Dictionary of Living Religions.* Nashville, TN: Abingdon, 1981.

David, A. Rosalie. *The Ancient Egyptians: Religious Beliefs and Practices.* London: Routledge & Kegan Paul, 1982.

Davies, Horton. *The English Free Churches.* London: Oxford University Press, 1963.

Davies, Douglas, ed. *Mormon Identities in Transition.* London: Cassell, 1996.

Davis, Mary B. *Native America in the Twentieth Century: An Encyclopedia.* New York: Garland, 1954.

Dayton, Donald W. *The Roots of Pentecostalism.* Peabody, MA: Hendrickson Press, 1987.

dc Bary, Theodore, ed. *Sources of Chinese Tradition.* 2 vols. New York: Columbia University Press, 1960.

DeJong, J. W. *A Brief History of Buddhist Studies in Europe and North America.* Viranasi, India: Bharat-Bharati, 1976.

De Lange, Nicholas, ed. *The Illustrated History of the Jewish People.* New York: Harcourt Brace & Company, 1997.

Dimont, Max I. *Jews, God and History.* New York: Mentor, 1994.

Eban, Abba. *Heritage: Civilization and the Jews.* New York: Summit Books, 1984.

Bibliography

Eliade, Mircea, ed. *Encyclopedia of Religion*. 16 vols. New York: Macmillan, 1986.

Eliade, Mircea and Joan P. Couliano with Hillary S. Wiesner. *The Eliade Guide to World Religions*. New York: Harper Collins, 1991.

Ellis, Peter B. *The Druids*. London: Constable, 1994.

Ellwood, Robert S., Jr. *The Eagle and the Rising Sun: Americans and the New Religions of Japan*. Philadelphia: Westminster Press, 1974.

Embree, Ainslie T., ed. *Sources of Indian Tradition. Volume One: From the Beginning to 1800*. New York: Columbia University Press, 1988.

Embree, Ainslie T., ed. *Encyclopedia of Asian History*. 4 vols. New York: Charles Scribner's Sons, 1988.

Ferrell, Robert H. and Joan Hoff, eds. *Dictionary of American History, Supplement*. New York: Charles Scribner's Sons Reference Books, 1996.

Fey, Harold E., ed. *A History of the Ecumenical Movement: 1948–1968*. Philadelphia: The Westminster Press, 1970.

Flood, Gavin. *An Introduction to Hinduism*. Cambridge: Cambridge University Press, 1996.

Fodor, Nandor. *An Encyclopedia of Psychic Science*. Secaucus, NJ: Citadel Press, 1966.

Fogarty, Robert S. *Dictionary of American Communal and Utopian History*. Westport, CT: Greenwood Press, 1980.

Ford, David F., ed. *The Modern Theologians: An Introduction to Christian Theology in the Twentieth Century*. Oxford: Basil Blackwell, 1989.

Gibetz, Judah, Edward L. Greenstein and Regina Stein. *The Timetables of Jewish History*. New York: Simon & Schuster, 1993.

Girardot, N. J. *Myth and Meaning in Early Taoism*. Berkeley: University of California Press, 1983.

Gorman, Robert F. and Edward S. Mihalkanin. *Historical Dictionary of Human Rights and Humanitarian Organizations*. Lanham, MD: Scarecrow Press, 1997.

Hamilton, Clarence H. *Buddhism in India, Ceylon, China, and Japan*. Chicago: University of Chicago Press, 1931.

Hardacre, Helen. *Shinto and the State, 1868–1989*. Princeton: Princeton University Press, 1989.

Haskins, James. *The Methodists*. New York: Hippocrene Books, 1992.

Hay, Hope. *The Quakers*. London: Ward Lock Educational, 1981.

Heelas, Paul *The New Age Movement*. Oxford: Blackwell, 1996.

Hillerbrand, Hans, ed. *Oxford Encyclopedia of the Reformation*. New York: Oxford University Press, 1996.

Hinnells, John R. *Who's Who of World Religions*. New York: Simon & Schuster, 1991.

Hinnells, John R., ed. *A New Handbook of Living Religions*. London: Penguin, 1997.

Hirschfelder, Arlene and Martha Kreipe de Monta–o. *The Native American Almanac*. New York: Prentice Hall, 1993.

Hirschfelder, Arlene and Paulette Molin. *The Encyclopedia of Native American Religions*. New York: Facts On File, 1992.

Holmes, George. *Oxford Illustrated History of Medieval Europe*. Oxford: Oxford University Press, 1988.

Holtom, D. C. *The National Faith of Japan: A Study in Modern Shinto*. (1938; reprint, New York: Paragon Book Reprint Corp., 1965).

Hopple, Lee C. "A Religious and Geographical History of the Shakers." *Pennsylvania Folklife* (1989) 39: 57–72.

Hostetler, John A. *Hutterite Society*. Baltimore: Johns Hopkins University Press, 1974.

Hostetler, John A. *Amish Society*. 3rd ed. Baltimore: Johns Hopkins University Press, 1980.

Humphreys, Christmas. *Buddhism*. Harmondsworth, England: Penguin Books, 1951.

Hussey, J. M. *The Orthodox Church in the Byzantine Empire*. Oxford: Clarendon Press, 1986.

Iliffe, John. *Africans: The History of a Continent*. Cambridge: Cambridge Univesity Press, 1995.

Jacobs, Sylvia M., ed. *Black Americans and the Missionary Movement in Africa*. Westport, CT: Greenwood Press, 1982.

Jain, Muni Uttam Kamal. *Jaina Sects and Schools*. Delhi: Concept Publishing Co., 1975.

Jehovah's Witnesses: Proclaimers of God's Kingdom. New York: Watch Tower Bible and Tract Society of Pennsylvania, 1993.

Jones, Alison *The Wordsworth Dictionary of Saints*. Ware, England: Wordsworth Reference, 1992.

Jordan, Michael. *Witches: An Encyclopedia of Paganism and Magic*. London: Kyle Cathie, Ltd., 1996.

Kane, Steven M. *Snake Handlers of Southern Appalachia*. Ann Arbor, University Microfilms International, 1986.

Kaplan, Jeffrey. *Radical Religion in America: Millenarian Movements from the Far Right to the Children of Noah*. Syracuse, NY: Syracuse University Press, 1997.

Karatnycky, Adrian, et al. *Freedom in the World: The Annual Survey of Political Rights & Civil*

Bibliography

Liberties, 1996–1997. New Brunswick, NJ: Transaction Publishers, 1997.

Kato, Genichi. *A Historical Study of the Religious Development of Shinto*. Translated by Shoyu Hanayama. New York: Greenwood Press, 1988 (1973).

Kehoe, Alice B. *North American Indians: A Comprehensive Account*. Englewood Cliffs, NJ: Prentice-Hall, 1981.

Kew, Clifford W. *The Salvation Army*. Oxford, England: Religious Education Press, 1977.

Kitagawa, Joseph Mitsuo and Mark D. Cummings. *Buddhism and Asian History*. New York: Macmillan, 1989.

Klostermaier, Klaus. *A Survey of Hinduism*. Albany: State University of New York Press, 1989.

Knipe, David M. *Hinduism: Experiments in the Sacred*. San Francisco: HarperSanFrancisco, 1991.

Kohn, Livia. *The Taoist Experience: An Anthology*. Albany, NY: State University of New York Press, 1993.

Kumar, Bhuvanendra. *Jainism in America*. Mississauga, Ontario: Jain Humanities Press, 1996.

Lambert, Malcolm. *Medieval Heresy: Popular Movements from the Gregorian Return to the Reformation*. 2nd ed. Oxford: Blackwell, 1992.

Lapidus, Ira M. *A History of Islamic Societies*. Cambridge: Cambridge University Press, 1988.

Layman, Emma McCloy. *Buddhism in America*. Chicago: Nelson-Hall, 1976.

Lenman, Bruce P., ed. *Larousse Dictionary of World History*. Edinburgh: Larousse, 1994.

Levinson, David. *Religion: A Cross-Cultural Dictionary*. New York: Oxford University Press, 1998.

Levinson, David. *Ethnic Groups Worldwide*. Phoenix, AZ: Oryx Press, 1998.

Levinson, David and Melvin Ember, eds. *American Immigrant Cultures: Builders of a Nation*. New York: Macmillan Reference USA, 1997.

Lewis, James and J. Gordon Melton, eds. *Perspectives on the New Age*. Albany: State University of New York Press, 1992.

Lewis, Bernard. *The Middle East: A Brief History of the Last 2,000 Years*. New York: Scribner, 1995.

Lincoln, C. Eric and Lawrence H. Mamiya. *The Black Church in the African American Experience*. Durham: Duke University Press, 1990.

Lippy, Charles H. and Peter W. Williams, eds. *Encyclopedia of the American Religious Experience: Studies of Traditions and Movements*. New York: Charles Scribner's Sons, 1988.

Ludlow, Daniel H., ed. *Encyclopedia of Mormonism*. 4 vols. New York: Macmillan, 1992.

Lynch, Joseph. *The Medieval Church: A Brief History*. Longman: New York 1992.

Marini, Stephen A. *Radical Sects of Revolutionary New England*. Cambridge: Harvard University Press, 1982.

Marsden, George M. *Fundamentalism and American Culture*. New York: Oxford University Press, 1980.

Marty, Martin E. *Pilgrims in Their Own Land: 500 Years of Religion in America*. Boston: Little, Brown and Company, 1984.

Marwick, Max, ed. *Witchcraft and Sorcery*. London: Penguin, 1970.

Maspero, Henri. *Taoism and Chinese Religion*. Trans. Frank A. Kiernan Jr. Amherst, MA: University of Massachusetts Press, 1981.

McLeod, Hew. *Sikhism*. London: Penguin, 1997.

Melton, J. Gordon, Jerome Clark, and Aidan A. Kelly. *New Age Encyclopedia*. Detroit: Gale Research, 1990.

Mehta, Mohan Lal. *Jaina Culture*. Parshvanath Vidyashram Series, No. 13. Varanasi, India: P.V. Research Institute, 1969.

Metzger, Bruce M. and Michael D. Coogan, eds. *The Oxford Companion to the Bible*. New York: Oxford University Press, 1993.

Meyendorff, John. *The Orthodox Church: Its Past and Its Role in the World Today*. Trans. John Chapin. New York: Pantheon Books, 1962.

Milisauskas, Sarunas. *European Prehistory*. New York: Academic Press, 1978.

Moen, Matthew C. and Lowell S. Gustafson, eds. *The Religious Challenge to the State*. Philadelphia: Temple University Press, 1992.

Mother Jones. November/December, 1997. Special Issue: *Believe It or Not: Spirituality Is the New Religion*.

Murakami, Shigeyoshi. *Japan's Religion in the Modern Century*. Trans. by H. Byron Earhart. Tokyo: University of Tokyo Press, 1968.

Nielsen, Niels C. Jr., et al. *Religions of the World*. New York: St. Martin's Press, 1983.

Nies, Judith. *Native American History: A Chronology of a Culture's Vast Achievements and Their Links to World Events*. New York: Ballantine Books, 1996.

Nigosian, S. A. *World Faiths*. New York: St. Martin's Press, 1994.

Newman, Cathy. "The Shaker's Brief Eternity." *National Geographic*. September 1989.

Bibliography

Norwood, Frederick A. *Strangers and Exiles: A History of Religious Refugees*. Vol. 1. Nashville: Abingdon Press, 1969.

Noss, David S. and John B. Noss. *A History of the World's Religions*. New York: Macmillan, 1990.

Numbers, Ronald L. *The Creationists: The Evolution of Scientific Creationism*. New York: Alfred A. Knopf, 1992.

O'Dea, Thomas F. *The Mormons*. Chicago: University of Chicago Press, 1957.

Olson, James S. *An Ethnohistorical Dictionary of the Russian and Soviet Empires*. Westport, CT: Greenwood Press, 1994.

Pas, Julian F., in cooperation with Man Kam Leung. *Historical Dictionary of Taoism*. Lanham, MD: Scarecrow Press, 1998.

Peiris, William. *The Western Contribution to Buddhism*. Delhi: Motil Banarsidass, 1973.

Pelikan, Jaroslav, ed. *The World Treasury of Modern Religious Thought*. Boston: Little, Brown and Company, 1990.

Pennick, Nigel. *The Celtic Cross*. London: Blanford, 1997.

Prokurat, Michael, Alexander Golitzin, and Michael D. Peterson. *Historical Dictionary of the Orthodox Church*. Lanham, MD: Scarecrow Press, 1996.

Quebedeaux, Richard. *The New Charismatics: The Origins, Development, and Significance of Neo-Pentecostalism*. Garden City, NY: Doubleday & Company, 1976.

Queen, Edward L. II, Stephen R. Prothero, and Gardiner H. Shattuck, Jr. *The Encyclopedia of American Religious History*. 2 vols. New York: Facts On File, 1996.

Reat, Noble Ross. *Buddhism: A History*. Berkeley, CA: Asian Humanities Press, 1994.

Riley, Dorothy Winbush. *The Complete Kwanzaa: Celebrating Our Cultural Harvest*. New York: HarperCollins, 1995.

Robbins, Thomas and Susan J. Palmer, eds. *Millennium, Messiahs, and Mayhem: Contemporary Apocalyptic Movements*. New York: Routledge, 1997.

Robinet, Isabelle. *Taoism: Growth of a Religion*. Trans. Phyllis Brooks. Stanford, CA: Stanford University Press, 1997.

Rogerson, John and Philip Davies. *The Old Testament World*. Cambridge: Cambridge University Press, 1989.

Rosenberg, Roy A. *Everything You Need to Know about America's Jews and Their History*. New York: Plume, 1997.

Ross, Floyd Hiatt. *Shinto: The Way of Japan*. Boston: Beacon Press, 1965.

Rouse, Ruth and Stephen Charles Neill, eds. *A History of the Ecumenical Movement: 1517–1948*. 2nd ed. Philadelphia: Westminster Press, 1967.

Roux, Georges. *Ancient Iraq*. 3rd ed. London: Penguin, 1992.

Sacher, Howard. *A History of Jews in America*. New York: Knopf, 1992.

Saunders, Kenneth J. *Epochs in Buddhist History*. Chicago: University of Chicago Press, 1924.

Saletore, Bhasker Anand. *Mediaeval Jainism—With Special Reference to the Vijayanagara Empire*. Bombay: Publishing House, 1939.

Scarre, Christopher and Brian M. Fagan. *Ancient Civilizations*. Reading, MA: Longman, 1997.

Schweitzer, Frederick M. *A History of the Jews since the First Century A.D.* New York: Macmillan, 1971.

Shah, Shantilal. "The Traditional Chronology of the Jainas." *Bonner Orientalistische Studien*, Heft 9. Stuttgart: Kohlhammer, 1935.

Siegel, Richard and Carl Rheins. *The Jewish Almamac*. New York: Bantam Books, 1980.

Simpson, George E. *Black Religions in the New World*. New York: Columbia University Press, 1978.

Singh, Ram Bhushan Prasad. *Jainism in Early Medieval Karnataka (c. AD 500–1200)*. Delhi: Motilal Banarsidass, 1975.

Smith, Peter. *The Babi and Baha'i Religions: From Messianic Schism to a World Religion*. Cambridge: Cambridge University Press, 1987.

Spitz, Lewis W. *The Renaissance and Reformation Movements*. Revised Edition.

St. Louis, MO: Concordia House, 1987.

Stein, Gordon. *The Encyclopedia of the Paranormal*. Amherst, NY: Prometheus Books, 1996.

Stein, Stephen J. *The Shaker Experience in America*. New Haven: Yale University Press, 1992.

Strayer, Joseph, ed. *Dictionary of the Middle Ages*. 13 vols. New York: Charles Scribner's Sons. 1982–1989.

Stroup, Herbert H. *The Jehovah's Witnesses*. New York: Russell & Russell, 1967.

Sullivan, Bruce M. *Historical Dictionary of Hinduism*. Lanham, MD: Scarecrow Press, 1997.

Swatos, William H. Jr., ed. *Encyclopedia of Religion and Society*. Walnut Creek, CA: Altamira Press, 1998.

Tester, S. J. *A History of Western Astrology*. Bury St. Edmunds, Britain: Boydell Press, 1987.

Thompson, F. M. L., ed. *The Cambridge Social History of Britain*. 3 vols. Cambridge: Cambridge University Press, 1990.

Bibliography

Thompson, Laurence G. *Chinese Religion: An Introduction*. 5th ed. Belmont, CA: Wadsworth Publishing Company, 1996.

Toews, John A. *A History of the Mennonite Brethren Church*. Freson, CA: Board of Christian Literature, 1975.

Twitchett, Denis, ed. *The Cambridge History of China*. Vol. 3, Sui and T'ang China, Part 1. Cambridge, England: Cambridge University Press, 1979.

Twitchett, Denis and Michael Loewe, eds. *The Cambridge History of China*. Vol. 1, The Ch'in and Han Empires. Cambridge, England: Cambridge University Press, 1986.

Utter, Glenn H. and John W. Storey. *The Religious Right: A Reference Handbook*. Santa Barbara, CA: ABC-Clio, 1995.

Walker, Benjamin. *Gnosticism: Its History and Influence*. Wellingborough, England: Aquarian Press, 1983.

Washington, Peter. *Madame Blavatsky's Baboon*. New York: Schocken Books, 1995.

Weber, Max. *The Religion of China*. New York: Macmillan, 1964.

Whalen, Lucille. *Human Rights: A Reference Handbook*. Santa Barbara, CA: ABC-Clio, 1989.

Wistrich, Robert S. *Antisemitism: The Longest Hatred*. New York: Pantheon Books, 1991.

Woodard, William P. *The Allied Occupation of Japan 1945–1952 and Japanese Religions*. Leiden, the Netherlands: E. J. Brill, 1972.

Wright, Arthur F. *The Confucian Persuasion*. Stanford, CA: Stanford University Press, 1960.

Yates, Timothy. *Christian Mission in the Twentieth Century*. Cambridge: Cambridge University Press, 1994.

Youngs, J. William T. *The Congregationalists*. Westport, CT: Greenwood Press, 1990.

INDEX

A

A Course in Miracles, 583, 629
Abbasid dynasty, 131, 133, 139, 141, 144, 145, 149, 151, 154, 195
Abduh, Muhammad, 419, 429
Abelard, Peter, 170
Abingdon v. Schempp, 555
Abiodun, Christianah, 488
abolition movement, 373
Aboriginal Christian Uniting Church, 591
abortion, 579, 586, 595, 596, 602, 613, 614, 627, 628, 633
Abraham, 8
Abrahamites, 327
Absolute Established Maori Church of Aotearoa, 513
Abyssinian Baptist Church, 457
Acheh, 236, 242, 284
Acropolis, 20, 28
Act Concerning Religion, 292
Act of Settlement, 312
Act of Supremacy, 251
Act of Uniformity, 299
Action Française, 440
Adejobi, Adeleke, 496
Adena/Hopewell cultural tradition, 50
Adi Granth, 324
Adler v. Duval County School Board, 651
Advices and Queries, 306
Aetherius Society, 540
African Apostolic Church of John Maranke, 516
African Baptist Church, 330
African Basketmaker Church, 552
African Charter on Human and People's Rights, 599
African Communion, 466
African Feast cult, 525
African Greek Orthodox Church, 494, 559
African Independent Churches, 440, 481, 496, 542
African Israel Church Nineyah, 513
African Methodist Episcopal Church, 341, 358, 361, 363, 392
African Methodist Episcopal Zion Church, 385
Afro-Brazilian religions, 363

Agatha, 74
Agbebi, Mojola, 466
Age of Aquarius, 548
Age of Reason, The, 345
agnosticism, 405
Agonshu, 594
Ahmad, Muhammad, 420
Ahmadiya sect, 418, 458
Aiyetoro, 522
Ajanata cave temples, 93
Ajuoga, Abednego Matthew, 542
Akbar, 261, 268, 270
Akiva, Rabbi, 332
Akkadians, 7
Aksum, 63
Aladura, 473
Albanian Orthodox Church, 482
Al-Azhar University, 419, 602, 636
al-Banna, Hasan, 493
al-Ghazzai, 169
al-Hajj, Umar, 390
al-Hilal, 458
al-Kindi, 144
al-Ma'mun, 139
al-Malik, Abd, 122
al-Mustafa Saghunughu, Muhammad, 337
al-Qadir, Abd, 372
al-Sadat, Anwar, 586, 598
al-Sadiq, Ja'far, 133
al-Shaf'i, 139
al-Tijani, Ahmad, 338
al-Wahhab, Muhammad bin 'Abd, 326
Albigenses (Albigensians), 155, 174, 185, 188
alchemy, interior
    See Quanzhen
Alexander the Great, 36
Algerian Manifesto, 515
Ali, 117
Ali, Muhammad, 352
Ali, Noble Drew, 466
Aliens Bill, 453
Alinestoué, 515
Aliyah, 421, 451, 476, 487, 503
All Africa Council of Churches, 553
All-Muslim Nation Union, 543
Allen, Richard, 341, 350, 358

World Hindu Council, 644
World Missionary Conference, 461
World Sikh Organization, 604
World Vision, 530
World's Christian Fundamentals Association,
    475, 477
World's Parliament of Religions, 434, 435
Worldwide Church of God, 503, 589
Worshipers of Shang-ti movement, 385, 386
Wounded Knee massacre, 431
Wounded Knee II, 578
Wovenu, C. K. N., 509
Wovoka, 407, 428
Wu, Empress, 122
Wyclif, John, 208, 216, 219, 222
Wycliffe Bible Translators, 503

X

X case, 627
Xavier, Francis, 255, 257
!Xhosa cattle sacrifice, 393
Xu Daozang, 277
Xu Shoucheng, 293
Xun-zi, 38, 40

Y

Yahweh ben Yahweh, 572
Yali movement, 531
Yamaga, Soko, 294, 313
Yamazaki, Ansai, 281, 292, 302
Yan, Yuan, 308
Yazid, 121
Year of Duputations, 113
Yellow Turban rebellion, 67
Yen-Li school of Confucianism, 309
Yeshiva University, 440
Yi, Hwang, 257
Yi, I, 257
Yiddish, 146, 234, 440
Yiddish Book Center, 641
YIVO Institute for Jewish Research, 488
yoga, 27, 49, 50, 80, 136, 410, 506

Yogananda, Paramahansa, 477, 489, 564
Yom Kippur War, 578
Yoro Code, 127
Yoshido Shinto, 231, 297
Yoshikawa, Koretaru, 293
Young, Brigham, 380
Young Christian Workers, 464
Young Israel movement, 465
Young Men's Christian Association, 381, 388
Young Men's Hebrew Association, 391, 412
Young Tunisians, 456
Young Turks, 429, 442, 457
Young Women's Christian Association, 392, 395
Young Women's Hebrew Association, 428

Z

Zayanid dynasty, 198
Zen (Chan) Buddhism, 96, 120, 121, 171, 181,
    182, 190, 194, 202, 209, 493, 496, 532, 550,
    572
Zeng, Guofan, 399
Zeus, 4
Zevi, Shabbetai, 301
Zhen Gao, 95
Zhou dynasty, 13, 14
Zhou, Lianxi, 157
Zhouyi, 26
Zhu Xi, 171–3, 177–9, 184, 193, 194, 217, 234,
    255, 274, 281, 297, 332
Zhuangzi, 37
ziggurat, 7
Zion Christian Church, 487
Zion, city of, 442, 443
Zion College, 459
Zion religion, 397
Zionism, 406, 407, 438, 443, 582, 585, 617
Zoar, 359
Zoe movement, 442
Zohar, 202
Zoroaster, 12, 17
Zoroastrianism, 12, 40, 71, 72, 97, 116, 127,
    320, 328, 421, 422, 594, 596
Zwingli, Huldrich, 249, 250